The best one-volume introduction to point-based graphics ever, it addresses virtually every aspect of computer graphics from a point-based perspective: acquisition, representation, modeling, animation, rendering–everything from the history of point-based graphics to the latest research results. A broad and deep book destined to be the standard reference for years to come, edited and written by leaders in the field.

Dr. Henry Fuchs
Federico Gil Professor, Department of Computer Science, University North Carolina, Chapel Hill

Point-based representations have recently come into prominence in computer graphics across a range of tasks, from rendering to geometric modeling and physical simulation. Point-based models are unburdened by connectivity information and allow dynamically adaptive sampling, according to the application needs. They are well-suited for modeling challenging effects such as wide-area contacts, large deformations, or fractures. The lack of manifold connectivity and regularity among the samples, however, presents many new challenges in point-based approaches and requires the development of new toolkits to address them. This book, in a series of well-written chapters, covers all essential aspects of using point-based representations in computer graphics, from the underlying mathematics to data structures to GPU implementations—providing a state-of-the-art review of the field.

Prof. Leonidas J. Guibas
Computer Science Department, Stanford University

There is no simpler object than a zero dimensional point. Yet somehow, armed with millions of such simple primitives, researchers have constructed complex 3D models that we can see and manipulate on the screen. Point-Based Graphics brings us the rich history of work that has been done in this area of computer graphics. Editors Markus Gross and Hanspeter Pfister and their contributing authors present a complete set of all the detailed work that has exploded over the past decade resulting in many of the images we see today. This book provides both the theoretical foundations as well as the practical elements needed to build new applications with point-based graphics.

Michael F. Cohen
Principal Researcher, Microsoft Research

This book offers much more than what its title advertises. It provides not only an in-depth coverage of the new field of point-based graphics, but also a solid introduction to most modern techniques in computer graphics, from acquisition to rendering and animation. Written by leading experts on the topic, chapters include the introduction of fundamental tools as well as in-depth case studies of state-of-the-art algorithms. I learned a lot reading the book and I expect to use it often as a reference.

Frédo Durand
Associate Professor, Computer Science and Artificial Intelligence Laboratory, Massachusetts Institute of Technology

Point-based graphics has seen a significant rebirth, which greatly changes the graphics arena. This book, focusing on the major, recent advances in point-based graphics, provides an excellent introduction and overview of the state of the art. It is particularly impressive for its breadth and depth, covering the foundations of the point primitive, modeling, processing, and rendering, as well as advanced topics, such as physics- based animation. Other distinctive features of the book are its world-renowned editors, Markus Gross and Hanspeter Pfister, and the high academic caliber of the contributors. Professionals and students alike will find the book intriguing and stimulating with sound and practical advice. It is a required reading for anyone who wants to keep pace with the rapid progress in this re-emerging and important area of research.

Dr. Arie E. Kaufman
Distinguished Professor & Chair, Computer Science Department, Stony Brook University (SUNY), Stony Brook, NY

Point-Based Graphics

The Morgan Kaufmann Series in Computer Graphics

Point-based Graphics

Edited by

MARKUS GROSS AND HANSPETER PFISTER

AMSTERDAM • BOSTON • HEIDELBERG • LONDON
NEW YORK • OXFORD • PARIS • SAN DIEGO
SAN FRANCISCO • SINGAPORE • SYDNEY • TOKYO

Morgan Kaufmann Publishers is an imprint of Elsevier

ELSEVIER

Publisher	Denise E. M. Penrose
Acquisitions Editor	Tiffany Gasbarrini
Publishing Services Manager	George Morrison
Senior Production Editor	Dawnmarie Simpson
Assistant Editor	Michele Cronin
Cover Design	Chen Design
Composition	diacriTech
Technical Illustration	diacriTech
Copyeditor	Multiscience Press
Proofreader	Multiscience Press
Indexer	Multiscience Press
Interior printer	Hing Yip Printing Co.
Cover printer	Hing Yip Printing Co.

Morgan Kaufmann Publishers is an imprint of Elsevier.
30 Corporate Drive, Suite 400, Burlington, MA 01803, USA

This book is printed on acid-free paper.

© 2007 by Elsevier Inc. All rights reserved.

Library of Congress Cataloging-in-Publication Data
Gross, Markus, 1963-
  Point-based graphics / Markus Gross, Hanspeter Pfister.
     p. cm.
  Includes bibliographical references and index.
  ISBN 978-0-12-370604-1 (hardcover : alk. paper) 1. Computer graphics . 2. Three-dimensional display systems. I. Pfister, Hanspeter. II. Title.
  T385.G769 2007
  006.6–dc22   2007010612

ISBN: 978-0-12-370604-1

For information on all Morgan Kaufmann publications,
visit our Web site at *www.mkp.com* or *www.books.elsevier.com*

Printed and bound by CPI Group (UK) Ltd, Croydon, CR0 4YY

Transferred to Digital Print 2011

To Lisa, Jana, and Adrian.

M. G.

To Jennifer, Lilly, and Audrey.

H. P.

About the Editors

DR. MARKUS GROSS

 Dr. Gross is a professor of computer science, chair of the institute of computational science, and director of the Computer Graphics Laboratory of the Swiss Federal Institute of Technology (ETH) in Zürich. His research interests include point-based graphics, physically-based modeling, multiresolution analysis, and virtual reality. He has published more than 130 scientific papers on computer graphics and scientific visualization, and he authored the book "Visual Computing", Springer, 1994. He holds various patents on core graphics technologies. Gross has taught courses at major graphics conferences including ACM SIGGRAPH, IEEE Visualization, and Eurographics. He serves as a member of international program committees of many graphics conferences and on the editorial board of various scientific journals. Gross was a papers co-chair of the IEEE Visualization '99, the Eurographics 2000, and the IEEE Visualization 2002 conferences. He was chair of the papers committee of ACM SIGGRAPH 2005. Gross received a Master of Science in electrical and computer engineering and a PhD in computer graphics and image analysis, both from the University of Saarbrucken, Germany. From 1990 to 1994, Gross worked for the Computer Graphics Center in Darmstadt, where he established and directed the Visual Computing Group. He is a senior member of IEEE, a member of the IEEE Computer Society, a member of ACM and ACM Siggraph, and a member of the Eurographics Association. From 2002-2006 he was a member of the ETH research commission. Gross serves in board positions of a number of international research institutes, societies and government organizations. He is chair of the technical advisory committee of Ageia Corporation. Gross co-founded Cyfex AG, Novodex AG, and LiberoVision AG.

DR. HANSPETER PFISTER

Hanspeter Pfister is Associate Director and Senior Research Scientist at MERL—Mitsubishi Electric Research Laboratories—in Cambridge, MA. He is the chief architect of VolumePro, Mitsubishi Electric's real-time volume rendering hardware for PCs. His research interests include computer graphics, scientific visualization, and graphics architectures. His work spans a range of topics, including point-based graphics, appearance modeling and acquisition, computational photography, 3D television, and face modeling. Hanspeter Pfister received his Ph.D. in Computer Science in 1996 from the State University of New York at Stony Brook. He received his M.S. in Electrical Engineering from the Swiss Federal Institute of Technology (ETH) Zurich, Switzerland, in 1991. Dr. Pfister has taught courses at major graphics conferences including SIGGRAPH, IEEE Visualization, and Eurographics. He has been teaching introductory and advanced graphics ourses at the Harvard Extension School since 1999. He is Associate Editor of the IEEE Transactions on Visualization and Computer Graphics (TVCG), chair of the IEEE Visualization and Graphics Technical Committee (VGTC), and has served as a member of international program committees of major graphics conferences. Dr. Pfister was the general chair of the IEEE Visualization 2002 conference. He is senior member of the IEEE, and member of ACM, ACM SIGGRAPH, the IEEE Computer Society, and the Eurographics Association.

ABOUT THE CONTRIBUTORS

Adams, Bart   Bart Adams received the M.Sc. Degree in Computer Engineering (magna cum laude) from the Katholieke Universiteit Leuven, Belgium in 2002. In October 2002 he joined the Computer Graphics Group of Prof. Philip Dutré and started a Ph.D. at the Computer Science Department of the Katholieke Universiteit Leuven funded by the National Fund for Scientific Research, Belgium. His current research focuses on the use of point-based surface representations and techniques for computer graphics applications and has lead to two publications so far at the annual ACM SIGGRAPH conference. He has worked together with the Computer Graphics Lab at ETH Zürich on various projects and was a visiting scholar at Stanford University in the summers of 2004 and 2005.

Adamson, Anders   Anders Adamson is a research associate, teaching assistant and PhD student at the Department of Computer Science of the TU Darmstadt,

Germany. He holds Dipl.-Informatiker (MSc) Degree in Computer Science. His research interests are the reconstruction and rendering of surfaces defined by points.

Alexa, Marc   Marc Alexa is a Professor in the Faculty of Electrical Engineering and Computer Science at the Technical University of Berlin and heads the Computer Graphics group. He is primarily interested in representing shapes and their deformation, using point sampled geometry, implicit surfaces, explicit representations, and linear spaces of base shapes. For his earlier work on morphing he received a PhD in Computer Science from Darmstadt University of Technology.

Amenta, Nina   Nina Amenta is an Associate Professor of Computer Science at the University of California at Davis. She got her PhD from the University of California at Berkeley, and was a post-doc at The Geometry Center at the University of Minnesota, and at Xerox Palo Alto Research Center (PARC), and an Assistant Professor at the University of Texas at Austin. Professor Amenta studies computational geometry and computer graphics.

Barthe, Loïc   Loïc Barthe is an assistant professor at the computer graphics department of IRIT/UPS Toulouse, France since September 2003. From September 2000 to August 2003, he was a postdoctoral scholar first at IRIT/UPS Toulouse, then at Cambridge University and finally at RWTH Aachen. Before, he received his PhD in 2000 and hold a Master Degree in 1997. His is specially interested in shape representation, interactive and intuitive modeling.

Botsch, Mario   Mario Botsch is a post-doctoral research associate at the Computer Graphics Laboratory of ETH Zurich, Switzerland. After he received his M.S. degree in mathematics in 1999 from the University of Erlangen-Nürnberg, Germany, he worked as research associate at the Max- Planck Institute for Computer Science in Saarbrücken, Germany, until 2000. He then joined the computer Graphics group at RWTH Aachen, Germany, as research associate and Ph.D. candidate in 2001, from where he received his Ph.D. degree in Computer Science in July 2005.

Christensen, Per   Per Christensen is a senior software developer in Pixar's RenderMan group. His main research interest is efficient ray tracing and global illumination in very complex scenes. He received an M.Sc. degree in electrical engineering from the Technical University of Denmark and a Ph.D. in computer science from the University of Washington.

Dachsbacher, Carsten   Carsten Dachsbacher is a postdoctoral scholar at INRIA/Sophia-Antipolis, France (since May 2006). Before he has been at the Computer Graphics Group of the University of Erlangen-Nuremberg, Germany. He received his Ph.D. degree (summa cum laude) in 2006 and his diploma (with honors) in computer science in 2002 from the University of Erlangen-Nuremberg, Germany. His research focuses on interactive, hardware-assisted computer graphics; in particular he is working on interactive global illumination techniques, procedural models for rendering photo-realistic virtual terrains and point-based rendering.

Ertl, Thomas   Thomas Ertl is a full professor of computer science at the University of Stuttgart, Germany and the head of the Visualization and Interactive Systems Institute (VIS). He received a MS in computer science from the University of Colorado at Boulder and a PhD in theoretical astrophysics from the University of Tuebingen. His research interests include visualization, computer graphics, and human computer interaction.

Guennebaud, Gaël   Gaël Guennebaud is a postdoctoral scholar at the computer graphics department of IRIT/UPS Toulouse, France. He received his Ph.D. degree in 2005 and holds a Master Degree in 2002. His research interests include real-time rendering of complex scenes, point-cloud refinement and soft-shadow generation.

Kalaiah, Aravind   Aravind Kalaiah received a Ph.D. from the University of Maryland in 2005, a M.S. from Stony Brook University in 2000, and a B. Tech. degree from the Indian Institute of Technology, Bombay in 1998. His research interests are in point-based graphics, geometric modeling, and hardware accelerated rendering. Aravind is currently a Senior Engineer at Nvidia.

Keiser, Richard   Richard Keiser is a research associate and PhD student at the computer science department of ETH Zurich, Switzerland. He holds a Masters Degree in Computer Science and specializes in physics based animations using particles and deformable point-based surface modeling.

Klein, Thomas   Thomas Klein received his MS in computer science from the University of Stuttgart. He is a PhD Student at the Visualization and Interactive Systems Group in Stuttgart. His research interests include volume rendering, hardware-accelerated graphics and point-based rendering.

Kobbelt, Leif P.   Leif P. Kobbelt is a full professor of Computer Science and head of the Computer Graphics group at the RWTH Aachen University, Germany. His research interests include all areas of Computer Graphics and Geometry Processing with a special focus on 3D model acquisition and optimization, high-quality shape editing, and the efficient handling of complex geometric models. He previously worked at the Max-Planck Institute for Computer Science in Saarbrücken, Erlangen University, University of Wisconsin in Madison, and Karlsruhe University, where he got his Master and Ph.D. degrees.

Levoy, Marc   Marc Levoy is a Professor of Computer Science and Electrical Engineering at Stanford University. He received degrees in Architecture from Cornell University in 1976 and 1978 and a PhD in Computer Science from the University of North Carolina in 1989. His research interests include computer-assisted cartoon animation, volume rendering (for which he won the SIGGRAPH Computer

Graphics Achievement Award in 1996), 3D scanning, light field sensing and display, computational imaging, and digital photography.

Matusik, Wojciech   Wojciech is a research scientist at Mitsubishi Electric Research Labs. He received a B.S. in EECS from the University of California at Berkeley in 1997, M.S. in EECS from MIT in 2001, and Ph.D. in 2003. In 2004, he was named one of the world's top 100 young innovators by MIT's Technology Review Magazine. Wojciech's primary research lies in computer graphics, data-driven modelling, computational photography, and new display technologies.

Müller-Fischer, Matthias   Matthias Müller-Fischer received his Ph.D. on atomistic simulation of dense polymer systems in 1999 from ETH Zurich and changed fields to macroscopic physically-based simulations during his post-doc 1999-2001 with the MIT Computer Graphics Group.

In 2002 he co-founded NovodeX, now a subsidiary of AGEIA Inc., the company developing the world's first Physics Processing Unit (PPU) for games. He currently works for AGEIA as a principal software engineer responsible for the development of hardware accelerated simulation software for real-time effects such as fluids, cloth and rigid body animation.

Pajarola, Renato   Renato Pajarola received Dipl. Inf-Ing ETH and Dr. sc. techn. degrees in computer science from ETH Zürich in 1994 and 1998 respectively. After being a postdoctoral scholar at Georgia Tech for one year he was an Assistant Professor at University of California Irvine from 1999 to 2006 where he founded the Computer Graphics Lab. Since 2005 he has been a Professor in computer science at University of Zürich where he leads the Visualization and MultiMedia Lab, and his research interests include 3D graphics, multiresolution modeling, point based graphics, interactive scientific visualization, remote and parallel rendering.

Paulin, Mathias   Mathias Paulin is an associate professor at the computer science department of the université Paul Sabatier, Toulouse, France since november 2004. He his a member of IRIT, a join institute between french CNRS, Université Paul Sabatier and National Polytechnic Institute of Toulouse. His habilitation, defended in november 2004, was entittled "Rendering in computer graphics : from realism to real time". His research interests include real time rendering of complex scenes, multi-model and multiresolution shape and appearance modeling and physics-based lighting simulation.

Pauly, Mark   Mark Pauly is an assistant professor at the computer science department of ETH Zurich, Switzerland, since April 2005. From August 2003 to March 2005 he was a postdoctoral scholar at Stanford University, where he also held a position as visiting assistant professor during the summer of 2005. He received his Ph.D. degree (with highest distinction) in 2003 from ETH Zurich and his M.S. degree (with honors) in computer science in 1999 from the Technical University of Kaiserslautern, Germany. His research interests include geometry processing, multi-scale shape modeling and analysis, physics-based animation, and computational geometry.

Peikert, Ronald   Ronald Peikert is a senior researcher in the Institute of Computational Science at ETH Zurich. He received his PhD in mathematics at ETH in 1985, and from 1988 to 1995 he was head of the scientific visualization group of the Swiss Center for Scientific Computing. His research interests include flow visualization, feature extraction techniques, and industrial applications of visualization.

Reina, Guido   Guido Reina is a PhD Student at the Visualization and Interactive Systems Group in Stuttgart. He received his MS in computer science from the University of Stuttgart. His research interests include molecular visualization, hardware-accelerated graphics, point-based rendering and volume rendering.

Rusinkiewicz, Szymon   Szymon Rusinkiewicz is an assistant professor in the Computer Science Department at Princeton University. His work focuses on acquisition and use of the reflectance and 3D shape of real-world surfaces, including the design of scanning devices and data structures for efficient representation. He also investigates algorithms for processing of geometric and reflectance data, including registration, matching, completion, and sampling, as well as real-time rendering and perceptually-guided depiction.

Sadlo, Filip   Filip Sadlo is a research associate and PhD student at the computer science department of ETH Zurich, Switzerland. He holds a masters degree in computer science from ETH Zurich and his research topic is scientific visualization with focus on flow visualization.

Stamminger, Marc   Marc Stamminger is a professor for computer graphics at the University of Erlangen-Nuremberg, Germany, since 2002. After finishing his PhD thesis on finite element methods for global illumination in 1999, he was a PostDoc at the MPI Informatik in Saarbrücken Germany, and at the INRIA Sophia-Antipolis in France. His current research interests are interactive computer graphics, global illumination, and medical visualization.

Varshney, Amitabh   Amitabh Varshney is a Professor of Computer Science at the University of Maryland. He has served on several visualization and graphics conference committees and journal editorial boards. Varshney received the NSF CAREER award in 1995 and the IEEE Visualization Technical Achievement Award in 2004. Varshney received a B.Tech. in Computer Science from the Indian Institute of Technology Delhi in 1989 and a M.S. and Ph.D. in Computer Science from the University of North Carolina at Chapel Hill in 1991 and 1994.

Wand, Michael   Michael Wand is currently visiting assistant professor in the computer graphics laboratory at Stanford University. He has previously been member of the computer graphics group at University of Tübingen, Germany, from 2000 to 2005 where he received a PhD in computer science in 2004. He has studied computer science at University of Paderborn, Germany, where he received a Diploma in 2000. His current research interests include multi-resolution representations for complex geometry and statistical data analysis techniques for geometry processing.

Weyrich, Tim Tim Weyrich received his Diploma degree in computer science from the University of Karlsruhe (TU), Germany in 2001. He is currently PhD student in the Computer Graphics Laboratory of the Institute of Technology (ETH) in Zürich. His research interests are point-based graphics, 3D reconstruction, and appearance modeling. He is member of ACM SIGGRAPH and GI.

Wicke, Martin Born in 1979, Martin Wicke studied Computer Science at the University of Kaiserslautern, Germany. He currently works as a research associate and Ph.D. Student at the Computer Graphics Laboratory at ETH Zurich, Switzerland. His main research interests are physics based modeling and animation.

Würmlin, Stephan Dr. Stephan Würmlin is currently a post-doctoral researcher in the Computer Graphics Laboratory at ETH Zurich and head of the blue-c-II project. He received a PhD degree from ETH Zurich in 2004 on the design of the 3D video technology for the blue-c collaborative virtual reality system. His current research interests include 3D video, video-based rendering, point-based representations and rendering, virtual reality, and multimedia coding.

Wu, Jianhua Jianhua Wu is a research assistant and pursuing his Ph.D. Degree at Computer Graphics Group, RWTH Aachen University, Germany. He graduated in 2002 with a Master Degree in computer science from Tsinghua University, Beijing, China. His research interests mainly focus on efficient surface representations for geometry processing and efficient geometric data structures for distributed and mobile multimedia communications.

Zwicker, Matthias Matthias Zwicker is an Assistant Professor with the Department of Computer Science and Engineering at the University of California, San Diego. After receiving his Ph.D. from the Swiss Federal Institute of Technology Zurich in 2003, he was a Postdoctoral Associate with the Computer Graphics Group at the Massachusetts Institute of Technology until 2005. His research interests include signal processing for computer graphics, geometry processing, and data-driven modeling and animation.

Contents

CHAPTER 8. SELECTED TOPICS   389

Foreword

In any established field, doing something "different" presents a challenge. Even in computer graphics, an area that evolves rapidly, the notion of treating simple points as primitive modeling and display elements did not get off to a fast start. Nevertheless, every good idea has its time. Two timely factors that promote the idea of point-based graphics are procedural shape definition and automated shape acquisition. The former has the flexibility to produce as many or as few points as needed to accurately represent itself. The latter naturally produces a massive flood of points. The sheer complexity of such models begs for a representation that is inherently simple. Points are simple. However, effectively acquiring, editing, animating, rendering, and otherwise processing points requires a non-intuitive understanding of the representations and processes. That's why this book is necessary.

Twenty years ago, when my students were experimenting with point-based representations of surfaces and volumes, they repeatedly asked "what would happen if we tried this crazy idea?" As demonstrated in this text, today's discussions are conducted with more rigor and sophistication. While points themselves may be simple, a complete understanding of how they are processed and how collections of them should be interpreted requires sophisticated explanations. And there is no single "best" method for processing such point collections. The explanations in this book are broad; the authors cover a range of applications and techniques, and they cover these thoroughly.

The approaches described in this book may once have been considered outside the mainstream by experienced graphics practitioners. The editors and contributors themselves, however, are among the best and brightest in mainstream computer graphics research. To bring their expertise to bear on a single coherent volume is no small feat.

There are undoubtedly a few of us that enjoy ideas just because of their inherent beauty. Having migrated to computer graphics from a background in signal processing, I have a certain attachment to point-based graphics methods. Because of this interest, I have tracked the work of many of the book's contributors for several years.

Their perseverance and ingenuity are an inspiration. Seeing their work collected in one place is a tremendous personal pleasure. More importantly for the reader, this text is a unique and valuable resource for those who wish to understand and make use of point-based graphics technology.

Turner Whitted
Microsoft Research

Point-Based Graphics

CHAPTER ONE

Gross, Markus

Computer Graphics Laboratory
ETH Zürich
Haldeneggsteig 4 / Weinbergstrasse
CH - 8092 Zürich
grossm@inf.ethz.ch
Tel: +41-44-632 7114
Fax: +41-44-632 1596

Pfister, Hanspeter

MERL - Mitsubishi Electric Research Laboratories
201 Broadway
Cambridge, MA 02139
USA
pfister@merl.com
Tel: +1 617 621 7566
Fax: +1 617 621 7550

1 INTRODUCTION

Markus Gross and Hanspeter Pfister

1.1 OVERVIEW

Point primitives have experienced a major renaissance in recent years, and considerable research has been devoted to the efficient representation, modeling, processing, and rendering of point-sampled geometry. There are two main reasons for this new interest in points: on one hand, we have witnessed a dramatic increase in the polygonal complexity of computer graphics models. The overhead of managing, processing, and manipulating very large polygonal-mesh connectivity information has led many researchers to question the future utility of polygons as the fundamental graphics primitive. On the other hand, modern three-dimensional (3D) digital photography and 3D scanning systems acquire both geometry and appearance of complex, real-world objects. These techniques generate huge volumes of point samples, which constitute the discrete building blocks of 3D object geometry and appearance—much as pixels are the digital elements for images.

Over the past five years, point-based graphics has seen an amazing growth. By the time of publication of this book, three symposia on point-based graphics will have concluded, the first of which was started in Zürich, Switzerland, in 2004. The large number of submissions to these conferences shows the huge interest in this young and exciting field and its potential for research and teaching.

This interest in combination with the huge success of various tutorials on this topic and thousands of downloads of Pointshop3D, a freeware software package for point-based graphics, have motivated us to create this textbook. It presents a comprehensive collection of both fundamental and more advanced topics in point-based computer graphics. The book is based on a series of courses that we and some of the authors taught over the past five years at major graphics conferences. We have extended our material significantly and we have invited numerous prolific authors in the field to contribute to this publication.

The book assumes familiarity with the standard computer graphics techniques for surface representation, modeling, and rendering. No previous knowledge about point-based methods is required. The book is suitable for both classroom and professional use. The comprehensive coverage of the topic makes the book a reference and teaching tool, and the in-depth coverage of algorithms as well as the inclusion of the Pointshop3D open-source system makes it very attractive for developers.

The book is intended for researchers and developers with a background in traditional (polygon-based) computer graphics. They will obtain a state-of-the-art overview of the use of points to solve fundamental computer graphics problems such as surface data acquisition, representation, processing, modeling, and rendering. With this book, we hope to stimulate research and development of point-based methods in games, entertainment, special effects, visualization, digital content creation, and other areas. For instance, game developers will learn how to use point-based graphics for game characters and special effects (physics, water, etc.) employing real-time rendering on graphics processing units (GPUs). Developers in the movies and special effects industry will learn how to use points for offline, high-quality global illumination, character rendering, and physics. Engineers will learn how to process huge point clouds that naturally arise during object scanning. Architects of current GPUs (e.g., at NVIDIA and ATI) will learn what operations need to be implemented or accelerated to facilitate point-based graphics. Digital content creators and artists will use Pointshop3D for the creation of very complex models.

We believe that point-based graphics bear a huge potential for future research and development and might influence the way we will do computer graphics in the future. We hope that this book will stimulate new ideas in this rapidly moving field and that it will convince more graphics researchers and developers of the utility of point-based graphics.

1.2 BOOK ORGANIZATION

The book organization follows essentially the 3D content creation pipeline, as outlined in Figure 1.1.

Historically, points have received relatively little attention in computer graphics. Yet, there has been fundamental work that laid ground for the more recent developments. In Chapter 2, Marc Levoy will present an historical perspective on the topic. He will highlight early work on point-based modeling and rendering, and will point out how this work provided a basis for the subsequent chapters of this book.

The first stage in Figure 1.1 involves the acquisition of point clouds from real-world models through means of 3D scanning and reconstruction. Chapter 3 will give a comprehensive overview over the state-of-the-art in 3D acquisition and scanning methods for point-sampled models. The authors focus both on geometry and appearance acquisition. The discussed algorithms and systems will make the reader familiar with the essentials of scanning technology, including a practical guide to build a low-cost 3D scanning system. The final topic of this chapter is devoted to sophisticated appearance acquisition using 3D photography.

The next stage in the content creation pipeline includes mathematical methods to reconstruct surfaces from point clouds and to deal with the discrete nature of

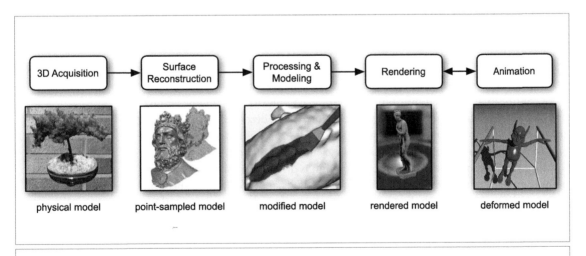

Figure 1.1: The 3D graphics content-creation pipeline serves as a model for the book's organization.

point sets. Chapter 4 acquaints the reader with the mathematical and algorithmic fundamentals of point-based surface representations. It describes the basic concepts of discrete differential geometry and topology as well as specific representations, such as the famous moving least squares (MLS) method. Other topics of the chapter are discretization and sampling and an overview over the most important data structures for point-based representations. The chapter concludes with a presentation of real-time, iterative refinement methods.

Once the surface representations are in place, the next step in the content creation pipeline is the digital processing, filtering, modeling, and editing of point models. Chapter 5 is devoted to the digital processing of point-sampled models. It demonstrates the versatility of point-sampled representations that combine the simplicity of conventional image editing operations with the power of advanced 3D modeling methods. The chapter includes a variety of preprocessing methods, such as model cleaning, filtering, and feature extraction, as well as photo editing operations. More advanced shape modeling operations, like deformations and constructive solid geometry (CSG), will also be discussed. The chapter is closely related to the core functions of Pointshop3D, the software accompanying the book.

The final stage in our content creation pipeline is high-quality and efficient display of the point model. Novel rendering pipelines and concepts had to be devised for point-based models. Chapter 6 presents a comprehensive overview of high-quality rendering methods for point-sampled geometry. It starts with a review of the fundamentals of surface splatting, one of the most widely used techniques for point rendering. More advanced and hardware-accelerated methods for point splatting will be discussed next. Finally, we explain ray-tracing methods for point-sampled geometry and acceleration structures for high-performance point rendering.

Very often, graphics models have to be animated; i.e., their shape and attributes have to be controlled and altered over time. Due to the complexity of the topic, animation cannot be treated comprehensively. But Chapter 7 will describe physically based animation using point-sampled representations. This topic has emerged recently as a promising alternative to conventional finite element simulation. It is inspired by so-called meshless methods, where the continuum is discretized using unstructured point samples. We will demonstrate that such methods allow for a wide spectrum of material simulations, including brittle fracture, elastic and plastic deformations, and fluids. Such physical point representations are combined with high-resolution point-sampled surface geometry.

The concluding Chapter 8 contains a collection of select topics related to point-based computer graphics. One such method is the dynamic representation, compression, and display of 3D video. A second one is the modeling and analysis of uncertainty in point clouds. A further topic discusses point-based visualization of attributed datasets. Another contribution addresses the computation of global illumination in point-sampled scenes and shows how such methods are used in a production environment. The chapter demonstrates the versatility and application potential of point-based methods.

1.3 COMMON ISSUES AND REOCCURRING PATTERNS

Points are clearly the simplest of all graphics primitives. Throughout the book, there are reoccurring issues inherent to point-based graphics that can be summarized as follows.

Points generalize pixels and voxels toward irregular samples of geometry and appearance. The conceptually most significant difference to triangles is that points—much as voxels or pixels—carry all attributes needed for processing and rendering. There is no distinction between vertex and fragment anymore.

As a sampled representation including geometry and (prefiltered) appearance, point representations allow one to carry over some of the computationally expensive fragment processing, such as filtering, to the preprocessing stage. Their very "sameness" of geometry and appearance creates the potential of designing leaner graphics pipelines. Of course, this simplified processing comes at a price. Straightforward framebuffer projection leaves holes in the image that have to be filled for close-up views. Point models also require a denser sampling compared to triangle meshes. The higher resolution of the representation potentially leads to increased bandwidth requirements between the computer processing unit (CPU) and GPU. In some sense, bandwidth has to be traded with processing speed.

Points, in their purest form, do not store any connectivity or topology. Since many 3D acquisition algorithms generate point clouds as output, points naturally serve as the canonical representation for 3D acquisition systems. In contrast, triangle meshes are the result of 3D reconstruction algorithms and require prior assumptions on topology and sampling. The lack of topology and connectivity, however, is strength and weakness at the same time. The atomic nature of a point sample gives the representation a built-in level of detail (LOD), making it possible, for instance, to stream and render point clouds progressively.

Points have proven their ability to model complex geometry. Their lack of connectivity enables one to conveniently resample without the need to restructure the representation on the fly. Resampling, one of the key ingredients of many point graphics algorithms, can be accomplished in many different ways. Continuous surface reconstructions are provided by the many versions of MLS. The lack of connectivity makes changes of model topology more accessible, but comes at a cost. k-nearest neighborhoods, needed for many surface processing algorithms, have to be computed on the fly. This, in turn, requires more elaborate data structures, including K-d-trees or spatial hashing. Also, improperly sampled point models do not give guarantees on topological correctness, which may or may not be a problem. The flexibility of dynamic adjacency computation is specifically efficient if the model size is large and the operations are local. Some researchers have resorted to cache strategies to retain some static adjacency in the representation.

Similar observations hold for physically based simulations. Meshless methods have successfully been applied to compute elastic and plastic deformations as well as fracturing of solid objects. It has been shown that the absence of a rigid mesh structure facilitates the modeling of phase transitions, for example, during melting. The proposed methods are robust and render visually plausible results. In addition to the use of points for the discretization of computational domains, some research has been done to reconstruct and animate the corresponding surfaces using point samples. Again, the previously discussed properties of point representations help to conveniently change topology (fracture, melting) or resample dynamically (deformation).

In summary, point primitives constitute a simple and versatile low-level graphics and visualization primitive. Representation points have different strengths and weaknesses compared to other graphics primitives. They are not going to replace the existing ones, but have proven their ability to complement them. Many technical issues related to point-based graphics boil down to reconstruction and resampling. As a sample-based approach to graphics, points stimulate us to take a signal processing view onto graphics and visualization.

1.4 ACKNOWLEDGMENTS

This book reflects a significant part of our own research and experience in this topic collected and carried out over the past years. There are many individuals who have contributed to its completion, in small and in large ways.

First, we would like to thank all authors for all the work and effort they have put into their contributions to bring the book to completion. We also thank all reviewers for providing very valuable feedback in various stages of the manuscript. In particular, Mario Botsch and Miguel Otaduy from the Computer Graphics Laboratory in Zürich helped greatly with the revision of the manuscript.

We were delighted that Turner Whitted from Microsoft Research, one of the pioneers of point based graphics, agreed to write the excellent foreword to our book. We were also very pleased to read the endorsements from some of the most distinguished senior researchers of our community, including Michael Cohen from Microsoft Research, Fredo Durand from MIT, Henry Fuchs from University of North Carolina, Leo Guibas from Stanford University, and Arie Kaufman from SUNY at Stony Brook.

Our special thanks goes to Rolf Adelsberger, who did an invaluable job in keeping the sources of the document consistent, tracking authors and changes, compiling the manuscript for the publisher, checking figures and references and assembling the Pointshop3D resources. Richard Keiser also helped in many ways to put together the ancillary materials accompanying this book. Martin Wicke and Doo-Young Kwon assisted us in setting up internal websites for communication with our authors. We also thank all the students and collaborators involved with the projects that are summarized in this book. Without their help and effort the presented results would not have been possible.

We thank our publisher, Elsevier, for accepting our proposal and everybody involved for bringing this book to life. Special thanks go to Tim Cox for his patience and support of the project, and to Dave Eberly for his encouragement and help. Our gratitude also goes to our production editors, Alan Rose and Darice Moore from Multiscience Press, our project managers, Dawnmarie Simpson, Michelle Ward and Michele Cronin, our acquisitions editor, Tiffany Gasbarrini, and our publisher, Denise E. M. Penrose.

Many thanks go also to our employers, ETH Zürich and Mitsubishi Electric Research Laboratories (MERL), for giving us the freedom and flexibility to work on this project. Finally, our work and careers would be meaningless without the love and support of our wives and children, Jennifer, Lilly, and Audrey Pfister, and Lisa, Jana, Adrian Gross.

CHAPTER TWO

Levoy, Marc

Stanford University
Computer Graphics Laboratory
Stanford, CA 94305
USA
levoy@cs.stanford.edu
Tel: +1 650 725 4089
Fax: +1 650 723 0033

2 THE EARLY HISTORY OF POINT-BASED GRAPHICS

Marc Levoy

Why is it worthwhile to study where an idea came from? Thomas Kuhn, writing in *The Structure of Scientific Revolutions*, notes that scientists like to see their discipline's past "developing linearly toward its present vantage" [Kuh62]. As a result, textbooks often discard or obscure the origins of ideas, thereby robbing students of the experience of a scientific revolution. This in turn makes them unable to realize when one is upon them and ignorant about how to act in these circumstances. I do not claim that point-based rendering was a scientific revolution, at least not in 1985 when Turner Whitted and I wrote our first paper on the topic. However, that paper was written in response to a scientific crisis, which bears some of the same characteristics. As a technical achievement, our paper was a failure. However, as a story of crisis and response it is instructive. In this spirit I offer the following historical account.

2.1 SAMPLE-BASED REPRESENTATIONS OF GEOMETRY

Since the beginning of computer graphics, a creative tension has existed between representing scenes as geometry versus as collections of samples. Early sample-based representations included textures, sprites, range images, and density volumes.

More recent examples include light fields, layered depth images, image caches, and so on. Points are another such representation, often used to approximate curved surfaces as this book amply demonstrates. In each case researchers faced a common set of challenges: how to edit the scene by manipulating its samples, how to store and compress these samples, how to transform and shade them, and how to render them with correct sampling, visibility, and filtering.

However, to understand the early history of point rendering, we must understand a different tension that existed in the early history of computer graphics, one between image-order and object-order algorithms for displaying geometric primitives. It was in response to this tension that Turner Whitted and I proposed points as a way to display curved surfaces [LW85]. And it was on the shoals of sampling, visibility, and filtering that our idea ran aground. Let us see why.

2.2 IMAGE-ORDER VERSUS OBJECT-ORDER VISIBILITY AND ANTIALIASING

In their seminal paper on hidden-surface algorithms [SSS74], Ivan Sutherland et al. showed that visibility is tantamount to sorting. As any student of computing knows, sorting N objects into P bins can be done using a gather or a scatter. In computer graphics, the gather strategy leads to an image-order algorithm. One example is ray tracing [Whi80]; for the viewing ray associated with each image pixel, search among the geometric primitives in a scene for the frontmost primitive intersecting that ray. By contrast, the scatter strategy leads to an object-order algorithm. The most common of these is the Z-buffer [Cat74]; create an array as large as the screen, and for each primitive decide which pixel it falls into. While building such an array was expensive in the 1970s, causing Sutherland et al. [SSS74] to dismiss the Z-buffer algorithm as hopelessly impractical, a steady decline in semiconductor memory prices eventually made this and other image-order algorithms both practical and attractive. Image-order traversal is particularly easy to implement because the number of samples that should be taken of the primitive is obvious: one per pixel. For an object-order algorithm, enough samples must be taken to avoid leaving any pixels uncovered, but not so many that the algorithm becomes inefficient.

To avoid aliasing artifacts in computer-generated images, each pixel should be assigned not a point sample of the scene but instead a sample of the convolution of the scene by a filter function. Repeating this process for every pixel in a two-dimensional (2D) image, and assuming the filter is a discrete 2D function, we obtain four nested loops. Since convolution is linear, these loops can be rearranged so that the outer loop is over image pixels, leading to an image-order algorithm, or over points on the scene primitives at some resolution, leading to an object-order algorithm. As was the case for visibility, antialiasing poses fewer problems if implemented in image order. In an influential early paper, Edwin Catmull [Cat78] observed that to compute a correct color in a pixel, only those primitives or portions of primitives that lie frontmost within the filter kernel centered at the pixel should be included in the convolution. This is easy in an image-order algorithm, because all primitives that might contribute to the pixel are evaluated at once. In an object-order algorithm, solving this problem requires retaining subpixel geometry for every primitive in every pixel. To avoid this difficulty, researchers have proposed computing visibility at a higher resolution than the pixel spacing (by supersampling and averaging down), approximating subpixel geometry using a bitmask [Car84] or summarizing it as a scalar value (called alpha), leading to digital compositing [Wal81, PD84]. In some rendering algorithms, sub-pixel geometry has been used as both an alpha value and a filter weight, leading to problems of correctness to which I will return later.

2.3 THE CHALLENGE POSED BY PROCEDURAL MODELING

If it is easier to render scenes in image order, why did researchers develop object-order algorithms? The answer lies in the convenience of procedural modeling, which may be loosely defined as the generation of scene geometry using a computer algorithm (rather than interactively or by sensing). Examples of procedural modeling include fractal landscapes [Car80], clouds [Gar85], plants [PL90], and generative surface models [Sny92]. Although some cite Levoy and Whitted [LW85] as introducing points as primitives, procedurally generated points or particles had already been used to model smoke [CHP+79], clouds [Bli82b], fire [Ree83], and tree leaves and grass [Ree85].

To render a procedurally defined object using favored image-order algorithms, one must be able to compute for a given pixel which part of the object (if any) lands there. If the procedure is expensive to invert in this sense, or even uninvertible, then an object-order algorithm rendering must be used. During the 1970s and early 1980s, researchers invested considerable effort in resolving this conflict between rendering order and geometry traversal order. As an example, Reeves [Ree85] modeled tree leaves as circular particles with semitransparent fringes. To decide how many particles to draw for each tree, he examined its approximate size on the screen. He rendered these particles using an image-order algorithm. In this algorithm, transparency could be used either as a filter weight or a compositing alpha, but not both, as noted earlier. To resolve this ambiguity, Reeves sorted his particles into buckets by screen location and Z-depth, treated transparency as weight, and additively accumulated color and weight in each pixel. When a bucket was finished, it would be combined with other buckets using digital compositing, with the accumulated weight in each pixel now serving as its alpha value. While not exact, this algorithm worked well for irregular geometry like trees and grass.

Another important class of procedurally defined objects are parametric surfaces. For given values of the parameters s and t, it is straightforward to evaluate the surface functional, yielding an (x, y) position on the screen. However, for a given pixel position it may be difficult to determine whether the surface touches it. For parametric bicubic surfaces, some researchers attacked this inverse problem head-on, developing scanline algorithms that directly gave these curves of intersection [Bli78, Whi78]. However, these algorithms were fragile and difficult to implement efficiently. Others proposed an object-order approach, subdividing the surface recursively in parametric space into patches until their projection covered no more than one pixel [Cat74]. Still others proposed hybrid solutions, subdividing the surface recursively until it was locally flat enough [Cla79, LCWB80] (or detailed enough in the case of fractal surfaces [Car80]) to represent using a simpler primitive that could be rendered using an image-order algorithm. Another hybrid solution was to partially evaluate the procedural geometry, producing an estimate of its spatial extent in the form of an image space decomposition [RW80] or collection of bounding boxes [Kaj83]; the overlap between these extents and screen pixels could then be evaluated in image order.

This struggle, which had to be repeated each time a new geometric primitive was proposed, was perceived by many as a crisis in the field. Kuhn [Kuh62] states that when such a crisis arises in a scientific paradigm, and "normal science" is no longer fruitful, there is a gradual loosening of the rules for research, leading researchers to propose solutions that were previously considered outlandish. Before we make that jump, there is one procedural modeling method that so severely broke the dominant display paradigm that it requires special mention.

2.4　THE CURIOUS CASE OF DISPLACEMENT MAPPING

One of the most important single advances in the realism of computer imagery was texture mapping, first used by the GE lunar lander simulator in 1968, then described and analyzed by Catmull [Cat74]. By associating a tabular two-dimensional array of colors with each geometric primitive, the visual complexity of a scene could far exceed its shape complexity. Bump mapping [Bli78] generalized texture mapping by using a tabular array to locally modify surface orientation.

In his paper on shade trees, Cook proposed using textures to locally modify surface position [Coo84] (Figure 2.1). Although a powerful idea, displacement mapping

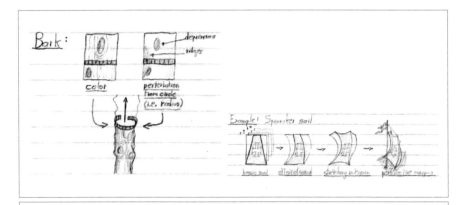

Figure 2.1: Levoy and Whitted envisioned modeling complex objects from points, represented as textures and compounded using simple rules. At left, a tree trunk is modeled using two textures—giving color and X,Y,Z-displacement from the surface of a cylinder. At right, a trapezoidal texture is warped using a sequence of mappings, each defined as a texture or procedure. If the compound mapping is uninvertible, then rendering can only be done in object order. These sketches are from Marc Levoy's research notebook of September 1984.

badly broke the accepted image-order graphics pipeline. In this pipeline the set of pixels covered by a primitive was independent of whatever textures were associated with it; a primitive could be rasterized without regard to its textures, and once a pixel was selected by the rasterizer for rendering, its textures could be considered when computing its color. In Cook's method a texture was allowed to move a primitive and thereby change the set of pixels it covered.

For the restricted case of a flat plane displaced in one direction only (i.e., a terrain model), this problem could be fixed by changing the screen traversal order, as described by Fishman and Schachter [FS80] and Max [Max81]. However, if the displacement could be in any direction, or the underlying geometric primitive was curved, then the problem became harder. Moreover, since displacement maps could be generated procedurally, interactively, or by sensing, their displacement function was often uninvertible. This made the problem insoluble except by abandoning image-order rendering.

2.5 POINTS AND MICROPOLYGONS TO THE RESCUE

The notion of using points and an object-order rendering algorithm to display smooth (i.e., continuous) primitives was first proposed for lines and curved strokes by Whitted [Whi83] (based on Alvy Ray Smith's earlier Z-paint brush [Smi79]), and for displacement-mapped surfaces by Levoy and Whitted [LW85] (Figure 2.2). Although the latter paper advertised points as a universal metaprimitive, having in mind the rather ambitious modeling paradigm described in Figure 2.1, they only demonstrated its use for rendering displaced surfaces.

The notion of using points to display continuous surfaces was not an obvious idea when proposed, nor was it obviously a good idea once proposed. Indeed, the method immediately ran into exactly the problems enumerated at the beginning of this chapter. The first of these was how to vary the density of points locally to match the pixel spacing. If this density was too high, the algorithm would be slow; if it was too low, the surface would contain holes. To solve this problem, Levoy and Whitted used the determinant of the Jacobian of a unit-sized surface patch after transformation to screen space, an idea that resurfaced in Heckbert's analysis of texture mapping [Hec89].

Harder to resolve was the conflict between visibility and antialiasing. For this Levoy and Whitted proposed (concurrently but independently from Reeves) a *moving surface cache* composed of depth buckets that were dynamically created and destroyed as the surface was traversed. Like Reeves, points were rendered with antialiasing, whose weights were combined additively within a bucket and multiplicatively (via digital compositing) between buckets. Unfortunately, while Reeves got away with this approximation because he was rendering irregular objects, Levoy and Whitted did not. Their use of a moving cache was clever, but it was also fragile; narrow surfaces, highly curved surfaces, and surfaces that folded over on themselves sometimes exhibited holes, almost regardless of the density of points employed.

The REYES algorithm [CCC87] solved this same problem—of rendering displacement-mapped surfaces—by traversing them in object order, dicing each into micropolygons about the size of a pixel, and rendering these using an image-order algorithm with stochastic sampling [Coo86]. Although arguably more expensive than point rendering, Cook's micropolygons fit snugly against each other. An image-order algorithm could render such a mesh of micropolygons without creating holes. In retrospect, Levoy and Whitted's mistake was to discard the natural connectivity between points on a surface. In so doing, they made reconstruction of a continuous surface difficult.

Not to belabor our story, the publication and obvious success of the REYES algorithm caused Levoy and Whitted to abandon their work on point-based rendering. Points might still be advantageous, they reasoned, but their advantages must lie elsewhere. Indeed, researchers continued throughout the 1980s experimenting with pointlike approaches in other domains. For example, under the name *splatting* [Wes90], antialiased points briefly became one of the two dominant methods for rendering volume

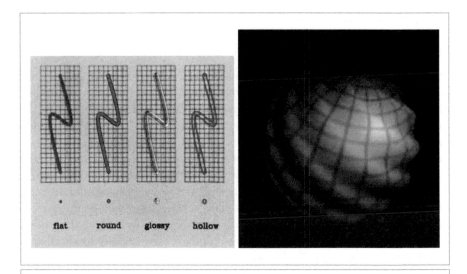

Figure 2.2: At left, Whitted [Whi83] rendered continuous curves as a sequence of brush stamps in 3D, each represented as a pixel array having color, opacity, and Z-depth. At right, Levoy and Whitted [LW85] rendered displacement-mapped surfaces (i.e., surfaces with relief) as a collection of points in 3D, each represented as a pixel array having the same characteristics.

data, the other two being ray tracing [Lev88] and planar texture mapping [DCH88]. For the special case of displaying isosurfaces from volume data, a pointlike algorithm called *dividing cubes* was proposed by Cline and Lorensen [CLL⁺88], whereby a volume was subdivided into subvolumes until their projection covered no more than a pixel. Although implemented in hardware, this algorithm was eventually overshadowed in popularity by the same authors' marching cubes algorithm [LC87].

2.6 THE CURRENT RENAISSANCE IN POINT GRAPHICS

Kuhn says that crises in science end in one of three ways: (1) the existing paradigm proves capable of handling the crisis, (2) the problem is set aside for future generations having better tools, or (3) there is a transition to a new paradigm. Although I have argued here that the crisis in rendering algorithms in the 1980s was adequately resolved without a switch to point-based rendering, this is not to say that all the difficulties posed by the dominant paradigm were resolved. Micropolygon rendering is slow and parallel poorly, and the out-of-order evaluation demanded by displacement maps still causes headaches to the designers of graphics hardware. Nevertheless, except for one paper in the mid-1990s on a hardware system for point-based rendering [GD98], the idea was more or less forgotten for a decade.

By the time point-based rendering was resurrected (contemporaneously by Rusinkiewicz and Levoy in their QSplat system [RL00] and by Pfister et al. in their surfels system [PZvBG00]), the graphics landscape had changed considerably. The number of pixels covered by a typical polygon had been shrinking for a decade, and hardware antialiasing was becoming commonplace. These developments made connectivity less important than it was in 1984, and they made antialiased points a more attractive primitive. At the same time, display screen resolution was rising slowly, which made accurate antialiasing less critical than it was 15 years earlier. In addition, the 1990s saw the development of several new ways to create points, including 3D scanning and particle-based physics simulations. In some cases these point sets included connectivity information, but in other cases they did not, leading to so-called point-cloud data. Finally, new techniques had been invented for discretely approximating the operators of differential geometry, enriching the set of operations that could be applied to point-based representations of surfaces.

With the lesson of the rise and fall of point-based rendering in the 1980s in mind, and in my unenvious position as the author of this rise and fall, I encourage the new generation of researchers in this field, many of whom are represented in this book, to learn from my mistake by clearly distinguishing those things points can do but so can other representations, those things points can do that other representations cannot, and those things points cannot do or will never do well.

CHAPTER THREE

Rusinkiewicz, Szymon

Princeton University
Department of Computer Science
35 Olden Street
Princeton, NJ 08544
USA
smr@princeton.edu
Tel: +1 609 258 7479
Fax: +1 609 258 1771

Weyrich, Tim

ETH Zürich
Computer Graphics Laboratory
Haldeneggsteig 4
8092 Zürich
Switzerland
weyrich@inf.ethz.ch
Tel: +41 44 632 03 56
Fax: +41 44 632 15 96

Matusik, Wojciech

MERL - Mitsubishi Electric Research Laboratories
201 Broadway
Cambridge, MA 02139
USA
matusik@merl.com
Tel: +1 617 621 7500
Fax: +1 617 621 7550

Sadlo, Filip

ETH Zürich
Computer Graphics Laboratory
Haldeneggsteig 4
8092 Zürich
Switzerland
sadlo@inf.ethz.ch
Tel: +41 44 632 71 44
Fax: +41 44 632 15 96

Peikert, Ronald

ETH Zürich
Computer Graphics Laboratory
Haldeneggsteig 4
8092 Zürich
Switzerland
peikert@inf.ethz.ch
Tel: +41 44 632 55 69
Fax: +41 44 632 15 96

Pfister, Hanspeter

MERL - Mitsubishi Electric Research Laboratories
201 Broadway
Cambridge, MA 02139
USA
pfister@merl.com
Tel: +1 617 621 7566
Fax: +1 617 621 7550

3 ACQUISITION

INTRODUCTION

This chapter provides a comprehensive overview of state-of-the-art 3D acquisition and scanning methods for point-sampled models. The chapter will focus both on geometry and appearance acquisition. The discussed methods and systems are intended to make the reader familiar with the essentials of scanning technology. Section 3.1 gives an overview of 3D geometry acquisition and introduces the basic concepts of 3D scanning. Section 3.2 demonstrates how the presented methods can be utilized in practice to design and build a low-cost 3D scanning system. The chapter concludes with the more advanced topic of 3D digital photography. Section 3.3 presents a method and system for appearance acquisition.

The field of 3D acquisition has emerged as an important source of both challenges and applications for point-based techniques. The high detail and ease of acquisition of 3D models of real-world objects have driven their acceptance in computer graphics productions, but the size and density of these datasets have required the development of efficient representations and processing algorithms. In this chapter, we present both the background of 3D scanning technology and related algorithms, as well as a complete example of a 3D model acquisition pipeline built around point-based techniques. Note that in this chapter we deal exclusively with 3D *surface* scans and scanners, as opposed to the volumetric data (representing density as a function of position in space) produced by devices including computed tomography (CT) and magnetic resonance imaging (MRI) scanners.

Among the reasons for the natural affinity of 3D scanners and points are:

- *Size*: 3D scans can be large and detailed, with models in the range of 10^6 to 10^9 samples becoming commonplace. As argued throughout this book, point-based methods achieve greater efficiency in storage and certain kinds of geometric processing, and these advantages are put to greatest effect on scanned models.
- *Noise*: All scans have noise, and depending on the particular scanner design this noise can be on the order of the sample spacing. This makes it difficult to infer and preserve mesh connectivity, leading to a strong preference for techniques that defer or avoid inferring adjacency information and compute surface properties such as normals, when required, by considering variable-sized neighborhoods in space.
- *Sparseness*: Some 3D acquisition techniques, especially passive methods, can only return reliable geometry at a few locations on the surface (essentially, at "features" or "texture" resulting from color variation). This makes it error prone to estimate the connectivity of points within a scan, and mistakes can lead to difficulty in combining multiple scans of the same object. Even for those scanning technologies that return "dense" point clouds, establishing the connectivity of nearby samples must rely on a heuristic to avoid connecting across the depth discontinuities visible from a single view. Point-based techniques, by omitting or deferring the estimation of connectivity, can avoid such difficulties.

3.1 ACQUISITION OF POINT-SAMPLED GEOMETRY

Szymon Rusinkiewicz

This section presents an overview of 3D scanning hardware, focusing on the resolution, noise, and point density achievable by the different available technologies.

In addition, it describes the algorithms for registration and scan merging necessary to go from raw 3D *data* to finished *models*. To see the need for such algorithms, we begin with an overview of the 3D model acquisition pipeline, some version of which appears in every research and commercial scanning system.

3.1.1 OVERVIEW OF THE 3D ACQUISITION PIPELINE

To begin, let us discuss the important distinction between *3D scanners* and *3D model acquisition systems*. The former refers simply to devices capable of returning the shape of (some portion of) surfaces visible from one viewpoint. These data are useful in a variety of contexts including robot navigation, metrology (e.g., for quality control), and cases in which the complete surface actually can be captured from one direction (e.g., terrain). In addition, single scans may be used together with color images for image-based modeling and rendering (IBMR) applications, such as view interpolation or foreground/background segmentation. For almost all objects, however, a single "scan" can only capture part of the surface. Thus, for most applications in graphics it is necessary to combine the information in 3D scans taken from multiple (usually overlapping) viewpoints, making necessary the development of a "pipeline" of algorithms that operate on multiple 3D scans and attempt to produce a single, integrated 3D model. We shall refer to this use of scanning as *3D model acquisition*.

A basic 3D model acquisition pipeline may include the following stages:

- *3D scanning*: A scan is taken at some viewpoint.
- *Registration*: The transformation of the newest scan relative to other scans is computed. This may include a combination of tracking the position of the scanner, user input, feature detection and matching, or iterative minimization of scan-to-scan distance. After all scans have been acquired, a *global registration* algorithm may be used to simultaneously minimize misalignment errors over all pairs of overlapping scans.
- *Merging*: The aligned scans frequently contain significant regions in which many scans overlap. Merging these logically separate scans into a single model both reduces storage and averages away some of the scanning noise (while, hopefully, keeping the "signal"). Many merging algorithms are possible, of which the most popular approaches include averaging of implicit functions [HDD⁺92, CL96, Kaz05]; stitching or "zippering" of the original range images [TL94]; moving least squares [Lev04, ABCO⁺03, AA04b, AK04, DS05]; and directly triangulating the union of the point clouds of all scans [EM94, ABK98, ACK01a, DG04]. Some of these methods are described in detail elsewhere in this book.
- *View planning*: A decision is made about where to position the scanner relative to the object in order to perform the next scan. In most systems, this decision is left to the user, though there has also been research on automated view

planning systems [MB93, SA98]. In any case, view planning usually requires the availability of partial results from the above stages, in order to detect holes or undersampled regions in the data. In cases in which the view planning is performed by the user, these partial results must be in a form that can be efficiently rendered [RHHL02].

- *Postprocessing*: Depending on the final use for the model, the output of the merging step may undergo further processing [WPK⁺04], including noise or outlier reduction, automated filling of small remaining holes [DMGL02, SACO04, PR05], and curvature-adaptive resampling or decimation.

The form of the data that is passed among these stages can have a significant influence on the efficiency of the algorithms. Since it is the goal of this book to describe and advocate the use of point-based methods, we will confine ourselves to describing two possible representations for these points.

1. One possibility is to represent the data as *unorganized point clouds*. That is, the data consist of an unordered list of 3D point locations, together with any other per-point properties that are necessary or relevant.
2. A second possibility is to represent the data using *range images*. This is a data structure, analogous to a regular image, in which one stores not a color but a *depth* along each of a regularly spaced set of rays in space. Range images go by many names, and are also called range surfaces, depth images, depth maps, height fields, 2 ½D images, etc.

While unorganized point clouds are conceptually simple and are appropriate for all scanners and all stages of the pipeline, it is nevertheless the case that many 3D scanners naturally return a range image as their fundamental data type, and there are some advantages to maintaining the range image organization (at least until the merging stage of the pipeline). First, range images implicitly store information about empty space (i.e., the portion of each ray between the center of projection and the sample on that ray is known to be empty), which is used by some registration and merging algorithms. In addition, there is an implicit and easily calculated notion of adjacency or connectivity provided by a range image that, with some caveats, may be used to accelerate local computations such as determining normals. Of course, merely looking at neighbors in the range image does not provide connectivity directly, since one must be careful to avoid considering points lying across a depth discontinuity as being adjacent. In practice, this decision of whether or not to consider neighboring points as being adjacent is made on the basis of a heuristic, based either on a fixed depth difference threshold or a threshold on the ratio of depth difference (e.g., in z) to sample spacing (in x and y).

Because algorithms for the merging and processing stages of the 3D model acquisition pipeline are described elsewhere in this book, the remainder of this section will focus on 3D scanning technologies and registration algorithms. For the 3D scanners, our goal is not to provide a complete description of how each possible technology is implemented (such details may be found in sources such as computer vision books [Fau93, TV98, FP03a]), but to describe enough of the process to be able to understand the characteristics of the resulting data.

3.1.2 TRIANGULATION-BASED 3D SCANNERS

We begin our look at 3D scanning technologies by considering the scanners based on the principle of triangulation. All of these scanners have the common element of possessing two (or more) viewpoints on the object being scanned, and determining *correspondences* between rays from those viewpoints. That is, they are able to find rays from the two viewpoints that intersect at a common 3D point on the surface of the object, and find the coordinates of that point by computing the intersection of the rays (Figure 3.1). This, of course, requires calibration: it is necessary to know the mapping of pixels from the two views to rays in space [Tsa86, HS97].

The above description is deliberately vague about what exactly the two "viewpoints" represent. In fact, there are many possible variants of triangulation systems, differing largely in what type of device is present at the two viewpoints. Conceptually, the simplest setup is *passive stereo*, in which the viewpoints contain cameras and no controlled light is introduced into the scene. In this case, the correspondence

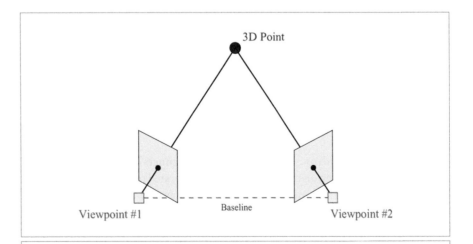

Figure 3.1: Triangulation-based 3D scanners find the positions of points on a surface by computing corresponding pixels from two viewpoints. The correspondence defines a pair of rays in space, and the intersection of the rays determines a 3D position.

problem requires finding pixels (or local neighborhoods of pixels) in one image that are as similar as possible to pixels or neighborhoods in the other. This problem proves to be difficult in many cases, so *active stereo* systems augment the setup with a spatially or temporally varying projected pattern designed to introduce features into the scene that make the correspondence problem easier to solve. This leads naturally to *structured-light* systems, in which one of the viewpoints for triangulation is replaced with a projector of known patterns of light. One important variant of structured light, namely *single-light-stripe* scanning, has been frequently implemented in commercial systems, largely because of its potentially low cost and the ability to optimize it for very high precision. Finally, *multibaseline stereo* and *structure from motion* systems rely on more than two viewpoints on the scene to obtain advantages such as higher robustness or fewer calibration requirements.

As might be guessed from the above description, there are many qualitative differences in the kinds of data that may be obtained using each of the possible triangulation setups. Some, such as passive stereo, return data that are sparse and often noisy. In contrast, light-stripe scanners return dense, high-quality data with relatively few outliers, but do so at the cost of introducing light into the scene, as well as their long acquisition time (since the stripe must be swept across the scene). There are, however, certain advantages and disadvantages shared by all triangulation-based scanners. Among the advantages are

- *Flexible working volume*: The working volume (i.e., region of space in which the object being scanned must be contained) is a function of parameters such as the field of view of the camera(s), but most importantly is directly proportional to the baseline (i.e., the distance between the two viewpoints used for triangulation). Because of this, it is relatively straightforward to design triangulation-based scanners covering a wide range of working volumes, ranging from millimeters to tens of meters. At the low end, the limits are the same as those present in all scanners that rely on light, namely that they are inappropriate when the object being scanned begins to approach the wavelength of light (400–700 nm). The limits on the high end are discussed below.

- *Low complexity and cost*: Triangulation-based scanners require calibrated cameras and, depending on the design, possibly calibrated projectors, light sources, and/or motors. These are items that are readily available in both research and commercial settings, and are less expensive and easier to work with than some of the exotic devices necessary for designs based on principles such as time of flight. In particular, the rapid technological progress in electronic imager technology in the past several years has dramatically increased the resolution and decreased the cost of digital cameras, while the development of DLP "micromirror" chips has led to speed and precision gains for light projectors.

- *Precision scales with camera resolution*: Since triangulation-based scanners rely on ordinary cameras, and since the resolution of consumer-grade cameras had advanced considerably in the past decade, it is becoming easier than ever to design scanners that have both high precision and larger working volumes.

Some of the common disadvantages are

- *Two-line-of-sight problem*: In order to return the 3D position of a point, triangulation scanners must observe that point from two separate viewpoints. Depending on the specifics of the scanner, this may cause one of two different problems. For active systems, this merely implies that the patch of surface acquired from one scanner position will typically not cover one complete side of the surface: it will have missing data in regions shadowed from one view or the other. In extreme cases, such as a deep indentation in the surface, there may not be *any* position in which the scanner may be placed such that the deepest part of the indentation is unshadowed from both views simultaneously. This is then an ultimate limitation on scannable surface geometry that cannot be overcome without changing the design (e.g., by reducing the baseline and hence the triangulation angle). For passive systems, the two-line-of-sight problem is potentially even more serious. In particular, the fact that there are regions of the surface visible from one camera but not the other can lead to difficulties in recognizing that the correspondence problem does not have a solution for those points. Special techniques, often relying on global regularization, are necessary to prevent the correspondence algorithm from returning outliers in such cases.
- *Sensitivity to shiny or translucent objects*: Essentially all triangulation systems make the implicit assumption that a diffuse, opaque surface is being scanned. Specular reflection and subsurface scattering violate this assumption and lead to errors in the returned depth estimates. For specular reflection, these errors can be arbitrarily large, as interreflection of light from multiple surfaces can lead to false correspondences between the reflections. These problems are exacerbated if the ratio of specularly reflected light to diffuse reflection is large, as is the case for dark objects. The effects of translucency on triangulation are less serious, and typically show up as a bias in the estimated depth (i.e., the scanned model is some distance *inside* the correct surface [GBR⁺01]). Of course, for completely transparent objects it is difficult to acquire depth using any optical means.
- *Difficulties for large scenes*: Although triangulation systems scale to different scene sizes better than many other designs, the practicality of scanning large scenes is limited by the difficulty of constructing and calibrating a system with a large baseline. Active triangulation systems face an additional difficulty in

that the light they introduce must be detectable over any ambient light that is present. This leads to difficulties in using active systems for outdoor scanning during daylight.

We now describe the most popular triangulation scanner designs in more detail. Note that although we present these systems in something of a logical progression, emphasizing the similarities between them, this in fact has not been how these systems have traditionally been considered in the research literature. Indeed, there has been relatively little communication and exchange of ideas between, for example, the stereo and light-stripe scanner communities. This is beginning to change, however, with the development of some hybrid scanner designs that combine ideas originally explored in different research communities.

Passive Stereo

Constructing an effective 3D scanner based on stereo is essentially synonymous with solving the correspondence problem between images taken with two cameras. Passive stereo begins with the immediate recognition that it is hopeless to solve this problem by looking at individual pixels, hence it is necessary to match *regions* in one image against the other. Depending on the amount of texture in the scene, the optimal size of the patches may range from 3×3 pixels to, for example, 25×25 pixels or even larger.

In the simplest cases, the correspondence is computed merely by evaluating some *matching cost function* between a window of pixels in one image, known as the *reference image*, and windows of pixels in the other image at various *disparities*, or displacements in pixel location. The match having the lowest cost is taken as the correct one. The matching cost function ψ may be as simple as the sum of squared differences (SSD):

$$\psi_{SSD}(\delta) = \sum_i \left(I_1(i) - I_2(i + \delta) \right)^2, \qquad (3.1)$$

where I_1 and I_2 are the two images, δ is the disparity, and the sum is overall pixels in the matching window.

Although the SSD metric corresponds strongly to the intuitive notion of similarity, several other functions are common. For example, the sum of absolute differences (SAD) function replaces the square with an absolute value, leading to less sensitivity to outliers. The normalized cross-correlation (NCC) incorporates terms that make the function sensitive only to brightness differences within the window, ignoring any overall difference in brightness between the two images:

$$\psi_{NCC}(\delta) = -\sum_i \frac{\left(I_1(i) - \bar{I}_1 \right) \left(I_2(i + \delta) - \bar{I}_2 \right)}{\sigma_1 \sigma_2}. \qquad (3.2)$$

Here, $\bar{I}$ and σ are the mean and standard deviation of pixel values in the window, as evaluated in both the left and right images. Note that, for consistency with other matching functions, the sum is negated so that lower matching cost scores indicate higher similarity.

Although a naive implementation of stereo correspondence would require, for a window in the reference image, evaluating this similarity function at all possible windows in the other image, there is an important property of multiview or *epipolar* geometry that reduces the search space greatly. This is based on the observation that the correspondence to a point in one image must lie along the projection of the ray of that pixel into the other image. Thus, given any pixel in the reference image, it is possible to compute the *epipolar line* in the other image along which the match must lie.

In fact, in many stereo systems an additional shortcut is used to simplify this search even further. This is based on the observation that any plane through the baseline connecting the centers of projection of the two cameras intersects the two image planes in a pair of lines. Any points on one of the lines must have correspondences on the *conjugate epipolar line* in the other image plane (Figure 3.2). The process of *rectification* involves warping the two images such that conjugate epipolar lines lie, for example, along horizontal scanlines, and in fact may be done such that correspondences lie along the *same* scanline in both images [Fau93]. The warps necessary for rectification may be computed from the intrinsic and extrinsic calibration of the two cameras (i.e., the field of view and relative position and orientation), and performing the warps is typically relatively fast compared to the rest of the correspondence-finding process.

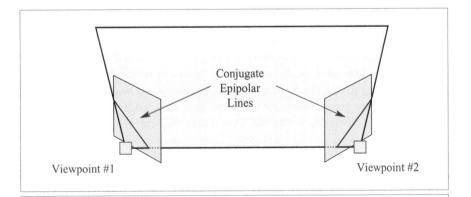

Conjugate
Epipolar
Lines

Viewpoint #1   Viewpoint #2

Figure 3.2: Each plane passing through the baseline intersects the two image planes in a pair of *conjugate epipolar lines*. All matches to points on the line in one image must lie on the conjugate line in the other image.

So, finding the correspondence between windows can be reduced to considering one window in the rectified reference image and evaluating the matching function for windows in the other rectified image, considering all possible horizontal disparities. The disparity yielding the highest similarity is chosen as the correct one (possibly with some threshold on the similarity value used to eliminate false matches), and rays corresponding to the two corresponding points are triangulated to find a 3D location. Many things can still go wrong, however. First, it is certainly the case that two image windows at the location of the correct match can look dissimilar. This can be because of the presence of nondiffuse materials, or because the surface is tilted a different amount relative to the two cameras, leading to a difference in the amount of foreshortening present in the two views. To address the first of these problems, one may use a matching metric such as NCC, which tends to be more robust to small differences in appearance, or a technique such as Helmholtz stereopsis (an active method), which relies on the reciprocity of Bidirectional Reflectance Distribution Functions (BRDFs) to compensate for non-Lambertian reflectance [ZBK02]. To address the problem of differential foreshortening, a common method is to use an iterative technique in which a first round of correspondence finding is used to estimate the shape of the surface, which in turn is used in a second round to warp the images of windows to account for the estimated foreshortening [LK81]. The process may be repeated a few times to obtain more precise correspondence estimates.

The above problems are, however, minor compared to the major weakness of passive stereo, which is the presence of ambiguous matches. Since the correspondence finding is at the mercy of the brightness variations that occur naturally in the scene, the presence of either regions of constant color or repeated texture can lead to equally low matching cost at multiple disparities. Of the many methods that have been developed to address this problem, here we will consider two.

One method for dealing with ambiguous matches involves adapting the window size, shape, and weighting to the data themselves. The basic idea is that larger windows can reduce ambiguity, but also lead to more blurring in the estimated shape. Thus, windows should be expanded locally, and only in regions in which this is necessary to provide unambiguous correspondence. Moreover, the pixels near the center of the window should be given more weight than pixels near the edge, in an effort to preserve local detail when this is possible. One system implementing this approach is described by Scharstein and Szeliski [SS98]. They propose to start with the matching score for single-pixel windows and "diffuse" a fraction of the matching score from neighboring pixels in cases in which this reduces the matching certainty. The latter property is measured using metrics such as winner margin (i.e., what is the difference in the matching score between the best match and the next-best match) or entropy of the matching scores across all disparities.

An alternate method for reducing the errors due to ambiguous matches relies on regularization. That is, a scoring function is constructed that considers not only the matching score at each location, but also the extent to which the computed disparities are smooth across the scene. The latter is measured locally, as the difference between the disparity at each location and at its neighbors, but in practice it should be a non-linear function of the disparity difference to prevent excessive blurring across true depth discontinuities. For example, a function such as the following is often used:

$$V(i,j) = \min(|\delta_i - \delta_j|, K), \tag{3.3}$$

where a penalty V is assigned to the disparities δ found at neighboring pixels i and j. The threshold K represents the disparity difference considered to be a true depth discontinuity, and no additional penalty is applied for greater jumps in disparity.

One may thus construct an energy function consisting of both matching and regularization terms, and attempt to compute a global assignment of disparities that minimizes the energy. Unfortunately, such an energy function invariably contains many local minima and minimizing it is provably NP-hard. Most practical algorithms use heuristics to find approximate minima of this function, using methods such as simulated annealing. Recent work by Boykov et al., for example, has demonstrated how to use graph min-cut algorithms to compute excellent approximations to the minimum of this function [BVZ01], while work of Meltzer et al. has shown that in some cases it is possible to compute the global minimum of the energy function in reasonable time, though of course there are no guarantees of fast running time [MYW05].

Ultimately, both the variable window-size and regularization approaches serve to return dense depth estimates by interpolating and extrapolating information from locations at which the correspondences are truly unambiguous. This motivates an alternative general approach to correspondence finding that first performs *feature detection* to locate regions in the image likely to have unambiguous matches, then simply tries to match those features between the two images. Although these methods return sparse correspondences, such matches are often of consistently high quality and, depending on the application, may be more useful than the dense but low-quality matches returned by correlation-based approaches. One such system is the Marr-Poggio method, which is based on the proposition that image edges, in conjunction with the epipolar constraint, make good features for matching [MP79]. The edges are detected and matched using a dynamic programming algorithm, which includes a regularization component that attempts to preserve the relative ordering of matches between the two images. The entire process is repeated in a coarse-to-fine manner, leading to coarse matching of the most important edges at early rounds followed by smaller-scale matches of the fine details in the later rounds (during which less smoothing is performed).

Characteristics   Passive methods differ from most of the other techniques considered in this section in that most of the characteristics of the datasets they produce, including density, accuracy, and presence of outliers, depend almost exclusively on the object or scene being acquired, rather than on the cameras and setup of the scanner itself. In the best case, namely scenes with significant texture, stereo can return accurate estimates of depth, and has the advantages of lowest equipment cost and the ability to return depth from a pair of frames taken at a single time instant. The depth maps in this case are also relatively dense, though the maximally accurate matches are still restricted to brightness or color edges in the scene. For this reason, in many applications the output of stereo is best suited to the unorganized point cloud representation. As scene contrast decreases, of course, so do data density and accuracy.

Active Stereo

In situations that permit additional light to be introduced into the scene, significant gains in robustness, accuracy, and data density may be obtained by moving to an active-stereo method. The typical assumption is that a pattern of light is projected into the scene, though the projector or other device used to introduce the light is not itself calibrated with respect to the cameras. The purpose of the projected light is, therefore, purely to reduce the ambiguity of stereo matching by introducing additional visible features in the scene.

The simplest way to incorporate an active element into stereo is to project a static pattern consisting of a high-frequency texture, such as an array of dots, a grid of lines, or even a random binary pattern. A traditional passive-stereo algorithm is run without modification on the resulting images, retaining the advantages described above while minimizing the presence of ambiguous matches. Alternatively, special algorithms that take advantage of knowledge of the projected pattern may be used. This is especially popular with patterns that are regular grids or arrays of dots [PGO96], and algorithms that take advantage of surface continuity to look for neighboring dots or corners are possible. Algorithms such as these are especially effective when acquiring relatively smooth objects with few depth discontinuities, and a popular application is scanning of faces. More complex spatial patterns are also possible, with some based, for example, on arrays of colored dots having specified uniqueness properties. We will look at such patterns in greater detail in the section on structured light.

An alternative way of extending passive stereo to include active lighting is to consider the time dimension. The idea behind temporal active stereo is to project a time-varying pattern into the scene, permitting the stereo matching functions to be evaluated over windows that have *temporal*, rather than spatial, extent [DC01, DNRR05]. As long as each pixel accumulates a unique pattern of lighting over time, the correspondences may be computed robustly using windows that have spatial extent of a single pixel. This leads to greater precision in the reconstruction, and typically reveals significantly more surface detail than methods using spatial windows greater than one pixel.

In fact, with good temporal illumination the ultimate limit on the accuracy of surface reconstruction relies heavily on the ability to perform good *subpixel estimation* of correspondence. A simple implementation of this is to find the best integer match, then consider the matching cost for the two immediately neighboring pixels. By fitting a parabola to the three samples of the matching-cost-versus-position function, one may analytically find the minimum of the parabola and take its (noninteger) location as the best match. More complex schemes for subpixel matching are possible, and Nehab et al. [NRD05] show that it is necessary to simultaneously refine subpixel positions in both images to avoid bias and noise in the estimates.

While active stereo with static patterns operates on one frame at a time, hence allowing for moving objects, temporal stereo requires the object to remain still for many frames. Using matching with windows having both spatial and temporal extent, however, allows for systems that balance between the high precision of temporal stereo and the tolerance to movement of spatial stereo. Such *spacetime stereo* systems can be tuned for different speeds of motion, by adjusting the relative widths of the matching window in space and time [DNRR05], and, by estimating the motion that is present, can use diagonal windows through space-time to obtain the highest robustness and accuracy [ZCS03]. Recent work has demonstrated the ability of such systems to capture moving objects such as faces [ZSCS04].

Characteristics   The data returned by active stereo systems can be of high quality, and it is not uncommon to have noise in depth less than one-tenth of the sample spacing. The scanning also tends to be robust, with few outlier points (with some exceptions near depth discontinuities). The points returned are dense on the surface (though subject to the two-line-of-sight problem, or even a three-line-of-sight problem if the illumination source is shadowed), meaning that some algorithms can take advantage of the space carving and implicit connectivity provided by a range image representation. Relative to passive stereo, therefore, active stereo systems tend to return better data, at the cost of the requirement to introduce light into the scene and the inability to acquire the color of objects simultaneously with their shape.

Structured Light

Conceptually, structured-light systems may be thought of as active stereo systems in which the second camera is eliminated and the source of illumination is itself considered to be one of the viewpoints on the scene. This has a few disadvantages relative to active stereo, in that it imposes requirements on how precise the active light must be, and requires that it be calibrated (for both intrinsics and extrinsics). This precludes the use of space- or time-varying, yet uncontrolled illumination (which has been referred to as "unstructured light"), and requires full control over the light (and, for temporal systems, synchronization to the camera). On the other hand, structured-light systems have the advantage of reducing the amount of equipment that is required and, more importantly, allowing for algorithms that take advantage of the epipolar constraints between the camera and projector.

It is this latter characteristic that has driven the development of structured-light systems based on "light codes" [PA82, Bes88]. These are spatial or temporal (or, indeed, space-time) patterns of projected light that are carefully designed so that every point visible from the camera is guaranteed to correspond uniquely to one ray from the projector. For example, a spatial light code may consist of an array of colored dots [DN96] having the property that every local subset of $n \times n$ dots has a different pattern of colors from every other. Alternatively, the code may consist of *stripes* perpendicular to the camera-projector baseline [BK87, CKS98], with the property that any n adjacent stripes have a unique color pattern. In this case, the epipolar constraint between the camera and projector is implicitly used: the triangulation proceeds by intersecting a *ray* from the camera with a *plane* from the projector (Figure 3.3). Because stripe codes are easier to design and easier to detect

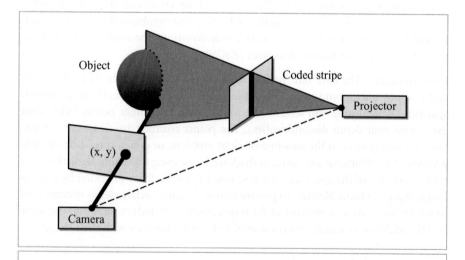

Figure 3.3: Structured-light systems frequently code only stripes of light from the projector, and perform ray-plane intersection to find 3D geometry.

than codes of dots, most structured-light systems, whether spatial or temporal, use some type of stripe coding.

Temporal structured-light systems provide perhaps the most "bang for the buck" in that they return high-quality 3D data for static objects while being easy and inexpensive to build. Indeed, homemade structured light scanners are frequently found in research labs, and they make excellent student projects. Section 3.2 describes a practical scanning system based on temporal structured light.

The most popular temporal structured-light scanners are based on binary stripe coding (i.e., each stripe is either on or off at each frame in time), and the most popular scheme for coding the stripes is based on the *binary Gray code* [BER76]. The latter is a way of arranging the 2^n binary numbers of n bits such that adjacent codewords differ only in one bit (this property leads to greater robustness in "decoding" the observed pattern). The reflected code, the most popular way of constructing a Gray code, arises from the following simple recipe:

- The reflected code for one bit is 0, 1.
- The reflected code for n bits consists of the code for $n - 1$ bits, prefixing each element by a 0, followed by the *reverse* of the code for $n - 1$ bits, prefixing each element by a 1.

Each codeword is assigned to a stripe, and at frame k, each stripe is colored black or white depending on the value of its k-th bit. The resulting pattern consists of a series of wide stripes on early frames, with the stripes becoming progressively narrower with each frame (Figure 3.4). Additional all-white and all-black frames are frequently included to allow compensation for surface reflectance and ambient illumination. Even with these additional frames, scanning is usually relatively fast, with the number of required frames being logarithmic in the number of projector stripes.

Two other temporal structured-light codes are frequently encountered, and are worthy of mention. The *phase-shifting* code augments a low-resolution Gray code with a sequence of black-and-white stripes, each several projector pixels wide. The stripes are shifted by one pixel on successive frames, leading to greater robustness and better subpixel matching than is achievable with full-resolution Gray codes (which may include very narrow stripes, several of which can fall on the same camera pixel). The cost for this is the requirement for slightly more total frames in order to uniquely code a fixed number of projector stripes. Moving away from binary codes, the *gray wedge* technique uses only two frames: an all-white frame and a frame in which stripe intensity smoothly varies from black on one side to white on the other [CH85]. The identity of the stripe is found by dividing the intensities observed on the two frames.

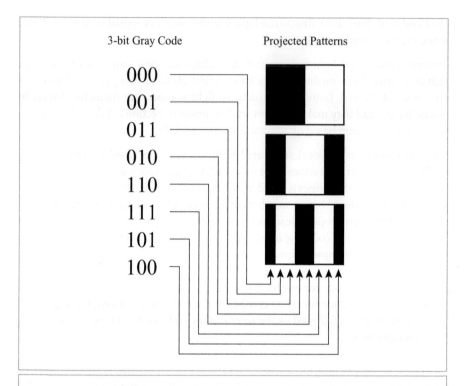

Figure 3.4: Example of a Gray code and the resulting frames that would be projected in a structured-light system.

Most structured-light systems are either purely spatial or purely temporal, but there has been some work on spatiotemporal codes as well. For example, Hall-Holt and Rusinkiewicz introduced a code in which each *pair* of adjacent stripes, as seen over *n* frames, is unique [HHR01]. As with spacetime stereo techniques, adjusting the relative spatial and temporal extent of the code-carrying windows provides for a natural trade-off between the degree of spatial continuity (i.e., surface smoothness) and temporal continuity (i.e., motion) that is assumed. In this case, the method allows for slow motion of the object while assuming relatively little surface continuity. The stripe pairs (or, more specifically, the stripe boundaries) are tracked over time to provide robust and relatively dense 3D estimates at video rates. The scanner may be combined with real-time alignment, merging, and point-rendering methods to enable the entire 3D model acquisition pipeline to run in real time [RHHL02]. More recent research by Koninckx and van Gool has shown how structured-light codes may be adapted to the scene in real time, providing for both higher accuracy and greater robustness [KPDG05].

Characteristics   The data returned by structured-light systems qualitatively share many features with active stereo. Datasets tend to be accurate, dense, and large. Outliers are few, and are mostly caused by depth discontinuities or specular reflections. One interesting difference is the role played by surface texture (i.e., reflectance variation): as opposed to active stereo systems, which are often helped by texture, the data returned by structured-light systems are usually degraded by variations in reflectance. Phenomena such as "texture embossing," in which reflectance variations show up as systematic biases in estimated depth, are often observed [CL95]. In addition, structured-light systems often suffer from missing data in dark regions of the surface, where the projected light patterns cannot be detected.

Light Stripe

A simple way of thinking about light-stripe scanners is that they are structured-light scanners with a pattern that illuminates only one stripe per frame. The visual effect is that of a stripe being swept slowly across the surface, tracing out a single 2D "slice" of geometry at each point in time. This description should make it clear that light-stripe triangulation scanners are significantly slower than, for example, Gray code structured-light systems, but the single-stripe configuration allows for greater optimization of the physical scanner setup, leading to greater accuracy.

The first major optimization performed on light-stripe systems is to use a laser as the light source. This allows the stripe to be made bright and consistent, leading to lower sensitivity to ambient light (especially if a narrow-band filter is used in front of the camera). The use of a laser also allows the stripe to be focused to a very narrow width, leading to high resolution. Next, the laser-stripe generator and camera are often mounted to each other, with the scanning motion consisting of moving the laser and camera as a rigid assembly (Figure 3.5a). This configuration can simplify calibration, but more importantly it results in a working volume with a more useful shape and more uniform sample spacing than the intersection of two pyramids typical of structured-light systems (Figure 3.5b–c). There is no reason to restrict the motion to be purely translational, and configurations based on rotation of either the laser-camera scanhead or of the object itself are common. Finally, the optics of the camera in a laser-stripe system may be optimized to ensure that the image of the laser stripe is in focus, by tilting the sensor relative to the optical system (the "Scheimpflug principle"). In addition, cylindrical lenses may be used to effect the desired trade-off between depth of working volume and depth resolution. Manufacturers of high-quality laser scanners, such as Cyberware Corp., typically use all of these principles.

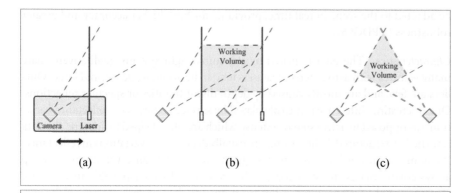

Figure 3.5: (*a*) Laser-stripe scanners are frequently designed with the laser and camera mounted rigidly on a translating assembly. This results in a working volume with a more useful shape and even sampling (*b*), as compared to the working volume of a structured-light scanner (*c*).

The processing to extract depth from a light-stripe scanner may broadly proceed along either spatial or temporal lines. The "spatial" approach to processing treats each frame in time separately, and finds the peak of the light stripe along each scanline. The peakfinding can be based simply on maximum intensity, but it is more stable to use the mean of a Gaussian fit to the intensity profile along a scanline. Temporal processing, in contrast, treats each camera pixel independently, and finds the time instant at which it achieves the highest intensity. Temporal processing in general tends to result in fewer artifacts than spatial, but as shown by Curless and Levoy the optimal processing is in fact spatiotemporal, in which peaks are found along paths angled through space-time [CL95]. Despite this, many laser triangulation systems today use spatial processing because it is the simplest and least computationally expensive (data are naturally gathered and organized spatially, so temporal processing requires transposing the data and spacetime processing requires a more complex rotation).

Characteristics   The data produced by light-stripe scanners are among the highest in quality, and the use of laser light results in little missing data (other than due to occlusion of the camera or laser) and few outliers. Datasets are dense, and are most naturally organized as range images.

Multiview Triangulation and Structure from Motion

Any of the above techniques can be combined with additional calibrated cameras, leading to multiview techniques. Multiview stereo (both active and passive) has been explored in greatest detail, due to the ability of the additional cameras to reduce the ambiguity inherent in stereo matching [OK93]. This relies on the observation that an incorrect match from a pair of cameras, leading to an incorrect 3D position, will not in general appear to match when projected to a third viewpoint. Incorrect matches may appear consistent between pairs (or small subsets) of cameras, but only the true matches are likely to be consistent between all cameras. Passive multiview systems therefore suffer from significantly fewer false correspondences between regions that appear similar, though of course the introduction of additional cameras does nothing to improve the situation in textureless regions. Single-pattern *active* multiview stereo systems are fairly popular, and can return relatively dense 3D estimates with high reliability.

In one sense, structure from motion (SfM) represents a limiting case of multiview stereo: there are many "cameras" placed densely together. In practice, the many views are acquired with a video camera that is moved throughout a scene. Features are detected in the video stream and are tracked over many frames, thus establishing correspondence. The major difference, however, between multiview stereo and SfM techniques is the portion of the algorithm that is considered to be difficult. For stereo, the difficulty is in finding correspondences; for SfM, the feature-tracking problem is relatively easy, and the challenge is performing the 3D reconstruction.

The interesting feature of most SfM techniques is that they do not require the camera to be calibrated (some methods require intrinsic calibration, however): they solve for the camera parameters simultaneously with solving for the 3D positions of the tracked features. The reason this is possible becomes clear if we consider the number of knowns and unknowns. Assume that we have p feature points that have been tracked for n frames. At each frame, we know the 2D position of each point in the image, leading to $2np$ knowns. In contrast, the unknowns for which we must solve are the 3D positions of the points, as well as the camera parameters (which, considering only the extrinsics, are the camera position and orientation at each frame). Thus, there are only $3p + 6n$ unknowns, which given enough points and enough frames can be fewer than the number of knowns. Of course, there are certain global unknowns that can never be solved for, such as the absolute scale of the scene. Methods for solving the SfM problem include a popular linear method [TK92] that assumes weak perspective (i.e., assumes that the scale of the scene is small relative to the distance to the camera), as well as full nonlinear bundle adjustment algorithms [PGV+04].

Characteristics Both structure from motion and multiview stereo systems return sparse, though accurate, depth estimates. In addition, SfM, in contrast with most of the techniques considered here, can return points from all around an object, rather than just from one direction. Unorganized point clouds are therefore the appropriate representation.

3.1.3 OTHER 3D SCANNING TECHNOLOGIES

There exist several methods for 3D shape acquisition that are based on technologies fundamentally different from triangulation. While they are sometimes less accurate than triangulation scanners, they are also more appropriate in certain regimes such as very large or very small scenes. Here we consider some of the most popular alternative scanning technologies.

Pulsed and Modulated Time of Flight

Although SONAR and RADAR are both relatively well-known methods for obtaining 3D distances at large scales, there is a smaller-scale cousin, LIDAR (light detection and ranging), that uses the round-trip time of light between the scanner and the scene to estimate depth. One way to use the LIDAR principle involves firing a short (often on the order of picoseconds) pulse of light, and timing how long it takes to return. A rotating mirror is used to change the direction of the pulses, and so a depth map is built up one point at a time. Pulsed time-of-flight scanners are usually expensive, require long scanning times, and have poor accuracy in absolute terms (many millimeters or larger, with slow progress on the technology to reduce this—after all, this requires picosecond-level timing). Nevertheless, they have some significant strengths. First, these scanners have large working volumes, often measured in tens or hundreds of meters. Thus, their *relative* depth accuracy can be quite significant. In addition, they require only a single line of sight to the surface point being scanned, since the light pulse returns along the same path along which it was projected. Therefore, these systems can both acquire geometry that may be impossible to scan using triangulation systems, and are significantly more practical for large scenes since they do not require a long, calibrated baseline. For this reason, pulsed time of flight is the dominant scanning technology used for large objects such as building interiors or exteriors.

The other main technology that makes use of time of flight relies on modulation. A continuous beam of laser light is projected, with its intensity modulated at a high frequency. The reflected light is then modulated at the same frequency, allowing the measurement of a signal that depends on the phase difference between the outgoing and reflected beams. Since this phase difference depends on the distance between the scanner and the scene, it may be converted to a depth measurement. Different variants of this scheme may measure either a single point or a complete 2D array of range pixels at a time. The choice of modulation frequency is important: too low a frequency will give poor depth accuracy, while too high a frequency will allow for only a shallow range of depths before the depths "wrap around" (because of the 2π ambiguity in phase). To improve on this, a series of sweeps using different modulation frequencies can be used to disambiguate the depths while retaining high accuracy.

In practice, most of these systems are optimized for working volumes of a few meters (i.e., room-sized) and are a natural choice for measuring people, furniture, etc.

Shape from Silhouettes and Other Space-carving Methods

The idea behind most space-carving methods is to maintain an estimate of which portions of space are occupied and which are not. This estimate is initialized to mark the whole working volume as occupied, and as information about empty space is acquired it is used to "carve off" regions. The effect is not unlike sculpting, in that material may only be removed, not added, to the shape estimate.

While some 3D scan-merging methods, such as VRIP [CL96], make use of space carving in addition to traditional depth estimates, there have been some 3D acquisition systems that rely purely on space carving. The most popular rely on the ability to distinguish the object's exterior silhouette (i.e., the boundary between the object and the background) in each of a set of calibrated views [MTSA97, MBR+00]. Space carving is performed based purely on this information, resulting in a final model that is a superset of the original object. The intermediate model representation used during the carving may be a binary voxel (occupancy) grid or a polyhedron, or for image-based applications, the 3D model might not be reconstructed directly (with the method relying on mapping candidate points into the original images and testing them against the silhouettes). In all cases, there is a restriction on the types of objects whose shape may be recovered: there are some features such as spherical concavities that silhouette carving cannot recover. In general, with a sufficient number of views, the reconstruction converges to the *line hull* of the original shape. The strength of shape from silhouettes, therefore, is not in precise reconstruction but rather in obtaining a rough 3D model with little effort.

A related technique, sitting somewhere between space carving and multiview triangulation, is *voxel coloring* [SD99]. In this system, the shape being recovered is represented as a voxel grid and is carved from the outside in. Each voxel on the currently outermost layer is considered in turn, and is projected into all of the available views. A consistency metric is evaluated across all the views, testing whether the colors visible from the different cameras are the same. If the colors are inconsistent, the voxel is carved away. This algorithm results in reconstructions that have the character of multiview stereo in regions with significant texture, but that look more like space-carving results in regions of constant color.

One fact that should be noted about all carving methods is that they, by definition, produce a watertight surface as output. This property is important for many applications including rendering, simulation, and 3D hardcopy output. In contrast, most other 3D acquisition methods do not produce watertight surfaces automatically and require special support in the scan merging or holefilling stages of the pipeline.

Shape from Shading and Photometric Stereo

The brightness of a surface depends on its orientation relative to light sources, and there exist techniques that use this to estimate surface normals. Although this is different from obtaining 3D positions directly, the normals may be "integrated" to obtain shape, possibly with some additional stability provided by sparse or rough depth estimates obtained using a different method. Although passive shape from shading is of some interest, especially since it is clear that the human visual system uses such shading cues, most practical systems are active methods that rely on multiple calibrated, controlled light sources. These are known generally as *photometric stereo* [Woo80, RTG97]. Note that, despite the use of the word stereo, this is a single-view method and it is the lights of which there are two or more.

The most direct photometric stereo methods assume Lambertian reflectance and three light sources of known direction and radiance. The object is imaged under each light source in turn, and at each pixel we know that

$$I_i = L_i \, \rho \, (\mathbf{n} \cdot \mathbf{l}_i), \tag{3.4}$$

where I_i is the observed pixel intensity, L_i is the radiance of the light source, and $\mathbf{l}_i$ is the direction to the i-th light source. The unknowns are ρ, the diffuse albedo of the surface, and the surface normal $\mathbf{n}$. Given three such measurements, we can write

$$\begin{pmatrix} l_{1,x} & l_{1,y} & l_{1,z} \\ l_{2,x} & l_{2,y} & l_{2,z} \\ l_{3,x} & l_{3,y} & l_{3,z} \end{pmatrix} \begin{pmatrix} \rho n_x \\ \rho n_y \\ \rho n_z \end{pmatrix} = \begin{pmatrix} I_1/L_1 \\ I_2/L_2 \\ I_3/L_3 \end{pmatrix} \tag{3.5}$$

and solve for the vector $\rho\mathbf{n}$. Since we know that the normal is unit length, we obtain both it and the albedo (in practice, the albedos are determined up to a constant, and finding them in absolute terms requires calibrating the gain of the camera, vignetting in the lens system, etc.). If there are more than three light sources, the resulting overconstrained system may be solved using least squares, or the most reliable three lights may be used, eliminating shadowed regions and specular highlights [RTG97]. In order to avoid singularities in the solution, the three lights plus the camera must be noncoplanar.

As we have mentioned, photometric stereo is very well suited for use in combination with other techniques that return noisy, inaccurate, or sparse depth estimates. When used in combination with scanners returning dense depths, such as those based on structured light, the normals may be associated one to one with the 3D points, for use in rendering or accurate surface reconstruction. The noise present in these normals is generally lower than in the surfaces obtained from triangulation, though photometric stereo is susceptible to systematic low-frequency bias resulting from non-Lambertian surfaces or imperfect estimation of light source radiance and position.

Nehab et al. have demonstrated that by combining the high-frequency information obtained using photometric stereo with the low-frequency information from triangulation, the benefits of both types of scanners may be obtained while avoiding their drawbacks [NRDR05].

A somewhat related technique to shape from shading is shape from texture, which relies on either the variation in density of texture elements or the foreshortening of individual elements to estimate surface orientation. Another similar technique is shape from specularity, which uses the presence of specular highlights to obtain (usually sparse) orientation measurements.

Shape from Focus and Defocus

It is possible to construct systems that determine depth based on the focus distance at which a lens must be set to observe objects with greatest clarity ("shape from focus") or based on *how* out-of-focus objects appear at a fixed lens setting ("shape from defocus"). Real-time systems have been demonstrated using active depth from defocus, which relies on a projected pattern of dots [NN94].

3.1.4 SCAN ALIGNMENT

Since most types of scanners return data from only one part of the object at a time, it is necessary to obtain multiple scans and align them together. The alignment stage is not necessary, of course, if the motion of the scanner and object relative to each other are calibrated, but in many instances this is not possible. However, provided the geometry or color of the object is sufficiently distinctive, and provided there is sufficient overlap in the scanned regions, the data themselves may be used to align the different scans to each other. Alignment based on color is conceptually similar to image feature matching, and many of the same techniques that are used for stereo correspondence are applicable. Here we focus on alignment techniques that use geometric information, splitting them into methods that obtain an initial rough estimate for the alignment, methods that refine the alignment between a pair of scans, and methods that attempt to balance the pairwise registration errors across all pairs of overlapping scans.

Initial Alignment

The simplest method for obtaining an initial alignment, of course, is to ask the user. A typical user interface displays a pair of scans, then either provides the capability for directly moving the scans, using, for example, a virtual trackball interface, or allows the user to click on at least three pairs of corresponding points and solves for the optimal transformation. Despite the fact that this manual method does not sound particularly elegant or exciting, it should not be overlooked: automated methods for computing initial alignment can be slow, not robust, and tricky to implement correctly. Even for a large scanning session, manual initial alignment can be the fastest and most reliable technique.

In situations in which automated initial alignment is desirable, the general technique is as follows:

1. **Find distinctive feature points** on each scan.
2. **Compute local *shape descriptors*** characterizing the surface geometry around the features [Kaz04].
3. **Propose correspondences** between features by matching similar descriptors.
4. **Compute the rigid-body transform** that best aligns corresponding features.
5. **Verify** that the proposed alignment is reasonable, by checking the scan-to-scan distance at a large number of points. If the alignment does not seem plausible, repeat using a different set of proposed correspondences.

There are many possible variations on this broad outline, and to a large extent greater sophistication in one stage may compensate for simplicity in another. For example, if the feature points are particularly distinctive and are consistently found in similar locations on different scans, there may not be a need for a shape descriptor: all triplets of feature correspondences may simply be tried [CH99]. Conversely, if a sophisticated shape descriptor is used it may be sufficient to compute that descriptor at random locations on the surface [JH99, HH03]. Finally, in many situations it is not unreasonable to simply use a brute-force algorithm, testing a sparse sampling of possible rotations and translations.

Iterative Pairwise Registration Using ICP

The ICP (originally iterative closest point, though iterative corresponding point is perhaps a better expansion for the abbreviation) algorithm has become the dominant method for pairwise alignment of 3D models based purely on the geometry, and sometimes color, of the meshes. ICP starts with two meshes and an initial guess for their relative rigid-body transform, and iteratively refines the transform by repeatedly generating pairs of corresponding points on the meshes and finding the transformation that minimizes an error metric, such as the sum of squared point-to-point distances. The original ICP algorithm computed the "correspondences" as being, for each point on one mesh, the *closest* point on the other mesh (Figure 3.6).

Since the introduction of ICP by Besl and McKay [BM92], many variants have been introduced on the basic ICP concept. We may classify these variants as affecting one of six stages of the algorithm:

1. **Selection** of some set of points in one or both meshes.
2. **Matching** these points to samples in the other mesh.
3. **Weighting** the corresponding pairs appropriately.

Figure 3.6: In the ICP algorithm, points on one scan (blue) are selected and matched to the *closest* points on the other scan (red). One of the scans is moved such as to minimize the distances between pairs of points and the process is iterated until convergence.

4. **Rejecting** certain pairs based on looking at each pair individually or considering the entire set of pairs.
5. Assigning an **error metric** to the current alignment, based on the point pairs.
6. **Minimizing** the error metric.

A survey of many of these variants is available [RL01a], so here we will restrict the description to variants generally regarded as current "best practice."

Point Selection   A reasonable method for selecting points at each iteration is simply random sampling of points on *both* scans, with a few hundred to a few thousand points usually sufficient for good stability. However, in difficult cases in which some components of the transform are restricted by features on a relatively small portion of the mesh, greater care must be taken to sample points that do a good job of constraining the transformation. A simple option is to estimate normals on the scan, then sample points having as uniform a distribution of normals as possible. A more theoretically well-grounded method, proposed by Gelfand et al., directly considers the error metric being minimized, performs an eigenanalysis on the linear system being solved, and uses the eigenvalues of the system to determine which eigenvectors are most underconstrained. Sampling according to these criteria ensures that all components of the transformation are well constrained [GIRL03].

Matching   Although the distinguishing feature of ICP-like algorithms is that they use the closest point (given the current best estimate of the transformation) as the approximation for the corresponding point at each iteration, greater stability and faster convergence may be achieved by instead matching to the *closest compatible* point, using some compatibility criterion. Criteria based on color, normals, curvature, etc. have been proposed, and all improve performance in certain cases [GRB94, Pul99, SLW02]. A simple condition, such as that normals should be within 45° of each other, can improve convergence at minimal cost. In all cases, a spatial data structure such as a K-d-tree may be used to accelerate the closest-point computations.

Weighting   Although many weighting schemes based on uncertainty, compatibility, point-to-point distance, and other criteria have been proposed, in most cases the effect of weighting on convergence rate tends to be small and highly data dependent.

Rejection   Since ICP is fundamentally a least squares approach, it is necessary to perform outlier rejection to avoid contamination of the results by incorrect matches. A good, all-purpose approach is to reject pairs whose point-to-point distance is larger than some small multiple of the median distance. In cases in which ICP is being performed on meshes or range images, such that it is possible to determine which points are on mesh boundaries, we additionally recommend rejecting all pairs containing such edge points (Figure 3.7). This strategy avoids erroneous pairings (that cause a systematic bias in the estimated transform) in cases when the overlap between scans is not complete [TL94].

Error Metric   The original ICP algorithm minimized the sum of squared point-to-point distances among corresponding pairs of points, but a variant by Chen and Medioni proposed using point-to-plane distances instead [CM92] (Figure 3.8). That is, the algorithm minimizes the distance from one point to the plane containing the other point and perpendicular to its normal. This has the effect of making it easy to move the scans "along" the surface, leading to dramatically (order of magnitude) faster convergence in many cases.

Mitra et al. have also proposed precomputing a piecewise-quadric approximation for the function representing the distance to one of the scans and evaluating the function at locations on the other scan [MGPG04]. A special data structure is used

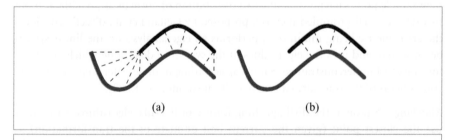

(a)   (b)

Figure 3.7: (*a*) When two meshes to be aligned do not overlap completely (as is the case for most real-world data), allowing correspondences involving points on mesh boundaries can introduce a systematic bias into the alignment. (*b*) Disallowing such pairs eliminates many of these incorrect correspondences.

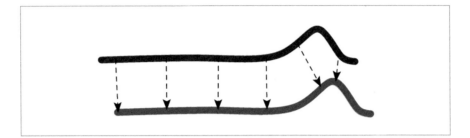

Figure 3.8: The point-to-plane metric for ICP captures the notion that sliding two planes along each other does not affect the distance between them. In this example, the two scans are mostly planar, with only the small bump at right constraining the left-to-right component of the translation. Using the original point-to-point minimization, however, the point pairs in the flat region will prevent the scans from "sliding along each other" to reach the correct transformation (it is useful to think of them as small springs that are attempting to contract). In this situation, using the point-to-plane metric will lead to significantly faster convergence.

to store this approximation, and the parameters of the quadric are used directly during a Newton's method-style minimization. This provides the stability of point-to-point minimization far away from the correct minimum while retaining the high convergence rate of point-to-plane minimization once the transformation is close to correct.

Minimization   While there exist closed-form solutions for the rotation and translation that minimize point-to-point distance [ELF97], there are no analogous methods for the recommended point-to-plane minimization. Instead, the recommended method is as follows.

Assume we have a collection of points $(\mathbf{p}_i, \mathbf{q}_i)$ with normals $\mathbf{n}_i$. We want to determine the optimal rotation and translation to be applied to the first collection of points (i.e., the $\mathbf{p}_i$) to bring them into alignment with the second (i.e., the $\mathbf{q}_i$). Thus, we want to minimize the alignment error

$$\varepsilon = \sum_i \left[(\mathbf{R}\mathbf{p}_i + \mathbf{t} - \mathbf{q}_i) \cdot \mathbf{n}_i \right]^2 \qquad (3.6)$$

with respect to the rotation $\mathbf{R}$ and translation $\mathbf{t}$.

The rotation is a nonlinear function, incorporating sines and cosines of the rotation angles. If, however, we assume that incremental rotations will be small, it is possible to linearize the rotations, approximating $\cos\theta$ by 1 and $\sin\theta$ by θ. For example, in the case of rotation in x,

$$
\mathbf{R}_x \;\; = \;\;
\begin{pmatrix}
1 & 0 & 0 \\
0 & \cos r_x & -\sin r_x \\
0 & \sin r_x & \cos r_x
\end{pmatrix}
\;\; \approx \;\;
\begin{pmatrix}
1 & 0 & 0 \\
0 & 1 & -r_x \\
0 & r_x & 1
\end{pmatrix}.
\tag{3.7}
$$

Thus, the full rotation may be approximated as

$$
\mathbf{R} \approx
\begin{pmatrix}
1 & -r_z & r_y \\
r_z & 1 & -r_x \\
-r_y & r_x & 1
\end{pmatrix},
\tag{3.8}
$$

for rotations r_x, r_y, and r_z around the x, y, and z axes, respectively.

Defining

$$
\mathbf{c} = \mathbf{p} \times \mathbf{n}, \qquad
\mathbf{r} =
\begin{pmatrix}
r_x \\
r_y \\
r_z
\end{pmatrix}
\tag{3.9}
$$

and substituting Equation (3.8) into (3.6), we obtain

$$
\varepsilon = \sum_i \left[(\mathbf{p}_i - \mathbf{q}_i) \cdot \mathbf{n}_i + \mathbf{t} \cdot \mathbf{n}_i + \mathbf{r} \cdot \mathbf{c}_i \right]^2.
\tag{3.10}
$$

We now minimize ε with respect to r_x, r_y, r_z, t_x, t_y, and t_z, leading to the following linear system:

$$
\left[\sum_i \begin{pmatrix} \mathbf{c}_i \\ \mathbf{n}_i \end{pmatrix} (\mathbf{c}_i \;\; \mathbf{n}_i) \right]
\begin{pmatrix} \mathbf{r} \\ \mathbf{t} \end{pmatrix}
= - \sum_i ((\mathbf{p}_i - \mathbf{q}_i) \cdot \mathbf{n}_i)
\begin{pmatrix} \mathbf{c}_i \\ \mathbf{n}_i \end{pmatrix}.
\tag{3.11}
$$

This is a linear matrix equation of the form $\mathbf{Cx} = \mathbf{b}$, where $\mathbf{C}$ is the 6×6 "covariance matrix" accumulated from the $\mathbf{c}_i$ and $\mathbf{n}_i$, $\mathbf{x}$ is a 6×1 vector of unknowns, and $\mathbf{b}$ is a 6×1 vector that also depends on the data points. The equation may be solved using standard methods ($\mathbf{C}$ is symmetric, so Cholesky decomposition is the preferred algorithm), yielding the optimal incremental rotation and translation.

As mentioned above, this 6×6 covariance matrix plays a critical role in the stability sampling, since it encodes the increase in the alignment error when the transformation is moved away from its optimum:

$$
d\varepsilon = \left(d\mathbf{r} \;\; d\mathbf{t} \right) (C) \begin{pmatrix} d\mathbf{r} \\ d\mathbf{t} \end{pmatrix}.
\tag{3.12}
$$

The larger this increase the greater the stability of ICP, since the error landscape will have a deep, well-defined minimum. On the other hand, if there are incremental transformations that cause only a small increase in alignment error, ICP will be relatively unstable with respect to these degrees of freedom.

By expanding $\mathbf{C}$ in terms of its eigenvectors we may see directly the effect of various incremental transformations. If all eigenvalues of $\mathbf{C}$ are large, any transformation away from the minimum will result in a large increase in alignment error. If, on the other hand, one or more eigenvalues are small, the corresponding eigenvectors are transformations that do not increase error much, and therefore represent directions in transformation space along which the error landscape is shallow.

Global Registration

Although it is sometimes possible to build complete 3D models just by aligning each scan to one other, this can be unstable. Consider the situation in which there is a chain of scans stretching all the way around an object. Simply aligning each scan to the one immediately before it can lead to an accumulation of any pairwise alignment errors that might have been caused by noise, miscalibration, or some other cause. As a result, the final scan can end up quite a distance away from the first. As a result, some method of "spreading out" the alignment error is necessary, so it is not concentrated in just one pair of scans. This is the goal of so-called "global registration" algorithms.

One global registration approach that is sometimes used is to take a special scan that covers a large part of the surface. This might be a "cylindrical scan" that goes all around the object, and some commercial laser-triangulation scanners have the capability of taking such scans in addition to the more-common linear scans. If such a scan is available, it certainly makes sense to take advantage of it by aligning all the other scans to it, rather than to each other [TL94]. In many cases, however, it is impossible or impractical to obtain such a scan.

The simplest "true" global registration technique is the brute-force solution: bring all scans into the ICP iteration loop. That is, at each ICP iteration we compute correspondences from points on one scan to the closest point on *all* overlapping scans, then find the transformation for that scan that minimizes all the pairwise transformations [BSGL96]. While this approach works, it requires holding all the scans in memory at once and can be computationally impractical.

A simple way of speeding up the previous idea is to precompute pairwise alignments between all overlapping scans. The final global registration step then just has to solve for a set of transformations that are as consistent as possible with all the pairwise ICPs. The advantage of this is that the global registration step does not need all the scans themselves in memory, just some data computed during the pairwise registrations. This makes it much more practical for models with many scans.

Pulli's algorithm is a combination of the two previous ideas: the result of the pairwise ICPs is a small set of precomputed point correspondences between the scans, never to be computed again, and these are the only thing that is used during the global registration. The final global step itself involves repeatedly considering each scan and finding the transformation that minimizes its precomputed point correspondences with respect to all other scans [Pul99]. Faster convergence is achieved by considering scans in decreasing order of the number of other scans that they overlap. Sharp has proposed a different variant on the same theme, which focuses specifically on "spreading out" the mutual inconsistency between pairwise alignments [SLW05]. Specifically, the algorithm looks for cycles within the graph of scan overlaps. For each cycle, the net alignment error is spread out equally among all pairs of scans within that cycle. Scans belonging to multiple cycles receive the average transformation.

Finally, Krishnan et al. have proposed an SVD-based method that can solve for the optimal transformations directly, given precomputed pairwise transformations for a set of scans [KLMV05]. The method is an extension of one of the closed-form solutions for pairwise point-to-point alignment, and is exact in the absence of noise. Otherwise, the SVD provides an initial estimate, and the global registration proceeds via a Newton iteration.

3.1.5 CONCLUSION

Scanning hardware, based on technologies such as triangulation and time of flight, has emerged as an important source of detailed 3D models and has partially driven the development of point-based methods. Depending on the method, data are produced as either unorganized point clouds or range images and are processed by further stages in a 3D model acquisition pipeline, including registration (described in this section) and merging (described later in this book). While the scanning technologies are mature and capable of producing high-quality models for most objects, research continues to improve the speed and accuracy of scanning hardware, the ability to scan specular and translucent objects, and the ease and automation of creating complete 3D models. The following section describes a case study based on the principles surveyed in this chapter: a complete system for acquiring 3D models with color using a structured-light scanner.

3.2 A PRACTICAL LOW-COST SCANNER FOR GEOMETRY AND APPEARANCE

Filip Sadlo, Tim Weyrich, and Ronald Peikert

3.2.1 OVERVIEW

The previous section gave an overview of state-of-the-art acquisition techniques. This section describes in detail an implementation of a temporal structured-light system based on binary Gray codes. It allows robust and accurate acquisition of objects with arbitrary geometry and a wide range of materials. A benefit of this method is that geometry and texture can be acquired with the same camera, resulting in texture that is consistent with the geometry. As stated in Section 3.1.2, another benefit is the low cost compared to other systems, since video projectors are often available and because only a single camera is needed. During the whole acquisition stage, the data are represented and processed in point-based format, resulting in an unorganized point-cloud model.

The object is rotated in small known steps by a turntable and for each position the view is reconstructed using structured light. Unlike many approaches, the demanding and error-prone task of mutually registering the single reconstructions is avoided. Instead, precise calibration of the projector, the camera, and the axis of the turntable is assured. This allows them to produce consistent multiview reconstructions (rings of overlapping views). Then some methods for the removal of artifacts are applied. After that, an efficient method for merging the overlapping reconstructions into a single-layered surfel representation is applied. For the reconstruction of texture, photometric calibration is added to the already computed geometric calibration of the projector. This way, a calibrated light source is obtained that is used for the per-surfel reconstruction of either Lambertian texture or texture according to the Phong reflectance model. At the end of this section a method for analyzing the geometric accuracy of the system is described.

3.2.2 SYSTEM OVERVIEW

The acquisition system (Figure 3.9) consists of custom hardware, namely a video projector that projects the structured-light patterns, a turntable that rotates the object, a camera that takes images of the projections, and a computer that controls the hardware and does the reconstruction.

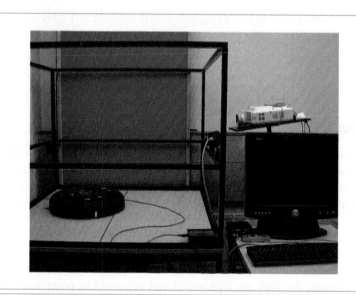

Figure 3.9: System overview: turntable, camera, projector, and control computer (from *left to right*).

In our setup, the system contains an analog-input $1,024 \times 768$ DLP video projector. It is beneficial if the projector allows for disabling features such as automatic synchronization and image size adaption. This way the calibration is not lost when the projector is turned off between scans. Another aspect is the projector's minimal image diagonal, or in other words, the minimal focal distance. This becomes important if small objects have to be acquired. Currently, an IEEE-1394 video camera with a resolution of uncompressed $1,024 \times 768$ pixels is used to acquire the images. It is preferred to use monochrome cameras and to illuminate the object (or calibration pattern) with red, green, and blue projector light in order to acquire colors. The reason is that cameras using a Bayer pattern for color acquisition (each pixel has a red, green, or blue filter attached) exhibit increased blur and artifacts due to under-sampling and interpolation. This complicates calibration, smoothes the reconstruction, and can produce artifacts comparable to those in Figure 3.14 shown later. For similar reasons, it is also avoided to rectify the images and instead the lens distortion is modeled.

Often several rings of reconstructions are needed in order to get a complete reconstruction. This is accomplished by either tilting the object, or by moving projector and camera to a new position between the scans. The optimal solution would be to perform these transformations again around a calibrated axis.

But since this tends to be mechanically demanding, the object is tilted by hand and each time a ring of reconstructions is acquired by rotation of the turntable. Therefore, the resulting rings have to be mutually registered, treating each ring as a separate rigid model. Some methods for mutual registration of reconstructions are geometry based, such as iterated closest points (ICP) described in Section 3.1.4, and others are image based, such as that by Bernardini et al. [BMR01]. The current system uses ICP for registration. Some challenges of registration, such as error accumulation, play a minor role in this case because the rings are already consistent at high accuracy, leading to a simpler registration problem. After the rings have been merged to a single-layered surfel representation, reflectance samples for each surfel are collected into *lumitexels* [LGK+01] and used for texture reconstruction according to the Phong reflectance model, which is then rendered and edited using Pointshop3D [ZPKG02] as described in Section 5.2.

3.2.3 CALIBRATION

Although often underestimated, precise calibration of the structured-light system is one of the main prerequisites for a successful and accurate reconstruction. This is especially true for multiview reconstructions, where a given surface point is reconstructed several times and the corresponding reconstructions have to match. In order to increase accuracy and to ease calibration, separate intrinsic calibration of camera and projector is performed and then an extrinsic calibration step is applied.

For intrinsic and extrinsic calibration of the camera and projector, the Zhang calibration method [Zha00] is used as implemented by OpenCV's cvCalibrateCamera. This calibration model consists of focal length with respect to pixel widths and heights, the principal point, and a radial and a tangential lens distortion modeled by two parameters each. As proposed by OpenCV, a chessboard pattern is used for calibration. However, the pattern detection algorithm of OpenCV fails under difficult lighting or oblique viewing conditions. This conflicts with the experience that strong perspective views at oblique angles increase the accuracy of intrinsic and especially extrinsic calibration. It also conflicts with the need to detect a printed pattern and a (distorted) chessboard projection in the same view (for intrinsic projector calibration). Therefore, an alternative detection procedure based on projective geometry is applied.

Calibration Patterns

OpenCV's detection of the calibration pattern inside the images is done in two steps. First, approximative guesses of the chessboard corners are computed. Then, the corners are detected at subpixel accuracy from the guesses. The second step works well, but the first step fails under difficult light or viewing conditions.

To ease the pattern detection, identical color marks are attached onto the four corners of the chessboard pattern and an additional one for defining the origin. It has been chosen to use colors instead of spatial marks because of the invariance of color with respect to projective transforms. A detailed description of the detection procedure and the subsequent calibration steps is given in Sadlo et al. [SWPG05].

Intrinsic Camera Calibration

The camera is calibrated using different views of a printed chessboard pattern as described above. The pattern is illuminated by the projector in order to create similar lighting conditions as in the case of projector calibration. This allows the use of identical camera settings and HSV segmentation ranges for detection in all calibration steps.

Intrinsic Projector Calibration

The projector is calibrated as an inverse camera. This means that instead of taking pictures of a chessboard with known geometry and detecting the corners inside the images, a chessboard pattern with known geometry is projected to different orientations and positions of a plane and the projections are measured with the calibrated camera.

Extrinsic Calibration

The orientation of projector and camera relative to each other is determined in a similar way as in the projector calibration, but with a single camera image. This time both projector and camera are calibrated extrinsically. The reference coordinate frame is also determined in this step.

Turntable Axis Calibration

Calibration of turntables is approached in different ways, such as using markers permanently attached to the turntable [SPMS04], or by fitting an axis to rotated reconstructions. A color-marked chessboard pattern is put horizontally on the turntable and a full rotation is done in a given number of steps, typically 12. For each step, the position and orientation of the camera relative to the pattern is computed by extrinsic calibration. Then a circle is fitted to the resulting ring of virtual camera positions. The rotational axis of the circle represents the axis of the turntable.

Luminous Projector Calibration

Because the object is illuminated by the projector for texture acquisition, the irradiance from the projector has to be known at a given point in space. For each new projector, the luminous intensity I of the projector pixels is to be initially calibrated. This could be done using a calibrated reflection target, for example, Spectralon.

As our application does not require absolute physical quantities, a gray cardboard is used instead and I is scaled to map color intensities into a useful range. Two calibration modes have been implemented. I is either assumed to be identical for all pixels, or I is determined on a per-pixel basis, capturing spatial intensity variations at the cost of more noise. The irradiance E at a given surface point is then computed as follows: $E = I/d^2$, with d its distance to the projector's center of projection.

3.2.4 GEOMETRY RECONSTRUCTION

Geometry is reconstructed using structured light according to the Gray code and phase-shifting method described below. Normals are computed from the weighted positions of neighboring samples by plane fitting. They are computed separately for each view before merging the reconstructions. This avoids influence of registration errors.

Gray Code and Phase Shifting

Structured-light methods make use of a projection device to determine the z-depth of every illuminated camera pixel. This is done by optical triangulation of the camera ray with the corresponding projector ray that illuminated the surface element. There are many possibilities to structure light in order to allow the identification of a projector pixel by its light. It has been chosen to do time-multiplexing of gray level codes. This allows a wide range of materials but limits the system to static objects.

In the standard Gray code algorithm (see Section 3.1.2), the ray defined by a camera pixel is intersected with the plane defined by the corresponding projector column. However, this assumes no lens distortion inside the projector because otherwise the plane would be distorted. To make the reconstruction process more robust against lens distortion and decoding errors, both projector columns and rows are encoded. The plane-ray intersection problem becomes an overdetermined ray-ray intersection problem that also allows for the removal of artifacts by the ray skew criterion as described below.

Since the projected Gray codes are binary, the achievable precision is limited to integer projector coordinates. Therefore, the detected pixel relations are subsequently improved using a variant of the phase-shifting technique (Section 3.1.2) based on a grayscale sine pattern as shown in Figure 3.10. This also reduces decoding errors in the least significant bits of the Gray code. In addition, phase-shift reconstruction even allows to determine the projector coordinates at subpixel accuracy. It has also been experimented with line-shifting [GBBF00], which achieves subpixel accuracy in camera coordinates rather than in the projector domain. However, in our setup it generally produced inferior results.

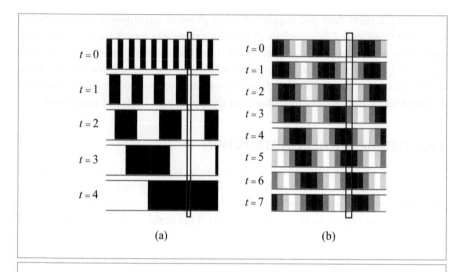

Figure 3.10: (*a*) Gray-coded structured light. The temporal signal (blue box) at a given object point represents the column of the corresponding projector pixel. The procedure is repeated with horizontal stripes to also encode the projector rows. (*b*) Phase shifting. Shifted sinusoidal stripe patterns are projected to the object, producing a temporal sine signal on a given object point. The phase of this signal represents the projector column. The procedure is repeated with horizontal stripes to also encode the projector rows.

Due to errors in calibration and decoding, the two corresponding rays usually do not intersect. The method presented by Guehring [Gue01] addresses the problem by nonlinear least squares and analysis of the residual, while Hartley and Sturm [HS94] give an overview and introduce a polynomial method. In our system the point of intersection is computed as the point on the camera ray that is closest to the projector ray. The solution is constrained to the camera ray because its calibration can be assumed more accurate than that of the projector rays. This way the projector only contributes depth information, which meets the original intention. The distance between the intersecting rays (ray skew) is used for the removal of artifacts as described below. The ray skew is also visualized by color coding the reconstructions for visual verification of the quality of calibration. Figure 3.11 shows an example.

Artifact Removal

Here some of the implemented methods for the elimination of geometric artifacts are described. They are all applied to the single-view reconstructions before they are merged.

Figure 3.11: Single-ring reconstruction colorized by the ray skew for verification of calibration quality. Red means small skew; surfels with ray skew larger than 0.6 mm (outliers) have already been removed.

Signal Strength   A black reference image with all projector pixels set to black and a white reference image with all projector pixels set to white are taken for each view. They are used for elimination of camera pixels that receive no or too weak signals and they are also used for normalization of the structured-light signal. A camera pixel is eliminated if the white reference differs from the black reference by less than a user-defined threshold. The threshold is chosen in order to reject mainly background and part of the shadows.

Ray Skew   This method detects artifacts caused by decoding errors as well as artifacts that are produced by reflected or scattered codes. Assuming accurate calibration, it is unlikely that the projector ray corresponding to the falsely decoded code intersects with the camera ray as well as the correct projector ray would do. In other words, the ray skew tends to increase on decoding errors. A threshold for the minimal distance between intersecting rays is used and the reconstruction is rejected if the threshold is exceeded (Figure 3.12).

Subpixel Variance   This method addresses artifacts that originate during phase shifting from object regions with varying reflectance and curved (or discontinuous) surface as described by Curless and Levoy [CL95]. The phase-shift signal is spatially integrated over the area of each camera pixel during acquisition. Assuming that the

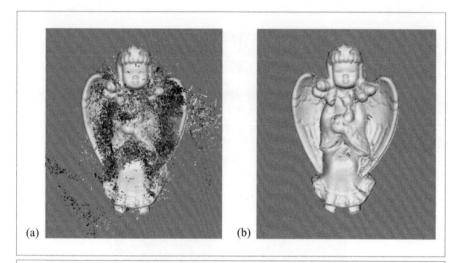

Figure 3.12: Removal of artifacts based on ray skew and component size. (*a*) Ray skew and component size are unlimited (2,527,362 surfels). (*b*) Ray skew is limited to 0.6 mm and connected component size to six surfels (2,053,543 surfels). Only the last few outliers were eliminated by component size.

left half of the camera pixel looks, say, at black material, while the right half observes a bright material, the signal integrated over the pixel will contain only codes from the right half, leading to wrong projector rays usually visible as depth errors. As overlapping views have been acquired, it is possible to address this problem by eliminating surfels that lie on edges in image space. The pixel corresponding to the surfel is resampled at subpixel resolution using Lanczos interpolation, and its variance is computed. It is rejected if its variance exceeds a threshold. The method also removes sharp shadow boundaries.

Outliers are also removed based on other geometric criteria, such as small connected component size of surfels, and photometric criteria, such as saturated pixels.

View Merging

After the rings of reconstructions have been registered, we want to merge the overlapping reconstructions into a single-layered surfel representation in order to reduce storage and visualization cost. Doing so, care has to be taken that texture quality and geometric accuracy remain as high as possible.

Blending of the overlapping textures and averaging the overlapping surfel positions would require that the reconstructions fit together at subpixel accuracy, otherwise the resulting reconstruction would get blurred or doubled. Therefore, combining original patches of the overlapping reconstructions, as described later in this section, is tried to preserve detail. This method relates to Turk and Levoy [TL94] and it also has a thinning effect because the patches have original resolution.

Bounded Projective Nearest Neighbors   The system does a nearest-neighbor search to get the overlapping surfels of a given surface element of the object. Instead of performing a standard nearest-neighbor search, it is more efficient to perform the search in the M camera images. Because every point is reconstructed by a corresponding camera pixel, one can make use of the calibrated setup. To find for a given point $\mathbf{p}$ and a given search radius r the nearest (or all) point reconstructions, $\mathbf{p}$ is projected to all camera images, yielding a $\mathbf{p}'_i$ for each view i. Then all point reconstructions that have been reconstructed by camera pixels within a search radius r'_i around $\mathbf{p}'_i$ in image space are tested for whether they lie within distance r to $\mathbf{p}$ in world space. The search radius r'_i is computed from r by projection.

The complexity of the search is $O(M \cdot r'^2)$, where M is the number of camera images (r'^2 is limited by the number of pixels per image). In the current application, the search radius is small and constant. Therefore r' has a small upper bound, resulting in an algorithmic complexity of $O(M)$.

Best Surfels   A simple greedy approach is used to select patches from overlapping reconstructions in order to get a single layer of points and for each object region the best patch regarding the quality of geometry and texture. The current approach is purely surfel based, hence it does not maintain a volumetric representation such as by Pulli et al. [PDH$^+$97].

The algorithm defines and selects the patches implicitly in two steps. First, the homologous surfels representing the same point on the surface are determined using the nearest-neighbor search just presented. Then the best of these candidates is chosen for the resulting reconstruction.

The method is based on a simple idea: for each object point, take the surfel that has been reconstructed most orthogonally by its camera (regarding the surface normal computed from its neighbors). This addresses the fact that texture and geometry usually have the highest resolution when acquired by perpendicular view. At the same time, this simple criterion generates the patches. Figure 3.13 shows an example result. There are holes due to the greedy nature of the algorithm. However, the holes are small enough to disappear when the surfels are rendered.

A modification is applied to the described algorithm in order to remove outliers (additionally to the methods described above). This is achieved by modification of the nearest-neighbor search. Instead of computing the search range in image space r'_i using projection, it is set by the user to a smaller range. This way, the region

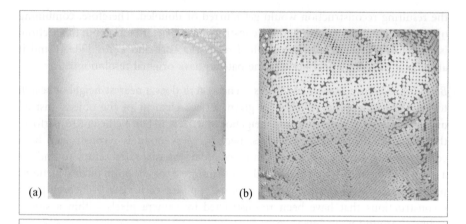

(a)   (b)

Figure 3.13: Best surfels. (*a*) Before merging (2,053,543 surfels). (*b*) After merging (226,664 surfels). Search radius in world space = 1.2 mm. Search radius in image space = 1 pixel in order to remove outliers.

where best surfel candidates are sampled is not spherical any more (as would result from a true 3D distance test); instead, the search range is restricted in directions perpendicular to the views. This eliminates outliers because it allows us to choose a larger search radius that captures the outliers without thinning out too many neighboring surfels. Figure 3.13 shows an example result.

3.2.5 TEXTURE RECONSTRUCTION

Most materials exhibit a certain amount of specular reflection. In the case of strong specular reflection, the effects are confined to a small region on the object for a given view and illumination by the projector. Since many overlapping reconstructions are acquired, one could remove the specularly reflecting parts in all of them before view merging. Theoretically this would lead to consistent diffuse reconstructions of specular objects. However, the specular information would be lost. Additionally, many materials have moderate specular reflection that leads to specular effects that cover large parts of the object. There it would not be possible to remove them without producing holes. Consequently, a specular reflectance model has to be fitted in these cases.

The diffuse reflectance model can however be used to generate high-resolution reconstructions of objects that do not possess too strong of a specular reflection. The surfel reconstruction preserves the subpixel information discretized by the camera if the surfels are located on the viewing rays of the camera pixels and if each surfel gets its uniform color only from the corresponding pixel. This can be achieved for the diffuse reflectance model, because it can be robustly fitted to a single reflectance sample.

Shadow Removal

The acquisition system can generally not acquire shadowed object regions, because the structured light does not reach these parts. However, the reconstruction still may yield points in shadows if they are indirectly illuminated by interreflection, subsurface scattering, and other effects. It is important to detect and remove shadows when computing texture. Furthermore, structured-light reconstruction of indirectly illuminated regions and at shadow boundaries leads to geometric artifacts (see Figure 3.14a). These artifacts include texture embossing (see Section 3.1.2) and additional depth error from indirect illumination. The texture embossing phenomena can be reduced by avoiding Bayer tiling in the camera and by the above subpixel variance method.

The shadows are detected using a depth test relative to the projector. For each position of the turntable a reconstruction with corresponding viewpoint and projector position is obtained. After view merging, the remaining surfels are projected into each virtual view of the projector. Projector pixels that get more than one surfel projection are tested for shadow. If the surfel producing the projection belongs to the same depth map as the virtual view and if it is not nearest to the camera, it is removed. In order to preserve surfels at silhouettes, the surfel is only removed if it is farther away from the nearest surfel than a user-defined small threshold.

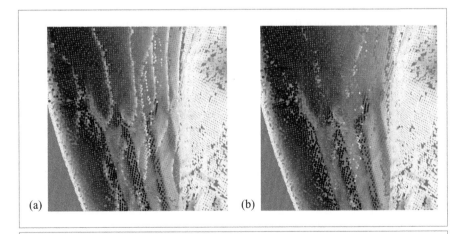

(a)   (b)

Figure 3.14: Removal of shadows (seam artifacts). (*a*) No removal. (*b*) Local range = 1 and minimal distance = 2 mm (18,452 surfels removed).

The generated holes are filled with other surfels by repeating the view-merging procedure.

Although some shadow surfels are eliminated by the described method, there are usually shadow surfels remaining due to calibration errors, reconstruction errors, and the fact that the sampled surface elements have an extent. Therefore, instead of projecting each surfel to the projector and storing it only in the corresponding projector pixel, it is stored to a user-defined range around that projector pixel. This way the sensitivity for depth discontinuities is increased, and at the same time, surfels that have been reconstructed at grazing angles are removed.

Reflectance Sampling

In order to reconstruct the texture, it is necessary to collect for each surface point all available and reliable reflectance samples from the acquired texture views. Reflectance is computed from the image intensities using the calibrated illumination model described in Section 3.2.3. According to Lensch et al. [LGK+01], a surface point together with the corresponding samples is called a *lumitexel*. Not all views contribute a sample for a given surface point. There might be effects like occlusion and insufficient illumination or shadows that invalidate a sample in a given view. Insufficient illumination is detected using a user-defined threshold that rejects samples illuminated at grazing angles, in addition to the signal strength threshold described above.

The shadow and occlusion tests are based on the surfel representation. Only surfels that belong to the final merged reconstruction represent surface points and hence lumitexels. Therefore, the points that are removed by the merging procedure are only marked as such, since they are needed for sample selection.

Occlusion/Shadow Test The structured-light method already performs a kind of implicit occlusion test in the sense that it can only acquire surface points that are visible by the camera. The same holds for the light source, so theoretically no shadows can be acquired. Therefore, it can be decided if a point $\mathbf{p}$ gets occluded in a given view v_i by projecting $\mathbf{p}$ to that view (onto the camera pixel $\mathbf{p}'_i$) and by examining the surfel $\mathbf{s}_{\mathbf{p}'_i}$ that has been reconstructed by the pixel $\mathbf{p}'_i$ of view v_i. Possible cases are:

- There has been no $\mathbf{s}_{\mathbf{p}'_i}$ reconstructed. This means that reconstruction failed for that pixel or that it has been removed by one of the presented methods. Another possibility is that it has been removed by the shadow removal process. In any case, the corresponding sample is rejected.
- $\mathbf{s}_{\mathbf{p}'_i}$ has been reconstructed (and either selected as best surfel or not). This means either that v_i has an unobstructed view to the point $\mathbf{p}$ or that $\mathbf{s}_{\mathbf{p}'_i}$ represents a surface point different to $\mathbf{p}$. To test if $\mathbf{s}_{\mathbf{p}'_i}$ represents a different

point, the distance between $\mathbf{p}$ and $\mathbf{p}_{v_i}$ ($\mathbf{p}_{v_i}$ is the camera position of v_i) is measured as well as the distance between $\mathbf{s}_{\mathbf{p}'_i}$ and $\mathbf{p}_{v_i}$. If the difference $|\|\mathbf{p} - \mathbf{p}_{v_i}\| - \|\mathbf{s}_{\mathbf{p}'_i} - \mathbf{p}_{v_i}\||$ exceeds a user-defined threshold, the points are assumed to be distinct and the sample is rejected due to occlusion.

Lambertian Texture

Diffuse texture is computed from a single reflectance sample according to the Lambertian reflectance model:

$$\rho_d = \frac{L}{\mathbf{n}^T \mathbf{l} E},$$

(3.13)

with, for a given object point, ρ_d the diffuse albedo, L the radiance observed by the camera, E the irradiance from the projector at that point, $\mathbf{n}$ its normalized surface normal, and $\mathbf{l}$ the normalized vector toward the light source. The surface normal is actually computed from the neighbors of the reconstructed point. The direction $\mathbf{l}$ is computed from the geometric projector calibration and E from the luminous projector calibration. Figures 3.15 and 3.16a show respective results.

Figure 3.15: Single view reconstruction, Lambertian texture.

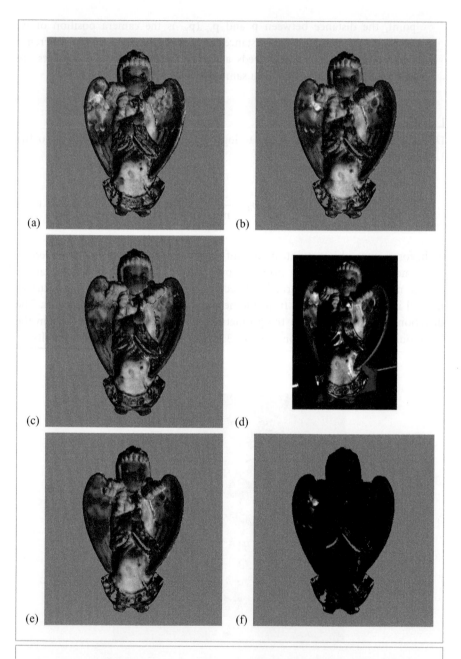

Figure 3.16: Reconstructed Lambertian texture (*a*), Phong texture (*b*), blended overlapping reconstructions (*c*), region of original camera view (*d*), diffuse component of Phong texture (*e*), and specular component (*f*).

Phong Texture

Alternatively, the diffuse term is used together with a specular Phong lobe as the reflectance model:

$$\frac{L}{E} = \rho_d \mathbf{n}^T \mathbf{l} + \rho_s (\mathbf{l}^T (2\mathbf{n}\mathbf{n}^T - \mathbf{I})\mathbf{v})^n,$$ (3.14)

with ρ_s the maximum specular albedo, $\mathbf{v}$ the normalized vector toward the camera, and n the specular exponent. Nonlinear least squares fitting of Equation (3.14) to the reflectance samples is done simultaneously for red, green, and blue ρ_d and ρ_s, but with a single exponent n using the Levenberg-Marquardt method as suggested by Lafortune et al. [LFTG97]. An initial estimate is computed by linear fitting. This is achieved by fixing n for optimization and by solving the resulting linear least squares problem. This is repeated for exponentially increasing n and each time the residual is computed. The fit leading to the smallest error is chosen as a result of the linearized fitting. Linear fitting can also be used as fall back to nonlinear fitting.

Figure 3.16 shows a result of the Phong fit. The reconstruction still shows some artifacts in regions of sparse sampling and at points with erroneous normals due to outliers. However, the diffuse part of the specular fit provides a significantly improved texture compared to the Lambertian fit, as the Lambertian fit overestimates brightness in specular regions.

Further improving the Phong fit is difficult due to the limited number of samples per lumitexel. One way to come around this would be to apply material clustering as presented by Lensch et al. [LGK+01]. Another possibility is to improve the accuracy of the normals by including them into the texture-fitting process, but this also requires a well-distributed reflectance sampling.

3.2.6 RESULTS

Figure 3.17 shows a single-ring reconstruction of a clay pot acquired from only 15 views. Figure 3.18 shows a telephone also reconstructed from 15 rotated views using the same setup. It can be seen that the clay pot produces better quality regarding texture and geometry because its material is mostly diffuse, in contrast to plastic material of the telephone.

Because the chosen objects contain both diffuse and specular materials and relatively much occlusion, the achieved results still contain artifacts such as outliers, false normals, and holes. These are addressed by the postprocessing stage as described by Weyrich et al. [WPK+04], although in our case, most of the holes originate from suboptimal setup and could be addressed by interactive control of the turntable and more appropriate tilting of the object in order to generate optimal views.

Figure 3.17: Clay pot reconstructed from 15 rotary views (384,492 surfels). Lambertian texture (*a*) and synthetic Phong texture (*b*) for showing geometric detail. The Lambertian texture exhibits stripe artifacts due to specular reflection of the clay surface.

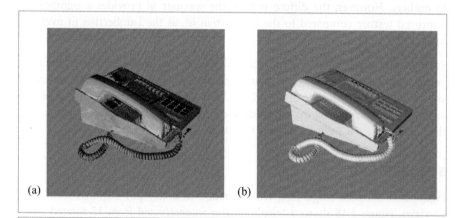

Figure 3.18: Telephone reconstructed from 15 rotary views (317,681 surfels). Lambertian texture (*a*) and no texture (*b*).

Accuracy

The accuracy of the system is evaluated using a steel sphere of 150 mm in diameter that had been manufactured with a tolerance of 0.1 mm and painted in white color. A single ring of 10 partial reconstructions at a uniform angular step was taken and merged according to Section 3.2.4. For the merged reconstruction, a center was computed by fitting a least squares sphere to the surfels. The mean distance to the center was 74.947 mm and the maximal errors were less than 0.5 mm, which is roughly the surfel spacing (red histogram in Figure 3.19a). For further analysis of these errors, a sphere of the same radius was fitted to each partial reconstruction. The resulting centers (Figure 3.19b) reveal a small systematic error in the turntable calibration, plus a mechanical effect happening between the first two scans. The blue histograms show the higher accuracy of each partial reconstruction. The green histogram is obtained by translating the partial reconstructions to a common center. This step cannot be done for general objects, it just illustrates that there is some potential left in the merging process. However, registration of surfel objects based on geometry or texture to extreme subsurfel precision is difficult.

Performance

The angel figurine of 180 mm height was reconstructed from 3 × 30 views. Each view contributed in average 28,082 surfels, leading to a raw reconstruction consisting of 2,527,362 surfels. From these, 473,819 erroneous surfels were removed by the ray skew criterion or because they formed too-small connected components (outliers). Another 1,826,879 surfels were discarded during merging. Finally, 18,452 surfels got discarded by the shadow removal process. Removing the shadows is the computationally most expensive step—it took 38 minutes. Texture reconstruction took 16 minutes and computation of the normals another 6 minutes. The best surfels merging procedure took again 6 minutes and the cost of the remaining operations is negligible.

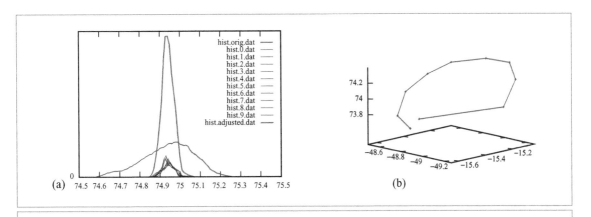

Figure 3.19: (a) Histograms of surfel distances to sphere center (red: full reconstruction; blue: partial reconstruction; green: partial reconstructions merged by optimal translations). (b) Centers of least squares fits for partial reconstructions. All units given in millimeters.

3.2.7 CONCLUSION

This section described a completely point-based acquisition system for geometry and texture. The system consists of a projector as a calibrated light source, a single grayscale camera, and a turntable. Methods for robust reconstruction and removal of artifacts have been presented as well as methods for merging multiple point-based reconstructions into a single-layered representation. Additionally, to the Lambertian reflectance model, the Phong model was fitted to the reflectance samples, utilizing the underlying structured-light approach.

The described system is oriented for low cost, simple operation, and arbitrary object geometry, and can handle cavities due to the structured-light approach. The next section presents a high-end system based on the visual hull method, aiming at the acquisition of objects with difficult surface properties, such as fuzzy and highly specular objects.

3.3 POINT-BASED 3D PHOTOGRAPHY

Wojciech Matusik and Hanspeter Pfister

3.3.1 OVERVIEW

The point-based acquisition systems described in the previous two sections, including most commercial systems, cannot scan very complex geometries and appearances, such as glass, fur, hair, cloth, leaves, or feathers. In this section we describe a robust, completely automated point-based scanning system that can capture objects with arbitrary geometric complexity and appearance. It automatically creates object representations that produce high-quality renderings from arbitrary viewpoints, either under fixed or novel illumination. The system is built from off-the-shelf components. It uses digital cameras, leveraging their rapid increase in quality and decrease in cost. It is easy to use, has simple setup and calibration, and scans objects that fit within one cubic foot volume. The acquired objects can be accurately composited into synthetic scenes.

3.3.2 PREVIOUS WORK

There are many approaches for acquiring high-quality 3D shape from real-world objects, including contact digitizers, passive stereo depth-extraction, and active light-imaging systems. The previous two sections discuss passive and active scanning systems. To acquire objects with arbitrary materials, we use an image-based modeling and rendering approach. Image-based representations have the advantage of capturing and representing an object regardless of the complexity of its geometry and appearance.

Early image-based methods [MB95, CW93] allowed for navigation within a scene using correspondence information. Light field methods [LH96, GGSC96] achieve similar results without geometric information, but with an increased number of images. Gortler et al. [GGSC96] combine the best of these methods by including a visual hull of the object for improved ray interpolation. These methods assume static illumination and, therefore, cannot accurately render objects into new environments.

An intermediate between purely model-based and purely image-based methods is the view-dependent texture mapping systems described by Pulli et al. [PCD$^+$97] and Debevec et al. [DYB98, DTM96]. These systems combine simple geometry and sparse texture data to accurately interpolate between the images. These methods are extremely effective despite their approximate 3D shapes, but they have some limitations for highly specular surfaces due to the relatively small number of textures.

As noted in Debevec et al. [DYB98], surface light fields [GMP98, WAA$^+$00, NSI99a, CBCG02] can be viewed as a more general and more efficient representation of view-dependent texture maps. Wood et al. [WAA$^+$00] store light field data on accurate high-density geometry, whereas Nishino et al. [NSI99a] use a coarser triangular mesh for objects with low geometric complexity. Chen et al. [CBCG02] use a decomposition of surface light fields that can be efficiently rendered on modern graphics hardware. Surface light fields are capable of reproducing important global effects such as interreflections and self-shadowing. Our system is capable of surface light field acquisition and rendering.

Images generated from a surface light field always show the object under a fixed lighting condition. To overcome this limitation, inverse rendering methods estimate the surface BRDF from images and geometry of the object. To achieve a compact BRDF representation, most methods fit a parametric reflection model to the image data [SWI97, YDMH99, LGK$^+$01]. Sato et al. [SWI97] and Yu et al. [YDMH99] assume that the specular part of the BRDF is constant over large regions of the object, while the diffuse component varies more rapidly. Lensch et al. [LGK$^+$01] partition the objects into patches and estimate a set of basis BRDFs per patch.

Simple parametric BRDFs, however, are incapable of representing the wide range of effects seen in real scenes. As observed in Hawkins et al. [HCD01], objects featuring glass, fur, hair, cloth, leaves, or feathers are very challenging or impossible to represent this way. Reflectance functions for points in highly specular or self-shadowed areas are very complex and cannot easily be approximated using smooth basis functions. In our work we make no assumptions about the reflection property of the material we are scanning.

An alternative is to use image-based, nonparametric representations for object reflectance. Marschner et al. [SHWC99] use a tabular BRDF representation and measure the reflectance properties of convex objects using a digital camera. Their method is restricted to objects with a uniform BRDF, and they incur problems with geometric errors introduced by 3D range scanners. Georghiades et al. [GBK99] apply image-based relighting to human faces by assuming that the surface reflectance is Lambertian.

More recent approaches [MGW01, DHT$^+$00, HCD01, BKMK01] use image databases to relight objects from a fixed viewpoint without acquiring a full BRDF. Debevec et al. [DHT$^+$00] define the *reflectance field* of an object as the radiant light from a surface under every possible incident field of illumination. They use a light stage with few fixed camera positions and a rotating light to acquire the reflectance field of a human face [DHT$^+$00] or of cultural artifacts [HCD01]. The polynomial texture map system described in [MGW01] uses a similar technique for objects with approximately planar geometry and diffuse reflectance properties. Belhumeur et al. [BKMK] use essentially the same method as Debevec et al. [DHT$^+$00] to render objects with arbitrary appearance. These reflectance field approaches are limited to renderings from a single viewpoint.

3.3.3 SYSTEM OVERVIEW

Our system uses a point-sampled visual hull [MBR$^+$00] as the underlying geometric model. The visual hull can be computed robustly using active backlighting. We augment the point-sampled visual hull with view-dependent opacity to accurately represent complex silhouette geometry, such as hair. We call this new shape representation the *opacity hull*. To construct the opacity hull we use the multibackground matting techniques similar to Smith and Blinn [SB96].

Our system can acquire a surface light field of the object. It can also acquire reflectance fields of the object from multiple viewpoints. We call this representation a *surface reflectance field*, because the data are parameterized on the surface of the visual hull of the object. Surface reflectance fields can be rendered from any viewpoint under new illumination. We use images from the same viewpoints to compute the opacity hull and the surface reflectance field. This avoids any registration inaccuracies and has proven to be extremely robust.

Laurentini [Lau94] introduced the visual hull as the maximal volume that is consistent with a given set of silhouettes. The visual hull cannot represent surface concavities. Yet, due to its hull property, it provides a conservative estimate of an object's structure. The opacity hull and surface reflectance field extend the utility of visual hull considerably by faithfully representing complex silhouettes and materials.

Instead of relying on accurate geometry, our representation relies heavily upon acquired radiance information to produce accurate renderings of the object. We can adaptively acquire more images for objects with concavities or high specularity, and fewer images for objects with simple geometry and mostly diffuse surfaces. Naturally, this approach is not useful for applications where geometric fidelity is required. In this Chapter we demonstrate that the combination of opacity hull geometry and the image-based surface-reflectance field leads to an effective representation for rendering applications. Our system is capable of acquiring and rendering objects that are fuzzy, highly specular, or that contain any mixture of materials.

3.3.4 HARDWARE SETUP

Figure 3.20 (left) shows an overview of our hardware setup. Objects are placed on a plasma monitor that is mounted onto a rotating turntable. An array of light sources is mounted on an overhead turntable. The lights are spaced roughly equally along the elevation angle of the hemisphere.

During object scanning, the lights can be fixed, rotate around the object for a fixed point of view, or made to rotate with the object. Six video cameras are pointed at the object from various angles. To facilitate consistent backlighting we mount the cameras roughly in the same vertical plane. A second plasma monitor is placed directly opposite of the cameras. Figure 3.20 (right) shows a picture of our third-generation scanner. The two plasma monitors have a resolution of 1,024 × 768 pixels.

We use six QImaging QICAM cameras with 1,360 × 1,036 pixel color CCD imaging sensors. The cameras are photometrically calibrated. They are connected via FireWire to a 2 GHz Pentium-4 PC with 1 GB of RAM. We alternatively use 15 mm or 8 mm C-mount lenses, depending on the size of the acquired object. The cameras are able to acquire full resolution RGB images at 11 frames per second.

The light array holds four to six directional light sources. Each light uses a 32-watt HMI halogen lamp and a parabolic reflector to approximate a directional light source at infinity. The lights are controlled by an electronic switch and individual dimmers. The dimmers are set once such that the image sensor is not oversaturated for viewpoints where the lights are directly visible.

In many ways, our setup is similar to the enhanced light stage that has been proposed as future work in Hawkins et al. [HCD01]. A key difference is that our

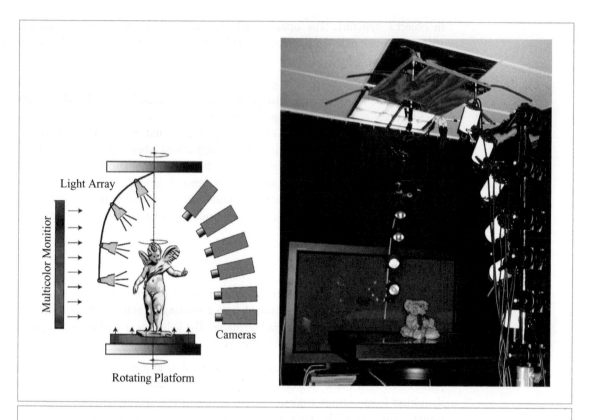

Figure 3.20: Our 3D digitizing system combines both active and passive imaging methods. Objects are rotated on a turntable while images are acquired. Plasma monitors are used to extract high-quality alpha mattes. An overhead array of light sources can be rotated to acquire surface reflectance fields. A system diagram is shown on the left and the photograph is shown on the right.

system uses multicolor backlights for alpha matte extraction and construction of the opacity hull. As we will show, the availability of approximate geometry and view-dependent alpha greatly extends the class of models that can be captured.

3.3.5 DATA ACQUISITION PROCESS

Calibration

The scanning sequence starts by placing the object onto the turntable and, if necessary, adjusting the position and aperture of the cameras. If any camera adjustments are required, we must first acquire images of a known calibration object, a patterned cube in our case. An image of the calibration target is taken from each of the viewpoints. Intrinsic and extrinsic camera parameters are computed using a special calibration procedure for turntable systems with multiple cameras [Bea02]. Calibration can be computed reliably given the fixed rotation axis and the large numbers of images.

Reference Images

Next, the plasma monitors are turned on and we acquire images of patterned backdrops used for multibackground matting. For each viewpoint, each patterned backdrop is photographed alone without the foreground object. As in Zongker et al. [ZWCS99], we call these images the *reference images*. Reference images only have to be acquired once after calibration. They are stored and used for subsequent object scans.

Object Images

The object is then put on the turntable and a sequence of images is automatically acquired. The number of turntable positions is user specified and depends on the object. During this first rotation, both plasma monitors illuminate the object from below and behind with the patterned backdrops. As in Zongker et al. [ZWCS99], we call the images of the foreground object in front of the backdrops *object images*. The object images and reference images are used to compute alpha mattes and the opacity hull. We depend on good repeatability of the turntables to ensure that the reference images and the object images are well registered.

Radiance Images

We then switch off the plasma monitors and turn on one or more directional lights of the array. We found that we get the best results when using additional fill light to avoid dark shadows and high contrast in the images. We avoid specular reflections from the monitors by covering the vast majority of the display surface with black felt without upsetting the object position. We acquire a set of *radiance images* of the illuminated object during the second rotation of the turntable. The radiance images are used for surface light-field rendering. The directional lights can be fixed or made to rotate with the object. The coupled rotation case leads to greater coherence of radiance samples in each surface point.

Reflectance Images

If we want to relight the acquired object, we acquire an additional set of images used to construct the surface reflectance field. The array of lights is rotated around the object. For each rotation position, each light in the light array is sequentially turned on and an image is captured with each camera. We use four lights and typically increment the rotation angle by 24° for a total of 4 × 15 images for each camera position. This procedure is repeated for all viewpoints. We call the set of all images the *reflectance images*. They are used to construct the surface reflectance field.

Environment Mattes

If we would like to relight highly specular or refractive objects, we additionally acquire environment mattes from multiple viewpoints. Environment mattes are a compact representation for high-resolution surface reflectance. The acquisition process involves taking multiple images of the scanned object in front of a backdrop with a 1D Gaussian profile that is swept over time in horizontal, vertical, and diagonal directions. We capture environment mattes using three of the six cameras, roughly spaced 10° apart in elevation and 5° in angular turntable increments. For a full 360° view of the object this corresponds to $3 \times 72 = 432$ viewing positions.

HDR Images

All radiance and reflectance images are captured using a high dynamic range technique similar to that of Debevec and Malik's [DM97]. Since raw output from the CCD array of the cameras is available, the relationship between exposure time and radiance values is linear over most of the operating range. For each viewpoint, we take four pictures with exponentially increasing exposure times and use a least squares linear fit to determine the response line. Our imager has 10 bits of precision. Due to nonlinear saturation effects at the extreme ends of the scale we only use values in the range of 5 to 1,000 in our least squares computation. We can ignore the direct current (DC) offset of this calculation and store only the slope of the response line as one floating point number per pixel. This image representation allows for the specification of a desired exposure interval at viewing time.

Alpha Mattes

To construct the image-based visual hull on which we parameterize the opacity hull, we extract silhouette images from various viewpoints. Earlier versions of our system use fluorescent lights to acquire silhouette views. Backlighting is a common segmentation approach that is often used in commercial 2D machine vision systems. The backlights saturate the image sensor in areas where they are visible. We then threshold the silhouette images to establish a binary segmentation for the object.

However, binary thresholding is not accurate enough for objects with small silhouette features, such as hair. It also does not permit subpixel accurate compositing of the objects into new environments. An additional problem is color *spill* [SB96], the reflection of backlight on the foreground object. Spill typically happens near object silhouettes because the Fresnel effect increases the specularity of materials near grazing angles. With a single color active backlight, spill is particularly prominent for highly specular surfaces, such as metal or ceramics.

We use a variant of the multibackground matting technique of Smith and Blinn [SB96] to solve these problems. We acquire alpha mattes of the object from each viewpoint. An alpha matte of a foreground object can be extracted by imaging the object against two background images with different colors. We display the following sinusoidal background patterns on the plasma monitors:

$$I_j(x, y, n) = \left(1 + n \sin\left(\frac{2\pi(x + y)}{\phi} + j\frac{\pi}{3}\right)\right) \times 127. \qquad (3.15)$$

$I_j(x, y, n)$ is the intensity of color channel $j = r, g, b$ at pixel location (x, y). To maximize the per-pixel difference between the two backdrops, the patterns are phase shifted by 180° ($n = -1$ or 1). The user defines the period of the sinusoidal stripes with the parameter ϕ.

Using the multibackground matting equation from Smith and Blinn [SB96], the per-pixel object alpha α is computed as

$$\alpha = 1 - \frac{\sum |O_{n=1} - O_{n=-1}|}{\sum |R_{n=1} - R_{n=-1}|} \qquad (3.16)$$

where $R_{n=1}$ and $R_{n=-1}$ are per-pixel background colors of the reference images, and $O_{n=1}$ and $O_{n=-1}$ are per-pixel foreground colors for $n = \pm 1$, respectively.

If we measure the same color at a pixel both with and without the object for each background, Equation (3.16) equals zero. This corresponds to a pixel that maps straight through from the background to the sensor. The phase shifts in the color channels of Equation (3.15) assure that the denominator of Equation (3.16) is never zero. The sinusoidal pattern reduces the chance that a pixel color observed due to spill matches the pixel color of the reference image. Nevertheless, we still observed spill errors for highly specular objects, such as the teapot or the bonsai pot.

To reduce these errors we apply the same procedure multiple times, each time varying the parameter ϕ of the backdrop patterns. For the final alpha matte we store the maximum alpha from all intermediate mattes. We found that acquiring three intermediate alpha mattes with relatively prime periods $\phi = 27, 40$, and 53 is sufficient. The overhead of taking the additional images is small, and we need to store only the final alpha matte. Figure 3.21 shows two alpha mattes acquired with our method. We found that in practice this method works very well for a wide variety of objects, including specular and fuzzy materials.

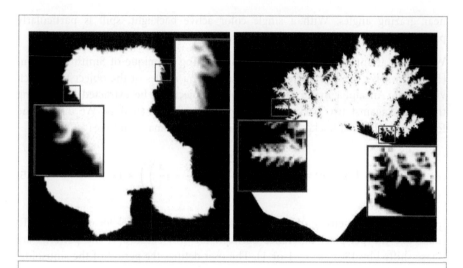

Figure 3.21: Alpha mattes acquired using our backdrops.

Opacity Hull Construction

Using the alpha mattes of the object from various viewpoints, we construct the opacity hull. First, we use binary thresholding on the alpha mattes to get binary silhouette images. Theoretically, each pixel with $\alpha > 0$ (i.e., not transparent) belongs to the foreground object. We use a slightly higher threshold because of noise in the system and calibration inaccuracies. We found that a threshold of $\alpha > 0.05$ yields a segmentation that covers all of the object and parts of the background.

The binary silhouettes are then used to construct the Image-Based Visual Hull (IBVH) [MBR+00]. The IBVH algorithm can be counted on to remove improperly classified foreground regions as long as they are not consistent with all other images. We resample the IBVH into a dense set of surface points as described in Section 3.3.6. Each point on the visual hull surface is projected onto the alpha mattes to determine its opacity from a particular observed viewpoint.

The opacity hull is similar to a surface light field, but instead of storing radiance it stores opacity values in each surface point. It is useful to introduce the notion of an *alphasphere A*. If ω is an outgoing direction at the surface point $\mathbf{p}$, then $A(\mathbf{p}, \omega)$ is the opacity value seen along direction ω.

Figure 3.22 shows the observed alpha values for three surface points on an object for all 6×36 viewpoints. Each pixel has been colored according to its opacity. Black color corresponds to $\alpha = 0$, white color corresponds to $\alpha = 1$, and gray

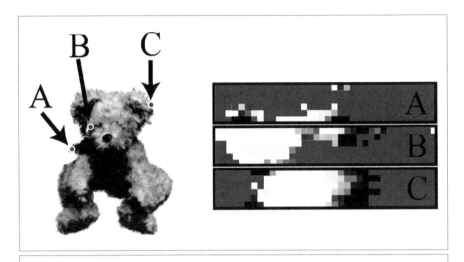

Figure 3.22: Observed alpha values for points on the opacity hull. Red color indicates invisible camera views.

color corresponds to values in between. Red color indicates camera views that are invisible from the surface point.

The function A is defined over the entire direction sphere. Any physical scanning system acquires only a sparse set of samples of this function. As is done for radiance samples of lumispheres in Wood et al. [WAA+00], one could estimate a parametric function for A and store it in each alpha sphere. However, as shown in Figure 3.22, the view-dependent alpha is not smooth and not easily amenable to parametric function fitting. Consequently, we store the acquired alpha mattes and interpolate between them to render the opacity hull from arbitrary viewpoints.

It is important to keep in mind that the opacity hull is a view-dependent representation. It captures view-dependent partial occupancy of a foreground object with respect to the background. The view-dependent aspect sets the opacity hull apart from voxel shells, which are frequently used in volume graphics [UO93]. Voxel shells are not able to accurately represent fine silhouette features, which is the main benefit of the opacity hull.

Recognizing the importance of silhouettes, Sander et al. [SGG+00] use silhouette clipping to improve the visual appearance of coarse polygonal models. However, their method depends on accurate geometric silhouettes, which is impractical for complex silhouette geometry like fur, trees, or feathers. Opacity hulls are somewhat similar to the concentric, semitransparent textured shells that Lengyel et al. [LPFH01] used to render hair and furry objects. They use geometry—called *textured fins*—to improve the appearance of object silhouettes. A single instance of the fin texture is used on all edges of the object. In contrast, opacity hulls can be looked at as textures with view-dependent alphas for every surface point of the object. They accurately render silhouettes of high complexity using only visual hull geometry.

Surface Light Fields and Reflectance Fields

Similar to constructing the opacity hull, we reparameterize the acquired radiance images into rays emitted from surface points on the visual hull. This representation is a surface light field as described by Miller et al. [RMP98] and Wood et al. [WAA+00]. However, our surface light fields are created on the surface of the visual hull rather than on the surface of the object.

Surface light fields can only represent models under the original illumination. To address this limitation we acquire surface reflectance fields from multiple viewing positions around the object. Debevec et al. [DHT+00] define the reflectance field under directional illumination as a six-dimensional function $R(\mathbf{p}, \omega_i, \omega_r)$. For each surface point $\mathbf{p}$, it maps incoming light directions ω_i to reflected color values along direction ω_r. Thus, for each point $\mathbf{p}$ we have a four-dimensional function $R_{\mathbf{p}}(\omega_i, \omega_r)$.

During acquisition, we sample the four-dimensional function $R_{\mathbf{p}}(\omega_i, \omega_r)$ from a set of viewpoints Ω_r and a set of light directions Ω_i. In previous reflectance field approaches [DHT+00, HCD01, BKMK01], the sampling of light directions is dense (e.g., $|\Omega_i| = 64 \times 32$ in [DHT+00]), but only a single viewpoint is used. In our system, we sample the reflectance field from many directions ($|\Omega_r| = 6 \times 36$). To limit the amount of data we acquire and store, our system uses a sparse sampling of light directions ($|\Omega_i| = 4 \times 15$). Thus, our illumination environment has to be filtered down substantially, and our re-illumination is accurate only for relatively diffuse surfaces [RH01a].

Reconstruction of an image from a new viewing direction under a new lighting configuration is a two-pass process. First, we reconstruct the images from the original viewpoints under novel illumination. Once we have computed these images, we interpolate the image data to new viewpoints. For a particular image from the original viewpoint, it is useful to define a slice of the reflectance field called a *reflectance function* $R(x_o, \omega_i)$ [DHT+00]. It represents how much light is reflected toward the camera by pixel x_o as a result of illumination from direction ω_i. We can reconstruct the image $L(x_o)$ from the original viewpoint under novel illumination as a weighted linear combination of the light sources as we will show in Section 3.3.8.

Environment Mattes

We observe that using a high-resolution environment matte in a particular viewing direction is superior to using only the light array to provide incident illumination. For example, Debevec et al. [DHT+00] use 2,048 light positions, which corresponds to a 32 × 64 pixel environment map. Using only our light array effectively constrains us to illumination from a 4 × 15 pixel environment map. These resolutions are not nearly enough to accurately capture and represent transmissive and refractive effects. For example, looking straight through a glass window shows the background in its full resolution. On the other hand, using a high-resolution illumination environment is only feasible with environment matting. The alternative would be to store a very large number of reflectance images for each viewpoint, which is impractical. Environment mattes are in essence a very compact representation for high-resolution surface reflectance fields.

To acquire environment mattes, we are using the high-quality procedure by Chuang et al. [CZH+00]. The acquisition process involves taking multiple images of the foreground object in front of a backdrop with a 1D Gaussian profile that is swept over time in horizontal, vertical, and diagonal directions. Using the nonlinear optimization procedure described by Chuang et al. [CZH+00], we then solve for a and the parameters of the 2D Gaussian's G.

To save storage and computation time for the nonlinear parameter estimation, we identify and remove areas outside the object silhouette. The environment matte is subdivided into 8 × 8 pixel blocks. Each surface point on the opacity hull that is visible from this view is projected into the image. Only those blocks that contain at least one back-projected surface point are stored and processed.

For certain positions in the camera array, the rim of the plasma monitors is visible through a transparent object, which makes much of the field of view unusable. Consequently, we only use the lower and the two uppermost cameras for acquisition of environment mattes. The lower camera is positioned horizontally, directly in front of the background monitor. The two upper cameras are positioned above the monitor on the turntable. Using our environment matte interpolation (see Section 3.3.8), we can render plausible results for any viewpoint.

3.3.6 POINT-SAMPLED DATA STRUCTURE

We use an extended point representation based on the layered depth cube (LDC)-tree [PZvBG00] as our shape model on which we parameterize the view-dependent appearance data. In a preprocess, we compute the octree-based LDC-tree from the IBVH. The creation of the LDC-tree starts with the sampling of the visual hull from three orthogonal directions. The sampling density depends on the model complexity and is user specified. The layered depth images are then merged into a single octree model. Since our visual hulls are generated from virtual orthographic viewpoints, their registration is exact. This merging also insures that the model is uniformly sampled.

Point samples have several benefits for 3D scanning applications. From a modeling point of view, the point-cloud representation eliminates the need to establish topology or connectivity. This facilitates the fusion of data from multiple sources, as pointed out by Levoy and Whitted [LW85]. They also avoid the difficult task of computing a consistent parameterization of the surface for texture mapping. We found that point models are able to represent complex organic shapes, such as a bonsai tree or a feather, more easily than polygonal meshes. In particular, it would be hard to represent the view-dependent opacity values at each point of the opacity hull using polygonal models and texture mapping.

Each surfel (surface element) in the LDC-tree stores depth, normal, and a camera-visibility bit vector. The visibility vector stores a value of one for each camera position from which the surfel was visible and zero if it was not visible. It can be quickly computed during IBVH construction using the visibility algorithm described in Matusik et al. [MBR^{+}00]. Our representation stores all of the acquired radiance and reflectance images with irrelevant information removed. This is accomplished by dividing each source image into 8 × 8 blocks and removing those blocks that lie outside the object's silhouette. For each image, we compute a simple mask by back-projecting all surfels from which this view is visible. Only the 8 × 8 pixel blocks that contain at least one back-projected surfel are stored. This simple scheme typically reduces the total amount of image data by a factor of 5 to 10, depending on the geometry of the model.

A relightable model requires more than 20 GB of raw image data. In order to make these data more manageable, we have implemented a simple compression scheme for reflectance images. For each original viewpoint, we apply principal component analysis (PCA) to corresponding 8 × 8 image blocks across the varying 4 × 15 illumination directions taken from a common viewpoint. We set a global threshold for the root mean square (RMS) reconstruction error and store a variable number of principal components per block. As shown in Section 3.3.8, the average number of components per block is typically four to five. PCA compression typically reduces the amount of reflectance data by a factor of 10.

Figure 3.23 shows a depiction of our data structure for surface reflectance fields, simplified for clarity. The figure shows the first six PCA images for two original views. These images are combined into new radiance images from the same viewpoints under new illumination using the method described in Section 3.3.8. During rendering, points on the opacity hull of the object are projected into the radiance images based on their visibility. Each surfel's color is determined using

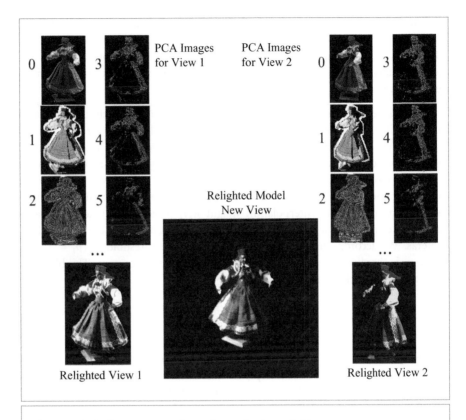

Figure 3.23: Data structure for surface reflectance fields.

interpolation among the four closest views. Note that the figure shows the two closest views.

3.3.7 SURFACE LIGHT FIELDS

Surface Light Field Rendering

To render our point-sampled models we use the elliptical weighted average (EWA) surface-splatting approach of Zwicker et al. [ZPvG01] (see Section 6.1). First, the opacity and color of each surfel are interpolated from the radiance images as discussed below. A hierarchical forward-warping algorithm projects the surfels onto the screen. A screen-space EWA filter reconstructs the image using the opacity, color, and normal stored per surfel. A modified A-buffer provides order-independent alpha blending and edge antialiasing.

To interpolate the radiance images from the original viewpoints to arbitrary viewpoints, we use the unstructured lumigraph interpolation of Buehler et al. [BBM+01]. For each surfel, we use k-nearest neighbor interpolation to reconstruct view-dependent alpha and radiance values. This assures continuous transitions between camera views.

For each frame, we compute the normalized direction $r_c(i)$ from each surfel position to each visible camera i using the visibility bit vector and a global array of camera positions. We also compute the normalized viewing direction r_v from the surfel position to the center of projection of the current view. We then assign a penalty $p(i) = 1 - \cos \theta_i$ to each visible camera, where $\cos \theta_i = r_c \cdot r_v$. We consider only the $k = 4$ cameras with smallest penalty $p(i)$ when interpolating a value. All other cameras are assigned an interpolation weight $w(i)$ of zero. We take care that a particular camera's weight falls to zero as it leaves the set of the closest four cameras. We accomplish this by defining an adaptive threshold $\cos \theta_t = r_4 \cdot r_v$, where r_4 is the direction of the surfel to the fourth closest camera. The blending weight $w(i)$ for each camera is

$$w(i) = \frac{\cos \theta_i - \cos \theta_t}{1 - \cos \theta_t}. \qquad (3.17)$$

This weight function has its maximum value of one for $\cos \theta_i = 1$, and it falls off to zero at $\cos \theta_i = \cos \theta_t$. To ensure epipole consistency, we multiply $w(i)$ by $1/p(i)$. This ensures that rendering the object from original camera viewpoints reproduces exactly the original images. We also normalize all $w(i)$ so that they sum up to one.

Surface Light Field Examples

We have collected a wide range of objects and surface types with our system. We have acquired many difficult surfaces including those of various genuses, with concavities, and with fine scale features. We have also captured a wide range of materials, including fuzzy and highly specular materials. A variety of different models are shown in Figure 3.24.

For all objects, we use 6 cameras and 36 turntable positions. We acquire 6 object images for alpha matting from each viewpoint (over three ϕ values with $n = \pm 1$). For surface light fields, we capture 1 radiance image from each viewpoint for a total of $6 \times 36 \times (4 \times 1 + 6) = 2{,}160$ images. The entire digitizing process takes about one hour for a surface light field. The whole process is fully automated without any user intervention. All of our models are created from a single scan.

We resampled all of our visual hull models to 512×512 resolution of the LDC-tree. The processing time to segment the images, compute the opacity hull, and build the point-based data structure is less than 10 minutes.

Figure 3.25 shows the visual hull, opacity hull, and final composite rendering of a bonsai tree. Notice the coarse shape of the visual hull and the much improved rendition using the opacity hull, despite the fact that their geometry is identical. The opacity hull also allows high-quality compositing over complex backgrounds without edge aliasing.

Figure 3.24: Surface light fields of several objects from new viewpoints. Note the alpha compositing with the textured backgrounds.

Figure 3.25: (*a*) Photo of the object. (*b*) Rendering using the opacity hull. (*c*) Visual hull. (*d*) Opacity hull.

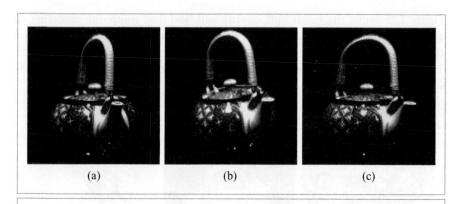

Figure 3.26: Rendering from arbitrary viewpoints. (*a and c*) Original images. (*b*) Interpolated view.

Unstructured lumigraph interpolation for viewpoints other than those seen by reference cameras introduces small artifacts, most notably for specular or concave areas. Figure 3.26 shows acquired images of an object (Figures 3.26a and c). Figure 3.26b shows the object from an intermediate viewpoint. Note that the figure shows only the two closest views, although we use the four closest views for interpolation. As can be seen in the figure, the artifacts are generally small. The animations show that the k-nearest neighbor interpolation leads to nice and smooth transitions.

To evaluate the number of images required to compute the visual hull, we instrumented our code to compute the change in volume of orthographic visual hulls as each silhouette is processed. We then randomized the processing order of the images and repeated the IBVH calculation multiple times. The plots shown in Figure 3.27 illustrate the rather typical behavior.

Generally, the visual hull converges to within 5% of its final volume after processing around 20 images, and seldom is this plateau not reached by 30 images. Collecting data over the entire hemisphere ensures that this volume closely approximates the actual visual hull. This implies that the visual hull processing time can be dramatically reduced by considering fewer images to compute the hull model. However, dense alpha mattes are still important for representing view-dependent opacity. These view-dependent opacities and radiance measurements dramatically improve the final renderings.

3.3.8 RELIGHTING

Light Transport Model

We first develop our model for how light scatters at the object surface following the exposition of Chuang et al. [CZH+00] and Debevec et al. [DHT+00]. Assuming

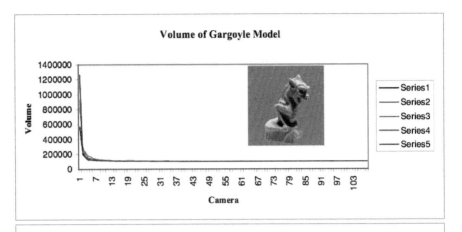

Figure 3.27: The volume of the visual hull as a function of the number of images used to construct the visual hull.

that the incident radiation originates infinitely far away from the object surface, the light arriving at a camera pixel can be described as

$$L(x_o) = \int_\Omega R(x_o, \omega_i) L(\omega_i) d\omega_i. \qquad (3.18)$$

$L(x_o)$ is the recorded radiance value at each camera pixel, and $L(\omega_i)$ is the environment illumination from direction ω_i. $R(x_o, \omega_i)$ is a weighting function that comprises all means of light transport from the environment through the foreground object to the camera. Debevec et al. [DHT+00] call it the reflectance function. The integration is carried out over the entire hemisphere Ω and for each wavelength. We will drop the wavelength dependency in the rest of this Chapter, assuming that all equations are evaluated separately for r, g, and b.

Given a measured radiance $L(x_o)$ at a pixel and an environment $L(\omega_i)$, we want to estimate the function $R(x_o, \omega_i)$ for the point x_o on the object surface corresponding to the ray through that pixel. Our scanning system provides two different illumination fields for the environment: illumination from a high-resolution 2D texture map behind the object (displayed on the plasma monitors), and illumination by the overhead light array from a sparse set of directions on the remaining hemisphere. Figure 3.28 shows the basic setup.

We call the sector of the environment hemisphere covered by the high-resolution texture map Ω_h, and the remaining sector covered by the light array Ω_l. Furthermore, we are making the simplifying assumption that light transport in Ω_h can be described by two components (see Figure 3.28a). As shown in the figure, we are approximating the (potentially complicated) paths of light through the object

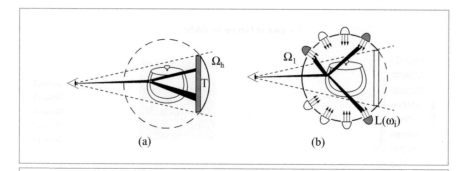

Figure 3.28: Illumination environment and light propagation model in our system. (*a*) High-resolution sampling across Ω_h. (*b*) Low-resolution sampling across Ω_l.

by two straight light bundles from the ray-surface intersection to the background monitor. On the other hand, light from one or more directional light sources $L(\omega_i)$ in Ω_l is refracted and reflected by the object before arriving at pixel x_o (see Figure 3.28b). Here we assume that the incident light field in Ω_l can be sampled at substantially lower resolution than light in Ω_h coming directly from behind the object. Thus, Equation (3.18) becomes

$$L(x_o) = \int_{\Omega_h} R_h(x_o, \omega_i)L(\omega_i)d\omega_i + \int_{\Omega_l} R_l(x_o, \omega_i)L(\omega_i)d\omega_i. \qquad \text{(3.19)}$$

As proposed by Chuang et al. [CZH$^+$00], we use a sum of 2D Gaussians to describe $R_h(x_o, \omega_i)$. We restrict ourselves to a maximum of two Gaussians per surface point x_o. Thus,

$$R_h(x_o, \omega_i) = \sum_{j=1}^{2} a_j(x_o)G_j(\omega_i, x_o). \qquad \text{(3.20)}$$

G_j are elliptical, oriented 2D unit-Gaussians, and a_j are attenuation factors. Each Gaussian G_j is parameterized by the center C_j, its standard deviation σ_j, and its orientation θ_j.

Since we are sampling Ω_l with a discrete set of n light positions L_j, we can rewrite Equation (3.19) as

$$L(x_o) = \int_{\Omega_h} \sum_{j=1}^{2} a_j(x_o)G_j(\omega_i, x_o)L(\omega_i)d\omega_i + \sum_{j=1}^{n} R_jL_j. \qquad \text{(3.21)}$$

Using the environment matting and reflectance field procedures outlined in Section 3.3.5, we estimate the parameters for a_j, G_j, and R_j. For each viewpoint, the estimated parameters a_j and G_j are stored in an environment matte T and R_j is stored in n reflectance images.

Discussion   Equation (3.21) is a compromise between high-quality environment matting [CZH$^+$00] and the practical limitations of our 3D acquisition system. Ideally, one would surround the object with high-resolution monitors and acquire the parameters of an arbitrary number of weighting functions W distributed over multiple monitors. Instead, we assume that most of the refracted and reflected rays arriving at a pixel originate from the incident light field behind the object. This is true for most objects with a strong reflected component (mostly at grazing angles) and a strong refracted component. It is not necessarily correct for transparent objects with large-scale internal structure or surface facets, such as a crystal glass. However, in practice we found this approach to work reasonably well.

It is important to note that, despite the term surface *reflectance* field, we are capturing a much wider array of effects, including refraction, dispersion, subsurface scattering, and nonuniform material variations. These effects, which are typically costly or impossible to simulate, can be rendered from our model in a reasonable amount of time. As noted by Debevec et al. [DHT$^+$00], the surface reflectance field is almost equivalent to the Bidirectional Surface-Scattering Distribution Function (BSSRDF). The main differences are that we do not know the exact physical location of a ray-surface intersection, and that the incoming direction of light is the same for any point on the surface. The first problem could potentially be addressed by improving the visual hull geometry using methods of stereopsis. Solving the second problem would require illuminating the object with a dense set of laser-point light sources.

Equation (3.21) differs from Equation (3.12) in Chuang et al. [CZH$^+$00] by restricting the number of incoming ray bundles from the monitors to two, and by replacing the foreground color F with a sum over surface reflectance functions R_i. The first assumption is valid if reflection and refraction at an object causes view rays to split into two distinct ray bundles that strike the background (see Figure 3.28a). The second assumption results in a more accurate estimation of how illumination from Ω_l affects the object's foreground color. Chuang et al. [CZH$^+$00] make up for this by capturing additional environment mattes using monitors on each side of the object.

Surface Reflectance Field Rendering

We start with a new environment map, for example, a spherical high-dynamic range light probe image of a natural scene. We first reconstruct the low-resolution reflectance function for the original viewpoints using this new illumination environment. Next we interpolate these relit images to the new viewpoint. The high-resolution reflectance function is reconstructed by first interpolating the parameters of the Gaussians for a new viewpoint. Then we integrate the Gaussians with the environment map to compute the outgoing radiance. (Note the difference between environment "mattes" and "maps.") Finally, we sum the low- and high-resolution components. We now discuss these steps in more detail.

Low-resolution Reflectance Function   During rendering, we compute the k-nearest ($k = 4$) visible original viewpoints used for each surface point. As mentioned in Section 3.3.5, visibility is determined during opacity hull construction and stored in the visibility vector. We compute the interpolation weights w_i for the four closest viewpoints according to unstructured lumigraph interpolation [BBM+01]. The weights ensure continuous transitions between camera views and epipole consistency; in other words, rendering the object from original camera viewpoints exactly reproduces the original images. Using the global camera parameters, each surface point is then projected into its k-nearest alpha mattes. We use the interpolation weights w_i to interpolate the view-dependent alpha from the alpha mattes.

Now we describe how we compute images that show the object under the new environment map illumination for each of the k-nearest original viewpoints. The environment map must be down-sampled to match the light positions used during acquisition. In our case it contains only 4×15 positions. The original reflectance images for a viewpoint are compressed using PCA as described in Section 3.3.6. This allows us to express the reflectance function R_j of a specific incoming light direction for the low-resolution lighting environment as

$$R_j \approx \tilde{R}_j = \sum_{i=1}^{m} \gamma_{ij} e_i,$$
(3.22)

where e_i are the eigenvectors corresponding to the the largest m eigenvalues. Each e_i is a 64-element vector corresponding to an 8×8 pixel block. Given a new set of n directional lights $\tilde{L}_j$, we can compute the outgoing radiance L_{Ω_i} for the relit image as

$$L_{\Omega_i} = \sum_{j=1}^{n} \tilde{R}_j \tilde{L}_j = \sum_{j=1}^{n} (\sum_{i=1}^{m} \gamma_{ij} e_i) \tilde{L}_j$$
(3.23)
$$= \sum_{i=1}^{m} (\sum_{j=1}^{n} \gamma_{ij} \tilde{L}_j) e_i.$$

The inner summation over n is the same for each of the 8×8 pixels and can, therefore, be computed only once. Finally, we use the interpolation weights w_i to interpolate the k relit images to obtain the image from the novel viewpoint.

High-resolution Reflectance Function   Our acquired environment mattes are parameterized on the plane T of the background monitor. However, for rendering they need to be parameterized on the global environment map Ω. Figure 3.29 shows a 2D drawing of the situation.

During system calibration we determine the position of each monitor plane T with respect to each viewpoint. This information is globally stored per viewpoint. Ω is the parameterization plane of the new environment map. The mapping from T to Ω may be nonlinear, for example, for spherical environment maps. A 3D surface point **p** on the object is projected onto a pixel of the environment matte E, which stores the parameters of the 2D Gaussian G. We compute the Gaussian $\tilde{G}$ that best approximates the projected Gaussian G on the parameterized surface $\tilde{T}$.

We represent the new Gaussian $\tilde{G}$ using the following parameters: a (the amplitude of G), $\tilde{C}$ (a 3D vector), (α, β) (the opening angles), and $\tilde{\theta}$ (the new rotation angle). This projection is performed for each change of the environment map.

To compute the radiance contribution from the environment mattes involves two steps: interpolating the new Gaussian $\hat{G}$, and convolving it with the environment map to compute the resulting colors.

We first interpolate the parameters of $k = 4$ reprojected Gaussian $\tilde{G}_i$. Using w_i, we compute linear combinations for the amplitudes a_i and the directional vectors $\tilde{C}_i$. The angular parameters (α_i, β_i) and $\tilde{\theta}_i$ are blended using quaternion interpolation. The result is a new Gaussian $\hat{G}$ that is an interpolated version of the Gaussian $\tilde{G}_i$, morphed to the new viewpoint.

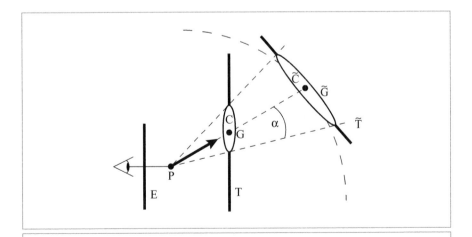

Figure 3.29: Reprojection of the environment matte Gaussian G from the monitor plane T into the environment map Ω.

Note that this interpolation needs to be performed on matching Gaussians from the environment mattes. Figure 3.30 shows a simplified 1D drawing of the matching process. We are only storing two Gaussians G_i per environment matte pixel, where each pixel corresponds to a viewpoint ray V_i in the figure. The two Gaussians per pixel are classified as *reflective* ($\tilde{G}_{ir}$) or *transmissive* ($\tilde{G}_{it}$). We compute the angle ϕ of their center vectors $\tilde{C}_{ir}$ and $\tilde{C}_{it}$ with the surface normal N. If $\phi > 90°$, we classify the Gaussian as transmissive. If $\phi <= 90°$, we classify it as reflective. If both Gaussians are reflective or refractive, we only store the one with the larger amplitude a. This computation has to be performed for each change of the environment map, after computing the reprojected Gaussian $\tilde{G}$.

During interpolation, we match up refractive and reflective Gaussians. In other words, new Gaussians $\hat{G}_r$ and $\hat{G}_t$ are interpolated from $\tilde{G}_{ir}$ and $\tilde{G}_{it}$, respectively. Note that this matching would be much more difficult if we had stored more than two Gaussians per environment matte pixel, as proposed by Chuang et al. [CZH+00].

To compute the outgoing radiance L_{Ω_h} for a new viewpoint we integrate the interpolated Gaussian $\hat{G}_{r,t}$ with the novel high-resolution illumination $L(\omega_i)$:

$$L_{\Omega_h} = \int_{\Omega_h} \sum_{j=r,t} a_j(x_o)\hat{G}_j(\omega_i, x_o)L(\omega_i)d\omega_i. \qquad (3.24)$$

The final pixel color C according to Equation (3.21) is the sum of the low-resolution reflectance field (Equation 3.23) and the high-resolution reflectance field (Equation 3.24).

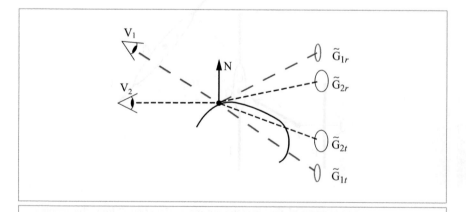

Figure 3.30: Matching of reflective and refractive Gaussians.

Surface Reflectance Field Examples

Low-resolution Illumination   First, we present the results and analysis of relighting using only low-resolution reflectance fields. For low-resolution surface reflectance fields, we acquire reflectance images using 4×15 light directions from each viewpoint for a total of $6 \times 36 \times (4 \times (4 \times 15)) + 6) = 53{,}136$ images. The entire digitizing process takes about 14 hours for a surface reflectance field.

Figure 3.31 shows a model under new illumination. Figure 3.32 shows several scanned objects composited into real environments. We acquired spherical light probe images [DM97] at the respective locations to capture the illumination. All objects shown in this paper are rendered from novel viewpoints that are not part of the acquired image sequence.

In the process of acquiring models, we have made many interesting measurements and observations. Figure 3.33 shows plots of the measured low-resolution reflectance field data for three surface points on an object. We chose the surfels to be in specular and self-shadowed areas of the object. The dark parts of the plots are attributable to self-shadowing. The data lack any characteristics that would make them a good fit to standard parametric BRDF models or function approximation techniques. This is typical for the data we observed.

Figure 3.34 shows a visualization of the number of PCA components per 8×8 pixel block of the reflectance images from an original viewpoint. We set the global RMS reconstruction error to be within 1% of the average radiance values of all high dynamic range (HDR) reflectance images. Note that areas with high texture frequency require more components than areas of similar average color. The maximum number of components for this view is 10, the average is 5. This is typical for all of our data.

High-resolution Illumination   Next, we present the results of using the combined low-resolution reflectance fields and high-resolution environment mattes. Figures 3.35 and 3.36 show different models in new illumination environments.

Figure 3.31: Relightable model under novel illumination.

Figure 3.32: A combination of scanned and real objects in real environments. The scanned objects were illuminated using surface reflectance fields.

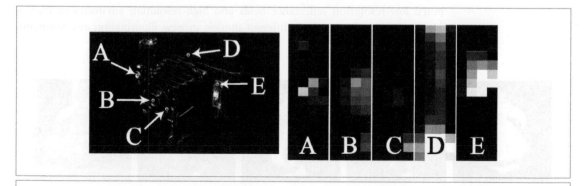

Figure 3.33: Measured reflectance function data for several surface points.

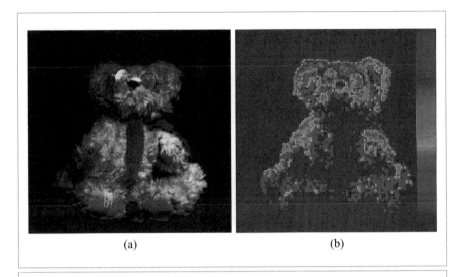

(a)   (b)

Figure 3.34: (*a*) Original view. (*b*) Visualization of the number of PCA components per block (Max. = 15, Mean = 5).

Figure 3.35: *Left*: High-resolution reflectance field from the environment mattes. *Middle*: Low-resolution reflectance field from the reflectance images. *Right*: Combined.

Figure 3.36: Frames from an animation with rotating viewpoint.

We used the light-probe images available from Paul Debevec's website as environment maps. All objects are rendered from novel viewpoints that are not part of the acquired image sequence.

Figure 3.35 shows renderings using only the environment mattes (left), using only the reflectance images (middle), and combining the two (right). Note that the environment mattes, storing the high-resolution reflectance field, mostly capture refractions, while the reflectance images, storing the low-resolution reflectance field, mostly capture reflections.

Figure 3.36 shows a few frames from an animation with a rotating viewpoint. Note how the specular highlights and refractive effects are accurately preserved by our interpolation procedure.

In addition to low-resolution surface reflectance fields we need to acquire environment mattes from different viewpoints. For each viewpoint we capture 300 images to estimate an environment matte. Because the aspect ratio of our monitor is 16:9, we use a different number of backdrop images for each direction: 125 in diagonal, 100 in horizontal, and 75 in vertical direction. We capture environment mattes using only three of the six cameras. The cameras are roughly spaced 10° apart in elevation and 5° angular turntable increments. For a full 360° view of the object, this corresponds to $3 \times 72 = 432$ viewing positions. All environment matte and reflectance images are captured using the HDR technique. For each viewpoint, we take four pictures with different exposure times. The total number of pictures is $3 \times 72 \times 300 \times 4 = 259{,}200$. The additional acquisition time is about 18 hours, or 5 minutes per viewpoint.

3.3.9 CONCLUSION

This section described a fully automated and robust 3D photography system optimized for the generation of high-quality renderings of objects. The basic premise of our scanning approach is to use large amounts of radiance and opacity information to produce accurate renderings of the object instead of relying on accurate geometry. We have also presented a method for acquisition and rendering of transparent and refractive objects. Using a point-based 3D scanning system with color monitor backdrops, we are able to scan transparent objects that would be extremely difficult or impossible to scan with traditional 3D scanners.

We have introduced the opacity hull, a new shape representation that stores view-dependent alpha parameterized on the visual hull of the object. Opacity hulls combined with surface reflectance fields allow us to render objects with arbitrarily complex shape and materials under varying illumination from new viewpoints. We have shown that a parameterization of surface reflectance fields into high- and low-resolution areas offers a practical method to acquire high-quality models.

CHAPTER FOUR

Amenta, Nina

University of California
Department of Computer Science
2063 Engineering II
One Shields Avenue
Davis, CA 95616
USA
amenta@cs.ucdavis.ed
Tel: +1 530 754 5377
Fax: +1 530 752 4767

Wu, Jianhua

RWTH Aachen
Lehrstuhl für Informatik VIII
52056 Aachen
Germany
wu@informatik.rwth-aachen.de
Tel: +49 241 8021814
Fax: +49 241 8022899

Pauly, Mark

ETH Zürich
Computer Graphics Laboratory
Haldeneggsteig 4
8092 Zürich
Switzerland
pauly@inf.ethz.ch
Tel: +41 44 632 06 68
Fax: +41 44 632 15 96

Guennebaud, Gaël

IRIT - CNRS UMR 5505
Université Paul Sabatier
118, Route de Narbonne
31 062 Toulouse Cedex
France
guenneba@irit.fr
Tel: +33 56 155 83 29

Paulin, Mathias

IRIT - CNRS UMR 5505
Université Paul Sabatier
118, Route de Narbonne
31 062 Toulouse Cedex
France
Mathias.Paulin@irit.fr
Tel: +33 56 155 83 29

Alexa, Marc

TU Berlin
Computer Graphics
Sekretariat EN 7-1
Einsteinufer 17
10587 Berlin
Germany
marc@cs.tu-berlin.de
Tel: +49 30 314 73100
Fax: +49 30 314 23596

Kobbelt, Leif

RWTH Aachen
Lehrstuhl für Informatik VIII
52056 Aachen
Germany
kobbelt@informatik.rwth-aachen.de
Tel: +49 241 8021 801
Fax: +49 241 8022 899

Pajarola, Renato

Department of Informatics
University of Zürich
Binzmühlestrasse 14
8050 Zürich
Switzerland
pajarola@acm.org
Tel: +41 44 635 4370
Fax: +41 44 635 6809

Barthe, Loïc

IRIT - CNRS UMR 5505
Université Paul Sabatier
118, Route de Narbonne
31 062 Toulouse Cedex
France
lbarthe@irit.fr
Tel: +33 56 155 74 31

4 FOUNDATIONS AND REPRESENTATIONS

INTRODUCTION

This section acquaints the reader with the mathematical and algorithmic fundamentals of point-based surface representations. The chapter starts with a comprehensive overview of point-based surface representation and reconstruction methods presented in Section 4.1. It discusses major results from graphics, geometric modeling, and computational geometry. Section 4.2 is devoted to moving least squares surface representations (MLS) which are of fundamental importance in point-based computer graphics. The issue of point-cloud sampling and resampling is addressed in Section 4.3. Very often, point-based algorithms require fast access to

neighbored samples. The aspect of efficient spatial data structures will be elaborated in Section 4.4. Section 4.5 concludes this chapter with a presentation of real-time point model refinement, a somewhat more advanced topic which is important for efficient, high-quality rendering and display.

4.1 SURFACE RECONSTRUCTION

Nina Amenta

4.1.1 OVERVIEW

Converting a point-cloud representation of an object into a more explicit one, such as a triangle mesh, a collection of parametric patches, or the zero-set of a function on space, is known as *surface reconstruction*. For a point cloud dense enough to serve as a surface representation, the desired surface should be fairly unambiguous and most any computational technique one tries will produce a reasonable surface. This accounts for the wide variety of approaches that have been taken to the surface reconstruction problem. Rather than a single dominant method, there are many different approaches that are used depending on properties of the input, the desired output, the availability of software, the philosophy of the user, and so on.

Certainly which method is best depends in part on the input. For a noisy input point cloud with many outliers, for instance one captured using a stereo camera, it is important to filter the outliers and extract as much information as possible from the noisy data. A point cloud produced by a series of modeling operations, on the other hand, will be essentially noise free and a method that interpolates the input points could be used. Point clouds captured using commercial laser range scanners fall somewhere in between, with few outliers but some noise, mostly caused by scanner artifacts at sharp edges and, more significantly, alignment error between scans. The desired output also of course affects the choice of algorithm. Many applications require a watertight surface, that is, a surface bounding a closed solid, or, better yet, a closed manifold (disallowing points of contact of the surface with itself). This is necessary if the output solid is to be used for finite element analysis, rapid prototyping, parameterization, and many other purposes. In addition, the added constraint that the output surface needs to be watertight often makes for easier, or more robust, algorithms; the fewer choices the algorithm has the opportunity to make incorrectly, the better. On the other hand, some input point clouds, for instance a scan of a human face, cannot reasonably be interpreted as the boundary of a solid object. For such inputs, methods that produce a watertight surface have to "hallucinate" large portions of the output. In these cases, a method that produces surfaces with boundaries is preferable. Another way algorithms have been compared is by theoretical analysis. For the most part this kind of analysis has been applied to algorithms that use computational geometry, probably because of the theoretical history of that field. Most of the theoretical results use the following framework: assume that the input point set is sampled "densely enough" from the surface of an object, and then prove that some algorithm produces an output surface that recovers the correct topology and approximate geometry of the object surface. These proofs include a precise enough definition of what it means for a sample to be dense enough so that we get a very good sense of when the algorithm is guaranteed to work, which has been a strong aspect of this line of work. In this chapter, we will survey several of the approaches that have been taken to the surface reconstruction problem.

4.1.2 NORMAL ESTIMATION

We preface this survey by briefly considering the closely related problem of estimating normals vectors at or near an input point cloud $\mathcal{P}$. Surface reconstruction from a set of surfels with reliable normal directions is an easier problem than surface reconstruction from points alone; in essence, each surfel provides a local reconstruction of the surface. Finding normals is the first step in some reconstruction algorithms; others simply assume that reliable normals are available. Like surface reconstruction itself, the quality of the normals that can be computed for a point cloud depends on its distribution.

An approach first used by Hoppe et al. [HDD$^+$92] in the context of surface reconstruction is to find the k-nearest neighbors of point $\mathbf{p}$, the set $\mathcal{N}_k(\mathbf{p})$, and take the normal of the total least squares best-fitting plane to $\mathcal{N}_k(\mathbf{p})$ as the surface normal at $\mathbf{p}$. This method might lead to trouble when the points are not uniformly distributed. An example of particular concern is that when the points are distributed in rows or slices on the surface, then all of the points of $\mathcal{N}_k(\mathbf{p})$ are likely to lie in the same slice, and the total least squares best-fit plane might be perpendicular to the surface rather than an approximate tangent plane, as intended. An alternative is to use all points within distance r of $\mathbf{p}$. Using a fixed radius r leads to the same difficulties as using a fixed number of neighbors k, although one method or the other might work better on specific inputs.

Mitra et al. [MNG04] studied methods for choosing r adaptively at different points of $\mathcal{P}$. They observed that there is generally not a single best choice of r for a given input $\mathcal{P}$: the error of the best-fit plane increases with r in areas of high curvature, while it decreases with r where the noise is high. Assuming a random noise model, they gave analytic methods for bounding the error of the normal as a function of r, and proposed an algorithm for estimating the local curvature and noise level from the data and using them to choose an optimal r.

The Voronoi diagram of P can also be used to give a good estimate of the surface normal for points near the boundary of P. Assuming that P is fairly dense, the Voronoi cells of a point $\mathbf{p}$ on the exterior of P are elongated in the direction perpendicular to the surface. Call the vertex of the Voronoi cell of $\mathbf{p}$ farthest from $\mathbf{p}$ the *pole* of $\mathbf{p}$ [ABK98]. The vector from $\mathbf{p}$ to its pole is a good estimate of the surface normal. Dey and Goswami [DG04] bounded the error of this estimate, again assuming a specific noise model. Dey et al. [DLS04] compared this method experimentally to the total least squares approach above, and found it to be more accurate, although much more time consuming.

Whatever method is used to produce normals, some algorithms then expect them to be oriented so as to agree with each other about which is the inside and which is the outside of the surface. Sometimes (e.g., with laser range scanner data) this can be determined from the input. Finding a consistent orientation is also easy when the input densely samples a closed surface that cleanly divides the surrounding space into interior and exterior. With noisy and incomplete surface data, however, finding a consistent orientation can be difficult, especially if parts of the surface are very close to one another or if there are sharp creases that might be mistaken for surface boundaries.

4.1.3 IMPLICIT SURFACE METHODS

Many surface-reconstruction algorithms are based on the idea of using the input sample to produce a function $f()$ on all of 3D space. The function $f()$ is designed to be negative inside the object and positive outside the object, so that the desired surface S can be extracted as the zero level-set of $f()$. The *signed distance function*, representing the oriented distance from the surface, is one possible candidate for $f()$, but any function such that S is the zero-set can be used. There is a huge variety of techniques for representing and handling such implicit surfaces, and many of them have been applied to surface reconstruction.

Implicit function methods have the advantage that the output surface is always the watertight boundary of a solid (the set of points x such that $f(x) \leq 0$). In the generic case in which the zero-set avoids singularities of f, the resulting surface is also a manifold. To produce a manifold surface, the function $f()$ should be computed on a domain large enough to surround the input point set P and contain the entire zero-set of $f()$, as for instance in Turk and O'Brien [TO99]. An alternative is to instead take the domain to be a thin shell surrounding P, as for instance in Curless and Levoy [CL96]. This produces the subset of the surface that lies near P, which is typically a partial surface with boundary. While the output is not watertight, this approach is often more efficient.

Voxel-based Methods

The implicit surface method was implemented on a voxel grid by Hoppe et al. [HDD+92] in an influential paper that popularized the surface reconstruction problem in the graphics community. Their algorithm first estimates the normal direction at each point $\mathbf{p}$ by fitting a plane through $\mathbf{p}$'s k-nearest neighbors, the set $\mathcal{N}_k(\mathbf{p})$. The resulting directions are unoriented (see Section 4.1.2). We then traverse a spanning tree of $\mathcal{P}$ assigning a consistent orientation to the normals. The value of the function $f()$ at a point x in space is defined to be the distance from x to the tangent plane associated with the point $\mathbf{p} \in \mathcal{P}$ nearest to x. Finally, a piecewise-linear surface is extracted from the zero-set of $f()$ using marching cubes. Notice that this function $f()$ is discontinuous; the marching cubes process plasters over most of the discontinuities in the zero-set, but the resulting surfaces can suffer from holes. The implicit function representations discussed below, based on blending (rather than just switching between) locally defined approximations to the distance function, could remedy this problem at the cost of some additional computation.

Curless and Levoy [CL96] focused on the problem of surface reconstruction from laser range data. Their algorithm is remarkable for its efficiency and the quality of the output, and an implementation is available. Recall that a single laser range scan is a depth map: a grid of points in the $x - y$ plane, each associated with a depth value in the z-direction, all in some coordinate system related to the position and orientation of the scanner relative to the object. Rather than assigning point normals, patches of surface are reconstructed from individual input scans by simply connecting points adjacent in the $x - y$ grid if their distance from the scanner does not differ too greatly. Each such patch is then associated with a directional distance function in the z-direction associated with the coordinate system of that particular scan. These directional distance functions are then blended, using normalized Gaussian weights, to form the function $f()$, and again the surface is extracted using marching cubes. While each of the individual directional distance functions is itself continuous, the fact that two functions with very different directions might be blended together seems to lead to a noisier function F than might at first be expected, and some subsequent work has addressed the problem of cleaning up the "topological noise" in the output surfaces [WHDS04]. Efficiency is gained by limiting the domain on which $f()$ is computed to a thin shell around the input points, and only dealing with voxels within the shell. The algorithm returns a surface with boundaries, which tends to have holes where $\mathcal{P}$ has gaps. Curless and Levoy's algorithm is one of the few that treats scanner noise carefully. Each point of $\mathcal{P}$ is assigned a confidence. Points at which the scanner z-direction is nearly tangent to the surface patch are assigned lower confidence than points at which the scanner z-direction is nearly normal to the patch. Points near sharp features and near the edges of the patch are assigned lower confidence.

Probably because of this careful weighting of the input, this algorithm manages to produce good outputs from very difficult inputs involving many outliers and a lot of noise. See Figure 4.1.

The VripPack software, available at the Stanford Graphics website, implements this reconstruction method. It takes individual laser range scans as input.

Basis Functions

Implicit surfaces are also commonly represented by a weighted sum of basis functions, most commonly radial basis functions. Given the value of $f()$ at a set of constraint points in space, we center a radial basis function at each constraint point, and then solve for the choice of weights that causes the function to interpolate or approximate the constraints. For a number of natural measures of "smoothness or regularity" of the function $f()$, the optimal $f()$ satisfying the constraints is given by the interpolation using a particular radial basis function related to the smoothness measure [Dyn87]. This optimality is a very appealing property, both theoretically and in practice. Although it is the 3D function $f()$ that is optimized, not the zero-set S that is the actual output, nonetheless the surfaces produced tend to be very smooth and attractive. One important detail is that if all of the constraint points are surface points, then they have function value zero, since they are intended to lie on the

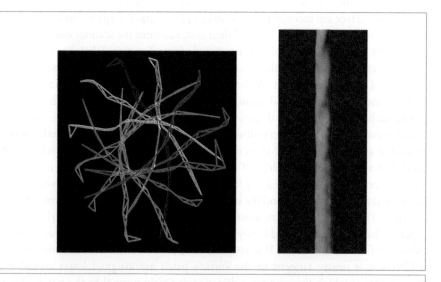

Figure 4.1: Reconstruction of a drillbit from Curless and Levoy [CL96]. (*Left*) A cross-section of the noisy input data, including a lot of scatter from the sharp corners. (*Right*) The reconstructed surface of the drillbit, extracting the spiral shape from the noisy data.

zero-set of $f()$. But the smoothest function fitting a set of points all with value zero is just the constant function zero. So it is necessary to provide constraint points in the interior of the object, with negative values, and outside the object, with positive values, as well as surface points.

In some situations such points are naturally available, and in others they can be generated. For instance, if points with normals are supplied, then for every surface point we can place additional off-surface points offset from it in both normal directions, and provide them with negative and positive values [TO99, CBC+01]. In this case it is important to ensure that the offset is small enough that the constructed points are not placed near other surface points. Turk and O'Brien [TO99] and Dinh et al. [DTS02] have applied implicit surfaces based on radial basis functions to a number of problems in computer graphics, including surface reconstruction. They show that radial basis functions can be used both with dense, fairly clean inputs like laser range scanner data, and also for sparse and noisy inputs that arise often in computer vision. Solving for the weights or other parameters associated with radial basis functions can be quite demanding computationally. Carr et al. [CBC+01] used multiscale methods developed by Beatson to efficiently compute radial basis function surfaces for inputs consisting of hundreds of thousands of input points, and also explored methods for iteratively adding basis functions until sufficient resolution is achieved.

Indicator Function

Another choice for $f()$ is the indicator function, which is one inside the object and zero outside. Kazhdan [Kaz05, KBH06] has proposed a clever algorithm, based on the observation that the gradient of the indicator function has a particularly simple form: it is zero everywhere except at the object surface, where it is equal to the surface normals. A continuous representation of the gradient field is easily computed from an input set of oriented surfels. The computation of $f()$ from its gradient field is a Poisson problem. Initially, this was solved in the Fourier domain, while the more recent paper with Bolitho and Hoppe [KBH06] gives a much more efficient solution using radial basis functions to represent both the gradient field and $f()$ itself. This surface reconstruction method produces a global function, like the radial basis function (RBF) methods of the previous section, but it is computationally much more efficient. It produces excellent looking results, and should be a very competitive method in practice.

MLS and MPU with Local Functions

Some recent implicit surface representations are based on the idea of constructing many "little" implicit functions locally near the point cloud, and then blending them together to form $f()$. Each function $f_i()$ is associated with a point $\mathbf{p}_i$ in space. To evaluate $f()$ at an arbitrary point x in space, we blend the $f_i()$, using weights that are designed to form a partition of unity, as follows. We associate a weight function w_i with each $\mathbf{p}_i$ that decreases monotonically with the distance from $\mathbf{p}_i$ (often all the w_i are the same, but this is not necessary). Then the value of $f()$ at point x is computed as:

$$f(x) = \frac{\sum_i w_i(||x - \mathbf{p}_i||)f_i(x)}{\sum_i w_i(||x - \mathbf{p}_i||)}. \tag{4.1}$$

This blending function produces the value for $f(x)$ that minimizes

$$\sum_i \frac{w_i(||x - \mathbf{p}_i||)}{\sum_i w_i(||x - \mathbf{p}_i||)}(f(x) - f_i(x))^2. \tag{4.2}$$

This idea of finding an optimum with respect to the local weights is the definition of the moving least squares function approximation (as opposed to the MLS projection method). If the weights can be chosen so that for any x, most of the weights $w_i(||x - \mathbf{p}_i||)$ are zero, $f()$ can be computed efficiently. In the common case in which the w_i are chosen to be Gaussian, usually the functions associated with points $\mathbf{p}_i$ sufficiently far from x can be disregarded.

The multilevel partition of unity (MPU) surface representation [OBA+03] is one implementation of this idea. It is built on an octree decomposition of space around the point cloud. Each octree leaf contains a constant number of points, each with an associated normal. A low-degree polynomial function that approximates the distance function to the points within the cell is used as $f_i()$, and the center of the cell is used as $\mathbf{p}_i$. Functions are also associated with interior nodes in the tree, giving lower-resolution approximations of the surface that fill in holes and ensure that the function is represented everywhere in space. Three different surface representations are used at the nodes, depending on the number of points and whether their normals agree or not: a parametric function (normals agree); an implicit quadric (many points, varying normals); or a piecewise-parametric function (few points, varying normals). Because of the quadtree, MPU does not require a uniform distribution of input points, but the possibility of octree artifacts (especially induced by outliers far from the data points) is a drawback.

A preliminary version of the software for MPU surface reconstruction is currently available from Ohtake's website at MPI-SB. It takes a list of points, followed by a list of normals, as input. The MPU code is quite fast, and can handle hundreds of thousands of input points.

Other applications of this idea are formulated in terms of the MLS function approximation rather than partitions of unity. Xie et al. [XWH03] compute approximating quadric polynomials $\mathbf{f}_i$ to cover homogenous patches of surface. These patches are grown from seeds and expanded as long as the points included can be well approximated by a quadric. Orientations are assigned to the patches in a final step, and the final surface representation is formed by locally blending the polynomials. The surfaces used by Nielson [Nie04] and Shen et al. [SOS04] for converting polygonal surfaces to implicit surfaces also fall into this category. In both cases local functions are defined for the facets of the polygonal model, and associated with points on the facets.

Such a function can also be defined given an input point set P with normals: we define the function $f_i()$ at each input sample $\mathbf{p}_i$ to be the distance from the plane through $\mathbf{p}_i$ with its normal $\mathbf{n}_i$. Kolluri [Kol05] showed that using such functions to define an MLS implicit function $f()$ gives a provably correct surface reconstruction algorithm. His analysis is similar to some of the results for algorithms based on Voronoi diagrams discussed in Section 4.1.4. Kolluri's proof requires the sample points to be distributed nearly uniformly on the surface. Dey and Sun [DS05] recently gave a similar definition that they show gives a correct reconstruction, even when the sampling density varies, so long as it is everywhere sufficiently dense. The influence of an input point s on the function at a point x in space is weighted both by the sampling density near x and the sampling density near s.

4.1.4 VORONOI METHODS

Algorithms for surface reconstruction developed in the computational geometry community have for the most part been based on the Voronoi diagram and its dual, the Delaunay triangulation. A particular strength of these algorithms is the emphasis on providing proofs of correctness, which usually take the following form: first assume that a smooth surface S is sampled "sufficiently densely" by set P, and then show that the output of the algorithm on P is a good approximation of S. The definition of a sufficiently dense sample must depend on some property of the surface; computational geometry algorithms use the distance from the medial axis. The *local feature size* lfs(x) at a point x in space is defined as the minimum distance from x to the medial axis. The distance between samples is then required to be proportional to lfs(x). Specifically, a set of sample points on the surface is an ϵ-sample if, for every point x on the surface, there is a sample within distance $\epsilon f(x)$ of x. The idea of this definition is that while the samples must be dense in more intricate parts of the surface, featureless areas can still be sampled sparsely. The radius of curvature of the surface is an upper bound on lfs(x), so this definition is related to sampling according to curvature, but lfs(x) can be small even when the curvature is zero, if two sheets of the surface lie near each other. One unfortunate feature of this definition is that lfs(x) is zero at a sharp corner, requiring infinitely dense sampling. Thus most of the results below are only valid for a smooth surface S. An ϵ-sample remains an ϵ-sample when more sample points are added; any kind of oversampling is allowed. Another drawback is that the sampling is usually assumed to be noiseless, and many of the

Voronoi diagram-based surface-reconstruction algorithms do not in fact do well on very noisy samples; current work is beginning to address this issue [CL05, DG04].

Algorithms

Surface reconstruction has been a topic in computational geometry since the 1980s, although the analytic framework is more recent. Jean-Daniel Boissonnat proposed "sculpting the shape from the 3D Delaunay tetrahedralization" [Boi84]. Tetrahedra likely to be outside the object are identified by their shape and removed one by one, in such a way that the remaining solid is always a sphere. Edelsbrunner and Mücke used a filtration of the Delaunay triangulation, the alpha shape, which is based on the interpoint distances [EM94]. Triangles for which small circumspheres can be found are retained as possible surface triangles.

Delaunay Filtering

The analytic framework and the sampling model were introduced in conjunction with the crust algorithm of Amenta and Bern [AB99, ABK98]. This algorithm is based on explicitly using the the Voronoi diagram to estimate the medial axis. The Voronoi cells of an ϵ-sample have a distinctive shape: they are long, thin, and perpendicular to the surface S; see Figure 4.2. The two "ends" of these long thin cells have to lie

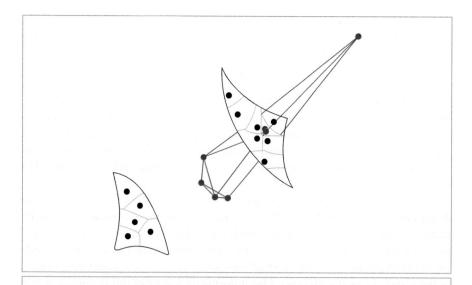

Figure 4.2: The 3D Voronoi diagram of points sampled from a smooth 2D surface. The intersection of the 3D cells with the surface is shown in black, and the edges of one Voronoi cell, belonging to the blue point, are shown in red. Notice that the Voronoi cell is long and skinny, with its long axis perpendicular to the surface. The ends of the Voronoi cell are located near the medial axis.

near the medial axis [ACK01b]. We call these Voronoi vertices the *poles*. The crust algorithm used the poles to eliminate triangles from the Delaunay tetrahedralization that cannot belong to the surface. The co-cone algorithm [ACDL02] simplifies and improves on this idea. The essential observation is that the vector from a sample point p to either of its poles should be close to the surface normal, so Delaunay triangles lying on the surface can be recognized by comparing their normals with the vectors to the poles. This algorithm was extended in various ways by Dey and others, to handle surfaces with sharp features and boundaries [DG01] and to produce watertight models [DG03]. Software for these algorithms is available. A recent algorithm of Dey and Goswami [DG04] generalizes the definition of poles to include all Voronoi vertices far from the surface, which can be determined from noisy as well as smooth data, to give an algorithm that works well on quite noisy inputs.

Distance Function and Gradient Flow

Another family of algorithms based on the Voronoi diagram and Delaunay triangulation uses the structure as an approximation of the distance function of S, from which a surface can be extracted. The Voronoi diagram of a point set P is the set of singularities of the squared distance function of P. The value of the distance function should be low near P and high near the medial axis. Unfortunately this function is only zero at the points themselves, and bumpy nearby, so it is not obvious how to extract an approximate surface directly from the Voronoi diagram. Two different algorithms, one due to Edelsbrunner [Ede05] and another to Giesen and John [GJ03], extract a 3D solid from the Delaunay triangulation by constructing a discrete flow corresponding to the gradient flow on the squared distance function; the two algorithms differ in the details of how the discrete flow is defined. In a discrete flow, a Delaunay tetrahedron flows into its neighbor across a face, or not, depending on the gradient of the Voronoi edge dual to the face. The part of the Delaunay tetrahedralization that flows to infinity is discarded as the exterior of the object. Interior portions flow to maxima in the interior of the object. Unfortunately, there can also be maxima corresponding to pockets exterior to the object. Resolving which maxima are interior or exterior to the object requires some user input, or other information.

Rather than the squared distance function, Boissonnat and Cazals [BC02b] interpolate a signed distance function. To get the sign, they need points with normals as input. They use Sibson's interpolation method, which is based on the Voronoi diagram. Sibson's interpolation adapts well to irregularities in the distribution of the input points, so that the zero-set of the resulting smooth function is used to select a set of Delaunay triangles to represent the surface.

Power Crust

The power crust algorithm of Amenta et al. [ACK01a, ACK01b] also constructs a 3D solid, but it uses the weighted Voronoi diagram of the poles, known as a *power diagram*, rather than the Delaunay triangulation of the sample points P. Instead of meeting at the medial axis, the cells of the power diagram meet at the object's surface. Power diagram cells belonging to the interior of the object can be cleanly separated from those belonging to the outside of the object by traversing the structure and looking at the connections between the cells. The resulting algorithm is quite robust. The output is the surface separating the interior and exterior cells, and it passes through the set P of input sample points (at least in the noise-free case). A drawback is that the output facets are convex polygons rather than triangles, and unfortunately this algorithm produces overly dense tessellated surfaces, even given nice inputs. Software for this algorithm is available, but it only works on moderately sized (tens of thousands of points) inputs.

Advantages and Disadvantages

All of these algorithms begin by computing the Delaunay triangulation of the input points. While Moore's Law and the sporadic improvement of 3D Delaunay codes make this feasible for increasingly large inputs, the current maximum seems to be somewhere in the tens of millions of points, and the computation is expensive in time and space. Then most of the triangulation is thrown away. Computing only the necessary part of the Delaunay triangulation would be much better. The ball-pivoting algorithm of Bernardini et al. [BMR+99] does this. Intuitively, the algorithm rolls a ball of fixed radius around the outside of the point cloud. Every time the ball comes to rest on three input samples, we connect those samples with a triangle. This works well for fairly uniformly sampled surfaces, such as laser range scanner data. It is not as robust as the algorithms that compute the entire Delaunay triangulation, however.

One advantage of these Voronoi/Delaunay algorithms is that most of them do not require surface normals as part of the input; the poles provide a very good approximation of the surface normals, and they generally relay on the global structure of the Voronoi diagram and the Delaunay triangulation to find a consistent orientation of the normals.

4.1.5 SURFACE EVOLUTION METHODS

Yet another class of methods is based on surface evolution. The idea is to gradually deform a simple input surface, using rules to maintain its structure and also rules to attract it to the input data. Since the initial placement of the evolving surface defines the inside or the outside of the object, typically these methods do not require normals for the input points.

An early straightforward implementation of this idea is due to Chen and Medioni [CM94]. They initialize the surface as a small ball inside the input point cloud, and allow it to expand using "balloon forces" until it reaches the input points. This is an example of a Lagrangian approach to surface evolution, in which the the evolving surface is represented explicitly, in this case by a triangle mesh. The forces include an inflation force in the normal direction and spring forces between neighboring vertices. When a sample point is detected close to a surface vertex and nearly in its normal direction, the vertex is "anchored" and no longer moved. Triangles that remain active and grow too large are subdivided. This has the effect of allowing the surface to change shape and adapt to non-star-shaped objects. A major drawback of this algorithm is that it only can be used to reconstruct objects homeomorphic to a sphere. Also the balance of the spring forces and edge subdivision seems like it might require some calibration for different inputs.

The level-set method of Osher and Sethian [OS88] has revolutionized surface evolution algorithms over the last decades. The level-set method is a Eulerian approach, meaning that the evolving surface is represented by a level-set in an implicit 3D function represented on a voxel grid. Changes in the implicit function can induce topological changes in the evolving surface, so that the topological genus of the output surface need not be known in advance. The level-set method was applied to surface reconstruction by Zhao et al. [ZOMK00], and the efficiency of the method was improved by Zhao et al. [ZOF01].

To use the level-set method, it is necessary to formulate the problem in terms of a PDE describing the evolution of the surface. This is then translated into the problem of evolving an implicit function $f()$ on the space, with the surface represented by the zero-set $f(x) = 0$. Finally this evolution is solved numerically.

To apply this, we assume that the evolving surface Γ is trying to minimize the surface quality functional:

$$E(\Gamma) = \left[\int_{x \in \Gamma} d^m(x, \mathcal{P}) ds \right]^{1/m}. \tag{4.3}$$

Here ds indicates a surface area element, and typically the exponent $m = 1$ or $m = 2$. Notice that the functional is reduced both by bringing the surface closer to the sample set $\mathcal{P}$ and by reducing the surface area. The reconstructed surface is thus something like a minimal surface spanning the samples.

Since there is no explicit requirement on the topology of the surface, and we only measure the distance from the surface to the samples, not the distance from the samples to the surface, the global minimum Γ is the empty set. But there are also locally minimal solutions, and if we choose our starting surface well, we can end up at a local minimum that is a good approximation to the surface. Because the level-set method can introduce topological changes in the surface when they locally result in a reduction of the quality functional, the evolving surface can usually handle

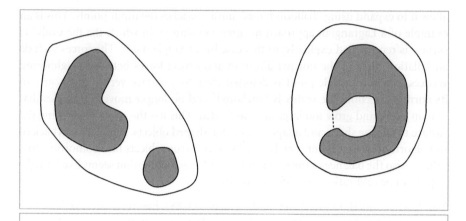

Figure 4.3: Surface evolution starting from a bounding surface. Most topological changes are handled gracefully, but sometimes it can get stuck in an undesired local minimum. (**Left**) The outer surface is attracted to the object boundary. At some moment, it covers both the connected components, and the connecting channel shrinks to have zero volume, and then disappears, leaving a correct surface representation. (**Right**) The shrinking outer surface will get stuck in a local minimum including the dotted line and not the interior of the cavity; moving the dotted line into the cavity increases the surface area and requires more energy.

situations in which a handle should be introduced or two connected components should be separated, as in Figure 4.3 (left). In other situations, as in Figure 4.3 (right), even a topologically correct starting surface might get stuck in other local minima before reaching the surface points. Starting from a good initial estimate generally avoids such problems; for instance, a connected component of a small isocontour often works well [ZOF01].

4.1.6 CONCLUSION

Surface reconstruction is applied to point clouds in different contexts. Point clouds captured by laser range scanners are large, too dense in many areas, and somewhat irregular and noisy. Taking more processing time to do a better job of integrating noisy data is a very appropriate trade-off in this case. The method of Curless and Levoy (Section 4.1.3) does a good job of integrating information available from the scanning process into the reconstruction process, but other methods have for the most part not addressed this important issue. Memory efficiency is probably more important than speed for handling really large inputs. The MPU method (also in

Section 4.1.3) handles quite large inputs, and the Poisson surface method of Kazhdan et al. seems very promising.

In point-based modeling, the point sets are synthetically generated, and so can be nearly uniform or sampled according to some appropriate criterion, and are essentially noise free. This presents a great opportunity to develop very fast surface reconstruction algorithms that depend on having good input data available. An improved understanding of the point distributions required by different reconstruction methods will be helpful here, for which the sampling theory developed in the context of the Voronoi/Delaunay algorithms (Section 4.1.4) should be useful.

4.2 MOVING LEAST SQUARES–BASED SURFACE REPRESENTATIONS

Marc Alexa

4.2.1 OVERVIEW

Representing the surface with points is slightly different from the problem of reconstructing a surface from point samples: the basic idea of representation is to use the points as the main source of information about the shape. Efficient algorithms are applied to the points to determine if a certain point in space is inside or outside of the shape or how far it is from the surface, to project this point onto the surface or to intersect other primitives with the surface. In contrast, reconstruction is typically concerned with converting the point set into another representation, where these algorithmic goals are potentially easier to perform.

A consequence of this view is a focus on local algorithms. Specifically, we'd like to avoid the construction of a global connectivity structure among the points. Doing this could lead to very good reconstruction results, as it considers all of the data at once. At the same time, looking at all the data has the severe drawback that gathering information about some part of the shape always requires all of the data to be considered. For example, examining the face of a large scanned statue would require processing all points including those of the lower torso, which hardly seem relevant. In addition, effective global solutions would require to keep all data in main memory, which is impossible for the current size of large datasets in comparison to available memory.

Only local algorithms have the premise to be efficient when used to perform certain local operations on very large point sets. Despite the lack of global structure, we wish that putting all the local computations together would result in a nice surface. Nice in this context means that the surface is smooth, in other words, contains no visible kinks and is (where reasonable) manifold (locally equivalent to a disk). In fact, we will construct surfaces that are locally equivalent to parametric surface patches, which is an even stronger property.

In particular, this section introduces methods that are related to locally weighted least squares approximations for defining a surface from points—the so-called moving least squares (MLS) approach.

We start by discussing some common methods to interpolate or approximate functional data. To compute a surface from points is different as the parameterization of the surface is unknown. This requires additional data, which we usually find by considering the normals in the points. These normals are either available with the data or have to be computed. We discuss some simple techniques to estimate normals.

Using the normals, the techniques for fitting to functions can be extended to fitting surfaces to scattered points in space. We feel that the most advanced method in terms of desirable properties is the MLS method for surface. We derive two variants in the end of this section, where the latter one exceeds in terms of computational ease.

4.2.2 NOTATION AND TERMS

We assume that the points $\mathcal{P} = \{\mathbf{p}_i \in \mathbb{R}^3\}, i \in \{1, \ldots, N\}$, are sampled from an unknown surface $\mathcal{S}$, and that they might contain some noise due to the imperfect sampling process. Some sampling processes additionally provide normal information in each point, which we assume to be represented as $\mathcal{N} = \{\mathbf{n}_i \in \mathbb{R}^3, \|\mathbf{n}_i\| = 1\}$. We assume that data are *irregular* (i.e., that the points are not sampled from a regular lattice in space).

Our goal is to define computational methods for the interrogation or manipulation of a point $\mathbf{x} \in \mathbb{R}^3$. These computational tools indirectly define a surface $\hat{S}$ from the points $\mathcal{P}$ (and possibly the normals $\mathcal{N}$). We understand the term *locality* as the extent of space or the number of points that is necessary to perform the computations for $\mathbf{x}$. A *global* method will potentially require all points in $\mathcal{P}$ to perform the computations.

The reconstructed surface is said to be *interpolating* if $\mathcal{P} \in \hat{S}$, otherwise it is approximating (see Figure 4.4). We will almost exclusively look at the case of approximation. Approximating the points takes into account that the surface is assumed to be not too wiggly and that the points contain some noise. An approximation allows smoothing this noise and providing a reasonably behaved surface.

Before we approach the general surface representation problem, we'll recall some basic methods for the interpolation or approximation of functional data. For this,

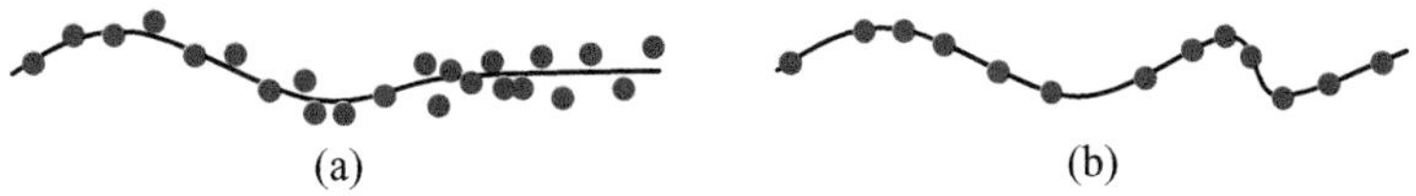

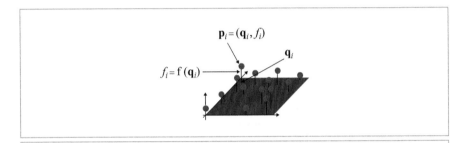

Figure 4.4: A point set is (*a*) respectively approximated by a curve and (*b*) interpolated.

$$\mathbf{p}_i = (\mathbf{q}_i, f_i)$$

$$\mathbf{q}_i$$

$$f_i = \mathrm{f}(\mathbf{q}_i)$$

Figure 4.5: The notation for the functional (parameterized) setting.

we assume that each point $\mathbf{p}_i = (\mathbf{q}_i, f_i)$ is composed of a position $\mathbf{q}_i$ in parameter space ($\mathbb{R}^2$ in our setting) and a value f_i at this position (see Figure 4.5 for an illustration). Note that in the general case of computing a surface from a set of points we don't have the distinction of parameter values and function values (i.e., the surface is not parameterized). That makes the problem harder, and we discuss concepts for solving it once the basic solutions for the simpler problem are introduced.

4.2.3 INTERPOLATION AND APPROXIMATION OF FUNCTIONAL DATA

For now, our goal is to determine a function f that interpolates or approximates the given constraints $\mathbf{p}_i = (\mathbf{q}_i, f_i)$ (i.e., $\hat{f}(\mathbf{q}_i) \approx f_i$). Defining such a function means to describe an algorithm that computes for every $\mathbf{x} \in \mathbb{R}^2$ a function value $\hat{f}(\mathbf{x})$.

We start with a very simple approach: given $\mathbf{x}$, find the closest location for which a function value is defined (i.e., $\min_j \|\mathbf{q}_j - \mathbf{x}\|$). If the minimum is not unique, choose the one with smallest index j. Then set $\hat{f}(\mathbf{x})$ to f_j. More formally, we define

$$\hat{f}(\mathbf{x}) = \mathbf{q}_j, 0 < j < i \Rightarrow \|q_j - \mathbf{x}\| < \|\mathbf{q}_i = \mathbf{x}\|, i < j < N \Rightarrow \|q_j - \mathbf{x}\| \le \|\mathbf{q}_i = \mathbf{x}\|. \quad (4.4)$$

The result is a function that interpolates the points but is not continuous.

The obvious idea to improve the continuity of $\hat{f}$ is to combine the values of several close points. In general, our approach looks like this:

$$\hat{f}(\mathbf{x}) = \sum_i w_i(\mathbf{x}) f_i, \quad (4.5)$$

where $w_i(\mathbf{x})$ are weight functions appropriate to combine the values of several points in a location $\mathbf{x}$.

Depending on how the set of "close" points is identified and how the weight functions are computed based on the set of close points, several methods with different properties can be derived. We consider the following ideas:

- **Voronoi techniques.** Identify the regions for which the location of data point $\mathbf{q}_i$ is closest and exploit the adjacency of these regions. The Voronoi decomposition in two or more dimensions is a global problem, so we won't cover this approach here. It was briefly discussed in the previous section.
- **Radial basis functions.** Attach a (radial) function to each data point that describes how it influences space.
- **Shepard.** Collect points in a certain radius and weight them based on distance.
- **Moving least squares.** Collect points in a certain radius and weight them so that polynomials are reproduced.

Radial Basis Functions

A basic and very general approach is to model the weight functions as radial functions:

$$w_i(\mathbf{x}) = \frac{c_i}{f_i} \theta(\|\mathbf{x} - \mathbf{q}_i\|) \Leftrightarrow w_i(\mathbf{x}) f_i = c_i \theta(\|\mathbf{x} - \mathbf{q}_i\|), \quad (4.6)$$

where θ is a function that describes the influence of $\mathbf{q}_i$ on $\mathbf{x}$ based on the distance between the two locations (see Figure 4.6 for an illustration and [Dyn89, Buh03]).

In this approach, all weight functions w_i are essentially the same and only differ by a linear factor. Note that the method is already fully defined for a fixed function θ in case we ask for interpolation: Requiring $\hat{f}(\mathbf{q}_j) = f_j$ leads to

$$\hat{f}(\mathbf{q}_j) = \sum_i c_i \theta(\|\mathbf{q}_j - \mathbf{q}_i\|) = f_j, \quad (4.7)$$

which is, in fact, a system of linear equations:

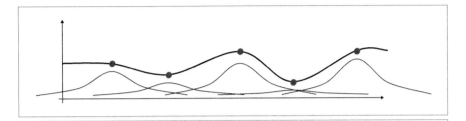

Figure 4.6: The RBF approach to interpolating functional data. A radial weight function is attached to each data point. The coefficients for each weight function are computed by solving a linear system of equations, resulting from asking for interpolation in each of the data points.

$$
\begin{pmatrix}
\theta(\|\mathbf{q}_0 - \mathbf{q}_0\|) & \theta(\|\mathbf{q}_0 - \mathbf{q}_1\|) & \theta(\|\mathbf{q}_0 - \mathbf{q}_2\|) & \cdots \\
\theta(\|\mathbf{q}_1 - \mathbf{q}_0\|) & \theta(\|\mathbf{q}_1 - \mathbf{q}_1\|) & \theta(\|\mathbf{q}_1 - \mathbf{q}_2\|) & \cdots \\
\theta(\|\mathbf{q}_2 - \mathbf{q}_0\|) & \theta(\|\mathbf{q}_2 - \mathbf{q}_1\|) & \theta(\|\mathbf{q}_2 - \mathbf{q}_2\|) & \cdots \\
\vdots & \vdots & \vdots & \ddots
\end{pmatrix}
\begin{pmatrix}
c_0 \\ c_1 \\ c_2 \\ \vdots
\end{pmatrix}
=
\begin{pmatrix}
f_0 \\ f_1 \\ f_2 \\ \vdots
\end{pmatrix}
\tag{4.8}
$$

So, before we are able to compute the weights we first need to solve this linear system. This requires that the system has a solution, which means the data points allow being interpolated with the given functions. As the matrix depends only on values of θ, solvability obviously depends on the choice of θ.

Standard choices for the radial function θ are $\theta(\delta) = \delta^{-u}$, $u \in \mathbb{N}$ [Dyn87] or the Gaussian $\theta(\delta) = \exp(\delta^2/h^2)$ [Dyn89]. However, another concern makes these functions impractical: each point influences every other point, making the approach global. This can also be recognized from the fact that a dense linear system has to be solved before $\hat{f}$ could be evaluated in any point.

In an attempt to make the solution local we should use locally supported radial functions. This means we can choose a distance parameter ϵ. If two points are farther apart than ϵ the function θ attached to either of them vanishes in the other point (i.e., $\delta > \epsilon \Rightarrow \theta(\delta) = 0$).

Popular choices with good properties are Wendland's radial functions [Wen95], because they consist of polynomial pieces with low degree (i.e., they are easy to compute) and lead to solvable linear systems. The particular function to be used depends on the space in which the locations $\mathbf{q}_i$ live.

Using these locally supported functions leads to sparse linear systems, which can be solved in almost linear time (e.g., using multiresolution methods [FI96]. Nevertheless, strictly speaking this is a global solution, as the inverse of a sparse matrix is not necessarily sparse. Practically speaking this means moving one point could potentially influence points farther away than ϵ by a cascade of effects on other points.

On the other hand, the sparse linear system has to be solved only once. This defines the linear factors $\{c_i\}$, which in turn define the weight functions $w_i(\mathbf{x})$. Evaluating $\hat{f}(\mathbf{x})$ is typically very cheap, as θ has to be evaluated only for few close points.

Least Squares Fitting

Most readers will be familiar with the idea of least squares fitting a polynomial to given data (Figure 4.7 shows fitting a quadratic function to univariate data). Here, we will rediscover this method in our setting, by introducing the concept of a precision set. This presentation aims at helping with the understanding of the following techniques.

As before, we represent $\hat{f}$ at $\mathbf{x}$ as $\sum_i w_i(\mathbf{x}) f_i$. We ask that $\hat{f}$ has a certain precision, which is described by a precision set $\mathcal{G}$: if the pairs $(\mathbf{q}_i, f_i)$ happen to be sampled from a function contained in the precision set (say, $g \in \mathcal{G}$), then we wish that $\hat{f}$ results to be exactly that function. We can formalize this requirement as follows: for every $g \in \mathcal{G}$ the weight functions have to satisfy

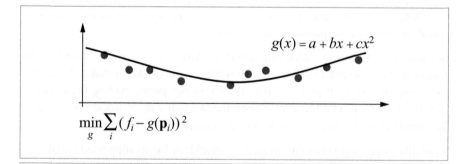

$$g(x) = a + bx + cx^2$$

$$\min_g \sum_i (f_i - g(\mathbf{p}_i))^2$$

Figure 4.7: Least squares: Fitting a (here: quadratic) function $\hat{f}$ by minimizing the squares of differences between the given function values f_i and the values of the quadratic function at the corresponding locations $\mathbf{q}_i$. The standard approach is to minimize among all quadratic functions $\hat{f}(x) = a + bx + cx^2$ (i.e., $\min_{a,b,c} \sum_i (f_i - \hat{f}(\mathbf{q}_i))^2$); here we rediscover the same solution starting from different assumptions (see text).

$$g(\mathbf{x}) = \sum_i w_i(\mathbf{x}) g(\mathbf{q}_i). \tag{4.9}$$

As a more concrete example, consider the precision set of quadratic polynomials $g(\mathbf{x}) = a + \mathbf{b}^T\mathbf{x} + \mathbf{x}^T\mathbf{C}\mathbf{x}$. Look at the following system of equations:

$$1 = \sum_i w_i(\mathbf{x})1$$

$$x_0 = \sum_i w_i(\mathbf{x})q_{i_0}$$

$$\vdots \tag{4.10}$$

$$x_0^2 = \sum_i w_i(\mathbf{x})q_{i_0}^2$$

$$\vdots$$

Note that the set of linear combinations of these equations,

$$a + \mathbf{b}^T\mathbf{x} + \mathbf{x}^T\mathbf{C}\mathbf{x} = \sum_i w_i(\mathbf{x})\left(a + \mathbf{b}^T\mathbf{q}_i + \mathbf{q}_i^T\mathbf{C}\mathbf{q}_i\right), \tag{4.11}$$

is, in fact, the requirement of reproducing any function from the precision set of quadratic polynomials.

We can write the system of equations in matrix form as

$$\mathbf{Q}\mathbf{w}(\mathbf{x}) = \mathbf{z}. \tag{4.12}$$

Typically, we will have more points than dimensions in the space of polynomials (i.e., the system is underdetermined). We need to restrict the weights further. A common way to do this would be to ask that the sum of squared weights is minimal, in other words

$$\min_{\{w_i(\mathbf{x})\}} \sum_i (w_i(\mathbf{x}))^2 = \min_{\mathbf{w}(\mathbf{x})} \mathbf{w}(\mathbf{x})^T\mathbf{w}(\mathbf{x}). \tag{4.13}$$

How could we find this minimum, subject to the linear constraints given in Equation (4.12)? Assume we know the solution vector $\mathbf{w}(\mathbf{x})$. Now look at the polynomial $(a, b_0, \dots)\mathbf{Q}\mathbf{w}(\mathbf{x})$. We can certainly choose the polynomial coefficients $(a, b_0, \dots)$ so that this polynomial attains a minimum or a maximum for the given weight vector $\mathbf{w}(\mathbf{x})$. So instead of minimizing only squared weights, we try to minimize

$$\mathbf{w}(\mathbf{x})^T\mathbf{w}(\mathbf{x}) - (a, b_0, \dots)\mathbf{Q}\mathbf{w}(\mathbf{x}), \tag{4.14}$$

where we have the polynomial coefficients as additional degrees of freedom. This approach helps to include the linear constraints in the minimization, at the cost of additional variables to solve for. A necessary condition for the minimum is that all partial derivatives are identical to zero. Taking all partial derivatives with respect to the weights and setting to zero leads to

$$\mathbf{w}(\mathbf{x})^\mathsf{T} - (a, b_0, \ldots)\mathbf{Q} = 0 \iff \mathbf{w}(\mathbf{x}) = \mathbf{Q}^\mathsf{T}(a, b_0, \ldots)^\mathsf{T}. \tag{4.15}$$

Using that in Equation (4.12) yields

$$\mathbf{Q}\mathbf{Q}^\mathsf{T}(a, b_0, \ldots)^\mathsf{T} = \mathbf{z}, \tag{4.16}$$

which is identical to the normal equation for least squares fitting a polynomial and also shows that the solution is independent of the location $\mathbf{x}$. Once the polynomial coefficients are determined one could indeed solve for the weights at $\mathbf{x}$, however, in this case it is easier to compute $\hat{f}$ using the representation as a polynomial.

Notice that the solution we have presented works for any precision set that could be represented as a finite linear space.

Moving Least Squares

We will follow the basic ideas of the last section. The only modification is that we localize weights. We do this by incorporating a separation measure into the minimization of squared weights:

$$\min_{\{w_i(\mathbf{x})\}} \sum_i w_i^2(\mathbf{x})\eta(\|\mathbf{q}_i - \mathbf{x}\|) = \min_{\mathbf{w}(\mathbf{x})} \mathbf{w}(\mathbf{x})^\mathsf{T}\mathbf{E}(\mathbf{x})\mathbf{w}(\mathbf{x}). \tag{4.17}$$

The separation measure $\eta(\|\mathbf{q}_i - \mathbf{x}\|)$ penalizes the influence of points at $\mathbf{q}_i$ far away from $\mathbf{x}$ (i.e., the function increases with the distance between $\mathbf{q}_i$ and $\mathbf{x}$).

The solution to this constrained minimization is similar to the uniform situation. Now one has to solve

$$\mathbf{w}(\mathbf{x})^\mathsf{T}\mathbf{E}(\mathbf{x}) - (a, b_0, \ldots)\mathbf{Q} = 0, \tag{4.18}$$

which leads to

$$\mathbf{w}(\mathbf{x}) = \mathbf{E}(\mathbf{x})^{-1}\mathbf{Q}^\mathsf{T}(a, b_0, \ldots)^\mathsf{T}. \tag{4.19}$$

This can be inserted into the constraint equation $\mathbf{Q}\mathbf{w}(\mathbf{x}) = \mathbf{z}$ to get the polynomial coefficients:

$$\left(\mathbf{Q}\mathbf{E}(\mathbf{x})^{-1}\mathbf{Q}^\mathsf{T}\right)(a, b_0, \ldots)^\mathsf{T} = \mathbf{z}. \tag{4.20}$$

We see that the polynomial coefficients result from a weighted least squares system. The weighting comes from the η^{-1}, which we call θ for convenience. It depends on the location $\mathbf{x}$, because η depends on $\mathbf{x}$.

The resulting approach could also be interpreted like this: in each location $\mathbf{x}$ determine a locally weighted least squares fitting polynomial and use the value of this polynomial at $\mathbf{x}$ (a moving least squares approximation [LS86, Lev98]). This is illustrated in Figure 4.8. In this interpretation it seems the approximating values of $\hat{f}(\mathbf{x})$ are computed independently for different locations, so it might not be imme-diately clear that $\hat{f}$ is a continuously differentiable function. Our derivation of $\hat{f}$, however, reveals that it is, if η (or, better, $\mathbf{E}(\mathbf{x})$) is continuously differentiable.

If θ is locally supported (i.e., vanishes for large distances between $\mathbf{x}$ and $\mathbf{q}_i$) the com-putations for $\mathbf{x}$ are also local, as they depend only on the data points that are within the support. For $\eta(0) = 0$ (i.e., $\theta(0) = \infty$) the resulting function $\hat{f}$ interpolates the points. Notice that the statements about the continuity of $\hat{f}$ hold also for the case of local support and/or interpolation.

The coefficients of the polynomial could be used to find the weights as

$$\mathbf{w}(\mathbf{x}) = \mathbf{E}(\mathbf{x})^{-1}\mathbf{Q}\left(\mathbf{Q}\mathbf{E}(\mathbf{x})^{-1}\mathbf{Q}^{\mathsf{T}}\right)^{-1}\mathbf{z}. \qquad (4.21)$$

Now we take a closer look at the special case of asking only for constant precision. Then, $\mathbf{Q}$ is a row vector containing only ones and $\mathbf{z} = 1$. Then $\mathbf{E}(\mathbf{x})^{-1}\mathbf{Q}$ is a row vector containing the terms $\theta(\|\mathbf{q}_i - \mathbf{x}\|)$, and $\mathbf{Q}\mathbf{E}(\mathbf{x})^{-1}\mathbf{Q}^{\mathsf{T}}$ is the sum of these terms. This means we get the following weights for location $\mathbf{x}$ when asking only for constant precision:

$$w_j(\mathbf{x}) = \frac{\theta(\|\mathbf{q}_j - \mathbf{x}\|)}{\sum_i \theta(\|\mathbf{q}_i - \mathbf{x}\|)}. \qquad (4.22)$$

This type of weight is commonly called a *partition of unity*, because the weights sum up to one everywhere. Using $\theta(\delta) = \delta^{-r}, r > 0$ we rediscover a particular and well-known instance of partition of unity: Shepard's interpolation method [She68, FN80].

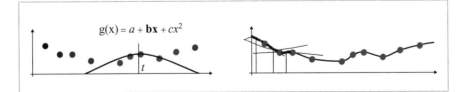

Figure 4.8: Moving least squares: In each location $\mathbf{x}$ a polynomial is computed using the least squares method, however, weighting the influence of the data points based on their distance. The value of this polynomial at $\mathbf{x}$ yields the functional approximation (*left*). The set of locally approximated function values, together, forms the approximated curve (*right*).

4.2.4 NORMALS

So far we have considered functional data. Now we turn to the problem of approximating a surface represented by points P in space. In this setting, we don't have a suitable parameter domain to directly apply the techniques explained above. It turns out that almost all approaches compensate for this lack of information by using approximating tangent planes or normals on or close to the point set.

Normals might be part of the data or not. If normals are missing, we can try to estimate them as follows. Assume we want to compute the normal $\mathbf{n}$ in a location $\mathbf{q}$ in space. The points close to $\mathbf{q}$ describe the surface around $\mathbf{q}$. A tangent in $\mathbf{q}$ should be as close as possible to these close points.

Determining a tangent plane around $\mathbf{q}$ can be formulated as a least squares problem (see Figure 4.9). We search a plane $H(\mathbf{x}) : \mathbf{n}^\mathsf{T}\mathbf{q} = \mathbf{n}^\mathsf{T}\mathbf{p}_i, \|\mathbf{n}\| = 1$ passing through $\mathbf{q}$ that minimizes the squares $(\mathbf{n}^\mathsf{T}(\mathbf{q} - \mathbf{p}_i))^2$. However, we want to consider only a few points $\mathbf{p}_i$ close to $\mathbf{q}$. We could do this by either using only the k-nearest neighbors of $\mathbf{q}$ or by weighting close points with a locally supported weight function θ. Because the k-nearest neighbor approach could be simulated by using a hat function with appropriate radius for θ, we will only detail the locally weighted version. Then, $\mathbf{n}$ is defined by the following minimization problem:

$$\min_{\|\mathbf{n}\|=1} \sum_i \left(\mathbf{n}^\mathsf{T}(\mathbf{p}_i - \mathbf{q})\right)^2 \theta(\|\mathbf{p}_i - \mathbf{q}\|). \qquad (4.23)$$

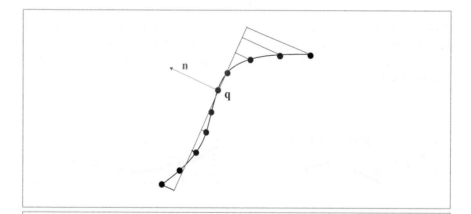

Figure 4.9: Estimating the normal direction close to a point $\mathbf{q}$: A unit normal $\mathbf{n}$ is computed so that the plane orthogonal to $\mathbf{n}$ minimizes the squared distances to the points. The extra constraint $\|\mathbf{n}\| = 1$ makes this a nonlinear problem that can be solved, however, by an eigenvalue/eigenvector computation.

This is a nonlinear optimization problem, because of the quadratic constraint $\|\mathbf{n}\| = 1$. To arrive at a computable solution, we use the outer product matrices $(\mathbf{p}_i - \mathbf{q})(\mathbf{p}_i - \mathbf{q})^\mathsf{T}$ and rewrite the functional to be minimized as

$$m(\mathbf{n}) = \mathbf{n}^\mathsf{T}\left(\sum_i (\mathbf{p}_i - \mathbf{q})(\mathbf{p}_i - \mathbf{q})^\mathsf{T}\theta(\|\mathbf{p}_i - \mathbf{q}\|) \right)\mathbf{n}, \tag{4.24}$$

and inspect the eigenvalue/eigenvector decomposition of the sum of outer products:

$$\sum_i (\mathbf{p}_i - \mathbf{q})(\mathbf{p}_i - \mathbf{q})^\mathsf{T}\theta = \mathrm{E}\,\mathrm{diag}(\lambda_0, \lambda_1, \dots)\mathrm{E}^\mathsf{T}. \tag{4.25}$$

Using this decomposition we see that in transformed coordinates $\mathbf{E}^\mathsf{T}\mathbf{n}$ the functional $m(\mathbf{n}) = \mathbf{n}^\mathsf{T}\mathrm{E}\,\mathrm{diag}(\lambda_0, \lambda_1, \dots)\mathbf{E}^\mathsf{T}\mathbf{n}$ has only pure quadratic terms, and each of these quadratic terms has an eigenvalue as coefficient. Let $\lambda_0 \le \lambda_1, \dots$, then $m(\mathbf{n})$ clearly attains its minimum among all unit-length vectors for $\mathbf{E}^\mathsf{T}\mathbf{n} = (1, 0, 0, \dots)^\mathsf{T}$. This means, $\mathbf{n} = \mathbf{e}_0$ (i.e., the eigenvector corresponding to the smallest eigenvalue).

Fitting a tangent plane will only yield a normal direction, not an orientation. We assume that the correct orientation can be derived from inside-outside information generated using scanning of the object.

4.2.5 IMPLICIT SURFACES FROM POINTS AND OFFSET POINTS

The basic idea of approaches based on implicit surfaces is to assume that all points on the surface have zero value; in other words, the surface is implicitly defined by

$$S = \{\mathbf{x} \mid \hat{f}(\mathbf{x}) = 0\}. \tag{4.26}$$

In this setting, the point set delivers a set of constraints of the form

$$\hat{f}(\mathbf{p}_i) = 0. \tag{4.27}$$

Now, our approach is to apply the techniques for local function estimation presented in the preceding section. However, all of these methods would result in $\hat{f} = 0$, as this perfectly satisfies all constraints. We obviously need additional nonzero constraints. These additional constraints have to be generated based on the given point data.

The normals can be used to generate additional point constraints for $\hat{f}$. A standard trick is this: move a small step (say, δ) from $\mathbf{p}_i$ in the normal direction outward from the surface. This point is $\mathbf{p}_i + \delta\mathbf{n}_i$. Require $\hat{f}$ to be δ at this point. The surface could be additionally supported by also moving to the inside and requiring that the value at $\mathbf{p}_i - \delta\mathbf{n}_i$ is $-\delta$.

A potential danger of this approach is that the location $\mathbf{p}_i + \delta\mathbf{n}_i$ is less than δ away from the surface, because the step is so large that we have moved toward some other part of the surface. A good strategy to check and avoid this is to compute the closest point to $\mathbf{p}_i + \delta\mathbf{n}_i$. If this is not $\mathbf{p}_i$, the step size δ has to be reduced until this holds true.

If a spatial subdivision is used to organize the points this is another good way to add nonzero constraints (Figure 4.10). In each of the corners and centers of a cell the distance to the surface is approximated as the smallest distance to any point of the set. A sign for the distance can be computed from inside-outside information. For small distances, the distance to the closest point becomes less reliable. We propose to rather compute the distances to the k-nearest points ($k = 3$) and check that they all have the same sign.

The result of either procedure is a set of additional constraints of the form

$$\hat{f}(\mathbf{p}_{N+i}) = d_i. \tag{4.28}$$

Together with the constraints $\hat{f}(\mathbf{p}_i) = 0$ they can be used to approximate a function $\hat{f}$ using any of the techniques for approximating functions as described in the last section.

Several works discuss the details of using RBF for approximating the implicit function [Mur91, MYR+01, CBC+01, DST01, TO02, DTS02, OBS03]. Spatial subdivisions have been used together with partition of unity weights, either RBF approximations in a K-d-tree [TRS04], or local polynomial and specific sharp edge functions in the cells of an octree [OBA+03].

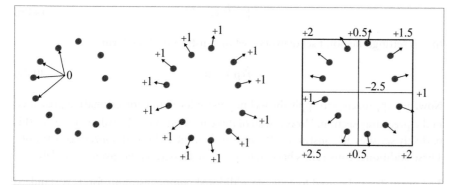

Figure 4.10: Fitting an implicit function to the data. An implicit surface is defined as the zero-set of a scalar function in space. Consequently, at the data points the function should be zero (*left*). Using normals or a spatial subdivision helps provide the necessary additional nonzero modeling constraints.

4.2.6 IMPLICIT SURFACE FROM POINTS AND TANGENT FRAMES

Rather than generating additional point constraints to make the standard function approximation techniques applicable we could also try to adapt them to the more general setting. An underlying idea of several approaches in this direction is to estimate local tangent frames and then use a standard technique in this local tangent frame.

Hoppe's and Related Approaches

A straightforward approach to generate an implicit function $\hat{f}$ based on the normals is due to Hoppe et al. [HDD$^+$92]. For a point in space $\mathbf{x}$ compute the closest point $\mathbf{p}_i$ in $\mathcal{P}$. Then set $\hat{f}(\mathbf{x})$ to $\mathbf{n}_i(\mathbf{p}_i - \mathbf{x})$; in other words, the signed distance to the tangent plane through $\mathbf{p}_i$ (see Figure 4.11). This yields a piecewise linear approximation of signed distances to the surface. The set of points in space associated to the same point $\mathbf{p}_i$ forms the Voronoi cell around $\mathbf{p}_i$. So, another viewpoint on this is that we use local linear approximations, however, for Voronoi cells we use a local frame based on the tangent plane.

One can compute a smoother surface approximation by exploiting the Voronoi cells around the points and using Voronoi interpolation as explained in the preceding section. This has been exploited by Boissonnat and Cazals [BC00].

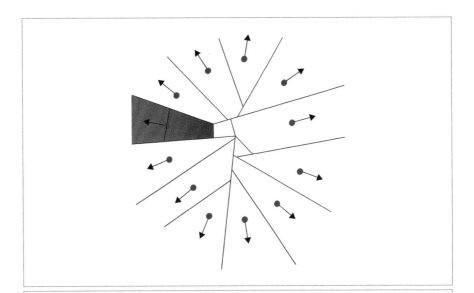

Figure 4.11: Hoppe's approach to defining an implicit function from local tangent frames. Each point in space is associated to the closest data point. The distance value is then computed as the distance from the tangent plane associated to the data point.

MLS Surfaces

The MLS surface S_P of $\mathcal{P}$ is defined implicitly by a projection operator. The basic idea for projecting a point $\mathbf{r}$ onto S_P is based on two steps. First, a locally tangent reference domain H is computed. Then, a local bivariate polynomial is fitted over H to the point set (Figure 4.13).

However, to compensate for points with some distance to the surface, we don't restrict the tangent plane to pass through the point $\mathbf{r}$ (Figure 4.12). Yet, we still want to weight the influence of points based on the distance to the origin of the tangent frame. This leads to a more complex minimization problem, however, yields the desired projection property.

Specifically, the local reference domain $H = \{\mathbf{x} | \langle \mathbf{n}, \mathbf{x} \rangle - D = 0, \|\mathbf{n}\| = 1$ is determined by minimizing

$$\sum_{i=1}^{N} (\langle \mathbf{n}, \mathbf{p}_i - \mathbf{r} - t\mathbf{n} \rangle)^2 \, \theta(\|\mathbf{p}_i - \mathbf{r} - t\mathbf{n}\|) \qquad (4.29)$$

among all normal directions $\mathbf{n}$ and offsets t (see Figure 4.12).

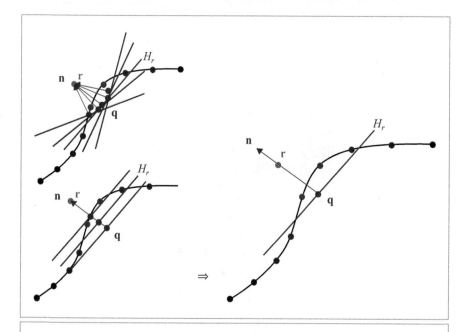

Figure 4.12: The reference plane for the first step of the MLS projection is found by optimizing over all normal directions $\mathbf{n}$ and all offsets t.

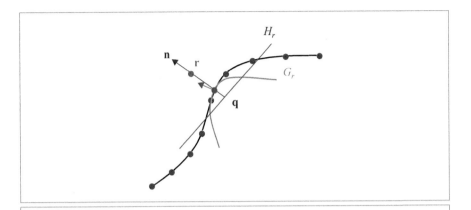

Figure 4.13: The reference plane is then used to compute a polynomial least squares approximation. The value at the origin of the reference frame is used as the projection of **q**.

Let $\mathbf{q}_i$ be the projection of $\mathbf{p}_i$ onto H, and f_i the height of $\mathbf{p}_i$ over H (i.e., $f_i = \mathbf{n} \cdot (\mathbf{p}_i - \mathbf{q})$). The polynomial approximation g is computed by minimizing the weighted least squares error:

$$\sum_{i=1}^{N} (g(x_i, y_i) - f_i)^2 \, \theta(\|\mathbf{p}_i - \mathbf{r} - t\mathbf{n}\|). \tag{4.30}$$

The projection of **r** is given by (see Figure 4.13)

$$MLS(\mathbf{r}) = \mathbf{r} + (t + g(0,0))\mathbf{n}. \tag{4.31}$$

Formally, the surface S_P is the set of points that projects onto itself. We can also define the surface in the standard notation using

$$\hat{f}(\mathbf{x}) = \|(t + g(0,0))\mathbf{n}(\mathbf{x})\|. \tag{4.32}$$

The projection procedure itself has turned out to be a useful computational method for computing points on the surface. The reader might want to look up [Lee00, ABCO+01, PGK02a, PKG02, ABCO+03, FCOAS03, Lev03, PKKG03] for details on the properties, extensions, and implementations of this approach. The method detailed in the following section presents another view on the same idea and results in simpler computations.

Surfaces from Normals and Weighted Averages

Inspired by MLS surfaces, we can also define the surface implicitly based on normal directions and weighted averages. What makes the MLS projection procedure complex is the nonlinear optimization problem for computing the reference plane. An alternative way of computing a projection is as follows (see Figure 4.14 and [AA03a]). Given $\mathbf{x}$, a tangent frame is computed in $\mathbf{x}$. This tangent frame is used to approximate the data with a locally weighted least squares polynomial. The intersection of the normal through $\mathbf{q}$ and the polynomial is the result $\mathbf{x}'$ of the first step. The procedure is then repeated starting from $\mathbf{x}'$ yielding $\mathbf{x}''$, and so on, until convergence.

The process is particularly simple when constant polynomials are used for the approximation, because a constant approximation passes through the locally weighted average $\mathbf{a}(\mathbf{x})$ of the points (Figure 4.15). In each step, a local normal approximation $\mathbf{n}(\mathbf{x})$ (see Section 4.2.4) and the locally weighted average

$$\mathbf{a}(\mathbf{x}) = \frac{\sum_{i=0}^{N-1} \theta(\|\mathbf{x} - \mathbf{p}_i\|)\mathbf{p}_i}{\sum_{i=0}^{N-1} \theta(\|\mathbf{x} - \mathbf{p}_i\|)} \tag{4.33}$$

are computed, and then

$$\mathbf{x}' = \mathbf{x} - \mathbf{n}(\mathbf{x})^{\mathsf{T}}(\mathbf{x} - \mathbf{a}(\mathbf{x}))\,\mathbf{n}(\mathbf{x}), \tag{4.34}$$

repeating this computation until convergence is the projection operator. This simple to implement (see Figure 4.16 for pseudocode) and stable version has been derived independently by Amenta and Kil [AK04] as well as Alexa and Adamson [AA04b].

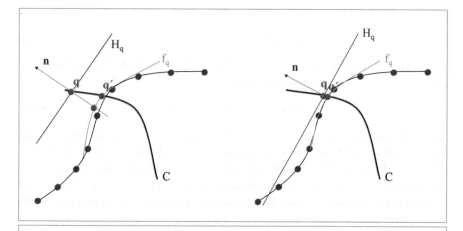

Figure 4.14: An alternative constructive definition of a projection. Reference planes are computed through **x** yielding the next point **x'**. The process is repeated until convergence.

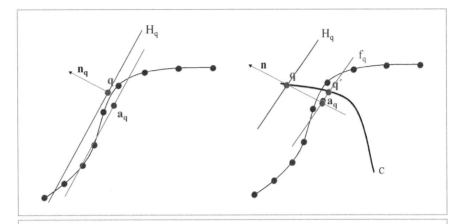

Figure 4.15: If constant polynomial approximations are used, the approximation passes through the locally weighted average of points $\mathbf{a}(\mathbf{q})$. A single step in the iteration then becomes $\mathbf{q}' = \mathbf{q} - \mathbf{n}(\mathbf{q})^{\mathsf{T}}(\mathbf{q} - \mathbf{a}(\mathbf{q}))\,\mathbf{n}(\mathbf{q})$, and repeating this assignment is the recommended projection operator. The stationary points of this operator also give rise to an interpretation of the surface defined by the implicit function $f(\mathbf{x}) = \mathbf{n}(\mathbf{x})(\mathbf{a}(\mathbf{x}) - \mathbf{x}) = 0$.

```
MLSProjection(x, ε)
    x = weightedAverage(x);
    do
        n = localNormal(x);
        a = weightedAverage(x);
        f = n · (x − a);
        x = x − fn;
    while (|f| > ε);
    return x;
```

Figure 4.16: Pseudocode for the projection operator. Note that $\mathbf{x}$ is first moved to the locally weighted average of the points to make the normal computation more reliable.

This constructive definition also gives rise to an alternative interpretation of the surface defined by an implicit function (see Figure 4.15). The implicit function $f : \mathbb{R}^3 \to \mathbb{R}$ describes the distance of a point $\mathbf{x}$ to the weighted average $\mathbf{a}(\mathbf{x})$ projected along the normal direction $\mathbf{n}(\mathbf{x})$:

$$\hat{f}(\mathbf{x}) = \mathbf{n}(\mathbf{x}) \cdot (\mathbf{a}(\mathbf{x}) - \mathbf{x}). \tag{4.35}$$

Note that this interpretation does not allow analyzing the properties of the surface as the sign of $\hat{f}$ is undefined. Amenta and Kil [AK04] define the surface more rigorously as a product space. This way they can show that the surface is smooth. Figure 4.16 gives the pseudocode of the projection operator, which exploits the idea that $\hat{f}$ tends to zero as points get close to the surface.

If θ is locally supported one has to make sure to compute $\hat{f}$ only in the support of the weights. Computing the weighted average and the local tangent frame also allows to one define boundaries of the surface in a natural way (see Figure 4.17). We inspect the relative location of the weighted average $\mathbf{a}(\mathbf{x})$ in the points. For points far away from the point set the distance $\|\mathbf{x} - \mathbf{a}(\mathbf{x})\|$ increases, while we expect this distance to be rather small for locations close to (or inside) the points. The main idea for defining a boundary is to require $\|\mathbf{x} - \mathbf{a}(\mathbf{x})\|$ to be less than a user-specified threshold. More details can be found in Alexa and Adamson [AA04a].

4.2.7 CONCLUSION

The moving least squares method and its variants are a versatile approach for generating and finding points on a surface that is given by a set of sample points. The methods presented here will be used throughout the book.

After looking at several reconstruction methods and this detailed look at one particular method that is of importance for many of the techniques presented later, as well as being used in Pointshop, it is important to generate well-behaved samplings of given surface models. This is described next.

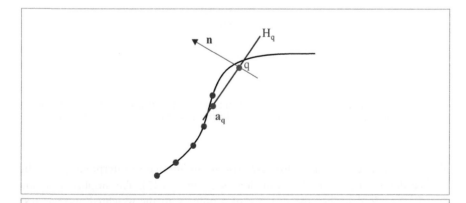

Figure 4.17: Boundaries of the surfaces can be defined by evaluating the distance of the weighted average $\mathbf{a}(\mathbf{q})$ to $\mathbf{q}$.

4.3 SAMPLING OF POINT MODELS

Jianhua Wu, Leif Kobbelt, and Mark Pauly

Point-based surface representations are truly discrete in the sense that they only consist of a finite number of samples (position and/or normal). Since these samples are supposed to represent a continuous surface, questions arise about the appropriate sampling density to capture the relevant geometric details. Sampling techniques for point models typically come in two flavors. *Upsampling* increases the number of samples while *downsampling* decreases their number. If no metaknowledge about the underlying surface is available, the positions of the new samples during upsampling are determined based on some notion of surface smoothness. Downsampling usually serves the purpose of data reduction, which implies that some application-dependent criterion is required that rates the geometric significance of each sample.

In the literature, downsampling methods have received more attention than upsampling. The reason for this is that point models are usually obtained from laser scanning, which leads to rather dense point clouds. Hence the raw point data are already a highly detailed model that has to be decimated for efficient processing and display. On the other hand, upsampling becomes necessary whenever a given point model is modified (e.g., by local deformation). In this case the local surface stretch can reduce the sampling density below a critical threshold, which can be compensated by upsampling. A general framework for upsampling is presented in Section 4.5 and upsampling in the context of shape modeling is revisited in Section 5.3. The current section focuses on downsampling techniques.

4.3.1 OVERVIEW

Purely point-based surface representations as obtained with one of the techniques discussed in Chapter 3 correspond to piecewise constant interpolation functions, and approximation theory tells us that the approximation error in this case depends on first-order derivatives of the underlying continuous surface. Geometrically speaking, the approximation error between a continuous surface and discrete set of points is bounded by the (geodesic) distance between the points. In order to reduce the error by a factor of two we have to increase the number of point samples by a factor of four.

In order to fill the gaps in between the samples more efficiently, point-based representations are most often extended to splat-based representations [ZPvBG01b] where the surface is locally approximated by a little disk or ellipse. This is of special interest in the context of rendering (see Chapter 6), where a disk-based representation allows for efficient algorithms. Since these disks provide a first-order approximation to the surface (position and normal), the approximation error now depends on second-order derivatives. In fact, just like with other piecewise linear surface representations, we can use large splats in flat areas of the surface and a high sampling density with smaller splats is only necessary in highly curved regions. As a consequence, the approximation error can be reduced by a factor of two by approximately doubling the number of splats, which is the same convergence rate as with triangle meshes. The major difference, though, is that splat-based representations do not define a continuous surface and hence each splat stays an independent geometric object and the conceptual simplicity of point-based representations is preserved (see Figure 4.18).

Even though splat-based representations are commonly used in practice, there is a number of decimation schemes that only take the splat-center position into account. The idea is to first generate a set of surface samples whose density is adapted to the surface curvature. In a postprocessing step these samples are then converted into circular or elliptical splats by estimating their local normal orientation and splat size. Such algorithms are usually very efficient but the results are not optimal in terms of approximation quality (i.e., approximation error per number of splats). In contrast, splat decimation techniques exploit the full geometry of a disk or ellipse in order to find an optimal set splat covering the surface. The trade off is that splat decimation techniques are computationally more involved.

4.3.2 DECIMATION AND RESAMPLING TECHNIQUES

Point-simplification Methods

Linsen [Lin01] and Alexa et al. [ABCO+03] adopted greedy schemes to iteratively remove samples from the input point cloud yielding a subset of the input samples

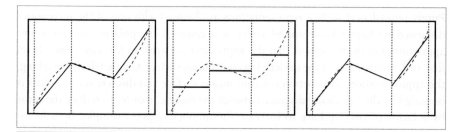

Figure 4.18: Comparison of the different shape approximations: piecewise linear C^0 polygons (*left*), piecewise constant C^{-1} points (*center*), and piecewise linear C^{-1} splats (*right*). Splats provide the same approximation order as triangle meshes, but due to the C^{-1} continuity they offer the same flexibility as pure point clouds.

as output. Moenning and Dodgson [MD03] use fast-marching farthest point sampling for point set simplification to generate the output samples. While these methods are simple and efficient, their greedy algorithmic nature cannot guarantee a globally uniform point distribution. Moreover, reliable error control is not supplied in these methods and seems not trivial to achieve.

A systematic exploration of different approaches to point simplification was proposed by Pauly et al. [PGK02a], where various established mesh-simplification techniques have been adapted to simplify point-sampled geometry. Specifically, these point-simplification algorithms include: *clustering methods*, which are fast and memory efficient; *iterative simplification*, which puts more emphasis on high surface quality; and *particle simulation*, which allows for intuitive control of the resulting sampling distribution.

Clustering methods have been used in many computer graphics applications to reduce the complexity of 3D objects. The standard volumetric strategy [RB93] cannot adapt to nonuniformities in the sampling distribution and can easily join unconnected parts of a surface for large grid cells. To alleviate these shortcomings, Pauly et al. [PGK02a] use a surface-based clustering approach, where clusters are built by collecting neighboring samples while regarding local sampling density. Two general approaches are distinguished for building clusters (Figure 4.19): an incremental approach, where clusters are created by region growing, and a hierarchical approach that splits the point cloud into smaller subsets in a top-down manner [BW00, SG01]. Both methods create a set $\{C_i\}$ of clusters, each of which

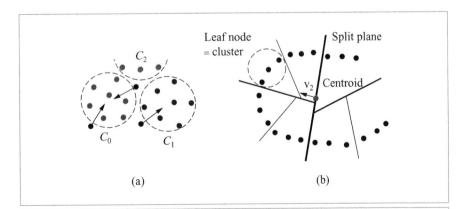

Figure 4.19: (*a*) Clustering by incremental region growing, where "stray samples" (black dots) are attached to the cluster with closest centroid. (*b*) Hierarchical clustering, where the thickness of the lines indicates the level of the BSP tree (2D for illustration).

is replaced by a representative sample, typically its centroid, to create the simplified point cloud $\mathcal{P}'$.

Clustering approaches attempt to group the input samples into patches that do not exceed a given upper bound for their size (in terms of diameter) or variation (in terms of normal cone angle or surface deviation in covariance analysis [PGK02a]). For clustering by region growing, starting from a random seed point $\mathbf{p}_0$, a cluster C_0 is built by successively adding nearest neighbors. This incremental region growing is terminated when the size or the variation of the cluster reaches an upper bound. The next cluster C_1 is then built by starting the incremental growth with a new seed chosen from the neighbors of C_0 and excluding all points of C_0 from the region growing. Due to fragmentation, this method creates many clusters that do not reach the maximum size or variation bound, but whose incremental growth was restricted by adjacent clusters. To obtain a more even distribution of clusters, the sample points of all clusters that did not reach a minimum size and variation bound (typically half of the maximum bound) are distributed to neighboring clusters (see Figure 4.19a).

Hierarchical clustering is a different method for computing the set of clusters recursively by splitting the point cloud using a binary space partition. The point cloud $\mathcal{P}$ is split if the size $|\mathcal{P}|$ is larger than the user-specified maximum cluster size or the variation of the point set is too large. The split plane is defined by the centroid of $\mathcal{P}$ and the eigenvector of the covariance matrix of $\mathcal{P}$ with the largest corresponding eigenvalue [PGK02a]. Hence the point cloud is always split along the direction of greatest variation according to the covariance analysis. If the splitting criterion is not fulfilled, the point cloud $\mathcal{P}$ becomes a cluster C_i. As shown in Figure 4.19b, hierarchical clustering builds a binary tree, where each leaf of the tree corresponds to a cluster.

Iterative point-simplification techniques proposed by Pauly et al. [PGK02a] consecutively reduce the number of points using a sequence of atomic decimation operators. This approach is very similar to the mesh-based simplification methods for creating progressive meshes [Hop96]. Decimation operators are usually arranged in a priority queue according to an error metric that quantifies the error caused by the decimation. The iteration is then performed in such a way that the decimation operation causing the smallest error is applied first. Point-pair contraction, an extension of the common edge collapse operator, is used, which replaces two points $\mathbf{p}_1$ and $\mathbf{p}_2$ by a new point $\bar{\mathbf{p}}$. An adaptation of the quadric error metric (QEM) presented for polygonal meshes in Garland and Heckbert [GH97] is used to rate the contraction operations.

In order to adapt the above technique to the simplification of unstructured point clouds the k-nearest neighbor relation is used to compose a dynamic topology for point sets [PGK02a], since manifold surface connectivity is not available. To initialize the error quadrics for every point sample $\mathbf{p}$, a tangent plane E_i is estimated for every *edge* that connects **p** with one of its neighbors $\mathbf{p}_i$. This tangent plane is spanned by the vector $\mathbf{e}_i = \mathbf{p} - \mathbf{p}_i$ and $\mathbf{b}_i = \mathbf{e}_i \times \mathbf{n}$, where **n** is the estimated normal vector at **p**. After this initialization the point-cloud simplification works exactly like mesh decimation [GH97] with the point $\bar{\mathbf{p}}$ inheriting the neighborhoods of its ancestors $\mathbf{p}_1$ and $\mathbf{p}_2$ and being assigned the error functional $Q_{\bar{\mathbf{v}}} = Q_{\mathbf{v}_1} + Q_{\mathbf{v}_2}$. Figure 4.20 shows an example of a simplified point cloud created by iterative point-pair contractions.

The third point-simplification method proposed by Pauly et al. [PGK02a] is the particle simulation approach that is adapted from the point repulsion algorithm for polygonal meshes [Tur91]. The desired number of particles is randomly spread across the surface and their positions are equalized using the same point repulsion algorithm. The particle simulation is initialized by adding more samples in regions of lower sampling density to ensure the uniformity of the initial sample distribution. The same linear repulsion force as in [Tur91] is used with a finite radius of influence. Point movement is restricted on the surface to ensure an accurate approximation of the original surface. To do so, a displaced particle **p** is kept on the surface by simply

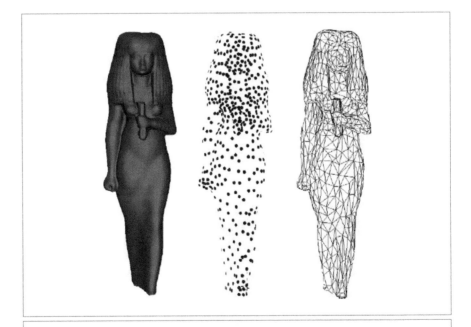

Figure 4.20: Iterative simplification of the Isis model from 187,664 (*left*) to 1,000 sample points (*middle*). The right image shows all remaining potential point-pair contractions indicated as an edge between two points. Note that these edges do not necessarily form a consistent triangulation of the surface.

projecting it onto the tangent plane of the point $\mathbf{p}'$ of the original point cloud that is closest to $\mathbf{p}$. Only at the end of the simulation, the full MLS projection (see Section 4.2) is applied, which does not change the sampling distribution noticeably.

The three point-simplification methods mentioned above provide wide range selections for high-quality point-sampling schemes. However, all cannot take an a priori approximation error tolerance into account. In addition, their pure greedy simplification produces results with small a posteriori error but also with nonuniform sampling density. Though this result can be postoptimized with the particle simulation scheme that, alas, tends to increase the approximation error.

Splat-Decimation Methods

As we have noted before, all of the above downsampling methods do not take the full splat geometry into account in the algorithmic design and hence require extra effort to estimate the actual splat spatial extent. More recent downsampling schemes use the complete geometry of elliptical splats (i.e., their outputs are no more pure point sets), but rather sets of elliptical splats with spatial extent (see Figure 4.21). We refer to these approaches as splat-decimation methods and comparisons (see Section 4.3.3) show that by considering the whole splat geometry throughout the decimation procedures, the resulting sampling quality can be largely improved.

Among these recent methods that can produce decimated surface splats directly, the first-generation approaches [RL00, BWK02, Paj03] are mainly based on hierarchical

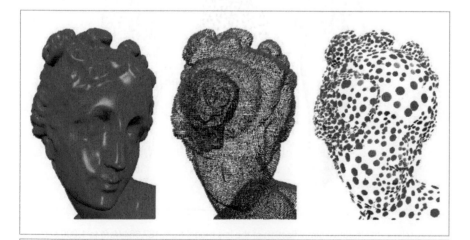

Figure 4.21: The original point model (*left and middle*, 352,000 points) is decimated to 30,000 circular surface splats (*right*).

clustering schemes. The input points are rearranged in a hierarchical spatial partitioning data structure like octrees and splats are created for every node by analyzing the local surface properties. This technique is simple and fast but since there is no optimization strategy involved, the results are usually overly conservative and tend to contain lots of redundant splats.

To produce higher-quality sampling results than the above straightforward hierarchical clustering approaches, Wu et al. [WZK05] have presented an iterative greedy-point decimation scheme to create progressive splat representations for efficient surface splatting (see Figure 4.22). Intuitively, this method that works directly on C^{-1} piecewise linear surface splats functions as the counterpart of the well-known progressive meshes [Hop96] in the C^0 piecewise linear polygonal meshes setting and the iterative point simplification [PGK20a] in the C^{-1} piecewise constant points setting. Its general procedures work in the following way. Given the input point set, initial splats are first created for all point samples. Then all possible splat merge operators are arranged in a priority queue according to an error metric measuring errors caused by respective operators with the top element having minimum error. Iterative operations are usually performed repeatedly with applying the top operator and updating possibly affected operator priorities in the queue until the desired number of splats is reached.

As usual, the input is a set of point samples $\mathcal{P} = \{\mathbf{p}_i\}$. Each output splat s_i is a general 3D ellipse given by its center $\mathbf{c}_i$, its unit normal vector $\mathbf{n}_i$, and two additional *nonunit* vectors $\mathbf{u}_i$ and $\mathbf{v}_i$ defining its major and minor axes. In the first initial splat-generation step, in order to analyze the local surface properties as well as the associated initial splat s_i of a point sample $\mathbf{p}_i$, the k-nearest neighbors $\mathcal{N}_k(\mathbf{p}_i)$ have to be computed beforehand. Then a least square plane H can be found for $\mathbf{p}_i$ and $\mathcal{N}_k(\mathbf{p}_i)$ defining the

Figure 4.22: Progressive splatting of Charlemagne model (600,000 points) from left to right with 2,000, 10,000, 70,000 and 600,000 surface splats.

normal $\mathbf{n}_i$ of s_i, with center $\mathbf{c}_i = \mathbf{p}_i$. As all initial splats are set to be circles, initial $\mathbf{u}_i$ and $\mathbf{v}_i$ can be any two orthogonal vectors parallel to H with same length r_i,

$$r_i = max_j \|(\mathbf{p}_j - \mathbf{c}_i) - \mathbf{n}_i^T (\mathbf{p}_j - \mathbf{c}_i) \mathbf{n}_i\|, \tag{4.36}$$

for all $\mathbf{p}_j \in \mathcal{N}_k(\mathbf{p}_i)$. Note that the above k-nearest neighbor relation is also used to compose the supporting dynamic topology [PGK02a] during the decimation procedure. An iterative splat merge operator Φ will merge two splats s_l and s_r associated with endpoints $\mathbf{p}_l$ and $\mathbf{p}_r$ of a virtual edge e into one larger splat s_m [WZK05]. In the decimation, the initialization and update of the ordering queue of splat merger operators are similar to the iterative point simplification in [PGK02a].

In order to utilize the full geometry of surface splats and to ensure similar approximation quality as that of the established mesh cases, two different error metrics measuring distance deviation and normal deviation, respectively, are also generalized and embedded into this splat decimation framework.

The first one, the L^2 error metric, is based on Euclidean distance measurement. To be able to compute the deviation error caused by a splat merge operator Φ with respect to the original point set, an additional array of indices $\{f_i\}$ to the original points is kept for each splat s_i and initialized with a single index $\{i\}$ referring to the initial point $\mathbf{p}_i$. When merging two splats, their index arrays will be united and assigned to the new splat. Then for a merge operator Φ, to merge splat s_l and s_r to new splat s_m, the approximation error is defined as

$$\varepsilon_\Phi = \|e\| \cdot \sum_{f \in \{f_m\}} |dist(\mathbf{p}_f, s_m)|^2, \; \{f_m\} = \{f_l\} \cup \{f_r\}. \tag{4.37}$$

Note that the above error metric has been weighted by the edge length to penalize merging two distant splats that otherwise would produce oversized splats.

Given the L^2 error metric (Equation 4.37) and two splats s_l and s_r to be merged, the new splat s_m can be determined by applying principle component analysis (PCA [Jol86]) to the point set $\mathcal{P}_m = \{\mathbf{p}_f\}, f \in \{f_m\}$ in 3D directly rather than the projected point set in 2D as in Pajarola [Paj03]. Afterward, there will be the average point $\bar{\mathbf{p}}$ as well as three real eigenvalues $\lambda_1 \geq \lambda_2 \geq \lambda_3$ and the corresponding eigenvectors $\mathbf{e}_1, \mathbf{e}_2, \mathbf{e}_3$. Then for s_m, center $\mathbf{c}_m = \bar{\mathbf{p}}$, normal $\mathbf{n}_m = \mathbf{e}_3$, and two axes $\mathbf{u}_m$ and $\mathbf{v}_m$ will have direction $\mathbf{e}_1$ and $\mathbf{e}_2$, respectively, with a length ratio $\sqrt{\lambda_1/\lambda_2}$. The final axis lengths are scaled simultaneously so that the elliptical splat e_m covers all points $\mathcal{P}_m$ in 2D when they are projected onto the splat plane (see Figure 4.23).

The $L^{2,1}$ error metric measures the deviation of normal directions and is extended from the original metric first presented in Cohen-Steiner et al. [CSAD04]. In this case, the error computation is simpler and there is no need to keep the index array

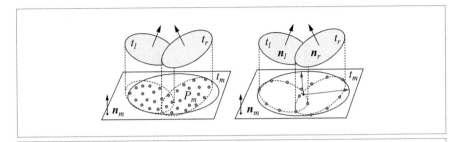

Figure 4.23: Splat merge operators according to L^2 error metric (**left**) and $L^{2,1}$ metric (**right**), which will merge splats t_l and t_r into a new splat t_m.

either. Given the splat merge operator Φ, the respective area $|s_l|$ and $|s_r|$ of two splats s_l and s_r to be merged, similar to Equation (4.37), the edge-length weighted error is calculated as

$$\varepsilon_\Phi = \|e\| \cdot (|s_l| + |s_r|) \cdot \|\mathbf{n}_l - \mathbf{n}_r\|^2. \qquad (4.38)$$

According to the $L^{2,1}$ metric, the geometry of new splat s_m is defined as center

$$\mathbf{c}_m = \frac{|s_l| \cdot \mathbf{c}_l + |s_r| \cdot \mathbf{c}_r}{|s_l| + |s_r|}; \qquad (4.39)$$

and normal

$$\mathbf{n}_m = \frac{|s_l| \cdot \mathbf{n}_l + |s_r| \cdot \mathbf{n}_r}{|s_l| + |s_r|}. \qquad (4.40)$$

The extent of splat s_m is computed in the same way as for the L^2 metric. The only difference is that rather than projecting the point set $\mathcal{P}_m$ (which is not kept), n points are uniformly sampled on both boundaries of splat s_l and s_r and projected to the splat plane of s_m to find the main axis directions and proper scaling (see Figure 4.23). With these error metrics and splat merge operators, the proposed greedy splat decimation framework [WZK05] is complete.

By investing more computation effort, the techniques of Wu and Kobbelt [WK04] obtain highest quality of the decimated splat models. Exploiting the flexibility brought by the point models without topology constraints, a global optimization scheme has been applied in their method to compute an approximately minimal set of splats that covers the entire surface while staying below a globally prescribed maximum error tolerance. Compared to previous work in this area, this subsampling scheme is able to obtain a significantly lower splat number for a given error tolerance while still having high splatting quality (see Figure 4.24).

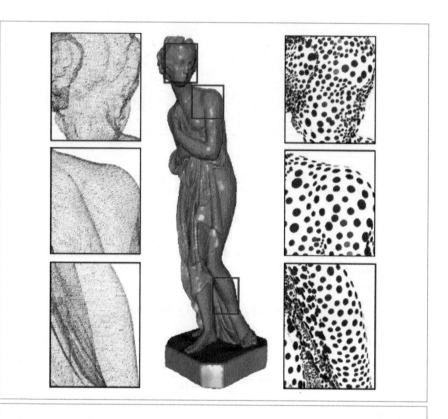

Figure 4.24: Optimized subsampling of the Iphigenie (*left*, 352,000 points) using 30,181 circular splats. The error tolerance is set to 0.05% of the bounding box diagonal. The center figure is rendered with EWA-filtered splats and the right zoom-in figures show the sample density and distribution.

The goal of the optimized subsampling algorithm is to to find a minimum set of surface splats $T = \{s_j\}$ that approximates $\mathcal{P}$ with an error below some prescribed tolerance ε. To initialize the algorithm along with k-nearest neighbors relations [PGK02a, WK04], for each point sample $\mathbf{p}_i$, its local surface properties like normals $\mathbf{n}_i$ and point sampling density ω_i (proportional to the distance between $\mathbf{p}_i$ and its farthest k-nearest neighbor) have to be computed. Depending on the application, the user can choose if *circular* or *elliptical* splats should be used. A circular splat s_j is given by its center $\mathbf{c}_j$, its normal vector $\mathbf{n}_j$, and its radius r_j. For elliptical splats, the radius r_j is replaced by two additional vectors $\mathbf{u}_j$ and $\mathbf{v}_j$ to define the major and minor axes.

In this optimized splat decimation algorithm [WK04], the splat subsampling problem has been formulated into a minimum dominating set problem [CLRS01].

In order to ensure the error tolerance constraint, a new point-splat distance metric also has been introduced. In other words, for a point sample $\mathbf{p}_i$, its distance to the splat set T is computed by orthogonal projection onto the splats s_j:

$$\text{dist}(\mathbf{p}_i, T) \;=\; \text{dist}(\mathbf{p}_i, s_j) \;=\; |\mathbf{n}_j^T (\mathbf{p}_i - \mathbf{c}_j)| \tag{4.41}$$

if

$$\| (\mathbf{p}_i - \mathbf{c}_j) - \mathbf{n}_j^T (\mathbf{p}_i - \mathbf{c}_j) \, \mathbf{n}_j \|^2 \;\leq\; r_j^2 \tag{4.42}$$

for circular splats or

$$\left(\mathbf{u}_j^T (\mathbf{p}_i - \mathbf{c}_j) \right)^2 \;+\; \left(\mathbf{v}_j^T (\mathbf{p}_i - \mathbf{c}_j) \right)^2 \;\leq\; 1 \tag{4.43}$$

for elliptical splats. If $\mathbf{p}_i$ projects into the interior of several splats, the minimum distance is chosen. If Equation (4.42) or (4.43) does not hold for any t_j, $\text{dist}(\mathbf{p}_i, T) = \infty$ is set.

For a given set T of splats and an error tolerance ε, conditions in Equations (4.42) and (4.43) imply a *coverage relation* $C_\varepsilon \subset P \times T$ that includes all pairs $(\mathbf{p}_i, s_j)$ for which Equation (4.42) or (4.43) holds and $\text{dist}(\mathbf{p}_i, s_j) \leq \varepsilon$. Then the *surface patch* $Q_j = C_\varepsilon(*, s_j)$ corresponding to a splat s_j can be defined as the set of all samples $\mathbf{p}_i$ for which the relation $(\mathbf{p}_i, s_j) \in C_\varepsilon$ holds. To measure the size of a patch, its approximative area can be given by

$$\Omega_j \;:=\; \sum_{\mathbf{p}_i \in Q_j} \omega_i. \tag{4.44}$$

The optimized subsampling task now can be formulated as a minimum dominating set problem for the two-colorable graph $(P \cup T, C_\varepsilon)$ whose connectivity is defined by the coverage relation C_ε. Since the dominating set problem is known to be NP-hard [CLRS01], Wu and Kobbelt have presented a three-step approximate optimization algorithm to solve the problem [WK04].

The first step is to compute a maximum splat s_i for each input sample $\mathbf{p}_i$ whose size is limited by the prescribed error tolerance ε. The splats in this initial set are centered at $\mathbf{p}_i$ in the sense that $\mathbf{p}_i$ projects to the center $\mathbf{c}_i$. Starting from a seed point $\mathbf{p}_i$, the splat s_i is grown by adding neighboring sample points in the order of their projected distances (Equation 4.42) to $\mathbf{p}_i$. For each new point $\mathbf{p}_j$ the signed distance $h_j \;=\; \mathbf{n}_i^T (\mathbf{p}_j - \mathbf{p}_i)$ is computed and the growing stops as soon as the interval $[h_{\min}, h_{\max}]$ becomes larger than $2\,\varepsilon$. The center of the splat is then set to

$$\mathbf{c}_i \;=\; \mathbf{p}_i + \frac{h_{\min} + h_{\max}}{2} \, \mathbf{n}_i, \tag{4.45}$$

and the radius is set to

$$r_i \;=\; \| (\mathbf{p}_j - \mathbf{c}_i) - \mathbf{n}_i^T (\mathbf{p}_j - \mathbf{c}_i) \, \mathbf{n}_i \|, \tag{4.46}$$

where $\mathbf{p}_j$ has the largest projected distance (Equation 4.42) before the prescribed error tolerance is violated (see Figure 4.25).

Afterward, this maximum *circular* splat can optionally continue the growing procedure into the minimum curvature direction to obtain an *elliptical* splat that better adapts to the local anisotropic surface curvature while still keeping the error tolerance. The (normalized) principal directions $\mathbf{e}_{min}$ and $\mathbf{e}_{max}$ are robustly estimated by the shape operator of [CSM03]. The minor axis of the elliptical splat will have the direction of $\mathbf{e}_{max}$ and the growing continues in the $\mathbf{e}_{min}$ direction. The growing procedure is similar to the above circular case with the different point ordering of increasing aspect ratios α (see Figure 4.26).

From the initial set of splats, an active subset that safely covers the whole surface is selected by a greedy procedure. The selection criterion guarantees that neighboring splats have sufficient overlap to provide a hole-free approximation of the input surface S. The rank of the splats is computed according to their incremental surface

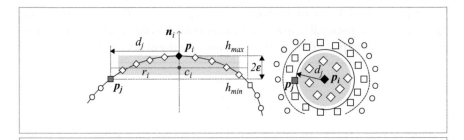

Figure 4.25: Growing a splat s_i initially centered at $\mathbf{p}_i$. Symbols ◊, □, and ○ stand for *conquered*, *front*, and *uncovered* samples, respectively. The left figure shows a view in tangent direction and the right figure is viewed in normal direction.

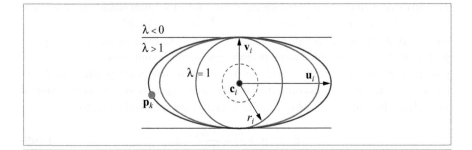

Figure 4.26: A circular splat with center $\mathbf{c}_i$ and radius r_i is extended into an elliptical splat with semi-axes $\mathbf{u}_i$ and $\mathbf{v}_i$.

area contribution Ω_i (Equation 4.44). In each step the splat that adds the maximum surface area is selected to the active set and the area contribution of the remaining candidates is updated. Since the error tolerance ε has been taken into account in the splat-generation step, any selection of splats s_j such that the union of their corresponding patches Q_j completely covers $\mathcal{P}$ automatically satisfies the approximation tolerance.

In the last phase, the greedy solution is further improved by a global relaxation procedure. The idea is to iteratively replace subsets of splats by new sets that have fewer elements or at least a better splat distribution as the greedy output based on local decisions is usually redundant and has a disturbing nonuniformity of the splat distribution [WK04]. The global optimization scheme exploits the fact that splat-based surface representations do not have to respect any consistency requirements. Hence splats can be added and removed in arbitrary order as long as they can preserve a full hole-free coverage of the input samples.

The above global relaxation procedure actually mimics the behavior of repulsing particles on the surface [Tur91]. The local movement of a splat particle s_i is achieved by removing s_i from the active set and replacing it with another neighboring splat s_j. The choice of the new splat s_j is controlled by a local relaxation force that is different from related approaches [Tur91, PGK02a]. This force is derived by taking the complete splat geometry into account and does not only consider the relation between splat centers. In this procedure, two operations have been used to improve the splat distribution and to remove redundant splats. In the first operation they iterate over all active splats and check if there is another splat in the vicinity that has less overlap with its neighbors. In the second operation, they check for each splat if it can be removed (i.e., if the hole resulting from its removal can be recovered by locally "moving" the neighboring splats). Readers are recommended to refer to the original paper, Wu and Kobbelt [WK04], for more details. Figure 4.27 shows the effects of the above global relaxation procedure and once this step is finished, the final optimized subsampling result can be generated.

Point Upsampling Techniques

All point-sampling methods we have introduced above belong to the class of downsampling techniques. On the other hand, point upsampling becomes necessary whenever a given point model is modified (e.g., by local deformations during the shape modeling (see Section 5.3). In this case, large deformations may cause strong distortions in the distribution of sample points on the surface that can lead to insufficient local sampling density.

To ensure a high surface quality for both rendering and approximation, Pauly et al. [PKKG03] have presented a dynamical upsampling technique to insert new point samples where the sampling density becomes too low. The basic idea is to first

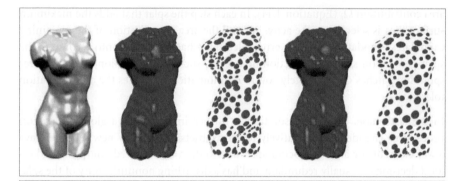

Figure 4.27: A female torso model (*left*, 171,000 sample points) is approximated by 422 circular splats after greedy selection (*middle two*). Global relaxation further reduces the number of splats to 333 (*right two*) while not increasing the approximation error. The figures show both EWA-filtered splats for approximation quality and smaller splats for distribution quality. The error tolerance is $\varepsilon = 0.47\%$ of the bounding box diagonal. Notice the improved splat distribution after the global relaxation step.

measure the surface stretch of point-sampled models after the deformation. Then those largely distorted surface splats are split to add new samples and their positions are determined by a relaxation filter (see Figure 4.33 later). Scalar function values for the newly generated samples are achieved with another interpolation filter. More details can be found in Section 5.3.

4.3.3 ANALYSIS AND COMPARISON

In this section, we will conduct comparative analysis of different representative point decimators in order to provide users a practical guide for the selection of application-specific downsampling techniques. Along with the progressive splatting algorithm (denoted as PSP) [WZK05], the comparisons also include the other two typical progressive point decimators, the level-of-details (LOD) point rendering [Paj03] and the iterative point simplification (IPS) [PGK02a], and the single-resolution optimal splat subsampling scheme (OSS) [WK04], respectively. We have to note that single resolution means models of different resolution have to be generated and maintained separately, and progressive means models of higher resolution can be easily generated or transformed from lower resolution ones. In order to have a fair comparison, for LOD, splats in the same octree levels will be collected, and for IPS, an extra step is necessary to convert its point-based output to the splat representation. Our comparisons focus on the two most relevant aspects, the quality and the speed, since flexible algorithms always have to provide good trade-offs between speed and quality according to the available computational power.

Quality

The result quality of different methods is estimated in the following aspects:

- *Error measurement* captures the statistical distances [CRS98] between decimated splat approximations and the original point model. Figure 4.29 (right) compares the three progressive splat decimators while in Figure 4.28,

Figure 4.28: Bunny model (see also Figure 4.30) decimated to similar number of splats by single-resolution OSS (*left*, 2,577) and progressive PSP (*right*, 2,591) algorithms. Although PSP and OSS have quite close errors (0.103% to 0.092%), being able to concentrate more splats on regions of high curvatures, OSS gives better splat shapes and distribution than PSP.

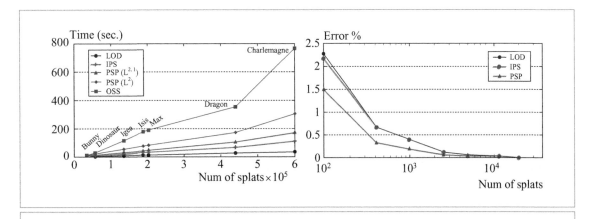

Figure 4.29: (*Left*) Computation times for different point decimation methods where for PSP, OSS, and IPS, times are measured for a simplification to 1% of the input model size and LOD is its whole structure creation time. (*Right*) Error comparisons on bunny model (35,000 points) for three different progressive splat decimators.

errors caused by the progressive PSP algorithm and discrete OSS scheme are reported.

- *Visual quality* depends on the rendering effects as well as the splat shapes and distribution (see Figures 4.28 and 4.30).
- *Area ratio* between the area sum of splat approximations and the mesh surface area of the original point model (see Table 4.1). With the same number of splats that can cover the whole surface (see Figure 4.30), the smaller the ratio, the smaller the area of splats to be rasterized in the fragment shader of the GPU, and the faster the rendering speed.

Considering all above three criteria in combination, it is not difficult to tell that, among the three *progressive* point decimators, the PSP algorithm always performs better than both the LOD and IPS. Especially on coarser scales, we find that because

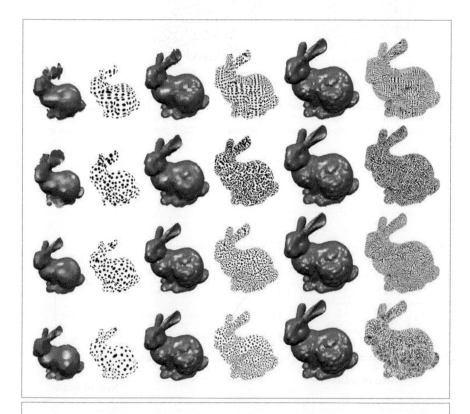

Figure 4.30: Visual comparisons of LOD (*top row*), IPS (*top middle*), PSP (*bottom middle*), and OSS (*bottom*) where the bunny model (35,000 points) is approximated with the same number of 415 (*left*), 2,591 (*middle*), and 11,588 (*right*) splats for LOD, IPS, and PSP, and 419, 2,577, and 11,564 splats for OSS, respectively.

Table 4.1: Area Ratio for Different Point Decimation Methods, Normalized to the Initial Surface Area of the Triangle Mesh. This Factor Measures How Much Overdraw Occurs in the Rasterization of the Splats.

n_{splat}	PSP	LOD	IPS	OSS
415	2.18	2.34	4.14	1.63
2,591	2.52	2.71	4.12	2.15
11,588	3.23	3.22	4.23	3.13

LOD merely adopts the octree space-partitioning scheme and IPS only considers splat centers rather than whole splats, they could not produce as promising results as PSP. In addition, the *single-resolution* OSS usually produces best quality due to its global optimization but OSS cannot create progressive splat representations. In some aspects (e.g., error measurement) the PSP method comes quite close to the best OSS solution.

Speed

Computation times of different point decimation methods are shown and compared in Figure 4.29 (left) as functions of input model size. No wonder that LOD runs fastest as it has a quite simple algorithmic structure. Although both use the same greedy framework, the PSP algorithm is slower than IPS, which has adopted the efficient quadric error metric (QEM) [GH97], as it has to compose and solve least square systems in each splat merge step. And it is not a surprise that the best-quality OSS needs the most running time because of its complex global optimization techniques. Nonetheless, since high computational costs have been traded with improved output quality, and since all point decimation schemes are preprocessing procedures, the amount of running time that has been reported is always endurable.

4.3.4 MULTIRESOLUTION REPRESENTATIONS

The point-sampling techniques can also lead to multiresolution representations for point-based geometry. In this section, we will introduce two conceptual different multiresolution representations. The first one is the *progressive incremental* representations, which refer to a set of surface approximations with varying sampling resolution, thus describing a surface at different levels of coarseness [RL00, WZK05]. These multiresolution progressive representations work as the established multiresolution *topological hierarchies* for the polygonal meshes [KCVS98] generated by mesh simplification algorithms. And they have been used successfully in the context of efficient rendering, surface compression, progressive transmission, and so on. The second one is the *multiscale hierarchical* representations, which describe a surface at different levels of smoothness, without any reference to a particular sampling distribution [PKG06]. These multiresolution hierarchical representations work as the multiresolution *geometric hierarchies* for polygonal meshes [KCVS98] and are largely motivated by the need for higher-level editing semantics, which allow for surface modifications at different scales.

Progressive Incremental Representations

One early multiresolution progressive incremental representation for point models is proposed with QSplat [RL00] where complete volumetric hierarchies of bounding spheres are built for the rendering of large models. The construction algorithm creates the hierarchy by splitting the set of vertices along the longest axis of its bounding box, recursively computing the two subtrees, and finding the bounding sphere of the two children spheres. During rendering, this bounding sphere hierarchy is traversed with recursive criteria like visibility culling, scree-space area, curvatures, normals, and others. Once deciding to stop recursing, a splat is drawn to represent the current sphere and when the traverse is over, all splats drawn will synthesize the final rendering image.

More natural multiresolution progressive representations can be derived from the progressive splat decimators [WZK05]. Specifically, the sequence of splat merge operators $\{\Phi_i\}$ can be recorded during the splat decimation procedure, and when the decimation is stopped, a coarse base splat set $\mathbf{T}_B$ will remain. Then similar to the well-known progressive meshes [Hop96], the progressive splat format is composed with the base splat set $\mathbf{T}_B$ and a set of continuous detail operators $\{\Psi_i\}$, the straightforward inverses of the splat merge operators $\{\Phi_i\}$. Each single detail operator Ψ_i is the inverse of the corresponding splat merge operator Φ_i and will contain three splat indices l, r, m, and the geometry of three splats s_l, s_r, s_m. The data storage amounts to 48 bytes per operator with single floating point precision.

This incremental progressive format can be traversed in both directions. For refinement, the splat of index m will be split and replaced with two smaller splats s_l and s_r. For coarsification, two splats of respective indices l and r will be merged and replaced with a larger splat s_m. Note that by utilizing this progressive splats format we can both increase and decrease the model resolution without any extra data storage, and thus can produce splat models of arbitrary resolution. This will also support efficient applications like progressive rendering and transmission of surface splats. Figures 4.22 and 4.31 show examples of using the progressive representations for progressive surface splatting.

Multiscale Hierarchical Representations

The multiscale hierarchical multiresolution representations are a set of successively smoother approximations of the input point-sampled surface and each level of the discrete multiscale representation is encoded as a normal displacement of its

Figure 4.31: Progressive splatting of dragon model (438,000 points) from top to bottom with 2,000, 6,000, and 20,000 splats.

immediate smoother approximation [PKG06]. The idea is derived from the general framework of multiresolution modeling [KCVS98] for polygonal meshes into the point setting where detail coefficients have to be encoded with respect to the local frames. As discussed in Kobbelt et al. [KCVS98], normal displacement is also used by Pauly et al. [PKG06] to perform the detail encoding. Thus, the formal discrete definition of the hierarchical representations can be as the following: Let $\mathcal{P} = \{\mathbf{p}_1, \dots, \mathbf{p}_n\}$ be a point cloud representing a surface S. Its discrete, point-based multiscale hierarchical representation is a sequence of point clouds $\mathbf{P} = \{\mathcal{P}^0, \dots, \mathcal{P}^k\}$, such that

- For all $l \in \{0, k-1\}$, the surface represented by $\mathcal{P}^l$ approximates S, and $\mathcal{P}^k = \mathcal{P}$.
- $|\mathcal{P}^l| = |\mathcal{P}| = n$, for all $l \in \{0, k\}$.
- For all $\mathbf{p}_i^l \in \mathcal{P}^l$ and all $l \in \{1, k\}$, there exists a $\mathbf{p}_i^{l-1} \in \mathcal{P}^{l-1}$ such that

$$\mathbf{p}_i^l = \mathbf{p}_i^{l-1} + d_i^{l-1} \cdot \mathbf{n}_i^{l-1},$$ (4.47)

where $\mathbf{n}_i^{l-1}$ is the surface normal and d_i^{l-1} a scalar-valued detail coefficient.

Thus, each sample $\mathbf{p}_i \in \mathcal{P}$ is represented by a point $\mathbf{p}_i^0 \in \mathcal{P}^0$ plus a sequence of normal displacement offsets $d_i^0, \ldots, d_i^{k-1}$. To reconstruct the position of $\mathbf{p}_i^l$ at a certain level l the point $\mathbf{p}_i^0$ is recursively displaced in normal direction:

$$\mathbf{p}_i^l = \mathbf{p}_i^0 + d_i^0 \mathbf{n}_i^0 + d_i^1 \mathbf{n}_i^1 + \ldots + d_i^{l-1} \mathbf{n}_i^{l-1}.$$ (4.48)

The inverse of the reconstruction operator is the decomposition operator that determines the detail coefficients of the normal displacement offset between two point clouds. Figure 4.32 shows a discrete multiscale hierarchical representation of the Max Planck model.

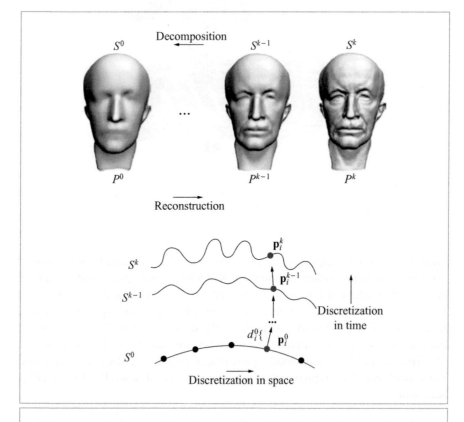

Figure 4.32: Discrete multiscale representation. *Top row:* 3D surface model; *bottom row:* 2D illustration.

In order to compose the above multiscale hierarchical representations, we require two main building blocks. The first is a fairing operator (i.e., a geometric low-pass filter that generates successively smoother approximation levels of a given input surface). For this purpose, the typical discrete fairing methods for polygonal meshes (e.g., Gaussian smoothing techniques [Tau95]) can be generalized to smooth the point-based geometry by replacing the one-ring neighborhood relation with a point neighborhood relation based on k-nearest neighbors.

The second component is a decomposition operator (i.e., a method to encode each level relative to the next smoother level using normal displacements to ensure intuitive detail preservation). In fact, this is equal to computing or encoding the detail coefficients between successive approximation levels. Two alternatives have been proposed that include the bottom-up encoding by ray-shooting (i.e., to shoot a ray from each sample in the smoother level and find the intersection point on the next finer level), and the top-down encoding by projection (i.e., to orthogonally project a sample on the finer level onto the surface of the next smoother level to create the correspondence [PKG06]).

The possible surface-editing applications for multiscale hierarchical point representations are diverse and may include multiscale spectral surface filtering, surface morphing, and multiscale surface deformation. Figure 4.33 shows an example of detail-preserving deformation.

4.3.5 CONCLUSION

The acquisition of point models (e.g., via laser scanning) usually yields highly oversampled point models that cannot be processed efficiently. Hence, techniques for the *subsampling* or *decimation* of point models are an important part of any point-based processing pipeline. In this section we have discussed several such techniques, starting with decimation methods for models consisting of points only. While this representation is simple, it has the drawback of rather weak geometry approximation capabilities. The more powerful splat-based representations are a popular extension to pure point data for which suitable decimation techniques have been presented as well. The last part of this section discussed the construction of multiresolution hierarchies for splat models, which allow for efficient processing (Section 5.1), editing (Sections 5.2 and 5.3), and level-of-detail rendering (Chapter 6).

Looking at the above methods from an implementation point of view it becomes clear that almost all operations need efficient access to the (geodesic) neighbors of given points or splats. Up to now, however, we have implicitly taken for granted that this access is possible. A discussion of data structures providing the required access is the topic of the next section.

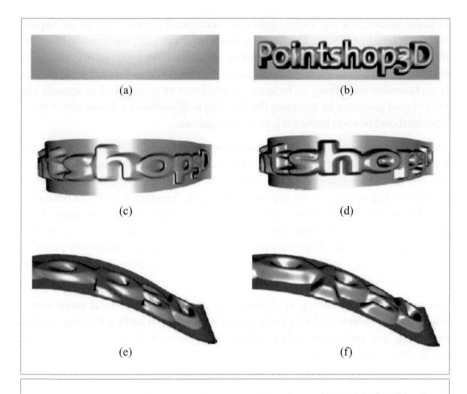

Figure 4.33: Multiscale versus single-scale modeling: (*a*) base surface, (*b*) surface with detail, (*c and e*) single-scale deformation of (*b*), (*d and f*) multiscale deformation of (*a*) with subsequent normal displacement.

4.4 EFFICIENT DATA STRUCTURES

Renato Pajarola

4.4.1 OVERVIEW

In all applications and systems where large data volumes must be managed and processed, the issue of efficient data organization and access methods has to be addressed carefully. This is particularly the point when processing large 3D point datasets (see also Chapter 5) that can reach sizes of several 100 million points or more (see also Chapter 3). Hence, for the design and implementation of an efficient 3D point data structure, the following three pivotal questions should be asked:

1. What classes of query requests to retrieve points must be supported?
2. What type of storage constraints are imposed to represent point splats?
3. What are the requirements for dynamic point insertions and deletions?

From traditional indexing problems we know that questions 1 and 2 may constitute conflicting targets. In general, compactness of data is of paramount significance. However, radical data reduction, *compression*, may not be desired if it comes at the expense of query performance, or ease of use and implementation of the data structure. Both aspects will be touched on in this section. In many cases we may ignore question 3 as the point data to be visualized is static, and for now we will concentrate on static point sets in this chapter. In addition, deformable objects and particles are addressed in Chapter 7 and dynamic (video) point representation in Section 8.1.

4.4.2 SPATIAL DATA ORGANIZATION

The goal of a spatial data structure is to index the space, meaning decompose it into cells and provide a mapping between these and the space occupied by an object [Nie89, GB90, Sam89b, NW97]. The query classes to be supported are spatial operations, such as intersection, containment, and distance, often coming in the form of a search request asking for all objects overlapping a given region (range search) or containing a given point (point search). In the context of 3D shape representation and display, these typically constitute of ray-object intersection, a modified point search,[1] and region (visibility) culling, a range search. Moreover, accessing different parts of an object at different level of detail (LOD) is another type of spatial range search methods to be supported as discussed in Section 4.4.3.

To index objects in 3D space, a spatial data structure can either organize the embedded space or the content itself. In the former case we are generally speaking of a *space partitioning*, in the latter of a *data-partitioning* index structure. While space partitioning guarantees to decompose space into disjoint cells, data partitioning usually generates fewer cells more tightly fitting around the data. Despite the fact that we are dealing with point-sampled surface objects given by a point set $\mathcal{P}$, these splats are not zero-dimensional elements but do have a spatial, planar extent as outlined earlier. Thus, each splat $\mathbf{p}_i \in \mathcal{P}$ has an associated (elliptical) disk of radius r_i. In general, objects with spatial extent require clipping and referencing from multiple cells in space partitioning or cause overlapping cells in data-partitioning approaches [Sam89b, Sam89a, NW97].

As we will see, however, a pragmatic solution to this dilemma is to combine an efficient space- or data-partitioning approach of the zero-dimensional points with

---

1   Stabbing query.

aggregate bounding information on their spatial extent attributes. The basic idea is to keep the cells of the spatial data structure disjoint and compact, and for each *bucket* of points $B_j = \{\mathbf{p}_{1_j}, \ldots, \mathbf{p}_{n_j}\}$ corresponding to a cell j to store bounding volume attributes, such as, for example, the center of mass $\hat{\mathbf{p}}_j = 1/n_j \sum \mathbf{p}_{i_j}$ and bounding sphere radius $\hat{r}_j = \max |\hat{\mathbf{p}}_j - \mathbf{p}_{i_j}| + r_{i_j}$ (see Figure 4.37 later). This allows the use of a spatial data structure to effectively bucketize points, and provides means to quickly find data buckets with potential candidates satisfying a spatial search query.

Effective bucketization improves *spatial selectivity*, which is important for coherent memory access; points in the same bucket are likely to be accessed at the same time when the corresponding region in space is queried. A basic spatial search query (e.g., find all points within region R) is carried out in that the cells of the spatial data structure are tested against the query region R. Given an intersection of cell j, its points B_j are then individually tested and reported if inside R.

For large point sets $\mathcal{P}$, a bucketization $\mathcal{P} = \bigcup_{j=1}^{m} B_j$ may still result in a large number m of buckets, which may in turn have to be organized with respect to their attributes $(\hat{\mathbf{p}}_j, \hat{r}_j)$. Hence, most spatial data structures employ some sort of subdivision of space and organize the buckets themselves in a hierarchical data structure, with the leaf nodes being the actual data buckets. The internal nodes represent cells of recursively grouped data buckets.

It is advisable to avoid excessive recursive subdivision down to a single data element per leaf node, and instead strive to have a bucket of up to k points per leaf of the hierarchy. Therefore, leaf node j stores a bucket of data points B_j together with its bounding sphere position $\hat{\mathbf{p}}_j$ and radius $\hat{r}_j$. An internal cell node j maintains some reference to its child nodes (assume their indices being $c_{1\ldots}$), and stores a tight bounding sphere centered at $\hat{\mathbf{p}}_j = 1/m \sum \mathbf{p}_i$ with radius $\hat{r}_j = \max |\hat{\mathbf{p}}_j - \mathbf{p}_i| + r_i$ from aggregating the information over all m points $\mathbf{p}_i$ covered by the subtree rooted at j. Alternatively, a *nested* bounding sphere hierarchy can be constructed by considering only the immediate child nodes, thus storing the center as $\hat{\mathbf{p}}_j = 1/k \sum \widehat{\mathbf{p}_{c_i}}$ and radius $\hat{r}_j = \max |\hat{\mathbf{p}}_j - \widehat{\mathbf{p}_{c_i}}| + \widehat{r_{c_i}}$ (for child nodes $i = 1\ldots k$).

Octrees

Hierarchical octree data structures [Sam84] are one of the most common choices to handle large point sets (e.g., for interactive rendering) [CH02, BWK02, Paj03, HE03, PSG04, SPL04, SP04]. Starting with a 3D bounding box cell, enclosing the entire data space, each (internal) cell containing data is recursively subdivided into up to eight nonempty octants. This recursion terminates if a cell contains less than a predetermined number of points that are then forming the data bucket of this (leaf) cell. As with quadtrees, there are two main strategies for performing the subdivision of one cell into octants: (1) regular binary subdivision of all dimensions—*region octree*, and (2) axis-aligned subdivision at an arbitrary point inside the cell—*point octree*. As shown in Figure 4.34 this may result in different subdivision hierarchies depending

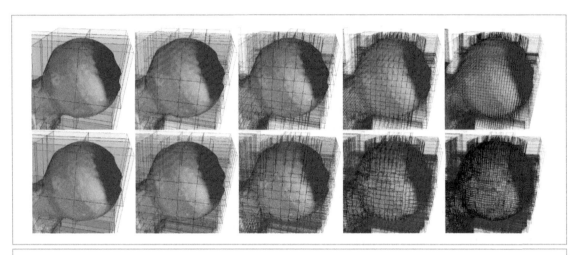

Figure 4.34: Examples of regular region octree subdivision, binary in each dimension (**upper row**), versus adaptive point octree subdivision at arbitrary split positions (**lower row**).

on the shape of the object and the point sample distribution. While the second strategy is more adaptive to the data distribution and may produce fewer octree nodes [Paj03], the first strategy has a simpler hierarchy structure and may require less information to be maintained per node.

An octree over a set $\mathcal{P}$ of n points $\mathbf{p}_{1\ldots n}$ can efficiently be generated in $O(n \log n)$ time. Below we outline a recursive top-down algorithm with tight bounding sphere attributes and data bucket size of up to k points per leaf node. Get_new_split_position() generates the (x, y, z) split coordinates, as a binary subdivision of the current bounding box's dimensions for a region octree or as the mean or median over the current point set $\mathcal{P}$. Get_octant() generates an octant code $(0 \ldots 7)$ for any point $\mathbf{p}_i$ with respect to the current split coordinates (x, y, z), for example, z-order given by $(p_{iz} > z) \cdot 4 + (p_{iy} > y) \cdot 2 + (p_{ix} > x)$.

Octree$(\mathcal{P})$
   if $|\mathcal{P}| \leq k$ **then**
      return New_leaf_node$(\mathcal{P})$

   $\mathbf{p}_{split} \leftarrow$ Get_new_split_position$(\mathcal{P})$
   for $i = 1$ **to** $|\mathcal{P}|$
      $r_{split} \leftarrow$ MAX$(|\mathbf{p}_{split} - \mathbf{p}_i| + r_i, r_{split})$
      $j \leftarrow$ Get_octant$(\mathbf{p}_{split}, \mathbf{p}_i)$

$$\mathcal{P}_j \leftarrow \mathcal{P}_j \cup p_i$$

for $j = 1$ **to** 8

    if $\mathcal{P}_j \neq \emptyset$ **then**

        $c_j \leftarrow \text{Octree}(\mathcal{P}_j)$

return New_octree_node($\mathbf{p}_{split}, r_{split}, c_{1\ldots 8}$)

In Pfister et al. [PZvBG00] a special-purpose octree-like data structure, based on the *layered depth cube* (LDC) [LR98], has been proposed to store point data. The LDC basically consists of three orthogonal, axis-aligned *layered depth images* (LDIs) [SGwHS98] completely enclosing the modeled object as illustrated in Figure 4.35a. This representation requires the 3D object to be resampled in a preprocess (i.e., by orthographic ray casting along all coordinate axes). The resampling records all surface intersections, including depth as well as shape and shade attributes (e.g., such as normal and color). A hierarchical LDC-tree [PZvBG00] is then generated as follows. The initial LDC is subdivided into blocks with user-specified dimension b (i.e., consisting of LDIs with b^2 image resolution). Subsampling by a factor of two and combining up to eight nonempty blocks at each step, an octree is built bottom-up. Figure 4.35b illustrates two levels of this LDC-octree hierarchy with $b = 4$.

K-d-trees

While octrees provide a simple hierarchical organization of space they can suffer from the fact that in general points in 3D cannot evenly be subdivided into eight octants. This may lead to an unbalanced and suboptimal data structure. In contrast, K-d-trees [Sam89b, Sam89a, NW97] can guarantee a fully balanced hierarchical data structure.

Similar to a binary search tree, each node represents a split key along one particular dimension. Starting with the bounding box enclosing all elements, in each recursion the current cell is split along one dimension into two subregions enclosing an equal number of elements. Instead of repeatedly cycling through the split dimensions, the

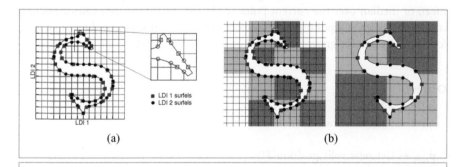

(a)   (b)

Figure 4.35: (*a*) Layered depth cube sampling based on orthogonal layered depth images. (*b*) Two LDC-tree levels with empty blocks shown in white (shown in 2D).

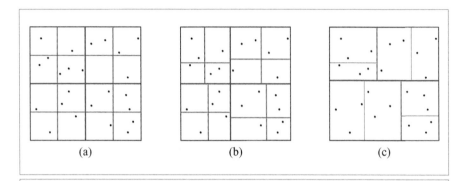

(a)	(b)	(c)

Figure 4.36: Comparison of a (*a*) regular region quadtree, (*b*) adaptive point quadtree, and (*c*) 2D-tree split organization, for a bucket size of three.

best results are achieved by splitting the dimension of largest spatial extent at each recursion step [DDG00].

Through the simple recursive binary subdivision of space, free choice of split key and flexible split dimension, the K-d-tree can generate a balanced binary search tree over a given set of input points. Figure 4.36 illustrates this advantage on the basis of comparing the 2D analog of an octree, and the quadtree [Sam84], with a K-d-tree (for $k = 2$). While a point octree may avoid empty cells and improve data distribution over a region octree, the K-d-tree can achieve a better fill rate using a minimal number of subdivisions.

A K-d-tree over an array of n points $P[1 \ldots n]$ can efficiently be built in logarithmic time as outlined below for a bucket size of k points. We assume that three additional sorted arrays $\mathcal{X}, \mathcal{Y}, \mathcal{Z}$ of indices—only references to points in P—have initially been generated. Each such array sorts the points (indices) according to the corresponding coordinate axis. Thus $\mathcal{X}, \mathcal{Y}, \mathcal{Z}$ have the same dimension and store the same indices, just in a different order. The recursive top-down K-d-tree construction algorithm proceeds by finding the longest bounding box side of the current point set (referenced by either $\mathcal{X}, \mathcal{Y},$ or $\mathcal{Z}$) in Dimension_of_largest_extent(). The points referenced by $\mathcal{X}, \mathcal{Y}, \mathcal{Z}$ are then equally subdivided with respect to the median coordinate of this dimension. Tight bounding sphere attributes can be maintained during the recursive subdivision procedure as indicated.

K-d-tree$(P, \mathcal{X}, \mathcal{Y}, \mathcal{Z})$
   $m \leftarrow |\mathcal{X}|$
   if $m \leq k$ **then**
      return New_leaf_node$(P, \mathcal{X}, m)$

$cutdim \leftarrow \text{Dimension\_of\_largest\_extent}(\mathcal{P}, \mathcal{X}, \mathcal{Y}, \mathcal{Z})$

$median \leftarrow$ **switch** $(cutdim)$

    $x : \mathcal{X}[m/2 + 1]$

    $y : \mathcal{Y}[m/2 + 1]$

    $z : \mathcal{Z}[m/2 + 1]$

$\mathbf{p}_{split} \leftarrow \mathcal{P}[median]_{xyz}$

$x1 \leftarrow x2 \leftarrow y1 \leftarrow y2 \leftarrow z1 \leftarrow z2 \leftarrow 1$

for $i = 1$ **to** m

    $r_{split} \leftarrow \text{MAX}(|\mathbf{p}_{split} - \mathcal{P}[\mathcal{X}[i]]_{xyz}| + \mathcal{P}[\mathcal{X}[i]]_r, r_{split})$

    if $\mathcal{P}[\mathcal{X}[i]]_{cutdim} < \mathbf{p}_{cutdim_{split}}$ **then**

       $\mathcal{X}1[x1] \leftarrow \mathcal{X}[i] ; x1 \leftarrow x1 + 1$

    else if $\mathcal{X}[i] \neq median$ **then**

       $\mathcal{X}2[x2] \leftarrow \mathcal{X}[i] ; x2 \leftarrow x2 + 1$

    if $\mathcal{P}[\mathcal{Y}[i]]_{cutdim} < \mathbf{p}_{cutdim_{split}}$ **then**

       $\mathcal{Y}1[y1] \leftarrow \mathcal{Y}[i] ; y1 \leftarrow y1 + 1$

    else if $\mathcal{Y}[i] \neq median$ **then**

       $\mathcal{Y}2[y2] \leftarrow \mathcal{Y}[i] ; y2 \leftarrow y2 + 1$

    if $\mathcal{P}[\mathcal{Z}[i]]_{cutdim} < \mathbf{p}_{cutdim_{split}}$ **then**

       $\mathcal{Z}1[z1] \leftarrow \mathcal{Z}[i] ; z1 \leftarrow z1 + 1$

    else if $\mathcal{Z}[i] \neq median$ **then**

       $\mathcal{Z}2[z2] \leftarrow \mathcal{Z}[i] ; z2 \leftarrow z2 + 1$

$left \leftarrow right \leftarrow \text{NULL}$

if $m/2 > 0$ **then**

    $left \leftarrow \text{K-d-tree}\ (\mathcal{P}, \mathcal{X}1, \mathcal{Y}1, \mathcal{Z}1)$

if $m/2 + 1 < m$ **then**

    $right \leftarrow \text{K-d-tree}\ (\mathcal{P}, \mathcal{X}2, \mathcal{Y}2, \mathcal{Z}2)$

return New K-d-tree_node $(\mathbf{p}_{split}, r_{split}, left, right)$

Bounding Volume Hierarchies

Bounding volume hierarchies (BVHs) have extensively been used in rendering since Clark and Rubin and Whitted [Cla76, RW80], to efficiently support spatial queries such as visibility culling or ray-object intersections. While being a data-partitioning approach to spatial indexing, unlike octrees and K-d-trees outlined above, a BVH does not have to be space partitioned. Thus, it removes any constraints on spatial subdivision and allows the use of more generic hierarchical organization of spatial data. In fact, a completely random hierarchical grouping of elements could be used, which, however, would not provide the necessary spatial selectivity critical to any good spatial indexing scheme. The only requirement in a BVH is that in each node the bounding volume (i.e., a bounding box or sphere) is known that encloses all elements in this subtree.

It is obvious that space-partitioning data structures can be extended to a BVH by just generating the necessary bounding volume attributes at each node as shown earlier. However, additional data-partitioning (but not space-partitioning), spatial packing, and grouping strategies for 3D points can be used alternatively. This could range from R-tree [Gut84] to k-means [Jai88] point-clustering techniques. An interesting approach is to consider proximity-preserving linearization of space [Pea90, His91, FR89] and exploit its implicit clustering properties [Jag90, ARR$^+$97, Pas00, KF94]. Consequently, points are linearly ordered according to a one-dimensional spatial key. Moreover, any bucketization and order-preserving hierarchical organization can be used to generate the BVH (e.g., a binary search tree or B-tree). This principal of spatial ordering and bucketization is also exploited in Pajarola et al. [PSL05] for accessing and rendering large point sets from out of core.

A bounding volume hierarchy based on this space-linearization concept can be formed with $O(n \log n)$ cost for a set $\mathcal{P}$ of n points with bucket size of k as follows. We assume that the one-dimensional spatial key has previously been assigned to each point. Given the current point set $\mathcal{P}$, Get_median_spatial_key_and_point() returns the median spatial key and the corresponding point $\in \mathcal{P}$, and Spatial_key() provides the spatial key of one point.

BoundingVolumeTree($\mathcal{P}$)
  if $|\mathcal{P}| \le k$ **then**
    return New_leaf_node($\mathcal{P}$)

  $(median, \mathbf{p}_{split}) \leftarrow$ Get_median_spatial_key_and_point($\mathcal{P}$)
  for $i = 1$ **to** $|\mathcal{P}|$
    $r_{split} \leftarrow$ MAX($|\mathbf{p}_{split} - \mathbf{p}_i| + r_i, r_{split}$)
    if $median >$ Spatial_key($\mathbf{p}_i$) **then**
      $\mathcal{P}_< \leftarrow \mathcal{P}_< \cup \mathbf{p}_i$
    else
      $\mathcal{P}_\ge \leftarrow \mathcal{P}_\ge \cup \mathbf{p}_i$

  $left \leftarrow right \leftarrow$ NULL
  if $\mathcal{P}_< \ne \emptyset$ **then**
    $left \leftarrow$ BoundingVolumeTree($\mathcal{P}_<$)
  if $\mathcal{P}_\ge \ne \emptyset$ **then**
    $right \leftarrow$ BoundingVolumeTree($\mathcal{P}_\ge$)
  return New_inner_node($\mathbf{p}_{split}, r_{split}, left, right$)

QSplat [RL00] is a hierarchical-point data structure based on a bounding sphere hierarchy. While a K-d-tree-like construction algorithm is proposed in Rusinkiewicz and Levoy [RL00], other hierarchical organizations can be used as well as long as the bounding sphere property is provided. In fact, due to the recursive quantization, which is applied to the bounding volume attributes as discussed in more detail in Section 4.4.4, the hierarchy actually has to preserve the nesting property as explained earlier.

4.4.3 MULTIRESOLUTION AND LEVEL OF DETAILS

Level of detail (LOD) and (view-dependent) multiresolution-modeling techniques have been established to adjust display quality and performance of large complex 3D objects and scenes to available rendering resources [LRC+03]. As LOD point rendering is discussed in more detail in Chapter 6 we only concentrate on the data structure aspects here.

As discussed earlier in this chapter, we know that each point $\mathbf{p}$ in fact represents a circular or elliptical disk with major radius r, and aspect ratio η for the ellipse, oriented with respect to the surface normal $\mathbf{n}$. Given the point splat's area $A = \pi \cdot r \cdot \eta r$ and the viewpoint $\mathbf{v}$, we can define the screen-space projected size of a point as $\varepsilon = f \cdot A/d$, with $d = |\mathbf{p} - \mathbf{v}|$ and $f \in [0, 1]$ being a correction factor taking the angular difference between $\mathbf{n}$ and $\mathbf{p} - \mathbf{v}$ into account [SPL04, SP04]. A basic LOD data structure can represent the 3D object at variable geometric complexity, thus using a varying number of LOD point splats. The fewer points used, the larger their splat size A has to be. Therefore, for a constant projection ε the choice of LOD depends on the distance d.

Besides computing specific LOD approximations (see also [PGK02b]), hierarchical representations are generally used for adaptive LOD-based interactive rendering (see also [PZvBG00, RL00, CH02, BWK02, Paj03, HE03, PSG04, GM04, SPL04, SP04]). Therefore, each node's attributes—to derive A and f—in the LOD hierarchy must represent the aggregate information of all points in its subtree. While the position is generally given by a median or mean aggregation (e.g., $\hat{\mathbf{p}} = 1/n \sum \mathbf{p}_i$), the splat size and normal deviation are based on a maximum operator. The splat size radius is commonly derived from a bounding sphere measure [Cla76, RW80] (e.g., $\hat{r} = \forall_i \max |\hat{\mathbf{p}} - \mathbf{p}_i| + r_i$). For efficient visibility culling and estimation of visible projected area, the normal cone concept [SAE93] is used to bound the angular deviation of surface normals (e.g., $\hat{n} = 1/n \sum n_i$ and $\hat{\theta} = \forall_i \max (\angle(\hat{\mathbf{n}}, \mathbf{n}_i) + \theta_i)$). Figure 4.37 illustrates this concept of maintaining bounding volume attributes.

4.4.4 EFFECTIVE REPRESENTATION

Due to their simplicity, missing any connectivity graph information, points are of particular interest to represent objects and surfaces at high resolutions, using very dense point samplings. The resulting large scale point sets ask for efficient

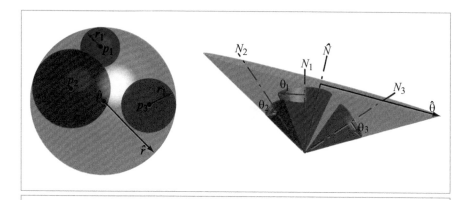

Figure 4.37: Illustration of (*a*) a bounding sphere and (*b*) a bounding normal cone formed from a group of three points.

representation formats. A major issue is the representation of the (minimal) point attributes such as position, normal, color, and the splat size radius. Rounding within the discrete sampling error, quantization and data compression are the general techniques applied here.

Attribute Quantization

An effective representation has been presented in QSplat [RL00], which is based on quantization and predictive encoding. The position $\mathbf{p}$ and radius r values of a point are quantized to $1/13$, relative to the diameter and radius of the parent node in the BVH. This quantization proceeds recursively top-down, which prevents unwanted propagation of quantization error. Given the parent's values $\mathbf{p}_P$ and r_P, the child's values are $\mathbf{p}_C = \mathbf{p}_P + (2/13 \cdot (i, j, k)^T - (1, 1, 1)^T) \cdot r_P$ and $r_C = t \cdot r_P/13$,[2] with i, j, k, t all being multiples of $1/13$. Since not all 13^4 of the possible (i, j, k, t) values are valid, a 13-bit lookup table is proposed to index the used ones.

The normals are quantized to 14 bits, corresponding to a 52×52 grid on each face of a (warped) cube around the origin. Again a lookup table provides run-time access to the quantized normal vectors. The bounding normal cone angle θ is quantized in QSplat to 2 bits, representing the angles having a $\sin(\theta)$ of $1/16$, $4/16$, $9/16$, and 1.

In Pajarola [Paj03] the normals are quantized as illustrated in Figure 4.38. The positive space octant is uniformly subdivided as shown in Figure 4.38a: subdividing the latitude angle into k values $i = 1 \ldots k$ starting at the z-axis pole, and subdividing the

2   Rounded up with respect to center and radius quantization to always enclose the original sphere.

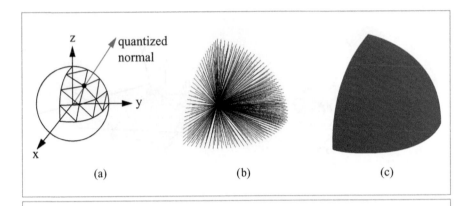

Figure 4.38: (*a*) Illustration of normal quantization in the positive-space octant. A 9-bit quantization leads to 31 subdivisions in latitude, resulting in (*b*) a well-sampled normal space and (*c*) excellent shading results.

longitude angle into values $j = 1\ldots i$ according to the latitude i, rotating from the x- to the y-axis. A $(k^2 + k)/2$ lookup table stores the corresponding normal vectors and a 3-bit octant code defines the normal coordinates' signs. A 9-bit quantization[3] of the positive normal space is shown in Figures 4.38b and c, which provides a well-sampled normal space without shading artifacts.

Colors are quantized in QSplat [RL00] to 5-6-5 bits, respectively, for red, green, and blue, but more savings could be achieved by also predicting colors from parent nodes in the hierarchy. In color theory it is known that human perception indicates a $40 : 20 : 1$ visual sensitivity to red, green, and blue [Hun93]. Therefore, quantization could be adjusted accordingly to improve color coding.

Coordinate Compression

Further space reduction beyond quantization may be required to deal with very large point sets. Compression of point coordinates has been proposed in the context of triangle mesh compression in Devilliers and Gandoin [DG00, GD02b]. The approach is based on a successive subdivision of a segment into two equal half segments, and encoding the number of points contained in one of them. For coordinates quantized to q bits this recursive subdivision stops after q steps when it reaches the quantization accuracy, as the corresponding segment can only contain one distinct point. The point coordinate is not explicitly encoded as the recursive binary subdivision down to the quantization accuracy implicitly defines the position (i.e., as the center of that

---

3   $k = 31$ and $\lceil \log_2(k^2 + k) \rceil - 1 = 9$.

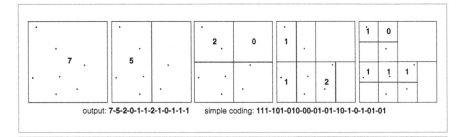

output: **7-5-2-0-1-1-2-1-0-1-1-1**   simple coding: **111-101-010-00-01-01-10-1-0-1-01-01**

Figure 4.39: Recursive binary subdivision of 2D segments and encoding of remaining number of elements in left half segment.

segment). At each step the number of points contained in one half segment (e.g., in the left child) is encoded using the minimal number of bits. That is, given the current segment contains n points, the number contained in one half segment can easily be coded in $\lceil \log_2(n+1) \rceil$ bits,[4] the number in the other half segment is given implicitly.

In higher dimensions the outlined approach only alternates the binary segment subdivision among the dimensions in a fixed order as illustrated in Figure 4.39. It also shows the resulting sequence of point numbers, and a simple $\lceil \log_2(n+1) \rceil$ bits encoding. Using arithmetic coding [CNW87] and prediction error coding as suggested in Devilliers and Gandoin [DG00, GD02b] further reduction can be achieved.

Controlling quantization and sampling density of a 3D surface S,[5] it is shown in Botsch et al. [BWK02] that a very efficient compression of point coordinates can be achieved using an encoding of the *space occupancy* of the surface. The bounding box of S is uniformly subdivided into $2^q \times 2^q \times 2^q$ cells (q-bit coordinate quantization) (i.e., forming the leafs of a regular region octree subdivision). Furthermore, a sample point $\mathbf{p}_i$ is placed at each center of a cell that is intersected by the surface S, resulting in the uniform sampling given the quantization. As only one sample point is defined by each nonempty cell, all points $\mathbf{p}_i$ can be recovered by identifying the nonempty cells.

An octree hierarchy is constructed bottom-up on the $2^q \times 2^q \times 2^q$ cells by recursively combining $2 \times 2 \times 2$ blocks. This generates q successively coarser space-occupancy levels of the surface S. To recover the space-occupancy information from a coarser to a finer level, a byte code indicating for each cell which of its eight subcells is nonempty is sufficient as illustrated in Figure 4.40a. Note that only the *nonzero* byte codes of all nonempty cells need to be stored. Thus starting with the nonempty cell of the

---

4   $\log_2(n+1)$ bits can be achieved using arithmetic coding as in Devilliers and Gandoin [DG00].
5   Which may need resampling or subsampling of the original surface model S or its point set.

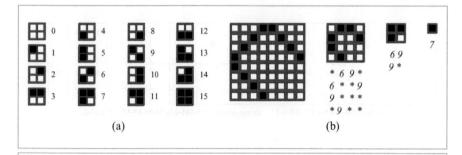

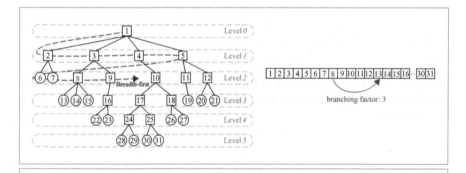

Figure 4.40: (*a*) Four-bit codes to recover space occupancy on the next finer grid level in two dimensions. (*b*) Hierarchical encoding of an 8 × 8 space-occupancy grid, with zero-codes * not being stored explicitly.

Figure 4.41: Breadth-first linear layout of a hierarchy using a *branching-factor* attribute per node and optionally a *first-child* index.

bounding box of S, a depth- or breadth-first traversal order of the octree's byte codes, skipping all emtpy cells, reconstructs the uniform point sampling of S. An example in 2D is given in Figure 4.40b. Assuming that on average each nonempty cell corresponds to four occupied cells on the next finer level, this approach encodes the point positions $\mathbf{p}_i$ with less than three bits per sample [BWK02].

Hierarchy Traversal

An efficient traversal of a hierarchical data structure can be achieved by linearization of its elements into an array representation (see also [SPL04, SP04]). This corresponds to replacing the parent-child pointer relation with array indexing where each node is referenced by its position in the array of all nodes instead of by a pointer. A breadth-first order linearization allows each nonleaf node to store the array index of its first child and the branching factor as illustrated in Figure 4.41. In fact, the branching factor itself is sufficient—and requires very few bits—to describe the hierarchy given a linear layout. This is useful for compact disk storage, however, at run-time the first-child index should be reconstructed and kept in memory for efficient traversal (i.e., allowing backtracking). This is also exploited in QSplat [RL00].

Given a regular region-octree hierarchy, the *model-view-projection* (MVP) can efficiently be computed during the traversal of the hierarchy as shown in [BWK02] as a number of vector additions. Let $\mathbf{M}$ be the MVP transformation matrix and $\mathbf{p}'$ a point derived from $\mathbf{p}$ by displacement of $\mathbf{d}$. Then it holds that

$$\mathbf{M}\mathbf{p}' = \mathbf{M}(\mathbf{p} + \mathbf{d}) = \mathbf{M}\mathbf{p} + \mathbf{M}\mathbf{d}. \tag{4.49}$$

Therefore, if we know the image $\widehat{\mathbf{p}} = \mathbf{M}\mathbf{p}$ we can find $\mathbf{M}(\mathbf{p} + \mathbf{d})$ by adding a precomputed displacement vector $\widehat{\mathbf{d}} = \mathbf{M}\mathbf{p}$ to $\widehat{\mathbf{p}}$. This can now be exploited by precomputing for each frame all possible displacement vectors $\widehat{\mathbf{d}}^l{}_{1\ldots 8}$ for each level l of the octree hierarchy and its 8 child-node displacements (note also that $\widehat{\mathbf{d}^{l+1}}_j = 2\widehat{\mathbf{d}^l}_j$). Now that each point is given by some sum $\mathbf{p} = \mathbf{p}_{root} + \sum_{i=1}^{k} \mathbf{d}^i_{j_i}$ we get its image by

$$\mathbf{M}\mathbf{p} = \mathbf{M}\mathbf{p}_{root} + \sum_{i=1}^{k} \widehat{\mathbf{d}^i}_{j_i}. \tag{4.50}$$

During octree traversal any single addition of a displacement image $\widehat{\mathbf{d}^i}_j$ is reused for all point samples in the subtree below the current node. Amortized for an average branching factor of four, this leads to four scalar additions per point sample (plus eventually two divisions for screen-space dehomogenization) [BWK02].

4.4.5 OUT-OF-CORE REPRESENTATION

An efficient representation is particularly important when manipulating and rendering datasets too big to fit into available physical main memory. Such an out-of-core representation must increasingly take into account memory access coherency because random access to memory locations in external memory is affecting performance unequally worse compared to doing so in main memory.

Clustering

In the *layered point clouds* approach [GM04] the idea of spatial data partitioning and organization is used to recursively cluster point data in a binary hierarchy. Starting at the root, each node stores a uniform subsampling $\mathcal{B}$, of size m, of all points $\mathcal{P}'$ corresponding to this node and its descendants. The remaining points $\mathcal{P}'' = \mathcal{P}' \setminus \mathcal{B}$ are equally (spatially) subdivided among its two subtrees. Hence without duplication of data the hierarchy exactly represents the input point set $\mathcal{P} = \bigcup_{\forall \text{nodes } j} \mathcal{B}_j$ in

$\log_2 |\mathcal{P}|/m$ LOD levels using data buckets of size m.[6] Each node can be seen as a local LOD refinement of its parent. The LOD information for each node j is determined by its average sample spacing r_j, corresponding to merging its points B_j with all parents. Additionally, bounding sphere and normal cone attributes are computed for each node.

The physical data are separated into a point-cloud repository and an index tree. The index tree is assumed to have a small enough memory footprint to be stored in main memory, depending on the choice of m, and each node references its point-cloud bucket through a 32-bit index. The point-cloud repository sorts the data buckets by a primary tree-level index key and a secondary Morton index key, thus combining LOD and spatial ordering. Moreover, storage cost is reduced in Gobbetti and Marton [GM04] by quantization of position and normal attributes as well as delta-predictive entropy encoding.

Linear Memory Layout

The linearization of a hierarchical (multiresolution) data structure as outlined earlier is itself a good starting point for an out-of-core data representation approach. Any hierarchical point representation, such as QSplat [RL00], or octrees such as in Botsch et al. [BWK02] or Confetti [PSG04], can be organized in a linear memory layout (array) and stored as such on disk. An out-of-core representation can directly be achieved by *memory mapping* this file from disk, allowing the application to traverse the hierarchy by accessing array elements. The operating system's virtual memory (VM) manager automatically takes care of which parts of the file have to be loaded into main memory at any time through VM paging and swapping mechanisms.

XSplat [PSL05] makes direct use of this approach and modifies the sequential point tree (SPT) representation [DVS03] described in Section 6.5. It takes advantage of the following two facts: (1) an SPT point is a self-contained LOD point that can independently be evaluated for LOD and culling, and rendered; and (2) SPT points can be processed for rendering in any desired order. Consequently, XSplat reorders all LOD points as illustrated in Figure 4.42, lexicographically with respect to a *layer* number and a spatial ordering index (i.e., the z-curve indexing). It then paginates the linear data into blocks of fixed size that are used as basic LOD selection and culling units. At run-time, the block header array—in main memory or separately mapped from the file—can be scanned and evaluated by the application, and LOD point data are accessed for rendering as required.

To avoid some of the major drawbacks of memory mapping (e.g., glitches in the frame rate when data are not present and the application has to wait), and to support a

---

6　The terminal leaf nodes have less than m points in general.

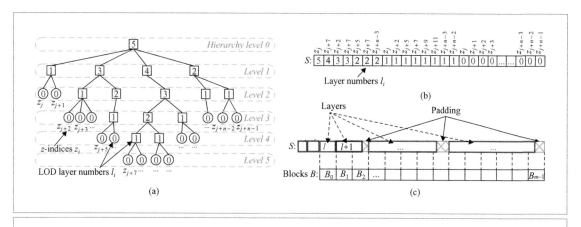

Figure 4.42: (*a*) Indexing of hierarchical nodes according to layer numbers and *z*-curve index. (*b*) Linearized ordering of hierarchy nodes into an array. (*c*) Blockification of on disk linearized LOD data.

client-server based remote rendering architecture, which requires more control over the data loading, streaming QSplat [RL01b] has its own format, which is outlined below.

Streaming

The definition of streaming we adopt here is to scan through and process data in a strict sequential order; in other words, read point data from a source (stream), move them through some processing stage, and eventually write them to a (new) destination. Representing points as a stream, and expressing a processing task as an operation on that stream, is a powerful out-of-core framework since the I/O streams can be from/to external memory and processing only requires little data active in main memory.

SPTs [DVS03] (Section 6.5) are basically a streaming point-rendering system. For each frame, the sequence of points is scanned, passed from the CPU to the GPU, and processed for LOD selection, culling, and finally display. In theory, SPTs could directly be memory mapped from disk files, and hence support out-of-core rendering. However, the problem is that SPTs perform a very conservative selection on the CPU; the range of points to be further processed is much larger than what is finally displayed and no visibility culling is supported. Thus, the CPU touches many points that will eventually be discarded by the GPU. In an out-of-core context this is critical as the primary directive is to limit data access from external memory. To be more useful, the SPT representation has to be extended in a way to allow fast (visibility and LOD) culling of sizable chunks of point data on the CPU without having to touch all points individually. One approach in this direction has been presented in Pajarola et al. [PSL05].

Streaming QSplat [RL01b] takes the linearized QSplat multiresolution hierarchy [RL00] and partitions it into chunks of 1 KB. In addition to the basic LOD selection procedure, the depth-first traversal now also terminates when data in a subtree of the LOD hierarchy are not (yet) available. A bit-mask on the rendering client indicates which data portions are already available, and a two-bit code per data block indicates if they are present, desired, requested, or not present. A prioritized queue manages the data requests from the client and fetches the most urgent data from a remote server. The client-side rendering algorithm of streaming QSplat, with its LOD hierarchy traversal, is not a streaming data representation and processing approach in the sense we outlined above. However, the server-to-client data request and transfer system surely is.

A stream-processing concept and implementation framework not for rendering but for general processing of point data has been proposed in Pajarola [Paj05]. The fundamental idea is to process data sequentially with only a very limited amount of data active at any time, resembling a sliding window over the data stream as illustrated in Figure 4.43. At any given time, only a small fraction of the entire dataset resides in in-core memory while the remainder rests out of core.

Given a stream of points, each point $\mathbf{p}_i$ is read once from the input stream, kept in an active working set $\mathcal{A}$ (a FIFO queue) for some time, and then written to the output stream. All data processing is limited to points in the working set $\mathcal{A}$. Whenever a new point $\mathbf{p}_j$ is passed by the sweep-plane, it is added to the working set $\mathcal{A}$. When the smallest point $\mathbf{p}_{j-m} \in \mathcal{A}$ cannot possibly contribute to any operation on subsequent points $\mathbf{p}_{i>j-m}$ it can safely be written to the output stream. Since the active set $\mathcal{A}$ is

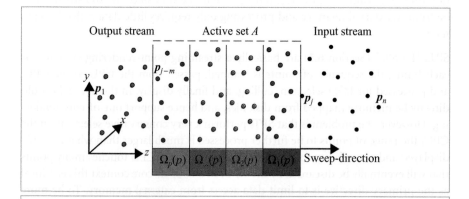

Figure 4.43: Conceptual stream-processing pipeline: A point $\mathbf{p}_i$ moves from right to left through the staged stream operators $\Omega_{1...p}$.

orders-of-magnitude smaller than the entire dataset, $|\mathcal{A}| = m \ll n$, it can efficiently be maintained in main memory even for very large datasets. Moreover, because input and output are streams of points this directly leads to an out-of-core framework for stream processing huge point sets.

In this stream-processing framework, a series of local operators $\Omega_{1...p}$ can be concatenated and applied in succession to a stream of points. In this context, each operator Ω_k also acts as a sequential FIFO queue buffer on the point stream. The class of functions supported includes local operators that perform a nonrecursive computation on a point and its locally (in space) restricted set of neighbors.

4.4.6 CONCLUSION

Processing and manipulating very large point datasets can be very resource intensive, in particular with respect to memory consumption and CPU processing time. Operating on 3D point data frequently encompasses random access to and computations on points coherently located in 3D space. Therefore, efficient spatial organization and compact representation of point data, as well as techniques for out-of-core data access, will significantly reduce the load on memory and CPU time cost. The spatial data structures outlined in this section coherently maintain the point data such that complex digital point-processing and -filtering operations, as discussed in the following Section 4.5, can be implemented efficiently.

Moreover, hierarchical spatial data structures provide the basic framework for most multiresolution representations that are chiefly used for interactive rendering of very large models (see Section 6.4). Most multiresolution data attributes can readily be combined and integrated with a spatial data structure. The basic space or data partitioning and hierarchical grouping properties of a spatial data structure can be exploited to define different levels of detail of the represented 3D shape.

4.5 REAL-TIME REFINEMENT

Gaël Guennebaud, Loïc Barthe, and Mathias Paulin

4.5.1 OVERVIEW

As stated in Section 4.3, both downsampling and upsampling techniques can be required by the processing of a point set. While Section 4.3 focuses on downsampling, this section focuses on upsampling. Even though point-set refinement techniques are necessary for high-quality rendering, multiresolution processing, modeling, etc., they received little attention so far. One reason is certainly the lack of connectivity information in point clouds that makes the neighborhood selection tedious and, hence, the refinement process very unstable. This section presents a general refinement framework for point-based geometry using a one-ring neighborhood selection [GBP05, GBP04]. The choice of a small one-ring neighborhood is motivated by two fundamental criteria. First, by comparison with subdivision surfaces on meshes, a one-ring neighborhood is sufficient to provide C^1 continuous interpolatory subdivision schemes [ZSS96] or C^2 continuous approximation schemes [Loo87, CC78, Kob00]. Secondly, keeping the neighborhood as small as possible is an important issue to maintain real-time performance as well as pertinent neighborhood selection. Based on this general one-ring selection, a $\sqrt{3}$-like refinement interpolating both points and normals and generating visually smooth surfaces at high rate is detailed. For instance, in the context of high-quality rendering, the purpose of this refinement procedure is to maintain a small screen space splat size by dynamically inserting new points where the point set is not dense enough (Figure 4.44). Other refinement possibilities such as interpolation or approximation with MLS, Kobbelt's $\sqrt{3}$, or Loop's subdivision schemes are also discussed.

General Settings

The refinement algorithm takes as input an initial point cloud $\mathcal{P}^0 = \{\mathbf{p}_i\}$ defining a smooth manifold surface where each point $\mathbf{p}_i \in \mathcal{P}^0$ is equipped with a normal $\mathbf{n}_i$ and a radius r_i describing the local density. In other words, the algorithm takes as input a set of splats. The radius of a point $\mathbf{p}_i$ must be at least greater than the distance from $\mathbf{p}_i$ to the farthest neighbor of its natural first-ring neighborhood.

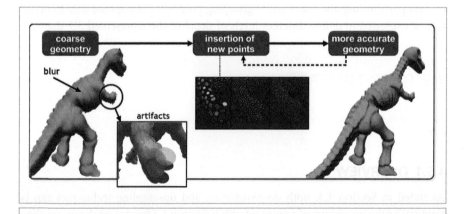

Figure 4.44: Illustration of the principle of the iterative refinement procedure.

The general refinement procedure of a single point $\mathbf{p}$ first requires the computation of a convenient one-ring neighborhood $\mathcal{N}(\mathbf{p})$ of $\mathbf{p}$ (Section 4.5.2) that implicitly forms a triangle fan. Next, this local topology allows us to decide where to insert new points. At this step, different insertion strategies (dyadic, $\sqrt{3}$, ...) and smoothing operators displacing the inserted points onto a smooth surface can be applied.

In a similar fashion to subdivision surfaces, the point set is iteratively refined, leading to a sequence of point sets $\mathcal{P}^0, \mathcal{P}^1, \ldots, \mathcal{P}^l, \ldots$. For interpolatory refinements (such as the $\sqrt{3}$-like refinement presented in Section 4.5.3), we have $\mathcal{P}^l \subset \mathcal{P}^{l+1}$ (only the radius of points varies between two steps), and the refined point set $\mathcal{P}^{l+1}$ is the union of the set $\mathcal{P}^l$ itself and the set of points resulting from the local refinement of each point $\mathbf{p} \in \mathcal{P}^l$.

4.5.2 ONE-RING NEIGHBORHOOD SELECTION

The selection of a pertinent one-ring neighborhood is a critical step in the refinement process. Indeed, it is from this selected set of points that new points are inserted around the refined point $\mathbf{p}$, and hence, the robustness of the refinement algorithm directly depends on the quality of this neighbor selection. Unfortunately, common neighborhood definitions, such as those presented previously in Sections 4.1 and 4.2, suffer from several drawbacks. On the one hand, k-nearest neighbors–based methods fix the number of neighbors while this number can vary significantly from one point to another. On the other hand, an orthogonal projection of the nearest neighbors onto the local tangent plane significantly reduces the accuracy. Indeed, the elevation information, which is crucial when dealing with low local density and high curvature areas, is lost.

For these reasons it is pertinent to use a more flexible neighborhood computation procedure significantly improving the tolerance to undersampled and/or scattered point sets. The computation of the neighborhood $\mathcal{N}(\mathbf{p})$ of the point $\mathbf{p}$ is performed using the three following steps.

Step 1: Coarse Selection

In order to accelerate further computations, let us start by computing the Euclidean neighborhood $\mathcal{N}_r(\mathbf{p})$ of $\mathbf{p}$ as the indices of all points $\mathbf{p}_i$ included in the ball of center $\mathbf{p}$ and radius r:

$$\mathcal{N}_r(\mathbf{p}) = \{i \mid \mathbf{p}_i \in \mathcal{P}^l, \mathbf{p}_i \neq \mathbf{p}, \|\mathbf{p} - \mathbf{p}_i\| < r\}. \tag{4.51}$$

Next, according to the a priori knowledge about the current point cloud, this subset can be reduced by applying several binary rules. For instance, the co-cone rule [ABK98] states that two points $\mathbf{p}_0, \mathbf{p}_1$ can be neighbors only if $\mathbf{p}_1$ (respectively, $\mathbf{p}_0$) is in the complement of the double cone (co-cone) of apex $\mathbf{p}_0$ (respectively, $\mathbf{p}_1$), axis $\mathbf{n}_0$ (respectively, $\mathbf{n}_1$), and angle θ_{cocone} (see Figure 4.45a):

$$C_{cocone}(\mathbf{p}_0, \mathbf{p}_1) \Leftrightarrow \mathrm{Cos}^{-1}\left(\left|\mathbf{n}_0^T \frac{\mathbf{p}_1 - \mathbf{p}_0}{\|\mathbf{p}_1 - \mathbf{p}_0\|}\right|\right) < \theta_{cocone}$$

$$\text{and } \mathrm{Cos}^{-1}\left(\left|\mathbf{n}_1^T \frac{\mathbf{p}_1 - \mathbf{p}_0}{\|\mathbf{p}_1 - \mathbf{p}_0\|}\right|\right) < \theta_{cocone}. \qquad (4.52)$$

A typical choice for the angle θ_{cocone} is $\frac{\pi}{4}$. Another heuristic is to include a maximal angle θ_{normal} criterion between the point normals:

$$C_{normal}(\mathbf{p}_0, \mathbf{p}_1) \Leftrightarrow \mathrm{Cos}^{-1}(\mathbf{n}_0^T \mathbf{n}_1) < \theta_{normal}. \qquad (4.53)$$

This criterion allows us to separate very close pieces of surface as illustrated in Figure 4.45a. Finally, a first approximation $\widetilde{\mathcal{N}}(\mathbf{p})$ of the neighborhood is computed with

$$\widetilde{\mathcal{N}}(\mathbf{p}) = \{i \in \mathcal{N}_r(\mathbf{p}) \mid C_{cocone}(\mathbf{p}, \mathbf{p}_i) \text{ and } C_{normal}(\mathbf{p}, \mathbf{p}_i) \text{ and } \dots\}. \qquad (4.54)$$

Step 2: Geodesic Projection

The goal is now to simplify the final one-ring selection step via a projection of the neighbor candidates onto the tangent plane of the refined point $\mathbf{p}$. However, in order to provide a more meaningful organization of the projected points, the standard orthogonal projection is replaced by a projection based on the geodesic

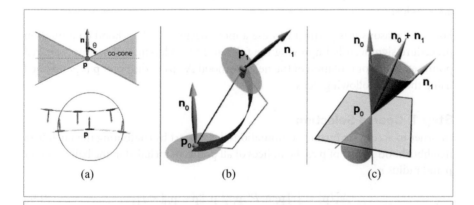

(a)   (b)   (c)

Figure 4.45: (a) *Top*: definition of a co-cone; *bottom*: a condition on the angle between normals can help to separate two close pieces of surface. (b) The relative positions and orientations of the points $\mathbf{p}_0$ and $\mathbf{p}_1$ are such that the construction of a Bézier curve by projection is inconsistent. (c) Given the position $\mathbf{p}_0$ and the two normals $\mathbf{n}_0$, $\mathbf{n}_1$, the point $\mathbf{p}_1$ must be outside the yellow cone.

distance between the current point **p** and its neighbors (Figure 4.46b). Because we
do not know the surface a priori, we can only compute a local approximation of the
distance along the surface. This is a reasonable approximation since the purpose is
just to improve the simple orthogonal projection and not to compute an accurate
geodesic distance.

A first approximation is given by the Euclidean distance. However, since the surface
normal is known at each point, a significantly more accurate approximation is given
by the length of a cubic Bézier curve $\mathbf{B}(u)$ interpolating the two points and their nor-
mals. Such a curve is defined by four control points $\mathbf{b}_0, \mathbf{b}_1, \mathbf{b}_2$, and $\mathbf{b}_3$. The two points
$\mathbf{b}_0$ and $\mathbf{b}_3$ define the extremities of the curve and must be respectively $\mathbf{p}_0$ and $\mathbf{p}_1$ while
the two others control the tangents of the curve and must only be in the respective
tangent plane of the points $\mathbf{p}_0, \mathbf{p}_1$. A solution easy to compute and providing a reasonable shape is to take for $\mathbf{b}_1$ the projection of $\mathbf{p}_1$ onto the tangent plane of $\mathbf{p}_0$ moved
such that the length of the vector $\mathbf{p}_0\mathbf{b}_1$ is equal to the third of the Euclidean distance
between the two extremities $\mathbf{p}_0, \mathbf{p}_1$ (see Figure 4.46a). Let $\mathbf{q}(\mathbf{p}_i, \mathbf{x})$ be the orthogonal
projection operator, projecting the point $\mathbf{x}$ onto the tangent plane of $\mathbf{p}_i$:

$$\mathbf{q}(\mathbf{p}_i, \mathbf{x}) = \mathbf{x} + \mathbf{n}_i^T(\mathbf{p}_i - \mathbf{x})\mathbf{n}_i. \tag{4.55}$$

We also define $\mathbf{t}_{i,j}$ as the pseudotangent vector going from $\mathbf{p}_i$ toward $\mathbf{p}_j$ as follows:

$$\mathbf{t}_{i,j} = \frac{\|\mathbf{p}_j - \mathbf{p}_i\|}{3} \frac{\mathbf{q}(\mathbf{p}_i, \mathbf{p}_j) - \mathbf{p}_i}{\|\mathbf{q}(\mathbf{p}_i, \mathbf{p}_j) - \mathbf{p}_i\|}. \tag{4.56}$$

Then $\mathbf{b}_1$ and $\mathbf{b}_2$ are simply given by:

$$\mathbf{b}_1 = \mathbf{p}_0 + \mathbf{t}_{0,1}.$$
$$\mathbf{b}_2 = \mathbf{p}_1 + \mathbf{t}_{1,0}. \tag{4.57}$$

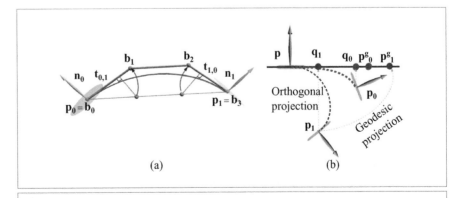

(a)   (b)

Figure 4.46: (a) Construction of a cubic Bézier curve interpolating two point normals.
(b) Illustration of the geodesic projection against an orthogonal projection.

Finally, because the exact computation of the length of a Bézier curve is too expensive for our purpose, we'd rather use a sufficient approximation given by the length of the control polygon:

$$\tilde{g}(\mathbf{p}_0, \mathbf{p}_1) = \frac{2}{3} \|\mathbf{p}_1 - \mathbf{p}_0\| + \|\mathbf{b}_2 - \mathbf{b}_1\| . \tag{4.58}$$

Note that a better approximation would be the average of the control polygon length and the Euclidean distance, but an overestimation is actually better suited when dealing with high-curvature areas.

Then, the geodesic projection $\mathbf{p}_i^g$ of a point $\mathbf{p}_i$ onto the tangent plane of $\mathbf{p}$ is the orthogonal projection moved such that the distance between $\mathbf{p}$ and $\mathbf{p}_i^g$ is equal to the geodesic distance between $\mathbf{p}$ and $\mathbf{p}_i$:

$$\mathbf{p}_i^g = \mathbf{p} + \tilde{g}(\mathbf{p}, \mathbf{p}_i) \frac{\mathbf{q}(\mathbf{p}, \mathbf{p}_i) - \mathbf{p}}{\|\mathbf{q}(\mathbf{p}, \mathbf{p}_i) - \mathbf{p}\|} . \tag{4.59}$$

Compared to a simple orthogonal projection, the geodesic projection allows us to correctly sort neighbors in the 2D domain even in case of high curvature, as illustrated Figure 4.46b.

Finally, note that the construction by projection of a cubic Bézier curve interpolating two point normals is not always consistent. Indeed, as illustrated in Figure 4.45b, certain configurations of the positions and normals of the two boundary extremities yield to an inconsistency with respect to the normal's orientation (inside/outside). This situation occurs when the point $\mathbf{p}_1$ is inside the infinite cone of apex $\mathbf{p}_0$ and axis $\mathbf{n}_0 + \mathbf{n}_1$ (Figure 4.45c). In this case, a specific (global) treatment could be applied in order to reestablish the normal consistency. However, this would mean that we try to reconstruct a highly undersampled surface from an r-sampling $\mathcal{P}^0$ with $r > 2$ (see the definition in Section 4.1) and, hence, it is more natural to consider that the points $\mathbf{p}_0$ and $\mathbf{p}_1$ are not neighbors. Thus, we can add the following generic condition when constructing $\tilde{\mathcal{N}}(\mathbf{p})$ (Equation 4.54):

$$C_{cone}(\mathbf{p}_0, \mathbf{p}_1) \Leftrightarrow \left| (\mathbf{n}_0 + \mathbf{n}_1)^T \frac{\mathbf{p}_1 - \mathbf{p}_0}{\|\mathbf{p}_1 - \mathbf{p}_0\|} \right| > 1 + \mathbf{n}_0^T \mathbf{n}_1 . \tag{4.60}$$

Step 3: Fuzzy BSP Selection

The purpose of this last step is to select a pertinent one-ring neighborhood by applying a fuzzy BSP filtering on the set of points $\mathbf{p}_i^g$, $i \in \tilde{\mathcal{N}}(\mathbf{p})$. Here, the intuitive idea is to remove all neighbors that are strongly "behind" another one or slightly "behind" two others. Inspired from the BSP neighborhood [Pau03], the notion of fuzzy discriminant plane is defined by a *badness* value w_{ij} stating to what extent the neighbor $\mathbf{p}_i$ is "behind" the neighbor $\mathbf{p}_j$ relatively to the current point $\mathbf{p}$ (see Figure 4.47).

The value of w_{ij} varies linearly from 0 to 1 as the angle $\beta_{ij} = \widehat{\mathbf{p}\mathbf{p}_j^g \mathbf{p}_i^g}$ varies from θ_0 to θ_1:

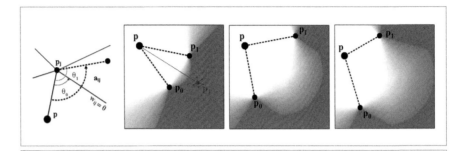

Figure 4.47: *Left*: Computation of the badness value w_{ij} between two points. The other pictures illustrate the blending of two fuzzy discriminant planes with different configurations. The gradient represents the badness value $w_i = w_{i,0} + w_{i,1}$ produced by the two points p_0 and p_1, at every point of the 2D space.

$$w_{ij} = \frac{\beta_{ij} - \theta_0}{\theta_1 - \theta_0},$$

(4.61)

and computations are simplified using the following approximation:

$$w_{ij} \approx \frac{\cos(\beta_{ij}) - \cos(\theta_0)}{\cos(\theta_1) - \cos(\theta_0)}.$$

(4.62)

The value w_{ij} defines a scalar field where the isovalue $v \in]0, 1[$ corresponds to a cone of angle $\theta_0(v - 1) + \theta_1 v$. In practice, these two angles must be chosen such that the isovalue 0.5 defines a cone with an angle greater than $\frac{\pi}{2}$ (i.e., $\frac{\theta_0 + \theta_1}{2} > \frac{\pi}{2}$) in order to provide a sufficient flexibility to the selection. A typical choice is $\theta_0 = \frac{3\pi}{8}$ and $\theta_1 = \frac{6\pi}{8}$.

Next, these fuzzy discriminant planes must be combined two by two (Figure 4.47). Let $Succ_i$ (respectively, $Pred_i$) be the set of successors (respectively, predecessors) of the point p_i, $i \in \tilde{\mathcal{N}}(p)$ such that $Succ_i = \{j \in \tilde{\mathcal{N}}(p) \mid 0 < \widehat{p_i^g p p_j^g} < \pi\}$ (respectively, $Pred_i = \{j \in \tilde{\mathcal{N}}(p) \mid -\pi < \widehat{p_i^g p p_j^g} < 0\}$). These definitions are illustrated Figure 4.48a. The badness value w_i, stating how the neighbor p_i is "behind" the whole neighborhood of p, is computed for each neighbor p_i. Then w_i is the sum of the two maximal badness values involved by the successors and predecessor of p_i:

$$w_i = \max_{j \in Succ_i}(w_{ij}) + \max_{j \in Pred_i}(w_{ij}).$$

(4.63)

This blending of two fuzzy planes is illustrated in Figure 4.47. Finally, as soon as a neighbor p_i has a badness value w_i greater than 1 it is removed from the neighborhood of p (Figure 4.48b) yielding the final one-ring neighborhood $\mathcal{N}(p)$ (Figure 4.48c):

$$\mathcal{N}(p) = \{i \mid i \in \tilde{\mathcal{N}}(p), w_i < 1\}.$$

(4.64)

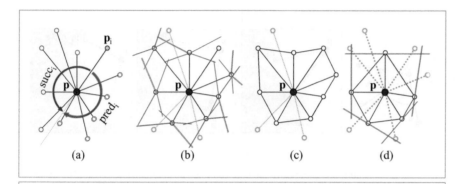

Figure 4.48: (*a*) Definition of the successors and predecessors of the point $\mathbf{p}_i$. (*b*) Application of the fuzzy BSP filtering on the neighborhood of the point $\mathbf{p}$. (*c*) The filtered neighborhood of $\mathbf{p}$ implicitly defines a triangle fan. (*d*) Comparison with the original BSP neighborhoods.

Figure 4.48d compares the result of the classical BSP neighborhoods against the fuzzy approach.

Symmetric Version

Note that a naturally symmetric version of the neighborhood can easily be obtained by avoiding the projection step (i.e., by taking $\mathbf{p}_i^g = \mathbf{p}_i$). On one hand, the symmetric property is very important for several operations, such as the analysis of the refinement procedure. On the other hand, avoiding the geodesic projection significantly reduces the robustness of the selection in case of low-sampling density or high curvature. A simple solution is to use the nonsymmetric version for the first difficult refinement steps and the symmetric one for the following steps.

4.5.3 REFINEMENT ALGORITHM

This section details the refinement of the current point $\mathbf{p}$ from its one-ring neighborhood $\mathcal{N}(\mathbf{p})$ computed with the method of the previous section. At this step, the neighbors $\mathbf{p}_i$, $i \in \mathcal{N}(\mathbf{p})$ are sorted by increasing angles of their projection $\mathbf{q}(\mathbf{p}, \mathbf{p}_i)$ onto the tangent plane of $\mathbf{p}$, so that this neighborhood implicitly forms a triangle fan around $\mathbf{p}$ (Figure 4.48d).

$\sqrt{3}$ Interpolation

In order to provide a visually smooth interpolating surface, the interpolation power of Bézier triangles is combined with a $\sqrt{3}$ refinement strategy. In a $\sqrt{3}$ refinement strategy new points are inserted close to the center of the selected triangle. Next these points are displaced onto a local smooth interpolating surface via the construction of a cubic Bézier triangle $\mathbf{B}(u, v)$ interpolating the three points and their normals (Figure 4.49a):

$$\mathbf{B}(u, v) = \sum_{i+j+k=3} \mathbf{b}_{ijk} \frac{3!}{i!j!k!} u^i v^j w^k, \ w = 1 - u - v. \qquad (4.65)$$

Given three points $\mathbf{p}_0, \mathbf{p}_1, \mathbf{p}_2$, and their respective normals $\mathbf{n}_0, \mathbf{n}_1, \mathbf{n}_2$, the nine control points $\mathbf{b}_{ijk}$ of the patch (Equation 4.65) are computed as follows:

1. The three extremities $\mathbf{b}_{300}, \mathbf{b}_{030}, \mathbf{b}_{003}$ are respectively $\mathbf{p}_0, \mathbf{p}_1, \mathbf{p}_2$.
2. The positions of the six boundary control points ($\mathbf{b}_{ijk}, i + j + k = 3, i \neq j \neq k$) only depend on the two extremities of their respective boundary and are computed in the same manner as for the cubic Bézier curves used to evaluate geodesic distances (see the previous section). For instance:

$$\mathbf{b}_{210} = \mathbf{p}_0 + \frac{\|\mathbf{p}_1 - \mathbf{p}_0\|}{3} \frac{\mathbf{q}(\mathbf{p}_0, \mathbf{p}_1) - \mathbf{p}_0}{\|\mathbf{q}(\mathbf{p}_0, \mathbf{p}_1) - \mathbf{p}_0\|} = \mathbf{p}_0 + \mathbf{t}_{0,1}. \qquad (4.66)$$

3. The central point $\mathbf{b}_{111}$ is set to be close to quadratic polynomials by setting $b_{111} = \mathbf{c} + \frac{3}{2}(\mathbf{a} - \mathbf{c})$ where $\mathbf{c}$ is the center of gravity of the three input points and $\mathbf{a}$ is the average of the six boundary control points.

This construction varies from the one of Vlachos et al. [VPBM01] only in one point. The difference is that after projection, the boundary points $\mathbf{b}_{ijk}$ ($i + j + k = 3$,

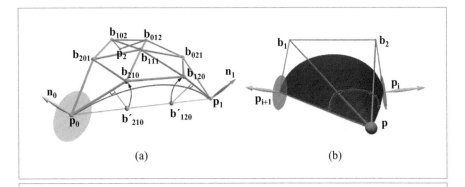

(a)   (b)

Figure 4.49: (a) Construction of the control polygon of a cubic Bézier triangle interpolating three splats. (b) The "curved angle" between two point normals $\mathbf{p}_i$, $\mathbf{p}_{i+1}$ relative to a third point $\mathbf{p}$ is specially useful for areas of high curvature. On this example there is a ratio of two between the geometric angle and the "curved angle."

$i \neq j \neq k$) are displaced in order to avoid the introduction of flat area in the reconstructed surface, especially in areas of high curvature.

Therefore, the smoothing operator ϕ is defined as the displacement of the center of gravity onto the Bézier triangle. The position of the new point $\mathbf{p}_{new}$ is

$$\mathbf{p}_{new} = \frac{1}{3}(\mathbf{p}_0 + \mathbf{p}_1 + \mathbf{p}_2) + \phi(\mathbf{p}_0, \mathbf{p}_1, \mathbf{p}_2), \qquad (4.67)$$

where ϕ is the average of the six pseudotangent vectors:

$$\phi(\mathbf{p}_0, \mathbf{p}_1, \mathbf{p}_2) = \frac{1}{6} \sum_{i=0}^{2} \mathbf{t}_{i,\,i+1} + \mathbf{t}_{i,\,i+2}. \qquad (4.68)$$

The normal of the new point is the cross product of the two tangent vectors at the center of the Bézier triangle ($u = v = \frac{1}{3}$):

$$\frac{\partial \mathbf{B}}{\partial u}\left(\tfrac{1}{3}, \tfrac{1}{3}\right) = 7(\mathbf{p}_1 - \mathbf{p}_0) + \mathbf{b}_{120} - \mathbf{b}_{102} + \mathbf{b}_{012} - \mathbf{b}_{210} + 2(\mathbf{b}_{021} - \mathbf{b}_{201})$$

$$\frac{\partial \mathbf{B}}{\partial v}\left(\tfrac{1}{3}, \tfrac{1}{3}\right) = 7(\mathbf{p}_2 - \mathbf{p}_0) + \mathbf{b}_{102} - \mathbf{b}_{120} + \mathbf{b}_{021} - \mathbf{b}_{201} + 2(\mathbf{b}_{012} - \mathbf{b}_{210}). \qquad (4.69)$$

Other attributes of the points, like the texture color, are simply linearly interpoled from the three initial points.

Sampling Control

In order to avoid oversampling and/or redundancy, new points must not necessarily be inserted at the center of each triangle. Relevant new points are those that optimize the uniformity of the new neighborhood of $\mathbf{p}$ by taking into account the relative position of neighbors and the new points of $\mathcal{P}^{l+1} - \mathcal{P}^l$ already inserted. Thus, the challenge is to build a new neighborhood $\mathcal{N}'(\mathbf{p})$ around $\mathbf{p}$, corresponding to one refinement step that must both fill holes and regularize the sampling.

First the set $\mathcal{N}'(\mathbf{p})$ is initialized with the indices of the points of $\mathcal{P}^{l+1}$, which can be considered as newly inserted points; in other words, the points that are at a distance from $\mathbf{p}$ smaller than λr with $\lambda = 1/\sqrt{3}$ (Figures 4.50a and b). The value of λ is set according to the scale factor of a $\sqrt{3}$ refinement in the regular case [Kob00].

The refinement of $\mathbf{p}$ is complete as soon as the maximal angle between two consecutive points of $\mathcal{N}'(\mathbf{p})$ is smaller than a given threshold $\theta_c = \frac{\pi}{2}$. Hence, while $\mathcal{N}'(\mathbf{p})$ is not complete, new points are inserted. To do so, three terms are defined (Figures 4.50b and c):

- $\mathcal{Y}(\mathbf{p})$ is the set of points already inserted that are sufficiently close to $\mathbf{p}$ but not close enough to be selected in $\mathcal{N}'(\mathbf{p})$:

$$\mathcal{Y}(\mathbf{p}) = \{i \,|\, \mathbf{p}_i \in \mathcal{P}^{l+1}\mathcal{P}^l, \lambda r < \|\mathbf{p}_i - \mathbf{p}\| < r\}. \qquad (4.70)$$

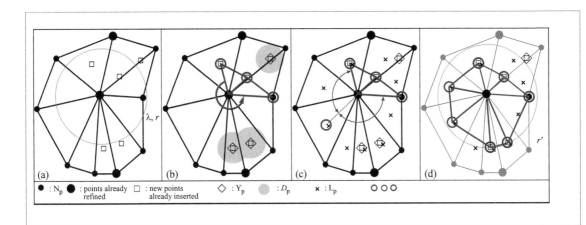

Figure 4.50: Local refinement of the current point **p**. (*a*) The neighborhood of the point **p** before its own refinement. Two of its neighbors have already been refined: new points are represented by squares. (*b*) Initialization of the new neighborhood $\mathcal{N}'(\mathbf{p})$ (in green). (*c*) Selection of a point to insert. (*d*) The new neighborhood $\mathcal{N}'(\mathbf{p})$ is complete.

- $\mathcal{D}(\mathbf{p})$ is the discard space avoiding oversampling and redundancy. It is the union of the spheres of radius $\frac{1}{2}\lambda r$ centered on the points of $\mathcal{Y}(\mathbf{p})$:

$$\mathcal{D}(\mathbf{p}) = \{\mathbf{x} \mid i \in \mathcal{Y}(\mathbf{p}), \|\mathbf{x} - \mathbf{p}_i\| < \frac{1}{2}\lambda r\}. \tag{4.71}$$

- $\mathcal{L}(\mathbf{p})$ is the set of all possible new points; in other words, it is the set of points resulting from the application of the smoothing operator (Equation 4.68) on the center of gravity of all triangles of the implicit triangle fan formed by the sorted neighborhood $\mathcal{N}(\mathbf{p})$:

$$\mathcal{L}(\mathbf{p}) = \left\{ \frac{1}{3}(\mathbf{p} + \mathbf{p}_i + \mathbf{p}_{i+1}) + \phi(\mathbf{p}, \mathbf{p}_i, \mathbf{p}_{i+1}) \mid i \in \mathcal{N}(\mathbf{p}) \right\}. \tag{4.72}$$

The insertion procedure is the following:

While the neighborhood $\mathcal{N}'(\mathbf{p})$ is not complete **repeat.**

1. Select the pair of consecutive points $\mathbf{p}_j$, $\mathbf{p}_{j+1}$ in $\mathcal{N}'(\mathbf{p})$ forming the maximal angle (Figure 4.50b).
2. Select the new point in $\mathcal{L}(\mathbf{p})$ which best balances point sampling (Figure 4.50c). A good candidate is the point $\mathbf{p}_k \in \mathcal{L}(\mathbf{p})$ such that the minimum of the two angles $\widehat{\mathbf{p}_j\mathbf{p}\mathbf{p}_k}$ and $\widehat{\mathbf{p}_k\mathbf{p}\mathbf{p}_{j+1}}$, is maximal.
3. If this point is not too close to an already inserted point (i.e., $\mathbf{p}_k \notin \mathcal{D}(\mathbf{p})$), then it is inserted in $\mathcal{P}^{l+1}$ and $\mathcal{N}'(\mathbf{p})$. Otherwise no new point is inserted in $\mathcal{P}^{l+1}$ and

the closest point to $\mathbf{p}_k$ in $\mathcal{Y}(\mathbf{p})$ is inserted in $\mathcal{N}'(\mathbf{p})$ (Figure 4.50d). Thus, if the samples are locally dense enough, no new point is inserted.

When this process terminates, the radius of the point $\mathbf{p}$ is updated according to its new neighborhood $\mathcal{N}'(\mathbf{p})$. The new radius r' is set to the maximum distance between $\mathbf{p}$ and the points of $\mathcal{N}'(\mathbf{p})$: $r' = \max_{j \in \mathcal{N}'(\mathbf{p})}(\|\mathbf{p} - \mathbf{p}_j\|)$ (Figure 4.50d). The radius r_j of each new neighbor $\mathbf{p}_j, j \in \mathcal{N}'(\mathbf{p})$ is set to the maximum of the four values: r_j, $\|\mathbf{p}_j - \mathbf{p}\|$, $\|\mathbf{p}_j - \mathbf{p}_{j-1}\|$, and $\|\mathbf{p}_j - \mathbf{p}_{j+1}\|$.

However, the angle criterion used to determine whether the new neighborhood is complete or not can be irrelevant in case of local high curvature (i.e., when the angle between the normals of neighbors is too large). Hence, it is more relevant to use a new angle measure taking into account the ratio of the Euclidean distance and the geodesic distance between the two points. Following the geodesic distance approximation, the "curved-angle" $\widetilde{\alpha}(\mathbf{p}, \mathbf{p}_0, \mathbf{p}_1)$ is defined as the sum of three angles taken along the control polygon of the boundary curve interpolating $\mathbf{p}_0, \mathbf{p}_1$ (Figure 4.49b):

$$\widetilde{\alpha}(\mathbf{p}, \mathbf{p}_0, \mathbf{p}_1) = \widehat{\mathbf{p}_0 \mathbf{p} \mathbf{b}_{210}} + \widehat{\mathbf{b}_{210} \mathbf{p} \mathbf{b}_{120}} + \widehat{\mathbf{b}_{120} \mathbf{p} \mathbf{p}_1}. \qquad (4.73)$$

Local versus Global Sampling Control

The strategy presented here uses the radius of the current point to locally equilibrate the sampling density. Therefore, an originally denser region will remain denser than another region after several refinement steps. A variant of this strategy is to use a global radius to control the sampling (i.e., the radius of the largest splats). This leads to a globally uniform sampling.

Smoothness and Robustness

In order to evaluate the robustness of the refinement method, it has been tested on several irregularly downsampled models: for instance in Figure 4.51 the refinement algorithm is applied to 3,500 points randomly selected from a set of 150,000 points representing a statue of Isis. Figure 4.52 illustrates the use of the refinement on an especially large hole. To fill this hole only the radius of points has been adjusted such that they overlap the hole and the refinement algorithm has been applied several times. In this case the alternate refinement strategy leading to a global uniform sampling (see above) is especially useful. Figure 4.53 illustrates the usefulness of the "geodesic projection" and the "curved angle" on a highly undersampled area. In this example, the boundary of the *David*'s eye exhibits holes if these tools are not used. Figure 4.54 illustrates the superiority in the reconstructed surface smoothness of the $\sqrt{3}$ refinement algorithm over the butterfly mesh-based interpolatory subdivision scheme [ZSS96] (C^1 surface but with large oscillations) and a dyadic refinement method [GBP04](high-frequency oscillation artifacts). Even though some insights

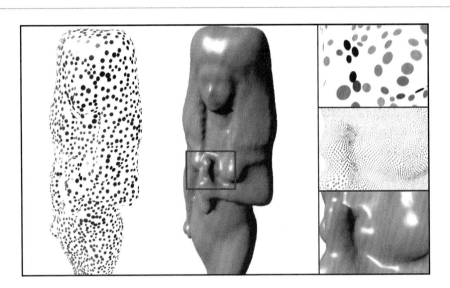

Figure 4.51: Illustration of the smooth reconstruction capabilities of the $\sqrt{3}$-like refinement procedure on the Isis model irregularly sampled with 3,500 points (*left*). The right images focus on a particularly undersampled area; from *top to bottom*: the initial sampling, after four, then six refinement steps.

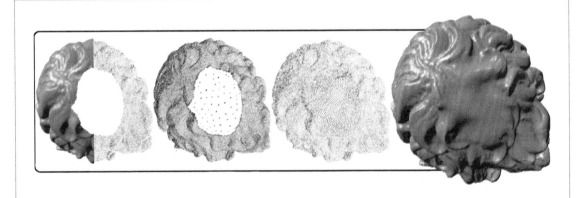

Figure 4.52: Illustration of the hole-filling capability of the refinement algorithm. A large hole in the *David*'s hair is filled by adjusting the radius of boundary points such that they are greater than the hole and applying the refinement algorithm. The final image is obtained after eight refinement steps while the two others show intermediate steps.

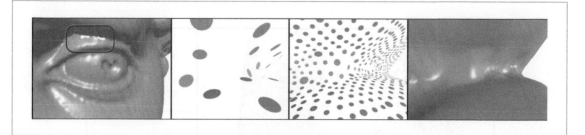

Figure 4.53: Illustration of the usefulness of the geodesic projection and the curved angle. *Left*: If they are both disabled, high-curvature areas are not reconstructed (holes appear). The three other images are close views of the refinement process when the geodesic projection and curved angle are enabled. Then from *left to right*: The initial sampling, intermediate step, and final refinement step where the previous holes are smoothly reconstructed.

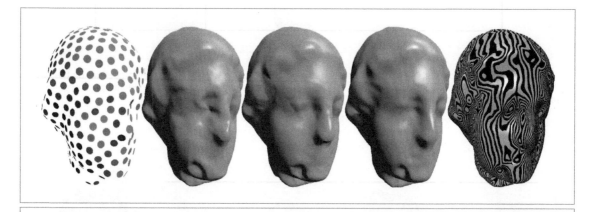

Figure 4.54: *Right*: The Igea model uniformly sampled by 600 points is refined to 150,000 points with various techniques. Then, from *left to right*: The butterfly (after a meshing step), a dyadic refinement of point clouds [GBP04], and the $\sqrt{3}$-like refinement. The last picture is rendered with reflexion lines showing normal and curvature variations.

are given in Guennebaud et al. [GBP05], the analysis of the limit surface continuity remains an open problem.

4.5.4 REFINEMENT OF SHARP FEATURES

So far, we have assumed that the initial point cloud represents a smooth manifold surface. In this section we show how to refine sharp creases and boundaries. A common and efficient way to handle sharp creases with point-based geometry is to use clipped splats. Although clipped splats are sufficient for the rendering, geometry processing requires, in addition, that splats share the same center. Thus, in our case, a crease splat is a single point with two different normals and a corner splat has three different normals.

Detection and Interpolation of Creases

Refining a crease requires first its detection and then its reconstruction. For the detection step, let us remind that the interpolating operator is based on the computation of tangent vectors $t_{0,1}$ going from one point p_0 toward another point p_1 (Equation 4.56). Since points can now have multiple normals we have to distinguish three cases to construct $t_{0,1}$:

1. p_0 has a unique normal: no change, $t_{0,1}$ is obtained by projecting p_1 onto the tangent plane of p_0.
2. p_0 has two normals n_0^1, n_0^2, and p_1 that satisfy the following condition:

$$\left| v_0^T \frac{p_1 - p_0}{\|p_1 - p_0\|} \right| > \cos(\theta_{edge}), \tag{4.74}$$

where v_0 is the tangent vector of the edge curve: $v_0 = \frac{n_0^1 \times n_0^2}{\|n_0^1 \times n_0^2\|}$. This condition defines a cone of apex p_0, axis v_0, and angle θ_{edge}. This allows us to test whether the point p_1 is on the crease or not. The choice for the value θ_{edge} actually depends on the status of p_1. If p_1 also represents an edge, then θ_{edge} is large in order to ensure the connection of edges (e.g., $\frac{3\pi}{8}$). Otherwise, the crease must be extended only if p_1 is very close to the edge, implying a small angle threshold (e.g., $\frac{\pi}{6}$).
In this case we take for:

$$t_{0,1} = \begin{cases} \frac{1}{3}\|p_1 - p_0\| v_0 & \text{if } v_0^T(p_1 - p_0) > 0 \\ \\ -\frac{1}{3}\|p_1 - p_0\| v_0 & \text{otherwise.} \end{cases} \tag{4.75}$$

3. If p_0 has two normals and the condition (Equation 4.74) is not satisfied, then the tangent vector $t_{0,1}$ is computed by projecting p_1 onto the two tangent planes of p_0. The closest projection to p_1 is selected to define $t_{0,1}$. In this case, the edge will be blended with a smooth surface.

If p_0 represents a corner (i.e., p_0 has three different normals), the normal associated to the farthest tangent plane from p_1 is simply ignored and the point is treated as in the case 2 or 3. Then six possibilities remain for the construction of an interpolating curve between two points. From those, only three combinations (i.e., 2-2, 3-2, and

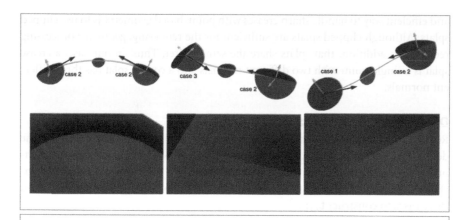

Figure 4.55: Illustration of the refinement of sharp features. The three combinations 2-2, 3-2, 1-2 are explicitly shown.

1-2) involve a sharp crease (see Figure 4.55). When an edge is detected between two points, it is reconstructed by a cubic Bézier curve $\mathbf{B}(u)$ built as in Equation (4.58) with the tangent vectors computed as shown above. When a new point is inserted on such a curve, its two normals must also be computed. However, a curve does not define a surface, and the only requirements are that these normals must be orthogonal to the tangent vector $\frac{\partial \mathbf{B}}{\partial u}(u)$ of the curve and that normals must smoothly vary from one extremity to the other. Hence, a reasonable solution is to linearly interpolate extremity normals and to take the closest orthogonal vectors to the curve (i.e., the projections of the interpolated normals onto the plane of normal $\frac{\partial \mathbf{B}}{\partial u}(u)$). For instance, the unnormalized normal $\mathbf{n}^1(u)$ of a point $\mathbf{B}(u)$ that corresponds to the extremity normals $\mathbf{n}_0^1$ and $\mathbf{n}_1^1$ is computed as follows:

$$\widetilde{\mathbf{n}}^1(u) = (1 - u) \cdot \mathbf{n}_0^1 + u \cdot \mathbf{n}_1^1$$
$$\mathbf{n}^1(u) = \widetilde{\mathbf{n}}^1(u) - \widetilde{\mathbf{n}}^1(u)^T \frac{\partial \mathbf{B}}{\partial u}(u) \cdot \frac{\partial \mathbf{B}}{\partial u}(u). \tag{4.76}$$

Application to the $\sqrt{3}$-like Refinement

However, since with a $\sqrt{3}$-like refinement strategy, new points are never directly inserted between two points, a particular attention must be paid. With the mesh-based $\sqrt{3}$ subdivision scheme Kobbelt [Kob00] proposes the insertion of two vertices on each boundary and crease segment at each even refinement step only. Since no connectivity information is stored, after two refinement steps, the crease (or boundary) points will probably not be neighbors anymore so that no special treatment can be applied between them, and the crease will not be reconstructed. Since we cannot wait for an even refinement step to detect and treat creases, the idea is to refine creases early. At each odd refinement step, two new points are inserted on each detected and reconstructed crease curve at respective positions 1/3 and 2/3. In order to avoid the modification of the neighborhood selection at the next refinement step (even step), such early inserted points are not taken into account in the neighborhood selection procedure. Note that boundaries can be handled in the same manner except that a boundary is detected only between two boundary points. Figure 4.56 shows an example of the refinement of sharp creases with a $\sqrt{3}$-like strategy.

4.5.5 IMPLEMENTATION AND APPLICATIONS

Closest Point Query

As in a lot of point-based processing methods, a critical time-consuming part of the refinement is the closest points query necessary to compute the Euclidean neighborhood $\mathcal{N}_r(\mathbf{p})$ (Equation 4.51). To improve efficiency, points must be spatially sorted into a data structure, like a K-d-tree or a 3D grid, with a fine granularity (see also Section 4.4).

Moreover, the local refinement step of a single point $\mathbf{p} \in \mathcal{P}^l$ also requires us to find the closest points already inserted into $\mathcal{P}^{l+1}$ (to compute the sets $\mathcal{N}'(\mathbf{p})$ and $\mathcal{Y}(\mathbf{p})$). Assuming that new points are sequentially inserted into a list of points, a solution is to associate to each point $\mathbf{p} \in \mathcal{P}^l$ the indices of the first and last new points inserted during its own refinement. These points are called the *children* of $\mathbf{p}$. Thus, the set of new points already inserted into $\mathcal{P}^{l+1}$ close to $\mathbf{p}$ is inferred from all children of all

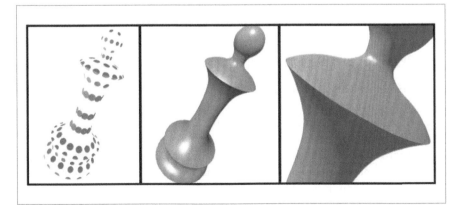

Figure 4.56: Illustration of the refinement of creases.

neighbors $\mathbf{p}_i$, $i \in \mathcal{N}_r(\mathbf{p})$ of $\mathbf{p}$. This solution has the advantage that it naturally creates a hierarchy of bounding spheres (a radius is associated with each point) that is also used to perform efficient closest points queries with a very low memory consumption: only the first index (three bytes) and the number of children (one byte) are stored. In addition, the initial point set $\mathcal{P}^0$ has to be structured once with a classical static data structure (e.g., a K-d-tree). A closest points query around the current point $\mathbf{p}$ at a level l is done by performing a recursive traversal of the bounding spheres hierarchy while the starting bounding spheres (points of the set $\mathcal{P}^0$) are found by performing a closest points query using the initial data structure.

Progressive Rendering

A typical application of a refinement algorithm is real-time high-quality rendering. Here, the refinement procedure is used on top of a splatting technique to maintain a screen space splat size smaller than a given threshold (e.g., two pixels). The progressive rendering algorithm presented in Guennebaud [GBP04, GBP05] is an extension of classical multiresolution point-rendering systems (see Sections 4.5, 6.4, and 6.5). A typical scenario is to store points in a coarse hierarchical data structure allowing to select appropriate levels of detail according to the relative position of the view point. Now, if a node of the hierarchy is an insufficiently dense leaf, then this node is split and refined, yielding to the insertion of new points that are stored in a cache. The memory cache is managed by a "last recently used" strategy (i.e., outdated generated points are removed when the cache is full). Note that even though the data structure presented above already provides a dynamic and hierarchical partition of the point model, its granularity is much too fine to be suitable for efficient LOD selection. Hence, it is preferable to use a second coarse hierarchical data structure such as the dynamic tree presented in Guennebaud [GBP05].

Finally, in order to provide best performance, when the point cloud is relatively well sampled and/or after a few refinement steps, a lot of expensive operations of the refinement procedure can be safely optimized:

1. Approximate the "curved angle" by the simple geometric angle:
   $\widetilde{\alpha}(\mathbf{p}, \mathbf{p}_0, \mathbf{p}_1) \approx \widehat{\mathbf{p}_0 \mathbf{p} \mathbf{p}_1}$.
2. Approximate the geodesic distance by the Euclidean distance:
   $\widetilde{g}(\mathbf{p}_0, \mathbf{p}_1) \approx \|\mathbf{p}_1 - \mathbf{p}_0\|$.
3. Approximate the position of a new point by the center of gravity during the refinement process and apply the smoothing operator if and only if the new point is effectively inserted.

In practice, these optimizations allow to significantly improve the performance of the algorithm (by a speedup factor from 1.5 to 2).

4.5.6 CONCLUSION

Even though the refinements algorithm has been presented with a $\sqrt{3}$-like interpolatory refinement it is important to notice that several other strategies can be placed on top of the one-ring neighborhood selection (Figure 4.57). For instance, the smoothing operator can easily be replaced by an MLS projection operator (see

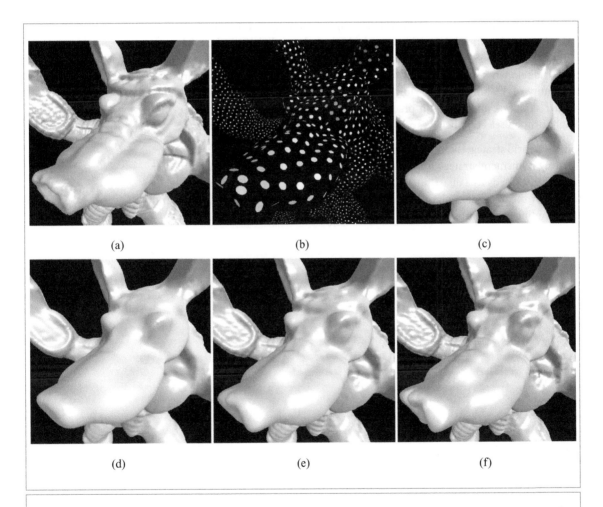

(a)	(b)	(c)
(d)	(e)	(f)

Figure 4.57: The Armadillo model (*a*) is downsampled to 10,000 points (*b*) and next upsampled with an MLS operator (*c*), the approximating $\sqrt{3}$ rules (*d*), a hybrid interpolating/approximating $\sqrt{3}$ (*e*), and the interpolating $\sqrt{3}$-like refinement (*f*).

Section 4.2 and Figure 4.57c). Note that, if the MLS operator is set to approximate rather than interpolate the point cloud, initial points must first be duplicated and projected onto the underlying MLS surface. The refinement is then used to sample the MLS surface defined by the initial point set and hence either a dyadic or a $\sqrt{3}$ insertion strategy is relevant. MLS projection operators require both a second larger neighborhood search and an orthogonal projection step reducing the reconstruction capabilities when handling low-sampling density in regions of high curvature.

Other interesting refinements are classical approximating subdivision schemes. Indeed, once the one-ring neighborhood is selected, subdivision rules of Loop's dyadic scheme [Loo87] or Kobbelt's $\sqrt{3}$ [Kob00] can easily be applied (Figure 4.57d). Since the selected triangle fans may overlap inconstantly we cannot yet guaranty the continuity of the limit surface. However, these subdivision schemes provide highly regular sampling and hence, in practice, after a few refinement steps the one-ring neighborhood selection behaves as if it were guided by an explicit connectivity.

Finally, hybrid strategies can also be employed. For instance, using the $\sqrt{3}$-like interpolating refinement strategy for the first steps followed by the approximating $\sqrt{3}$ for the last steps leads to a quasi-interpolating surface (Figure 4.57e). The main advantages over the pure interpolating strategy is that the surface is slightly smoother and the sampling more uniform.

CHAPTER FIVE

Weyrich, Tim
ETH Zürich
Computer Graphics Laboratory
Haldeneggsteig 4
8092 Zürich
Switzerland
weyrich@inf.ethz.ch
Tel: +41 44 632 03 56
Fax: +41 44 632 15 96

Zwicker, Matthias
Department of Computer Science and Engineering
University of California, San Diego
9500 Gilman Drive
La Jolla, CA 92093-0404
USA
mzwicker@ucsd.edu
Tel: +1 959 922 4720

Pauly, Mark
ETH Zürich
Computer Graphics Laboratory
Haldeneggsteig 4
8092 Zürich
Switzerland
pauly@inf.ethz.ch
Tel: +41 44 632 06 68
Fax: +41 44 632 15 96

Gross, Markus
Computer Graphics Laboratory
ETH Zürich
Haldeneggsteig 4 / Weinbergstrasse
CH - 8092 Zürich
grossm@inf.ethz.ch
Tel: +41-44-632 7114
Fax: +41-44-632 1596

Wicke, Martin
ETH Zürich
Computer Graphics Laboratory
Haldeneggsteig 4
8092 Zürich
Switzerland
wicke@inf.ethz.ch
Tel: +41 44 632 74 58
Fax: +41 44 632 15 96

Kobbelt, Leif
RWTH Aachen
Lehrstuhl für Informatik VIII
52056 Aachen
Germany
kobbelt@informatik.rwth-aachen.de
Tel: +49 241 8021 801
Fax: +49 241 8022 899

5 DIGITAL PROCESSING

INTRODUCTION

This chapter is devoted to the digital processing of point-sampled models. It demonstrates the versatility of point sampled representations which combine the simplicity of conventional image editing operations with the power of advanced 3D modeling methods. Section 5.1 starts with a variety of preprocessing methods, such as model cleaning and filtering, that can be utilized to improve the quality of 3D scan data. More advanced 3D editing, such as rubber stamping and texturing, is presented in Section 5.2. This section also provides an overview of the core functionality of PointShop3D, an open-source software accompanying this textbook. The chapter concludes with advanced shape modeling operations like deformations and CSG, that will be discussed in Section 5.3.

5.1 PREPROCESSING AND FILTERING OF POINT MODELS

Tim Weyrich and Markus Gross

5.1.1 OVERVIEW

With growing demand for realism in computer graphics and interactive techniques, we experience a steady increase in the geometric complexity of digital 3D surface models. Ab initio design of such shapes thus becomes increasingly time consuming and expensive. Most designers, therefore, rely on 3D scanning devices to acquire complex digital models from real-world objects. Accurate 3D acquisition also plays an important role in reverse engineering, rapid prototyping, biomedicine, architecture, cultural heritage acquisition, or the entertainment industry.

This diversity in application fields is reflected in a great variety of 3D imaging techniques: CT and MRI scanners are widely used in medical and engineering applications to acquire volumetric representations of real-world objects. Optical devices, such as laser range scanners or structured-light scanners, are primarily employed for surface and appearance acquisition.

This latter class of scanning devices typically produces a dense set of surface points, where each point samples a 3D position and possible additional attributes, such as normal information, color, or material properties. A respective acquisition pipeline and an exemplary scanner setup have been described in Sections 3.1 and 3.2. Depending on the specific acquisition method, the acquired data usually contain a number of typical scanning artifacts as illustrated in Figure 5.1:

- Physical limitations of the sensor lead to noise in the acquired dataset. Sample points can also be corrupted by quantization or motion artifacts. The latter occur when the scanned object moves during the acquisition process, a common problem when scanning humans or animals.
- Multiple reflections and heavy noise can produce off-surface points (outliers).
- Holes and undersampling in the model surface occur due to occlusion, critical reflectance properties, constraints in the scanning path, or limited sensor resolution.
- Many scanners tend to create displaced geometry when the scanned object is textured.

The raw point-cloud data produced by the scanner thus need to be processed before subsequent modeling operations can be performed. Commercial scanners are usually equipped with rudimentary scan-cleaning software that uses built-in heuristics for

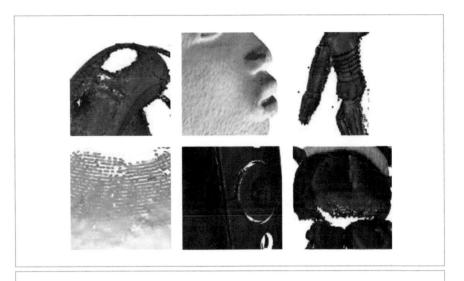

Figure 5.1: Typical artifacts of raw scanner data. ***Top row***: Holes due to sensor restrictions, noise, outliers. ***Bottom row***: Low sampling density due to gracing sensor views, low sampling density at delicate surface details, and holes due to critical reflectance properties.

outlier removal and noise reduction. These are often difficult to control as they are optimized for the specific scanner configuration.

More sophisticated data processing can only be applied by exporting the acquired surface model from the proprietary scanner software, typically in the form of a triangle mesh. However, if the aforementioned data imperfections have not been successfully removed from the dataset, the meshing process itself is fragile and can even introduce further artifacts. Therefore, postprocessing of scanned data should be performed directly on the acquired point cloud, before sophisticated surface reconstruction algorithms or advanced modeling operations are applied.

To this end, in Weyrich et al. [WPK⁺04] we propose a purely point-based scan-cleaning toolbox, consisting of a selection of user-guided tools that address the different scanning artifacts mentioned above. These include an eraser tool, low-pass filters for noise removal, a set of outlier detection methods, and various resampling and hole-filling tools.

Since many scan artifacts are strongly coupled, these tools should be applied in an interleaved fashion. Identification of artifacts is difficult and often requires human interpretation. Therefore, user guidance is a necessary prerequisite to achieve optimal results. All algorithms are specifically designed to support rapid feedback during an interactive scan-cleaning session.

The toolbox has been integrated as a plug-in into Pointshop3D, an open-source 3D editing tool for point-sampled surfaces [ZPKG02a, Poi]. In combination with a 3D scanning front end, the plug-in bridges the gap between 3D acquisition and high-level shape and appearance modeling, thus providing in a single application a complete point-based content creation pipeline (Figure 5.2).

The remainder describes the toolbox and its constituents. Section 5.1.2 discusses design criteria of the toolbox, while Section 5.1.3 presents the underlying techniques. Sections 5.1.4 and 5.1.5 present the resulting set of interactive tools. It is explained how the underlying techniques have been extended and combined to realize the different tools. The integration of the tools in a common user interface is presented.

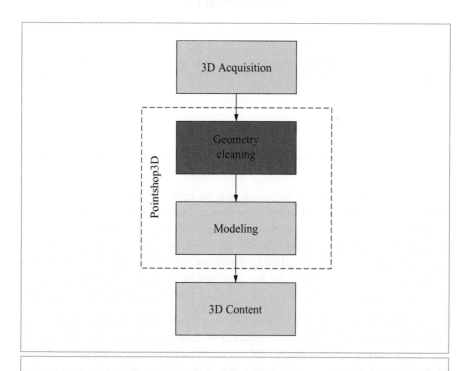

Figure 5.2: Geometry cleaning bridges the gap between 3D acquisition and higher-level modeling. We present an interactive cleaning toolbox implemented within Pointshop3D.

5.1.2 AN INTERACTIVE APPROACH

The central motivation of the toolbox has been to open up modeling techniques to be used for the cleaning of raw scan data. The modeling tools make extensive use of basic techniques (Section 5.1.3), which are well known in the point graphics community or adapted from triangle-based graphics, respectively.

The toolbox was designed to allow for the removal of typical scan artifacts, as depicted in Figure 5.1. In order to support an efficient scan-cleaning process, three design goals have been pursued:

1. *Predictability*: In order to allow a rapid workflow, it is important that each tool's effect is predictable under most circumstances. That is, if the user chooses a tool for a certain purpose, the outcome should meet the user's expectations.
2. *Controllability*: The range of application must be well controllable. Where possible, each tool should provide a set of parameters to tune its behavior.
3. *Intuitive handling*: The tools should rest upon intuitive editing metaphors. Any parameters should correspond to meaningful traits.

Following these criteria, the goal has been to make the tools as powerful as possible. However, making a tool powerful usually implies the use of higher-level automatisms, which are likely to fail when applied to raw scanner data. This would contradict predictability. Increasing the number of parameters to make the outcome more controllable would lead to an unintuitive handling.

Accordingly, the final set of tools comprises operations of different complexity (see Figure 5.3). Simpler, more robust tools allow for direct editing, especially in the presence of severe scanning artifacts. More complex and powerful tools can be applied at a later point in the scan-cleaning process, when a certain sampling quality has already been achieved.

In order to address controllability, all tools provide an exhaustive set of parameters that can be set using the user interface. Each tool comes with a set of reasonable default parameters.

For most of the tools it makes sense to apply them locally. Consequently, they are defined to work on a set of selected surfels.

Pointshop3D provides a selection mechanism. However, the Pointshop3D selection tool requires a well-sampled surface and cannot e.g., select scattered points, as they frequently appear in real-world scans. Hence, a volumetric brush has been introduced to facilitate the selection of surfels in areas where no properly sampled surface exists. The brush, box-shaped or ellipsoidal, can freely be moved in space, or, alternatively,

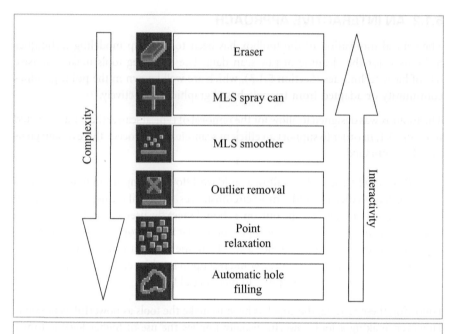

Figure 5.3: The toolbox contains tools of different complexity. Higher complexity goes with less interaction.

follow the object surface (see Figure 5.4). By resizing and rotating the brush, its shape can be adapted to the local object geometry.

The brush is designed to follow the object surface even in poorly sampled regions. This is achieved by analyzing the depth values of all surfels visible around the mouse pointer. The brush's depth is set to a robust mean of the different depth values.

All tools that support the volumetric selection can be applied to a set of surfels that were selected in a separate step. Alternatively, they are simultaneously applied to all points within the volumetric brush during navigation.

5.1.3 UNDERLYING TECHNIQUES

The presented toolbox internally utilizes a set of basic geometric modeling techniques. This section describes the respective techniques and explains their adaption to point clouds.

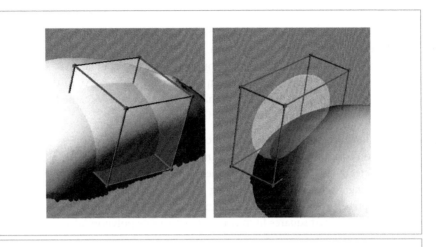

Figure 5.4: The volumetric brush. (*a*) A box-shaped selector following the object surface. (*b*) An ellipsoidal selector freely positioned in space.

Search Data Structures

Dealing with point clouds, there is no explicit connectivity information. This means that all computations are based on spatial proximity between point samples instead of geodesic proximity between mesh vertices. In this section we present two data structures for fast nearest-neighbor searches and range queries. A more elaborate description of search data structures can be found in Section 4.4.

A very well-known search data structure is the K-d-tree (e.g., [Ben75, FBF77, AM93]). A K-d-tree can be searched efficiently in $O(\log n)$, while it takes time $O(n \log n)$ to build it. Therefore, and because it is costly to maintain a K-d-tree after an insertion, deletion, or displacement of points, it is suitable for static data only. If the same point is queried more than once, it might be useful to cache the neighbors. In this case, a nearest-neighbor graph is built, storing the nearest neighbors for each point.

For querying dynamic data a hash data structure similar to Teschner et al. [THM⁺03] has been used. The coordinates of an arbitrary point in space are mapped to a cell. If the cell size is chosen smaller or equal to the maximal query range, all points within this range can be found by searching the adjacent cells to a query point (i.e., 27 cells have to be queried). Note that also k-nearest-neighbor queries can be performed efficiently if a maximal range can be given. However, while insertion of a point can be done in $O(1)$, querying takes $O(q)$, where q is the maximum number of points in a cell. In practice, with a sufficient number of cells q will be small.

MLS Projection

To compute a smooth surface that approximates a set of scattered data points, Levin [Lev01a] introduced a projection operator based on moving least squares (MLS) optimization. Using this projection procedure, Alexa et al. [ABCO⁺01] presented a high-quality rendering algorithm for point set surfaces. An in-depth discussion of the MLS method is provided in Chapter 4. Because the MLS method is crucial for the following algorithms, we will briefly review it here.

Given an unstructured set of sample points, the MLS projection as used in the cleaning toolbox takes a point **x** in space and projects it onto a polynomial that locally approximates the underlying surface in the vicinity of **x**. This polynomial is computed by first fitting a reference plane H using weighted least squares optimization. The reference plane provides a local parameterization of the sample points, which is used in a second least squares fit to compute a bivariate polynomial approximation.

Both the computation of the reference plane and the polynomial use a radially symmetric Gaussian weight function $\omega_i = e^{-\|\mathbf{x}_r - \mathbf{p}_i\|^2 / h^2}$, where $\mathbf{x}_r$ is the projected point of **x** onto H and h is a scaling factor. Since ω_i drops quickly with increasing distance, the least squares optimization is typically applied in a local neighborhood around the point of interest. The scaling factor h can either be a global constant or proportional to local sample spacing, estimated from a k-neighborhood as described in Pauly et al. [PGK02a]. More details on the MLS method can be found in Section 4.2.

Point Relaxation

In [Tur92], Turk uses particle simulation for resampling polygonal surfaces. Pauly et al. [PGK02a] adapted this method to point-sampled surfaces.

To achieve a uniform distribution of the particles, neighbored particles are let to repel each other. Every particle **p** exerts a force $\mathbf{f}_i(\mathbf{p})$ on its neighbored particles $\mathbf{p}_i$. The summation of all forces that act on a particle gives the resulting force. Finally, the new positions of the particles are computed by explicit Euler integration.

The presented work uses the same repulsion force **f** as in Turk and Pauly et al. [Tur92, PGK02a]:

$$\mathbf{f}_i(\mathbf{p}) = k(r - \|\mathbf{p} - \mathbf{p}_i\|)\frac{\mathbf{p}_i - \mathbf{p}}{\|\mathbf{p}_i - \mathbf{p}\|}, \qquad\qquad (5.1)$$

where k is a force constant and r is the repulsion radius. For finding the nearest neighbors within the radius r the hash data structure described above is used.

After each iteration, the particles are projected back onto the surface by applying the MLS projection described above. In the cleaning toolbox, the particle simulation is performed locally for a selected region. To ensure that the selected surfels keep within this region, for each selected surfel its n-nearest neighbors are computed, and the neighbors that are not selected are added to a list. While these surfels repel the selected surfels, their positions are fixed.

5.1.4 OUTLIER REMOVAL

Erroneous points outside the object surface are outliers that have to be removed. However, it is hard to specify a general criterion to detect outliers, if the real object surface is unknown. Noise further complicates the detection of outliers. In many cases, the scan quality has to be judged by the user in order to tell a noisy surface point from an outlier.

Weyrich et al. [WPK+04] developed an interactive tool for outlier removal incorporating the user into the outlier detection. The tool provides three outlier classification heuristics that have to be weighted by the user to obtain an appropriate classification (see Figure 5.5). Outliers are finally removed by applying a threshold to the resulting outlier classification.

The threshold can be chosen manually. Alternatively, it is automatically set to discard a certain percentage of the points. Outlier classification can be confined to the volumetric brush.

We now present the three underlying outlier criteria. All criteria deliver an estimator $\chi(\mathbf{p}) \in [0, 1]$ assigning the likelihood for a point sample $\mathbf{p}$ to be an outlier. To prevent any bias from an intermediate surface representation, all criteria are based only on analysis of $\mathbf{p}$'s k-nearest neighbors $\mathcal{N}_k(\mathbf{p})$.

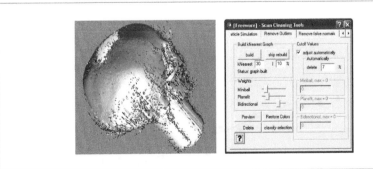

Figure 5.5: Outlier classification. The three classifiers can be weighted using the depicted sliders. Probable outliers, scheduled for removal according to the resulting classification and a given threshold, are rendered in red.

Plane Fit Criterion

An intuitive criterion is the point's deviation from a manifold approximating its neighbors. The *plane fit criterion* considers a plane H that minimizes the squared distances to $\mathbf{p}$'s neighbors:

$$\min_H \sum_{\mathbf{q} \in \mathcal{N}_k(\mathbf{p})} \text{dist}(\mathbf{p}, H)^2 \tag{5.2}$$

(see Figure 5.6). Let d be the distance of $\mathbf{p}$ to H, and $\bar{d}$ the mean distance of points from $\mathcal{N}_k(\mathbf{p})$ to H. The plane fit criterion is defined as

$$\chi_{\text{pl}}(\mathbf{p}) = \frac{d}{d + \bar{d}} . \tag{5.3}$$

Normalization by $\bar{d}$ relates d to possible noise and surface deviations.

Instead of H, it would be possible to use higher-order approximations of $\mathcal{N}_k(\mathbf{p})$. The plane fit criterion has been chosen to achieve a maximum of robustness.

Miniball Criterion

A point comparatively distant to the cluster built by its k-nearest neighbors is likely to be an outlier. This observation leads to the following criterion.

For each point $\mathbf{p}$ consider the smallest enclosing sphere S around $\mathcal{N}_k(\mathbf{p})$ [Wel91] (see Figure 5.7). S can be seen as an approximation of the k-nearest-neighbor cluster. Comparing $\mathbf{p}$'s distance d to the center of S with the sphere's diameter yields a measure for $\mathbf{p}$'s likelihood to be an outlier. Consequently, the *miniball criterion* is defined as

$$\chi_{\text{mb}}(\mathbf{p}) = \frac{d}{d + 2r/\sqrt{k}} . \tag{5.4}$$

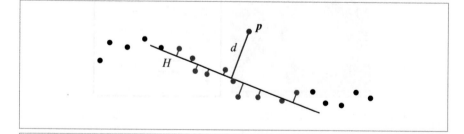

Figure 5.6: The plane fit criterion compares $\mathbf{p}$'s distance d to a least squares plane H with the average distance of its neighbors to H. $\mathbf{p}$'s k-neighbors are denoted in blue.

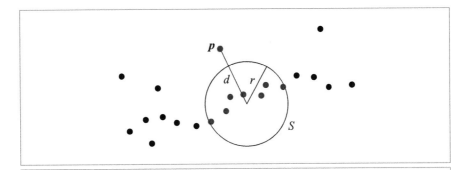

Figure 5.7: The miniball criterion. A miniball S approximates the cluster of **p**'s neighbors. The criterion compares **p**'s distance to S with the diameter of the sphere.

Normalization by $\sqrt{k}$ compensates for the diameter's increase with increasing number of k-neighbors at the object surface.

Nearest-neighbor Reciprocity Criterion

This criterion is based on the following observation: potential outliers draw their k-nearest neighbors from a larger vicinity than points in a well-sampled environment. In particular, a "valid" point sample **q** may be in the k-neighborhood of an outlier, but the outlier will most likely not be part of **q**'s k-neighborhood.

This relationship can be expressed by means of a directed graph G of k-neighbor relationships (see Figure 5.8). Outliers are assumed to have a high number of unidirectional exitant edges (i.e., asymmetric neighbor relationships). Consequently the criterion considers the ratio between unidirectional and bidirectional exitant edges in G.

The unidirectional neighbors are defined as $\mathcal{N}_{k,\mathrm{uni}}(\mathbf{p}) = \{\mathbf{q}\,|\,\mathbf{q} \in \mathcal{N}_k(\mathbf{p}), \mathbf{p} \notin \mathcal{N}_k(\mathbf{q})\}$, while the bidirectional neighbors build a set $\mathcal{N}_{k,\mathrm{bi}}(\mathbf{p}) = \{\mathbf{q}\,|\,\mathbf{q} \in \mathcal{N}_k(\mathbf{p}), \mathbf{p} \in \mathcal{N}_k(\mathbf{q})\}$. The classifier is expressed as follows:

$$\chi_{\mathrm{bi}}(\mathbf{p}) = \frac{\|\mathcal{N}_{k,\,\mathrm{uni}}(\mathbf{p})\|}{\|\mathcal{N}_{k,\,\mathrm{bi}}(\mathbf{p})\| + \|\mathcal{N}_{k,\,\mathrm{uni}}(\mathbf{p})\|} = \frac{\|\mathcal{N}_{k,\,\mathrm{uni}}(\mathbf{p})\|}{k} \,. \tag{5.5}$$

Classification

The final outlier classification is computed using weights $w_1, \dots, w_3$, $\sum_i w_i = 1$, interactively defined by the user:

$$\chi(\mathbf{p}) = w_1 \chi_{\mathrm{pl}}(\mathbf{p}) + w_2 \chi_{\mathrm{mb}}(\mathbf{p}) + w_3 \chi_{\mathrm{bi}}(\mathbf{p}) \,. \tag{5.6}$$

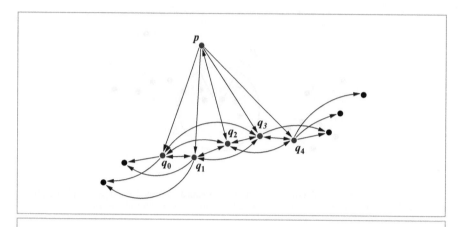

Figure 5.8: Nearest-neighbor graph. Depicted are the five nearest-neighbor relations for **p** and its five neighbors $\mathbf{q}_0, \ldots, \mathbf{q}_4$. Note that only $\mathbf{q}_2$ shares a reciprocal neighbor relationship with **p**.

As all outlier criteria are based on the k-nearest-neighbor graph, χ_{pl}, χ_{mb}, and χ_{bi} are computed once and cached during the computation of χ.

Depending on the scanning technique, outliers may occur in small clusters. In this case, χ_{pl} and χ_{mb} tend to fail to detect the clustered outliers correctly. In order to make them suitable for clustered outliers, a maximum cluster size l can be defined by the user. Subsequently, all k-nearest-neighbor queries will discard the first l neighbors, returning the $(l + 1)$-st to $(l + k)$-th neighbor instead. This effectively increases the robustness against clustered outliers while maintaining the basic functionality of the outlier criteria.

Performance Evaluation

When applying the outlier removal tool, the three different elementary outlier criteria show to be differently suited depending on the situation (see Figure 5.9). The plane fit criterion is best suited to detect outliers in a noisy reconstruction of a smooth surface. It produces poor results around small features and creases, as the orientation of the fitted plane becomes instable. The miniball criterion proved to be more robust, even around high-frequency details, but in contrast to the plane fit criterion, it shows a poor outlier detection for points that hover close to a smooth surface.

In comparison with the previous two, the criterion based on nearest-neighbor reciprocity shows the most robust outlier classification. It is equally sensitive around smooth and detailed regions. However, it consistently yields erroneous outlier classifications around manifold borders (see Figure 5.10). Obviously, each criterion is advantageous in different situations. The outlier removal tool allows us to confine the outlier detection to certain areas for the model and to weight the criteria according to the local situation.

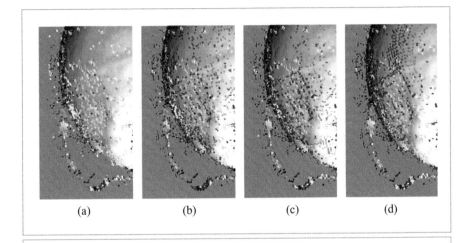

(a)   (b)   (c)   (d)

Figure 5.9: Three different outlier classifiers. Potential outliers marked in red. (*a*) Raw scanned geometry. (*b*) Classification using the miniball criterion. (*c*) Plane fit criterion. (*d*) *k*-nearest-neighbor graph criterion. All criteria were thresholded to classify 7% of the surfels as outliers.

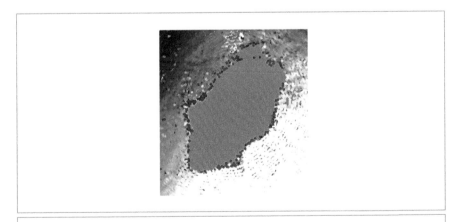

Figure 5.10: The nearest-neighbor outlier criterion performs poor around manifold borders.

5.1.5 HOLE FILLING AND SMOOTHING

After outliers have been removed, there is usually still inherent noise in the surface samples. Additional holes further complicate surface analysis and reconstruction.

Noise can be removed by applying a spatial low-pass filter to the 3D point data. Alternatively, noise can implicitly be handled during a surface reconstruction stage (see Sections 4.1 and 4.3). Alexa et al., Carr et al., and Ohtake et al. [ABCO+01, CBC+01, OBA+03] smooth surface by approximating the sample points. However, most automatic surface reconstruction algorithms fail in the presence of severe noise.

In the past, various hole-filling techniques have been proposed to address this problem. These methods mostly use implicit representations to define the underlying surface. Verdera et al. [VCBS03] extend image-inpainting techniques to 3D surfaces by solving anisotropic partial differential equations defined on the surface. Carr et al. [CBC+01] and Ohtake et al. [OBA+03] exploit the extrapolation properties of radial basis functions to fill regions of sparse sampling. Davis et al. [DMGL02] propose a method that applies a diffusion operator on the signed distance field of an incomplete triangle mesh.

The remainder of this section presents noise removal and hole-filling tools of the presented toolbox.

MLS Smoother

Smoothing is an elementary editing operation. It can be used for noise reduction, to smooth out high-frequency details, such as small artifacts like spikes and ripples, or to soften creases created during the editing process. Various smoothing operators have been proposed, partly with feature-preserving properties.

Given the unpredictable quality of input data, it had been decided against locally adapting filters, as they still tend to amplify scanning artifacts. Instead, a simple, more robust filter based on MLS projection has been implemented, leaving the treatment of features to the user's control by confining the operation to the volumetric brush selection.

The *MLS smoother tool* works by shifting point positions toward the corresponding MLS surface. For each point $\mathbf{p}$, its MLS projection $\mathbf{p}'$ is computed. A user-adjustable blending parameter α defines how far $\mathbf{p}$ is to be moved toward its "smoothed" position $\mathbf{p}'$. The point is finally set to

$$\mathbf{p}_{\text{smoothed}} = (1 - \alpha)\mathbf{p} + \alpha\mathbf{p}'. \tag{5.7}$$

An associated normal is filtered analogously, blending the original normal with the normal of the MLS surface. Parameterization of the MLS kernel function, as described in Section 5.1.3, allows the user to adjust the depth-pass characteristic of the MLS projection.

An additional user parameter D allows to attenuate the tool's effect toward the selection border. Within distance D to the border, α is weighted by a blending polynomial to vanish at the border. A point's distance to the border is defined as the distance to its nearest neighbor outside the selection.

α is usually set to values within $[0, 1]$, corresponding to strong or no smoothing, respectively (see Figure 5.11b). Alternatively, following the concept of USM filtering [Jai89], one may set α to negative values, corresponding to a detail (and noise) enhancement (see Figure 5.11c). This is a useful feature, however, for larger absolute values of α, surface self-penetration can occur.

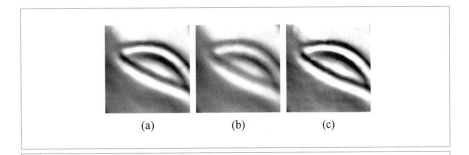

(a)   (b)   (c)

Figure 5.11: The MLS smoother tool. (*a*) Fine surface details. (*b*) Smoothing with $\alpha = 0.8$. (*c*) Detail enhancement for $\alpha = -0.75$.

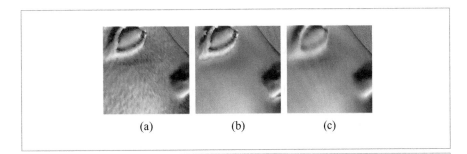

(a)   (b)   (c)

Figure 5.12: Selective noise removal using the MLS smoother. (*a*) Noisy input surface. (*b*) Smoothing of a subset of surfels, excluding high-frequency details. (*c*) Subsequently, global smoothing of the model.

Point Relaxation

Scanned models may contain regions of uneven point distribution. While some editing operations may change the point distribution directly, raw scan data will be unevenly sampled wherever point samples are missing due to scanning artifacts. Merging of depth maps also produces an uneven point distribution. Most applications, however, would benefit from a uniform distribution of the surfels.

To achieve an even distribution of the surfels a particle simulation as described in Section 5.1.3 is employed. The attributes of the relaxed surfels, such as the color, are interpolated from the attributes of the k-nearest original surfel neighbors.

The particle simulation can also be used to close small holes, as the repelling force will distribute the surfels over uncovered areas.

MLS Spray Can

Complementary to an eraser tool for point removal, the *MLS spray can tool* was introduced in order to fill small holes in the geometry. It randomly creates points inside the brush volume and projects them onto the MLS surface in the brush's vicinity.

A projected point **p** is added to the surface whenever the surrounding splat coverage is below a certain threshold. The local coverage is estimated by determining the ratio between the average distance $\bar{d}$ of **p** to its k-neighbors and the mean splat radius $\bar{r}$ of its neighbors. **p** is added if

$$\frac{\bar{r}}{\bar{d}} < 1. \tag{5.8}$$

Consequently, the MLS spray can relies on valid splat radii. When importing a model, initial splat radii are computed using a local surface analysis as proposed in Pauly [Pau03], based on a Voronoi diagram of the point cloud (see also Section 4.1.2).

If a new point is added to the surface, its normal is adopted from the MLS surface. All other surfel attributes (e.g., color and reflectance properties) are determined by interpolating attributes from neighboring surfels.

Application of the spray can tool may result in a roughly uniform point distribution (see Figure 5.14 later). Eventually, the point distribution has to be relaxed using the point relaxation tool.

Volumetric Diffusion

While the MLS spray can tool introduced above is very effective for filling small holes, it still remains a tedious process to create a complete watertight model when larger and more complex holes occur in the acquired point cloud. This is frequently the case, however, as line-of-sight constraints, difficult surface reflectance properties, or extensive noise and outlier removal, can lead to a highly incomplete representation of the model surface (see also Figure 5.16 later). As previously stated, many automatic hole-filling algorithms exist.

We extend the volumetric diffusion method by Davis et al. [DMGL02] to point-sampled models by replacing the distance field estimation of Davis et al. [DMGL02] by an MLS projection step as proposed in Pauly et al. [PKKG03]. The distance field is computed on a regular 3D grid that encloses the model surface (see Figure 5.13a). At each grid point we compute the signed distance to the MLS surface defined by the given input point set. To efficiently represent this volumetric grid an octree data structure similar to Frisken and Perry [FP03b] is used. This method makes use of binary location codes to address octree cells, allowing for fast point location and efficient neighborhood queries.

Memory and computation costs are further reduced by only representing the distance field in a narrow band around the surface, similar to level-set methods [OS88]. Holes in the distance field are detected using the classification method of Davis et al. [DMGL02]. Distance values on the boundary of holes can then be extrapolated by applying an iterative convolution operator until all holes of a user-specified size are filled. More details on this diffusion process can be found in Davis et al. [DMGL02].

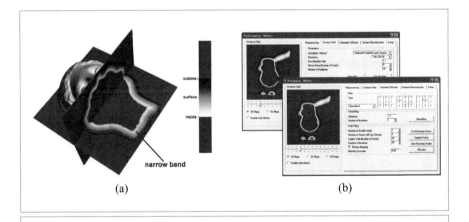

(a)   (b)

Figure 5.13: Volumetric diffusion. (*a*) Slices of the distance volume reveal the narrow band. (*b*) The user interface of the automatic hole-filling tool allows us to fine-tune the algorithm. The volumetric representation can be previewed before surface reconstruction.

To convert the distance field back to an explicit point-sampled representation the tool either applies a contouring method similar to marching cubes [LC87], or uses a particle simulation as described in Section 5.1.3. In the latter case, the MLS projection that keeps the particles on the surface is replaced by a projection based on gradient descent that moves particles to the zero-set of the signed distance field. Normals of the newly generated points can also be directly estimated from the distance field gradient.

The user interface supports fine-tuning of the algorithm (see Figure 5.13b). Though, using the default parameters, the automatic hole-filling tool is robust and easy to use.

Performance Evaluation

The hole-filling and smoothing tools have extensively been used to clean various models acquired with different scanning technologies. They have been used with models acquired by a CyberWare laser range scanner, a single-shot structured-light scanner by 3Q Technologies Ltd., and a phase-shift structured-light scanner similar to the system presented in Section 3.2. This section shows some exemplary situations as they occur during the model-cleaning process.

The general experience is that the simpler, more interactive tools are typically used at the beginning of the cleaning process, whereas the more complex, semi-automatic tools are applied toward the end of the procedure.

It turns out that the simpler tools are often used in combinations to achieve a desired effect. Figure 5.14 shows how the MLS spray can tool and point relaxation are used to manually fill a hole in a surface.

A similar combination can be used to remove undesired bumps from a surface. Figure 5.15 shows how the eraser, the MLS spray, point relaxation, and the MLS smoother work together to remove a bump from a surface.

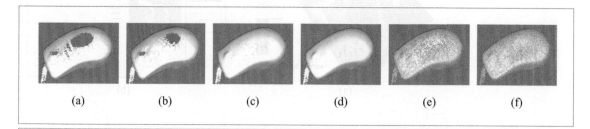

(a)   (b)   (c)   (d)   (e)   (f)

Figure 5.14: Manual hole filling using the MLS spray can tool. (*a*) A poor scan of a computer mouse, containing a hole in the surface. (*b and c*) Gradually filling the hole using the MLS spray can. (*d*) Point relaxation improves the point distribution. (*e and f*) Versions of (*c*) and (*d*) with reduced splat radii to reveal the point distribution.

In combination with the selection tool, the MLS smoother can also be used to smooth selected surface parts while preserving details (see Figure 5.12).

The robustness of the automatic hole-filling tool has been tested using a structured-light scan of a furry toy reindeer (see Figure 5.16). Fur is one of the most difficult materials to be scanned with optical methods. Consequently, the scan shows severe noise and a lot of outliers. Outlier removal leads to a very sparse object

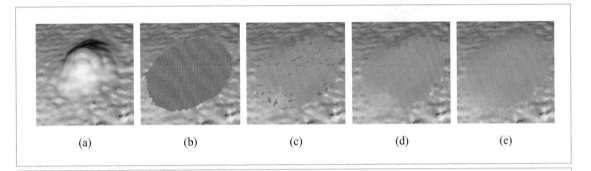

(a)   (b)   (c)   (d)   (e)

Figure 5.15: Removal of an undesired bump. (*a*) Close-up of the original data. (*b*) The eraser is used to stamp out a hole. (*c*) Using the MLS spray can, the hole is filled. (*d*) Point relaxation redistributes points. (*e*) Locally applying the MLS smoother, attenuating its strength toward the border of the hole. Note the smooth transition of the novel surface to the noisy surrounding.

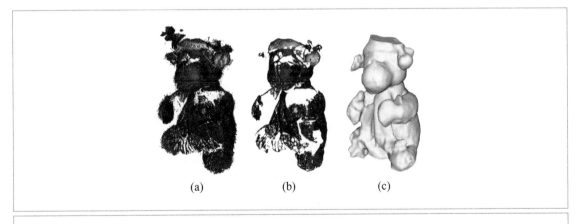

(a)   (b)   (c)

Figure 5.16: Robustness of the volumetric diffusion tool. (*a*) The furred object surface produces severe noise and outliers. (*b*) After the outlier removal, only little object points are left. (*c*) The volumetric diffusion tool still reconstructs a watertight model.

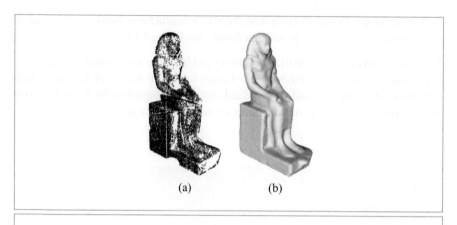

(a)   (b)

Figure 5.17: Egyptian sculpture scanned at the British Museum. (*a*) Input scan with varying sampling density. (*b*) Application of the volumetric diffusion tool.

reconstruction. However, as shown in Figure 5.16, the hole-filling tool is still capable of producing a watertight model. Only above the top of the model, the volumetric diffusion had to be constrained in order to get a closed surface.

Figure 5.17 shows an application of the automatic hole-filling tool to a scan with largely varying sampling density. The model has been scanned by INSIGHT [INS] at the British Museum, London.

5.1.6 CONCLUSION

In this section we presented a cleaning toolkit for the postprocessing of raw scanner data. It is entirely based on point-based modeling techniques, which are given at hand in the form of simple, interactively controllable tools. We introduced the underlying techniques and discussed the design principles leading to the presented set of tools.

The tools include an eraser tool, low-pass filters, and various resampling and hole-filling tools. We propose three different outlier criteria that are incorporated in an outlier detection tool. An adaption of the volumetric diffusion algorithm to point-sampled data is used to build an automatic hole-filling tool.

We evaluated the toolbox, cleaning various objects acquired with different scanner technologies. It proves to be versatile and well adaptable, as the tools can interactively be recombined depending on the situation. Most operations are robust against sampling artifacts and do not impose any topological constraints on the data. Future experiences will show whether the toolbox has to be extended. Possible extensions may be additional filter tools or the integration of texture synthesis into the MLS spray can. As a Pointshop3D plug-in the toolbox rounds off a point-based work-flow for the processing of scanned 3D surface data. The plug-in can be found on the accompanying website (www.pointbasedgraphics.com).

5.2 3D EDITING AND PAINTING

Matthias Zwicker and Martin Wicke

5.2.1 OVERVIEW

In this section we show how to generalize 2D photo editing to make it amenable to 3D point-sampled geometry. A point-based system for surface painting and edit-ing, such as Pointshop3D [ZPKG02b], is aimed at similar applications as commercial 3D content-creation tools based on polynomials [Ali01], triangle meshes [ABL95, Rig01], implicits [Ped95, PF01], or images [OCDD01]. However, by generalizing 2D image pixels toward 3D surface pixels (or surfels [ST92, PZvBG00]), we strive to com-bine the simplicity and effectiveness of 2D photoprocessing with the functionality of 3D geometry-based painting and editing.

The main challenges to the design of point-based 3D photo-editing tools are the absence of local topology in combination with the irregularity of the sampling patterns in point-based surfaces. We identify two key ingredients required for over-coming these difficulties: *interactive parameterization* and *dynamic resampling*. For instance, distortion minimal retexturing or surface carving both demand a flexi-ble parameterization of the point cloud. In addition, points discretize geometry and appearance attributes at the same rate. Thus, fine-grain surface detail embossing of an existing object with a high-resolution depth map can lead to heavy aliasing and requires a dynamic adaptation of the sampling rate.

Our editing framework originates from the motivation to provide a wide range of editing and processing techniques for point-sampled 3D surfaces, similar to those found in common photo-editing tools for 2D images. To give an overview of our system we will first describe a typical photo-editing operation on an abstract level. Then we will explain how these concepts can be transferred to surface editing, commenting on the fundamental differences between images and surfaces. This will serve as a motivation for the techniques and algorithms described in the following sections.

A 2D image can be considered a discrete sample of a continuous image function, which contains image attributes such as color or transparency. Implicitly, the dis-crete image always represents the continuous image, and image-editing operations are performed directly on the discrete image. The continuous function can be computed using a reconstruction operator whenever necessary. We describe a general image-editing operation as a function of an original image and a *brush* image. The brush image is used as a general tool to modify the original image. Depending on the considered operation, it may be interpreted as a paintbrush or a discrete filter, for example.

The editing operation involves the following steps. First, we need to specify a coordinate transformation, or a *parameterization*, that aligns the image with the brush. For example, the parameterization can be defined as the translation that maps the pixel at the current mouse position to the center of the brush. Next, we have to establish a common sampling grid for the image and the brush, such that there is a one-to-one correspondence between the discrete samples. This requires a *resampling* operation that first reconstructs the continuous image function and then samples this function on the common grid. Finally, an *editing* operation combines the image samples with the brush samples using the one-to-one correspondence established before.

Our goal is now to generalize this procedure to irregular point-sampled surfaces, as illustrated in Figure 5.18. Formally, we do this by replacing the discrete image by a point-based surface. As summarized in Table 5.1, each point stores appearance attributes, including color, transparency, or material attributes, and shape attributes, such as position and normal. Let us now consider what effects the transition from images to surfaces has on the individual operations involved in the editing procedure.

Parameterization

For photo editing, the parameter mapping from brush to image coordinates is usually specified by a simple, global 2D to 2D affine mapping, for example, as a combination of translation, scaling, and rotation. Mapping a manifold surface onto a 2D domain is much more involved, however. In a 3D editing system, the user interactively selects subsets, or *patches*, of the surface that are parameterized on the fly, as described in Section 5.2.3. In general, such a mapping exhibits distortions that cannot be avoided completely. Hence we propose an efficient method that automatically minimizes these distortions, and at the same time lets the user intuitively control the mapping.

Resampling

Images are usually sampled on a regular grid, hence signal-processing methods can be applied directly for resampling. However, the sampling distribution of surfaces is in general irregular, requiring alternative methods for reconstruction and sampling. We apply a scattered data approximation approach for reconstructing a continuous

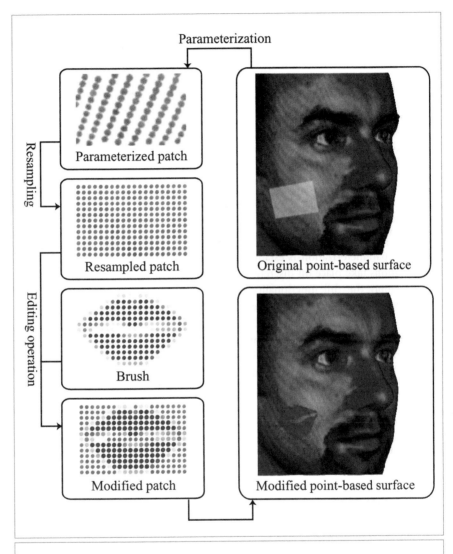

Figure 5.18: Overview of the framework for point-based surface editing.

function from the samples, as described in Section 5.2.4. We also present a technique for resampling our modified surface function onto irregular point clouds. A great benefit of our approach is that it supports adaptive sampling (i.e., works on a dynamic structure). This allows us to concentrate more samples in regions of high textural or geometric detail, while smooth parts can be represented by fewer samples.

Table 5.1: Attributes of 3D Surface Points.

Attribute	Abbreviation
Position	$\mathbf{p}_i$
Normal	$\mathbf{n}_i$
Color	$\mathbf{c}_i$
Transparency	α_i
Material properties	$\mathbf{m}_i$

Editing

Once the parameterization is established and resampling has been performed, all computations take place on discrete samples in the 2D parameter domain. Hence, we can apply the full functionality of photo-editing systems for texturing and texture filtering. However, since we are dealing with texture and geometry, the scope of operations is much broader. Additional editing operators include sculpting, geometry filtering, and simplification. As will be described in Section 5.2.5, all of these tools are based on the same simple interface that specifies a tool by a set of bitmaps and few additional parameters. For example, a sculpting tool is defined by a 2D displacement map, an alpha mask, and an intrusion depth.

5.2.2 INTERACTION MODES

We propose two user interaction schemes to manipulate the appearance attributes of a point-sampled model: brush interaction and selection interaction.

Brush Interaction

In the brush interaction mode the user moves a brush device over the surface and continuously triggers editing events, such as painting operations. The brush is positioned using the mouse cursor and aligned with the surface normal at the current interaction point. In terms of the editing framework described above, this means that the parameterization is continuously and automatically recomputed and resampling is performed for each editing event. A complete editing operation is then performed using a fixed brush image. Brush interaction is illustrated in Figure 5.19.

Selection Interaction

Here the user first selects a subset of the surface called a *patch*. He then defines the parameter mapping by imposing correspondence constraints for a set of feature

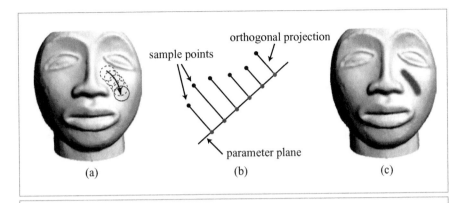

Figure 5.19: Brush interaction: (*a*) brush movement, (*b*) parameterization by orthogonal projection onto the brush plane, and (*c*) painted surface. This figure is from Pauly's thesis [Pau03].

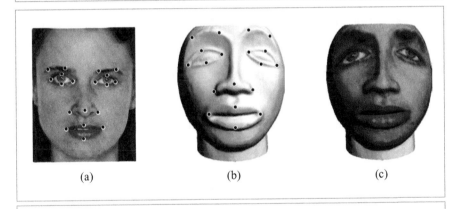

Figure 5.20: Selection interaction: (*a*) feature points in the parameter domain, (*b*) corresponding feature points on the selected surface patch, and (*c*) textured surface. This figure is from Pauly's thesis [Pau03].

points. Based on this fixed parameterization, various editing operations can be applied. Hence parameterization and resampling operators are evaluated once, while different editing operators can be applied successively to the selected patch. Selection interaction is illustrated in Figure 5.20.

5.2.3 SURFACE PARAMETERIZATION

This section describes two different methods to compute a parameterization for a point-sampled surface patch. The two approaches correspond to the two interaction schemes defined above. For brush interaction the parameter mapping will be computed by a simple orthogonal projection (Figure 5.19), while an optimization method is applied for computing a constrained minimum distortion parameterization for selection interactions (Figure 5.20).

Parameterization by Projection

A simple method for computing a parameter mapping is to project the sample points orthogonally onto a plane that represents the parameter domain. This plane can either be specified by the user, or computed automatically according to the distribution of the sample points (e.g., as a least squares fit). Using covariance analysis (see Section 4.2), the normal vector of the parameter plane would then be chosen as the eigenvector of the covariance matrix with smallest corresponding eigenvalue. In general, such a mapping will exhibit strong distortions and discontinuities, leading to inferior editing results as shown in Figure 5.21a. However, if the surface patch is sufficiently small, distortions will be small too and no discontinuities will occur. Thus, orthogonal projection is a suitable parameterization method for brush interactions, where the parameter plane is defined by the surface normal at the tool cursor and the surface patch is defined by the projection of the brush onto the surface.

Constrained Minimum-distortion Parameterization

Often a user desires to perform sophisticated texturing operations, such as mapping the image of a human face onto a point-based surface of a different face. To obtain an intuitive mapping, a user needs to be able to specify the correspondence of

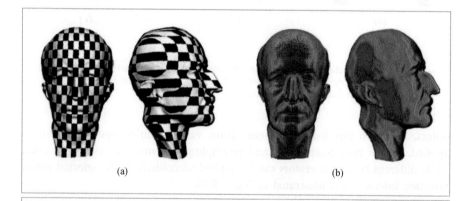

(a)   (b)

Figure 5.21: Parameterization by orthogonal projection is not suitable for large patches (*a*). The distortion visualization (*b*) exhibits large distortions. We color-code the first derivative, or the stretch, of the parameterization. Red corresponds to maximum, blue to minimum stretch. This figure is from Pauly's thesis [Pau03].

feature points. For example, the tip of the nose in the image should be mapped onto the tip of the nose on the surface, etc. In this section, we present a parameterization algorithm that respects user-specified feature correspondences while simultaneously minimizing distortions [Lev01b, ZPKG02b]. It is based on an optimization approach using an objective function that penalizes both correspondence errors and distortions. By discretizing the objective function we obtain a system of linear equations that can be solved efficiently using conjugate gradient methods.

Objective Function   We define a continuous parameterized surface by a mapping

$$P : \Omega \to S_P \subset \mathbb{R}^3, \tag{5.9}$$

where $\Omega = [0, 1] \times [0, 1]$ is the parameter domain. The mapping P is called a parameterization of the surface. For each parameter value $\mathbf{u} = (u, v) \in \Omega$ it determines a point

$$\mathbf{p} = P(\mathbf{u}) = (x(\mathbf{u}), y(\mathbf{u}), z(\mathbf{u}))^T \in S_P \tag{5.10}$$

on the surface S_P. We will also use the inverse mapping $U = P^{-1}$, which assigns parameter coordinates $\mathbf{u}$ to each point on the surface $\mathbf{p} \in S_P$. We measure the distortion of the parameter mapping using an energy functional

$$C_{dist}(P) = \int_{\Omega} \gamma(\mathbf{u}) d\mathbf{u}. \tag{5.11}$$

Here, $\gamma(\mathbf{u})$ is defined as the integral of the squared second derivative of the parameterization in each radial direction at a parameter value $\mathbf{u}$:

$$\gamma(\mathbf{u}) = \int_0^{2\pi} \left(\frac{\partial^2}{\partial r^2} P_{\mathbf{u}}(\theta, r) \right)^2 d\theta, \tag{5.12}$$

where we express the parameterization locally in polar coordinates:

$$P_{\mathbf{u}}(\theta, r) = P \left(\mathbf{u} + r \begin{bmatrix} cos(\theta) \\ sin(\theta) \end{bmatrix} \right). \tag{5.13}$$

If $\gamma(\mathbf{u})$ vanishes, the parameterization is arc length preserving (i.e., it defines a polar geodesic map at $\mathbf{u}$ [O'N66, WW94]).

A user obtains fine control over the parameterization by specifying a set $\mathcal{M}$ of feature correspondences, such that a point $\mathbf{p}_j$ of the point cloud corresponds to a location $\mathbf{u}_j$ in the parameter domain for $j \in M$. We incorporate these constraints using a second energy functional:

$$C_{fit}(P) = \sum_{j \in M} \left(P(\mathbf{u}_j) - \mathbf{p}_j \right)^2. \tag{5.14}$$

We combine the two cost functions C_{dist} and C_{fit} into the objective function

$$C(P) = C_{fit}(P) + \beta \cdot C_{dist}(P), \tag{5.15}$$

where the parameter β allows the user to control the relative weight of the fitting error and the distortion energy. We obtain the desired parameterization by computing the minimum of the objective function. This requires the discretization of the continuous formulation in Equation (5.15), which we describe next.

Discrete Formulation   Given a surface patch with points $\{\mathbf{p}_i\}$, our goal is to assign to each point $\mathbf{p}_i$ a parameter coordinate $\mathbf{u}_i$, such that the objective function is minimized. This means we are solving for the unknown discrete mapping $U: \mathbf{p}_i \mapsto \mathbf{u}_i$, hence, we reformulate Equation (5.15) by substituting the unknown P for its inverse U. For discretization of the distortion energy we construct piecewise linear parameterizations along a set of normal sections as shown in Figure 5.22.

We approximate the second derivatives in Equation (5.12) as the difference of the first derivatives between two neighboring segments on the normal section.

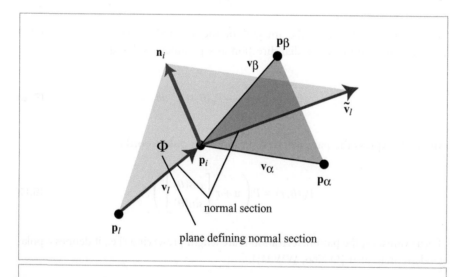

Figure 5.22: Normal section for discretizing second derivatives.

In addition, the integral is replaced by a sum over the normal sections. This yields the discrete objective function

$$\tilde{C}(U) = \sum_{j \in M} \left(\mathbf{p}_j - \mathbf{u}_j \right)^2 + \beta \sum_{i=1}^{n} \sum_{l \in N_i} \left(\frac{dU(\mathbf{p}_i)}{d\mathbf{v}_l} - \frac{dU(\mathbf{p}_i)}{d\tilde{\mathbf{v}}_l} \right), \qquad (5.16)$$

where n is the number of points in the patch, N_i specifies the set of normal sections, and $\mathbf{v}_l$ and $\tilde{\mathbf{v}}_l$ are unit vectors on the surface representing the two segments of the normal section.

Derivatives Along Normal Sections   We compute the derivatives along the normal sections $dU(\mathbf{p}_i)/d\mathbf{v}_l$ and $dU(\mathbf{p}_i)/d\tilde{\mathbf{v}}_l$ as illustrated in Figure 5.22. At each point $\mathbf{p}_i$, we collect a set N_i containing the indices of its k-nearest neighbors, typically $k = 9$. For each neighbor $\mathbf{p}_l$, $l \in N_i$, we define a normal section as the plane Φ that is given by the normal $\mathbf{n}_i$ at $\mathbf{p}_i$ and the vector $\mathbf{v}_l = \mathbf{p}_i - \mathbf{p}_l$. We then find two points and $\mathbf{p}_\alpha$ and $\mathbf{p}_\beta$, $\alpha, \beta \in N_i$, such that the angles between $\mathbf{v}_\alpha = \mathbf{p}_\alpha - \mathbf{p}_i$ and $\mathbf{v}_\beta = \mathbf{p}_\beta - \mathbf{p}_i$ and the plane Φ are minimal. In addition, the angles between $\mathbf{v}_l$ and $\mathbf{v}_\alpha$, and between $\mathbf{v}_l$ and $\mathbf{v}_\beta$ need to be bigger than $90°$. If we cannot find two points that satisfy these criteria, the normal section crosses the boundary of the patch, and we ignore it. This procedure is sufficient to handle patches with boundaries. Next, we compute the intersection line of the plane Φ and the plane given by $\mathbf{p}_i$, $\mathbf{p}_\alpha$, and $\mathbf{p}_\beta$ (see Figure 5.22), which we call $\tilde{\mathbf{v}}_l$.

The derivative of the parameterization along $\mathbf{v}_l$ is simply

$$\frac{dU(\mathbf{p}_i)}{d\mathbf{v}_l} = \frac{\mathbf{u}_i - \mathbf{u}_l}{\|\mathbf{v}_l\|}. \qquad (5.17)$$

Likewise, we compute the derivative along $\tilde{\mathbf{v}}_l$ by assuming a piecewise linear mapping on the triangle defined by the points $\mathbf{p}_i$, $\mathbf{p}_\alpha$, $\mathbf{p}_\beta$. This leads to a linear expression of the form

$$\frac{dU(\mathbf{p}_i)}{d\tilde{\mathbf{v}}_l} = a_i \mathbf{u}_i + a_\alpha \mathbf{u}_\alpha + a_\beta \mathbf{u}_\beta, \qquad (5.18)$$

where the coefficients a_i, a_α, a_β are determined by the points $\mathbf{p}_i$, $\mathbf{p}_\alpha$, $\mathbf{p}_\beta$, as presented in detail in the papers by Levy and Mallet [LM98, Lev01b] and in Zwicker's thesis [Zwi03].

Nested Iteration Least Squares Solver   The discrete objective function of Equation (5.16) is now a sum of squared linear relations of the general form

$$\tilde{C}(U) = \sum_j \left\| \mathbf{b}_j - \sum_{i=1}^{n} a_{j,i} \mathbf{u}_i \right\|^2 = \| \mathbf{b} - \mathbf{A}\mathbf{u} \|^2, \qquad (5.19)$$

where **u** is a vector of all unknowns and the coefficients $a_{j,i}$ result from Equations (5.17) and (5.18). We solve this linear least squares problem using normal equations and conjugate gradient methods [AMS90]. The convergence of such iterative solvers can be further accelerated by efficient multilevel techniques. To this end, we designed a hierarchical strategy as illustrated in Figure 5.23. In a top-down pass, we contract the system by recursively clustering the unknowns. The clustering is driven

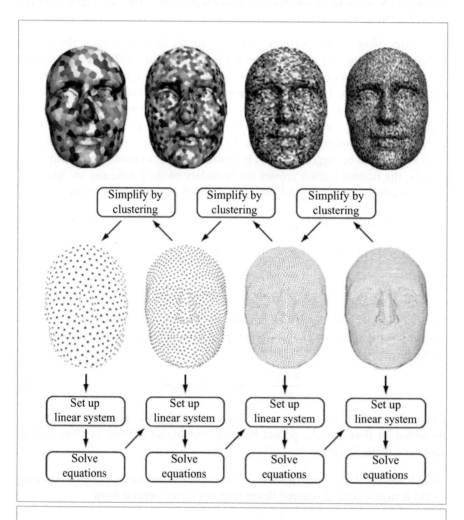

Figure 5.23: Spatial hierarchy for nested iteration. The **top row** shows the surface point clusters color coded on the original point cloud. This figure is from Pauly's thesis [Pau03].

by the spatial proximity of the corresponding surface points, and each cluster yields one unknown on the current level. In a bottom-up pass, we solve Equation (5.19) starting with the coarsest level. The solution is then prolonged by assigning it as an initial value to the next higher resolution level. This process is repeated recursively up to the original resolution.

5.2.4 RESAMPLING

Conceptually, a set of sample points and their attributes $\{\mathbf{p}_i, \mathbf{n}_i, \mathbf{c}_i, \alpha_i, \mathbf{m}_i\}$, as in Table 5.1, represent a continuous surface. The resampling operator strives to generate new samples $\{\mathbf{p}_i, \mathbf{n}_i, \mathbf{c}_i, \alpha_i, \mathbf{m}_i\}$ of this continuous surface and its attributes.

Our resampling approach is based on a surface parameterization, which can be computed, for example, with the methods described in Section 5.2.3. Resampling consists of two separate steps. First, we reconstruct a smooth approximation of the continuous surface, including all its shape and appearance attributes. The actual sampling step then evaluates the continuous surface at new sampling locations, such that a subsequent editing operation can be applied as described in Section 5.2.5. We present a number of different strategies to determine the sampling locations at the end of this section.

Reconstruction

The parameterization techniques presented in Section 5.2.3 determine a parameter value $\mathbf{u}_i$ for each 3D point $\mathbf{p}_i$ in a patch. However, for surface resampling we need a continuous mapping

$$P^* : \mathbf{u} \in \Omega \rightarrow [\mathbf{p}, \mathbf{n}, \mathbf{c}, \alpha, \mathbf{m}] (\mathbf{u}), \qquad (5.20)$$

which lets us evaluate all surface attributes at any point $\mathbf{u}$ in the parameter domain. For this purpose, we define a local reconstruction kernel $r_i(\mathbf{t}^i)$ on the tangent plane of each point. Here, $\mathbf{t}^i$ denotes a parameterization of the tangent plane of point i, which we determine as described in Section 4.2. We choose a Gaussian reconstruction kernel:

$$r_i(\mathbf{t}^i) = g_{\mathbf{R}_i}(\mathbf{t}^i) = \frac{1}{2\pi\sqrt{|\mathbf{R}_i|}} e^{-\frac{1}{2}(\mathbf{t}^i)^T \mathbf{R}_i^{-1} \mathbf{t}^i}. \qquad (5.21)$$

We also introduce local attribute functions $[\mathbf{p}_i, \mathbf{n}_i, \mathbf{c}_i, \alpha_i, \mathbf{m}_i] (\mathbf{t}^i)$. For simplicity, all these functions are constant (i.e., $\mathbf{n}_i(\mathbf{t}^i) = \mathbf{n}_i$, etc.) except for the surface position, which is reconstructed linearly:

$$\mathbf{p}_i(\mathbf{t}^i) = \begin{bmatrix} \mathbf{u}_i & \mathbf{v}_i & \mathbf{p}_i \end{bmatrix} \begin{bmatrix} \mathbf{t}^i \\ 1 \end{bmatrix}. \qquad (5.22)$$

Here, $\mathbf{u}_i$ and $\mathbf{v}_i$ are orthogonal unit vectors on the tangent plane. By defining mappings $m_i : \mathbf{t}^i \to \mathbf{u}$ from the local tangent planes to the global parameter domain, we define the continuous surface and its attributes as

$$P^*(\mathbf{u}) = \sum_i \frac{[\mathbf{p}_i, \mathbf{n}_i, \mathbf{c}_i, \alpha_i, \mathbf{m}_i]\left(m_i^{-1}(\mathbf{u})\right) r_i\left(m_i^{-1}(\mathbf{u})\right)}{\sum_i r_i\left(m_i^{-1}(\mathbf{u})\right)}. \tag{5.23}$$

We describe two different techniques to compute the mappings $m_i(\mathbf{t}^i)$:

- *Mapping by optimization*: Let us denote the set of the k-nearest neighbors of point $\mathbf{p}_i$ by $\mathcal{N}_k(\mathbf{p}_i)$. We introduce local tangent coordinates $\mathbf{t}_l^i$ for points $l \in \mathcal{N}_k(\mathbf{p}_i)$, which are given by orthogonally projecting the neighbors $\mathbf{p}_l$ onto the tangent plane of $\mathbf{p}_i$. We define the mapping m_i as

$$m_i(\mathbf{t}^i) = \min_{m_i} \sum_{l \in \mathcal{N}_k(\mathbf{p}_i)} \left(\mathbf{u}_l - m_i(\mathbf{t}_l^i)\right)^2. \tag{5.24}$$

We restrict the mappings to be affine, such that Equation (5.24) becomes a linear least squares problem. We use this approach preferably with the minimum distortion parameterization described in Section 5.2.3.

- *Mapping by projection*: In the case of parameterization by projection (Section 5.2.3), an alternative approach to compute the mappings $m_i(\mathbf{t}^i)$ is to use the same projection to map the tangent planes to the parameterization domain. This is also related to point-rendering approaches based on splatting described in Section 6.1.

Sampling

We discuss three different strategies to determine the resampling locations. A user selects one of them depending on the editing operation he or she wishes to perform and on the detail that is represented in the original surface and the brush.

- *Brush resampling*: In this method, we use the original surface points as the resampling grid. Hence we have to resample the brush, which is done using the same reconstruction approach as described above. The advantage of this method is that we do not have to insert any new surface points, and there is no loss of detail in the original surface due to resampling.
- *Surface resampling*: In many operations, such as texture mapping, we want to resample the surface to avoid any loss in texture quality. Therefore, the user can choose to resample the surface at the sampling distribution of the brush.
- *Adaptive resampling*: If the sampling density of the surface or the brush varies significantly, it occurs that in some areas in a patch the surface-sampling

distribution is finer, and in others the brush-sampling density. In this case, both of the above strategies fail to preserve detail of either the brush or the surface. An adaptive resampling operator locally decides whether to use samples of the surface or the brush. The decision is based on the comparison of the radii of the Gaussian reconstruction functions, since these radii directly correspond to the local sampling density.

5.2.5 SURFACE EDITING

The resampling technique of Section 5.2.4 provides a one-to-one correspondence between samples of the surface and samples of the brush. We can thus combine corresponding samples by applying an editing operation such as painting, carving, displacement mapping, or filtering.

Painting

Painting operations modify appearance attributes by alpha-blending corresponding surface and brush samples. For example, the diffuse color of a surface sample can be modified by alpha-blending it with the diffuse color of the corresponding brush sample. Similarly, painting can be applied to other attributes such as transparency or material reflectance properties.

Normal Displacements

We can also apply normal displacements to the positions of the surface samples. The new position $\mathbf{p}_i'$ is given as $\mathbf{p}_i' = \mathbf{p}_i + d_i \cdot \mathbf{n}_i$, where $\mathbf{p}_i$ is the original position, d_i is a scalar coefficient given by the corresponding brush sample, and $\mathbf{n}_i$ is the surface normal at $\mathbf{p}_i$. As illustrated in Figure 5.25 later, this type of editing operation is particularly suitable for embossing or engraving.

Carving

Carving subtracts a shape specified by the brush from the surface in a fashion that is similar to constructive solid geometry (CSG) operations described in Section 5.3. The shape of the brush is given by a reference plane and the brush values d_i that are interpreted as a distance from the reference plane. The reference plane is defined by the surface position and normal at a user-specified location. The new sample positions are then given by

$$\mathbf{p}_i' = \begin{cases} \mathbf{b}_i + d_i \cdot \bar{\mathbf{n}} & \|\mathbf{p}_i - \mathbf{b}_i\| < d_i \\ \mathbf{p}_i & \text{otherwise} \end{cases}, \tag{5.25}$$

where $\mathbf{b}_i$ are points on the reference plane corresponding to the brush values d_i. Further, $\bar{\mathbf{n}}$ is the reference plane normal, corresponding to the surface normal at the

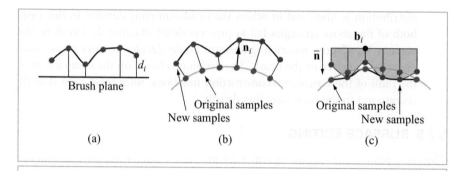

Figure 5.24: Comparison between normal displacements and carving: (*a*) brush, (*b*) normal displacement, and (*c*) carving.

user-specified location. The difference between displacement mapping and carving is illustrated in Figure 5.24.

Filtering

For filtering operations the brush is interpreted as a discrete convolution matrix. During filtering, the convolution is computed by multiplying and adding up corresponding surface and brush values. We can, therefore, implement arbitrary discrete linear filters by simply choosing the appropriate filter kernel values. Filters can be applied to any surface attribute (e.g., color) normal or also distance from the reference plane for geometric offset filtering.

It is straightforward to combine the above operations with alpha-blending. Alpha-blending computes a weighted average of the original surface sample and the modified sample (i.e., $\xi'_i = \alpha_i \cdot \bar{\xi}_i + (1 - \alpha_i) \cdot \xi_i$). Here, α_i is the alpha value stored in the brush that controls the blending, ξ_i is the original surface attribute, $\bar{\xi}_i$ is the surface attribute after one of the above operations has been applied, and ξ'_i is the output value. Alpha-blending allows us, for example, to generate smooth transitions between modified and unaltered surface areas. These editing operations are also described in more detail in Zwicker [Zwi03].

We illustrate the different editing operations in Figure 5.25. On the left we show a texturing operation with alpha-blending, in the middle we depict displacement mapping on a sphere, and the right image illustrates carving on a rough surface. All these operations can be performed interactively with Pointshop3D [ZPKG02b]; in other words, the user gets immediate visual feedback within tenths of a second (depending on the brush size) on a PC-class computer (e.g., Pentium IV processor at 2 GHz).

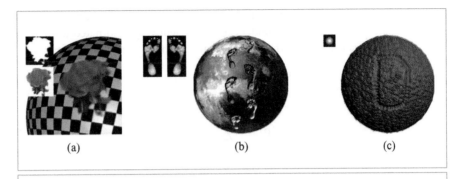

Figure 5.25: Examples of surface painting (*a*), displacement mapping (*b*), and carving (*c*).

5.2.6 PAINTING WITH VIRTUAL BRUSHES

Building upon the techniques discussed above, we now describe an approach to paint on three-dimensional objects using a virtual paintbrush. A haptic input device is used to control the brush, and makes it possible to give haptic feedback to the user. To complete the interaction metaphor, a paint model controls the transfer of attributes from brush to surface and vice versa. A more detailed description is given in a paper by Adams et al. [AWD+04].

Additional to the resampling algorithms discussed above, a fast collision detection algorithm is needed that allows us to give haptic feedback to the user, and evaluate penetration depths for carving.

Brush Model

Contrary to Section 5.2.2, the virtual brush that is used to paint the model is not an image, but it is another point-sampled object. In order to closely mimic a real brush, the brush tip should be modeled as a deformable object. A simple mass-spring skeleton with a geometrically defined point-sampled surface already offers a sufficient amount of realism; however, more elaborate models can be used. Thus, the brush model consists of two parts: a physical model that is used to simulate deformation, and a surface model. We will now turn to the physical model; the surface model will be treated in more detail in the next section.

Collision detection with the point-sampled model to be painted has to be fast in order to fulfill the hard real-time requirements of haptic feedback. For a penalty-based collision-handling method, it is sufficient to compute penetration depth for all constituting points of the physical model (e.g., in a mass-spring system, the mass points). For any point $\mathbf{p}$, penetration depth $d(\mathbf{p})$ and penetration direction $\mathbf{n}(\mathbf{p})$ with respect to a point-sampled model can be efficiently approximated using only the $\mathcal{N}_k(\mathbf{p})$-nearest-neighbor surfels s_i with center points $\mathbf{p}_i$ and normals $\mathbf{n}_i$:

$$d(\mathbf{p}) = \sum_{i \in \mathcal{N}_k(\mathbf{p})} w_i\, \mathbf{n}_i \cdot (\mathbf{p}_i - \mathbf{p}), \quad \text{and} \tag{5.26}$$

$$\mathbf{n}(\mathbf{p}) = \sum_{i \in \mathcal{N}_k(\mathbf{p})} w_i\, \mathbf{n}_i. \tag{5.27}$$

The weights w_i are defined such that they vanish for the neighboring point that is farthest away:

$$w_i = \frac{d_{\max} - d_i}{\sum_{j \in \mathcal{N}_k(\mathbf{p})} d_{\max} - d_j}, \tag{5.28}$$

where $d_i = \|\mathbf{p}_i - \mathbf{p}\|$ and $d_{\max} = \max d_i$. This makes $d(\mathbf{p})$ and $n(\mathbf{p})$ a smooth function of position. Using an acceleration structure for nearest-neighbor searches such as described in Chapter 4, this type of collision query can be computed fast enough to allow for haptic feedback. If the models to be painted are large, collision detection can be computed on a simplified model.

The physical model of the brush takes the collision information as input and computes the dynamic behavior of the brush, giving haptic feedback to the user if necessary. The loop updating the haptic feedback has to run at 1 kHz. See Figure 5.26a for an illustration. The brush dynamics loop is completely separated from the paint transfer loop, in which the actual painting takes place.

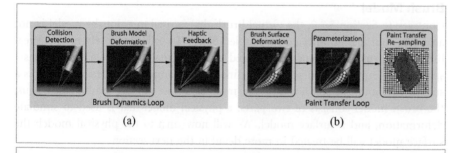

Figure 5.26: The two loops necessary for painting with a haptic device. (a) the brush dynamics loop computes collision detection, deforms the physical model of the brush accordingly, and gives haptic feedback to the user. (b) The paint transfer loop computes surface deformation and performs the actual paint transfer.

Paint Transfer

Paint transfer is computed between the surface of the brush and the surface of the object to be painted. In our setting, both surfaces are point sampled. The brush surface is geometrically deformed by the physical brush model. Then, a common parameterization of brush surface and object surface is computed. In this common domain, paint is transferred between the two surfaces. If necessary, the surfaces are then resampled to be able to represent the new surface attributes accurately. Figure 5.26b shows the paint transfer loop.

The common parameterization of the two surfaces is computed by orthogonal projection (see Section 5.2.3). As already noted, this can lead to substantial distortions. Since the brush is typically small, this is not a problem in most cases. In regions of high curvature, however, the distortion can become a problem. Here, the physical brush model allows the brush to split, and each of the brush parts is treated separately. This further reduces the size of the surface patches to be parameterized. Figure 5.27 illustrates brush splitting. Instead of using only one projection for parameterization, several projections are used. This greatly reduces the distortion problems. Using this technique, parameterization by orthogonal projection is a viable alternative to more costly approaches.

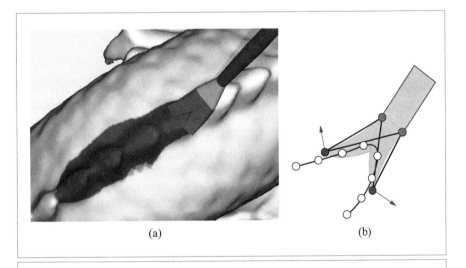

(a)   (b)

Figure 5.27: In regions of high curvature, the brush splits in order to alleviate problems with parameterization distortion. (*a*) A brush splitting in two parts on the back of the dragon model. (*b*) Schematic of a split brush. Both parts are treated independently, and two projections are used for parameterization.

Once the brush surface and the object surface have a common parameterization, bidirectional paint transfer is computed in the parameter domain. Therefore, both the object surface and the brush surface samples are splatted into a planar *paint buffer*. (Refer to Section 6.1 for more details on splatting). The paint buffer is an image with a resolution defined by the sampling density of the brush or object, whichever is higher. By carefully choosing the resolution of the paint buffer, we can ensure that no detail present on either the object surface or the brush is lost. The paint buffer contains not only colors, but also other paint attributes needed to compute the paint transfer, like wetness, diffusion coefficients, and the penetration depth of the brush at a specific point.

There are many possible choices for a paint model [AWD+04, BLL03, BSLM01, BWL04]. These usually work on images, such that we can apply these models directly to the paint buffer. The paint transfer is bidirectional, such that both the brush and the surface are affected by the computation. Once the new paint distribution in the paint buffer is known, this information has to be remapped onto object's and brush's surfaces and stored there. Since we now have an image (the paint buffer) and the point-sampled object surface, we can use the resampling strategy as described in Section 5.2.4. Since all necessary information is available in the paint buffer, it is straightforward to do carving, embossing, or similar, geometry-altering operations using the virtual brush. Figure 5.28 shows some 3D models painted using a haptic interface.

5.2.7 CONCLUSION

In this section, we presented a versatile framework for appearance and shape editing of point-based models. Our approach strives to generalize the functionality and ease of use of 2D image-editing tools to 3D surface editing. The key ingredients of our technique comprise a flexible and powerful point-cloud parameterization and a dynamic resampling scheme based on a continuous reconstruction of the model surface. We described the implementation of various painting and editing operations, such as texturing, filtering, carving, and displacement mapping. In addition, we presented an extension of our system toward an intuitive virtual paintbrush interface with haptic feedback. Our approach also includes a physically motivated paint transfer simulation. The main limitation of the framework presented in this section is that it is restricted to small-scale modifications of the surface geometry. We introduce powerful shape-modeling tools that enable more general modifications of object geometry in the next section.

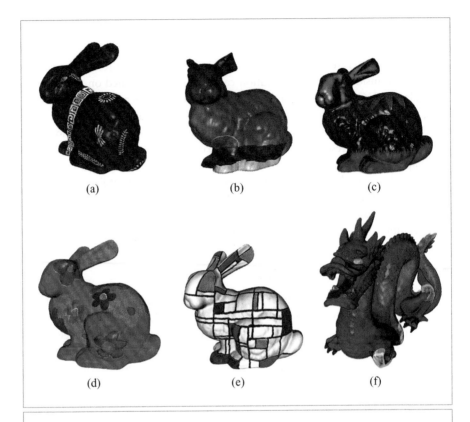

(a)   (b)   (c)

(d)   (e)   (f)

Figure 5.28: Models painted using a haptic interface. (*a–e*) Different painted bunny models. (*f*) A painted dragon model.

5.3 SHAPE MODELING

Mark Pauly and Leif Kobbelt

5.3.1 OVERVIEW

Modeling the shape of 3D objects is one of the central techniques in geometry processing. This section discusses two fundamental modeling approaches for point-sampled geometry: Boolean operations and free-form deformation. While the former are concerned with building complex objects by combining simpler shapes

[Hof89], the latter defines a continuous deformation field in space to smoothly deform a given surface [SP86] (see Figure 5.29).

Boolean operations are most easily defined on implicit surface representations, since the required inside-outside classification can be directly evaluated on the underlying scalar field. On the other hand, free-form deformation is a very intuitive modeling paradigm for explicit surface representations. For example, mesh vertices or NURBS control points can be directly displaced according to the deformation field. For point-based representations, the hybrid structure of the surface model defined in Chapter 4 can be exploited to integrate these two modeling approaches into a unified shape-modeling framework. Boolean operations can utilize the approximate signed distance function defined by the MLS projection (see Section 4.2) for inside-outside classification, while free-form deformations operate directly on the point samples.

5.3.2 BOOLEAN OPERATIONS

A common approach in geometric modeling is to build complex objects by combining simpler shapes using Boolean operations [Hof89] (see Figure 5.30). In constructive solid geometry (CSG), objects are defined using a binary tree, where each node corresponds to a union, intersection, or difference operation and each leaf stores a primitive (e.g., sphere, cylinder, or cone). Operations such as ray tracing, for example, are then implemented by traversing this tree structure. More commonly, surfaces are defined as boundary representations (BReps) of solids. Here Boolean operations have to be evaluated explicitly, which requires an algorithm for intersecting two surfaces. Computing such a surface-surface intersection can be quite involved, however, in particular for higher-order surfaces (see for example Kirshnan and Manocha [KM97]).

As will be demonstrated below, the MLS projection operator (see Section 4.2) can be used both for inside-outside classification as well as for explicitly sampling the

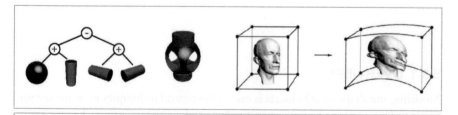

Figure 5.29: Boolean operations (*left*) and free-form deformation (*right*).

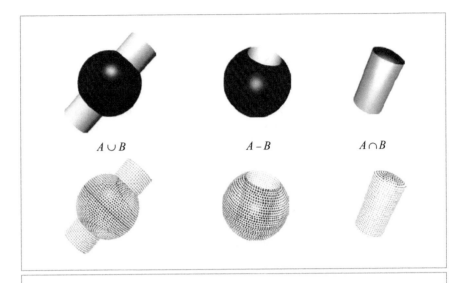

Figure 5.30: Boolean operations applied to a sphere A and a cylinder B: (*a*) union $A \cup B$, (*b*) difference $A - B$, (*c*) intersection $A \cap B$. The ***bottom row*** illustrates the sampling distribution.

intersection curve. The goal is to perform a Boolean operation on two orientable, closed surfaces S_1 and S_2 that are defined by two point clouds P_1 and P_2, to obtain a new point cloud P_3 that defines the resulting surface S_3. Since Boolean operations typically produce sharp creases at the intersection of the two surfaces S_1 and S_2, P_3 consists of two subsets $Q_1 \subseteq P_1$ and $Q_2 \subseteq P_2$ plus a set of newly generated sample points that explicitly represent the intersection curves. Thus, in order to perform a Boolean operation for point-sampled geometry, the following techniques are required:

- A classification predicate to determine the two sets Q_1 and Q_2.
- An algorithm to find samples on the intersection curve.
- A rendering method that allows the user to display crisp features curves using point primitives.

Classification
The goal of the classification stage is to determine which points of P_1 are inside or outside the volume enclosed by the surface S_2 and vice versa. For this purpose a classification predicate Ω_P is defined such that for $\mathbf{x} \in \mathbb{R}^3$,

$$\Omega_P(\mathbf{x}) = \begin{cases} 1 & \mathbf{x} \in \mathcal{V} \\ 0 & \mathbf{x} \notin \mathcal{V} \end{cases}, \tag{5.29}$$

where $\mathcal{V}$ is the volume bounded by the MLS surface S defined by the point cloud $\mathcal{P}$.

Let $\mathbf{y} \in S$ be the closest point on S from $\mathbf{x}$. It is known from differential geometry that, if S is continuous and smooth, the vector $\mathbf{x} - \mathbf{y}$ is aligned with the surface normal $\mathbf{n}_y$ at $\mathbf{y}$ [dC76]. If surface normals are consistently oriented to point outward of the surface, then $(\mathbf{x} - \mathbf{y}) \cdot \mathbf{n}_y > 0$ if and only if $\mathbf{x} \notin \mathcal{V}$. Since only a discrete sample $\mathcal{P}$ of the surface S is given, the closest point $\mathbf{y}$ on S is replaced by the closest point $\mathbf{p} \in \mathcal{P}$. Thus, $\mathbf{x}$ is classified as outside, if $(\mathbf{x} - \mathbf{p}) \cdot \mathbf{n}_p > 0$; in other words, if the angle between $\mathbf{x} - \mathbf{p}$ and the normal $\mathbf{n}_p$ at $\mathbf{p}$ is less than $\pi/2$ (see Figure 5.31, left). This discrete test yields the correct inside-outside classification of the point $\mathbf{x}$ if the distance $\|\mathbf{x} - \mathbf{p}\|$ is sufficiently large with respect to the local sample spacing η_p at $\mathbf{p}$ (see Chapter 4). If $\mathbf{x}$ is extremely close to the surface, the classification could fail, as illustrated in the right image of Figure 5.31. In this case the exact closest point is computed using the method described in Section 4.2.

Since for classification only an inside-outside test is of interest, the performance can be significantly improved by exploiting local coherence: $\Omega_P(\mathbf{x}) = \Omega_P(\mathbf{x}')$ for all points $\mathbf{x}'$ that lie in the sphere around $\mathbf{x}$ with radius $\|\mathbf{x} - \mathbf{p}\| - \eta_p$. Thus, the number of closest point queries and MLS projections can be reduced drastically, in practice up to 90%.

Given the classification predicate Ω, the subsets $\mathcal{Q}_1$ and $\mathcal{Q}_2$ can be computed as shown in Table 5.2. As Figure 5.32 illustrates, the resulting inside-outside classification is very robust and easily handles complex, nonconvex surfaces. Observe that Boolean operations can easily create a large number of disconnected components (i.e., can lead to a significant change in genus).

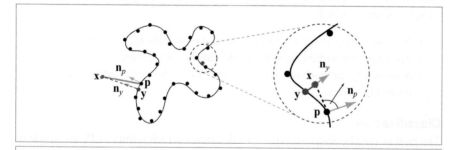

Figure 5.31: Inside-outside test. For $\mathbf{x}$ very close to the surface, the closest point $\mathbf{p} \in \mathcal{P}$ can yield a false classification (*right*). In this case, $\mathbf{x}$ is classified by computing the true closest point on the surface S.

Table 5.2: Classification for Boolean Operations.

	Q_1	Q_2
$S_1 \cup S_2$	$\{\mathbf{p} \in \mathcal{P}_1 \mid \Omega_{\mathcal{P}_2}(\mathbf{p}) = 0\}$	$\{\mathbf{p} \in \mathcal{P}_2 \mid \Omega_{\mathcal{P}_1}(\mathbf{p}) = 0\}$
$S_1 \cap S_2$	$\{\mathbf{p} \in \mathcal{P}_1 \mid \Omega_{\mathcal{P}_2}(\mathbf{p}) = 1\}$	$\{\mathbf{p} \in \mathcal{P}_2 \mid \Omega_{\mathcal{P}_1}(\mathbf{p}) = 1\}$
$S_1 - S_2$	$\{\mathbf{p} \in \mathcal{P}_1 \mid \Omega_{\mathcal{P}_2}(\mathbf{p}) = 0\}$	$\{\mathbf{p} \in \mathcal{P}_2 \mid \Omega_{\mathcal{P}_1}(\mathbf{p}) = 1\}$
$S_2 - S_1$	$\{\mathbf{p} \in \mathcal{P}_1 \mid \Omega_{\mathcal{P}_2}(\mathbf{p}) = 1\}$	$\{\mathbf{p} \in \mathcal{P}_2 \mid \Omega_{\mathcal{P}_1}(\mathbf{p}) = 0\}$

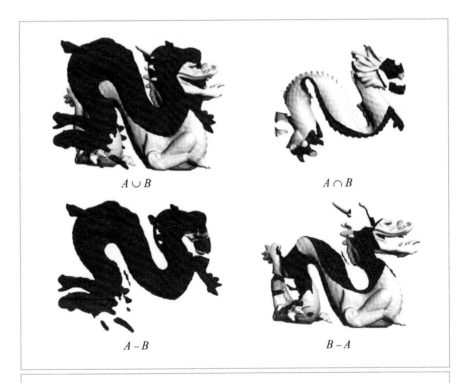

$A \cup B$ $A \cap B$

$A - B$ $B - A$

Figure 5.32: Boolean operations of a blue dragon A and a white dragon B: (**a**) Union $A \cup B$, (**b**) intersection $A \cap B$, (**c**) difference $A - B$, and (**d**) difference $B - A$.

Intersection Curves

Taking the union of Q_1 and Q_2 will typically not produce a point cloud that accurately describes the surface S_3, since the intersection curve of the two MLS surfaces S_1 and S_2 is not represented adequately. Therefore, a set of sample points that lie on the intersection curve is explicitly computed and added to $Q_1 \cup Q_2$, to obtain the point cloud P_3. First, all points in Q_1 and Q_2 are identified that are close to the intersection curve by evaluating the approximate distance function induced by the MLS projection operator (see Section 4.2). From all closest pairs ($q_1 \in Q_1, q_2 \in Q_2$) of these points a new sample q on the intersection curve is computed using a Newton-type iteration. This is done as follows (see Figure 5.33a–d): Let r be the point on the intersection line of the two tangent planes of q_1 and q_2 that is closest to both points (i.e., that minimizes the distance $\|r - q_1\| + \|r - q_2\|$). The point r is the first approximation of q and can now be projected onto S_1 and S_2 to obtain two new starting points q_1' and q_2' for the iteration. This procedure can be repeated iteratively until the points q_1 and q_2 converge to a point q on the intersection curve. The sample point is discarded if the projection does not monotonically approach the intersection curve, for instance, if either q_1' is farther away from S_2 than q_1 or q_2' is farther away from S_1 than q_2.

Local-sampling density estimation is used to detect whether the sampling resolution of the two input surfaces differs significantly in the vicinity of the intersection curve.

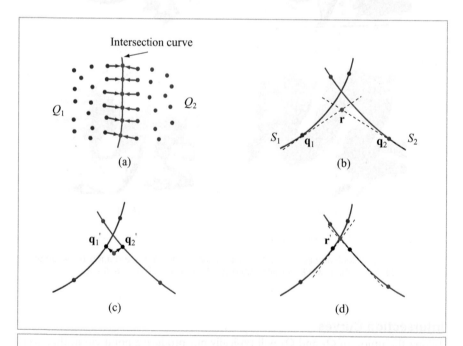

Figure 5.33: Sampling the intersection curve: (*a*) closest pairs of points in Q_1 and Q_2, (*b*) first estimate r, (*c*) reprojection, and (*d*) second estimate r'.

To avoid a sharp discontinuity in sampling density, the coarser model is upsampled
in this area to match the sampling density of the finer model, using the dynamic
sampling method of Section 5.3.4.

Note that the above Newton scheme also provides an easy mechanism for adaptively upsampling the intersection curve. A simple subdivision rule can be evaluated to create a new starting point for the Newton iteration (e.g., the average
of two adjacent points on the curve). Applying the iteration then yields a new
sample on the intersection curve as illustrated in Figure 5.34. Figure 5.35 shows
union, intersection, and difference operations of the Max Planck model with a
spiral. The effect of dynamically upsampling the intersection curve is illustrated
for three levels of subdivision. Compared to other explicit surface representations,
such as polygonal meshes, the adaptive refinement of intersection curves requires no
complicated adaptations of the local connectivity graph. The implicit MLS surface
model automatically adapts to newly created sample points so that only updates
of the local search data structure are necessary. However, care needs to be taken
when evaluating the surface resulting from Boolean operations. To avoid smoothing any sharp creases created by the intersection of two surfaces, MLS or other
surface-approximation operators should be evaluated on the different surface parts
separately. Alternatively, a feature-sensitive surface-approximation scheme should
be used such as the MLS extension proposed in Fleishman et al. [FCOS05].

Rendering Sharp Creases

The accurate display of the intersection curves requires a rendering technique that
can handle sharp creases and corners. For this purpose an extension of the surface-
splatting technique presented in Zwicker et al. [ZPvBG01b] can be used. In this
method, each sample point is represented by a surfel, an oriented-elliptical splat

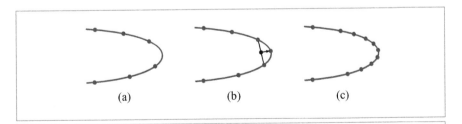

(a)   (b)   (c)

Figure 5.34: Adaptive refinement of the intersection curve: (*a*) original intersection
curve, (*b*) new point inserted in region of high curvature, and (*c*) final, adaptively
sampled intersection curve.

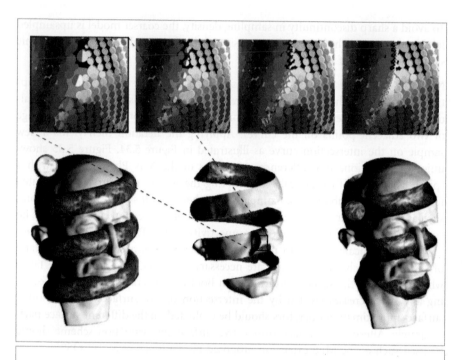

Figure 5.35: Upsampling the intersection curve to increase the accuracy of the representation. Three levels of uniform refinement are shown in the *top row*. The *bottom row* shows, from *left to right*, union, intersection, and difference operations of two point-sampled surfaces.

that is projected onto the screen to reconstruct the surface in image space (see also Chapter 6). A point on the intersection curve can now be represented by two surfels that share the same center, but whose normals stem from either one of the two input surfaces. During scan conversion, each of these surfels is then clipped against the plane defined by the other to obtain a piecewise linear approximation of the intersection curve in screen space (see Figure 5.35). Figure 5.36 shows an example of a difficult Boolean operation of two identical cylinders that creates two singularities. While the classification and intersection curve sampling work fine, the rendering method produces artifacts. This is due to numerical instabilities, since the clipping planes of two corresponding surfels are almost parallel. However, such cases are rare in typical computer graphics applications (e.g., digital character design). As such, the algorithms for Boolean operations are less suited for industrial manufacturing applications, where robust handling of degenerated cases is of primary concern.

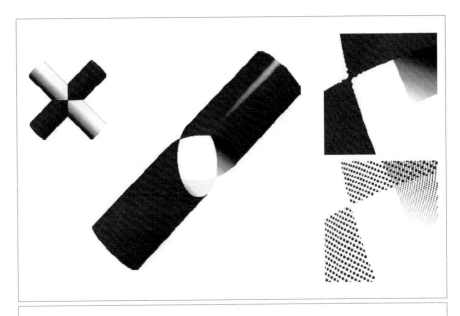

Figure 5.36: A difficult Boolean difference operation that creates two singularities.

Particle-based Blending

As illustrated in Figures 5.30 and 5.32, Boolean operations typically produce sharp intersections. In some applications it is more desirable to create a smooth blend between the two combined surface parts. To smooth out the sharp creases created by Boolean operations an adaptation of oriented particles [ST92] can be used. The idea is to define interparticle potentials $\Phi(\mathbf{p}_i, \mathbf{p}_j)$ in such a way that the minimum of the global potential function yields a smooth surface that minimizes curvature. Summing up these potentials yields a particle's total potential energy E_i. From this potential energy one can derive the positional and rotational forces that are exerted on each particle and compute its path of motion under these forces. Additionally, an interparticle repulsion force is applied to equalize the particle distribution (see also Section 4.3). All forces are scaled with a smooth fall-off function that measures the distance to the intersection curve to confine the particle simulation to a small area around the intersection curve without affecting other parts of the surface. A detailed discussion on implementation issues of the particle simulation method can be found in Keiser [Kei03].

Figure 5.37 shows the particle-based blending for the intersection of two planes, where the degree of smoothness can be controlled by the number of iterations of the simulation.

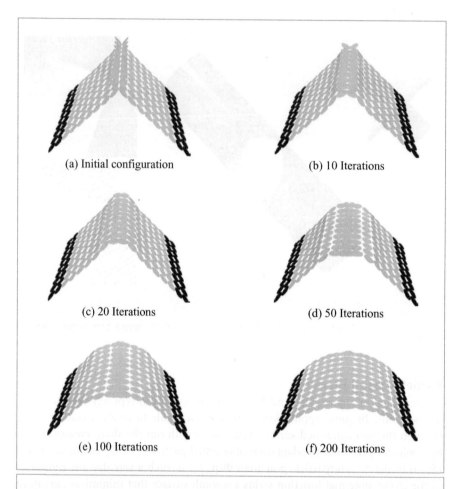

Figure 5.37: Particle simulation to blend two intersecting planes. Gray particles participate in the simulation, blue points indicate the fixed boundary.

In Figure 5.38, a more complex blending operation is shown. A union operation of three tori has created numerous sharp intersection curves as shown in (a). These can be blended simultaneously as illustrated in (b) using the particle simulation described above. The same blending technique can of course also be applied to the intersection and difference operations described in Section 5.3.2.

5.3.3 FREE-FORM DEFORMATION

Apart from composition of surfaces using Boolean operations, many shape design applications require the capability to modify objects using smooth deformations.

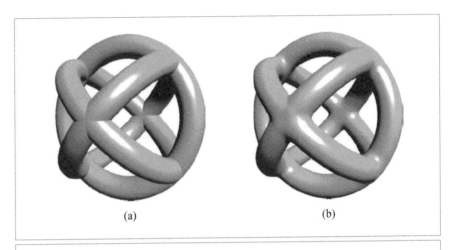

(a)   (b)

Figure 5.38: Boolean union of three tori: (*a*) reconstruction with sharp feature curves, and (*b*) feature curves have been blended using particle simulation.

These include bending, twisting, stretching, and compressing of the model surface. The idea of free-form deformation is to define a space-warping function $\mathbf{F} : \mathbb{R}^3 \rightarrow \mathbb{R}^3$ that deforms space and any embedded surface. Initially proposed in Barr [Bar84] and Sederberg and Parry [SP86] many different methods have been devised to specify the warping function $\mathbf{F}$. A fairly general approach makes use of the "handle" paradigm: the user first defines a deformable region $\chi_d \subset S$ on the model surface and marks parts of this region as a control handle. The surface can then be modified interactively by pushing, pulling, or twisting this handle. More specifically, the user defines an affine transformation of the control handle that together with the boundary of the deformable region imposes constraints for the computation of the continuous deformation function. Depending on the application, these constraints can include higher-order continuity, for example, the transition from the rigid part to the deformable part should be C^1 continuous [BK04].

Deformation Functions

One simple technique to define the deformation function is based on a continuously varying scale parameter $t \in [0, 1]$ that measures the relative distance of a point from the handle. The closer a point is to the handle, the stronger the deformation will be for that point. More precisely, let $\chi_1 \subset \chi_d$ be the handle, also called *one-region*, and $\chi_0 = S - \chi_d$ the *zero-region*, in other words, all points of the surface S that are not part of the deformable region. For both zero- and one-region distance measures d_0 and d_1, respectively, are defined as

$$d_j(\mathbf{p}) = \begin{cases} 0 & \mathbf{p} \in \chi_j \\ \min_{\mathbf{q} \in \chi_j}(\|\mathbf{p} - \mathbf{q}\|) & \mathbf{p} \notin \chi_j \end{cases} \tag{5.30}$$

for $j = 0, 1$. From these distance measures the scale parameter t is computed as $t = \beta(d_0(\mathbf{p})/(d_0(\mathbf{p}) + d_1(\mathbf{p})))$, where $\beta : [0,1] \rightarrow [0,1]$ is a continuous blending function with $\beta(0) = 0$ and $\beta(1) = 1$. Thus, $t = 0$ for $\mathbf{p} \in \chi_0$ and $t = 1$ for $\mathbf{p} \in \chi_1$. Using this scale parameter, the position of a point $\mathbf{p} \in \chi_d$ after the deformation is determined as $\mathbf{p}' = \mathbf{F}(\mathbf{p}, t)$, where $\mathbf{F}$ is a deformation function composed of a translational and a rotational part. The deformation function can be written as $\mathbf{F}(\mathbf{p}, t) = \mathbf{F}_T(\mathbf{p}, t) + \mathbf{F}_R(\mathbf{p}, t)$, where

- $\mathbf{F}_T(\mathbf{p}, t) = \mathbf{p} + t \cdot \mathbf{v}$ with $\mathbf{v}$ a translation vector, and
- $\mathbf{F}_R(\mathbf{p}, t) = \mathbf{R}(\mathbf{a}, t \cdot \alpha) \cdot \mathbf{p}$, where $\mathbf{R}(\mathbf{a}, \alpha)$ is the matrix that specifies a rotation around axis $\mathbf{a}$ with angle α.

Figure 5.39 shows a translational deformation of a plane, where the translation vector is equal to the plane normal. This figure also illustrates the effect of different choices of the blending function β. In Figure 5.40, two rotational deformations of a cylinder are shown, while a combination of both translational and rotational deformations is illustrated in Figure 5.45 later.

To perform a free-form deformation the user only needs to select the zero- and one-regions and choose an appropriate blending function. She can then interactively deform the surface by displacing the handle with a mouse or trackball device, similar to Kobbelt et al. [KCVS98]. This gives the method great flexibility for handling a wide class of free-form deformations, while still providing a simple and intuitive user interface. The deformable region and the handle can be specified using a simple paint tool that allows the user to mark points on the surface by drawing lines, circles, rectangles, etc. and applying flood filling and erasure.

Computing the scale parameter t requires an estimate for the distance of a point $\mathbf{p} \in \chi_d$ to the zero- and one-regions. Since both of these regions are represented by point sets, an approximation of $d_j(\mathbf{p})$ can be computed by searching for the closest point in the respective region. This, however, yields a nonsmooth deformation field, since the distance function to a point set has many discontinuities in its gradient. A more practical approximation for the distance values can be obtained by computing a weighted average of the distance to the k-nearest neighbors (all the figures in this section use $k = 20$). While this approach yields smoother deformation fields, it still cannot guarantee higher-order continuity.

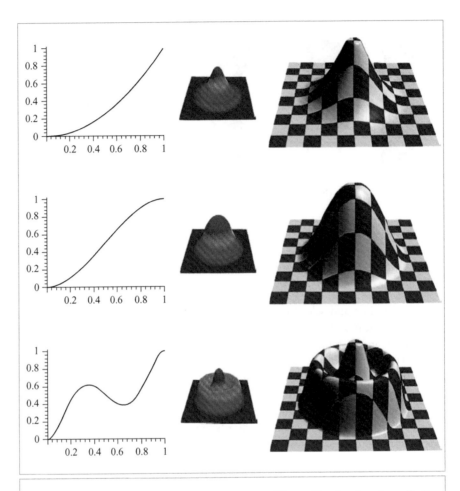

Figure 5.39: Deformations of a plane for three different blending functions: (*Left*) blending function, (*middle*) color-coded scale parameter, where blue indicates the zero-region ($t = 0$) and red the one-region ($t = 1$), and (*right*) final textured surface.

A different scheme that provides such guarantees has been proposed in Botsch and Kobbelt [BK05]. The editing metaphor is essentially the same; in other words, the user specifies a deformable region and a control handle and deforms the surface by applying an affine transformation to the handle. Since the method computes a space deformation, it can be applied to point-sampled surfaces as well as any other explicit surface representation. The displacements of the control handle define constraints for a system of triharmonic radial basis functions (RBFs). Additional fix-point constraints are specified on the boundary of the deformable region. Combining

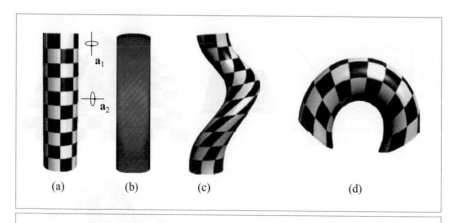

Figure 5.40: Rotational deformations of a cylinder: (*a*) original, (*b*) color-coded scale parameter, (*c*) rotation around axis $\mathbf{a}_1$, and (*d*) rotation around axis $\mathbf{a}_2$.

these constraints and selecting the constraint locations as RBF centers lead to a symmetric linear system. The number of unknowns depends on the number of constraints and is typically of order $m = \sqrt{n}$, where n is the size of the point cloud. However, since the triharmonic radial basis function $\phi(r) = r^3$ has global support, the system is dense and its solution has cubic complexity $O(m^3) = O(n^{1.5})$. Thus, Botsch and Kobbelt [BK05] present an efficient method to solve the system incrementally, using basis function precomputation to further enhance performance. The final resulting displacement function supports C^2 boundary constraints and has optimal fairness as it is the solution of a constrained energy minimization.

Topology Control

An important issue in shape design using free-form deformation is the handling of self-intersections. During deformation, parts of the deformable region can intersect other parts of the surface, which leads to an inconsistent surface representation. A solution to this problem requires a method for detecting and resolving such collisions.

Collision Detection   Similar to Boolean operations (Section 5.3.2), this requires an inside-outside classification to determine which parts of the surface have penetrated others. Thus, the classification predicate defined in Section 5.3.2 can be used for computing collisions between the deformable region χ_d and the zero-region χ_0.

First, the closest point $\mathbf{q} \in \chi_0$ to each sample point $\mathbf{p} \in \chi_d$ is computed. This defines an empty sphere s_p around $\mathbf{p}$ with radius $\|\mathbf{p}-\mathbf{q}\|$. If the point $\mathbf{p}$ only moves within this sphere during deformation, it is guaranteed not to intersect with the

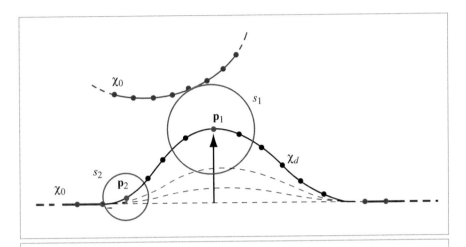

Figure 5.41: Temporal coherence for accelerating collision detection during deformation. The points $\mathbf{p}_1$ and $\mathbf{p}_2$ can move within the spheres s_1 and s_2, respectively, without the risk of an intersection with the zero-region.

zero-region (see Figure 5.41). So, in addition to exploiting spatial coherence as for Boolean classification, this approach also exploits the temporal coherence induced by the continuous change of deformation field during interactive editing. The classification predicate Ω has to be reevaluated only when $\mathbf{p}$ leaves s_p, which at the same time provides a new estimate for the updated sphere s_p. Note that this method for collision detection does not consider self-intersections of the deformable region χ_d.

Collision Handling   There are different ways to respond to a detected collision. The simplest solution is to undo the last deformation step and recover the surface geometry prior to the collision. Alternatively, the penetrating parts of the surface can be joined using a Boolean union operation to maintain the validity of the surface. Figure 5.42 shows an editing session, where a deformation causes a self-intersection. After performing a Boolean union, a sharp intersection curve is created as shown in (d). In the context of free-form deformation it is often more desirable to create a smooth transition between the two combined surface parts. Thus, the particle simulation described in Section 5.3.2 can be used to blend the intersection region.

5.3.4 DYNAMIC SAMPLING

Large deformations may cause strong distortions in the distribution of sample points on the surface that can lead to an insufficient local-sampling density. To

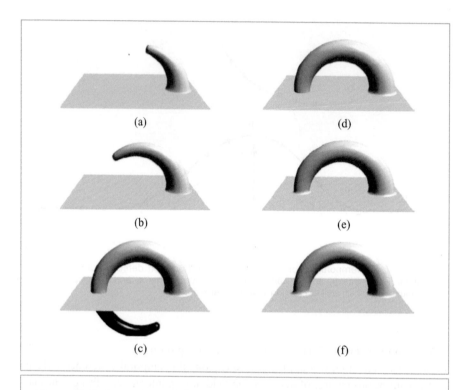

Figure 5.42: Interactive modeling session with collision detection: (*a–b*) intermediate steps of the deformation, (*c*) collision detection, where the blue part has been detected as self-intersecting, (*d*) Boolean union with sharp intersection curve, and (*e–f*) particle-based blending with different fall-off functions.

prevent the point cloud from ripping apart and to maintain a high surface quality, new samples have to be included where the sampling density becomes too low. This requires a method for measuring the surface stretch to detect regions of insufficient sampling density. Then new sample points have to be inserted and their position on the surface determined. Additionally, scalar attributes (e.g., color values or texture coordinates) have to be preserved or interpolated.

Measuring Surface Stretch

The first fundamental form known from differential geometry [dC76] can be used to measure the local distortion of a surface under deformation. Let **u** and **v** be two orthogonal tangent vectors of unit length at a sample point **p**. When applying a deformation, the point **p** is shifted to a new position **p**′ and the two tangent vectors are mapped to new vectors **u**′ and **v**′. Local stretching implies that **u**′ and **v**′ might no longer be orthogonal to each other nor do they preserve their unit length. The tangent vectors $\mathbf{u}'$ and $\mathbf{v}'$ are conjugate diameters of the ellipse defined by $\mathbf{x}^T\mathbf{Q}\mathbf{x} = 1$, where

$$\mathbf{Q} = \begin{bmatrix} \mathbf{u}'^2 & \mathbf{u}' \cdot \mathbf{v}' \\ \mathbf{u}' \cdot \mathbf{v}' & \mathbf{v}'^2 \end{bmatrix}^{-1} . \tag{5.31}$$

The eigenvalues λ_1 and λ_2 of this matrix yield the minimum and maximum stretch factors and the corresponding eigenvectors $\mathbf{e}_1$ and $\mathbf{e}_2$ define the principal directions into which this stretching occurs (see Figure 5.43).

The amount of this distortion can be measured by taking the ratio of the two eigenvalues of the matrix $\mathbf{Q}$ (local anisotropy) or by taking their product (local change of surface area). When the local distortion becomes too strong, new samples have

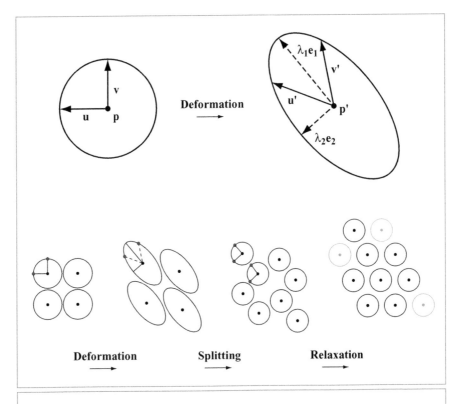

Figure 5.43: 2D illustration of local stretching after deformation and dynamic resampling.

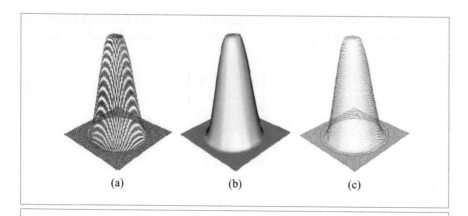

(a)   (b)   (c)

Figure 5.44: Dynamic sampling, and deformation of a plane: (*a*) local stretching, blue corresponds to zero stretch while red indicates maximum stretch, (*b*) surface after resampling, and (*c*) sampling distribution.

to be inserted to reestablish the prescribed sampling density. These new samples replace the existing point **p** and are positioned along the main axis of the ellipse defined by **Q** (see Figure 5.44).

Filter Operations

Whenever a splitting operation is applied, both the geometric position and the scalar function values for the newly generated sample points have to be determined. Both these operations can be described as the application of a filtering operator: a *relaxation filter* determines the sample positions, while an *interpolation filter* is applied to obtain the function values.

Relaxation   Introducing new sample points through a splitting operation creates local imbalances in the sampling distribution. To obtain a more uniform sampling pattern, a relaxation operator is applied that moves the sample points within the surface (see Figure 5.44). Similar to Turk [Tur92] (see also Section 4.3), a simple point repulsion scheme is used with a repulsion force that drops linearly with distance. This confines the radius of influence of each sample point to its local neighborhood, which allows very efficient computation of the relaxation forces. The resulting displacement vector is then projected into the points tangent plane to keep the samples on the surface.

Interpolation   Once the position of a new sample point **p** is fixed using the relaxation filter, the associated function values need to be determined. This can be achieved using an interpolation filter by computing a local average of the function values of neighboring sample points. The relaxation filter potentially moves all points of the neighborhood of **p**. This tangential drift leads to distortions in the associated scalar functions. To deal with this problem a copy of each point that carries scalar attributes is created and its position is fixed during relaxation. In particular, for each sample that is split a copy is maintained with its original data. These points will only be used for interpolating scalar values, they are not part of the current geometry description. Since these samples are *dead* but their function values still *live*, they are called *zombies*. Zombies will undergo the same transformation during a deformation operation as living points, but their positions will not be altered during relaxation. Thus, zombies accurately describe the scalar attributes without distortions. Therefore, zombies are only used for interpolation, while for relaxation only living points are considered. After an editing operation is completed, all zombies will be deleted from the representation.

Figure 5.45 illustrates this dynamic resampling method for a very large deformation that leads to a substantial increase in the number of sample points. While the initial plane consists of 40,000 points, the final model contains 432,812 points, clearly demonstrating the robustness and scalability of the method in regions of extreme surface stretch.

Downsampling
Apart from lower sampling density caused by surface stretching, deformations can also lead to an increase in sampling density, where the surface is squeezed. It might be desirable to eliminate samples in such regions while editing, to keep the overall sampling distribution uniform. However, dynamically removing samples also has some drawbacks. Consider a surface that is first squeezed and then stretched back to its original shape. If samples get removed during squeezing, surface information such as color will be lost, which leads to increased blurring when the surface is stretched again. Thus, instead of dynamic sample deletion, an optional garbage collection can be performed at the end of the editing operation. To reduce the sampling density, any of the simplification methods of Section 4.3 can be used.

5.3.5 CONCLUSION

The semi-implicit nature of point-based surface models has proven useful for inside-outside tests required for Boolean modeling operations and collision detection. Adaptive sampling of sharp intersection curves, which is important for high visual quality, can be implemented easily using an iterative procedure based on MLS projections.

Point-based representations are also suitable for interactive shape deformations, in particular when large edits require dynamic adaptations of the model discretization.

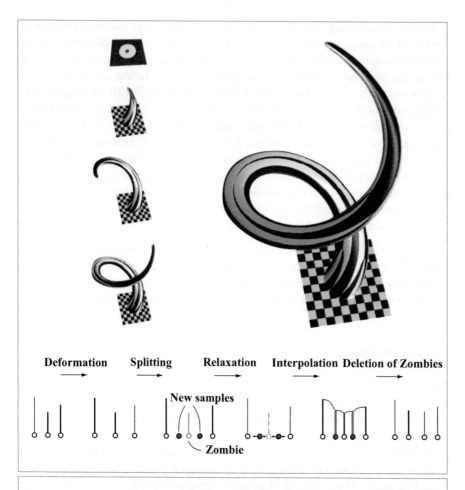

Figure 5.45: A very large deformation using a combination of translational and rotational motion. The *left column* shows intermediate steps with the *top* image indicating zero- and one-regions. Each point of the surface carries texture coordinates, which are interpolated during resampling and used for texturing the surface with a checkerboard pattern. The *bottom row* illustrates this interpolation process, where the function values are indicated by vertical lines.

The trade-off between efficient query time and light-weight updates to the search data structure used for nearest-neighbor computations is central in this context (see Section 4.4). Caching of local neighborhood information can substantially improve the performance, while still being conceptually simpler than consistent connectivity updates required for dynamic remeshing.

CHAPTER SIX

Zwicker, Matthias

Department of Computer Science and Engineering
University of California, San Diego
9500 Gilman Drive
La Jolla, CA 92093-0404
USA
mzwicker@ucsd.edu
Tel: +1 959 922 4720

Kobbelt, Leif

RWTH Aachen
Lehrstuhl für Informatik VIII
52056 Aachen
Germany
kobbelt@informatik.rwth-aachen.de
Tel: +49 241 8021 801
Fax: +49 241 8022 899

Adamson, Anders

TU Darmstadt
Interactive Graphics Systems Group
Fraunhoferstr. 5
64283 Darmstadt
Germany
anders.adamson@gris.informatik.tu-darmstadt.de
Tel: +49 6151 155 673
Fax: +49 6151 155 669

Dachsbacher, Carsten

Universität Erlangen - Nürnberg
Lehrstuhl Graphische Datenverarbeitung
Am Weichselgarten 9
91058 Erlangen
Germany
dachsbacher@cs.fau.de
Tel: +49 9131 852 9925
Fax: +49 9131 852 9931

Botsch, Mario

ETH Zurich
Computer Graphics Laboratory
Haldeneggsteig 4
8092 Zürich
Switzerland
mario.botsch@inf.ethz.ch
Tel: +41 44 632 74 46
Fax: +41 44 632 15 96

Adams, Bart

K.U. Leuven
Department of Computer Science
Celestijnenlaan 200A
3001 Heverlee
Belgium
Bart.Adams@cs.kuleuven.be
Tel: +32 16 327 830
Fax: +32 16 327 996

Wand, Michael

Stanford University
Max Planck Center VCC
Computer Graphics Laboratory
Computer Science Department
353 Serra Mall
Stanford, CA 94305-9025
USA
mwand@stanford.edu
Tel: +1 650 725 6532
Fax: +1 650 725 6528

Stamminger, Marc

Universität Erlangen - Nürnberg
Lehrstuhl Graphische Datenverarbeitung
Am Weichselgarten 9
91058 Erlangen
Germany
stamminger@cs.fau.de
Tel: +49 9131 852 9919
Fax: +49 9131 852 9931

6 RENDERING

INTRODUCTION

This chapter presents an overview and detailed discussion of high-quality rendering methods for point-sampled geometry. Section 6.1 starts with a review of the fundamentals of surface splatting (EWA), one of the most widely used techniques for advanced point rendering. Both the signal processing fundamentals are elaborated and practical implementations are presented. Section 6.2 focuses on improvements of point splatting as well as on implementations using state-of-the-art GPUs.

Section 6.3 introduces ray tracing of MLS surfaces as an alternative for high-quality point rendering. Rendering of very large point models is addressed in Section 6.4 where a multiresolution rendering algorithm is presented. A powerful acceleration structure for hardware-accelerated, high performance point rendering concludes this chapter with Section 6.5.

6.1 SPLATTING FUNDAMENTALS

Matthias Zwicker

6.1.1 OVERVIEW

Splatting is a simple and efficient technique for rendering high-quality images of point-sampled surfaces. In contrast to the ray-tracing algorithms described in Section 6.3, splatting is a forward-projection approach that uses a z-buffer algorithm to resolve visibility. Splatting can efficiently process unstructured point-sets without any additional acceleration structures such as spatial hierarchies, which are often required in ray-tracing approaches. It is, however, straightforward to combine splatting with hierarchical data structures, such as described in Section 4.4, to obtain progressive or level-of-detail (LOD) rendering. In addition, splatting achieves high image quality by including a principled texture antialiasing technique.

The basic idea of splatting is illustrated in Figure 6.1. A naive approach to point rendering would perspectively project each 3D point to the image plane as in Figure 6.1a, and assign the color of the point to the closest pixel. Obviously, this leads to holes in the rendered image if the surface is not sampled with sufficient density. On the other hand, if more than one point projects to the same pixel, the rendering result is dependent on the order in which the points are projected. Splatting, as shown in Figure 6.1b, solves these problems by distributing the color of each projected point among its neighboring pixels. Each point is associated with a *footprint* function $\rho_i(\mathbf{x})$ that weighs the color contributions to the neighboring pixels.[1] Footprint functions are usually smooth, decay quickly with increasing distance from the center, and have local support as indicated by the ellipses in Figure 6.1b. The same fundamental approach is also popular for volume rendering [Wes90, MC98, MMC99, ZPvBG01a].

Let us denote an image by a function $\phi(x, y)$ of 2D image coordinates (x, y). To simplify the notation, we assume the function is scalar-valued (i.e., it represents a

---

1   Early point-rendering algorithms used a different approach based on image space filtering [GD98, PZvBG00].

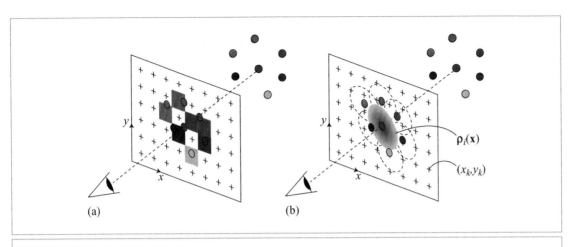

Figure 6.1: Point rendering by splatting. (*a*) Naive forward projection and rendering of point samples. (*b*) By splatting footprint functions each point sample distributes its contribution among neighboring pixels.

grayscale image). For color images, we would simply use three independent channels, for example, representing red, green, and blue color components. An image of a point-sampled surface rendered with a splatting algorithm can be represented as

$$\phi(x, y) = \sum_i c_i \rho_i(x, y), \tag{6.1}$$

where summation is over the indices i of all points $\{\mathbf{p}_i\}$ of the surface, ρ_i are individual footprint functions, and c_i are grayscale values associated with each point.

Unfortunately, Equation (6.1) does not reproduce surfaces with constant values $c_i \equiv c$, which can lead to visible artifacts. Hence, we extend the basic splatting formulation by normalizing Equation (6.1):

$$\phi(x, y) = \frac{\sum_i c_i \rho_i(x, y)}{\sum_i \rho_i(x, y)}. \tag{6.2}$$

This guarantees that constant surfaces are reproduced exactly, independent of the footprint function.

Equation (6.2) suggests a two-pass algorithm for rendering, which is summarized in Figure 6.2. In the first pass, we iterate over all points and compute their splat footprints ρ_i and shaded values c_i. The footprints are evaluated at each pixel, or *rasterized*, and their contributions are accumulated in a framebuffer. At each pixel (x, y), the framebuffer stores the sum of the weighted contributions $c(x, y) = \sum_i c_i \rho_i(x, y)$,

```
splat_rendering(p[], c[], w[], z[]) {

  for(all points i in p[]) {
    rho_i = footprint(p[i]);
    c_i = shade(p[i]);
    rasterize(rho_i, c_i, c[], w[], z[]);
  }
  for(all pixels [x,y]) {
    c[x,y] /= w[x,y];
  }
}
```

Figure 6.2: Pseudocode of the splatting algorithm.

the sum of the weights $w(x, y) = \sum_i \rho_i(x, y)$, and a depth value $z(x, y)$ for z-buffering. In the second pass, we iterate over all pixels and normalize the accumulated colors by dividing by the sum of the weights.

At the core of the splatting algorithm described in this section is a thorough approach to designing suitable footprint functions for high-quality rendering. We show that splatting is best understood as a resampling process in terms of signal processing. A point-based surface is interpreted as a discrete set of surface samples in 3D, which is mapped to a new set of image samples located at pixel positions during rendering. However, resampling is prone to visually disturbing *aliasing* artifacts if the resampled surface does not obey the *Nyquist limit* of the discrete pixel grid. Much of this section is dedicated to providing an understanding of these effects.

We review fundamental results from the signal-processing theory in Section 6.1.2 and explain aliasing in Section 6.1.3. We present a framework for ideal resampling with antialiasing in Section 6.1.4. Completing the necessary background for the following sections, we summarize the characteristics of Gaussian filters in Section 6.1.5. In Section 6.1.6, we describe how resampling with Gaussian filters can be applied to splatting, and we present an efficient algorithm that is based on high-quality antialiased footprint functions. We show results of our approach and compare it to other texture-filtering techniques in Section 6.1.7.

6.1.2 SIGNAL-PROCESSING BASICS

While, conceptually, computer graphics often deal with continuous representations of graphics models, in practice, computer-generated images are represented by a discrete array of samples. Digital image synthesis [Gla95] involves the conversion between continuous and discrete representations, which requires reconstructing and sampling multidimensional signals such as 2D textures, 3D point-sampled surfaces, 3D volume data, or animated image sequences. This may cause aliasing artifacts that appear as visually disturbing effects including moiré patterns and jagged edges, or flickering in animations.

The signal-processing theory precisely characterizes the relation between discrete and continuous signals, where a discrete signal is a signal that is represented by individual signal values, or samples, on a uniform grid. The main operations derived from this theory are *sampling*, which is the conversion of a continuous signal into a discrete signal, and *reconstruction*, which is the conversion of a discrete signal into a continuous signal. The key tool in signal processing is the *Fourier transform*, which is applied to represent continuous and discrete signals in the *frequency domain*. In this section, we review basic definitions and results from the signal-processing theory and Fourier analysis. We use these results in Section 6.1.3 to analyze the effects of sampling and to understand the aliasing phenomenon. For a more detailed introduction to signal processing we refer the reader to standard textbooks [DM84].

Linear Filtering, Convolution, and the Fourier Transform

A filter is an operator that takes a signal[2] as an input and generates a modified signal or a response as an output. The easiest class of filters to understand is linear space invariant filters. Mathematically, a filter is L linear if

$$L\{af + bg\} = aL\{f\} + bL\{g\} \qquad (6.3)$$

for any two scalars a and b, and any two signals $f : \mathbb{R} \to \mathbb{R}$ and $g : \mathbb{R} \to \mathbb{R}$. It is space invariant if

$$f(x) = L\{g(x)\} \Leftrightarrow f(x - s) = L\{g(x - s)\} \qquad (6.4)$$

for any spatial shift s. A linear space invariant filter L is uniquely characterized by its *impulse response* $h(x)$ (i.e., its output resulting from an impulse input δ). The impulse function δ is defined as

$$\delta(x) = 0 \quad \text{if} \quad x \neq 0 \quad \text{and} \quad \int_{-\infty}^{\infty} \delta(x)dx = 1. \qquad (6.5)$$

---

2   The term *signal* is synonymous to the term *function*.

It can be shown that, as a consequence [Gla95], the response of a linear space invariant filter to any input signal $f(x)$ is given by the *convolution* of $f(x)$ and $h(x)$:

$$L\{f(x)\} = \int_{-\infty}^{\infty} f(t)h(x - t)dt = (f \otimes h)(x). \tag{6.6}$$

Convolution is as a *linear operator* on the signal, denoted by the symbol $\otimes$.

We can analyze the properties of a filter by computing its eigenfunctions and eigenvalues. The eigenfunctions of linear space invariant filters are *complex exponentials*, and the eigenvalues are given by the *Fourier transform* of its impulses response, which is called its *frequency response*. The Fourier transform of a signal $f(x)$ is called the spectrum of the signal, denoted by $F(\omega)$. It is defined as

$$F(\omega) = \int_{-\infty}^{\infty} f(x)e^{-j\omega x}dx, \tag{6.7}$$

where ω is the angular frequency. Likewise, the inverse Fourier transform describes the signal in terms of its spectrum:

$$f(x) = \frac{1}{2\pi} \int_{-\infty}^{\infty} F(\omega)e^{j\omega x}d\omega. \tag{6.8}$$

We write $f(x) \leftrightarrow F(\omega)$ to relate the *spatial* and the *frequency domain* representation of the signal. One of the most useful properties of the Fourier transform is that the Fourier transform of the convolution of two signals is the product of their Fourier transforms (i.e., $f \otimes g \leftrightarrow FG$) and vice versa (i.e., $fg \leftrightarrow F \otimes G/(2\pi)$) [Gla95].

6.1.3 FREQUENCY ANALYSIS OF ALIASING

To study aliasing we interpret images, surface textures, point-sampled surfaces, or volume data as multidimensional signals. In the following discussion, we will focus on one-dimensional signals to clarify the explanations, implying that the same concepts also hold in the multidimensional setting. We analyze the sampling of a continuous signal using the Fourier transform and frequency domain representations, shown in Figures 6.3 and 6.4.

Sampling a continuous signal $a_c(x)$ is performed by multiplying it with an impulse train $i^T(x)$ (Figure 6.3b), which is a sum of impulse distributed with uniform spacing T:

$$i^T(x) = \sum_n \delta(x/T - n). \tag{6.9}$$

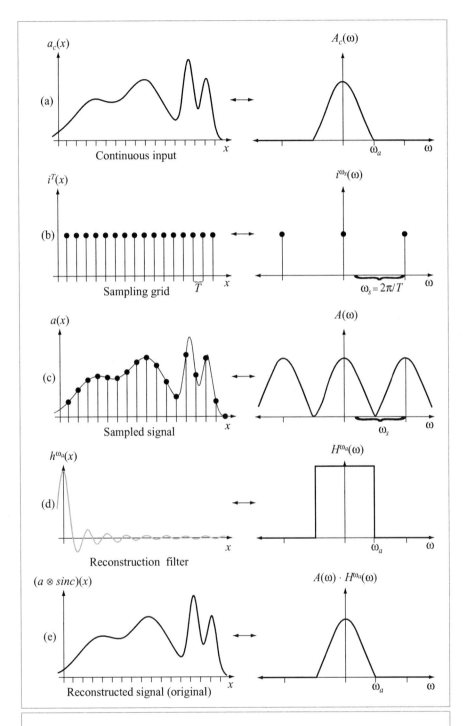

Figure 6.3: Frequency analysis of aliasing: aliasing free reconstruction. (*a*) Continuous input signal, (*b*) sampling grid, (*c*) sampled signal, (*d*) reconstruction filter, (*e*) reconstructed signal.

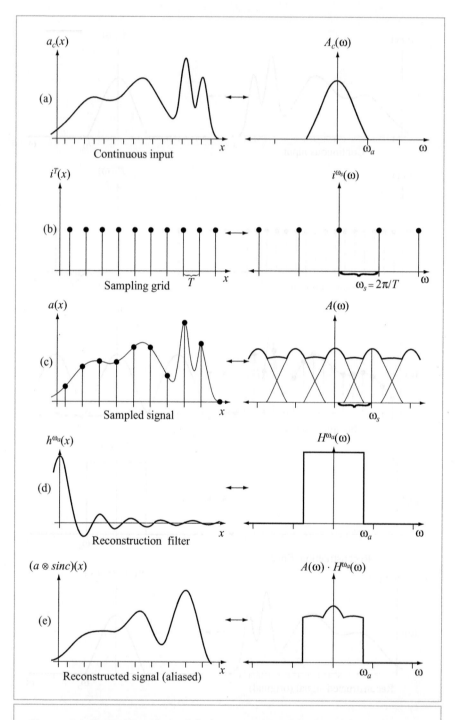

Figure 6.4: Frequency analysis of aliasing: occurrence of aliasing. (*a*) Continuous input signal, (*b*) sampling grid, (*c*) sampled signal, (*d*) reconstruction filter, (*e*) reconstructed signal.

Therefore, we obtain the discrete signal as $a(x) = a_c(x)i^T(x)$. In the frequency domain the spectrum of the discrete signal $A(\omega)$ is given by the convolution $A(\omega) = A_c(\omega) \otimes I^{\omega_s}(\omega)$. Here, $A_c(\omega)$ is the spectrum of the continuous signal $a_c(x)$. Furthermore, I^{ω_s} is the Fourier transform of the impulse train $i^T(x)$, which is another impulse train $I^{\omega_s}(\omega) = \omega_s i^{\omega_s}(\omega)$. The sample distance in the frequency domain ω_s is inversely proportional to the sampling distance T in the spatial domain (i.e., $\omega_s = 2\pi/T$). Since multiplication in the spatial domain corresponds to convolution in the frequency domain, the spectrum of the discrete signal consists of a superposition of replicas of the spectrum of the continuous signal spaced at a distance ω_s (Figure 6.3c).

To reconstruct the spectrum of the continuous signal, we have to eliminate all replicas of A_c from A except the central one. This is achieved by multiplying $A(\omega)$ with a box function $H^{\omega_a}(\omega) = 1$ for $\omega \leq \omega_a$ and 0 otherwise, where ω_a is the maximum frequency occurring in a_c or A_c, respectively. H^{ω_a} is called an *ideal low-pass filter* with cutoff frequency ω_a (Figure 6.3d, right), since it passes low frequencies $\omega \leq \omega_a$ unchanged and suppresses high frequencies $\omega > \omega_a$ completely. In the spatial domain, the impulse response of H^{ω_a} is a *sinc* function:

$$H^{\omega_a}(\omega) \leftrightarrow h^{\omega_a}(x) = 2\omega_a \frac{sin(2\pi\omega_a x)}{2\pi\omega_a x}. \qquad (6.10)$$

Since the reconstructed spectrum $A(\omega)H^{\omega_a}(\omega)$ in Figure 6.3e is identical to the original spectrum $A(\omega)$ (Figure 6.3a), the inverse Fourier transform perfectly reconstructs the original signal (Figure 6.3e, left).

However, if the maximum frequency ω_a in the spectrum of A_c is higher than half the sampling distance in the frequency domain (i.e., $\omega_a > \omega_s/2$), the replicas overlap, as shown in Figure 6.4c on the right.

In this case, it is impossible to reconstruct the original spectrum A_c from A. When A is multiplied with the low-pass filter (see Figure 6.4d), high frequencies from the replicas appear as low frequencies in the original spectrum (Figure 6.4e), which is called *aliasing*: the high frequencies in the original signal masquerade, or alias, as low frequencies in the reconstructed signal (Figure 6.4e, left).

Aliasing need not occur if the continuous input signal is band-limited to a *bandwidth* ω_a; in other words, it has no frequencies above ω_a, or $A_c(\omega) = 0$ for $\|\omega\| \geq \omega_a$. A continuous signal with bandwidth ω_a can be reconstructed exactly if the sampling frequency ω_s is at least twice the bandwidth (i.e., $\omega_s \geq 2\omega_a$). This fact is known as the *sampling theorem*, and $\omega_s = 2\omega_a$ is called the *Nyquist frequency* of the signal. Equivalently, the frequency $\omega_s/2$ is also called the *Nyquist limit* of the sampling grid. Sampling a signal that contains frequencies above the Nyquist limit produces aliasing.

6.1.4 RESAMPLING

Resampling is the process of transforming a sampled input signal from a *source* to a *destination* domain, and representing the signal in the destination domain on a given uniform sampling grid. In general, the sampling positions in the source domain are not mapped to sampling positions in the destination domain in a one-to-one fashion. Hence, resampling includes four steps. First, a continuous signal is *reconstructed* in the source domain; second, the continuous signal is *mapped* from source to destination domain; third, the continuous signal in the destination domain is *band-limited* to the Nyquist limit of the output sampling grid; and fourth, the band-limited signal is *sampled*. By band-limiting the transformed signal *before* sampling, aliasing artifacts due to the subsequent sampling step are avoided. Band-limiting before sampling is also called *prefiltering*.

Resampling was first introduced to computer graphics by Paul Heckbert in the context of texture mapping and image warping [Hec89]. In texture mapping, the source domain is a texture image, the destination domain is the output image plane, and the mapping from the source to the destination domain is a concatenation of a 2D to 3D parameterization of the texture onto a surface followed by perspective 3D to 2D projection. Resampling procedures have also been applied to volume rendering [ZPvBG01a] and to ray tracing [Ige99]. We will describe a resampling algorithm for point-based rendering in Section 6.1.6.

We illustrate the resampling procedure in the 1D setting in Figure 6.5. The generalization to higher dimensions is straightforward. Note also that we remove the restriction that the input signal be sampled on a uniform grid. Therefore, we will not use convolution, but a slightly more general approach to signal reconstruction.

Resampling consists of four steps:

1. In the first step, we reconstruct a continuous signal from the input samples. The continuous input signal is a weighted sum of sample values c_i and reconstruction kernels r_i in source space coordinates t:

$$f(t) = \sum_i c_i r_i(t). \tag{6.11}$$

   Here, the samples c_i may be located at *nonuniform* sampling positions, and the reconstruction kernels r_i may be different for each sample. Hence, Equation (6.11) does not correspond to a convolution. We show in Section 6.1.6 how to choose suitable kernels for surface splatting.

2. We denote the mapping from source to destination domain by $x = m(t)$, and $t = m^{-1}(x)$ is its inverse. Here, x denotes destination space coordinates.

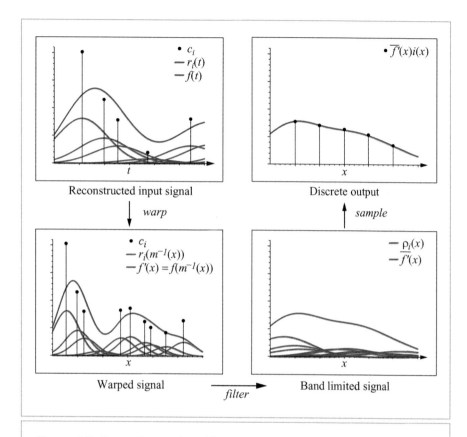

Figure 6.5: Resampling consists of four steps: reconstruction, warping, filtering, and sampling.

Applying this mapping to the input function yields the continuous function in the destination domain:

$$f'(x) = (f \circ m^{-1})(x) = f(m^{-1}(x)). \tag{6.12}$$

3. Now $f'(x)$ is prefiltered using a low-pass filter $h(x)$, resulting in the continuous output function

$$\bar{f}'(x) = (f' \otimes h)(x) = \int_{-\infty}^{\infty} f'(\xi)h(x - \xi)d\xi. \tag{6.13}$$

4. Finally, the continuous output signal is sampled by multiplying it with an impulse train i to produce the discrete output $\bar{f}'(x)i(x)$.

This procedure suggests a multipass approach, in which we first reconstruct, then warp, and convolve the input signal. However, we can avoid the explicit construction of the continuous signal by reordering the above operations. We derive an expression for the warped continuous output function by expanding the operations in reverse order:

$$\bar{f}'(x) = \int_{-\infty}^{\infty} h(x - \xi) \sum_i c_i r_i(m^{-1}(\xi))d\xi$$

$$= \sum_i c_i \rho_i(x), \tag{6.14}$$

where

$$\rho_i(x) = \int_{-\infty}^{\infty} h(x - \xi) r_i(m^{-1}(\xi))d\xi. \tag{6.15}$$

We call the warped and filtered reconstruction kernel $\rho_i(x)$ a *resampling filter*, which is expressed as a convolution in the destination space here. Equation (6.14) states that we can first warp and filter each reconstruction kernel individually to construct the resampling filters and then sum up the contributions of these filters in the destination space. This allows us to implement an efficient resampling scheme for interactive rendering as we show in Section 6.1.6.

6.1.5 GAUSSIAN FILTERS

Gaussian functions play an important role in many areas of applied mathematics, in particular in statistics. For digital-signal processing they are attractive because they provide a unique combination of reasonable spectral characteristics and analytical properties. We start by introducing 1D Gaussians and analyzing their filter characteristics. It is straightforward to generalize Gaussians to higher dimensions. In this section, we summarize the properties of 2D filters that are prerequisite for our techniques described in Section 6.1.6.

One-dimensional Gaussian Filters

A one-dimensional Gaussian function is defined as

$$g_{\sigma^2}(x) = \frac{1}{\sigma\sqrt{2\pi}} e^{-\frac{1}{2}\frac{x^2}{\sigma^2}}, \tag{6.16}$$

where σ^2 is called the *variance*, and σ the *standard deviation*. In this form, the Gaussian is normalized to have a unit integral:

$$\int_{-\infty}^{\infty} g_{\sigma^2}(x)dx = 1. \tag{6.17}$$

The Fourier transform of the 1D Gaussian is another Gaussian:

$$g_{\sigma^2}(x) \leftrightarrow G_{\sigma^2}(\omega) = e^{-\sigma^2\omega^2/2} = \sigma\sqrt{2\pi}g_{1/\sigma^2}(\omega). \tag{6.18}$$

However, note that the Gaussian in the frequency domain is not normalized to have a unit integral.

Figure 6.6 illustrates the relation of 1D Gaussians in the spatial and the frequency domain. A narrow impulse response in the spatial domain corresponds to a wide response in the frequency domain, and vice versa. For comparison, we also show the box function of an ideal low-pass filter in the frequency domain. Assuming that the sampling grid has unit spacing, the cutoff frequency of the box is set to $\omega = 1/2$. Hence, the box filter band limits the signal to the Nyquist limit of the grid. Clearly, choosing a suitable standard deviation for the Gaussian is a trade-off between blurriness and aliasing in the output signal (i.e., a trade-off between a deficiency of high frequencies in the pass band and leakage in the stop band).[3] For image-processing applications, values between $1 < \sigma < 2$ are often appropriate.

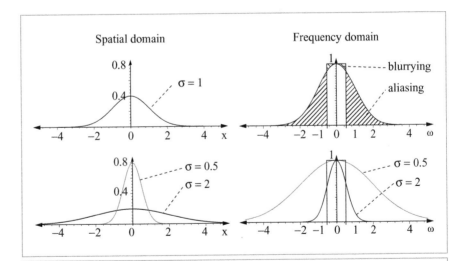

Figure 6.6: Gaussians in 1D: the spatial domain representation is on the *left*, with the corresponding frequency domain representation on the *right*.

---

3   The book by Glassner [Gla95] is a good reference for more details on filter design in computer graphics.

Two-dimensional Gaussian Filters

It is straightforward to generalize Gaussians to higher dimensions. For our applications, we are most interested in 2D Gaussians defined as

$$g_V(\mathbf{x}) = \frac{1}{2\pi\sqrt{|V|}} e^{-\frac{1}{2}\mathbf{x}^T V^{-1} \mathbf{x}}. \tag{6.19}$$

Here, $\mathbf{V}$ is the symmetric 2×2 *variance matrix*, with $|\mathbf{V}|$ its determinant, and $\mathbf{x}$ is a 2×1 column vector. As in 1D, the 2D Gaussian is normalized to unit integral analogous to Equation (6.17). $\mathbf{V}$ is called the variance matrix because it plays the role of the scalar variance σ^2 of a 1D Gaussian. The variance matrix of 2D Gaussian low-pass filters is usually chosen to be a 2×2 identity matrix for a balanced trade-off between aliasing and blurriness.

The Fourier transform of a 2D Gaussian is again a 2D Gaussian, with a scaling factor similar to the 1D case in Equation (6.18):

$$g_V(\mathbf{x}) \leftrightarrow G_V(\omega) = e^{-\frac{1}{2}\omega^T V \omega} = 2\pi\sqrt{|V|}g_{V^{-1}}(\omega). \tag{6.20}$$

Gaussians offer a number of analytical properties that make them attractive as digital filters for image synthesis. We summarize how *linear mappings* and *convolution* of Gaussians can be evaluated efficiently.

A 2D linear mapping is defined as $\mathbf{y} = \mathbf{M}\mathbf{x}$, where $\mathbf{M}$ is a 2×2 matrix, and $\mathbf{x}$ and $\mathbf{y}$ are column vectors. We apply this mapping to the 2D Gaussian in Equation (6.19) by substituting $\mathbf{x} = \mathbf{M}^{-1}\mathbf{y}$, yielding

$$
\begin{aligned}
g_V(\mathbf{M}^{-1}\mathbf{y}) &= \frac{1}{2\pi\sqrt{|V|}} e^{-\frac{1}{2}(M^{-1}y)^T V^{-1}(M^{-1}y)} \\
&= \frac{|M|}{2\pi\sqrt{|MVM^T|}} e^{-\frac{1}{2}(M^{-1}y)^T V^{-1}(M^{-1}y)} \\
&= |M|g_{MVM^T}(\mathbf{y}).
\end{aligned} \tag{6.21}
$$

Hence, under the linear mapping $\mathbf{M}$, the Gaussian with variance matrix $\mathbf{V}$ is transformed into a Gaussian with variance matrix $\mathbf{MVM}^T$. However, the transformed Gaussian is not normalized to unit integral anymore, but it is scaled with the determinant $|\mathbf{M}|$ (see also [Hec89]).

The convolution of two Gaussians is easily computed in the frequency domain, since convolution in the spatial domain corresponds to multiplication in the frequency domain [Hec89]. With Equation (6.20), we have

$$(g_V \otimes g_W)(\mathbf{x}) \leftrightarrow G_V(\omega) \cdot G_W)(\omega) = e^{-\frac{1}{2}\omega^T V\omega} \cdot e^{-\frac{1}{2}\omega^T W\omega}$$
$$= e^{-\frac{1}{2}\omega^T(V+W)\omega}$$
$$= G_{V+W}(\omega). \qquad (6.22)$$

Therefore, variances are added when two Gaussians are convolved:

$$(g_V \otimes g_W)(\mathbf{x}) = g_{V+W}(\mathbf{x}). \qquad (6.23)$$

6.1.6 SURFACE SPLATTING

Surface splatting renders point-sampled surfaces using a splatting approach as introduced in Section 6.1, and it applies the resampling framework described in Section 6.1.4 to compute antialiased splat footprints [ZPvBG01b]. The key to an efficient implementation for interactive rendering is the use of Gaussian kernels for reconstruction and low-pass filtering. The surface-splatting algorithm is illustrated in Figure 6.7. It proceeds in the following steps, which are described in detail in this section:

- First, we compute suitable 2D Gaussian reconstruction kernels associated with the points of a 3D point-sampled surface. The 2D kernels will be defined on the tangent plane (i.e., source space) at each point.
- Next, we map the Gaussian kernels to 2D image (i.e., destination) space. In contrast to Equation (6.12), each kernel will have its individual mapping function from the corresponding tangent plane to image space.
- We then combine the projected reconstruction kernels with Gaussian low-pass filters in image space to obtain antialised footprints, or resampling kernels.
- Finally, we sample the footprints at pixel locations in image space. The footprints are weighted with the shaded color value of each point. We use a z-buffering algorithm to restrict accumulation of resampling kernels (as in Equation 6.14) to visible surface regions. This process is also called *footprint rasterization*.

Tangent Space Reconstruction Kernels

Let us denote the 3D position of points of a point-sampled surface by column vectors $\mathbf{p}_i$ with elements $(p_{i\{x\}}, p_{i\{y\}}, p_{i\{z\}})$. As shown in Section 4.2, we can compute a tangent plane at each point, which is defined by two orthogonal vectors $\mathbf{u}_i$ and $\mathbf{v}_i$. We use the tangent vectors to specify a 2D parameterization of the tangent plane, and we denote tangent coordinates by column vectors $\mathbf{t} = (t_0, t_1)^T$. Tangent coordinates $\mathbf{t}$ correspond to 3D points $\Phi(\mathbf{t})$ as follows:

$$\Phi(\mathbf{t}) = \left[\mathbf{u}_i \ \mathbf{v}_i \ \mathbf{p}_i \right] \begin{bmatrix} \mathbf{t} \\ 1 \end{bmatrix}. \qquad (6.24)$$

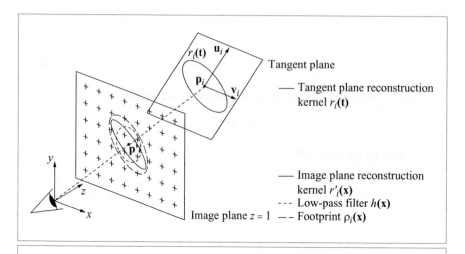

Figure 6.7: Surface splatting overview.

As described in Section 4.3, we can compute ellipses on the tangent plane of each point such that the union of all ellipses forms a watertight surface. We represent these ellipses as quadratic forms in tangent coordinates:

$$\mathbf{t}^T \mathbf{R}_i \mathbf{t} = 1. \tag{6.25}$$

Using this representation, we define Gaussian reconstruction kernels on the tangent plane of each point as

$$r_i(\mathbf{t}) = g_{\mathbf{R}_i}(\mathbf{t}) = \frac{1}{2\pi\sqrt{|\mathbf{R}_i|}} e^{-\frac{1}{2}\mathbf{t}^T \mathbf{R}_i^{-1} \mathbf{t}}. \tag{6.26}$$

This choice of Gaussian reconstruction kernels is a heuristics. In terms of signal-processing theory, Gaussian filters are an approximation of ideal low-pass filters. When using Gaussians, we always strive to find an optimal balance between aliasing and blurriness. However, it is difficult to analyze Gaussians with nonuniform sampling. The above construction is inspired by the use of Gaussians for uniform reconstruction as described in Section 6.1.5. There, a typical choice for the variance matrix is the identity matrix, such that the value of the exponent of the Gaussian is $-1/2$ at the closest neighboring sample. Our approach is an approximation of this behavior in the nonuniform case.

Projection to Image Space

We assume the position of points $\mathbf{p}_i$ and their tangent vectors $\mathbf{u}_i$ and $\mathbf{v}_i$ are expressed in a canonical camera coordinate system as shown in Figure 6.7. Here, the center of projection lies at the origin, and the plane $z = 1$ is the *image plane*.[4] For notational simplicity, let us denote the 2D image coordinates by $\mathbf{x} = (x, y)$. The mapping from tangent to image coordinates is derived from Equation (6.24). Points on the tangent plane are projected to the image plane by dividing by the z-coordinate:

$$\mathbf{x} = m_i(\mathbf{t}) = \begin{bmatrix} \frac{u_{i\{x\}} t_0 + v_{i\{x\}} t_1 + p_{i\{x\}}}{u_{i\{z\}} t_0 + v_{i\{z\}} t_1 + p_{i\{z\}}} \\[2mm] \frac{u_{i\{y\}} t_0 + v_{i\{y\}} t_1 + p_{i\{y\}}}{u_{i\{z\}} t_0 + v_{i\{z\}} t_1 + p_{i\{z\}}} \end{bmatrix}. \tag{6.27}$$

Unfortunately, it is not useful to apply the perspective projection as defined by Equation (6.27) to Gaussian reconstruction kernels. The perspective projection of a Gaussian results in a kernel that is not a Gaussian anymore and that cannot easily be band-limited as in Equation (6.15). Therefore, we use an *affine approximation* of the perspective projection. A linear Taylor series expansion of $m_i(\mathbf{t})$ at $\mathbf{t} = 0$ is given by

$$\mathbf{x} = \tilde{m}_i(\mathbf{t}) = m_i(0) + \mathbf{J}_i \mathbf{t}. \tag{6.28}$$

Here, $\mathbf{J}_i$ is the Jacobian of $m_i(\mathbf{t})$ evaluated at $\mathbf{t} = 0$:

$$\mathbf{J}_i = \frac{1}{p_{i\{z\}}^2} \begin{bmatrix} u_{i\{x\}} p_{i\{z\}} - p_{i\{x\}} u_{i\{z\}} & v_{i\{x\}} p_{i\{z\}} - p_{i\{x\}} v_{i\{z\}} \\ u_{i\{y\}} p_{i\{z\}} - p_{i\{y\}} u_{i\{z\}} & v_{i\{y\}} p_{i\{z\}} - p_{i\{y\}} v_{i\{z\}} \end{bmatrix}. \tag{6.29}$$

We also denote the projection of point $\mathbf{p}_i$ to the image plane by

$$\mathbf{p}_i' = \begin{bmatrix} p_{i\{x\}} / p_{i\{z\}} \\ p_{i\{y\}} / p_{i\{z\}} \end{bmatrix} = m_i(0). \tag{6.30}$$

The inverse of Equation (6.28) is an affine approximation of the mapping from image to tangent space:

$$\mathbf{t} = \tilde{m}_i^{-1}(\mathbf{x}) = \mathbf{J}_i^{-1}(\mathbf{x} - \mathbf{p}_i'). \tag{6.31}$$

With Equation (6.31) and using Equation (6.21), we express the Gaussian reconstruction kernel in image space as

$$r_i(\mathbf{J}_i^{-1}(\mathbf{x} - \mathbf{p}_i')) = r_i'(\mathbf{x} - \mathbf{p}_i') = |\mathbf{J}_i| g_{\mathbf{J}\mathbf{V}_i\mathbf{J}^T}(\mathbf{x} - \mathbf{p}_i'). \tag{6.32}$$

The main advantage of this equation is that it describes the image space reconstruction kernel, again, as a Gaussian. This will allow us to efficiently low-pass filter rendered surfaces as shown in the next section.

---

4   Given that objects are initially specified in some local object coordinate system, object coordinates can be converted to canonic camera coordinates using an appropriate linear transformation.

Low-pass Filtering

We could use the Gaussian reconstruction kernels in image space given by Equation (6.32) directly as the splat footprint functions. However, this would lead to aliasing artifacts because the rendered signal would not be band-limited to the Nyquist frequency of the pixel grid (as explained in Section 6.1.4). Instead, we rewrite Equation (6.15) using the affine approximation $\tilde{m}^{-1}$ from Equation (6.31):

$$
\begin{aligned}
\rho_i(\mathbf{x}) &= \int_{\mathbf{R}} h(\mathbf{x} - \xi) r_i(\mathbf{J}_i^{-1}(\xi - \mathbf{p}_i')) d\xi \\
&= \int_{\mathbf{R}} h(\mathbf{x} - \mathbf{p}_i' - \tau) r_i{}'(\tau) d\tau \\
&= (r_k' \otimes h)(\mathbf{x} - \mathbf{p}_i').
\end{aligned}
\tag{6.33}
$$

Equation (6.33) shows that the resampling kernel can be expressed as a convolution of a reconstruction kernel and a low-pass filter in image space. To obtain an explicit expression for this resampling filter, we choose a Gaussian low-pass filter:

$$
h(\mathbf{x}) = g_{\mathbf{H}}(\mathbf{x}) = \frac{1}{2\pi \sqrt{|\mathbf{H}|}} e^{-\frac{1}{2} \mathbf{x}^T \mathbf{H}^{-1} \mathbf{x}},
\tag{6.34}
$$

where $\mathbf{H}$ is usually a 2×2 identity matrix. Using Gaussian reconstruction and low-pass kernels, Equation (6.33) can be expanded to

$$
\begin{aligned}
\rho_i(\mathbf{x}) &= \frac{1}{|\mathbf{J}_i^{-1}|} (g_{\mathbf{J}_i \mathbf{R}_i \mathbf{J}_i^T} \otimes g_{\mathbf{H}})(\mathbf{x} - \mathbf{p}_i') \\
&= \frac{1}{|\mathbf{J}_i^{-1}|} g_{\mathbf{J}_i \mathbf{R}_i \mathbf{J}_i^T + \mathbf{H}}(\mathbf{x} - \mathbf{p}_i'),
\end{aligned}
\tag{6.35}
$$

where we used Equation (6.22) to evaluate the convolution. Finally, we substitute Equation (6.35) into Equation (6.14) to obtain the rendered, band-limited surface:

$$
\bar{f}'(\mathbf{x}) = \sum_i c_i \frac{1}{|\mathbf{J}_i^{-1}|} g_{\mathbf{J}_i \mathbf{R}_i \mathbf{J}_i^T + \mathbf{H}}(\mathbf{x} - \mathbf{p}_i').
\tag{6.36}
$$

Here, the coefficients c_i are shaded point samples. We use a scalar value to simplify notation; in practice, three color channels are rendered independently. Shading can be performed using any local illumination model. We also discuss more advanced shading approaches in Section 6.2.

Footprint Rasterization

Rasterization is the process of evaluating, or sampling, the footprint functions given by Equation (6.35) at output pixel locations, and accumulating their contributions in a framebuffer. We use a z-buffer to discard contributions from hidden surfaces.

Because Gaussian kernels have an infinite support, in theory, we have to evaluate each kernel at each pixel. However, in practice this is not necessary since the values of the Gaussians decrease quickly as we move away from their centers. Therefore, we evaluate the kernels only in an area where the absolute value of their exponents are smaller than a given threshold. Let us denote the inverse variance matrix of the Gaussian resampling kernel in Equation (6.35) by

$$\mathbf{Q}_i = (\mathbf{J}_i \mathbf{R}_i \mathbf{J}_i^T + \mathbf{H})^{-1},\qquad(6.37)$$

and the value of its exponent by $\mathbf{q}_i(\mathbf{x})$. We evaluate the kernel in the region

$$q_i(\mathbf{x}) = \frac{1}{2}(\mathbf{x} - \mathbf{p}_i')^T \mathbf{Q}_i(\mathbf{x} - \mathbf{p}_i') < \frac{1}{2}r^2,\qquad(6.38)$$

where r is the *cutoff radius*. Typically, r is chosen in the range $1 < r < 2$ for surface splatting. Larger values for r lead to smoother reconstructions, but can also cause visual artifacts and slow down rendering speed. If r is chosen too small, discontinuities or holes may appear in the rendered image.

We compute an axis-aligned bounding box of the area specified by Equation (6.38) to efficiently evaluate the Gaussian kernel. The extents of the bounding box x_{min}, x_{max}, and y_{min}, y_{max} are given by the solutions of the quadratic equations, illustrated in Figure 6.8:

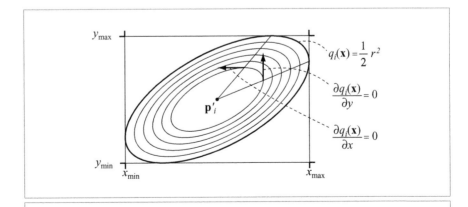

Figure 6.8: Bounding-box calculations for the resampling kernel.

$$x_{min}, x_{max} = \left\{ \frac{\partial q_i(\mathbf{x})}{\partial x} = 0, \quad q_i(\mathbf{x}) = \frac{1}{2}r^2 \right\}, \tag{6.39}$$

and

$$y_{min}, y_{max} = \left\{ \frac{\partial q_i(\mathbf{x})}{\partial y} = 0, \quad q_i(\mathbf{x}) = \frac{1}{2}r^2 \right\}. \tag{6.40}$$

With the discriminant $\Delta = Q_{i\{0,0\}} Q_{i\{1,1\}} - Q_{i\{0,1\}}^2$, the solutions of Equation (6.39) are given by

$$x_{max}, x_{min} = p'_{i\{x\}} \pm r\sqrt{\frac{Q_{i\{1,1\}}}{\Delta}}, \tag{6.41}$$

and

$$y_{max}, y_{min} = p'_{i\{y\}} \pm r\sqrt{\frac{Q_{i\{0,0\}}}{\Delta}}. \tag{6.42}$$

We also need to evaluate the z-coordinate of the tangent plane at each pixel to perform z-buffering. For efficiency reasons, we use the affine approximation of the mapping from image to tangent coordinates as given in Equation (6.31) and combine it with Equation (6.24) to determine a 3D point on the tangent plane:

$$\Phi'(\mathbf{x}) = \Phi(\tilde{m}_i^{-1}(x)) = \begin{bmatrix} \mathbf{u}_i & \mathbf{v}_i & \mathbf{p}_i \end{bmatrix} \begin{bmatrix} \tilde{m}_i^{-1}(\mathbf{x}) \\ 1 \end{bmatrix}. \tag{6.43}$$

Since the footprints usually cover only a few pixels in the image plane, this affine approximation works well in practice. For fast incremental evaluation of Equation (6.43), we note that $\Phi'(\mathbf{p}'_i)_z = p_{i\{z\}}$ and

$$\frac{\partial \Phi'(\mathbf{x})_z}{\partial x} = u_{i\{z\}} J_{i\{0,0\}}^{-1} + v_{i\{z\}} J_{i\{1,0\}}^{-1}, \tag{6.44}$$

and

$$\frac{\partial \Phi'(\mathbf{x})_z}{\partial y} = u_{i\{z\}} J_{i\{0,1\}}^{-1} + v_{i\{z\}} J_{i\{1,1\}}^{-1}. \tag{6.45}$$

In general, the depth complexity of point-sampled scenes we would like to render will be greater than one. However, the summation of resampling kernels at each pixel should be restricted to visible parts of the scene. Therefore, we apply an ϵ-z-buffering scheme to determine visibility of individual splat contributions. The idea is that all splat contributions within an ϵ-depth range should be considered part of the same surface. The threshold ϵ should be chosen proportionally to the depth range spanned by the footprint, for example,

$$\epsilon = \max \left\{ \left\| (x_{max} - x_{min}) \frac{\partial \Phi'(\mathbf{x})_z}{\partial x} \right\|, \left\| (y_{max} - y_{min}) \frac{\partial \Phi'(\mathbf{x})_z}{\partial y} \right\| \right\}. \tag{6.46}$$

Our framebuffer stores depth values $z(x, y)$, accumulated colors $c(x, y)$, and kernel weights $w(x, y)$. Given a new splat contribution with depth z_{new}, color c_{new}, and weight w_{new} at pixel (x, y), the framebuffer is updated as follows:

- If $|z_{new} - z(x, y) < \epsilon|$ the new value is considered part of the visible surface, and its contributions are added to the current framebuffer values (i.e., $c(x, y) = c(x, y) + c_{new}$, and $w(x, y) = w(x, y) + w_{new}$). If in addition $z_{new} < z(x, y)$, the depth buffer is updated too (i.e., $z(x, y) = z_{new}$).
- If $z_{new} < z(x, y) - \epsilon$ the new value lies in front of the visible surface. Hence, its values replace the current framebuffer values (i.e., $z(x, y) = z_{new}$, $c(x, y) = c_{new}$, and $w(x, y) = w_{new}$).
- Otherwise, the new contribution belongs to a hidden surface behind the visible surface and, hence, is discarded.

We summarize the splat rasterization algorithm with ϵ-z-buffering in Figure 6.9. This function should be called in a general splatting framework as described in Section 6.1. The input of the rasterization algorithm is the point position $\mathbf{p}_i$ and tangent vectors $\mathbf{u}_i$ and $\mathbf{v}_i$, the inverse of the Jacobian $\mathbf{J}_i^{-1}$ (Equation 6.29), the conic matrix $\mathbf{Q}_i$ (Equation 6.37), the shaded color c_{new}, and the cutoff radius r. Rasterization updates the framebuffer arrays storing accumulated colors $c(x, y)$, weights $w(x, y)$, and depth values $z(x, y)$. We use efficient incremental computation of the z-value and the exponent of the Gaussian kernel at each pixel.

6.1.7 RESULTS AND COMPARISON

In Figure 6.10, we illustrate the behavior of surface-splatting footprints in the image plane in different situations. We visualize isocontours of the footprint functions at $q_i(\mathbf{x}) = 1/2$. Note that the low-pass filter in the image plane always has the same shape. It only depends on the output sampling grid, but it is independent of the mapping function. Its variance matrix is an identity matrix, hence the visualized isocontour is a unit circle. Under minification, as shown on the left in Figure 6.10, the footprint shape is dominated by the low-pass filter. Considering the variance matrix of the resampling filter in Equation (6.35), this is intuitively clear: when the mapping is minifying the input function, its Jacobian scales down the reconstruction filter, and the variance matrix is dominated by the contribution of the low-pass filter. On the other hand, the resampling filter is largely determined by the reconstruction filter under magnification, as shown in the middle of Figure 6.10. In this case, the Jacobian scales up the reconstruction filter, and the variance matrix of the resampling filter is dominated by the enlarged reconstruction filter. Moreover, under anisotropic minification-magnification, the Jacobian anisotropically scales the reconstruction filter, as shown on the right in Figure 6.10. The scaling guarantees that the resampling filter is always wider than both the reconstruction and low-pass filter, so it is impossible that the filter falls between samples of the output grid.

```
rasterize(p[], u[], v[], inv_J[], Q[], c_new, r, c[], w[], z[]) {
x_p = p[0]/p[2];
y_p = p[1]/p[2];
Delta = Q[0,0]*Q[1,1]−*Q[0,1]*Q[1,0];
x_min = floor(x_p − r*sqrt(Q[1,1]/Delta));
x_max = ceil(x_p + r*sqrt(Q[1,1]/Delta));
y_min = floor(y_p − r*sqrt(Q[0,0]/Delta));
y_max = ceil(y_p + r*sqrt(Q[0,0]/Delta));
dzdx = u[2]*inv_J[0,0]+v[2]*inv_J[1,0];
dzdy = u[2]*inv_J[0,1]+v[2]*inv_J[1,1];
ddq = 2*Q[0,0];
dx = x_min−x_p;
epsilon = max(abs((x_max−x_min)*dzdx,abs((y_max−y_min)*dzdy)));

for(y = y_min; y <= y_max; y++) {
  dy = y − y_p;
  dq = 2*(dx*Q[0,0]+dy*Q[0,1]);
  q = (Q[1,1]*dy+2*Q[0,1]*dx)*dy+Q[0,0]*dx*dx;
  z_new = p[2]+dx*dzdx+dy*dzdy;

  for(x = x_min; x<= x_max; x++) {
    if(q < r*r) {
      w_new = f*exp(−1/2*q);
      if(z_xy < z[x,y]−epsilon) {
        w[x,y] = w_new;
        c[x,y] = c_new;
        z[x,y] = z_new;
      } else if(abs(z_new−z[x,y]) < epsilon) {
        w[x,y] += w_new;
        c[x,y] += c_new;
        if(z_new<z[x,y]) z[x,y] = z_new;
      }
    }
    q += dq; dq += ddq; z_xy += dzdx;
  }
}
}
```

Figure 6.9: Pseudocode for splat rasterization.

We compare the image quality of different texture-filtering approaches in Figure 6.11. The zebra texture has a resolution of 768 × 768 points and is rendered to an image with 768 × 190 pixels. We first compare surface splatting to *ellipse splatting*, which is based on the same splatting framework. However, ellipse splatting uses footprints that are projected reconstruction kernels only (i.e., they do not include the

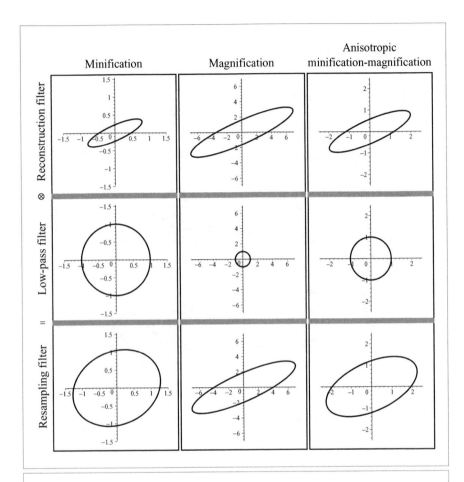

Figure 6.10: The behavior of surface-splatting footprints in the image plane under minification (*left*), magnification (*middle*), and anisotropic minification-magnification (*right*).

low-pass filter). Because the rendered texture is not band-limited, disturbing aliasing artifacts appear as shown in Figure 6.11b. We also compare surface splatting to bilinear interpolation, which is a common approach for texturing in triangle rendering [WNDS99]. Similar to ellipse splatting, bilinear interpolation does not include a low-pass filter and produces aliasing artifacts (Figure 6.11c). Trilinear interpolation, or *trilinear MIPmapping* [WNDS99], improves upon bilinear interpolation by adding a third interpolation step using prefiltered textures (so-called *mipmaps*). However, prefiltering is *isotropic* and performed in a preprocess. In contrast, surface splatting leads to *anisotropic* texture filtering. Because trilinear mipmapping filters textures isotropically based on the worst-case direction, it exhibits overly blurred edges along horizontal lines in Figure 6.11d.

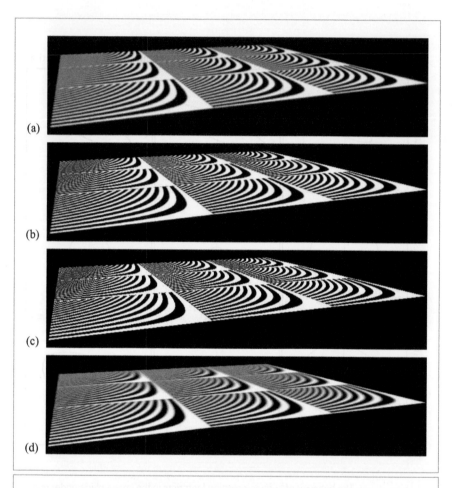

Figure 6.11: Image quality comparison of different texture-filtering approaches: (*a*) surface splatting, (*b*) ellipse splatting, (*c*) bilinear interpolation, and (*d*) trilinear interpolation (mipmapping).

More results of surface splatting are shown in Figure 6.12, illustrating high-quality texture filtering on arbitrary geometries.

6.1.8 CONCLUSION

We presented a splatting approach to point-based rendering that is based on a signal-processing framework. This allowed us to derive a high-quality rendering algorithm including anisotropic antialiasing. We achieved this by projecting reconstruction kernels to image space and analytically band-limiting each individual footprint

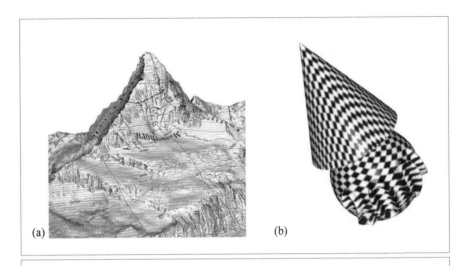

(a)   (b)

Figure 6.12: Surface-splatting examples: (*a*) Matterhorn digital elevation model with a texture taken from a topographic map 4, 782, 011 points and (reproduced by permission of swisstopo, BA067710), (*b*) cone and displacement mapped sphere with a checkerboard texture, 352, 467 points.

function. In addition, we showed how projection and low-pass filtering can be evaluated efficiently using Gaussian kernels. We compared our results to conventional texture mapping and demonstrated that our image quality is superior to isotropic texture filtering, such as trilinear mipmapping. Because of its simplicity, our algorithm is amenable to hardware implementation using programmable graphics processors, which is the topic of the following section.

6.2 GPU SPLATTING

Mario Botsch and Leif Kobbelt

6.2.1 OVERVIEW

The last section introduced the fundamental surface-splatting approach, as it was proposed in Zwicker et al. [ZPvBG01b]. The implementation of this algorithm was purely CPU based, which on the one hand allows for high flexibility, but on the other hand limits its performance to about 2 million splats/sec measured on a 3.0 GHz Pentium4. To increase performance, Botsch et al. [BWK02] proposed a hierarchical rendering technique that is capable of up to 10 million splats/sec on the same hardware. However, these two software-based methods put a high load on the main CPU, which prevents it from doing other computationally expensive tasks besides rendering.

In contrast, traditional triangle-mesh rendering is nowadays delegated completely to the graphics hardware, since the specialized stream-processing design of current graphics processors (GPUs) provides much higher performance compared to a CPU-based solution. Compared to a 3.0 GHz Pentium4, which has a theoretical floating point performance of 6 Gflops (billions of floating point operations per second), NVIDIA GPUs increased their performance from 20 Gflops (NV35) to 53 Gflops (NV40) and further up to 165 Gflops (G70) within three years [OLG+05]. Hence, besides providing higher performance, the growth rate of GPUs is also faster: while the CPU performance improves with a factor of about 1.5 per year, GPUs more than double their performance during the same period.

However, due to the missing native support for splat primitives in today's graphics hardware and graphics libraries, exploiting the GPU's hardware acceleration for point-based rendering is not straightforward. Fortunately, GPUs became more and more flexible during the last few years, thanks to the introduction of programmable vertex and fragment shader units in 2001 and 2002, respectively. Moreover, the latest GPU generation supports full floating-point precision throughout the whole rendering pipeline, thereby allowing for high-quality rendering without discretization artifacts. This increased flexibility finally enables the implementation of surface splatting on the GPU, as we will show in this section.

We will first give a brief introduction to the OpenGL rendering pipeline and pro-grammable shader models in Section 6.2.2, and afterward discuss the splat rendering in three stages, which basically follows the description of Section 6.1. *Rasterization* accounts for projecting splats into the image plane and determining the pixels covered by them (Section 6.2.3). *Shading* refers to the evaluation of a lighting model—either per splat or per pixel—combined with blending of overlapping neighboring splats (Section 6.2.4). *Antialiasing* is performed by applying a combination of an object-space reconstruction filter and a screen-space band-limiting prefilter (Section 6.2.5).

6.2.2 OPENGL AND GPU PROGRAMMING

When rendering 3D geometry into a 2D window, the underlying graphics library performs the standard transformation, lighting, and rasterization operations that can be found in any graphics textbook. We will focus on the OpenGL graphics API [SWND03] because of its high availability and its independence of hardware platforms as well as operating systems.

The OpenGL geometry rendering pipeline is outlined in Figure 6.13. When rendering a 3D model, the model-view transformation first maps its vertices from model coordinates into the camera coordinate system, where the viewer is located at the origin and looks down the negative z-axis. After performing lighting computations in camera space, the (homogeneous) projective mapping further transforms vertices into normalized device coordinates ($\in [-1, 1]^3$), where clipping is done. After dehomogenization by dividing each point by its homogeneous component, the window-to-viewport mapping computes the vertices' final 2D window position ($\in [0, \text{width} - 1] \times [0, \text{height} - 1]$). These coordinate systems are also depicted in Figure 6.14.

The projected primitives are then rasterized to window pixels using 2D homogeneous coordinates. For each resulting pixel, texture mapping can be applied by computing texture coordinates, fetching color values from textures, and combining them to the pixel's final color. Pixels that pass the fragment tests (scissor, stencil, alpha, and depth test) can then optionally be alpha-blended, and their color and depth values are finally written into the color buffer and depth buffer, respectively.

The dark boxes in Figure 6.13 depict which parts of the rendering pipeline can be customized using vertex and fragment shaders. The input data for both kinds of shaders consist of a small number of global read-only variables and data associated with the currently processed vertex or fragment, respectively. The latter can, for instance,

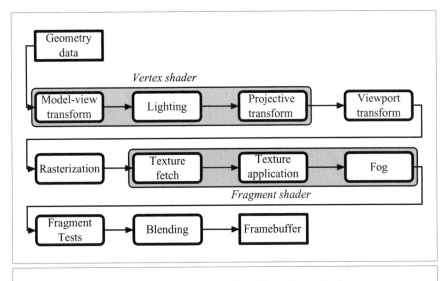

Figure 6.13: Programmable shaders in the OpenGL rendering pipeline.

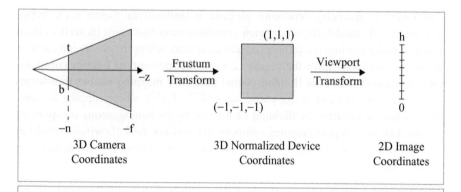

Figure 6.14: Using the frustum and viewport transformations, 3D points are mapped from camera coordinates over normalized device coordinates to 2D viewport coordinates.

be 3D position, normal, color, or texture coordinates for a vertex, or 2D window position, color, and texture coordinates for a fragment. In addition to that, fragment shaders can read textures, which can therefore be used to store any kind of precomputed values. Notice that due to the parallel stream-processing design of GPUs each vertex/fragment is processed individually (i.e., there is no way to access other vertices sharing the same triangle or pixels neighboring to the current fragment).

The typical output of a vertex shader is the position after model-view and projection transformations and a color value resulting from lighting computations. There are more optional output registers, like, for instance, texture coordinates or a point size. Most of the output registers of a vertex shader are transferred to the input registers of fragment shaders, such that data can be passed between vertex and fragment, for instance, by texture coordinates. The output of the fragment shader finally is the fragment's color and depth value.

Both vertex and fragment shaders use a rather small instruction set for their computations, which is accessible through different programming languages. The most low-level and, therefore, also the most efficient option, is assembler programs as provided by the ARB_vertex_program and ARB_fragment_program extensions. The language Cg ("C for graphics") provides higher-level shader programming [FK03, MGAK03], as does the OpenGL shading language (GLSL) [Ros04], which should be an integral part of any OpenGL implementation from version 2.0 on.

Performance Considerations

One of the reasons for employing point-based rendering techniques is the huge complexity of today's massive datasets, for instance, like those acquired by laser range scanning [LPC$^+$00]. Such models easily contain several millions of triangles, which, when projected onto the image plane, may cover only a few pixels. Because the rather expensive triangle-rasterization setup does not pay off for pixel-sized triangles, rendering massive triangle meshes becomes inefficient, such that in this case points (or splats) seem to be the conceptually more suitable rendering primitive. However, also when rendering complex point-based datasets, the following OpenGL performance optimization techniques should be taken into account.

- *Interleaved vertex arrays*: In order to minimize the number of function calls of the OpenGL API, the splat data (positions $\mathbf{p}_i$, normals $\mathbf{n}_i$, colors $\mathbf{c}_i$, radii r_i, etc.) should be stored in one large array. By this all the splats can be rendered using just one call of glDrawArrays(). For better memory coherence the data should additionally be arranged in an interleaved manner (i.e., in an array of the form $[\mathbf{p}_1, \mathbf{n}_1, \mathbf{c}_1, r_1, \ \mathbf{p}_2, \mathbf{n}_2, \mathbf{c}_2, r_2, \dots]$).
- *Vertex buffer objects*: In each frame all the splat data have to be transferred to the GPU, which can easily become the performance bottleneck when rendering massive models. In many situations these data are static, such that the can be stored in the GPU's efficient video memory. This functionality can be accessed by the ARB_vertex_buffer_object extension and effectively reduces data transfer costs.
- *Quantization*: In order to reduce the consumption of GPU memory and to further decrease transfer costs, the splat data should be stored in a compact format. A simple and transparent quantization method is to represent values of bounded absolute value (like normal vectors) by 16-bit floating point numbers on GPUs supporting this feature (NV_half_float), and colors by 4 bytes for RGBA.
- *Backface culling*: For surface splats representing a closed 3D model, backfacing splats can safely be discarded from rendering since they are always occluded by front-facing surface parts. This can save rasterization and shading computations for about 40–50% of the splats. Backfacing splats can be detected in a vertex shader based on the angle between their normal and the viewing ray, and they are discarded by assigning them a homogeneous position at infinity ($w = 0$).
- *Precomputed lighting*: Since lighting computations are performed for each splat, they can also become too expensive if several light sources are used. A common simplification is to restrict to directional light sources and neglect the viewer's local position, such that the lighting no longer depends on positional information and hence becomes a function of surface normals only. For static light sources this function can be precomputed and stored in a cubical texture map, such that complex lighting computations simplify to texture fetches.

- *Shading language*: While high-level shading languages are definitely more convenient to use, low-level assembler-like shader programs obviously are more efficient. Experiments showed that this performance gap can be quite significant (a factor of about 2–5), which might partially also be due to the immaturity of current drivers' GLSL support. An alternative can be using Cg for shader design, followed by a manual optimization of the Cg compiler's output.

These general performance optimization techniques apply to all the splat-rendering approaches discussed in the following, no matter how splats are represented, rasterized, or shaded.

6.2.3 SPLAT RASTERIZATION

The first step in splat rendering is splat rasterization (i.e., determining which image pixels are covered by the projected splats). Since there is no native support for splat primitives in current graphics libraries, splats have to be represented by other drawing primitives like points or triangles.

Polygonal Splats

The first option is to represent each splat by a triangle onto which a special elliptical alpha-texture is mapped, such that each pixel within the splat ellipse is assigned a positive alpha value and all fragments outside the splat are assigned a zero alpha value. The OpenGL alpha test can then be used to efficiently discard all fragments that do not belong to the splat (see Figure 6.15). This technique was used, for instance, in Ren et al. and Pajarola et al. [RPZ02, PSG04]. Its obvious advantage is that it requires very basic OpenGL functionality only (rendering of textured triangles), which simplifies implementation and runs on older graphics hardware.

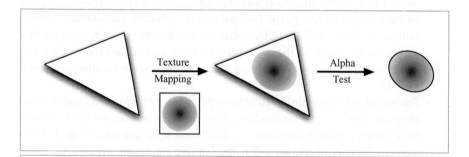

Figure 6.15: Splats can be rasterized by mapping an elliptical alpha-texture onto a triangle and setting up the alpha test to discard all fragments that do not belong to the splat's interior.

Notice, however, that the number of triangle vertices to be stored and processed is three times the number of splats in the model. When vertex arrays are to be used for performance reasons (Section 6.2.2), all the data associated with each splat (normal, color, etc.) have to be attached to each of its three triangle vertices, such that the total memory consumption is tripled. Since the original motivation for rendering points instead of triangles was the inefficient triangle setup for large datasets, rendering splats as textured triangles should usually not be considered efficient, neither in terms of memory consumption nor in terms of rendering performance.

Image-aligned Squares

For higher efficiency and more compact storage, splats should be rendered using one OpenGL point for each splat only, in other words, by using

```
glDrawArrays(GL_POINTS, &splats[0], splats.size());
```

As shortly mentioned in Section 6.2.2, an optional output of vertex shaders is the point size, which, when set to s, causes an $s \times s$ image-space square to be rasterized, centered at the current vertex's projected position. Instead of squares, image-aligned disks can be rendered by enabling point smoothing and alpha test:

```
glEnable(GL_POINT_SMOOTH);
glEnable(GL_ALPHA_TEST);
glAlphaFunc(GL_GREATER, 0.5);
```

The screen-space size of the projected OpenGL point has to be adjusted in a vertex shader to ensure that neighboring splats overlap in image space, such that a hole-free rendering is guaranteed. The complicated exact projected splat size [ZRB+04] is efficiently approximated by perspectively foreshortening the larger of the splat's ellipse radii r using the depth value of the splat center $\mathbf{p}$ in camera coordinates:

$$s = 2r \cdot \frac{n}{p_z} \cdot \frac{h}{t-b}, \tag{6.47}$$

where n, t, and b are the near/top/bottom parameters of the viewing frustum and h denotes the height (in pixels) of the viewport (see Figure 6.14). In this formula the term n/z corresponds to the projection onto the near plane, and $h/(t-b)$ scales the result from the near plane to image coordinates.

This simple splat-rasterization method was used in Dachsbacher et al. [DVS03], since it is extremely efficient and allows for splat rates of about 80 million splats/sec on current GPUs. On the downside, image-aligned squares or disks yield a rather poor approximation of the exact projected splat's shape, especially near the object's contour. Additionally, this method is not suitable for high-quality shading, because all pixels generated from one splat have the same depth value, which prevents correct blending of overlapping splats (see Section 6.2.4).

Affinely Projected Point Sprites

A better approximation to the elliptical projected splat shape in the case of *circular* object-space splats was presented in Botsch and Kobbelt [BK03]. One also starts by adjusting the point size in a vertex shader in order to render image-space squares. But in addition to the last method, for each of the squares' pixels a fragment shader determines whether or not it corresponds to the projection of a point inside or outside of the splat. Pixels outside the splat are then simply discarded using either the alpha test or the KILL shader command, resulting in an elliptical splat rasterization (see Figure 6.16).

The ARB_point_sprite extension can be used to achieve a parameterization of the screen-space square over $[-r, r]^2$, with r being the splat radius. For each of its pixels $(x, y) \in [-r, r]^2$, a depth offset δz from the splat center $\mathbf{p}$ can be computed as a linear function depending on the camera-space normal vector $\mathbf{n} = \left(n_x, n_y, n_z \right)^T$:

$$\delta z = -\frac{n_x}{n_z} \cdot x - \frac{n_y}{n_z} \cdot y. \tag{6.48}$$

This depth offset can then be used to compute the 3D distance from the splat center: the pixel (x, y) corresponds to a point inside the splat if $\left\| (x, y, \delta z) \right\| \leq r$.

One drawback of simple image-aligned points was the constant depth value per splat, which prevents correct occlusion and causes blending artifacts. Hence, the depth

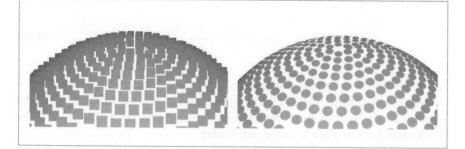

Figure 6.16: Adjusting the point size results in image-aligned squares to be rendered at the splat's center position (*left*). Computing the elliptical splat shape by an affine approximation to the projection leads to much better rendering, especially at the object's contours (*right*).

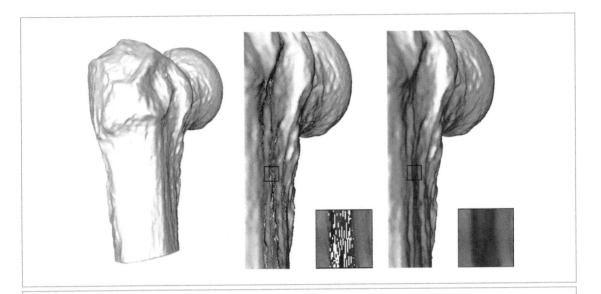

Figure 6.17: Local affine approximations to the projective mapping can cause holes for extreme viewing angles (*center*). These holes can be closed either by an affine approximation that correctly maps the outer splat contour or by perspectively correct per-pixel ray casting (*right*).

offset δz should also be used to correct the pixel's depth value. Starting from the adjusted camera-space depth value $z' := p_z + \delta z$, the frustum and viewport transformations yield the window-space depth buffer entry

$$\text{zbuffer}\,(x, y) = \frac{1}{z'} \cdot \frac{fn}{f-n} + \frac{f}{f-n}. \tag{6.49}$$

Compared to simple image-space squares or disks, the point-sprite method provides a much better approximation, especially noticeable at object contours (see Figure 6.16). However, notice that the depth offset δz is just an approximation, since it assumes a parallel projection in Equation (6.48), neglecting the angle between the viewing ray and the splat normal. This causes ellipses to become too thin when viewed under a flat angle, which might result in holes in the rendered image (see Figure 6.17).

Perspectively Correct Rasterization

The affine approximations to the splat projection used in the original EWA splatting [ZPvBG01b] and in the point-sprite approach [BK03] correctly transform the splat center, but not its outer contour, which can cause small holes in the rendered image.

The first approach proposed to handle these inaccuracies was the perspective accurate splatting of Zwicker et al. [ZRB⁺04]. They switched to an affine approximation that in contrast correctly transforms the outer contour of the splat, but has projective errors in the splat's interior. As Gaussians are closed under affine mappings, the use of local affine approximations enables the full EWA-filtering framework as described in Section 6.1. The drawback of this approach is its high computational complexity, which limits rendering performance to about 6 million splats/sec.

A more efficient and perspectively correct rasterization technique was presented in Botsch et al. [BSK04]. The main idea of this approach is to determine the 3D point corresponding to a 2D pixel based on local ray casting. As another advantage over point sprites besides the perspective correctness, this method also handles object-space elliptical splats. A splat s_i is, therefore, represented by a center $\mathbf{p}_i$ and two orthogonal axes $\mathbf{u}_i$ and $\mathbf{v}_i$, which are scaled according to their respective ellipse radii, such that splats can be represented by their local coordinates (u, v):

$$s_i = \left\{ \mathbf{p}_i + u\,\mathbf{u}_i + v\,\mathbf{v}_i \mid u^2 + v^2 \leq 1 \right\}. \tag{6.50}$$

The elliptical splats s_i are again rendered using GL_POINTS, and the larger of the ellipse radii $r_i := \max\{\|\mathbf{u}_i\|, \|\mathbf{v}_i\|\}$ is used to compute the point size in a vertex shader as described in the last subsections. Then, for each pixel (x, y) the *exact* corresponding 3D point $\mathbf{q}$ is computed by a local ray casting as described below. From this point $\mathbf{q}$ the local parameters (u, v) are computed, and the pixel is rendered or discarded if $u^2 + v^2 \leq 1$ or > 1, respectively.

Looking at the OpenGL transformation pipeline in Figure 6.14, the first step in computing $\mathbf{q}$ is to invert the window-to-viewport transformation, thereby mapping the pixel (x, y) to a 3D point $\mathbf{q}_n$ on the near plane:

$$\mathbf{q}_n = \begin{pmatrix} x \cdot \frac{r-l}{w} - \frac{r-l}{2} \\ y \cdot \frac{t-b}{h} - \frac{t-b}{2} \\ -n \end{pmatrix}, \tag{6.51}$$

where $b/t/l/r$ are the bottom/top/left/right parameters of the viewing frustum, and w/h denote the width/height of the viewport (see Figure 6.18).

Casting a ray from the origin (the eye) through the point $\mathbf{q}_n$ and intersecting it with the splat's supporting plane yield the corresponding point $\mathbf{q}$ as the solution of the 3×3 system:

$$\mathbf{q} = \lambda \mathbf{q}_n = \mathbf{p}_i + u\,\mathbf{u}_i + v\,\mathbf{v}_i. \tag{6.52}$$

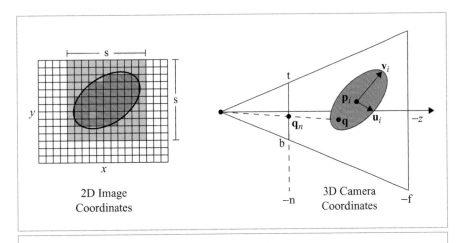

2D Image
Coordinates

3D Camera
Coordinates

Figure 6.18: Splat projection and ray casting.

Using Cramer's rule, computing the free parameters u, v, and λ simplifies to

$$\lambda = \mathbf{p}_i^T (\mathbf{u}_i \times \mathbf{v}_i) / \mathbf{q}_n^T (\mathbf{u}_i \times \mathbf{v}_i),$$
$$u = \mathbf{q}_n^T (\mathbf{p}_i \times -\mathbf{v}_i) / \mathbf{q}_n^T (\mathbf{u}_i \times \mathbf{v}_i), \qquad (6.53)$$
$$v = \mathbf{q}_n^T (-\mathbf{u}_i \times \mathbf{p}_i) / \mathbf{q}_n^T (\mathbf{u}_i \times \mathbf{v}_i),$$

where all terms except $\mathbf{q}_n$ do not depend on the current pixel (x, y), but are constant per splat, and thus can be precomputed in the vertex shader.

Based on the local parameters, the pixel is discarded if $u^2 + v^2 > 1$. Otherwise, its depth value is adjusted by inserting q_z as z' in Equation (6.49). Since the 3D point $\mathbf{q}$ is the *exact* preimage of the projective transform, this approach is actually perspectively correct for each pixel.

6.2.4 SPLAT SHADING

After determining the pixels that are covered by the projected splats in the rasterization stage, the second step in splat rendering involves the lighting and shading of surface splats.

Flat Shading

Since each splat is equipped with a normal vector (or with tangent axes from which a normal can be computed), for given material and reflectance properties a local lighting model can be evaluated on a per-splat basis. This results in a constant color $\mathbf{c}_i$

for each splat, similar to *flat shading* for polygonal meshes. However, since splats correspond to a C^{-1} surface representation, and since neighboring splats mutually intersect each other, simple flat shading leads to undesired shading discontinuities (see Figure 6.19, center left).

Gouraud Shading

To achieve a smoother rendering, the shading discontinuities can be blurred by Gaussian blending of the color values c_i of neighboring overlapping splats (see Section 6.1). Since lighting computations are still performed on a per-splat basis, this blending of colors conceptually corresponds to *Gouraud shading* for polygonal meshes (see Figure 6.19, center right).

To implement this kind of blending, each splat s_i is associated with a circular or elliptical Gaussian weight function—the object-space reconstruction kernel $r_i(\cdot)$. During rasterization the value of the projected reconstruction kernel $r_i'(x, y)$ at the pixel (x, y) is computed based on the distance of the corresponding 3D point to the splat center $\mathbf{p}_i$, or based on the local splat coordinates, leading to

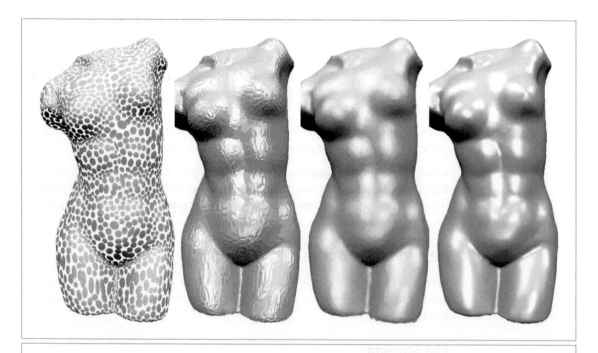

Figure 6.19: The same torso dataset of 3,000 splats (*left*) rendered using flat shading (*center left*), Gouraud shading (*center right*), and Phong shading (*right*).

$$r_i'(x, y) = r_i\left(\left\|x, y, \delta z\right\|\right) \tag{6.54}$$

for the point-sprite approach, and to

$$r_i'(x, y) = r_i\left(\sqrt{u^2 + v^2}\right) \tag{6.55}$$

for the perspective correct ray casting. The final color value for pixel (x, y) is the weighted average over all splats covering this pixel:

$$\mathbf{c}(x, y) = \frac{\sum_i r_i'(x, y)\, \mathbf{c}_i}{\sum_i r_i'(x, y)}. \tag{6.56}$$

This per-pixel averaging can be implemented in OpenGL using two render passes. First, additive alpha-blending is configured with separate blend functions for RBG and alpha components (EXT_blend_func_separate) by

```
glEnable(GL_BLEND);
glBlendFuncSeparateEXT(GL_SRC_ALPHA, GL_ONE, GL_ONE, GL_ONE);
```

Rendering the surface splats will then accumulate color values and weights in the RBG and alpha components of the framebuffer as $\left(\sum_i r_i'\,\mathbf{c}_i,\ \sum_i r_i'\right)$. For the final normalization each pixel's RBG components, therefore, have to be divided by its alpha component. This can be achieved by binding the result of the first render pass as a texture and rendering a window-sized rectangle with this texture mapped onto it. This trick sends each pixel through the OpenGL pipeline again, such that a simple fragment shader can perform the required per-pixel normalization, as proposed in Botsch and Kobbelt and Guennebaud and Paulin [BK03, GP03]. If supported by the GPU, this accumulation should be performed using floating-point render buffers and floating-point textures in order to avoid color saturation and discretization artifacts [BHZK05].

The missing component is a technique to restrict the blending to overlapping neighboring splats belonging to the same surface sheet. The custom ε-depth test employed in the CPU-based software renderer of Zwicker et al. [ZPvBG01b] has to be simulated by another rendering pass, the so-called *visibility splatting* [RL00]. For each frame, the *visibility pass* first renders the splats into the depth buffer only. Then the *blending pass* renders all splats again, but this time computes lighting and accumulates the resulting colors values using the additive alpha-blending as described above. Notice that this pass does not update the z-buffer from the visibility pass and adds a small offset ε to the fragments' depth values, which causes all splats within an ε-depth distance to be blended. The final *normalization pass* performs the required division by the alpha component as described above. The results of the three render passes are depicted in Figure 6.20, pseudocode is given in Figure 6.21.

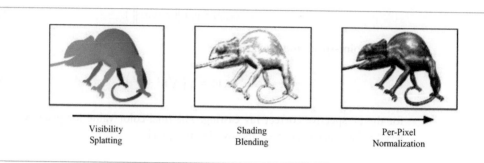

Visibility
Splatting

Shading
Blending

Per-Pixel
Normalization

Figure 6.20: The three-pass splat blending using visibility splatting, blending, and normalization render passes.

```
//  visibility splatting pass
glDepthMask(GL_TRUE);
glDisable(GL_BLEND);
bind_visibility_shaders();
glDrawArrays(GL_POINTS, &splats[0], splats.size());

//  blending pass
glDepthMask(GL_FALSE);
glEnable(GL_BLEND);
bind_blending_shaders();
glDrawArrays(GL_POINTS, &splats[0], splats.size());

//  normalization pass
glCopyTexSubImage2D(GL_TEXTURE_RECTANGLE_ARB, 0, 0, 0, 0, 0, w, h);
bind_normalization_shaders();
draw_rectangle();
```

Figure 6.21: Pseudocode for the three-pass splat blending.

Phong Splatting

When comparing the different shading techniques in Figure 6.19, Gouraud shading successfully removes the unwanted discontinuities of flat shading, but it also blurs the image noticeably. For the rendering of triangle meshes it is well known that per-pixel Phong shading yields results superior to Gouraud shading. Instead of computing lighting for each vertex and linearly interpolating the resulting color values within triangles, Phong shading interpolates vertex normals, followed by a per-pixel lighting based on the resulting piecewise linear normal field.

Hence, the key technique for high-quality point-based rendering is per-pixel Phong shading for surface splats [ZPvBG01b, KV01, KV03a, BSK04]. But since the missing connectivity information does not allow an interpolation of neighboring splats' normal vectors in object-space, the piecewise linear normal field has to be constructed in another way.

The *Phong splatting* approach of Botsch et al. [BSK04] explicitly assigns a linear normal field $\mathbf{n}_i(u, v)$ to each splat s_i instead of keeping its associated normal vector constant. During (perspectively correct) rasterization, the normal field is evaluated at each pixel based on the local splat parameters (u, v), and the normal vector $\mathbf{n}_i(u, v)$ is used for lighting computations. Since the resulting color values $\mathbf{c}_i(u, v)$ are still discontinuous between neighboring splats, they are accumulated and blended using the same three-pass rendering technique as for Gouraud shading. The remaining question is how to compute the splats' linear normal fields $\mathbf{n}_i(u, v)$.

The raw input data for a splat-based model usually is a set of surface samples $\hat{\mathbf{p}}_j$ with associated normal vectors $\hat{\mathbf{n}}_j$. Surface splats are then generated by least squares fitting of ellipses (defined by centers $\mathbf{p}_i$ and tangents $\mathbf{u}_i, \mathbf{v}_i$) to a small subset of sample points $\hat{\mathbf{p}}_j \in \mathcal{P}_i$ each, where $\mathcal{P}_i$ typically either consists of the sample $\hat{\mathbf{p}}_i$ and its k-nearest neighbors or is constructed by a splat subsampling process (see Section 4.3).

In an analogous way the linear normal field $\mathbf{n}_i(u, v)$ of the splat s_i is derived by a least squares fitting to the sample normals $\hat{\mathbf{n}}_j$ associated with $\hat{\mathbf{p}}_j \in \mathcal{P}_i$. The normal field is specified by a center normal $\bar{\mathbf{n}}_i$ and two scalar values α_i and β_i, such that the (unnormalized) normal of a point $\mathbf{q} \in s_i$ with local parameters (u, v) is

$$\mathbf{n}_i(u, v) = \bar{\mathbf{n}}_i + u\,\alpha_i\,\mathbf{u}_i + v\,\beta_i\,\mathbf{v}_i \qquad (6.57)$$

i.e., the center normal is tilted along the tangential directions. Due to this construction the method works best if the tangential directions are roughly aligned to the directions of minimum and maximum normal deviation of the sample normals $\hat{\mathbf{n}}_j$, i.e., to the principal curvature directions. If this is not already provided by the geometry-fitting scheme, the directions $\mathbf{u}_i$ and $\mathbf{v}_i$ can be estimated by the eigenvectors corresponding to the two smaller eigenvalues of the covariance matrix of sample normals $\sum_j \hat{\mathbf{n}}_j \hat{\mathbf{n}}_j^T$.

For the normal fitting the sample normals $\hat{\mathbf{n}}_j$ are represented w.r.t. the *local frame* spanned by the splat's tangents $(\mathbf{u}_i, \mathbf{v}_i)$ and its normal $(\mathbf{u}_j \times \mathbf{v}_j)$. Analogous to the normal tilting of Equation (6.57), the third local frame coordinate of $\hat{\mathbf{n}}_j$ is set to 1, such that each normal is actually represented by a point (x, y) on an offset tangent plane with distance 1, similar to homogeneous coordinates (Figure 6.22).

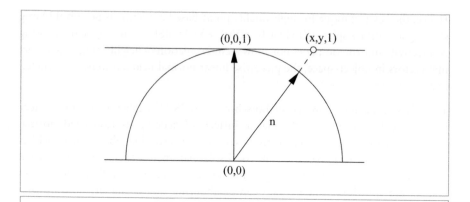

Figure 6.22: Normal vectors n are represented as homogeneous points $(x, y, 1)$ on an offset tangent plane.

If the center normal $\bar{\boldsymbol{n}}_i$ is represented by $(\bar{x}_i, \bar{y}_i)$, and if (u_j, v_j) denote the parameter values of the sample $\hat{\boldsymbol{p}}_j$ and (x_j, y_j) its local frame normal vector, then the normal fitting can be written as a set of linear equations

$$\begin{pmatrix} \bar{x}_i \\ \bar{y}_i \end{pmatrix} + \begin{pmatrix} u_j\,\alpha_i \\ v_j\,\beta_i \end{pmatrix} = \begin{pmatrix} x_j \\ y_j \end{pmatrix} \quad \forall \hat{\boldsymbol{p}}_j \in \mathcal{P}_i, \tag{6.58}$$

which are solved for $\bar{x}_i$, $\bar{y}_i$, α_i, and β_i in the least squares sense. Since in the above equations the x and y components are uncoupled, they can be further simplified to the solution of two 2×2 linear systems:

$$\begin{pmatrix} |P_i| & \sum_j u_j \\ \sum_j u_j & \sum_j u_j^2 \end{pmatrix} \begin{pmatrix} \bar{x}_i \\ \alpha_i \end{pmatrix} = \begin{pmatrix} \sum_j x_j \\ \sum_j x_j\,u_j \end{pmatrix}, \tag{6.59}$$

and

$$\begin{pmatrix} |P_i| & \sum_j v_j \\ \sum_j v_j & \sum_j v_j^2 \end{pmatrix} \begin{pmatrix} \bar{y}_i \\ \beta_i \end{pmatrix} = \begin{pmatrix} \sum_j y_j \\ \sum_j y_j\,v_j \end{pmatrix}, \tag{6.60}$$

where the summation is done over all $\hat{\boldsymbol{p}}_j \in \mathcal{P}_i$. The result of this fitting process is the desired linear normal field $\mathbf{n}_i(u, v)$, defined by center normal $\bar{\boldsymbol{n}}_i$ and two scalars α_i and β_i.

Phong splatting using precomputed normal fields yields a rendering quality that is clearly superior to Gouraud shading due to reduced blurring and sharper highlights (see Figures 6.19 and 6.23). Although additional normal fields have to be stored per splat, the ratio of memory consumption to rendering quality is still improved by Phong splatting, since it allows for high-quality shading even for very coarse models, as long as the normal fields have been derived from dense point samples (like in splat simplification, Section 4.3).

The main drawback of Phong splatting is the explicit precomputation of normal fields, which works well for static geometries, but is not applicable when datasets are dynamically deformed or resampled, like, for instance, in a shape-modeling application (see Section 5.3).

Deferred Shading

There are basically two options to generate smoothly interpolated per-pixel normal vectors. The first is the Phong splatting approach with its precomputed linear normal fields [BSK04], as discussed in the previous subsection. The second approach for normal interpolation was proposed for the CPU-based EWA splatting [ZPvBG01b]. Instead of color values, normal vectors and material properties are splatted into the framebuffer. This smoothly averages normals and colors of overlapping splats over the pixels they cover, with weights depending on the respective EWA filter kernels. In a final pass, *deferred* lighting is performed for each image pixel, based on

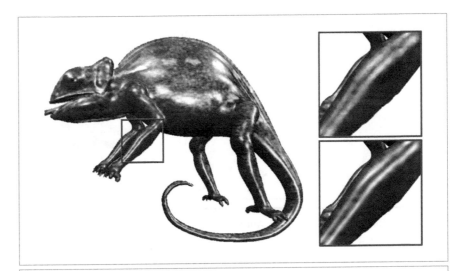

Figure 6.23: Comparison of Gouraud splatting (***top closeup***) and Phong splatting (***bottom closeup***) for the chameleon model consisting of 100,000 splats.

accumulated normal vectors and surface materials. The advantage of this approach over Phong splatting is that it also works for dynamically changing geometries.

Recent GPU generations provide all the hardware features required to implement this approach on the GPU. For instance, NVIDIA's NV40 GPU provides floating point precision at all necessary stages of the rendering pipeline (i.e., for shader arithmetic, alpha-blending, textures, and render targets). In combination with multiple render targets (ARB_DRAW_BUFFERS), which allow us to output up to four different RGBA color values within a single rendering pass, these features enable the implementation of accurate per-pixel deferred shading in the context of surface splatting, as demonstrated in Botsch et al. [BHZK05].

After the visibility pass (see Figure 6.24, left), two render targets are used to splat and accumulate normal vectors and material properties during the so-called *attribute pass* (see Figure 6.24, center). The rasterization pixel shader performs the computations outlined in Section 6.2.2, but instead of shading each accepted pixel, its (weighted) normal vector and color value are written to the two render targets. These buffers and the depth buffer are then used as textures for the normalization and shading pass, for which a window-size rectangle is rendered to send each pixel through the OpenGL pipeline again.

The *shading pass* (see Figure 6.24, right) corresponds to the normalization pass of Gouraud shading, but it additionally performs per-pixel lighting computations. For each pixel, an averaged normal and color can be computed by fetching the accumulated values from the textures and normalizing them. From the depth texture, the corresponding 3D position can be derived by inverting the viewing and projection mappings (see Figure 6.14). Having position, normal, and color information

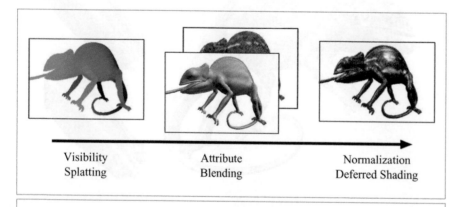

Visibility   Attribute   Normalization
Splatting   Blending   Deferred Shading

Figure 6.24: The deferred shading approach splats and accumulates surface attributes like colors and normals, followed by a normalization and shading pass.

at hand then enables *deferred* per-pixel shading computations [DWS+88]. The resulting Phong splatting again clearly improves the rendering quality over Gouraud shading.

Notice that lighting computations are performed only once for each pixel of the projected object. In contrast, nondeferred approaches incorporate lighting computations into the splat-rasterization process and perform a per-pixel blending of the resulting colors instead. Due to the required mutual overlap of individual splats, this multiplies the number of lighting computations by a factor of about 6–10 for typical splat datasets.

Depending on the complexity of the employed shaders, saving these unnecessary lighting computations yields noticeable performance improvements. The performance of the deferred shading approach is in fact almost independent of the actual surface shading. Incorporating more complex lighting computations into the rasterization pixel shader would in contrast significantly slow down the rendering, since profiling tests indicate that the pixel stage is the bottleneck of the splat rendering.

In addition to this, deferred shading also provides a clear separation between the splat rasterization process and the actual surface lighting or shading computations. This greatly simplifies the development of custom shaders, as the carefully optimized pixel shader for splat rasterization (Section 6.2.2) is left untouched. The deferred shading approach thus allows for a simple yet highly efficient implementation of custom shaders, of which Figure 6.25 shows several examples.

Figure 6.25: From *left to right*: The Phong-shaded octopus model, the NPR-shaded renderings of the dinosaur model, the Igea artifact, and the massive Lucy dataset from Botsch et al. [BHZK05]. All models are rendered with shadow mapping enabled and hence require one additional visibility rendering pass for the shadow-map generation.

Another important point to be considered is the precision of the render targets. A standard framebuffer offers eight bits for each of the four RGBA components, which as an additional constraint are clamped to $[0, 1]$. This leads to the frequently observed shading artifacts due to color saturation or discretization artifacts. Recent GPUs support the use of unclamped floating point values for render targets, which effectively avoids these problems. This is especially important since in addition to colors normal vectors also are accumulated, where noise due to discretization would immediately lead to shading artifacts.

6.2.5 ANTIALIASING

In the original EWA surface splatting [ZPvBG01b], two components are mainly responsible for high visual quality: per-pixel Phong splatting, which can be mapped to the GPU as shown in the last section, and anisotropic antialiasing provided by the EWA filter. It should be obvious that using no antialiasing technique at all, like in the case of simple flat shading, results in severe aliasing artifacts, which is clearly depicted in Figure 6.26, top left.

The EWA filter as described in Section 6.1 is composed of the projection $r_i'(x, y)$ of the object-space reconstruction kernel $r_i(u, v)$ and a band-limiting screen-space

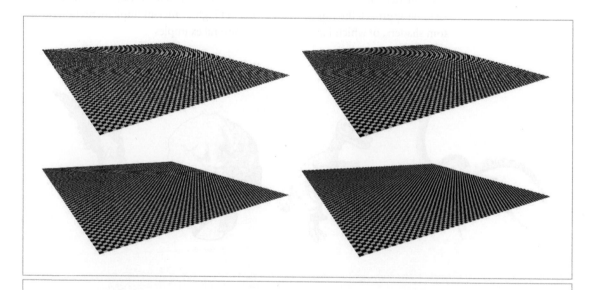

Figure 6.26: Without any filtering, both magnified and minified regions exhibit aliasing (***top left***). The object-space reconstruction filter alone cannot avoid aliasing in minification regions (***top right***). FSAA reduces aliasing to some degree, but the super-sampled image might still contain sampling artifacts (***bottom left***). The approximate EWA filter band-limits the signal before it is sampled and successfully removes the aliasing problems (***bottom right***).

prefilter $h(x, y)$. As the required convolution is computationally quite involved, many rendering approaches simply omit the screen-space filter and use the reconstruction kernel only. However, while this technique successfully removes aliasing in magnified regions, it cannot prevent aliasing in the case of minification when the size of projected splats falls below one pixel (see Figure 6.26, top right).

An appealing idea might be to diminish aliasing artifacts by full-screen antialiasing (FSAA), which is supported by any modern GPU. In general, FSAA redirects rendering to a higher resolution framebuffer in order to super-sample the image signal, and then down-filters this buffer to the actual framebuffer resolution. However, even the higher-resolution super-sampling buffer might suffer from aliasing, in which case a high-resolution *aliased* image will be down-scaled to the framebuffer. The resulting image will still contain alias artifacts, which are just shifted to a higher frequency band (see Figure 6.26, bottom left).

In [BHZK05], Botsch et al. proposed a simple and efficient approximation of the EWA filter. The footprint weight $\rho_i(x, y)$ is computed as the maximum of the projected reconstruction filter $r_i'(x, y)$ and the prefilter $h(x, y)$, instead of by a convolution of the two filters. For a pixel (x, y) the fragment shader computes a 3D radius $r_3(x, y) = \sqrt{u^2 + v^2}$, corresponding to the 3D distance from the splat center (see Section 6.2.3) and the (normalized) 2D distance $r_2(x, y)$ to the projected splat center. A given fragment is accepted if it lies within the union of the screen-space prefilter and the projected reconstruction filter (see Figure 6.27); i.e., if

$$\min\left\{r_2(x, y), r_3(x, y)\right\} \leq 1, \tag{6.61}$$

and its final footprint weight is computed as

$$\rho_i(x, y) = \text{Gauss}\left(\min\left\{r_2(x, y), r_3(x, y)\right\}\right) \tag{6.62}$$

$$\rho_i(x, y) = \max\left\{r_i'(x, y), h(x, y)\right\}. \tag{6.63}$$

This approximation to the EWA filter provides high-quality antialiasing in magnified and minified regions (see Figure 6.26, bottom right). Its results are comparable to those of the exact EWA filter, but in contrast the approximation is considerably easier to compute. If the projected splat center is passed from the vertex shader to the pixel shader, the screen-space filter requires a few additional instructions only (Figure 6.27).

Notice that for this approach the minimum size of projected splats has to be bounded to be at least 2×2 pixels in order to generate enough fragments for antialiasing

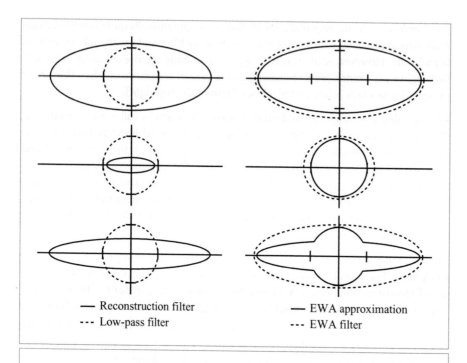

— Reconstruction filter
--- Low-pass filter

— EWA approximation
--- EWA filter

Figure 6.27: Comparison of the original EWA filter and its approximation. In the left column, three typical configurations of screen-size ratios between the projected reconstruction filter and the screen-space filter are shown. The right column compares the contours of the combined filter kernels.

purposes. This size restriction can easily be incorporated into the vertex shader. Limiting the minimal projected splat size obviously generates more fragments, which increases the average number of fragments contributing to each image pixel to about 15–30 for complex models with small projected splat sizes. As a consequence, the acceleration offered by the deferred shading approach (Section 6.2.3) is even more attractive in this case.

6.2.6 COMPARISON

The last section proposed several techniques for the three main components of a GPU-accelerated surface-splatting system (i.e., rasterization, shading, and antialiasing). In order to compare complexity and performance of these methods, some selected approaches are classified in Table 6.1.

Table 6.1:

	Rasterization	Shading	Antialiasing	Splats/sec
EWA splatting [ZPvBG01b]	Affine	Deferred	EWA	2M
Image-space squares	—	Flat	—	83M
Point sprites [BK03]	Affine	Gouraud	Object-space	27M
Persp. Accurate [ZRB⁺04]	Accurate	Gouraud	EWA	5M
Phong splatting [BSK04]	Correct	Phong	Object-space	6M
Deferred shading [BHZK05]	Correct	Deferred	Approximate EWA	23M

The rendering performances were determined by rendering several point-based models with complexities ranging from 150,000 to 14,000,000 splats into a 512 × 512 window, using a 3.0GHz Pentium4 equipped with a NVIDIA GeForce 6800 Ultra GPU. The performance for each model was computed based on three full 360° rotations around the three coordinate axes in steps of 5°, and the values given in Table 6.1 represent the averaged timings over all models. Notice that the GPU-based methods exploit all the performance-optimization techniques described in Section 6.2.1 except for quantization, and the shaders are implemented as ARB-assembler programs.

The deferred shading approach proposed in Botsch et al. [BHZK05] seems to represent the best trade-off between performance and rendering quality. Thanks to the combination of perspectively correct rasterization, flexible and efficient deferred shading, and approximate EWA filtering, this method yields the highest visual quality. At the same time this technique is almost as efficient as the high-performance but midquality point-sprite approach.

6.2.7 CONCLUSION

The steadily increasing performance and programmability of modern graphics hardware allow for efficient implementation of high-quality surface splatting. However, a major drawback is the need for the extra visibility splatting pass, which is caused by the missing programmability of the depth test. As a consequence, since the splat geometry has to be rendered twice, this effectively halves the rendering performance.

The deferred shading approach of Botsch et al. [BHZK05] has been implemented as a Pointshop3D plug-in and can be found on the Pointshop 3D Web site.

6.3 RAY TRACING OF POINT MODELS

Bart Adams and Anders Adamson

6.3.1 OVERVIEW

As discussed in the previous section, surface splatting has reached a mature state and it is the preferred algorithm to interactively render point-sampled objects. Although the state-of-the-art GPU algorithms produce high-quality images thanks to Phong splatting and EWA antialiasing, more advanced shading effects such as shadows, reflections, refractions, or even global illumination are hard to achieve. Also, surface splatting becomes costly for complex models consisting of millions of splats. In that sense, surface splatting can be compared to triangle rasterization, and thus shares many of its advantages and disadvantages [WS05].

With the upcome of physics-based animation algorithms that employ point-sampled surface representations (e.g., fracture (Section 7.2) or fluid (Section 7.3) animation), there is a high demand for realistic image synthesis from point clouds using the aforementioned complex shading effects. Computing these global effects eventually requires ray tracing (see [Gla89] and [Shi00] for good introductions) (i.e., one should be able to intersect a ray with the point-sampled surface in a consistent way).

One way to proceed could be to use the collection of splats as surface representation and intersect rays with the ellipses. The resulting surface is C^{-1} continuous and piecewise linear, which causes severe artifacts especially under complex lighting situations: the discontinuities are not only visible at the silhouettes, but they are also magnified by shadows cast; the planar patches lead to obvious distortions of specular reflections, and so on. Schaufler and Jensen [SJ00] overcome these problems by intersecting a cylinder around the ray with the splats and then computing the intersection as a weighted average of splats whose centers are inside the cylinder. Although this approach produces high-quality images, the resulting geometry depends on the particular rays used for intersecting the surface. Therefore, their ray-surface intersection algorithm does not define a consistent surface. This can be problematic, for example, when rendering subsequent frames of an animation sequence.

In Section 4.2 different variants of C^∞ surface definitions were discussed. The most popular one for ray-tracing point models is the definition of Adamson and Alexa [AA03a, AA04a]. This implicit surface definition is consistent and it can be shown to define smooth manifold surfaces from point clouds if certain natural sampling criteria are fulfilled [AA03a]. Due to these properties and its ease of implementation, several researchers have used this definition for ray-tracing point models [AA03a, AA04a, WS05, AKP+05]. See Figure 6.28 for an example.

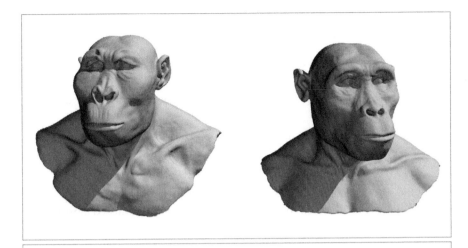

Figure 6.28: Ray tracings of point models acquired with a structured-light scanner. Both models are defined by approximately 200,000 points. Images taken from Adamson and Alexa [AA03a].

In this section, the basic ray-surface intersection algorithm based on this surface definition will be discussed. Together, we introduce extensions to handle sharp features such as edges and corners and bounded, nonorientable surfaces. Custom-tailored data structures are given together with various optimizations for static point clouds as well as free-form deforming point-sampled surfaces. We conclude the section with tips to efficiently implement the proposed algorithms.

6.3.2 RAY-SURFACE INTERSECTION ALGORITHM

Surface Definition

Given a set of points $\mathcal{P} = \{\mathbf{p}_i \in \mathbb{R}^3\}, i \in \{1, \dots, N\}$, sampled from a surface $\mathcal{S}$, define the neighborhood of $\mathcal{P}$ as the union of a set of balls centered at the points $\mathbf{p}_i$:

$$\mathcal{B} = \bigcup_i B_i, \ B_i = \{\mathbf{x} \mid \|\mathbf{x} - \mathbf{p}_i\| < r_B, \mathbf{x} \in \mathbb{R}^3\}. \tag{6.64}$$

It is assumed that $\mathcal{B}$ contains the surface $\mathcal{S}$ as well as the approximation $\hat{\mathcal{S}}$ that will be defined. For the approximation two functions will be defined on the neighborhood: the weighted average and the normal direction. The weighted average $\mathbf{a} : \mathcal{B} \to \mathcal{B}$ maps each point $\mathbf{x}$ onto the weighted average of the contributing points. The normal direction $\mathbf{n} : \mathcal{B} \rightarrow \mathbb{R}^3$ assigns each point in the neighborhood of the points a normal. Then, the approximating surface $\hat{S}$ is defined as

$$\hat{S} = \{\mathbf{x} \in \mathcal{B} \mid f(\mathbf{x}) = \mathbf{n}(\mathbf{x})^T(\mathbf{x} - \mathbf{a}(\mathbf{x})) = 0\}. \tag{6.65}$$

As in most cases the points $\mathbf{p}_i$ are equipped with normals $\mathbf{n}_i$, a commonly used definition of $\mathbf{a}$ and $\mathbf{n}$ is:

$$\mathbf{a}(\mathbf{x}) = \frac{\sum_{i=1}^N \theta(\|\mathbf{x} - \mathbf{p}_i\|/h)\mathbf{p}_i}{\sum_{i=1}^N \theta(\|\mathbf{x} - \mathbf{p}_i\|/h)}, \quad \mathbf{n}(\mathbf{x}) = \frac{\sum_{i=1}^N \theta(\|\mathbf{x} - \mathbf{p}_i\|/h)\mathbf{n}_i}{\|\sum_{i=1}^N \theta(\|\mathbf{x} - \mathbf{p}_i\|/h)\mathbf{n}_i\|}, \tag{6.66}$$

with h the support radius of the points. In the case the points do not carry surface normals, one could either first compute per-point normals as discussed in Section 4.2 or define a different mapping $\mathbf{n}$ based on the weighted covariance directions in $\mathbf{x}$ as discussed in Adamson and Alexa [AA03a].

Note that the summation is over all N points, but in practical implementations compactly supported weight functions $\theta : \mathbb{R} \rightarrow \mathbb{R}$ are used and, therefore, the summation is limited to the neighborhood of the point $\mathbf{x}$. Weight functions should be smooth, positive, and monotonically decreasing (have negative first derivatives).

If compactly supported functions are used, θ must return zero at distance h, the radius of support, in order to avoid discontinuities. Otherwise, a point sample entering the radius of support would immediately contribute to both $\mathbf{a}(\mathbf{x})$ and $\mathbf{n}(\mathbf{x})$. To further increase smoothness, it is desirable to have at least a zero first derivative at distance h.

A possible choice is to use a truncated Gaussian (Figure 6.29a):

$$\theta_g(r) = \theta_g(\|\mathbf{x} - \mathbf{p}_i\|/h) = \begin{cases} e^{-\frac{r^2}{\sigma^2}} & \text{if } r < 1, \\ 0 & \text{if } r \geq 1, \end{cases} \tag{6.67}$$

with σ a scaling parameter to ensure that the weights vanish sufficiently when approaching $r = 1$ (typically, σ is taken in the range $0.2 - 0.4$). Note also that all the higher-order derivatives get close to zero.

In practice the Gaussian is approximated by polynomial functions. A popular choice is the compactly supported Wendland function (Figure 6.29b):

$$\theta_w(r) = \theta_w(\|\mathbf{x} - \mathbf{p}_i\|/h) = \begin{cases} (1 - r)^4(4r + 1) & \text{if } r < 1, \\ 0 & \text{if } r \geq 1. \end{cases} \tag{6.68}$$

Here, the first three derivatives of θ_w yield zero at distance h. The computation requires only one addition, one subtraction, and four multiplications, which can be performed more efficiently than evaluating θ_g.

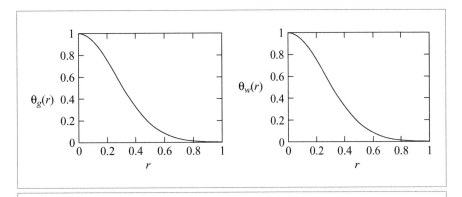

Figure 6.29: Weight functions. (*a*) truncated Gaussian θ_g (Equation 6.67, $\sigma = 0.378$); $\theta_g(1.0) = 0.00091$, $\theta_g'(1.0) = -0.0127$. For more accurate results a smaller σ has to be chosen. (*b*) Wendland function θ_w (Equation 6.68); θ_w and its first three derivatives yield zero at $r = 1$.

Remark 1   At first sight it seems that the function **n** defines the surface normal for points $\mathbf{x} \in S$. Alexa and Adamson [AA04b] prove, however, that in general this is not true. They show how to compute exact surface normals analytically from the implicit surface definition and it is shown that the exact surface normals in general differ from **n**. However, the difference is very small and in practice people avoid the computational complexity to compute exact surface normals and use **n** instead for shading computations.

Remark 2   If points carry additional attributes such as color, similar formulas as Equation (6.66) can be used to define the respective attributes at the surface.

Remark 3   Other surface definitions (such as Levin's MLS surface definition, for example [Lev98, Lev03]), could be used as well for ray-tracing point clouds. Often these surface definitions include a polynomial fitting step and might, therefore, be more robust in the presence of noise. In this section we will use the aforementioned surface definition. However, most of the discussions can be easily generalized to apply to other variants. We refer to Section 4.2 for more details on alternative point-based surface definitions.

Ray-surface Intersections

Computing ray-surface intersections amounts to finding points on the ray where the function $f(\mathbf{x})$ as defined in Equation (6.65) evaluates to zero. We propose three alternatives for finding such points on the ray. All alternatives proceed in two steps. In a first step, an initial guess or starting point $\mathbf{r}_0$ is computed. This point $\mathbf{r}_0$ is supposed to be close to the surface $\hat{S}$. In a next step, starting from this point $\mathbf{r}_0$, the actual intersection of the ray with the surface is constructed using, for example, an iterative procedure.

We first describe how to find the initial starting point $\mathbf{r}_0$, before describing the three different ray-surface intersection algorithms.

Finding an Initial Point Close to the Surface   By definition, the surface must be contained in $\mathcal{B}$, the union of balls B_i associated with the sample points. Thus, $\mathcal{B}$ defines a bounding volume of $\hat{S}$. The intersection points of the ray with the spheres B_i yield points close to the surface and can thus serve as initial starting points $\mathbf{r}_0$. Usually, the ray-sphere intersections are sorted front to back using the corresponding ray parameters.

Finding all $\mathbf{r}_0$ amounts to locating all B_i intersected by the ray. Iterating over all balls quickly becomes infeasible, as point models often consist of thousands or even millions of points. Therefore, the balls B_i should be stored in spatial data structures for quick intersection testing. Three popular acceleration hierarchies used in this context are *octrees* [AA03a], *bounding sphere hierarchies* [AA03b, AKP+05], and *K-d-trees* [WS05]. A general overview on acceleration data structures for ray tracing can be found in Glassner [Gla89] and Arvo and Kirk [AK89]. Examples of optimized acceleration hierarchies for static and deforming point models are given in Section 6.3.3.

Although the volume $\mathcal{B}$ effectively bounds the approximated surface $\hat{S}$, it is often too conservative: evaluating a compactly supported θ at the boundary of $\mathcal{B}$ yields no support at all. This could be corrected by moving some small ϵ into $\mathcal{B}$. However, performance of the ray-surface intersection algorithm is improved if starting points $\mathbf{r}_0$ are used that are closer to $\hat{S}$. Therefore, it is desirable to construct a different bounding volume that more tightly encloses the given input data.

One popular choice is to down-scale the B_i to an amount where no holes arise (see Figure 6.30a). The result is a tighter and more effective bounding volume for $\hat{S}$ that is contained in $\mathcal{B}$. Moreover, at intersection points with the down-scaled B_i, the weight functions now have bigger support and f can be evaluated without running into numerical problems.

If point normals are provided, it is also possible to use oriented-bounding boxes (see Figure 6.30b). As $\hat{S}$ is expected to be close to the planes formed by the samples and their normals, the boxes can be down-scaled in the normal direction. The union of the boxes yields an even smaller bounding volume for $\hat{S}$.

Starting with an adequate $\mathbf{r}_0$, we propose three ways to compute the actual ray-surface intersection point. The first alternative uses an iterative planar approximation and intersection procedure. The second alternative uses sphere tracing and the last alternative uses ray marching.

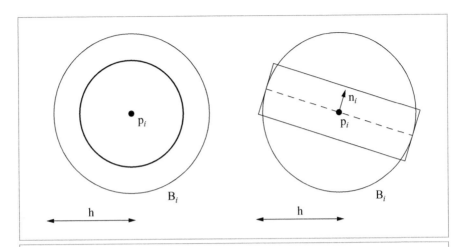

Figure 6.30: Different choices for a bounding volume corresponding to a sample $\mathbf{p}_i$, which contain a patch of $\hat{S}$. The union of these boundings encloses $\hat{S}$. (*a*) The support radius is down-scaled, in order to provide a starting point $\mathbf{r}_0$ with sufficient support. (*b*) A bounding box can be used if normals are provided. A plane normal to $\mathbf{n}_i$ through $\mathbf{p}_i$ is supposed to approximate $\hat{S}$ close to $\mathbf{p}_i$. Therefore, a box that is down-scaled in the normal direction still encloses $\hat{S}$.

Approximating and Intersecting the Surface   Given a point $\mathbf{r}_0 \in \mathcal{B}$ close to the surface $\hat{S}$, a local planar approximation to $\hat{S}$ is computed using $\mathbf{n}(\mathbf{r}_0)$ and $\mathbf{a}(\mathbf{r}_0)$ (see Figure 6.31a):

$$\mathcal{P}_0 : \mathbf{n}(\mathbf{r}_0)^T (\mathbf{x} - \mathbf{a}(\mathbf{r}_0)) = 0. \tag{6.69}$$

Intersecting the ray with the plane $\mathcal{P}_0$ yields a new point $\mathbf{r}_1$ (see Figure 6.31b) which, in theory, should be closer to the surface than $\mathbf{r}_0$. Proceeding in the same way (i.e., constructing and intersecting the planar approximation $\mathcal{P}_1$ from $\mathbf{r}_1$) yields a new point $\mathbf{r}_2$ again closer to the surface. This procedure can then be iterated until $\|\mathbf{n}(\mathbf{r}_j)^T(\mathbf{r}_j - \mathbf{a}(\mathbf{r}_j))\| < \epsilon$, which means that $\mathbf{r}_j$ is very close to the surface $\hat{S}$ and can thus be considered as an intersection of the ray with the surface according to Equation (6.65). Here, ϵ is a predefined error tolerance.

In the case where rays miss the surface, the sequence $\mathbf{r}_j, \mathbf{r}_{j+1}, \ldots$ does not converge to a point on the surface, as $\mathbf{r}_j$ starts to alternate on positions near the missed surface patch. The iteration has to be stopped and the procedure has to be restarted with the next location $\mathbf{r}_0$ resulting from intersecting the bounding volume. Otherwise, following intersections would be ignored (see Figure 6.32a).

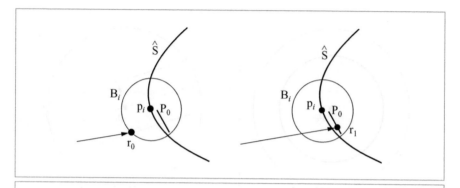

Figure 6.31: Intersecting a ray with the implicit surface. First, a starting point $\mathbf{r}_0$ is computed from which an average plane $\mathcal{P}_0 : \mathbf{n}(\mathbf{r}_0)^T(\mathbf{x} - \mathbf{a}(\mathbf{r}_0)) = 0$ is constructed. Next, the ray is intersected with that planar approximation yielding a new point $\mathbf{r}_1$. This procedure is repeated until convergence.

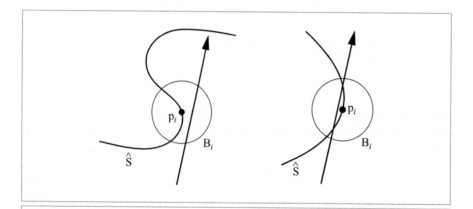

Figure 6.32: Special cases when intersecting the surface. (*a*) A ray missing $\hat{S}$. Further intersections are possible. (*b*) A ray hitting $\hat{S}$ close to the silhouette.

Special attention has to be paid if multiple intersections are contained in a single B_i, which is the case at silhouettes (see Figure 6.32b). If $\mathbf{r}_0$ is chosen to be at the front of the ray segment inside B_i, the procedure will converge to the relevant first intersection.

Note that for this intersection procedure the starting point $\mathbf{r}_0$ does not have to lie on the ray, nor does it have to lie in front of the actual intersection point. Therefore, one could alternatively use the center $\mathbf{p}_i$ of the intersected ball or even compute the intersection of the ray with a possible splat associated with $\mathbf{p}_i$. These choices are motivated by the fact that the iteration procedure converges faster if the initial guess $\mathbf{r}_0$ is closer to $\hat{S}$, which should be the case for the point $\mathbf{p}_i$ or the points on the splat associated with $\mathbf{p}_i$. However, care should be taken at silhouettes as discussed above.

Sphere Tracing   If the minimal distance $d(\mathbf{x}, \hat{S})$ of a point $\mathbf{x}$ to the surface $\hat{S}$ is known, we can construct a sphere of radius d around $\mathbf{x}$, which is assured not to contain $\hat{S}$. Then, we can move a step of size d in all directions, including the ray direction, without penetrating $\hat{S}$. If only a lower bound on d is available, we can move that distance instead. Iteratively performing such conservative steps until convergence is known as sphere tracing [Har96]. It can be applied to all implicit functions satisfying the condition $|f(\mathbf{x})| < d(\mathbf{x}, \hat{S})$, $\hat{S} = f^{-1}(0)$. Unfortunately, the surface definition given above does not have this property. However, $f(\mathbf{x})$ approximates $d(\mathbf{x}, \hat{S})$ very well, in particular when coming close to $\hat{S}$.

If normals are provided (i.e., $\mathbf{n}(\mathbf{x})$ is computed according to Equation 6.66), $f(\mathbf{x})$ approximates a signed distance to $\hat{S}$. In that case, a sign change indicates a penetration. In order to find the intersection, we simply have to move the signed distance, converging toward $\hat{S}$ from both sides.

If no normals are provided, the fact that $\hat{S}$ is locally orientable [AA04a] can be exploited to still detect penetrations. We assume that the steps are small enough, not to penetrate $\hat{S}$ more than once. Then, we simply have to orient successive normals consistently:

$$\mathbf{n}(\mathbf{r}_{j+1}) = \begin{cases} \mathbf{n}(\mathbf{r}_{j+1}) & \text{if } \mathbf{n}(\mathbf{r}_j)^T \mathbf{n}(\mathbf{r}_{j+1}) \geq 0, \\ -\mathbf{n}(\mathbf{r}_{j+1}) & \text{if } \mathbf{n}(\mathbf{r}_j)^T \mathbf{n}(\mathbf{r}_{j+1}) < 0. \end{cases} \tag{6.70}$$

To ensure that we start to move in the direction of the ray, we flip $\mathbf{n}(\mathbf{r}_0)$ if $f(\mathbf{r}_0) < 0$.

Computing ray-surface intersections using sphere tracing is slightly slower than applying the approximating and intersecting method. In contrast, it has the advantage that the tracing can be continued throughout several B_i, as long as there is support for the weight function θ.

Ray Marching with Linear Intersection Interpolation   Starting from the initial point $\mathbf{r}_0$, one could step and compute $f(\mathbf{r}_j)$ along the ray using fixed ray segments. A sign change in f then indicates that the surface should pass between consecutive $\mathbf{r}_j$'s and that an intersection point should lie somewhere on the ray between these evaluation points. Wald and Seidel [WS05] apply this approach in their interactive point-based ray-tracing framework. They use ray marching and compute several intersections simultaneously using SIMD (single instruction multiple data) optimizations. A multiple of the data amount that can be processed in parallel should be chosen (e.g., eight positions if four-way SIMD operations are available).

After a penetration is detected, the point of intersection should be interpolated to enhance precision. The two implicit values $f_{j+1} = f(\mathbf{r}_{j+1})$ and $f_j = f(\mathbf{r}_j)$ with differing signs indicate the approximate distance to $\hat{S}$. The resulting intersection point $\mathbf{x}$ from linear interpolation is then $\mathbf{x} = (1 - \alpha)\mathbf{r}_j + \alpha\mathbf{r}_{j+1}$, with $\alpha = |f_j|/(|f_j| + |f_{j+1}|)$.

Handling Sharp Features

The given surface definition and accompanying surface intersection algorithm produce C^∞ smooth manifold surfaces. Sometimes, however, sharp features such as edges and corners are desired. Examples include objects obtained by Boolean operations (Section 5.3) or fragments obtained by fracturing (Section 7.2). Defining the surface as in Equation (6.65) would smooth out all desired sharp features.

Fleishman et al. [FCOS05] propose an extension to Levin's moving least squares surface definition to handle sharp features (see Figure 6.33). They define a modified projection operator that accounts for C^1 discontinuities in the given point cloud. The core of the algorithm is a method to guide neighborhood creation using a technique from robust statistics called the *forward-search paradigm*. Using this technique they are able to locally classify regions of the point set to multiple outlier-free smooth regions. This classification allows them to project points on a locally smooth region rather than a surface that is smooth everywhere. By treating the points across the discontinuities as outliers, sharp features are easily defined. Their method is shown to be robust in the presence of noise and outliers.

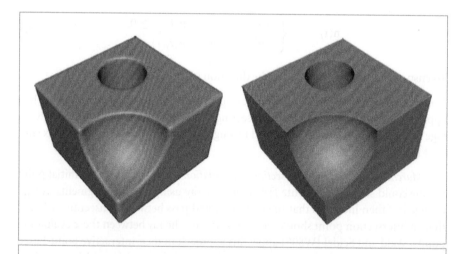

Figure 6.33: (*a*) Sharp edges are smoothed out. (*b*) Using the technique of Fleishman et al. [FCOS05] sharp features are preserved. Images taken from Fleishman et al. [FCOS05].

Pauly et al. [PKA⁺05] and Adams et al. [AKP⁺05] propose a way to ray trace point models with sharp features when the location of the features is known a priori. This is often the case in computer graphics applications such as when constructing Boolean operations (Section 5.3) or when fracturing solids (Section 7.2). The idea here is to store the points in separate collections (called surface sheets), and define *surface clipping* or *trimming relations* between the surfaces that intersect. For example, when computing the difference $A − B$ of two solids A and B, the resulting solid consists of a surface sheet S_A, containing points of object A and a surface sheet S_B, containing points of object B. During ray tracing, both surfaces are intersected separately (i.e., only point neighborhoods within the same surface sheet are used), and the resulting intersection point is trimmed if it lies outside the other surface. Pauly et al. [PKA⁺05] show how a similar technique can be used to render sharp edges and corners for fractured materials represented using point-based surfaces. Two examples of scenes ray traced using this technique are given in Figure 6.34.

Handling Bounded, Nonorientable Surfaces

So far we assumed that the represented surface is a solid and thus unbounded and globally orientable. Adamson and Alexa [AA04a] show how this surface definition can be easily extended to handle bounded and possibly nonorientable surfaces (such as the Klein bottle and Möbius strip in Figure 6.35).

Figure 6.34: (*a*) Sharp edges and corners in CSG models. Image taken from Adams et al. [AKP⁺05]. (*b*) Sharp features in fragments of a fractured object. Image taken from Pauly et al. [PKA⁺05]. Both images are ray traced using surface-surface clipping relations.

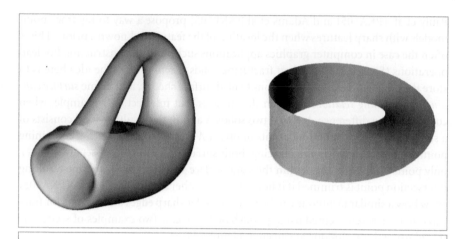

Figure 6.35: Renderings of nonorientable, bounded surfaces represented by unstructured point sets. Images taken from Adamson and Alexa [AA04a].

Handling nonorientable surfaces is straightforward, as the surface definition (Equation 6.65) is not altered when inverting $\mathbf{n}(\mathbf{x})$. The computation of $\mathbf{n}(\mathbf{x})$ is local and inside a ball. With sufficiently small radii the normals can be oriented consistently so that $\mathbf{n}(\mathbf{x})$ is indeed a smooth vector-valued function of $\mathbf{x}$ inside the ball.

To handle surfaces with boundaries, the surface definition of Equation (6.65) is altered to

$$\hat{S} = \{\mathbf{x} \in \mathcal{B} \mid f(\mathbf{x}) = \mathbf{n}(\mathbf{x})^T(\mathbf{x} - \mathbf{a}(\mathbf{x})) = 0 \ \wedge \ c(\mathbf{x}) = \|\mathbf{x} - \mathbf{a}(\mathbf{x})\| < \epsilon_c\}. \quad \text{(6.71)}$$

The added condition states that the point $\mathbf{x}$ should be within a small distance ϵ_c to the average of its neighbor positions $\mathbf{a}(\mathbf{x})$. The value $c(\mathbf{x})$ is called the off-center value of $\mathbf{x}$. The reasoning is that points on the surface should be surrounded by other points and, therefore, $c(\mathbf{x})$ is expected to be small. On the other hand, when $\mathbf{x}$ moves away from the surface, the off-center value becomes larger. It is shown in Adamson and Alexa [AA04a] that ϵ_c should be chosen relative to the radius r_B of the spheres associated with the points $\mathbf{p}_i$ and that following bounds result in well-defined boundaries:

$$\frac{2}{3}r_B < \epsilon_c < \frac{1 + 4\sqrt{3}}{9}r_B. \quad \text{(6.72)}$$

6.3.3 OPTIMIZATIONS FOR STATIC AND DEFORMING
POINT CLOUDS

In this section various optimizations for static (i.e., point models that do not deform, but only move rigidly with respect to the viewing position) and free-form deforming point models are given.

Ray-tracing Static Point Clouds

Wald and Seidel [WS05] build on the work of Adamson and Alexa [AA03a] and introduce various optimizations to achieve interactive frame rates. The performance is increased due to the combination of an efficient surface-intersection algorithm and a highly optimized K-d-tree acceleration structure. Interactive frame rates (on a single PC) are obtained of 7–30 frames per second at 512×512 image resolution for models consisting of over one million points.

The efficiency basically depends on a highly optimized K-d-tree that is built for the points $\mathbf{p}_i$ equipped with normals $\mathbf{n}_i$ and radius of influence h. In order to optimally place the split planes, they make use of the surface area heuristic (SAH). The goal is to produce large voxels that are completely empty. This does not only reduce the average number of voxels being traversed, it also encloses the surface as tightly as possible, reducing the number of surface interrogations. The nonempty cells of the K-d-tree are totally contained in $\mathcal{B}$, the union of the balls B_i. When traversing the K-d-tree, which can be done with few operations, the relevant ray segment is directly provided as the intersections of the voxels. This segment can be sampled using ray marching as described in Section 6.3.2.

To further tighten the nonempty K-d-cells, the following procedure is applied:

- The voxels are sliced into subcells: the average normal of the contained $\mathbf{p}_i$ is computed and used to construct a stack of equidistant slabs that are normal to that direction.
- Each subcell is sampled randomly to estimate its minimum and maximum implicit value.
- Only if these values have differing signs, the surface is expected to be contained in the subcell. All the others are removed.

Removing subcells enables the split planes of the K-d-tree to be moved toward the surface. In practice, 7–13 slices and 100–200 samples per cell have worked well. Two scenes rendered interactively using this algorithm are shown in Figure 6.36.

Ray-tracing Deforming Surfaces

In this section a framework is discussed for accelerated ray tracing of free-form deforming surfaces [AKP+05]. As opposed to Adamson and Alexa's and Wald and

Figure 6.36: Interactive ray tracing. (*a*) A scene consisting of 24 Iphigenias with a total of 24 million points with Phong shading and shadows rendered at two frames per second at 640 × 480 image resolution. (*b*) One Iphigenia rendered with precomputed global illumination at four frames per second for a resolution of 400 × 600 pixels. Images taken from Wald and Seidel [WS05].

Seidel's work, which is designed for static point clouds (i.e., only rigid movements are allowed), Adams et al. focus on free-form deforming point-sampled surfaces. Although the discussed optimizations are used for surfaces resulting from a particular animation framework [MKN+04] (Section 7.1), they can easily be generalized to fit in any animation method that applies the idea of an embedded surface (such as, for example, the point-based shell animation framework of Wicke et al. [WSG05]).

The key idea is to use a bounding sphere hierarchy (for quick intersection finding), which is updated in a lazy manner by looking at the deformation field only instead of looking at the deformed surface. In the animation framework of Müller et al. [MKN+04], the deformation field is defined at a relatively small number of simulation nodes $\{p_j\}$. These nodes are discrete point samples of the volume of the model and the displacements from their original position completely define the deformation of the object's surface. As the number of surface samples $\{s_i\}$ is usually much higher than the number of simulation nodes (usually up to two or three orders of magnitudes), updating the bounding sphere hierarchy from the simulation nodes is significantly faster than updating it from the surface points.

When deforming the material, the displacements of the surfels are determined from spatially adjacent simulation nodes using a free-form deformation approach. Initially, each surfel s_i is assigned a set of neighboring simulation nodes p_j (see

Figure 6.37, middle). After an animation step, the new position $\mathbf{x}'_{s_i}$ of s_i is computed using a first-order accurate approximation of the displacements $\mathbf{u}_{p_j}$ of the neighboring simulation nodes p_j as [MKN+04]:

$$\mathbf{x}'_{s_i} = \mathbf{x}_{s_i} + \sum_{p_j} \overline{\omega}^{h_i}_{\mathbf{x}_{s_i}, \mathbf{x}_{p_j}} (\mathbf{u}_{p_j} + \nabla^T \mathbf{u}_{p_j} \mathbf{d}_{\mathbf{x}_{s_i}, \mathbf{x}_{p_j}}), \tag{6.73}$$

where $\mathbf{d}_{\mathbf{x},\mathbf{y}} = \mathbf{y} - \mathbf{x}$, $\overline{\omega}^h_{\mathbf{x},\mathbf{y}} = \omega^h_{\mathbf{x},\mathbf{y}} / \sum_{\mathbf{y}} \omega^h_{\mathbf{x},\mathbf{y}}$, and $\omega^h_{\mathbf{x},\mathbf{y}}$ is a smoothly decaying weight function with support radius h (similar to the weight functions used in Section 6.3.2).

By decoupling the sampling of the simulation domain from the sampling of the boundary surfaces, this method allows efficient animation of highly detailed models using the smooth displacement field $\mathbf{u}$. This implicit spatial coherence can be exploited for efficient updates of the bounding sphere hierarchy, as will be discussed below.

The bounding sphere hierarchy is only built once for the undeformed object using a top-down strategy similar to the one used in QSplat [RL00]. Instead of rebuilding the hierarchy for each subsequent animation frame, it is updated dynamically from the deformation field to conform with the deformed object similar to James and Pai [JP04].

Updating the hierarchy requires computing new sphere centers and radii. Starting from the initial sphere center $\mathbf{x}_c$ and optimal radius R, the updated center $\mathbf{x}'_c$ and radius R' are computed from the simulation nodes p_j that define the displacements of the surfels s_i bounded by the sphere (see Figure 6.37c). The update proceeds by finding a new sphere position and radius so that the new sphere bounds the deformed

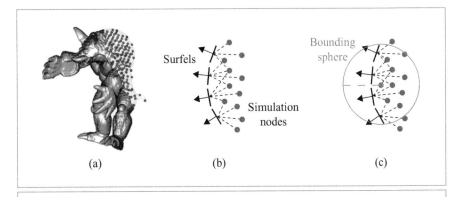

(a)   (b)   (c)

Figure 6.37: Point-based animations. (*a and b*) The surfels are embedded in the simulation domain defined by the simulation nodes. (*c*) Bounding sphere, which is updated by looking at the deformation of the associated simulation nodes.

surface. However, the update is done by only looking at the list of simulation nodes associated with the sphere.

Center Update   The displaced sphere center $\mathbf{x}_c'$ is computed in the same manner as the displaced surfel positions are computed:

$$\mathbf{x}_c' = \mathbf{x}_c + \sum_{p_j} \overline{\omega}_{\mathbf{x}_c,\mathbf{x}_{p_j}}^{R} (\mathbf{u}_{p_j} + \nabla^T \mathbf{u}_{p_j} \mathbf{d}_{\mathbf{x}_c,\mathbf{x}_{p_j}}) \tag{6.74}$$

$$\equiv \mathbf{x}_c + \mathbf{u}_c. \tag{6.75}$$

Radius Update   The new radius R' is conservatively estimated from the maximal distance between the deformed surfels (Equation 6.73) and the new sphere center (Equation 6.75) using basic linear algebra and the triangle inequality:

$$R' = \max_{s_i} \| \mathbf{x}_{s_i}' - \mathbf{x}_c' \|_2 \tag{6.76}$$

$$= \max_{s_i} \| (\mathbf{x}_{s_i} - \mathbf{x}_c) + \sum_{p_j} \overline{\omega}_{\mathbf{x}_{s_i},\mathbf{x}_{p_j}}^{h_i} (\mathbf{u}_{p_j} - \mathbf{u}_c) + \sum_{p_j} \overline{\omega}_{\mathbf{x}_{s_i},\mathbf{x}_{p_j}}^{h_i} \nabla^T \mathbf{u}_{p_j} \mathbf{d}_{\mathbf{x}_{s_i},\mathbf{x}_{p_j}} \|_2$$

$$\leq \max_{s_i} \| \mathbf{x}_{s_i} - \mathbf{x}_c \|_2 + \sum_{p_j} \max_{s_i} |a_{s_i,p_j}| \| \mathbf{u}_{p_j} - \mathbf{u}_c \|_2 + \sum_{p_j} \max_{s_i} \| \mathbf{b}_{s_i,p_j} \|_2 \| \nabla^T \mathbf{u}_{p_j} \|_F$$

$$\equiv R + \sum_{p_j} \mathbf{A}_j \mathbf{U}_j + \sum_{p_j} \mathbf{B}_j \nabla \mathbf{U}_j, \tag{6.77}$$

where $a_{s_i,p_j} = \overline{\omega}_{\mathbf{x}_{s_i},\mathbf{x}_{p_j}}^{h_i}$, $\mathbf{b}_{s_i,p_j} = \overline{\omega}_{\mathbf{x}_{s_i},\mathbf{x}_{p_j}}^{h_i} \mathbf{d}_{\mathbf{x}_{s_i},\mathbf{x}_{p_j}}$, and $\| \nabla^T \mathbf{u}_{p_j} \|_F$ is the Frobenius norm of the gradient of the displacement field. We can bring $\mathbf{u}_c$ into the summation since the weights $\overline{\omega}_{\mathbf{x}_{s_i},\mathbf{x}_{p_j}}^{h_i}$ sum up to 1 by construction. The entries $\mathbf{A}_j$ and $\mathbf{B}_j$ remain constant during the animation and can thus be precomputed once in the reference system. Note that the center and radius updates have time complexity linear in the number of simulation nodes associated with a bounding sphere, not in the number of bounded surfels. This is important as the number of simulation nodes is typically much smaller than the number of surfels. The radius update is always done with respect to the initial (optimal) bounding spheres (i.e., the radius can both increase and decrease over time). The sphere hierarchy thus maintains its tight fit even for highly elastic materials that expand and shrink significantly during an animation.

The resulting ray-tracing algorithm is roughly two times faster than the naive algorithm where each frame in the sequence is treated separately. Figure 6.38 shows example frames of animation sequences rendered using this dynamic data structure.

Figure 6.38: *Top row*: Three frames from the cannon ball armadillo sequence. Average rendering time was 8.5 seconds per frame (compared to 18.5 seconds per frame when not using any coherence). The armadillo is defined by 170,000 surface points and is animated using 453 simulation nodes. *Bottom row*: Three frames from the gymnastic goblin sequence. Average rendering time was 6 seconds per frame (compared to 12.8 seconds per frame when not using any coherence). The goblin is defined by 100,000 surface points and is animated using 502 simulation nodes. Images taken from Adams et al. [AKP+05].

6.3.4 IMPLEMENTATION TIPS

In this section we discuss some general tips that lead to a stable and efficient implementation of the above discussed ray-tracing algorithms.

Characteristics of the Weighted Covariance

If the covariance of the sample locations is used to compute $\mathbf{n}(\mathbf{x})$, one has to consider that the results are only approximately normal to $\hat{S}$, if $\mathbf{x}$ is close (i.e., within the sampling density). Otherwise, completely undesired directions result. To cope with this, one should use tight bounding volumes yielding $\mathbf{r}_0$ close to $\hat{S}$. Alternatively, one could use $\mathbf{n}(\mathbf{a}(\mathbf{x}))$ instead of $\mathbf{n}(\mathbf{x})$. The resulting surface:

$$\hat{S}' = \{\mathbf{x} \in \mathcal{B} \,|\, f'(\mathbf{x}) = \mathbf{n}(\mathbf{a}(\mathbf{x}))^T(\mathbf{x} - \mathbf{a}(\mathbf{x})) = 0\} \tag{6.78}$$

is almost identical to $\hat{S}$ and the normal calculation is as stable as averaging the $\mathbf{n}_i$.

Precomputing Neighborhoods

The heart of the ray-surface intersection algorithm consists of computing a weighted-average position and weighted-average normal from the neighboring points in the model. Thanks to the compactly supported weight functions, only the points within a small query ball around the current iteration point r_j need to be considered. As the different r_j are not known a priori, one has to perform a range query for each intermediate intersection point to obtain the neighborhood around r_j.

In case the scene remains static, references to all the potentially contributing samples can be stored in every bounding volume element (such as a voxel or sphere). These are the samples whose corresponding B_i intersect the bounding volume element. To evaluate $f(\mathbf{x})$ it is only necessary to determine the bounding volume element that contains $\mathbf{x}$ and loop over the contained samples. During traversal of the data structure this is usually known anyway.

Alternatively, the repeated neighborhood queries can be avoided by using the following observation. Assume the intersection algorithm starts with the guess r_0 that is obtained either as the intersection of the ray with the bounding sphere corresponding to a sample p_i, or as the sample itself (which actually means $r_0 = p_i$), or as the intersection of the ray with the splat associated with p_i. In all cases, r_0 is within a bounded distance to the point p_i. So it is possible to define a neighborhood for p_i that includes the neighborhood for r_0. Now, the positions p_i are known a priori, as they define our point model, and thus neighborhoods for these points can be precomputed once before ray tracing. We can now use p_i's neighborhood for r_0. If we assume that the subsequent intersection points r_j are all within a bounded distance to p_i (which is to be expected), we can use the same neighborhood during the whole intersection algorithm avoiding neighborhood queries altogether. Results show that using static neighborhoods of 10 to 16 points gives good results.

Adams et al. [AKP+05] go one step further and use this optimization even for deforming point clouds: neighborhoods are computed once and reused for the deformed surface in subsequent frames. This is only possible because the point models deform elastically and, therefore, neighborhoods are assumed to stay roughly constant.

Minimizing Bounding Volume Overlap

When building spatial data structures it is necessary to know the extents of the object to bound. Unfortunately, for implicit surfaces this is not a trivial task. Therefore, we build conservative bounding volumes for patches of the surface. In Section 6.3.2 two choices for such volumes are given that are located at the samples. In order to avoid holes, the volumes should overlap sufficiently. On the other hand, the overlap should be minimized as much as possible in order to improve performance. Indeed, a tighter bounding volume for $\hat{S}$ reduces the number of rays to be examined and reduces the number of invocations of the ray-surface intersection algorithm.

If we consider samples equipped with normals, these conditions are similar to the conditions desired for surface splatting (see Sections 4.3 and 6.1). In that context, Wu and Kobbelt [WK04] propose an algorithm to construct splats from a dense point cloud that satisfy the aforementioned conditions. If such adequate surfel splats are available, they can be expanded in normal direction (e.g., a factor one-fifth of their radius), to ensure all of the surface is contained. Instead of dealing with such cylinder caps, we propose to use oriented-bounding boxes for efficiency instead (refer to Figure 6.30).

Choosing the Radius of Support

The radius of support h has significant impact on the performance of the computations, even if the bounding volumes only have minimal overlap: each evaluation requires looping over all the contributing samples and computing the θ_i, $\mathbf{a}(\mathbf{x})$ and $\mathbf{n}(\mathbf{x})$. Therefore, h should be chosen as small as possible. However, we have to make sure the surface looks sufficiently smooth. Indeed, for small h the surface appears as piecewise linear patches that are blended together. In practice, choosing the support radius h so that the resulting neighborhoods consist of about 10 to 16 samples produces good results. Note that this criterion also works for irregularly sampled point clouds. Wald and Seidel [WS05] state that even four samples are sufficient.

Minimizing Ray-surface Intersection Tests

As computing the intersection of the ray with the surface is rather time consuming, it should be avoided as much as possible. Therefore, when implementing an acceleration data structure such as an octree, K-d-tree, or bounding sphere hierarchy, it is important to make sure that the first intersection on the ray is found as soon as possible. Adamson and Alexa [AA03a], for example, propose to first find *all* ray-sphere intersections and then sort the spheres front to back and perform the ray-surface intersection test for the nearest sphere first. This reduces the number of ray-surface intersection tests significantly, as the closest intersection is expected to be found in the nearest sphere.

Also, when tracing shadow rays, it is not important to find the closest intersection point as any as intersection point will do to block the ray. This has been used, for example, to increase performance in the framework of Adams et al. [AKP+05].

Speeding Up the Evaluation of f

Another interesting optimization was proposed by Wald and Seidel [WS05]. They exchange the function $f(\mathbf{x}) = \mathbf{n}(\mathbf{x})^T(\mathbf{x} - \mathbf{a}(\mathbf{x}))$ for a simpler one. The goal here is to find a function $F(\mathbf{x})$ that defines the same surface (i.e., it has the same roots) but which is simpler to intersect (i.e., less computations are needed for intersection testing).

This can be done by multiplying $f(\mathbf{x})$ with the denominators $D_1(\mathbf{x}) = \sum_{i=1}^{N} \theta_i$ and $D_2(\mathbf{x}) = \| \sum_{i=1}^{N} \theta_i \mathbf{n}_i \|$ of the expressions in Equation (6.66):

$$F(\mathbf{x}) = D_1(\mathbf{x})D_2(\mathbf{x})f(\mathbf{x}) \tag{6.79}$$

$$= (D_2(\mathbf{x})\mathbf{n}(\mathbf{x}))^T (D_1(\mathbf{x})\mathbf{x} - D_1(\mathbf{x})\mathbf{a}(\mathbf{x})) \tag{6.80}$$

$$= \Big(\sum_{i=1}^{N} \theta_i \mathbf{n}_i \Big)^T \Big(\Big(\sum_{i=1}^{N} \theta_i \Big)\mathbf{x} - \sum_{i=1}^{N} \theta_i \mathbf{p}_i \Big), \tag{6.81}$$

except for those $\mathbf{x}$ where $D_1(\mathbf{x}) = 0$ and $D_2(\mathbf{x}) = 0$ (for these points $f(\mathbf{x})$ was undefined anyway). It can be easily seen that $F(\mathbf{x})$ has the same roots and signs as $f(\mathbf{x})$ and, therefore, defines the same surface. The main advantage is that there are no divisions and no normalization anymore and, therefore, the intersection algorithm becomes much more efficient.

However, although the implicit surface remains the same, F does not approximate a distance field anymore, because a quadratic term was introduced. Ray marching with linear intersection interpolating is the only method of the tracing strategies described in Section 6.3.2 that can still be applied. The quality of the linear interpolation is considerably reduced by this optimization, which requires the step size to be sufficiently small. This is achieved by using extremely tight voxels, which only require very short ray segments to be examined.

To further speed up the computation, a simple linear function (or hat filter) θ_h can be used:

$$\theta_h(r) = \theta_h(\|\mathbf{x} - \mathbf{p}_i\|/h) = \begin{cases} 1 - r & \text{if } r < 1, \\ 0 & \text{if } r \geq 1. \end{cases} \tag{6.82}$$

However, this degrades the smoothness of the resulting surface.

6.3.5 CONCLUSION

Ray tracing of point-sampled surfaces is a relatively new research topic and only a handful of papers tackle this at first sight as a difficult problem. However, the surface definition proposed by Adamson and Alexa [AA03a] is very powerful and moreover it is very straightforward and easy to implement a ray-surface intersection algorithm for point models based on this definition. Other researchers [WS05, AKP+05] have picked up this work and propose various extensions and optimizations of the basic algorithm. The resulting algorithms have been used to visualize various animation sequences including the animation of elastic and plastic solids [AKP+05] (see Section 7.1), fracturing materials [PKA+05] (see Section 7.2), viscous fluids [KAG+05] (see Section 7.3), and point-based shells [WSG05]. The sequences show high-quality renderings of animated point-sampled surfaces including complex shading effects such as shadows, reflections, and refractions.

6.4 RENDERING OF VERY LARGE MODELS

Michael Wand

6.4.1 OVERVIEW

Point-based techniques can be used as a tool for rendering highly complex scenes, (i.e., scenes consisting of a large amount of primitives). The basic idea is easy to describe: instead of processing billions of primitives, only a small set of surface sample points are chosen to approximate the geometry. This sample set will be just dense enough to provide a sample for each pixel in the image. Then in a second step, an image is constructed using these sample points, hence neglecting most of the complex geometry. To make this work, the sampling density is chosen so that one obtains an approximately uniform distribution of points in the image plane. This guarantees that a sufficient, uniform level of information is obtained for all parts of the image.

Following this approach, one can create images using a number of points being roughly in the order of the number of image pixels, rather than being dependent on the number of primitives the scene consists of. A precomputed multiresolution point hierarchy will be employed to compute the sample sets in output-sensitive time (i.e., with time mostly dependent on the number of points needed only). Therefore, interactive walkthroughs of huge scenes consisting of vast amounts of geometric details can be rendered efficiently.

The main advantage of such a point-based rendering approach is its generality. Unlike other representations, the technique is applicable to virtually arbitrary scenes. A prominent example is the case of landscape scenes with trees and vegetation. Such scenes typically contain an exorbitant number of geometric primitives, which are arranged in highly nonuniform mesh topologies. This leads to significant problems for classic techniques such as simplification based on triangle hierarchies. Point-based multiresolution rendering techniques work as well in these cases as on simple smooth meshes, making them currently probably the most successful rendering techniques for such general classes of scenes.

This section of the book describes how to construct a point-based multiresolution rendering algorithm for large scenes. It consists of three parts. First, the general algorithmic approach and its variants are discussed. Second, a theoretical model of the performance characteristics of such techniques is summarized. This is not done for the sake of just being formal but will provide some interesting insights relevant for practical implementations. Accordingly, this section will conclude with a list of such recommendations. Lastly, a brief case study of one specific implementation is described, showing that the approach works in practice.

6.4.2 POINT-BASED MULTIRESOLUTION RENDERING

The Algorithm

As summarized above, the point-based multiresolution rendering algorithm consists of two main steps: *sample point selection* and *image reconstruction*. The goal of the first step is to create sample points that are more or less uniformly distributed on the projections of the objects in the image plane.[5] Obviously, such a set of sample points depend on the current viewpoint and thus change whenever the view position changes. To allow for interactive walkthroughs, precomputed hierarchical data structures are employed to extract such sample sets efficiently (as described in Section 4.4). The second step, image reconstruction, will then be performed using a splatting technique as discussed in Sections 6.1 and 6.2.

Before these two steps can be examined more in detail, it is first necessary to look at some properties of perspective projection.

Perspective Projection

How to create "uniformly distributed" sample sets in the image plane obviously depends on the employed camera model. In the context of large scenes, typically only a perspective type of camera model makes sense (e.g., an orthographic projection would be cluttered with lots of occluding details). For simplicity, a simple planar perspective projection is considered here, which is the natural model for a scene walkthrough. Figure 6.39a shows the setup. The camera is placed at a center of projection and the image is created on an image plane. Each object point is projected by intersecting the plane with a line through both the center of projection and the object point. Only a rectangular part of the image plane will be shown on the screen. Hence, a *view frustum* in space can be set up by four planes, defined by the center of projection and the four sides of the image rectangle in the image plane. Only geometry within the intersection of the four corresponding half spaces will project on the screen; anything else can be neglected for rendering. Additionally, a near-clipping plane in front of the center of projection is established. This fifth plane is necessary because the mapping is singular (infinite magnification) at the center of projection. Hence, all objects closer than a minimum distance will be excluded from rendering. The distance of the near clipping plane will become important later on for analyzing the efficiency of the rendering algorithm.

Given such a perspective projection, the *projection factor* can be defined: this is the scale factor by which an infinitesimally small piece of surface is scaled when

---

5   In this context, a "uniform" sampling might still allow for some local variations, for example, to adapt the sampling density to surface features such as curvature.

being projected to the screen. For a planar perspective projection (as defined above), the projection factor at a point $\mathbf{p}$ (within the view frustum) is given by (see also Figure 6.39b)

$$prj\,(\mathbf{p}) = \frac{d^2\,|\cos\beta|}{z^2\,\cos\alpha} \tag{6.83}$$

The projection factor is a product of multiple independent terms: The projected area of a surface fragment drops quadratically with depth ($\frac{1}{z^2}$). This term is called the *depth factor*. Additionally, the projected area depends on the orientation of the surface. The projected area is proportional to the cosine of the angle β between the surface normal and a vector toward the viewer. This term is called the *orientation factor*. The third factor, $\cos^{-1}\alpha$, is called the *distortion factor*. This factor leads to an increase of projected area if a surface fragment is visible in the outer regions of the image (rather than close to the center). The effect is only significant for camera settings with rather large viewing angles ("wide-angle lenses"), which is why it is often not taken into account. Finally, everything is scaled by d^2, which is just a constant accounting for the distance to the image plane (or, equivalently, the scaling of the pixels). Additionally, the projection factor is assumed to be zero outside the view frustum.

The goal is now to create sample sets with a density proportional to this projection factor. Currently, no algorithm being based on a reasonably sized precomputed data structure is known that can perform this task exactly without looking at every primitive of the scene (which would of course contradict the goal of efficient large scene

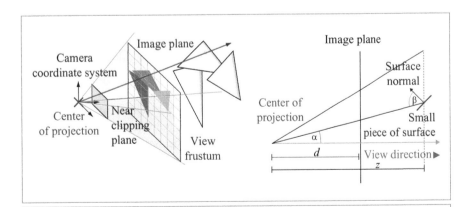

Figure 6.39: Perspective projection: (*a*) projection setup and (*b*) influence of orientation and distance.

rendering). Thus, an approximation strategy will be employed that will have to make some compromises:

- The sampling density will not be exactly proportional to the depth factor but allows variations up to a constant value. The same is true for the distortion factor.
- The orientation factor will just be neglected.
- The sampling density will be increased in discrete steps only (thus allowing for precomputed sample sets).
- View frustum culling will be performed only approximately.

The consequences of these approximations are discussed later, in Section 6.4.3. This will prove to be a critical point. The approximation is the reason that the whole approach works at all. At the same time it leads to some nonobvious trade-offs.

Selecting the Points

The sampling algorithm uses a precomputed multiresolution point hierarchy. The hierarchical data storage will support two important tasks: a good approximation of the depth factor and an approximate view frustum culling.

Data Structure   Section 4.4.3 describes several different variants of multiresolution point hierarchies based on a common idea: the space of the scene is partitioned into hierarchical clusters. For each cluster, a representative point set are chosen. The resolution of the representation increases with hierarchy depth. In order to unify the description here, using a multiresolution point hierarchy with the following properties is assumed (Figure 6.40a):

- The point hierarchy is an octree partition of the scene (similar results will also hold for other hierarchical partitions of the scene with bounded node degree and where the maximum diameters of the bounding boxes shrink exponentially with recursion depth).
- The sample spacing in each node is proportional to the side length of the bounding cube of the node. This means that within a closed surface, the maximum distance of a piece of surface to a sample point is no more than a fixed fraction of the side length of the bounding cube. Setting the fraction to one yields a data structure similar to QSplat; using a smaller fraction yields a data structure similar to an LDC-tree (see Section 4.4). Due to the octree subdivision, the resolution will double at each hierarchy level (Figure 6.40a).

For a faithful representation of arbitrary geometry with points, the hierarchy would need to have infinite depth. This is of course not realistic but there is a simple solution to this problem: the scene to be simplified itself must have been described by some set of original primitives. For conventional 3D models, these are typically triangles.

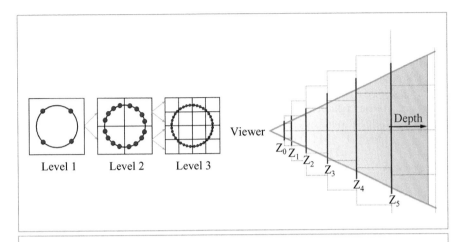

Figure 6.40: (*a*) Schematic view of a multiresolution point hierarchy: the space is partitioned using an octree hierarchy, and each node stores a precomputed set of representative points. (*b*) Estimation of the traversal costs the box sizes increase exponentially with depth, leading to logarithmic costs.

For geometry from 3D scanners, the representation could also be point-based itself, such as elliptical splats obtained from some preprocessing of the raw data (density estimation, normal estimation). The original geometry can now be included in the hierarchy to limit the size of the data structure. Whenever more than a small number of sample points from the same original primitive are necessary, the original primitive is stored at this hierarchy level and no further sampling is done in deeper levels. For example, if three points or more are representing a triangle, the original triangle itself can be used at similar costs. This limits the recursion depth necessary. Due to the exponential shrinkage of the point sets, one can expect (optimal) linear memory consumption (in practice, for nonpathological scenes).

The Point-selection Algorithm The points are selected by a simple recursive procedure, starting at the root node of the point hierarchy (see Figure 6.41 for pseudocode for this algorithm). First, the view frustum check is performed. This means, if the current bounding cube does not intersect with the view frustum, the recursion is terminated at this point. Otherwise, it must be checked whether the point resolution already meets the resolution demands. If the projected sample spacing is not larger than the desired point spacing in the image (typically, projected sample spacing below one pixel), the traversal is stopped and the points in the current node are projected to the image and rendered. If not, the algorithm is called recursively for all child nodes.

```
Procedure pointSelection(Node n, Camera c)
result :=∅
IF BoundingBox(n)∩viewFrustum(c)≠∅ Then
    z_min:=minimumDepth(BoundingBox(n), c)
    α_max:=maximumAlpha(BoundingBox(n), c)
    IF sampleSpacing(n) > requiredSampleSpacing(z_min, α_max) THEN
        FOR all children m of n DO
            result:=result∪ pointSelection(m, c)
    ELSE
        result :=points(n)
    ENDIF
ENDIF
```

Figure 6.41: Pseudocode for the hierarchy traversal algorithm. The procedure takes a node and the current camera parameters as input and returns a set of points with approximate uniform density.

The projected sample spacing is computed by a conservative estimate of the on-screen sampling density. First, the maximum sample spacing of the current node in object space is determined. Then, the maximum depth and distortion factors are computed. Next, the sample spacing is scaled accordingly and compared to the image pixel spacing. Orientation is not taken into account; implicitly, a worst-case, orthogonal view of all geometry is assumed. This procedure creates a *conservative* estimate: the point density might be too large, but it does not fall below the optimal uniform density.

Image Reconstruction

After the point-selection procedure, a set of points are obtained that cover the projections of objects in the image plane approximately uniformly. Now it remains to construct an image using this information. This procedure has just been described (Sections 6.1 and 6.2). It is assumed that each point is associated with a small circle or ellipse. The radii are chosen to reflect the sample spacing. For example, if the sample spacing of the computed point set in the image is guaranteed not to exceed two pixels, circular splats of two-pixel diameter could be used. Alternatively, ellipses in object space that cover the surfaces tightly at each level of resolution might be provided by the multiresolution hierarchy (Section 4.4). For rendering, the corresponding splats are drawn using a z-buffer algorithm (or some variant of this technique). Closer splats will overwrite splats that are farther away, yielding a closed surface with correctly reconstructed visibility. A blending or interpolation scheme is typically used to improve the image quality (Section 6.1).

6.4.3 RENDERING COSTS, QUALITY, AND OPTIMIZATIONS

In this section, the performance characteristics of the described point-based multiresolution rendering strategy are examined. The described algorithm still has open parameters (such as the number of points in each octree node) and it is nonobvious how these affect the rendering performance. Additionally, it still must be determined how fast the new rendering strategy will be for scenes of varying complexity. These questions should now be examined more in detail. Rendering costs are caused by two factors: processing hierarchy nodes and processing points. The final rendering costs (including image reconstruction) will be proportional to both of these costs. These two components of the rendering costs will now be examined subsequently.

Hierarchy Traversal

The key insight to bound the hierarchy traversal costs is the following. Boxes that are selected by the algorithm show a projected point spacing corresponding to the pixel spacing. In object space, this means that the side length of the box must be roughly proportional to its depth (because of perspective foreshortening). As the bounding box is a cube, this also applies to its depth. Let z_{min} be the minimum and z_{max} be the maximum depth of a node selected for rendering. Then, $z_{max} = z_{min} + \bar{c} \cdot z_{min} = c \cdot z_{min}$ with a constant $\bar{c} > 0$ and $c := 1 + \bar{c}$. Roughly speaking, for the next box, behind the previous one, its z_{min} value will be the z_{max} value of the previous box, and so on. Overall, this leads to an exponentially rising series of z values $z_i = z_{i-1}c = z_0 c^i$, with z_0 (roughly) being the distance to the near clipping plane (see Figure 6.40b). This leads to the following idea for bounding the number of hierarchy nodes extracted for rendering [CDL+96, WFP+01, Wan04]. The counting of boxes starts at the near clipping plane and covers the whole image with a constant number of boxes (this is possible, as the projection of the boxes is of fixed size, corresponding to the number of pixels per side length). Then, the next layer is added, with depth multiplied by a constant c. Each layer of boxes will have an exponentially increasing depth. Therefore, (the traversal costs grow at most logarithmically) with the size of the scene (the traversal must stop at last at the constructed set of boxes). Taking some more (minor) technical details into account, it can be shown [Wan04] that the hierarchy traversal costs are bounded by $O(\log \tau + h)$ where h is the height of the octree and τ is the *relative depth range*. The height of the octree is a very small quantity in practice so that this term does not have a significant impact on rendering performance. The relative depth range τ is the ratio of the depth value of the farthest piece of geometry to the depth of the nearest piece of geometry considered. This geometric quantity is always bound by the ratio of the maximum scene diameter to the depth value of the near clipping plane. τ can become very large. However, it affects the running time only logarithmically. Hence, the size of the scene does not severely limit the rendering performance. This is a very important result, because otherwise the proposed technique would be of little use for rendering large scenes.

Approximation Accuracy

Next, the point-processing costs are examined. These costs are directly linked to the approximation accuracy of the approximate sample selection scheme. The less accurate the (conservative) approximate sample selection algorithm chooses its sample points, the more points are necessary to cover the image, and thus, the higher are the point-processing costs.

The most important parameter affecting the accuracy is the "box size" (i.e., the number of points per box side length). The larger this value, the more points will be stored in one node at fixed sample spacing, reducing adaptivity. Two sources of inaccuracy are introduced. First, the view frustum culling is not precise. Nodes partially within the field of view may contain points that are not visible on-screen, causing unwanted overhead. Second, the sampling density will not strictly obey to depth and distortion factors, as these factors vary throughout the spatial extends of the node. It can be shown that the approximation accuracy for the depth factor is bounded by

$$\varepsilon(k) \leq \left(2\sqrt{3}k\frac{\tan\alpha_v/2}{I_h} + 1\right)^2 - 1. \tag{6.84}$$

In this expression, k is the number of points per box side length, I_h is the vertical image resolution, and α_v is the vertical viewing angle. $\varepsilon(k)$ is then the upper bound for the deviation to the ideal sampling density; in other words, the sampling density will not fall below the desired density and never exceed it by more than $1 + \varepsilon(k)$.

Similarly, the overestimation of the view frustum can be bounded. The projected on-screen size of the boxes is roughly constant. Thus, the relative error in view-frustum culling is fixed. This means that only a constant factor in running time is lost (assuming that geometry is distributed roughly uniformly in the view frustum). More specifically, this expected relative error can be bounded by

$$VF(k) \leq 1 + \frac{2\sqrt{3}kI_h(1 + R) + 12k^2}{RI_h^2} \tag{6.85}$$

for a screen with aspect ratio $R = width/height = I_w/I_h$. The influence of the distortion factor is usually rather small (see Wand [Wan04] for an analytic bound). All these quantities grow quadratically with k. However, the asymptotic behavior is of minor importance here as the fixed-image resolution renders arbitrary large values of k useless. More interesting is the value of these bounds for intermediate values of k, as

Table 6.2: Overestimation of the Depth Factor, the Projected View-frustum Area, and the Distortion Factor in Dependence of the Number of Sample Points per Box Side Length at an Image Resolution of 640 × 480 Pixels and 60° Vertical-viewing Angle.

Points per box side k	2	4	8	16	32	64	128	256
Depth app., $\varepsilon(k)$	0.017	0.034	0.068	0.14	0.28	0.60	1.35	3.27
View frus. app., $VF(k)$	0.025	0.051	0.10	0.21	0.44	0.97	2.25	5.79
Distortion app., $DF(k)$	0.042	0.084	0.017	0.034	0.069	0.14	0.30	0.63

arising in typical applications. Table 6.2 shows a few example values of these bounds. In practice, the dominant issue is the approximation accuracy for depth factor and view frustum; at the chosen vertical viewing angle (60°), the distortion factor is not important. For moderate values of k, the overhead is bounded by reasonably small constants. For k approaching the order of magnitude of the image resolution, the overhead becomes more substantial. Please note that the table shows upper bounds (upper bounds on the average overestimation in case of the view frustum). In practice, the overhead is typically smaller.

Sampling

Rendering performance is also affected by the choice of the (sub)sampling algorithm that is used to create the multiresolution point sets in the inner nodes of the hierarchy (different sampling strategies are discussed in detail in Section 4.3). A good sampling strategy should minimize the overlap of the corresponding splats associated with the sample points. The overlap must be minimized in object space as the view parameters are not known at the time of precomputing the sampling. There are two general sampling approaches: simple *uniform sampling* and *adaptive sampling*.

For uniform surface sampling, one can think of a small disk of constant radius attached to each sample point within one node of the hierarchy. The *oversampling* can then be quantified by the overlap of these discs. The optimum oversampling value for a (locally) flat surface is 1.21, corresponding to the well-known tightest coverage of the plane by circles [Wil79]. Such point sets can be approximated, for example, using the point-repulsion technique described in Section 4.3. However, such a numerical relaxation scheme is rather involved so that often simpler approximations are used. Common are random and grid-based representations [BWK02, SD01b, WFP+01]. For example, an LDC-tree (Section 4.4) uses a variant of grid-based sampling by ray-tracing geometry on regular grids from three orthogonal directions [PZvBG00]. In practice, it turns out that random sampling leads to oversampling factors of 8–20, depending on the probability of surface holes one is willing to tolerate. Sampling techniques that partition space with a regular grid, allowing only one surface sample from each grid cell, yield (empirical) oversampling ratios of 13.4 (unrestricted) and 3.45 (if points are quantized to grid cell centers). A very simple but effective strategy is to start with a random sample and then remove all points that are already "covered" by nearby neighbors (the empirical oversampling is 1.6, thus already close to the optimum [Wan04]). Oversampling factors can be quite significant. Consequently, employing a more elaborated sampling technique can substantially speed up rendering.

Adaptive sampling schemes improve on uniform sampling by adapting the point density to features such as curvature or color variance (see Sections 4.3 and 6.5 for details), potentially providing substantial savings. Adaptive sampling can easily be incorporated into the multiresolution rendering framework. Instead of storing point clouds with fixed sample spacing in each node, the sample spacing is allowed to vary according to surface features; it may exceed the base sample spacing in areas of little variance. The hierarchy traversal algorithm still selects nodes according to the base sample spacing, thus extracting fewer points in less important areas. Each sample point must now be tagged with the space it represents to allow correct image reconstruction later on. Storing little ellipses and using EWA surface splatting (Section 6.1) for image reconstruction is a canonical choice for solving this problem.

There is another source of oversampling that is often not taken into account: the octree hierarchy provides precomputed point clouds with point spacing increasing in powers of two. Thus, in the worst case, the number of points that are chosen is up to four times larger than the number needed. On the average, one could possibly roughly expect all densities being demanded with similar probability, leading to an oversampling factor of $\int_1^2 s^2 ds = 2\frac{1}{3}$. One can store multiple point clouds with varying density in each node, for example m clouds with sample spacing a factor of $\sqrt[m]{2}$ apart. This reduces this kind of oversampling, however, at the expense of more memory usage (which is increased by a corresponding constant factor).

Orientation

Up to now, the orientation factor has been ignored completely. What does this mean for oversampling? Assuming that all orientations of normals are equally likely, one can show that the average oversampling due to ignoring orientation is only a factor of two (by integrating over the orientation factor on a sphere). Accounting for back-face culling (i.e., assuming not to render back-facing surfaces), the factor is four. This factor is a constant (which is why this strategy works at all) but not really a small one. A simple improvement is storing normal cones in each hierarchy node that bound the possible values of normal orientations (see Section 4.4). This information can be used at least for back-face culling. Good estimates of orientation can be expected for smooth surfaces and close views of such surfaces. However, for strongly simplified, irregular geometry (e.g., think of trees), useful bounds on orientation are rarely obtained. Nevertheless, storing a normal cone at each hierarchy node and performing a quick back-face culling check before rendering basically comes for free, so there is little reason not to include this in an implementation.

Overall Rendering Time

Putting all the results above together, the overall asymptotic rendering time of point-based multiresolution rendering is $O(h + \log \tau + \bar{a})$, where h is the octree height, τ is the relative depth range, and $\bar{a}$ is the estimated projected area ("estimated" refers to the approximation of the projection factor). Assuming that geometry is distributed uniformly within the extended view frustum extracted by the approximation algorithm and assuming uniform probabilities for surface normals, this estimated projected area is expected to be in $O(a)$ where a is the real projected area of the scene for a given camera view. The height of the octree and the logarithmic additive constant referring to scene depth are typically quite small in practice. Hence, the rendering time is constant, being independent of the amount of details in the scene. This is a giant leap in comparison to a simple plain z-buffer rendering approach without a multiresolution data structure, where the rendering time grows linearly with the amount or primitives in the scene. However, the rendering time of the point-based approximation still depends linearly on the projected area, which, of course, includes the projected area from occluded parts of the scene. Thus, for scenes with much occlusion, a complementary occlusion-culling technique is needed. Most hierarchical occlusion-culling techniques [COCK+01] can easily be incorporated into the described hierarchy-traversal algorithm.

Image Quality Considerations

Of course, rendering performance is of no value if the rendering strategy does not provide an acceptable level of image quality. Hence, is the result of the point-based simplification really comparable to traditional rendering techniques even though heavy simplifications take place? At this point, only the principle limits of the multiresolution approach are discussed. Other issues, such as aliasing and shading, are discussed in Sections 6.1 and 6.2.

The basic idea of point-based simplification is to replace geometry by sample points. Some volume in space (potentially containing arbitrarily complex geometry) will be replaced by a sample point that only contains a fixed amount of information. Thus, there is an inherent loss of information that can become visible in the image. This is a general problem. It does not appear to be possible to represent the visual effect of complex geometry with a constant amount of information [CDL+96] as both light emission and transmission for different viewing angles can be arbitrarily complicated. A classic example is a Venetian blind (Figure 6.42a). Such a geometric configuration shows a light transmission that is zero for most angles and close to one for

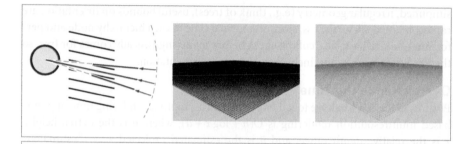

Figure 6.42: Principal accuracy limits of point-based simplification. In practice, often the opacity of simplified geometry is overestimated as subpixel occlusions cannot be captured faithfully. (*a*) Venetian blind: highly direction-dependent occlusion [CDL+96]. (*b*) Example: point-based rendering of many distant trees. (*c*) Reference image computed offline by distributed ray tracing.

a very small region in the angular domain. Furthermore, transfer through multiple pieces of geometry is also nontrivial. For correct compositing, the subpixel occlusion structure must be known. In general, an approximation, for example, by a simple transparency value does not yield correct results (think of compositing two Venetian blinds).

In practice, the color of a single sample point is usually considered to be constant as well as the light transmission (there are refined techniques, such as statistical models; see Section 8.2). The constant used for transparency has to be a conservative lower bound to avoid holes in closed surfaces. This easily leads to a significant overestimation of opacity and thus, strictly speaking, to wrong images. Nevertheless, renderings often appear quite plausible, despite being wrong in a strict formal sense. Figures 6.42b and c show an example: the opacity of the trees in the image is strongly overestimated by the point-based rendering algorithm, as revealed by the reference image created by (more expensive) stochastic ray tracing. Despite this, the depiction appears plausible (at least as long as one does not know the true solution).

6.4.4 EXAMPLE IMPLEMENTATION

This subsection shows some renderings produced by an example implementation of the point-based multiresolution rendering technique. The example scenes originally have consisted of triangle meshes and have been modeled using a scene graph data structure that provides hierarchical instantiation. It allows the formation of groups of objects and then a multiple "instantiation" of those groups in the scene (i.e., the replication of groups using different geometric transformations). The scene graph also allows hierarchical instantiation of groups of instances so that scenes of high geometric complexity can be described with reasonable memory consumption.

To apply the technique to precomputed point hierarchies, complete hierarchies are treated as ordinary geometric primitives that can be inserted into higher-level hierarchies. Using this technique, a very large "virtual" point hierarchy can be described that appears to contain billions of primitives and multiresolution representations of those. Please note that scene encoding is a significant problem. Finding an adequate description of a large scene that is compatible with memory and bandwidth restrictions might often be a more serious problem than rendering itself, and hierarchical instantiation is certainly not a general solution to this problem.

Figure 6.43 shows four application examples. The examples use octree hierarchies with $k = 48 - 64$ points per box side, which turned out to be optimal for the employed hardware (GeForce 5650go, 1.5 GHz Pentium-M, rendering using DirectX 9 managed vertex buffers). Using "large boxes" turned out to be critical for GPU-based rendering. Submitting many small batches is very expensive on current GPUs due to per-batch latency penalties [WH03]. As every node processed during rendering

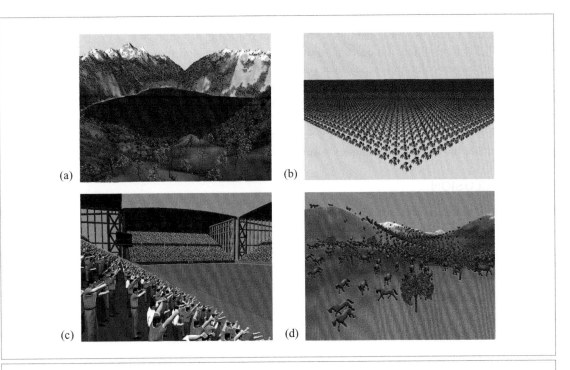

(a)   (b)   (c)   (d)

Figure 6.43: Example renderings (640 × 480 pixels). Frame rates for a 1.5 GHz Pentium-M notebook with nVidia GeForce FX 5650go graphics. (*a*) A landscape scene: 400 million triangles, frames per second; (*b*) a forest scene: 10^{15} triangles, 5–10 frames per second; (*c*) a stadium scene (105 million triangles), 10–20 frames per second; and (*d*) a herd of horses; 42 million triangles, 8–10 frames per second.

corresponds to a new batch, the rendering costs for "small boxes" (i.e., a large number of nodes) are completely dominated by latencies. For example, due to implementation limitations, scene (a) had to be rendered with smaller k ($k = 24$), which already results in significantly reduced performance. All scenes employ a uniform (nonadaptive) sampling technique (the neighborhood heuristic that approximates an optimal uniform sampling up to 30%). A single point cloud is stored per octree node (multiple resolution levels per hierarchy node are not employed). Image reconstruction is done by simply drawing single pixels in a z-buffering (no EWA surface splatting). Despite not employing all possible optimizations and using older hardware, interactive results can already be achieved for vastly complex scenes.

Figure 6.43a shows a landscape scene consisting of 400 million primitives (encoded by a scene graph by reusing six different tree models). The scene can be rendered at about four frames per second. Figure 6.43b shows a more drastic example: using five levels of 10×10 instantiations, six billion trees are encoded, amounting to about 10^{15} triangles. This scene can be rendered at about 10 Hz, permitting an interactive walkthrough. In comparison, a conventional z-buffer rendering without level-of-detail processing would have taken about half a year (using the same graphics hardware). Figures 6.43c and d show two more examples. The first is a rendering of a sports stadium with 16,500 football fans, amounting to over one hundred million triangles. Depending on the viewpoint, this scene can be displayed at frame rates of 10–20 Hz. The second image shows a similar scene but with a herd of horses (42 million triangles, 8–10 Hz). Due to the conceptual simplicity of the point-based approach, the rendering technique can easily be generalized. For example, the fans in the stadium and the herd of horses in the examples are actually animated; it is quite straightforward to generalize the described techniques to animated scenes [WH02].

6.4.5 CONCLUSION

Here is a list of conclusions and recommendations when using point-based rendering techniques for large scenes in practice:

- *Highly complex scenes can be rendered in real time*: Using the hierarchical point-based multiresolution rendering scheme described above, one can efficiently render highly complex scenes with a virtually unlimited number of primitives. The rendering time does *not* depend on the original level of detail; the geometric scene size (relative depth range) has only a minor influence.[6] Rendering is often more limited by memory constraints rather than rendering time.

---

6   The given results hold for most hierarchical techniques (LDC-trees, QSplat, and variants), as described previously. The analysis presented here does not apply to linearized hierarchies, as described in the next section.

- *Use big boxes*: Oversampling costs caused by using (moderately) larger point clouds per hierarchy node are quite reasonable in comparison to other sources of oversampling. Large clouds facilitate an efficient GPU implementation as the point cloud in every node can be submitted as one large batch. Thus, backed up by the theoretical analysis, one can recommend employing "big boxes" for GPU-based implementations. Hierarchies with few or even only one point per node are not optimal for GPU-based rendering. However, this might be the data structure of choice for various other applications, such as ray tracing or other CPU-based rendering techniques.
- *Sampling matters*: Unfavorable sampling patterns are a major cause of oversampling in practice. A well-designed sampling pattern can out perform an ad hoc or random version by about an order of magnitude. Adaptive sampling can decrease oversampling further. The quantization due to the hierarchy affects oversampling as well; data structures with branching factors larger than those of an octree are usually undesirable for this reason.
- *Point rendering can be expensive*: Hence, it should be used only when necessary. If the original geometry is not point based, it should be included in the multiresolution hierarchy at the high levels of detail. This assures both a faithful reproduction of the original data as well as the rendering algorithm to be never worse than simple rasterization of the original primitives in terms of rendering expenses.

The next section will describe how a point-based multiresolution rendering algorithm can be implemented entirely on a programmable GPU with almost no CPU intervention, and how to deal with the limitations of current graphics hardware by modifying the multiresolution data structure that represents the scene.

6.5 SEQUENTIAL POINT TREES

Carsten Dachsbacher and Marc Stamminger

6.5.1 OVERVIEW

Point clouds are a very useful representation for level-of-detail approaches. Their lack of topology information makes it easy to adapt the detail level by simply adding or removing points. No costly updates of topology information, as they are for example required for progressive meshes, are necessary. A typical example is the QSplat method ([RL00] and Section 4.4). The bounding box hierarchy is traversed top-down, and any branch can be skipped or rendered as a single point without considering neighboring branches, which makes the traversal efficient.

Nevertheless, due to its hierarchical nature, the top-down traversal of QSplat maps very badly to a current GPU. QSplat has a very fine granularity in its level-of-detail determination, and it generates the point cloud to be rendered point by point. As a consequence, if the points are rendered by a GPU, they have to be rendered in "immediate mode", (i.e., every single point is sent to the GPU separately). Thus, most of the power of current GPUs is unused, because the GPU is mainly waiting for new data. This bottleneck gets worse (in terms of memory bandwith), if more data is stored with every point (e.g., a normal, a color, a texture coordinate, etc.).

Memory traffic can be reduced by keeping all vertex data in video memory and only generating and sending vertex indices. Furthermore, recent computer architectures such as PCI Express provide much higher bandwidth. But current GPUs can still render many more points than the QSplat traversal can provide. So with QSplat on a current CPU roughly 10 million points can be generated per second, whereas a current GPU can easily render 100 million points per second and more.

Ideally, the QSplat point selection should happen directly on the GPU. This would solve the memory bandwidth problem, the computation power of the GPU can be better used, and the CPU is available for other tasks (e.g., game AI or physics simulation).

Sequential point trees [DVS03] achieve this goal by transforming the hierarchical traversal of the QSplat-like hierarchy to a sequential process. We first define a simple local point-selection criterion, with which we can decide for a single point of the hierarchy whether QSplat would select this point for a particular view or not, without having to look at its ancestors. We can then sequentially process all points and sort out the ones to be rendered. This processing can already be done by the GPU, at the cost that always all points have to be processed. The skipping of branches, that makes QSplat efficient, is not possible yet.

However, we can rearrange the nodes of a hierarchical point tree to a sequential list, so that all selected points are densely clustered in the list. This is demonstrated in Figure 6.44, where the Buddha model is rendered with increasing viewing distance. The bar below the Buddha visualizes the sequential point list with the selected points in red and the unselected points in green. The red points always form a cluster of varying size at the beginning of the list.

Furthermore, for any particular view, we can compute tight bounds on this cluster of selected points easily. We can then restrict the processing by the GPU to this bounded, yet sequential region. The majority of the points processed by the GPU is then also rendered, which dramatically increases performance. The CPU load is very low, the main process only has to compute the segment boundaries and pass them to the

Figure 6.44: Continuous detail levels of a Buddha generated in vertex programs on the GPU. The colors denote the LOD level used and the bars describe the selected amount of points selected for the GPU. CPU load is always below 1%.

GPU. The selection of the points inside this segment and the rendering are then done completely by the GPU, where the GPU can work at full power on the sequential data. Overhead arises due to the points that are culled by the GPU, but in our examples this fraction is in the range of only 10–40%. We thus achieve rates of about 60 million effectively rendered points per second on a Radeon 9700 and about 80 million on a GeForce 6800 GT, in each case with very low CPU load.

Note that our scenes are sets of objects. For each of the objects, a sequential point tree as described in the following is generated. With instancing, the same point tree can be rendered at different locations. This simple scene structure reflects the necessities of typical interactive applications, like games or rendering of outdoor scenes, for example. The goal is to render each visible object at a level of detail that is an optimal balance for the current point of view.

In the remaining chapter, we will first describe our local point-selection criterion. We then show how we rearrange the tree to a list and how we can efficiently bound the cluster of selected points. We then describe how additional error criteria, such as texture information, can be included. Finally, we extend our algorithm to a hybrid point and triangle representation, where for large, flat areas automatically the much better suited triangle-rendering primitive is selected.

6.5.2 SEQUENTIALIZATION

We start with a bounding sphere hierarchy, as it is used for QSplat and described in Section 4.4. QSplat traverses this hierarchy top-down. A bounding sphere is rendered, if its projection to the image is smaller than a threshold ϵ, usually with one or two pixels. The size r_p of the projection of a sphere (m, r) depends on the sphere's radius r and its distance d to the camera plane, which is the (maybe negative) z-coordinate of the point in camera space: $r_p = Fr/d$, where F is a scaling factor that accounts for image resolution. If r_p is above the threshold, the children bounding spheres are considered recursively.

This selection procedure is hierarchical. Points within skipped branches are not touched at all. If we want to switch to sequential processing, we need a local selection criterion that can decide for a single point whether it is to be selected or not, without knowing the history of the results of its ancestors.

In order to define such a local criterion, we first replace the hierarchical selection criterion $r_p < \epsilon$ by a similar, but for our purposes more intuitive, measure. We assume that ϵ is constant to make the formulation clearer. The recursive test for a sphere (m, r) checks whether $r_p = Fr/d < \epsilon$. We can rearrange this to $d > Fr/\epsilon$. We call the right side d_{min}. A sphere is now rendered if its camera distance d is larger than d_{min} (i.e., our new criterion is $d > d_{min}$). For now, d_{min} is just the scaled sphere radius, but in later sections we will extend d_{min} so that it also contains texture information and cannot be computed on the fly quickly. Thus we assume that d_{min} is stored with every bounding sphere.

Second, if the tree nodes are processed sequentially without hierarchy information, we need a *nonrecursive test* that also tests for every single point whether the current point and *none of its ancestors* are to be selected. To this end, we add a d_{max}-parameter to every node and use $d \in [d_{min}, d_{max}]$ as a nonrecursive test. Intuitively, we test with the lower bound whether the sphere is smaller than the threshold, and with the upper bound we check whether the distance is already so large that also one of the ancestors is selected; the d_{max} test thus replaces the recursive skip.

A first attempt for the selection of d_{max} is to use d_{min} of the direct parent or infinity for the root node. So when going up the hierarchy the intervals don't overlap and neither a node nor its children are selected. Examples with a simple point hierarchy and the node fronts selected by different values for d are shown in Figure 6.45.

The above approach assumes that d is the same for a bounding sphere and its children, which is generally only approximately true. If we use the correct d, it can happen for a sphere that d is just below d_{min}, but due to the different d for the children also above some childrens' d_{max}. These children are then incorrectly not selected, because it is incorrectly assumed that the parent sphere has been rendered. The result is holes in the rendering. We can account for this by increasing d_{max} by the distance between the child's and the parent's center. The resulting interval overlap ensures that no holes appear, but it also means that for some nodes both the node and some of its children are selected. This results in overdraw and slightly reduced performance, but we did not experience visible artifacts from it.

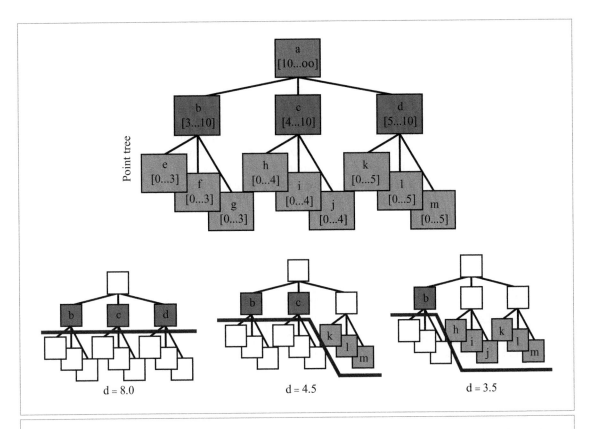

Figure 6.45: Point hierarchy with [d_{min}, d_{max}]-intervals (**upper left**) and selected tree cuts for three different view distances d.

Please note also that the accuracy threshold ϵ can easily be factored out, so that ϵ can be varied on the fly.

For fast rendering with a GPU, the spheres of the hierarchy are now stored as an array of point primitives. For every sphere, we store its center as a point coordinate, radius r, and d_{min} and d_{max} are stored as additional attributes (e.g., texture coordinates). Additionally, we can store colors, normals, or texture coordinates with these points. A simple vertex program first projects all points to camera coordinates. The z-coordinate of the camera coordinate gives us d, which is then compared with the [d_{min}, d_{max}]-interval of the point. If this test fails, the point is moved to infinity and thus culled. Otherwise a lighting computation is performed and the point is transformed to clip coordinates. Furthermore, we have to compute the splat size for the point, which is the radius of the sphere times a constant factor divided by d. The overhead for the interval test is only a few instructions. It slightly affects performance, because point rendering is usually vertex bound (if we do not apply expensive splatting techniques).

6.5.3 REARRANGEMENT

After transforming the recursive test to a simple distance-interval test, we store the spheres in a nonhierarchical list, which is processed sequentially. At this step, the $[d_{min}, d_{max}]$ test allows for an important optimization: After sorting the list by descending d_{max}, we can easily restrict the computation to a prefix of the list. Figure 6.46 shows the sequential version of the point tree of Figure 6.45 (upper left).

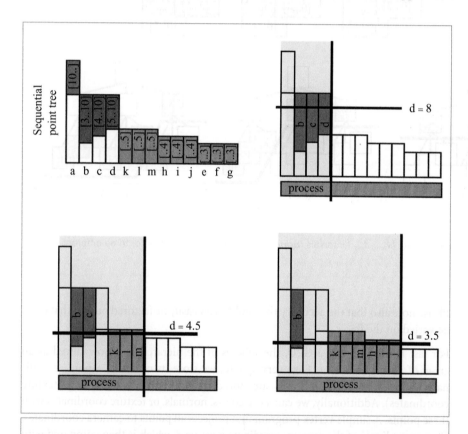

Figure 6.46: Conversion of the point tree of Figure 6.45 into a sequential point tree. *Upper left*: The sequential point tree sorted by d_{max}. The diagrams show $[d_{min}, d_{max}]$ for every node. *Upper right and bottom row*: The same tree cuts as in Figure 6.45, now within sequential point trees. The bars below denote the range that needs to be processed for rendering.

Furthermore, one can see the list points selected by a certain constant d. For $d = 8$, only the first four points can contribute, because for all later points $d_{max} < d$. If we decrease d, this boundary moves to the right.

Since the list is not sorted for d_{min}, a similar left bound is not easy to find. However, this is not really critical, because it is known that in a tree with a branching factor of, for example, four, only about one-fifth of the nodes are inner nodes, so the unselected points at the beginning of the list are only a small fraction. We thus simply use 0 as left bound.

In contrast to our assumption above, d is not constant for different points on an object. In general, d can vary over an interval with the extend of the object as size. In particular, if the camera is close to the object, this variation is significant in relation to the camera distance.

The resulting effect on the point selection is visualized in Figure 6.47. For constant d (left column), d defines a front in the point tree. In the sequential point tree list, this front cuts the list into two halves. If d varies, the resulting vertex front is enclosed by the vertex fronts defined by $\min\{d\}$ and $\max\{d\}$. In the list, this results in a fuzzy zone, where points are partially selected.

Thus, the entire algorithm goes as follows. First, a lower bound on d is computed from a bounding volume of the object. We then search the first list entry with $d_{max} \leq \min\{d\}$ by a binary search. The beginning of the list up to this entry is passed to the GPU.

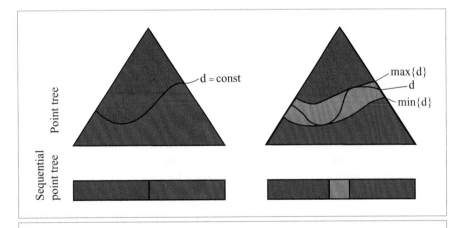

Figure 6.47: *Left*: For constant view distance r, the vertex front cuts the sequential point tree exactly. *Right*: If r varies, the border gets fuzzy.

With this simple approach, we efficiently combine coarse and fine granularity culling. The CPU does a first efficient preculling for d_{max} by selecting i and then passes the segment boundaries $[0, i]$ to the GPU (coarse granularity). The GPU processes the segment (which is ideally stored in video memory) sequentially at maximum efficiency and also does the fine granularity culling. The percentage of points culled by the GPU depends on the variation of d over the object. In typical examples, this fraction is 10–40%.

Also more sophisticated splatting techniques as described in Section 6.2 can be used in combination with sequential point trees. However, the slower the splatting, the smaller the advantage of our fast point selection. For expensive splatting techniques such as perspective-correct splatting, the sequential point trees provide no performance advantage, except for the fact that the CPU can be freed for other tasks.

Sequential point trees do not allow hierarchical visibility frustum culling *within* an object. Visibility culling creates unpredictable point fronts that cannot be considered during sorting.

6.5.4 BETTER ERROR MEASURES

Every node in our point-tree hierarchy represents a part of the object. As described in Section 4.4, it stores a center point $\hat{p}$, an average normal $\hat{n}$, and a radius $\hat{r}$ of a bounding sphere around the center for the represented object part. The generation of such hierarchies is detailed in Section 4.4.

Up to now, we assumed that, when rendering such a bounding sphere as a splat, the error is proportional to the projected sphere radius. This assumption is reasonable, but leaves room for improvement. In fact, our rearrangement scheme can handle any error measure that can be coded into a $[d_{min}, d_{max}]$ interval. In the following, we present two extensions that can also be used to generate an improved geometric error and also include color information.

Improved Geometric Error

In fact, a better error measure should be able to differentiate smooth regions that can be well handled by a single disk and detailed regions or boundary regions, where a disk is a bad approximation. In order to account for this, we define two different errors, perpendicular and tangential error, that can appear when a disk approximates a part of a surface. Both can be combined and coded to our $[d_{min}, d_{max}]$ criterion.

Perpendicular Error   The perpendicular error e_p is the minimum distance between two planes parallel to the disk that encloses the surrounding surface, and thus measures variance (see Figure 6.48, left). We compute this error bottom-up while building the hierarchy. If i iterates overall children of a node, we can compute e_p as

$$e_p = \max\{((\mathbf{p_i} - \mathbf{p})^T\mathbf{n}) + d_i\} - \min\{((\mathbf{p_i} - \mathbf{p})^T\mathbf{n}) - d_i\} \quad\quad (6.86)$$
$$\text{with}\quad d_i = r_i\sqrt{1 - (\mathbf{n_i}^T\mathbf{n})^2}.$$

During rendering, the perpendicular error projects into the image, resulting in an image error $\tilde{e}_p$. $\tilde{e}_p$ is proportional to the sine of the angle between the view vector $\mathbf{v}$ and the disk normal $\mathbf{n}$, and it decreases with $1/d$ and $d = |\mathbf{v}|$: $\tilde{e}_p = e_p\sin(\alpha)/d$ and $\alpha = (\mathbf{v}, \mathbf{n})$. $\tilde{e}_p$ captures the fact that errors along the silhouettes are less acceptable.

Tangential Error   The tangential error measures whether the parent disk covers an unnecessary large area, resulting in typical errors at surface edges (Figure 6.49). We measure this by fitting a number of slabs of varying orientation around the projected child disks. e_t is then the diameter of the disk minus the width of the tightest slab. Negative e_t are clamped to zero. e_t is projected to image space as

$$\tilde{e}_t = e_t\frac{\cos(\alpha)}{d}. \quad\quad (6.87)$$

Combined Geometric Error   Perpendicular and tangential error can be combined to a single geometric error

$$e_g = \max_{\alpha}\{e_p\sin\alpha + e_t\cos\alpha\} = \sqrt{e_p^2 + e_t^2}. \qu\quad (6.88)$$

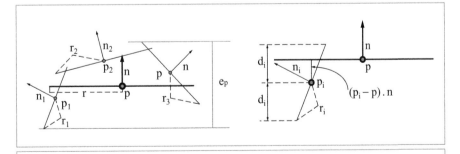

Figure 6.48: As perpendicular error for a disk we use the distance between the two planes parallel to the disk enclosing all children.

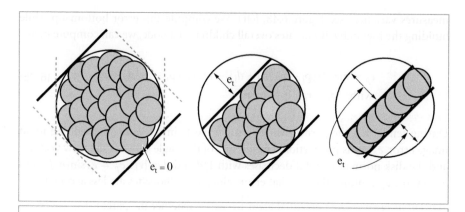

Figure 6.49: The tangential error measures how well a parent disk approximates the children's disks in the tangent plane.

The image space counterpart $\tilde{e}_g$ depends on the view distance d, but no longer on the view angle: $\tilde{e}_g = e_g/r$. This simplification is faster to compute, but also less adaptive. The maximal error e_g has the node's bounding sphere's diameter $2r$ as upper bound. When setting e_g to $2r$ we get the QSplat representation. Note that our error measure can be used both for closed surfaces and for unstructured geometry, like trees.

This combined geometric error fits well with our $[d_{min}, d_{max}]$ error criterion. For the computation of d_{min} we just replace the sphere radius r by the geometric error e_g. The resulting point tree representation adapts point densities not only to view distance d but also to local surface properties. Large, flat regions exhibit a small geometric error e_g and are thus rendered by large splats, whereas small splats are selected in geometrically or visually complex areas. The effect can be seen in Figure 6.44, where the different hierarchy levels are visualized with different colors.

Color, Texture, and Material

We can also use $[d_{min}, d_{max}]$ to account for color. Every leaf point of the point hierarchy represents a part of an object, so an average color can be assigned. If the object is textured, the texture color is also averaged and included in the point color. For inner nodes in the hierarchy the color of the children is averaged.

With the color averaging we have to reconsider our error measure. In flat regions we have small geometric error, but by rendering large splats the color and texture detail are washed out. To avoid this, we increase the point's error to the point's diameter when the color varies significantly. This enforces small splats and the blurring is reduced to the error threshold ϵ. With this measure, point densities adapt to texture detail, thus geometry is created to capture color detail.

The averaging corresponds to an object space-filtering operation. Since due to the above error criterion splats with texture detail all have roughly image size ϵ, this averaging operation implicitly is similar to image space-texture filtering. The filtering quality is not as good as sophisticated EWA-texture filtering (see Section 6.2), but aliasing is well reduced.

6.5.5 HYBRID POINT-POLYGON RENDERING

Sequential point trees can be extended to hybrid point-polygon rendering in the spirit of Cohen and Nguyen and Chohen et al. [CN01, CAZ01], where object parts are rendered by polygons when this is the faster option (Figure 6.50 shows an example). Rendering a triangle is probably the best solution as long as its longest side s has an image size above our error threshold: $s/d \geq \epsilon$, where d is the viewing distance. In this case, we need at least two splats to render the triangle, and no speed gain can be expected. Thus, we can compute a d_{max} value for triangles: $d_{max} = s/\epsilon$. If we render all triangles that are closer to the viewer than their d_{max}, we can remove all points, with a d_{max} smaller than the d_{max} of the original triangle, from the point list.

The goal is to do the triangle selection on the GPU, too. We thus sort all triangles for decreasing d_{max} values. At rendering time, for every object an upper bound on

Figure 6.50: *Left*: With hybrid rendering small triangles are replaced by points (red). *Right*: Hybrid rendering with normal lighting.

d is computed, and, analogously to the point list, the beginning of the triangle list with $d_{max} > \max\{d\}$ is passed to the GPU. A vertex program evaluates the condition $d < d_{max}$ for every vertex and puts the result into the alpha value of the vertex. Culling is then done by an alpha test. By this, triangles with differently classified vertices are rendered partially. Since this is a border case, the corresponding points are also rendered and resulting holes are automatically filled. Note that by resorting the triangle list, triangle strips are torn apart or triangle orders optimized for vertex caches get lost.

Additionally, we have to adapt our point-tree structure, and this is surprisingly simple with the $[d_{min}, d_{max}]$ test. Once we know the d_{max} values for all triangles, we traverse the point hierarchy. For all leaves, the d_{min} value for a point, which originally is zero, is replaced by the d_{max} value of the corresponding triangle (minus an offset to obtain the necessary overlap). The d_{max} values are propagated upward by updating d_{min} of the inner nodes accordingly. This can create negative intervals with $d_{min} > d_{max}$. They appear when large triangles obtain multiple sample points: in this case our algorithm considers it more efficient to render the triangle instead of multiple sample points. Because the render test will always fail, these points can simply be discarded. With this simple procedure, the point-tree hierarchy is automatically reduced to a size where point rendering is efficient.

6.5.6 IMPLEMENTATION AND RESULTS

An efficient implementation of sequential point trees of course requires a programmable geometry processing to perform the interval test and discarding point primitives. Optimal performance is achieved if the geometry data reside inside video memory to avoid slow bus transfers.

In Figure 6.51, we show a complex test scene with various models. The scene is rendered on an ATI Radeon 9700 using sequential point trees without splatting, that is with single-colored point primitives, for the statues and the trees. The ground, sky, and other models are rendered as triangles. With our implementation, a Radeon 9700 GPU can process 77 million points per second, if the sequential point tree data reside in video memory. *After* culling, 50 million points per second are rendered. All objects are textured, where the textures contain surface colors and light map information. The textures and geometry data are stored in the memory of the graphics card. The frame rates are in the range of 36–90 frames per second, with a CPU load of 5–15% on a 2.4 GHz Intel Pentium. As almost all work is offloaded to the GPU, the performance is only bound by memory bandwidth and geometry-processing power. Ideally, when the point sample data are stored in fast video memory, the number of points processed per second depends on the number of vertex shader units and the clock rate of the GPU.

Figure 6.51: Garden of SIG-GRAPH sculptures.

6.5.7 CONCLUSION

Sequential point trees are an algorithm for continuous level-of-detail control that is executed almost completely on the GPU. The algorithm is in the spirit of QSplat, but the hierarchical traversal is replaced by sequential processing, which can be done on the GPU with high efficiency. We extend the selection criterion of QSplat so that it also considers local curvature, boundary points, and textures. On the downside, our algorithm cannot gain efficiency by culling branches outside the view frustum. If the sequential point-tree data structure fits into video memory, a point throughput can be achieved that is an order of magnitude higher than a QSplat CPU implementation.

CHAPTER SEVEN

Müller-Fischer, Matthias

Ageia AG
Technoparkstrasse 1
8005 Zürich
Switzerland
mmueller@ageia.com
Tel: +41 44 445 21 49
Fax: +41 44 445 2147

Pauly, Mark

ETH Zürich
Computer Graphics Laboratory
Haldeneggsteig 4
8092 Zürich
Switzerland
pauly@inf.ethz.ch
Tel: +41 44 632 06 68
Fax: +41 44 632 15 96

Gross, Markus

Computer Graphics Laboratory
ETH Zürich
Haldeneggsteig 4 / Weinbergstrasse
CH - 8092 Zürich
grossm@inf.ethz.ch
Tel: +41-44-632 7114
Fax: +41-44-632 1596

Keiser, Richard

ETH Zürich
Computer Graphics Laboratory
Haldeneggsteig 4
8092 Zürich
Switzerland
keiser@inf.ethz.ch
Tel: +41 44 632 74 37
Fax: +41 44 632 15 96

Wicke, Martin

ETH Zürich
Computer Graphics Laboratory
Haldeneggsteig 4
8092 Zürich
Switzerland
wicke@inf.ethz.ch
Tel: +41 44 632 74 58
Fax: +41 44 632 15 96

7 PHYSICS-BASED ANIMATION

INTRODUCTION

Physically based animation using point-sampled representations has emerged recently as a promising alternative to conventional finite element simulation. It is inspired by so-called meshless methods, where the continuum is discretized using unstructured point samples. This chapter will demonstrate that such methods perform for a wide spectrum of material simulations including brittle fracture, elastic and plastic deformations, and fluids. Section 7.1 gives an introduction to meshless finite elements and demonstrates how they can be utilized to compute elastic and plastic deformations. This method serves as a basis for the simulation of fracture

using point-based surface representations in Section 7.2. It will be shown that the surface can be conveniently resampled without the need to restructure it, as it is required for triangle meshes. The chapter concludes with a discussion of methods for fluid simulation. The particle nature of fluids makes them ideally suited for point-based methods, but the proper reconstruction and animation of the fluid surface remains a challenge.

Physics-based animation using point-sampled representations has emerged recently as a promising alternative to conventional finite element method (FEM) simulation. It is inspired by so-called meshless methods, where the continuum is discretized using unstructured point samples. We will demonstrate that such methods allow for a wide spectrum of material simulations including brittle fracture, elastic and plastic deformations, and fluids. Such physical point representations are combined with high-resolution, point-sampled surface geometry.

7.1 MESHLESS FINITE ELEMENTS

Matthias Müller-Fischer

7.1.1 OVERVIEW

In computer graphics static objects are most often represented by two-dimensional surfaces only while their interior can safely be ignored. In this chapter, however, we will discuss ways to animate deformable objects using points. In order to solve the elasticity equations, the interior of an object needs to be modeled as well. The most popular approaches in computer graphics to simulate volumetric deformable objects are the use of mass spring systems or finite element meshes [NMK+05]. In recent years, meshless point-based approaches have become popular, both in computational sciences [BKO+96, Liu02, FM03] and in computer graphics [DC96, MKN+04]. Following the spirit of the book, we will discuss point-based approaches for the simulation of the object's volume. On the one hand, points will be used to represent the volume and the elastic properties of the material. As Müller et al. [MKN+04] we call these points *phyxels* as an abbreviation for *physics element*. In addition, a different set of points (the *surfels*) can be used to represent the surface of the deformable objects. These surfels passively follow the dynamic motion computed on the phyxels (see Section 7.1.9).

In this section we will present the basic method proposed in Müller et al. [MKN+04] for the simulation of elastic and plastic objects. This method is the basis for the simulation of fracturing material described in the next section. In contrast to mass spring systems, the method is based on continuum elasticity theory. The advantage of continuum-based approaches over simpler methods is the fact that they converge to the continuous solution as the granularity of the discretization goes to zero. In addition, the material stiffness is expressed in terms of Young's modulus E, which can be looked up in textbooks, in contrast to spring constants, which have to be tuned for a specific mesh. Continuum elasticity theory would cover an entire book in itself. Here we only explain the central ideas necessary to understand the method and refer the interested reader to Chung [Chu96] for more details on elasticity theory.

7.1.2 CONTINUUM ELASTICITY

Continuum elasticity theory describes the behavior of continuous (three-dimensional) objects. Hereby, the three quantities *displacement*, *strain*, and *stress* play a major role. In one-dimensional problems, these quantities are all one dimensional and have intuitive interpretations. Figure 7.1 depicts a beam with cross-sectional area A. When a force f_n is applied perpendicular to the cross section, the beam with original length l expands by Δl. The stress σ is the force applied per area f_n/A with unit $[N/m^2]$ while the strain ϵ is the relative elongation of the beam $\Delta l/l$ without unit.

Inside the beam, the displacement u varies linearly. It can be presented by a one-dimensional function $u(x) = x(\Delta l/l)$ as Figure 7.1 shows. The strain (i.e., the relative elongation of the material) can also be expressed in terms of the

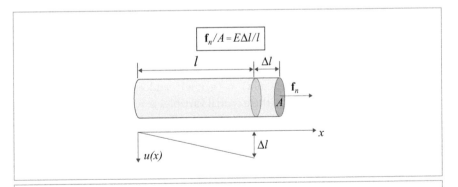

Figure 7.1: Hooke's law for a beam. The force per area applied on the cross section of area A (stress) is proportional to the relative elongation of the material (strain). The constant of proportionality E is Young's modulus. The displacement function $u(x)$ defines how far a material point originally at location x is moved to the right.

displacement function as $\epsilon_{const} = \frac{u(l)-u(0)}{l}$. This *global* expression, however, is only correct for linear displacement functions. For general displacement functions, the strain varies spatially. The strain at location x is then computed *locally* for an infinitesimal element of length dx as $\epsilon(x) = \frac{u(x+dx)-u(x)}{dx}$. This yields the more general expression $\epsilon(x) = \frac{d}{dx}u(x)$ for one-dimensional problems.

Hooke's law states that the strain depends linearly on the applied stress (i.e., $f_n/A = E\Delta l/l$ or $\sigma = E\epsilon$). This law is a good approximation of the behavior of so-called Hookean materials near the equilibrium. The constant of proportionality E is called Young's modulus. For steel, E is in the order of $10^{11} N/m^2$, while for rubber, it lies between 10^7 and $10^8 N/m^2$. A law that relates strain to stress like Hooke's law is called a *constitutive law*.

In three dimensions, continuum elasticity theory gets a bit more involved mathematically. The concepts, however, are exactly the same as in the one-dimensional case. A three-dimensional deformable object is typically defined by its undeformed shape (also called equilibrium configuration, rest, or initial shape) and by a set of material parameters that define how it deforms under applied forces. If we think of the rest shape as a continuous connected subset Ω of $\mathbb{R}^3$, then the coordinates $\mathbf{x} \in \Omega$ of a point in the object are called *material coordinates* of that point. In the discrete case Ω is a discrete set of points that sample the rest shape of the object.

When forces are applied, the object deforms and a point originally at location $\mathbf{x}$ (i.e., with material coordinates $\mathbf{x}$) moves to a new location $\mathbf{p}(\mathbf{x})$, the *spatial* or *world coordinates* of that point. Since new locations are defined for all material coordinates $\mathbf{x}$, $\mathbf{p}(\mathbf{x})$ is a vector field defined on Ω. Alternatively, the deformation can also be specified by the *displacement* field, which, in three dimensions, is a vector field $\mathbf{u}(\mathbf{x}) = \mathbf{p}(\mathbf{x}) - \mathbf{x}$ defined on Ω (see Figure 7.2).

The elastic strain ϵ is computed from the spatial derivatives of the displacement field $\mathbf{u}(\mathbf{x})$ as in the one-dimensional case. However, in three dimensions the displacement field has three components $\mathbf{u} = \mathbf{u}(\mathbf{x}) = (u, v, w)^T$ and each component can be derived with respect to one of the three spatial variables x, y, and z. Therefore, strain cannot be expressed by a single scalar anymore. For example, at a single point inside a three-dimensional object, the material can be stretched in one direction and compressed in another one at the same time. Thus, strain is represented in three dimensions by a symmetric 3×3 tensor:

$$\epsilon = \begin{bmatrix} \epsilon_{xx} & \epsilon_{xy} & \epsilon_{xz} \\ \epsilon_{xy} & \epsilon_{yy} & \epsilon_{yz} \\ \epsilon_{xz} & \epsilon_{yz} & \epsilon_{zz} \end{bmatrix}. \tag{7.1}$$

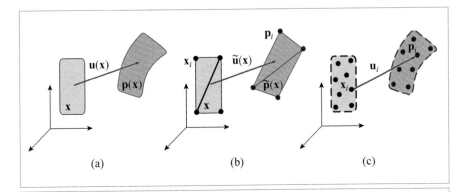

Figure 7.2: (*a*) A deformation is represented mathematically by a continuous vector field $\mathbf{u}(\mathbf{x})$ that describes the displacement of each material point $\mathbf{x}$. A point originally at location $\mathbf{x}$ ends up at location $\mathbf{p}(\mathbf{x}) = \mathbf{x} + \mathbf{u}(\mathbf{x})$ in the deformed shape. (*b*) In mesh-based approaches, the displacement field $\mathbf{u}(\mathbf{x})$ is approximated within an element by a field $\tilde{\mathbf{u}}(\mathbf{x})$ that interpolates the displacements of the corners of the element. (*c*) A mesh-free point-based approach represents the displacement field by a set of discrete samples $\mathbf{u}_i$ defined at locations $\mathbf{x}_i$. Displacement vectors between these locations are interpolated (e.g., with the moving least squares approach).

In computational sciences, several ways to compute the components of the strain tensor from the spatial derivatives of the displacement field are used. Popular choices in computer graphics are

$$\epsilon_G = \frac{1}{2}(\nabla\mathbf{u} + [\nabla\mathbf{u}]^T + [\nabla\mathbf{u}]^T\nabla\mathbf{u}), \tag{7.2}$$

and

$$\epsilon_C = \frac{1}{2}(\nabla\mathbf{u} + [\nabla\mathbf{u}]^T), \tag{7.3}$$

where the symmetric tensor $\epsilon_G \in \mathbb{R}^{3\times3}$ is Green's nonlinear strain tensor (nonlinear in the displacements) and $\epsilon_C \in \mathbb{R}^{3\times3}$ its linearization, Cauchy's linear strain tensor.

The gradient of the displacement field is a 3×3 matrix:

$$\nabla\mathbf{u} = \begin{bmatrix} u_{,x} & u_{,y} & u_{,z} \\ v_{,x} & v_{,y} & v_{,z} \\ w_{,x} & w_{,y} & w_{,z} \end{bmatrix}, \tag{7.4}$$

where the index after the comma represents a spatial derivative.

Now let us turn to the measurement of stress, the force per unit area applied to a plane. In three dimensions, the force and the orientation of the plane it is applied to are both three-dimensional vectors. The stress relating the two, therefore, is expressed by a symmetric 3 × 3 tensor:

$$\sigma = \begin{bmatrix} \sigma_{xx} & \sigma_{xy} & \sigma_{xz} \\ \sigma_{xy} & \sigma_{yy} & \sigma_{yz} \\ \sigma_{xz} & \sigma_{yz} & \sigma_{zz} \end{bmatrix}, \tag{7.5}$$

with the following interpretation:

$$\frac{d\mathbf{f}}{dA} = \sigma \cdot \mathbf{n}_A. \tag{7.6}$$

To get the force per area $\mathbf{f}/A$ with respect to a certain plain with normal $\mathbf{n}_A$, the stress tensor is simply multiplied by $\mathbf{n}_A$.

Hooke's law states that stress and strain are linearly related:

$$\sigma = \mathbf{E}\epsilon. \tag{7.7}$$

Both stress and strain are symmetric tensors so they have only six independent coefficients. The quantity $\mathbf{E}$ relating the two can, thus, be expressed by a 6 × 6-dimensional matrix. For isotropic materials (with equal behavior in all directions), Hooke's law has the following form:

$$\begin{bmatrix} \sigma_{xx} \\ \sigma_{yy} \\ \sigma_{zz} \\ \sigma_{xy} \\ \sigma_{yz} \\ \sigma_{zx} \end{bmatrix} = \frac{E}{(1+v)(1-2v)} \begin{bmatrix} 1-v & v & v & 0 & 0 & 0 \\ v & 1-v & v & 0 & 0 & 0 \\ v & v & 1-v & 0 & 0 & 0 \\ 0 & 0 & 0 & 1-2v & 0 & 0 \\ 0 & 0 & 0 & 0 & 1-2v & 0 \\ 0 & 0 & 0 & 0 & 0 & 1-2v \end{bmatrix} \begin{bmatrix} \epsilon_{xx} \\ \epsilon_{yy} \\ \epsilon_{zz} \\ \epsilon_{xy} \\ \epsilon_{yz} \\ \epsilon_{zx} \end{bmatrix}, \tag{7.8}$$

where the scalar E is Young's modulus describing the elastic stiffness and the scalar $v \in [0 \dots \frac{1}{2})$ Poisson's ratio, a material parameter that describes to which amount volume is conserved within the material. Figure 7.3 shows the difference between low- and high-volume conservation modeled via the Poisson's ratio.

We now turn to the question of how to simulate a dynamic elastic object. To this end, we apply Newton's second law of motion $\mathbf{f} = m\ddot{\mathbf{p}}$ to each infinitesimal volumetric element dV of the object. Since the mass of an infinitesimal element is not defined, both sides of the equation of motion are divided by the volume $dx \cdot dy \cdot dz$ of the

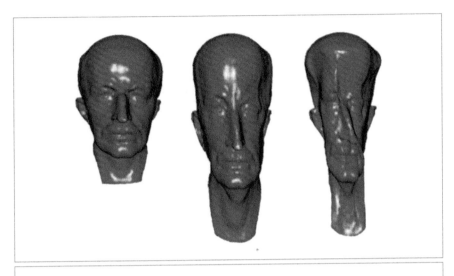

Figure 7.3: The effect of Poisson's ratio: the undeformed model (*left*) is stretched using a Poisson ratio of zero (*middle*) and 0.49 (*right*).

element. This turns mass $[kg]$ into density $[kg/m^3]$ and forces $[N]$ into body forces $[N/m^3]$. We get

$$\rho\ddot{\mathbf{p}} = \mathbf{f}(\mathbf{x}),\tag{7.9}$$

where ρ is the density and $\mathbf{f}(\mathbf{x})$ the body force acting on the element at location $\mathbf{x}$.

Figure 7.4 illustrates the forces that act on an element due to internal stress σ. Only those forces acting on the faces perpendicular to the x-axis are shown. The forces acting on the other faces of the element are computed analogously. According to Equation (7.6) the forces per unit area acting on the faces with normal $[-1, 0, 0]^T$ and $[1, 0, 0]^T$ are $-[\sigma_{xx}, \sigma_{xy}, \sigma_{xz}]^T_{x, y, z}$ and $[\sigma_{xx}, \sigma_{xy}, \sigma_{xz}]^T_{x+dx, y, z}$, respectively. To get forces, we multiply by the face area $dy \cdot dz$. Finally, the body forces are the forces divided by $dV = dx \cdot dy \cdot dz$. This yields $\mathbf{f} = ([\sigma_{xx}, \sigma_{xy}, \sigma_{xz}]^T_{x+dx, y, z} - [\sigma_{xx}, \sigma_{xy}, \sigma_{xz}]^T)/dx = [\sigma_{xx,x}, \sigma_{xy,x}, \sigma_{xz,x}]^T$ for the body forces, where the comma denotes spatial derivatives.

If we take the forces acting on the other faces into account as well, we arrive at the final expression for the body forces acting on an infinitesimal element due to internal stresses:

$$\mathbf{f}_{stress} = \nabla \cdot \sigma = \begin{bmatrix} \sigma_{xx,x} + \sigma_{xy,y} + \sigma_{xz,z} \\ \sigma_{yx,x} + \sigma_{yy,y} + \sigma_{yz,z} \\ \sigma_{zx,x} + \sigma_{zy,y} + \sigma_{zz,z} \end{bmatrix},\tag{7.10}$$

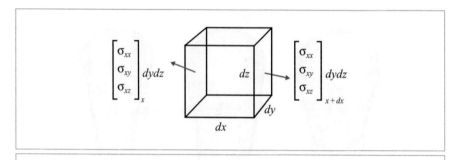

Figure 7.4: The elastic forces acting on the faces of an infinitesimal cube due to internal stresses. Only the forces acting on faces perpendicular to the x-axis are shown.

where, again, the commas represent a spatial derivative. We are now ready to write down the entire partial differential equation (PDE) governing dynamic elastic materials:

$$\rho \ddot{\mathbf{p}} = \nabla \cdot \sigma + \mathbf{f}_{\text{ext}}, \qquad (7.11)$$

where $\mathbf{f}_{\text{ext}}$ are externally applied body forces such as gravity or collision forces. This hyperbolic PDE describes the evolution of the world coordinates $\mathbf{p}$ of the elastic body since ρ and $\mathbf{f}_{\text{ext}}$ are known quantities, σ depends on ϵ via the constitutive law, and ϵ, in turn, is a function of the spatial derivatives of the displacements $\mathbf{u}(\mathbf{x})$ and, thus, of the world coordinates $\mathbf{p}(\mathbf{x}) = \mathbf{x} + \mathbf{u}(\mathbf{x})$.

A linear dependency of the stresses on the strains such as in a Hookean material is called *material linearity*. A linear measure of strain such as Cauchy's linear strain tensor defined in Equation (7.3) is called *geometric linearity*. Only with both assumptions, material and geometric linearity, Equation (7.11) becomes a linear PDE. Linear PDEs are easier to solve because discretizing them via finite differences of finite elements yields linear algebraic systems. However, for large deformations, the simplification of geometric linearity causes significant visual artifacts (see [MG04]).

Linearizing Equation (7.11) is only useful in connection with *implicit* time integration because in that case, either a linear or a nonlinear system of equations needs to be solved. However, in the explicit case it does not really matter whether the elastic forces are a linear or a nonlinear function of the displacements because they are evaluated explicitly at each time step.

7.1.3 MESHLESS DISCRETIZATION

In order to use the governing continuous PDE in a numerical simulation, the volume of an object needs to be discretized into regions of finite size. In mesh-based approaches, such as the finite element method (FEM), the volume is divided into disjoint volumetric primitives such as tetrahedra, which form a mesh. In contrast, in mesh-free methods the volume is sampled at a finite number of point locations without connectivity information and without the need of generating a volumetric mesh (see Figure 7.2).

In a point-based mesh-free model, all the simulation quantities, such as location $\mathbf{x}_i$, density ρ_i, deformation $\mathbf{u}_i$, velocity $\mathbf{v}_i$, strain ϵ_i, stress σ_i, and body force $\mathbf{f}_i$, are carried by the physically simulated points—the phyxels. For each simulated phyxel we have a position $\mathbf{x}_i$ in body space, defining what we call the *reference shape*, and their deformed locations $\mathbf{x}_i + \mathbf{u}_i$ the *deformed shape*.

Smoothed particle hydrodynamics (SPH) is a popular method for solving PDEs on point samples without connectivity. It was first proposed in the field of astronomy for the simulation of star clusters [Mon92]. In computer graphics it has been used to model highly deformable models [DC96] and fluids [MCG03]. One could also use SPH to solve the governing Equation (7.11) on the phyxels. However, as we will see later, the method is not accurate enough to get stable simulations of highly deforming and freely rotating objects. Still, one important idea can directly be adopted, namely how volumes and densities are assigned to the phyxels. In continuum mechanics, quantities are measured per unit volume. It is, thus, important to know how much volume each phyxel represents.

First, each phyxel is assigned a fixed mass m_i that does not change through the simulation. This mass is distributed in the neighborhood of the phyxel via a radially symmetric scalar-kernel function $\omega(r, h)$, where r is the distance from the phyxel position and h a cutoff distance after which the kernel is zero. The distance h is also called the *support* of the kernel. In order to properly convert an attribute into a body attribute the kernel needs to be normalized (i.e., $\int_{\mathbf{x}} \omega(|\mathbf{x} - \mathbf{x}_0|, h)d\mathbf{x} = 1$ with unit $[1/m^3]$). Müller et al. [MKN^{+}04] propose to use

$$\omega(r, h) = \begin{cases} \frac{315}{64\pi h^9}(h^2 - r^2)^3 & \text{if } r < h \\ 0 & \text{otherwise} \end{cases} \tag{7.12}$$

to distribute the masses of the particles. This normalized kernel can be evaluated efficiently because r only appears squared. The density at phyxel i can then be computed by smoothing the masses of all the phyxels as

$$\rho_i = \sum_j m_j \omega_{ij}, \tag{7.13}$$

where $\omega_{ij} = \omega(|\mathbf{x}_j - \mathbf{x}_i|, h_i)$. Finally, the volume represented by phyxel i is simply given by $v_i = m_i/\rho_i$. While the mass represented by a phyxel is fixed, the density and volume vary when the reference positions of the phyxels change in case of plastic deformation (Section 7.1.7).

The masses m_i and support radii h_i need to be initialized before the simulation starts. Here is a way to finding masses if the phyxels irregularly sample the initial volume. For each phyxel i compute the average distance $\bar{r}_i$ to its k (e.g., 10) nearest neighbors. The support radius h_i is chosen to be a multiple of (e.g., three times) $\bar{r}_i$. The masses are initialized as $m_i = s\,\bar{r}_i^3\,\rho$, where ρ is the material density and s is the same scaling factor for all phyxels, chosen such that the ρ_i resulting from Equation (7.13) are close to the material density ρ.

7.1.4 MOVING LEAST SQUARES INTERPOLATION

In order to compute strain, stress, and the elastic body forces, the spatial derivatives of the displacement field $\nabla \mathbf{u}$ are needed (see Equation 7.2). These derivatives can be estimated from the displacement vectors $\mathbf{u}_j$ of nearby phyxels.

The approximation of $\nabla \mathbf{u}$ must be first-order accurate in order to guarantee zero elastic forces for rigid body modes (global rotation and translation). Standard SPH approximation does not have this property. A method that is first-order accurate (i.e., that can reconstruct linear functions correctly) is the moving least squares formulation [LS81] with a linear basis (see also Section 4.2). Let us consider the x-component u of the displacement field $\mathbf{u} = (u, v, w)^T$. Using a Taylor approximation, the continuous scalar field $u(\mathbf{x})$ in the neighborhood of $\mathbf{x}_i$ can be approximated as

$$u(\mathbf{x}_i + \Delta \mathbf{x}) = u_i + \nabla u|_{\mathbf{x}_i} \cdot \Delta \mathbf{x} + O(\|\Delta \mathbf{x}\|^2), \tag{7.14}$$

where $\nabla u|_{\mathbf{x}_i} = (u_{,x}, u_{,y}, u_{,z})^T$ at phyxel i. Given u_i and the spatial derivatives ∇u at phyxel i, the values u_j at close phyxels j can be approximated as

$$\tilde{u}_j = u_i + \nabla u|_{\mathbf{x}_i} \cdot \mathbf{x}_{ij} = u_i + \mathbf{x}_{ij}^T \nabla u|_{\mathbf{x}_i}, \tag{7.15}$$

where $\mathbf{x}_{ij} = \mathbf{x}_j - \mathbf{x}_i$. A measure of the error of the approximation is given by the sum of the squared differences between the approximated values $\tilde{u}_j$ and the known values u_j, weighted by the kernel given in Equation (7.12):

$$e = \sum_j (\tilde{u}_j - u_j)^2\, \omega_{ij}. \tag{7.16}$$

The differences are weighted because only phyxels in the neighborhood of phyxel i should be considered and, additionally, fade in and out smoothly. Substituting Equation (7.15) into Equation (7.16) and expanding yields

$$e = \sum_j (u_i + u_{,x}\, x_{ij} + u_{,y}\, y_{ij} + u_{,z}\, z_{ij} - u_j)^2\, \omega_{ij}, \tag{7.17}$$

where x_{ij}, y_{ij}, and z_{ij} are the x-, y-, and z-components of $\mathbf{x}_{ij}$, respectively. Given the positions of the phyxels $\mathbf{x}_i$ and the sampled values u_i the best candidates for the derivatives $u_{,x}$, $u_{,y}$, and $u_{,z}$ are the ones that minimize the error e. Setting the derivatives of e with respect to $u_{,x}$, $u_{,y}$, and $u_{,z}$ to zero yields three equations for the three unknowns:

$$\left(\sum_j \mathbf{x}_{ij} \mathbf{x}_{ij}^T \omega_{ij} \right) \nabla u|_{\mathbf{x}_i} = \sum_j (u_j - u_i) \mathbf{x}_{ij} \omega_{ij}. \qquad (7.18)$$

The 3×3 system matrix $\mathbf{M} = \sum_j \mathbf{x}_{ij} \mathbf{x}_{ij}^T \omega_{ij}$ (the moment matrix) can be precomputed, inverted, and used for the computation of the derivative of v and w as well. If $\mathbf{M}$ is nonsingular we have the following formula for the computation of derivatives:

$$\nabla u|_{\mathbf{x}_i} = \mathbf{M}^{-1} \left(\sum_j (u_j - u_i) \mathbf{x}_{ij} \omega_{ij} \right). \qquad (7.19)$$

The components $\nabla v|_{\mathbf{x}_i}$ and $\nabla w|_{\mathbf{x}_i}$ are computed analogously using the same moment matrix $\mathbf{M}^{-1}$. If the number of phyxels within the support radius h in the neighborhood of phyxel i is less than four (including phyxel i) or if these phyxels are coplanar or colinear $\mathbf{M}$ is singular and cannot be inverted. This only happens if the sampling of the volume is too coarse. To avoid problems with singular or badly conditioned moment matrices, safe inversion via SVD (singular value decomposition [PTVF92]) should be used.

7.1.5 UPDATING STRAINS AND STRESSES

With Equation (7.19) the spatial derivatives of the deformation field at the phyxel's location $\mathbf{x}_i$ can be computed based on the displacement vectors $\mathbf{u}_j$ of neighboring phyxels j. Using Equations (7.2) and (7.7), the gradient of the displacement field, Green's strain ϵ_i, and the stress σ_i at phyxel i can all be computed from these derivatives:

$$\nabla \mathbf{u}_i \leftarrow \begin{bmatrix} \nabla u|_{\mathbf{x}_i}^T \\ \nabla v|_{\mathbf{x}_i}^T \\ \nabla w|_{\mathbf{x}_i}^T \end{bmatrix}, \quad \epsilon_i = \frac{1}{2}(\nabla \mathbf{u} + [\nabla \mathbf{u}]^T + [\nabla \mathbf{u}]^T \nabla \mathbf{u}), \quad \sigma_i \leftarrow \mathbf{E} \, \epsilon_i. \qquad (7.20)$$

7.1.6 COMPUTATION OF FORCES VIA STRAIN ENERGY

The last step before the set of phyxels can be animated is to derive internal elastic forces for each phyxel based on the internal stresses. These forces could be derived from Equation (7.10) by computing the divergence of the stress components. However, since the stresses σ_i are approximations of the real stresses and only available at the discrete locations of the phyxels, the resulting forces would, in general, violate

Newton's first law *actio = reactio* (i.e., they would not conserve linear and angular momentum). This, in turn, would introduce so-called *ghost forces* that cause linear and angular accelerations of the entire object.

Another way to derive elastic forces is to compute them as the gradients of the *strain energy*. Such forces automatically conserve both linear and angular momentum. The strain energy is the potential energy stored in a deformed material. The body strain energy (energy per unit volume) can be computed as

$$U = \frac{1}{2}\sigma \cdot \epsilon,$$

(7.21)

where the product $\sigma \cdot \epsilon$ is the componentwise dot product of all the components of the tensors (i.e., $\sigma \cdot \epsilon = \sigma_{xx} \cdot \epsilon_{xx} + \sigma_{xy} \cdot \epsilon_{xy} + \sigma_{xz} \cdot \epsilon_{xz} + \dots$). Intuitively, the strain energy is the energy built up by moving against the stresses along the strains. The unit test reveals stress $[N/m^2]$ times strain $[1]$ equals energy per unit volume $[Nm/m^3]$.

A phyxel i and all its neighbors j that lie within its support radius h_i can be considered a basic unit, analogous to a finite element in FEM (see Figure 7.5). Based on Equation (7.21) we estimate the strain energy stored around phyxel i as

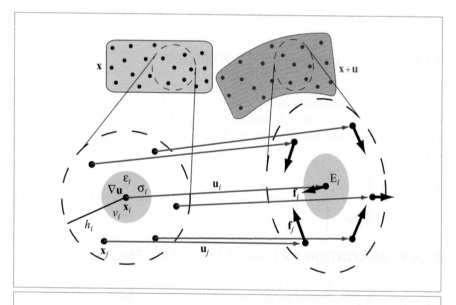

Figure 7.5: A basic unit in the point-based approach consists of a phyxel at $\mathbf{x}_i$ and its neighbors at $\mathbf{x}_j$ within distance h_i. The gradient of the displacement field $\nabla\mathbf{u}$ is computed from the displacement vectors $\mathbf{u}_i$ and $\mathbf{u}_j$, the strain ϵ_i from $\nabla\mathbf{u}$, the stress σ_i from ϵ_i, the strain energy U_i from ϵ_i, σ_i and the volume v_i, and the elastic forces as the negative gradient of U_i with respect to the displacement vectors.

$$U_i = v_i \frac{1}{2}(\sigma_i \cdot \epsilon_i), \tag{7.22}$$

assuming that strain and stress are constant within the rest volume v_i of phyxel i, equivalent to using linear shape functions in FEM. The strain energy is a function of the displacement vector $\mathbf{u}_i$ of phyxel i and the displacements $\mathbf{u}_j$ of all its neighbors. Taking the derivative with respect to these displacements yields the forces acting at phyxel i and all its neighbors j,

$$\mathbf{f}_j = -\nabla_{\mathbf{u}_j} U_i = -v_i \sigma_i \nabla_{\mathbf{u}_j} \epsilon_i, \tag{7.23}$$

as Figure 7.6 illustrates. The force acting on phyxel i turns out to be the negative sum of all $\mathbf{f}_j$ acting on its neighbors j. These forces conserve linear and angular momentum.

Using Equation (7.19), this result can be further simplified to the compact form

$$\mathbf{f}_i = -2v_i(\mathbf{I} + \nabla\mathbf{u}_i)\sigma_i\mathbf{d}_i = \mathbf{F}\mathbf{d}_i, \tag{7.24}$$
$$\mathbf{f}_j = -2v_i(\mathbf{I} + \nabla\mathbf{u}_i)\sigma_i\mathbf{d}_j = \mathbf{F}\mathbf{d}_j, \tag{7.25}$$

where

$$\mathbf{d}_i = \mathbf{M}^{-1}\left(-\sum_j \mathbf{x}_{ij}\omega_{ij}\right) \tag{7.26}$$

$$\mathbf{d}_j = \mathbf{M}^{-1}(\mathbf{x}_{ij}\omega_{ij}). \tag{7.27}$$

The detailed derivation of these equations can be found in Müller [MKN+04]. Using the definition of the vectors $\mathbf{d}_i$ and $\mathbf{d}_j$ we get for the total internal forces:

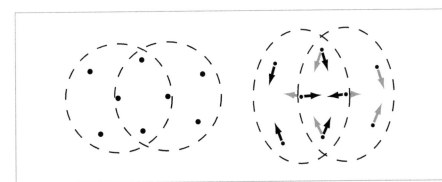

Figure 7.6: Each phyxel receives one force component from being the center phyxel and multiple force components from being a neighbor of other phyxels. The image shows the neighborhoods of two phyxels in the reference configuration (*left*) and the deformed configuration (*right*). The black and gray force components are induced by the left and right neighborhoods, respectively.

$$\mathbf{f}_i = \mathbf{FM}^{-1}\left(-\sum_j \mathbf{x}_{ij}\omega_{ij}\right),\tag{7.28}$$

$$\mathbf{f}_j = \mathbf{FM}^{-1}(\mathbf{x}_{ij}\omega_{ij}).\tag{7.29}$$

The matrix product $\mathbf{B} = \mathbf{FM}^{-1}$ is independent of the individual neighbor j and needs to be computed only once for each phyxel i.

7.1.7 ANIMATION OF ELASTIC OBJECTS

We are now ready to write down the entire simulation algorithm. Of course, the Euler integration steps in lines 20–23 could be replaced by any other (higher-order) explicit scheme.

(1) **forall** phyxels i
(2)   initialize $\mathbf{x}_i, \mathbf{u}_i = \mathbf{0}, \dot{\mathbf{u}}_i = \mathbf{0}, m_i, \rho_i, v_i,$
(3)   compute $\mathbf{M}_i^{-1} = \left(\sum_j \mathbf{x}_{ij}\mathbf{x}_{ij}^T\omega_{ij}\right)^{-1}$
(4) **endfor**
(5) **loop**
(6)   **forall** phyxels i **do** $\mathbf{f}_i = \mathbf{f}_{ext}(\mathbf{x}_i + \mathbf{u}_i)$
(7)   **forall** phyxels i
(8) $\nabla u_i = \mathbf{M}^{-1}\left(\sum_j (u_j - u_i)\mathbf{x}_{ij}\omega_{ij}\right)$
(9) $\nabla v_i = \mathbf{M}^{-1}\left(\sum_j (v_j - v_i)\mathbf{x}_{ij}\omega_{ij}\right)$
(10) $\nabla w_i = \mathbf{M}^{-1}\left(\sum_j (w_j - w_i)\mathbf{x}_{ij}\omega_{ij}\right)$
(11) $\nabla\mathbf{u}_i = [\nabla u_i, \nabla v_i, \nabla w_i]^T$
(12) $\epsilon_i = \frac{1}{2}(\nabla\mathbf{u} + [\nabla\mathbf{u}]^T + [\nabla\mathbf{u}]^T\nabla\mathbf{u})$
(13) $\sigma_i = \mathbf{E}\epsilon_i$
(14) $\mathbf{B}_i = -2v_i(\nabla\mathbf{u}_i + \mathbf{I})\sigma_i\mathbf{M}_i^{-1}$
(15)   **forall** neighboring phyxels j
(16) $\mathbf{f}_j = \mathbf{f}_j + \mathbf{B}_i(\mathbf{x}_{ij}\omega_{ij})$
(17) $\mathbf{f}_i = \mathbf{f}_i - \mathbf{B}_i(\mathbf{x}_{ij}\omega_{ij})$
(18)   **endfor**
(19)   **endfor**
(20)   **forall** phyxels i
(21) $\dot{\mathbf{u}}_i = \dot{\mathbf{u}}_i + \Delta t\,\mathbf{f}_i/m_i$
(22) $\mathbf{u}_i = \mathbf{u}_i + \Delta t\,\dot{\mathbf{u}}_i$
(23)   **endfor**
(24)   render configuration $\{\mathbf{x}_i + \mathbf{u}_i\}$
(25) **endloop**

After initialization in lines 1–4 the simulation loop is started. From the displacement vectors $\mathbf{u}_i$, the nine spatial derivatives of three scalar fields $u, v,$ and w are approximated using the moving least squares method in lines 8–11. From these derivatives, the strain and stress tensors are derived in lines 12 and 13. The forces acting at the center phyxel and all its neighbors are then computed as the negative gradient of the strain energy with respect to the displacements in lines 14–19. Finally, in lines 20–23 explicit Euler integration yields the new velocities and displacements of the phyxels.

7.1.8 PLASTICITY

So far, the set of phyxels returns completely to the rest shape (modulo rigid body transformations) if the external forces are released. This way, they simulate a perfectly elastic material. In contrast, a plastic material will store some of the deformation and will remain in a deformed state even if the applied forces are released. An elegant way of simulating plastic behavior is by using strain-state variables [OBH02]. Every phyxel i stores a plastic strain tensor $\epsilon_i^{\text{plastic}}$. The strain considered for elastic forces $\epsilon_i^{\text{elastic}} = \epsilon_i - \epsilon_i^{\text{plastic}}$ is the difference between measured strain ϵ_i and the plastic strain. Thus, in case the measured strain equals the plastic strain, no forces are generated. Since $\epsilon_i^{\text{plastic}}$ is considered constant within one time step, the elastoplastic forces are simply computed using Equations (7.24) and (7.25) with σ_i replaced by $\sigma_i^{\text{elastic}} = \mathbf{E}\epsilon_i^{\text{elastic}}$. The plastic strain is initialized with a zero 3×3 tensor. At every time step, it is updated as follows:

$$\epsilon^{\text{elastic}} \leftarrow \epsilon - \epsilon^{\text{plastic}}$$
$$\textbf{if } ||\epsilon^{\text{elastic}}||_2 > c_{\text{yield}} \textbf{ then } \epsilon^{\text{plastic}} \leftarrow \epsilon^{\text{plastic}} + c_{\text{creep}} \cdot \epsilon^{\text{elastic}}$$
$$\textbf{if } ||\epsilon^{\text{plastic}}||_2 > c_{\text{max}} \textbf{ then } \epsilon^{\text{plastic}} \leftarrow \epsilon^{\text{plastic}} \cdot c_{\text{max}}/||\epsilon^{\text{plastic}}||_2$$

First, the elastic strain is computed as the deviation of the actual strain from the stored plastic strain. The plasticity model has three scalar parameters c_{yield}, c_{creep}, and c_{max}. If the two-norm of the elastic strain exceeds the threshold c_{yield}, the plastic strain absorbs part of it. If $c_{\text{creep}} \in [0 \ldots 1]$ is one, the elastic strain is immediately and completely absorbed. Small values for c_{creep} yield slow plastic flow in the material. The parameter c_{max} defines the maximum plastic strain an element can store. If the two-norm of the plastic strain exceeds c_{max}, the plastic strain is scaled down accordingly.

In contrast to mesh-based methods, the mesh-free approach is particulary useful when the object deviates far from its original shape in which case the original mesh connectivity is not useful anymore. Using a mesh-free method, the reference shape can easily adapt to the deformed shape. However, changing the reference positions of phyxels is dangerous: two phyxels from two different objects having reference positions $\mathbf{x}_i$ and $\mathbf{x}_j$ might move within each other's support, even though their actual positions $\mathbf{x}_i + \mathbf{u}_i$ and $\mathbf{x}_j + \mathbf{u}_j$ are far from each other. This large displacement vector difference results in large strains, stresses, and elastic forces, causing the simulation to crash. Therefore, if the reference shape is changed, both reference shape and deformed shape need to be kept close to each other. There is a simple way to achieve this, with which highly plastic materials can be modeled, as well as melting and flow. After each time step, the deformation is completely absorbed by the reference shape while the built-up strains are stored in the plastic strain-state variable:

forall phyxels i **do**

$\quad \epsilon_i^{\text{plastic}} \leftarrow \epsilon_i^{\text{plastic}} - \epsilon_i$

$\quad \mathbf{x}_i \leftarrow \mathbf{x}_i + \mathbf{u}_i$

$\quad \mathbf{u}_i \leftarrow 0$

endfor

forall phyxels i **do**

$\quad$ update ρ_i, v_i and $\mathbf{M}_i^{-1}$

endfor

This way, both reference shape and deformed shape are identical after each time step. The strain is not lost, but stored in the plastic state variable. However, the original shape information is lost and small errors can sum up over time. Thus, this latter simulation method that changes the reference shape is only recommended for the simulation highly plastic objects that deviate far from their original shape.

Figure 7.7: The model presented in this chapter represents both the physical volume elements (phyxels in yellow) as well as the surface elements (surfels in blue) as point samples. It allows the simulation of elastic, plastic, melting, and solidifying objects (from *left to right*).

7.1.9 PASSIVE SURFEL ADVECTION

Often, a coarse sampling of the volume of an object with phyxels is sufficient to capture the object's elastic behavior. However, for rendering, a more detailed surface is needed. If this surface is represented by a set of surfels, the surfels need to be advected along the displacement field of the phyxels. To this end, the displacement vector $\mathbf{u}_{sfl}$ at a known surfel position $\mathbf{x}_{sfl}$ is interpolated from the displacements $\mathbf{u}_i$ of nearby phyxels as

$$\mathbf{u}_{sfl} = \frac{1}{\sum_i \omega(r_i, h)} \sum_i \omega(r_i, h)(\mathbf{u}_i + \nabla \mathbf{u}_i^T (\mathbf{x}_{sfl} - \mathbf{x}_i)), \qquad (7.30)$$

where $\omega(r_i, h) = \omega(\|\mathbf{x}_{sfl} - \mathbf{x}_i\|, h)$ is the weighting kernel defined in Equation (7.12). The $\mathbf{u}_i$ are the displacement vectors of phyxels at $\mathbf{x}_i$ within a distance h to $\mathbf{x}_{sfl}$.

If displacements are computed not only for the surfel center but also for the tips of the tangent axes, the deformation of the surfel as well as a transformed normal can be derived. Based on the elongations of the tangent axes, a surfel splitting and merging scheme can be applied to maintain a high surface quality in the case of large deformations (see Section 5.3.3 for details).

7.1.10 CONCLUSION

In this introductory chapter to physics-based animation, the basic concepts of continuum elasticity have been discussed. The equation of motion in the continuous case is a partial differential equation that has to be discretized in order to be solved numerically. In contrast to the finite element method where volumes of finite size are used, a meshless method discretizes continuous quantities on randomly distributed point samples (phyxels). Elastic forces are computed on those phyxels based on their displacements from the rest shape and the elastic properties of the material. Given the elastic forces, the point cloud can be integrated in time like a particle system.

The extension of the state of a phyxel by a strain-state variable allows the modeling of plasticity resulting in objects that do not return to the rest state when external forces are released. Finally, in order to enhance the visual quality of objects, the displacement field of the phyxels is used to advect a highly detailed point-based surface.

Section 7.2 discusses extensions to this basic model that allow the simulation of fracturing material.

7.2 ANIMATION OF FRACTURING MATERIAL

Richard Keiser and Mark Pauly

In the previous section, a framework for the animation of elastoplastic materials has been described. Here we will discuss how this framework can be extended for simulating fracturing solids [PKA$^+$05]. Central to the method is a highly dynamic surface- and volume-sampling method that supports arbitrary crack initiation, propagation, and termination, while avoiding many of the stability problems of traditional mesh-based techniques. Advancing crack fronts are modeled explicitly and associated fracture surfaces are embedded in the simulation volume. When cutting through the material, crack fronts directly affect the coupling between phyxels, requiring a dynamic adaptation of the nodal shape functions. Complex fracture patterns of interacting and branching cracks are handled using a small set of topological operations for splitting, merging, and terminating crack fronts. This allows continuous propagation of cracks with highly detailed fracture surfaces, independent of the spatial resolution of the phyxels, and provides effective mechanisms for controlling fracture paths. The method is applicable for a wide range of materials, from stiff elastic to highly plastic objects that exhibit brittle and/or ductile fracture.

7.2.1 OVERVIEW

Physically, fracturing occurs when the internal stresses and the resulting forces are so large that the interatomic bounds cannot hold the material together anymore. Fracturing has been studied extensively in the physics and mechanics literature. However, due to the complexity of the problem, the studies and simulation usually deal only with "simple" fractures, such as the creation or propagation of a single crack. In computer graphics, we often trade physical accuracy for visual realism. By simplifying the physical model, realistic animations of very complex fractures, such as the shattering of glass into hundreds of pieces, can be achieved. However, changing the topology of a simulated object is challenging for both the animation of the volume and the surface. When a solid fractures, the surface needs to adapt to the cracks that propagate through the volume of the solid. To achieve a high degree of visual realism, cracks should be allowed to start anywhere on the surface and move in any direction through the volume. Furthermore, cracks might branch into several cracks or different cracks can merge to a single crack within the solid. While fracturing, not only the topology of the surface changes, but also the discontinuities introduced by the cracks in the volume have to be modeled accordingly to achieve physically plausible fracture behavior.

The fracturing characteristics depend on the material. We differentiate between ductile and brittle fracture. While brittle material splits without experiencing significant irreversible deformation (i.e., only elastic deformation), ductile material experience some amount of plastic deformation before fracture [OBH02]. Two examples for brittle and ductile materials are shown in Figures 7.8 and 7.9. A force acting on the hollow stone sculpture in Figure 7.8 causes the model to explode. Due to the simulated brittle material this results in a shattering of the object into pieces. Figure 7.9 shows a ductile fracture of a highly plastic bubblegum-like material that is deformed beyond recognition before splitting along a single complex fracture surface.

Fracturing materials have been simulated using finite difference schemes [TF88], mass-spring models [HTK98], constraint-based methods [SWB00], finite-element methods (FEM) [OH99, MBF04], and meshless methods [BK0$^+$96]. Meshless methods have several advantages over finite element methods. Most importantly, meshless methods avoid complex remeshing operations and the associated problems of element cutting and mesh alignment sensitivity common in FEM. Maintaining a conforming mesh can be a notoriously difficult task when the topology of the simulation domain changes frequently [OP99]. Repeated remeshing operations can adversely affect the stability and accuracy of the calculations, imposing undesirable restrictions on the time step. Finally, meshless methods are well suited for handling large deformations due to their flexibility when locally refining the sampling resolution.

7.2.2 HISTORICAL BACKGROUND

In this section we will give a brief overview of fracturing methods in computer graphics. Terzopoulos et al. [TPBF87] pioneered physics-based animation of deforming objects using finite difference schemes to solve the underlying elasticity

Figure 7.8: Brittle fracture of a hollow stone sculpture. Forces acting on the interior create stresses that cause the model to fracture and explode. Initial/final sampling: 4.3*k*/6.5*k* phyxels, 249,000/310,000 surfels, 22 sec/frame.

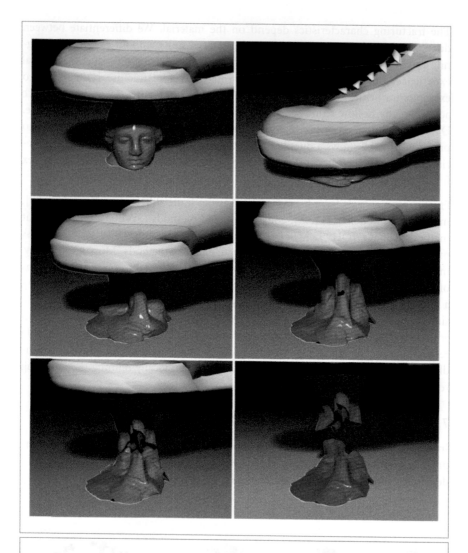

Figure 7.9: Highly plastic deformations and ductile fracture. The bubblegum-like material is first deformed beyond recognition. It is then stretched until the stress in the material is too high and it fractures along a complex fracture surface. Initial/final sampling: 2.2k/3.3k phyxels, 134,000/144,000 surfels, 2.4 sec/frame.

equations. This work has been extended in Terzopoulos and Fleischer [TF88] to handle plastic materials and fracture effects. Mass-spring models [HTK98] and constraint-based methods [SWB00] have also been popular for modeling fractures in graphics, as they allow for easy control of fracture patterns and relatively simple and fast implementations. Recent efforts have focused on finite element methods that directly approximate the equations of continuum mechanics [Chu96]. O'Brien et al. were the first to apply this technique for graphical animation in their seminal paper on brittle fracture [OH99]. Using element cutting and dynamic remeshing, they adapt the simulation domain to conform with the fracture lines that are derived from the principal stresses. O'Brien et al. [OBH02] introduce strain-state variables to model plastic deformations and ductile fracture effects. Element splitting has also been used in virtual surgery simulation, where Bielser et al. [BGTG03] introduced a state machine to model all configurations of how a tetrahedron can be split. Müller et al. [MMDJ01] and Müller and Gross [MG04] demonstrate real-time fracturing using an embedded boundary surface to reduce the complexity of the finite element mesh. The virtual node algorithm of Molino et al. [MBF04] combines the ideas of embedding the surface and remeshing the domain. Elements are duplicated and fracture surfaces are embedded in the copied tetrahedra. This allows more flexible fracture paths, but avoids the complexity of full remeshing and associated time-stepping restrictions.

7.2.3 MODELING OF DISCONTINUITIES

We will start by discussing how the discontinuity can be modeled that is introduced by a propagating crack into the domain of a simulated solid. For that, the so-called visibility criterion [BLG94] can be used where phyxels are allowed to interact with each other only if they are not separated by a surface. This is done by testing if a ray connecting two phyxels intersects the boundary surface, similar to ray tracing (see Section 6.3).

To see what happens when we use the visibility criterion we look at the discretization $\tilde{\mathbf{u}}$ of the continuous displacement field $\mathbf{u}$. This is typically approximated as $\mathbf{u}(\mathbf{x}) \approx \sum_i \Phi_i(\mathbf{x})\mathbf{u}_i$, where $\mathbf{u}_i$ are the displacement vectors at the material coordinates $\{\mathbf{x}_i\}$ of the phyxels and Φ_i are shape functions associated with these coordinates. For FEM, the Φ_i are constructed using a tessellation of the simulation domain into nonoverlapping elements. Meshless methods require no such spatial decomposition, but instead use techniques such as the moving least squares (MLS) approximation [LS81] to define the shape functions based on the location of the phyxels only. Given a complete polynomial basis $\mathbf{b}(\mathbf{x}) = [1 \ \mathbf{x} \ \dots \ \mathbf{x}^n]^T$ of order n and a weight function ω_i, the meshless shape functions can be derived as

$$\Phi_i(\mathbf{x}) = \omega_i(\mathbf{x}, \mathbf{x}_i)\mathbf{b}^T(\mathbf{x})[\mathbf{M}(\mathbf{x})]^{-1}\mathbf{b}(\mathbf{x}_i), \qquad (7.31)$$

where $[\mathbf{M}(\mathbf{x})]^{-1}$ is the inverse of the moment matrix defined as

$$\mathbf{M}(\mathbf{x}) = \sum_i \omega_i(\mathbf{x}, \mathbf{x}_i)\mathbf{b}(\mathbf{x}_i)\mathbf{b}^T(\mathbf{x}_i), \qquad (7.32)$$

and $\omega_i(\mathbf{x}, \mathbf{x}_i)$ is the weight function of Equation (7.12). A detailed account on how to construct shape functions for meshless methods can be found in Fries and Matthies [FM03].

Figure 7.10a shows the weight and shape functions when using the visibility criterion. The crack not only introduces a discontinuity along the crack surface, but also undesirable discontinuities of the shape functions within the domain. The transparency method proposed by Organ et al. [OFTB96] alleviates potential stability problems due to these discontinuities. The idea is to make the crack more transparent closer to the crack front. This allows partial interaction of phyxels in the vicinity of the crack front. Suppose the ray between two phyxels $\mathbf{x}_i$ and $\mathbf{x}_j$ intersects a crack surface at a point $\mathbf{x}_s$ (Figure 7.10c). Then the weight function ω_i (and similarly for ω_j) is adapted to $\omega_i'(\mathbf{x}_i, \mathbf{x}_j) = \omega_i(\|\mathbf{x}_i - \mathbf{x}_j\|/h_i + (2d_s/(\kappa h_i))^2)$, where d_s is the distance between $\mathbf{x}_s$ and the closest point on the crack front, and κ controls the opacity of the crack surfaces. Effectively, a crack passing between two phyxels lengthens the interaction distance of the phyxels until eventually, in this adapted distance metric, the phyxels will be too far apart to interact. As shown in Figure 7.10b this method avoids the discontinuities of the shape functions within the domain and thus leads to increased stability.

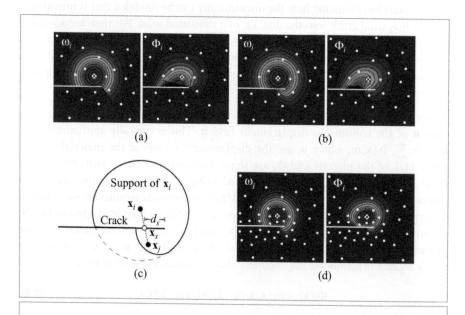

Figure 7.10: Comparison of visibility criterion (*a*) and transparency method (*b*) for an irregularly sampled 2D domain. The effect of a crack, indicated by the horizontal white line, on weight function ω_i and shape function Φ_i is depicted for phyxel $\mathbf{x}_i$ marked by the cross. A schematic view of the transparency method is shown in (*c*) and the effect of dynamic upsampling is illustrated in (*d*).

7.2.4 SURFACE MODEL

Introducing cuts into the model exposes interior parts of the solid that need to be bounded by new surface sheets. Previous approaches based on FEM define fracture surfaces using faces of the tetrahedral elements, which requires complex dynamic remeshing to avoid unnaturally coarse crack surfaces [OH99]. To simplify the topological complexity and avoid stability problems during the simulation, mesh-based approaches impose restrictions on where and how the material can fracture. These restrictions can be lifted by embedding a surface and explicitly creating new fracture surface sheets whenever the material is cut. Using a point-based representation as the boundary of a 3D solid allows simple and efficient creation of these surface sheets, since no explicit connectivity information needs to be maintained between surfels. Sharp creases and corners are represented implicitly as the intersection of adjacent surface sheets using the CSG method described in Section 6.3.2. The precise location of crease lines is evaluated at render time (see Figure 7.17 later), avoiding costly surface-surface intersection calculations during simulation.

A crack consists of a crack front and two separate surface sheets that are connected at the front to form a sharp crease. The crack front itself is defined by a linear sequence of crack nodes $c_1, \ldots, c_n$ that continuously add surfels to the fracture surfaces while propagating through the material. For surface cracks the end nodes of the front lie on a boundary surface or a fracture surface of a different crack. Interior cracks have circularly connected crack fronts; in other words, the two end nodes c_1 and c_n coincide (see Figures 7.11 and 7.12 later).

To animate the boundary surface of the solid, the free-form deformation approach described in Section 7.1.8 is used. To ensure that the displacement field is smooth at the crack front, the transparency weights described above are also used in Equation (7.30). because the changes of the transparency weights are localized to a small region around the crack front, only a small fraction of the weights needs to be updated in every time step, leading to an efficient implementation.

7.2.5 CRACK INITIATION AND PROPAGATION

Crack initiation is based on the stress tensor σ (see Equation 7.8). A new crack is created where the maximal eigenvalue of σ exceeds the threshold for tensile fracture (opening mode fracture [And95b]). This condition is evaluated for all phyxels. To allow crack initiation anywhere on the surface or in the interior of the model, a stochastic scheme can be applied to initiate crack fronts. A random set of surface and interior sample points are created and the stress tensor at these points is evaluated using weighted averaging from adjacent phyxels. The inherent smoothing is usually desired to improve the stability of the crack propagation. If a crack front is initiated at one of these spatial locations, the fracture thresholds of all neighboring samples are increased to avoid spurious branching.

A new crack is initialized with three crack nodes, each of which carries two surfels with identical position and radius but opposing normals. These surfels form the initial crack surfaces that will grow dynamically as the crack propagates through the solid (Figure 7.11). Crack propagation is determined by the propagation vectors $\mathbf{d}_i = \alpha_i \lambda_i (\mathbf{e}_i \times \mathbf{t}_i)$, where λ_i is the maximal eigenvalue of the stress tensor at $\mathbf{c}_i$, and $\mathbf{e}_i$ is the corresponding eigenvector. The vector $\mathbf{t}_i$ approximates the tangent of the crack front as $\mathbf{t}_i = (\mathbf{c}_{i+1} - \mathbf{c}_{i-1})/\|\mathbf{c}_{i+1} - \mathbf{c}_{i-1}\|$, where $\mathbf{c}_0 = \mathbf{c}_1$ and $\mathbf{c}_{n+1} = \mathbf{c}_n$ for surface cracks. The parameter α_i depends on the material and can be used to control the speed of propagation. The new position of a crack node $\mathbf{c}_i$ at time $t + \Delta t$ is then computed as $\mathbf{c}_i + \Delta t \mathbf{d}_i$, where Δt is the simulation time step. Additionally, the end nodes of surface cracks are projected back onto the surface that they originated from using the projection method described in Section 4.2. Since propagation alters the spacing of crack nodes along the front, the sampling resolution of the crack nodes is adjusted

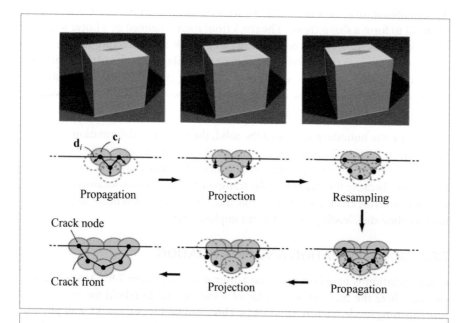

Figure 7.11: Front propagation and fracture surface sampling. The **upper row** shows a top view of an opening crack, the **lower part** shows a side view of a single fracture surface. After propagating the crack nodes $\mathbf{c}_i$ according to $\mathbf{d}_i$, end nodes are projected onto the surface. If necessary, the front is resampled and new surfels are added to the fracture surface sheets.

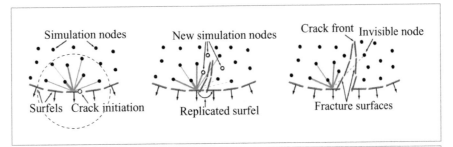

Figure 7.12: Transparency weights for embedding surfels in the simulation domain. The thickness of the lines indicates the influence of a phyxel on the displacement of a surfel. During crack propagation, new surfels and phyxels are created using dynamic resampling.

dynamically after each propagation step. If two adjacent crack nodes are farther apart than the radius of their associated surfels, a new node is inserted using cubic spline interpolation to determine the new node's position. Redundant crack nodes are removed when the distance to the immediate neighbors becomes too small. Fracture surface sheets are sampled by inserting new surfels if the propagation distance exceeds the surfel radius, indicating that a hole would appear in the surface. This spatially (along the crack front) and temporally (along the propagation vectors) adaptive sampling scheme ensures uniformly sampled and hole-free crack surfaces (see Figure 7.11).

During crack propagation, the simulation is adjusted automatically to the newly created fracture surfaces by adapting the shape functions using the transparency method described above. The transparency weight $\omega_i'(\mathbf{x}_i, \mathbf{x}_j)$ for a pair of phyxels is adapted by computing the intersection point on the fracture surface of the ray connecting the two phyxels (Section 7.2.3) using the method described in Section 6.3.2. The distance d_s to the crack front is approximated as the shortest Euclidean distance to the line segments defined by adjacent crack nodes. To avoid stability problems with curved fracture surfaces, weights are allowed to only decrease from one time step to the next.

7.2.6 TOPOLOGY CONTROL

The major challenge when explicitly modeling fracture surfaces is the efficient handling of all events that affect the topology of the boundary surface and the simulation domain. Apart from crack initiation, three fundamental events are sufficient to

describe the often intricate constellations that occur during fracturing: *termination,*
splitting, and *merging* of crack fronts:

- A crack is *terminated* if the crack front has contracted to a single point.
- *Splitting* occurs when a crack front penetrates through a surface as shown in
  Figure 7.13a. The signed distance of a crack node to a surface sheet can be
  estimated using the method described in Section 4.2. A splitting event is initiated when a sign change occurs from one time step to the next. The front is
  split at the edges that intersect the surface, discarding all nodes that are outside the solid, except the ones that are connected to an interior node. These

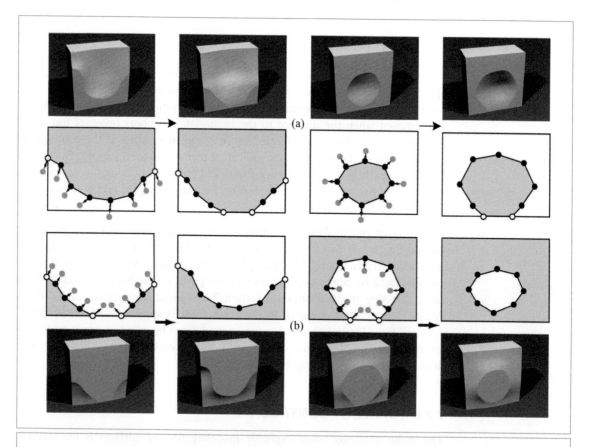

Figure 7.13: Topological events during crack propagation: (*a*) splitting and (*b*) merging. The ***top and bottom rows***
show a cutaway view with one crack surface exposed. The sketches in the ***center rows*** show this fracture surface
in gray, end nodes of crack fronts are indicated by white dots.

nodes become new end nodes by moving them to the intersection point with the surface. As shown on the left in Figure 7.13a, a surface crack is split into two new crack fronts that share the same crack surfaces (i.e., independently add surfels to the same fracture surface sheets during propagation). An interior crack becomes a surface crack after splitting, as illustrated on the right.

- A *merging* event is triggered when two surface end nodes of two crack fronts meet by creating the appropriate edge connections (Figure 7.13b). Two surface cracks are merged into a single surface crack (left), while a circular front is created if the two end nodes are from the same crack front (right). Typically, when cracks merge, their fracture surfaces create a sharp corner, so we maintain separate fracture surface sheets that intersect to create a crease.

As can be seen in Figure 7.13, splitting and merging are dual to each other. The former introduces two new end nodes, while the latter decreases the number of end nodes by two. Similarly, crack initiation and termination are dual topological operations. Note that the intersection of two crack fronts at interior nodes is handled automatically by first splitting both fronts and then merging the newly created end nodes.

One useful technique to improve the stability of the simulation is *snapping*. Snapping guarantees that problematic small features, such as tiny fragments or thin slivers, do not arise. It works by forcing nodes very near other nodes or very near surfaces to become coincident to ensure that any features present are of size comparable to the local node spacing. Similar methods have been proven to guarantee topological consistency with the ideal geometry in other settings [GM95]. Specifically, when a front intersects a surface, the crack nodes that are within snapping distance d to the surface are projected onto the surface. This avoids fragmenting the front into small pieces that would be terminated anyway within a few time steps. Furthermore, fronts are merged when the end nodes are within distance d by moving both end nodes to their average position. This avoids small slivers of material to be created, which would require a significant number of new phyxels to be added to the model (see Section 7.2.7). Similarly, the intersection of two crack fronts can lead to multiple splitting and merging events (Figure 7.14), which are combined into a single event to avoid the overhead of creating and subsequently deleting many small crack fronts. Snapping can also be applied to front termination, where a crack front is deleted when all its nodes are within distance d from each other.

7.2.7 VOLUMETRIC SAMPLING

One of the main advantages of meshless methods lies in the fact that they support simple and efficient sampling schemes. Initially, the volume V bounded by a surface S is discretized by sampling V with phyxels as described in Section 7.1.3. Similar to adaptive finite element meshing, we want a higher phyxel density close to the boundary surface and fewer phyxels toward the interior of the solid.

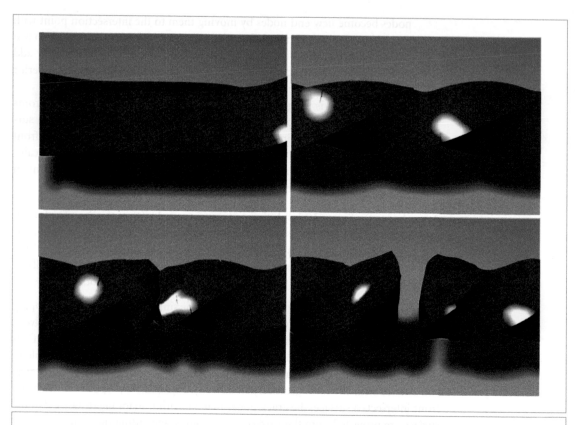

Figure 7.14: Crack merging. Four of a total 49 crack fronts merge in the center of the twisted bar to form a circular crack front. Initial/final sampling: 2,000/3,000 phyxels, 29,000/144,000 surfels, 10 sec/frame.

An appropriate sampling of the phyxels can be computed, for example, using a balanced octree hierarchy as shown in Figure 7.15. Starting from the bounding box of S, a cell of the octree is recursively refined, if it contains parts of S. The final number of phyxels is controlled by prescribing a maximum octree level at which the recursive refinement is stopped. Given this adaptive decomposition, a phyxel is created at each octree cell center that lies within V. To create a locally, more uniform, distribution, samples are displaced within their octree cell by applying a few iterations of point repulsion.

During simulation, the discretization of the simulation domain needs to be adjusted dynamically. Without dynamic resampling, frequent fracturing would quickly degrade the numerical stability of the simulation even for an initially adequately sampled model. New phyxels need to be inserted in the vicinity of the crack surfaces and in particular around the crack front. At the same time, strong deformations of the

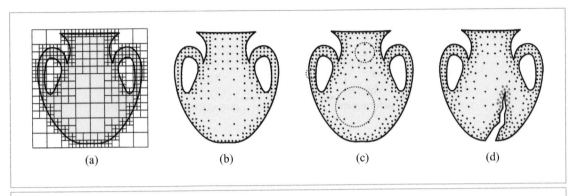

Figure 7.15: Volumetric sampling: (*a*) octree decomposition, (*b*) initial adaptive octree sampling, (*c*) sampling after local repulsion, where circles indicate 0.1 isovalue of weight function, and (*d*) dynamic resampling during fracturing.

model can lead to a poor spatial discretization of the simulation volume, which also requires a dynamic adaptation of the sampling resolution. This is particularly important for highly plastic materials, where the deformed shape can deviate significantly from its original configuration.

A simple local criterion can be used to determine undersampling at a phyxel $\mathbf{x}_i$. Let $\Omega_i = \sum_j \omega_i'(\mathbf{x}_i, \mathbf{x}_j)/\omega_i(\mathbf{x}_i, \mathbf{x}_j)$ be the normalized sum of transparency weights (see Section 7.2.3). Without visibility constraints, Ω_i is simply the number of phyxels in the support of $\mathbf{x}_i$. During simulation Ω_i decreases, if fewer neighboring phyxels are found due to strong deformations, or if the transparency weights become smaller due to a crack front passing through the solid. If Ω_i drops below a threshold $\Omega_{\min}$, $\lceil \Omega_{\min} - \Omega_i \rceil$ new phyxels are inserted within the support radius of $\mathbf{x}_i$ (see Figure 7.16), similar to Desbrun and Cani [DC96].

The mass associated with $\mathbf{x}_i$ is distributed evenly among the new phyxels and their support radius is adapted to keep the overall material density constant. Note that mass will not be strictly preserved locally in the sense that the mass distribution of phyxels after fracturing will not precisely match the correct distribution according to the separated volumes created by the fracture surface sheets. However, mass will be preserved globally and the local deviations are sufficiently small to not affect the simulation noticeably.

To prevent excessive resampling for phyxels very close to a fracture boundary, phyxel splitting is restricted by prescribing a minimal phyxel support radius. Note that resampling due to fracturing is triggered by the crack nodes passing through the solid, similar to adapting the visibility weights (see Section 7.2.4). Performing these checks comes essentially for free, since all the required spatial queries are already carried out during visibility computation. Figures 7.15d and 7.17 illustrate the dynamic

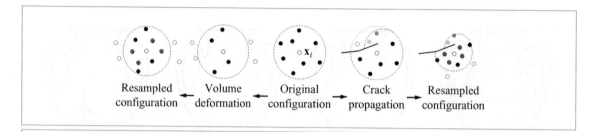

Figure 7.16: Dynamic resampling at the phyxel $\mathbf{x}_i$ due to strong deformation (*left*) and fracturing (*right*).

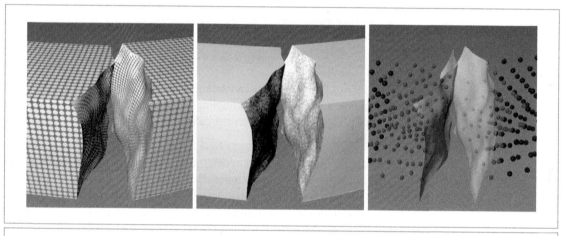

Figure 7.17: Surfels are clipped to create sharp creases with dynamically created fracture surfaces, whose visual roughness is controlled using 3D noise functions for bump mapping. The sampling of the simulation domain is shown on the right, where green spheres denote resampled phyxels.

adaptation of the sampling rates when fracturing. The effect on the shape functions is shown in Figure 7.10d.

7.2.8 FRACTURE CONTROL

By specifying material properties, the course of the simulation can be influenced. However, often direct control over the fracture behavior is crucial, especially in production environments and interactive applications where the visual effect is usually more important than physical accuracy. By exploiting the explicit point-based representation of the fracture surfaces, the fracture framework can be extended to support precise control of where and how a model fractures. One possibility is to use a painting interface as described in Section 5.2.4 that allows fast prototyping of fracture simulations by prescribing fracture patterns directly on the object boundary. The user can paint arbitrary networks of cracks on the surface and explicitly specify stress thresholds for these cracks. Additionally, a propagation history can be used to control the propagation of cracks through the material. The adjusted propagation vector at time t is computed as the weighted average $\bar{\mathbf{d}}_i^t = \gamma \mathbf{d}_i^{t-\Delta t} + (1-\gamma)\mathbf{d}_i^t$, where $\gamma \in [0,1]$ is the history factor. A purely stress-based propagation is achieved for $\gamma = 0$, while $\gamma = 1$ yields purely geometric cracks and fracture surfaces. Other possibilities include volumetric textures for adjusting the fracture thresholds within the material, and prescoring techniques, where the stress tensor is modified according to an embedded level set function [MBF04]. Figure 7.18 shows an example of an explicitly controlled fracture, using a combination of crack painting, propagation history, and adaptive fracture thresholds.

Figure 7.18: Controlled fracture. While the sphere blows up it fractures along the prescribed smiley face. Initial/final sampling: 4.6k/5.8k phyxels, 49,000/72,000 surfels, 6 sec/frame.

7.2.9 SIMULATION PIPELINE

Figure 7.19 shows a high-level overview of the simulation pipeline. An iteration step starts with the detection of collisions between two or several objects. Collision detection is based on the signed distance function of the boundary surfaces, see Section 4.2. Interpenetrations are resolved by computing an approximate contact surface that is consistent for both models [KMH+04]. The objects are separated by computing penalty forces from the contact surface. After resolving collisions and contacts, strains and stresses are computed as described in Section 7.1.2. Given the distribution of stress, new crack fronts are initiated and existing cracks propagated, and the spatial sampling of the fracture surfaces is adapted (Section 7.2.5). This stage is followed by the dynamic resampling of the simulation domain (Section 7.2.7). Finally, the forces are integrated (e.g., using an explicit leap-frog scheme) to obtain the new displacements.

7.2.10 CONCLUSION

With the meshless framework described above, deformable objects with material properties ranging from stiff elastic to highly plastic can be simulated. Extending this framework for fracturing is straightforward and shows several advantages compared to FEM simulation. Instead of maintaining a consistent volumetric mesh using continuous cutting and restructuring of finite elements, the shape functions of the phyxels are adjusted dynamically based on simple visibility constraints. The space discretization is continuously adapted using insertions of new phyxels. The simplicity of this dynamic resampling of the simulation domain highlights one of the main benefits of meshless methods for physics-based animation. Due to minimal consistency constraints between neighboring nodes, dynamic resampling is efficient and easy to implement, as compared to the far more involved remeshing methods used in FEM simulations. Similarly, a point-based representation is built for the boundary surface, which allows efficient dynamic sampling of fracture surfaces, and facilitates explicit control of the object topology. A general limitation of the meshless approach is that

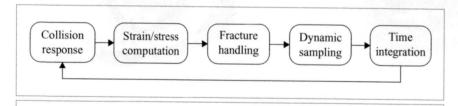

Figure 7.19: High-level overview of the meshless simulation pipeline.

even very small fragments must be sampled sufficiently dense in order to obtain a stable evaluation of the shape functions. This inflates the number of phyxels when an object is fractured excessively, which slows down the computations.

7.3 FLUID SIMULATION

Martin Wicke, Richard Keiser, and Markus Gross

7.3.1 OVERVIEW

Fluids constitute a large part of our visual surroundings. A fluid is defined as a material that cannot support shear stress in static equilibrium—it flows. This definition spans a wide range of material properties. Smoke and fire, as well as clouds and other natural phenomena based on the behavior of gases fall in the category of fluid simulation, but also the simulation of liquids such as water, oil, or lava.

While visualization of gaseous fluids is usually performed using volume-rendering techniques, liquids have a surface that needs to be extracted or tracked. The surface of a liquid is highly volatile and subject to frequent changes in topology.

This section presents meshless simulation methods that can be used for fluid simulation and compares those to other established algorithms. One particle method, *smoothed particle hydrodynamics* (SPH), will be considered in more detail. We will then turn to the problem of surface tracking and reconstruction.

7.3.2 SIMULATION METHODS

There are two distinct methods to discretize a physics problem in order to simulate it: *Lagrangian* and *Eulerian* methods. While Lagrangian methods discretize the material, Eulerian methods discretize the space in which the material moves. In other words, in a Langrangian simulation, the simulation elements move with the material, whereas in a Eulerian setting, the material moves through the simulation elements, which are fixed in space. Figure 7.20 illustrates the difference.

All Eulerian methods are mesh-based methods, for example the finite difference and finite volumes methods [FW60, And95a]. The simulation grid is a disjoint set of volume elements that cover the simulation domain. The volume elements do not necessarily form a regular grid, but for implementation and performance issues, this is often the first choice. Since the discretization of space does not depend on the material, it is easy for these algorithms to accommodate large deformations (such

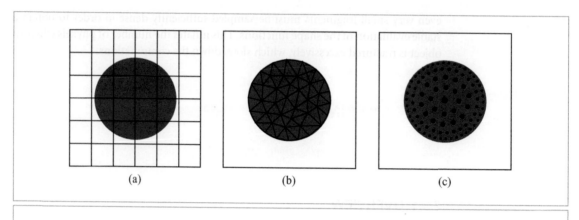

(a)   (b)   (c)

Figure 7.20: A 2D sphere of blue material discretized in a Eulerian mesh (*a*), Lagrangian mesh (*b*), and using particles (*c*). The Lagrangian elements discretize only the material, while the Eulerian elements discretize the embedding space. Only the meshes define a disjoint partitioning of space.

as those occurring in flow simulations). Hence, this class of simulation algorithms is well suited for fluid simulation, and they are still dominant in computer graphics (some examples include [FM97, Sta99, FF01, LGF04, FOA03]).

Since the discretization of the simulation domain does not change with the material shape, interface tracking and moving boundaries are problematic in Eulerian simulations. Also, mass loss can occur due to numerical dissipation.

In contrast to the Eulerian approach, Lagrangian methods discretize the material that is simulated, and the discretization moves during the simulation. Since each element of the discretization represents a part of the material, mass loss is not an issue for Lagrangian methods. Also complex moving boundaries and free surfaces are easier to handle, since the discretization moves along with the material.

Most prominent in this class of algorithms are mesh-based finite element methods, which are widely used in continuum mechanics. The numerical accuracy of these methods highly depends on the aspect ratio of the mesh elements used to cover the simulated material (most commonly tetrahedra). If the material undergoes large deformations, the mesh quality degrades and remeshing is needed. Therefore, mesh-based Lagrangian methods are rarely used for fluid simulation in computer graphics.

Particle methods are a Lagrangian discretization that do not require a mesh for simulation. These methods work on a set of samples (particles), without defining nearest-neighbor relationships. In practice, a set of neighbors are computed for each particle in each time step. Strictly speaking, this is only an optimization, exploiting the fact that the interpolation functions used usually have local support, and thus reducing the overall complexity from $O(N^2)$ to $O(N \log N)$ per time step, where N is the number of particles. Although, technically, these neighborhoods define a mesh, this mesh is not a disjoint partitioning of the domain, and explicit neighborhoods need not be stored.

Smoothed particle hydrodynamics [Luc77, GM77] was the first particle method, and is still the most popular in computer graphics. It was originally invented for astrophysics applications, where the particle metaphor is obvious. In Section 7.3.3, SPH will be discussed in detail.

Other methods include weakly coupled or spatially coupled particle systems. The former are popular methods for a wide range of special effects, like fire, clouds, or other fuzzy gaseous objects [Ree83, SF95]; waves [Pea86, Gos90]; or even animal flocking behavior [Rey87]. Here, particle behavior is usually determined by a procedural and/or stochastical process. These techniques are fast and easy to control while producing convincing animations for a large class of phenomena. They are, hence, ideally suited for movie productions and especially games.

Spacially coupled particle systems compute forces between pairs of particles in order to animate the particle system [Ton92]. Usually some potential is attached to each particle, defining the occuring interaction forces as the negative gradient of the potential field at each particle's position. Using functions like the Lennard-Jones potential known from molecular dynamics or variations thereof, different material properties can be modeled.

7.3.3 SMOOTHED PARTICLE HYDRODYNAMICS

The most popular particle method for fluid simulation in computer graphics is SPH. In this section, its basic formulation as a method for function interpolation will be derived. We will then go on to show how this framework can be applied to the problem of fluid simulation. For a more in-depth treatment of the topic, see Monaghan [Mon05] or Liu and Liu [LL03].

Elements of the SPH method have already been used in the MLS approximation described in Sections 7.1.3 and 7.1.4. SPH approximations are not first-order accurate, and thus not suitable for modeling general elasticity. However, this property is less critical for fluid simulation, and SPH is popular for its relatively low computational cost and good controllability.

In SPH, a number of particles represent the material, in our case, the fluid. Each particle carries mass, velocity, and other attributes. A kernel function $\omega_h(d)$ describes the influence of each particle on its surroundings, where the *smoothing length* h is a constant of the particle, and d is the distance from the particle. In almost all cases, the smoothing length is constant over all particles, and does not change during the simulation, yielding equal-sized particles that are much easier to handle algorithmically. The kernel function is generally defined to be a normalized and smooth function with local support, in particular $\omega_h(d) = 0 \quad \forall d > kh$ for some k.

Using the kernel, a continuous function $A(\mathbf{x})$ can be smoothed to obtain $A'(\mathbf{x})$:

$$A'(\mathbf{x}) = \int \omega_h(\|\mathbf{x} - \mathbf{x}'\|) A(\mathbf{x}') \, d\mathbf{x}'. \tag{7.33}$$

If we turn to the discrete setting, the function $A(\mathbf{x})$ is unknown, and only samples A_j at the particle positions $\mathbf{x}_j$ are accessible. Each particle represents a small volume element V_j, which is related to the particles' mass m_j and density ϱ_j by

$$V_j = \frac{m_j}{\varrho_j}. \tag{7.34}$$

Thus, the integral in Equation (7.33) can be approximated by a sum over the particles.

$$
\begin{aligned}
A'(\mathbf{x}) &\approx \sum_j \omega_h(\|\mathbf{x} - \mathbf{x}_j\|) \, V_j A_j \\
&= \sum_j \omega_h(\|\mathbf{x} - \mathbf{x}_j\|) \frac{m_j}{\varrho_j} A_j = \langle A(\mathbf{x}) \rangle.
\end{aligned}
\tag{7.35}
$$

We will call $\langle A \rangle$ the SPH approximation of the function A.

Note that the particle masses m_j are constant during the simulation, however, the densities ϱ_j are subject to change. Fortunately, the densities can be approximated by substituting ϱ for A in Equation (7.35):

$$\langle \varrho(\mathbf{x}) \rangle = \sum_j \omega_h(\|\mathbf{x} - \mathbf{x}_j\|) \varrho_j \frac{m_j}{\varrho_j} = \sum_j \omega_h(\|\mathbf{x} - \mathbf{x}_j\|) \, m_j. \tag{7.36}$$

By defining $\varrho_j := \langle \varrho(\mathbf{p}_j) \rangle$, Equation (7.35) can be used to interpolate any function from samples at the particle positions.

Approximations of Differential Operators in SPH

Differential operators can be directly applied to the SPH approximation $\langle A \rangle$. Since the sample values A_j are constants, we can write

$$\langle \nabla A(\mathbf{x}) \rangle = \sum_j \nabla \omega_h(\|\mathbf{x} - \mathbf{x}_j\|) \frac{m_j}{\varrho_j} A_j, \tag{7.37}$$

where the gradient $\nabla \omega_h(\|\mathbf{x} - \mathbf{x}_j\|)$ can be rewritten in terms of the kernel derivative:

$$\nabla \omega_h(\|\mathbf{x} - \mathbf{x}_j\|) = \frac{\mathbf{x} - \mathbf{x}_j}{\|\mathbf{x} - \mathbf{x}_j\|} \, \omega_h'(\|\mathbf{x} - \mathbf{x}_j\|). \tag{7.38}$$

Similarly, a Laplace operator for A and a divergence operator for a vector-valued function $\mathbf{A}$ can be defined:

$$\langle \Delta A(x) \rangle = \sum_j \frac{m_j}{\varrho_j} \, \omega_h''(\|\mathbf{x} - \mathbf{x}_j\|) \, A_i \tag{7.39}$$

$$\langle \nabla \cdot \mathbf{A}(\mathbf{x}) \rangle = \sum_j \frac{m_j}{\varrho_j} \, \nabla \omega_h(\|\mathbf{x} - \mathbf{x}_j\|) \cdot \mathbf{A}_j. \tag{7.40}$$

In a simulation, we mostly need SPH approximations at particle positions. We will therefore introduce the following shorthand notation. For the kernel weight of a particle at $\mathbf{x}_j$ with respect to $\mathbf{x}_i$, we write

$$\omega_{ij} = \omega_h(\|\mathbf{x}_i - \mathbf{x}_j\|), \tag{7.41}$$

and for any SPH approximation, evaluated at a point $\mathbf{x}_i$,

$$\langle A \rangle_i = \langle A(\mathbf{x}_i) \rangle. \tag{7.42}$$

Stability

The above approximations are derived using approximations to the integral in Equation (7.33). Their accuracy strongly depends on the distribution of particles in the region of interest. In practice, larger values of h provide more sample points and add stability to the simulation. This involves some computational cost and more smoothing, which might not be desirable.

The gradient operator is especially sensitive to a bad distribution of particles. If the distribution is not symmetric, Equation (7.37) can yield nonzero gradients even if the samples A_i are constant. Noting that the gradient of any function remains unchanged if we substract a constant function, we can rewrite the gradient approximation at the sample points $\mathbf{x}_i$ and obtain

$$\langle \nabla A \rangle_i = \sum_j \nabla \omega_{ij} \frac{m_j}{\varrho_j} (A_j - A_i). \tag{7.43}$$

Note that in order to compute the gradient, the constant field A_i is substracted everywhere. There are different methods to derive the above result; for a more general derivation, see Monaghan [Mon05]. The same method can be applied to obtain a better approximation to the divergence, yielding

$$\langle \nabla \cdot \mathbf{A} \rangle_i = \sum_j \frac{m_j}{\varrho_j} \, \nabla \omega_{ij} \cdot (\mathbf{A}_j - \mathbf{A}_i). \tag{7.44}$$

The approximations (7.43) and (7.44) are often superior to their counterparts (7.37) and (7.40), especially at the boundaries of the sampled region or in regions with high-density gradients.

The choice of interpolation kernel also influences the stability of the simulation. In the paper introducing SPH, Gingold and Monaghan used Gaussian kernels [GM77]. These, however, do not have local support and are rarely used nowadays. At the same time, Lucy used spline kernels [Luc77]. A good kernel has local support, is normalized, and has smooth derivatives. Depending on the problem, other properties may be desirable [MCG03]. Higher-order interpolation kernels that have positive and negative regions are problematic when the particles are not equidistant. An example for a (3D) kernel function is given in Equation (7.12). For use in more or less dimensions than three, the kernel has to be renormalized.

Fluid Simulation Using SPH

The motion of a fluid is determined by pressure forces, viscosity forces, and external forces:

$$\dot{\mathbf{v}} = \frac{\mathbf{f}_{pressure}}{\varrho} + \frac{\mathbf{f}_{viscous}}{\varrho} + \frac{\mathbf{f}_{external}}{\varrho}.$$

(7.45)

Here, the time derivative $\dot{\mathbf{v}}$ is a material derivative; in other words, the change of $\mathbf{v}$ in time when measuring $\mathbf{v}$ at the same point in the fluid, not the same point in space. In a Lagrangian setting, such as SPH, material derivatives are easy to compute, since the properties attached to the particles move along with the particles.

Pressure forces act against pressure differences:

$$\mathbf{f}_{pressure} = -\nabla P.$$

(7.46)

The direct translation of Equation (7.46) into an SPH approximation yields a working simulation, however, it cannot be guaranteed that linear and angular momentum are conserved exactly. Especially in computer graphics, where the simulations often use only a few particles to guarantee interactivity, this can be problematic. Several symmetric (and thus momentum-preserving) pressure forces have been proposed.

The derivation from Monaghan [Mon05] shall be presented here. Instead of interpolating the pressure gradient using $\frac{\mathbf{f}_{pressure}}{\varrho} = -\frac{\langle \nabla P \rangle}{\varrho}$, the acceleration is interpolated directly: $\frac{\mathbf{f}_{pressure}}{\varrho} = -\langle \frac{\nabla P}{\varrho} \rangle$. It can be easily verified that

$$\frac{\nabla P}{\varrho} = \nabla \left(\frac{P}{\varrho} \right) + \frac{P}{\varrho^2} \nabla \varrho.$$

(7.47)

Approximating this expression in SPH yields a symmetric term for the pressure force at the particles:

$$\frac{\mathbf{f}_{\text{pressure}}(\mathbf{p}_i)}{\varrho_i} = \langle \frac{\nabla P}{\varrho} \rangle_i = \langle \nabla \left(\frac{P}{\varrho} \right) + \frac{P}{\varrho^2} \nabla \varrho \rangle_i$$

$$= \sum_j \nabla \omega_{ij} \, m_j \left(\frac{P_j}{\varrho_j^2} + \frac{P_i}{\varrho_i^2} \right).$$

(7.48)

The pressure is a function of the density and the thermal energy. The latter is often ignored. A common choice for the pressure function is [Mon94]:

$$P = k\left(\left(\frac{\varrho}{\varrho_0} \right)^{\gamma} - 1 \right).$$

(7.49)

The parameter k is a measure for the incompressibility of the fluid. The higher k is, the higher the forces to counteract the density difference will be. Monaghan proposed $\gamma = 7$, whereas in computer graphics, a value of 1 is usually used [DC96, MCG03]. Low values of gamma make the fluid more compressible. Substracting 1 in Equation (7.49) removes artifacts at free boundaries.

High values of k provoke high pressure forces and limit the time step that a simulation can use. The speed of sound in the simulated medium is given by $c = \sqrt{\delta P / \delta \varrho}$, and the maximum safe time step for numerical simulation according to the Courant-Friedrichs-Lewy stability criterion is $\Delta t \leq \lambda h / c$, where λ is the Courant number. Thus, $\Delta t_{\max} \propto \sqrt{1/k}$. Viscosity further decreases the maximum time step [Mon92, DC96].

In computer graphics, viscosity effects due to compression are usually neglected. The viscosity force is often modeled after the viscosity term that applies to incompressible fluids [MCG03]:

$$\frac{f_{\text{viscous}}}{\varrho} = \mu \nabla^2 \mathbf{v} = \mu \Delta \mathbf{v}.$$

(7.50)

This term can again be approximated using SPH:

$$\frac{\mathbf{f}_{\text{viscous}}(\mathbf{x}_i)}{\varrho_i} = \mu \langle \Delta \mathbf{v} \rangle_i$$

$$= \mu \sum_j \Delta \omega_{ij} \frac{m_j}{\varrho_j} (\mathbf{v}_j - \mathbf{v}_i).$$

(7.51)

There are other ways of defining viscosity forces, see for example Monaghan [Mon05]. If viscosity is only used for numerical stability, the best approach is sometimes to simulate an inviscid fluid and add *artificial viscosity* later. One type of artificial viscosity is a variation of the XSPH technique [Mon92]. Here, after each time step, the velocity of a particle i is modified in the direction of the average velocity of its neighbors:

$$\Delta \mathbf{v}_i = \xi \sum_j \frac{m_j}{\varrho_j} \omega_{ij} (\mathbf{v}_j - \mathbf{v}_i). \tag{7.52}$$

Original XSPH uses the corrected velocities $\hat{\mathbf{v}}_i = \mathbf{v}_i + \Delta \mathbf{v}_i$ only for advection and stores the originally computed velocities for integration. If $\hat{\mathbf{v}}_i$ is also used for integration, the desired viscosity effect is stronger. In Equation (7.52), $0 \leq \xi \leq 1$ determines how strong artificial viscosity should be. This leads to better regularization of the particles, at the cost of higher viscosity. Even high values of ξ do not incur stability problems; on the contrary, stability increases as ξ gets closer to 1.

Algorithmic Summary

We now have all necessary ingredients to formulate a simple SPH fluid simulation algorithm:

(1) **loop**

(2)   **forall** particles $i \in \Omega$

(3)   find neighboring particles $\mathcal{N}_i \leftarrow \{j \in \Omega | \omega_{ij} > 0\}$

(4)   compute density $\varrho_i \leftarrow \sum_{j \in \mathcal{N}_i} \omega_{ij} \, m_j$

(5)   compute pressure $P_i \leftarrow k(\frac{\varrho_i}{\varrho_0} - 1)$

(6)   **forall** particles $i \in \Omega$

(7)   compute acceleration due to pressure forces
$$\mathbf{a}_i^p \leftarrow \sum_{j \in \mathcal{N}_i} \nabla \omega_{ij} \, m_j \left(P_i/\varrho_i^2 + P_j/\varrho_j^2 \right)$$

(8)   compute acceleration due to viscosity forces
$$\mathbf{a}_i^v \leftarrow \frac{\mu}{\varrho_i} \sum_{j \in \mathcal{N}_i} \Delta \omega_{ij} \frac{m_j}{\varrho_j} (\mathbf{v}_j - \mathbf{v}_i)$$

(9)   **forall** particles $i \in \Omega$

(10)   integrate accelerations $\mathbf{v}_i \leftarrow \mathbf{v}_i + \Delta t (\mathbf{a}_i^p + \mathbf{a}_i^v)$

(11)   integrate velocities $\mathbf{x}_i \leftarrow \mathbf{x}_i + \Delta t \, \mathbf{v}_i$

This algorithm needs three passes over the particles. In the first pass (steps 2 through 5), all densities and pressures in this time step are computed, which only depend on the particles' positions. The second loop computes the accelerations on the particles (steps 6 through 8). In the third pass (steps 9 through 11) the accelerations and velocities are integrated to obtain new positions of the particles. In the above example, the velocity Verlet integration scheme is used. Note that in

Verlet integration, velocities and positions are not in sync (i.e., the **v** and **x** that are stored with the particles are half a time step apart). At the end of a time step k, at simulation time $t = k\Delta t$, each particle stores $\mathbf{x}^t$ and $\mathbf{v}^{t-1/2\Delta t}$. Technically, the viscosity force is computed in an inconsistent state (with positions and velocities from different times). In practice, this effect is not noticeable.

In step 3, the *neighbors* of a particle are computed. A particle j is considered a neighbor of i if $\omega_{ij} > 0$. Thus, if the kernels have local support, most of the particles do not have to be considered in the inner loops. If the set of neighbors can be stored with each particle, it does not need to be recomputed for steps 7 and 8. In any case, appropriate acceleration structures such as hash grids or K-d-trees greatly speed up the simulation. Figure 7.21 shows snapshots from a small-scale simulation using the above algorithm.

7.3.4 SURFACE REPRESENTATION

So far, only the movement of the particles can be simulated. While this is sufficient for measurements, in the context of computer graphics, the visual appearance of the fluid is of interest.

For gaseous phenomena such as clouds or smoke, particles are often rendered as semitransparent spheres with a volumetric texture. The texture of the spheres can be chosen depending on density, temperature, or any other value from the underlying simulation (see for example [FOA03, Har03]). For liquids, the interfaces are more interesting. For nontransparent liquids, the interface is the only visible part of the simulation, and for transparent liquids, the surface is important for diffraction and reflection effects.

Figure 7.21: Snapshots from a small-scale SPH simulation. The particles are drawn as red spheres. The fluid is pulled into a box by gravity.

The easiest way to generate a surface around the particles is to use an implicit surface. Every particle is assigned a potential, and the surface of the fluid is taken to be an isosurface of the superposition of particle potentials [Bli82a]. Several variants to this approach have been proposed, for example Zhu and Bridson [ZB05]. This isosurface can be rendered directly (e.g., using ray tracing), or extracted using the marching cubes algorithm or a variant thereof. The resulting triangle mesh can be rendered with standard rendering algorithms—in the case of transparent liquids, ray tracing is the preferred solution for high-quality images—while hardware rendering can be used for simpler settings. See Figure 7.22 for an example of a ray-traced extracted surface (from [MSKG05]).

Since the particle potentials have no notion of connected components, and the potentials influence also distant particles, these simple isosurfaces do cause problems during topological changes of the surface. See Figure 7.23 for an illustration.

In order to avoid these problems, level sets are often used [OS88, FF01]. Level sets evolve an implicit function according to a velocity field given by the simulation. A PDE is solved on a computational grid in order to animate the surface. In their basic form, level sets suffer from severe volume loss, especially near detailed surface features. *Particle level sets* are a combination of level sets with tracker particles,

(a)   (b)

Figure 7.22: The particles from a particle simulation (*a*) and an isosurface of the particle potentials extracted using marching cubes and ray traced (*b*).

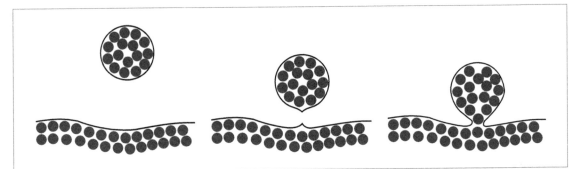

Figure 7.23: Artifacts occurring during topological changes using a purely implicit surface representation. Due to the purely spatial influence of the particle's potentials, the surface of the lower part is influenced by the particles in the drop—it anticipates the drop's arrival.

where the surface computed using level sets is corrected after each time step using tracker particles spawned around the surface [EMF02, ELF05].

7.3.5 SURFACE TRACKING USING POINT SAMPLES

Instead, the surface can be represented by surfels (for a more detailed discussion of this approach, see [KAG⁺05], Section 4). These surfels can then be rendered using either splatting or ray tracing (see Sections 6.2 and 6.3, respectively).

By using an explicit surface representation that is only guided by an implicit function, the advantages of explicit and implicit surfaces can be effectively combined. Splitting and merging operations, trivial for an implicit surface representation, remain simple. The unwanted effects of an implicit representation, like the artifacts due to long-range influence of the particle potentials (see Figure 7.23) can be avoided. By adding normal displacements of other means of detail encoding to the surface, a highly detailed surface can be represented and maintained. This can be used when modeling melting and freezing, or to reduce simulation complexity, when a physical model is used for large-scale movement of the liquid, and a simpler model generates the surface detail.

Initially, the surfels are samples of an implicit surface coating the particles. This implicit surface is an isosurface of a potential function depending on the particle positions alone. This potential function is called the *particle potential function*. Its nature may vary, and good results are obtained using blobbies [Bli82a].

In order to animate a surfel s_i, it is first moved using a first-order estimate of the displacement field defined by its neighboring particles j (see also Section 7.1.3):

$$\mathbf{p}_i^{t+1} = \mathbf{p}_i^t + \frac{\sum_j \omega_h(\|\mathbf{p}_i^t - \mathbf{x}_j^t\|) \left[\mathbf{u}_j^t + \nabla \mathbf{u}_j^t(\mathbf{x}_j^t - \mathbf{p}_i^t)\right]}{\sum_j \omega_h(\|\mathbf{p}_i^t - \mathbf{x}_j^t\|)}. \tag{7.53}$$

The gradient of the displacemtent field $\nabla \mathbf{u}$ is estimated for each particle using an MLS approximation. The surfel normal or tanges axes are also deformed.

Surface Potentials

After this first advection step, the surface is additionally deformed by minimizing a number of surface potentials in order to obtain a smooth and well-sampled surface at all times. There are four surface potentials: a guiding potential that pulls surfels toward an implicit function defined by the particles, a smoothing potential that prevents the typical bumpy surface structure of implicit functions, an attracting potential that keeps the surface close to the particles, and a repulsion potential that guarantees a well-sampled surface. Figure 7.24 shows the effect of these potentials. The potentials are weighted and a simple Eulerian integration is used to move the surfels to minimize the weighted sum of potential functions.

Guiding Potential   Similar to Desbrun and Cani-Gascuel [DCG98], the surfels are attracted to an isosurface of the particle potential function. Given a projection operator that projects onto the implicit function, a surface potential measuring the distance to the implicit function can be defined as

$$\phi_{s_i}^{\text{guiding}} = \frac{1}{2} \|\Gamma_I(\mathbf{p}_i) - \mathbf{p}_i\|^2. \tag{7.54}$$

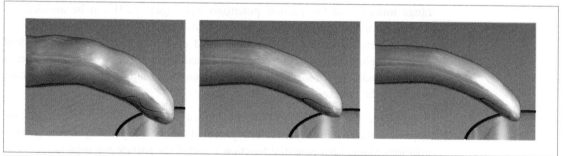

Figure 7.24: The effect of the different potential functions on the surface: (*a*) guiding potential, (*b*) smoothing potential, and (*c*) attracting potential.

Γ_I is a projection operator that projects onto the isosurface with isovalue I of the particle potential function.

Smoothing Potential   The implicit surfaces defined in Blinn [Bli82a] and similar approaches have the inherent property that the defined surface is "blobby." As the particle-sampling density increases, the blobbiness moves to higher frequencies and eventually becomes unnoticeable. Since the surfels are pulled toward an implicit surface, a smoothing potential to counteract the blobbiness is needed. This potential measures the difference between the surfel position $\mathbf{p}_i$ and its projection onto the least squares plane defined by its neighbors, $\Psi(\mathbf{p}_i)$:

$$\phi_{s_i}^{\text{smoothing}} = \frac{1}{2}\|\Psi(\mathbf{p}_i) - \mathbf{p}_i\|^2. \tag{7.55}$$

The forces introduced by this potential are constrained to act only normal to the surface.

Attracting Potential   Most physical interactions are computed on the particles alone. For a realistic visual impression, it is, therefore, necessary to keep the surface as close to the particles as possible. This is achieved using an attracting force pulling the surfels toward their nearest particles. Writing this as a potential, we obtain

$$\phi_{s_i}^{\text{attracting}} = \frac{\sum_j \omega_h(\|\mathbf{x}_j - \mathbf{p}_i\|)\,\|\mathbf{x}_j - \mathbf{p}_i\|^2}{2\sum_j \omega_h(\|\mathbf{x}_j - \mathbf{p}_i\|)}. \tag{7.56}$$

Repulsion Potential   The repulsion potential does not affect the movement of the surface, but only the sampling of the surface with surfels. Using repulsive forces between surfels if they are too close, a locally uniform sampling can be achieved. For a given target surfel distance d, the potential is defined as follows:

$$\phi_{s_i}^{\text{sampling}} = \frac{1}{2}\sum_{j \in \mathcal{N}(s_i)} (\|\mathbf{p}_i - \mathbf{p}_j\| - d)^2. \tag{7.57}$$

The index j runs over all surfels in the neighborhood of s_i. All these surfels hold $\|\mathbf{p}_i - \mathbf{p}_j\| < d$, so that the forces introduced by this potential are never attracting. The forces introduced by this potential are constrained to act only tangential to the surface. It is easily possible to locally vary d to achieve graded sampling of the surface, for example, for level of detail.

Topological Changes

Since our surface representation is not purely implicit, extra handling for topological changes needs to be implemented. Topological changes are characterized by two events: splitting and merging (Figure 7.25). In a particle setting, splitting occurs when particles are separated by a large enough gap. This criterion carries over to the

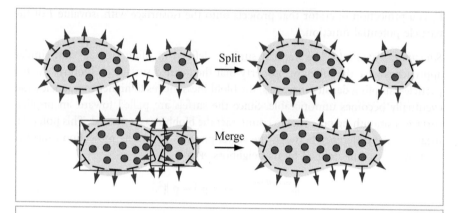

Figure 7.25: Splitting: when the isovalue at a surfel position is too low, the surfel is projected onto the minimum isovalue. Merging: if the isovalue is too high, the surfel is projected onto the maximum isovalue.

particle potential function. When splitting between two groups of particles occurs, there is a point between these groups where the potential function is lower than a threshold I_{min}. This minimum isovalue can be used to define which minimum distance between particles is needed in order to consider them separated. Conversely, if particles are close together, there will be no point between them with a potential lower than a threshold I_{max}.

This can be used to explicitly handle splitting and merging events. If the particle potential at any surfel position is lower than I_{min}, the surfel is reprojected onto the isosurface of the particle potential with isovalue $I_{min} : \mathbf{p}_i \leftarrow \Gamma_{I_{min}}(\mathbf{p}_i)$. For merging events, if the particle potential at the surfel position is too high, the surfel is projected onto the isosurface for isovalue $I_{max} : \mathbf{p}_i \leftarrow \Gamma_{I_{max}}(\mathbf{p}_i)$.

The surfels are free to move within the isorange $[I_{max}, I_{max}]$ of the particle potential, thus giving them the possibility to smooth out the blob artifacts in the isosurface and avoid the anticipating effects seen in purely implicit surface representations.

Since the potential functions rely on surfel and particle neighborhood relations, it is important to keep track of connected components. Flood-fill algorithms can be used to tag connected components. All neighborhoods are then restricted to the same connected component, such that different connected components cannot influence each other.

7.3.6 CONCLUSION

A particle-based fluid simulation has both advantages and disadvantages over alternative approaches, most prominently Eulerian fluid simulation methods.

In general, boundary conditions are easier to enforce in particle-based methods than in Eulerian simulations. Due to the discretization of space, boundary conditions in Eulerian simulation have to be aligned with the grid used to represent the simulation domain. For performance reasons, these meshes are usually regular grids, thus leading to artifacts when representing boundaries. Feldman et al. [FOK05] solve the problem by using adaptive meshes to discretize the simulation domain. Guendelman et al. [GSLF05] developed a method that couples a Eulerian fluid simulation to thin shells. The same technique could also be used to represent boundary conditions.

In particle-based simulations, the boundary condition can be applied to individual particles. For two-way interaction between fluids and other objects, the forces or impulses used to enforce the boundary conditions on the particles can be applied to the boundary [MST+04].

Another practical difficulty in Eulerian fluid simulations is the surface representation. Usually, the interface is tracked in the velocity field by integration. However, due to integration errors, the total volume of the fluid can change. In practice, this leads to mass loss, especially in thin sheets that cannot be resolved by the simulation grid. In contrast, in an SPH simulation, mass is carried by the particles, thus mass preservation is guarantueed.

A major disadvantage of SPH simulation, especially for fluids like water, is the inherent compressibility of the resulting material. In Eulerian simulations, it is relatively easy to enforce incompressibility by solving a global linear system. An analogous method exists for SPH simulation [KO96, PTB+03]. In practice, methods that use an auxiliary grid to solve for a divergence-free velocity field [Har64, BR86, ZB05] are more common.

Fluid simulation using particle methods is a topic of ongoing research. Until now, it has been used mainly in interactive or real-time settings with relatively few particles. Particle methods are relatively easy to implement, and the simple interaction with objects simulated using different simulation methods is an advantage for example in computer games. The surface tracking method discussed above, although not suitable for real-time environments, offers tangible advantages over level-set methods. Still, large simulations with photorealistic results have for the most part been left to Eulerian approaches, although recent work has produced results of visual quality comparable to Eulerian simulations [ZB05]. Depending on the application at hand, one should carefully choose which simulation method is most appropriate.

The next chapter will present selected applications of point-based representations in computer graphics.

CHAPTER EIGHT

Würmlin, Stephan

ETH Zürich
Computer Graphics Laboratory
Haldeneggsteig 4
8092 Zürich
Switzerland
wuermlin@inf.ethz.ch
Tel: +41 44 632 60 86
Fax: +41 44 632 15 96

Kalaiah, Aravind

NVIDIA Corporation
2701 San Tomas Expwy
Santa Clara, CA 94087
USA
akalaiah@nvidia.com
Tel: +1 408 557 0540
Fax: +1 408 486 2676

Reina, Guido

Universität Stuttgart
Visualization and Interactive Systems Institute (VIS)
Universitätsstraße 38
70569 Stuttgart
Germany
Guido.Reina@vis.uni-stuttgart.de
Tel: +49 711 7816 268
Fax: +49 711 7816 340

Ertl, Thomas

Universität Stuttgart
Visualization and Interactive Systems Institute (VIS)
Universitätsstraße 38
70569 Stuttgart
Germany
Thomas.Ertl@vis.uni-stuttgart.de
Tel: +49 711 7816 331
Fax: +49 711 7816 340

Gross, Markus

Computer Graphics Laboratory
ETH Zurich
Haldeneggsteig 4 / Weinbergstrasse
CH - 8092 Zürich
grossm@inf.ethz.ch
Tel: +41-44-632 7114
Fax: +41-44-632 1596

Varshney, Amitabh

University of Maryland
Department of Computer Science and UMIACS
College Park, MD 20742
USA
varshney@cs.umd.edu
Tel: +1 301 405 6761
Fax: +1 301 405 6707

Klein, Thomas

Universität Stuttgart
Visualization and Interactive Systems Institute (VIS)
Universitätsstraße 38
70569 Stuttgart
Germany
Thomas.Klein@vis.uni-stuttgart.de
Tel: +49 711 7816 263
Fax: +49 711 7816 340

Christensen, Per

Pixar Animation Studios
506 Second Avenue
Seattle, WA 98104
USA
per@pixar.com
Tel: +1 206 405 3961
Fax: +1 206 405 4027

8 SELECTED TOPICS

INTRODUCTION

This chapter contains a collection of selected topics and applications related to point-based computer graphics. The chapter aims at demonstrating its versatility and wide range of possible applications. Section 8.1 starts with point-sampled 3D video representations, where 3D points generalize 2D video for the dynamic representation,

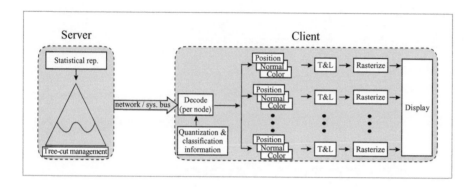

compression, and display of 3-dimensional video. A second application, presented in Section 8.2, includes the modeling and analysis of uncertainty in point clouds using statistical methods. Section 8.3 discusses the utility of irregular point samples for the visualization of irregular point data using so-called point glyphs. The final contribution in Section 8.4 addresses the computation of global illumination effects in point-sampled scenes and shows how such methods are employed in a production environment.

8.1 POINT-SAMPLED 3D VIDEO

Stephan Würmlin and Markus Gross

8.1.1 MOTIVATION

This section concentrates on three-dimensional or free-viewpoint video systems and shows that point samples—due to their unique spatio-temporal properties—feature many advantages as compared to other descriptions. Examples include both offline and online systems for capturing and resynthesizing 3D video objects. The final part is devoted to an outlook to 3D video of dynamic scenes with possibilities for convenient editing and authoring.

As one of the many promising emerging technologies for home entertainment and spatio-temporal visual effects, 3D video acquires the dynamics and motion of a scene during recording while providing the user with the possibility to change the viewpoint at will during playback. Free navigation regarding time and space in streams of visual data directly enhances the viewing experience and interactivity.

Nowadays, such effects (e.g., freeze-and-rotate) are pervasive in feature films like the *Matrix* trilogy, music videos, and commercials. Unfortunately, virtual viewpoint effects have to be planned precisely in most existing systems and changes are no more feasible after the scene has been shot, or involve a considerable amount of manual editing. As an example, Digital Air's *Movia*® systems comprise high-speed, high-definition digital cinema cameras that are placed accurately such that no software view interpolation is needed. But as a consequence, postprocessing and editing possibilities are restricted.

A key feature of 3D video is interactivity: A user should have the possibility to choose an arbitrary viewpoint within a visual real-world scene. No formal definition of 3D video is available to date. We define it as geometrically calibrated and temporally synchronized multiview video data. The broad field of 3D video can be categorized according to spatial camera configurations and application domains. While an arbitrary view configuration would permit all application domains, physical and algorithmic constraints typically lead to a reduced complexity of spatial camera configurations. They are typically tailored to specific application domains for 3D video and can be summarized as follows.

Three-dimensional television [MP04] marks a first line of recent research, aiming at view-independent video for dynamic scenes but in a very limited viewing range only. That is, users might experience changes in parallax but no fly-around effects are possible. It can provide stereoscopic display (one view for each eye) to produce a 3D impression for the viewer. Three-dimensional television is typically acquired using either stereo video captured with two cameras, or by a number of densely arranged cameras in parallel view. Dense means that the baseline between two cameras does not exceed 50 cm. Such configurations can also be used for spatio-temporal video effects with limited spatial scalability [ZKU$^+$04].

The concept of free-viewpoint video [WLG04, CTMS03], on the other hand, allows for truly free navigation in the spatial range of captured data (i.e., in the range covered by acquisition cameras). The scene is captured by a number of sparsely arranged cameras in a convergent setup. Sparse stands for cameras with a baseline that is in the range of 1 or 2 meters at an angle of 30°. Additional information about the scene geometry (e.g., disparity data) enables interactive and free navigation through the scene. Figure 8.1 shows an example of a free-viewpoint video re-rendering from a view in between the two original camera views [WLW$^+$05].

Omnidirectional video [SM04] is an extension of the conventional planar 2D video image plane toward other nonplanar videos (e.g., spherical, cubic, or cylindrical), like in the static but well-known QuicktimeVR [Che95] application. User interactions are limited to zoom and rotation around a predefined viewpoint. Video is captured at a certain viewpoint into every direction.

Figure 8.1: A 3D video re-rendering example: (*a and c*) synchronized video images from different viewpoints, and (*b*) re-rendered intermediate view.

8.1.2 DYNAMIC POINT SAMPLES

A point-sampled representation for free-viewpoint video features many advantages as compared to other descriptions. Firstly, it may be understood as a unified representation—quite contrary to approaches based on mesh and texture information that require handling of heterogeneous types of data (i.e., geometry and images). Dynamic point samples can be seen as a natural generalization of 2D video pixels toward 3D irregular point samples. Since the representation incorporates geometrical scene knowledge in terms of point-sample attributes we have to deal with less acquisition cameras for even broader viewing ranges as compared to purely image-based approaches in the spirit of light fields [LH96] or lumigraphs [GGSC96].

Each point sample can also store the reference to a pixel in an input video camera. This enables the use of efficient coding and compression schemes for free-viewpoint video by exploiting the correspondence between pixels in input images and 3D point samples. Consequently, when employed in 3D video, a dynamic point sample is necessarily generated from an input device (e.g., a digital video camera). Hence, a dynamic point sample can be seen as an extension to a traditional, static point sample or surfel (see Chapter 4). Figure 8.2 depicts the relationship between 2D pixels and 3D dynamic point samples.

8.1.3 3D VIDEO RECORDING

A 3D video recorder is a system capable of recording, processing, and playing three-dimensional video from multiple points of view. First, 2D video streams are recorded from several synchronized digital video cameras and preprocessed

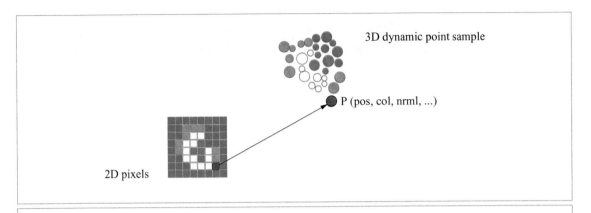

Figure 8.2: Relationship between 2D pixels and 3D dynamic point samples.

images are stored to disk. An offline processing stage converts these images into time-varying three-dimensional data and stores this 3D video to disk. We show two encoding techniques, one building a hierarchical point-based data structure and one that encodes the data in image space. The latter guides the way to the usage of conventional video coding techniques for 3D video.

As opposed to a traditional 2D video recorder comprising only two stages—recording and playback—a 3D video recorder features an additional stage: processing. It is clear that recording and playing need to be carried out in real time. There are no hard real-time constraints for the offline processing stage. Spending 60 times more time on offline processing than on online decompression is still acceptable. A 3D replay application in a broadcasting studio has stronger time constraints, since the replay needs to be available for broadcast only 10–20 seconds after the live action. The ultimate goal of a 3D video recorder is to process 3D information within these time limits. A typical 3D video recording pipeline is depicted in Figure 8.3.

For prerecorded data, the 3D video player provides interaction features known from video cassette recorders, like variable-speed forward, reverse, and slow motion. However, high-quality slow motion requires additional point-based shape morphing between consecutive frames, or the use of high-speed cameras. Three-dimensional video playback can then be enhanced with novel 3D video effects such as freeze-and-rotate and arbitrary scaling. The former can be realized easily by playing a sequence, pausing, rotating the viewpoint, and continuing playback again. In case the system is used for editing a 2D video from a 3D video sequence, the virtual camera path and the frame increments can be configured in a script file. To this end, a 3D video player typically implements a virtual trackball and, hence, arbitrary navigation and

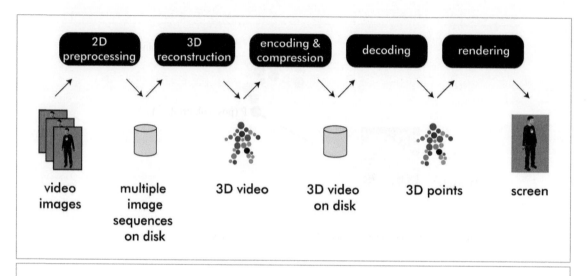

Figure 8.3: The 3D video recording pipeline.

scaling are possible and follow the popular interaction metaphors from other graphics renderers. Random access and decoding of individual frames of the 3D video is crucial for all these effects and interaction metaphors. Furthermore, every frame should be retrieved at different quality levels to accommodate different output devices.

Object-space Coding

Würmlin et al. [WLSG02] developed a 3D video-encoding approach that encodes the reconstructed 3D video sequences with a time-varying, three-dimensional hierarchical point-based data structure. A player software can then decode and render the encoded 3D videos from hard disk in real time, providing the afore-mentioned interaction features.

They use a hierarchical point-based data structure very similar to an octree with varying tree fanouts. Interframe coherence in object-space is not exploited and, hence, every 3D video frame is represented by an independent tree. These trees, which represent the reconstructed 3D video frames, can be stored using a space efficient and progressive representation. In order to achieve a progressive encoding, the tree is traversed in a breadth-first manner. Hence, the upper-level nodes are encoded first, and the nodes represent an averaged representation of the corresponding subtree. A succinct storage of the 3D representation can be achieved by considering separately the different data types it contains [Dee95]. The connectivity of the tree, which needs to be encoded without loss, is distinguished from the position of the points, color, and normal information. The number of allocated bits for storing these points can be traded against visual quality and lossy encoding is acceptable.

To encode the connectivity of the tree the algorithm from Jacobson [Jac89] is followed. Position information is encoded using a two-step process consisting of an approximation and a refinement step by encoding the error using a Laplace quantizer. The color data are encoded in YUV color space with a quantization scheme using twice as much bits for the Y component than for the U and V components, respectively. The normal vectors are encoded using quantized spherical coordinates. The vectors are normalized before encoding and then a certain amount of bits is allocated for each of the two angles. Table 8.1 summarizes the storage requirements for the different data types per node and compares them to the initial data size. For lossless encoding of the connectivity of the tree, a scheme is used that comes close to the information theoretic bound. The indicated values for the remaining data types are those that provided visually appealing results.

Figure 8.4 shows some example images from free-viewpoint video sequences encoded with the object-space approach. Encoding takes approximately 1 second per 3D video frame. Each frame leads to approximately 56,000 tree nodes and 48,000 significant point samples for high-quality decoding and rendering. The employed shape-from-silhouettes 3D reconstruction can lead to artifacts in regions occluded by all reference images, especially visible between the legs and under the arms. Furthermore, the normals (flat-shaded images in Figure 8.4c) from the 3D reconstruction method are not very precise due to the quality of the underlying surface representation (depth map in Figure 8.4d).

The framework allows encoding 3D video sequences of humans at a total bit rate of less than 7 megabits per second, the sequence running with 8.5 frames per second in

Table 8.1: Memory Requirements for One 3D Video Frame.

Name	Data Type	Raw (bits)	Compressed (bits)
position	float[3]	$3 \cdot 32$	$3 + 3 + 3$
color	char[3]	$3 \cdot 8$	$6 + 3 + 3$
normal	float[3]	$3 \cdot 32$	8
noOfChildren	unsigned char	8	$2 + 1 + \lceil lg\, 27 \rceil$
children	*PRkNode	$27 \cdot 32$	
Total		$1{,}088$	37

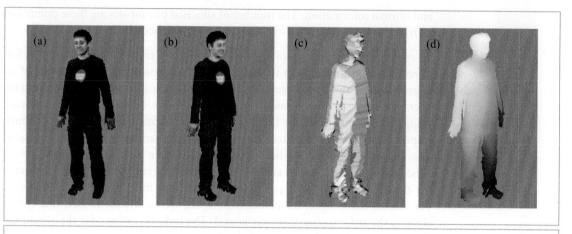

Figure 8.4: Images from object-space compressed 3D video sequences: (*a and b*) rendered views, (*c*) demonstrate the reconstructed normals by flat-shading the view from (*b*) without colors, and (*d*) the corresponding depth map.

normal playback with an average number of 45,000 point samples per frame. The total size for a sequence of 30 seconds is typically less than 30 megabytes. Compared to the memory requirements of the complete data structure, a compression ratio of 64:1 is achieved. Note that consecutive frames in a 3D video sequence contain a lot of redundant information (i.e., regions of the object remaining almost static), or changes that could be efficiently encoded using temporal prediction and motion compensation algorithms. However, efficient computation of 3D scene flows is nontrivial.

Image-space Coding

Alternatively, the free-viewpoint video data can be organized and compressed in image space [WLW+05]. To this end, an image-space representation and data format are used adopted by MPEG as an extension of the MPEG-4 AFX standard [ISO05]. Note that in the standard, this representation is named Depth Image-based Representations (DIBR) Version 2. Combined with suitable coding methods it is capable of streaming and displaying sparse multiview video data from arbitrary viewpoints. It is based on the fundamental concept of storing all information describing a scenes' visual appearance in multichannel video images. Each pixels' channels define different attributes of discrete point samples of observed surfaces. These include color, position, and optional data needed for high-quality rendering. Multichannel multiview video compression can be implemented with standard MPEG video coding tools and readily available video coding methods can thus be reused. Consequently, a complete free-viewpoint video system can be built using only MPEG-standardized tools—to our knowledge the first of its kind. Figure 8.5 illustrates this image-space free-viewpoint video framework.

Similar to our object-space coding scheme, the image space free-viewpoint video coding scheme is based on a dynamic point cloud as underlying 3D data structure. Since the point attributes are again separately stored and compressed, a referencing scheme that allows for the unique identification between points and their attributes is necessary. Using the camera images as building elements of the data structure, each point is uniquely identified by its position in image space and its camera identifier.

Furthermore, looking separately at each camera image, only foreground pixels are of interest—these contribute to the point cloud describing the 3D object. Thus, the segmentation mask from the camera images is used as reference for all subsequent coding schemes. In order to avoid shifts and wrong associations of attributes and points, a lossless encoding of the segmentation mask is required. This lossless segmentation mask must be at the disposal of all encoders and decoders. However, all pixel attributes can be encoded by a lossy scheme. Nevertheless, a lossless or almost lossless decoding should be possible if all data are available.

A great variety of image and video coding methods are available today, and more are under development. Of particular interest for 3D video systems are standard formats developed by MPEG and JPEG, since interoperable systems are targeted. Würmlin et al. [WLW+05] selected a few standard codecs for an extensive

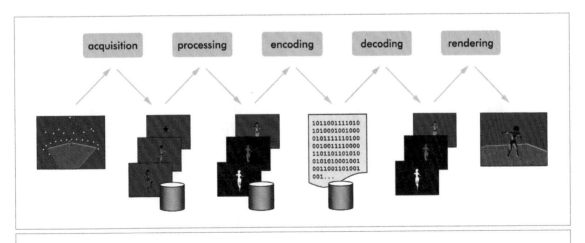

Figure 8.5: Overview of the image-space 3D video pipeline.

evaluation of different coding methods for image-space coding of 3D video data, namely MPEG-4 and JPEG-2000. They also present a novel progressive video coding method for this representation [LWW+04] that fulfills all requirements for unconstrained free-viewpoint video playback as defined by MPEG.

Figure 8.6 shows rendered image-space FVV results using MPEG-4 and JPEG-2000 as coding methods at different bit rates. Per-camera target bit rates are devised of 128 and 512 kbps and the available rate is allocated such that color uses twice as much bits than depth. The shape is encoded separately and accounts for approximately 25 kbps per camera. The rendered images in Figure 8.6 are composed of two reference cameras, so the total bit rates for these images are 306 and 1,074 kbps. MPEG-4 clearly outperforms JPEG-2000 due to motion compensation and its shape-adaptive nature. An extensive evaluation can be found in Würmlin [Wür04].

8.1.4 REAL-TIME 3D VIDEO

Würmlin et al. [WLG04] presented a real-time free-viewpoint video system based on dynamic point samples. A differential update stream inserts, deletes, or updates point samples on the fly in real time. It exploits the spatio-temporal coherence of individual 2D video streams by interframe prediction of input changes in image space. The prediction does not require expensive calculations like texture motion

Figure 8.6: Rendered FVV images with different coding methods: (*a*) uncompressed data, (*b*) JPEG-2000 at total bit rate of 512 kbps per camera, (*c*) MPEG-4 at total bit rate of 512 kbps per camera, and (*d*) MPEG-4 at total bit rate of 128 kbps per camera.

fields or 3D scene flows. While being conceptually simple the presented approach effectively cuts down the number of expensive 3D shape computations. By using a feedback loop that confines the number of active cameras, the acquisition process is dynamically controlled and can be scaled smoothly from view dependence to view independence. Moreover, virtual viewpoint- and resolution-driven sampling allows smooth transitions between a subset of the reference cameras and adapts to bandwidth or processing bottlenecks. The method features efficient rendering from arbitrary spatio-temporal positions and supports multiple viewers. This free-viewpoint video pipeline is designed and optimized for real-time applications and, hence, performance and quality are traded off at multiple stages. Figure 8.7 depicts a conceptual overview of this processing pipeline.

This real-time 3D video system is the enabling technology of the blue-c system [GWN+03]. The blue-c system combines the qualities of total immersion experienced in CAVE-like environments with simultaneous, real-time 3D video acquisition and rendering from multiple cameras. This concept enables a number of participants to interact and collaborate inside an immersive, virtual world, while perceiving the photorealistic three-dimensional human inlays of their collaboration partners in real time.

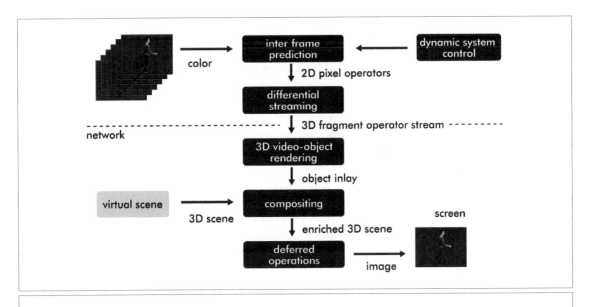

Figure 8.7: Conceptual components of the real-time 3D video processing pipeline.

Differential Coding

The correspondence between the point samples and the pixels in the input video camera allows for detecting changes in the input image and to propagate them to the point samples. Consequently, a dynamic point sample can be generated, updated, and deleted based on the changes in the camera image. The dynamic behavior of point samples can be described with three basic operators:

- NEW generates new point samples after they have become visible in one of the input cameras.
- KILL removes point samples from the representation once they vanish from the view of the input camera.
- UPDATE corrects appearance and geometry attributes of point samples that are already generated, but whose attributes have changed with respect to prior frames of the input camera.

The time sequence of these operators creates a differential operator stream that updates a 3D video data structure for a remote viewer. An INSERT operator results from the reprojection of a pixel with color attributes from image space into three-dimensional object space. Any real-time 3D reconstruction method that extracts depth and normals from images can be employed for this purpose (e.g., the image-based visual hull algorithm [MBR+00]). DELETE operators perform a lookup of the reference point sample and eliminate it. UPDATE operators are generated by all pixels that have been inserted in previous frames and that are still foreground pixels. They can be divided into three categories. The detection of *color changes* is performed during interframe prediction and leads to an UPDATECOL operator. UPDATEPOS operators take care of *geometry changes* and are analyzed on spatially coherent clusters of pixels in image space. If the differences to the previous depths exceed a threshold, 3D information is recomputed for entire blocks of points. Thus, the scheme proposes an efficient solution to the problem of uncorrelated texture and depth-motion fields. Note that position and color updates can be combined to an UPDATEPOSCOL operator. All other candidate pixels for updates remain *unchanged* and no further processing is necessary. A simple image-space interframe prediction mechanism is employed that derives the operators from the original video images by only using two functions for pixel classification, namely foreground/background segmentation and color differencing.

Results and Discussion

The current implementation of the real-time 3D video pipeline implemented in the blue-c system is able to deal with up to 85,000 INSERT or UPDATEPOS operations or more than 800,000 UPDATECOL and DELETE operations per second. A caching scheme ensures that the computation time for the costly INSERT and UPDATEPOS operations decreases logarithmically with the number of processed operations. The raw performance is sufficient for processing objects with less than 30,000 points.

Figure 8.8: Bidirectional transmission of real-time 3D video data in the blue-c: (*a*) portal view, and (*b*) rendering snapshot.

Figure 8.8 shows images of a bidirectional 3D video conference between two blue-c portals and illustrates user interaction. The small image in the lower left corner depicts an original camera view in the smaller portal. The big image in Figure 8.8a provides insight into the main portal and shows the rendered 3D video image of the other participant who can be controlled and viewed arbitrarily by the user. The big image in Figure 8.8b shows a rendered snapshot in a similar session.

Due to performance reasons only a coarse silhouette representation is used for 3D reconstruction. This results in a rough 3D shape approximation of the person. Temporarily visible geometry artifacts can be observed. These are due to the inherent nature of the visual hull reconstruction method that is not capable of properly reconstructing concave regions. During a live run of the blue-c system the mean bit rate of a differential 3D video sequence is 2.6 Mbps at nine frames per second. On average, more than 15,000 points were maintained in the 3D data structure. The peaks in the short-term bit rate are strongly correlated to the movements of the person and to the changes of the virtual viewpoint.

8.1.5 3D VIDEO OF DYNAMIC SCENES

Most of the systems presented earlier in this chapter are limited by the applied reconstruction algorithms to the capture of foreground objects or even humans only, and scalability in terms of camera configurations and data structures is not addressed. Moreover, most of the underlying representations and processes are still depth image based and typically do not allow for convenient editing. Waschbüsch et al. [WWC+05] presented a scalable 3D video system that captures and processes dynamic scenes based on point samples. They envision a system where also editing of the spatio-temporal streams is easy to perform. For this purpose, they rely on view-independent 3D geometry streams, which allow for similar authoring and editing techniques as carried out in common 3D content creation and modeling tools. Inserting novel objects to a scene or adding spatio-temporal effects is becoming straightforward with simple postprocessing methods, and one has no longer to cope with the common limitations of image-based representations.

The 3D video-acquisition system consists of several so-called 3D video bricks that are capturing high-quality depth maps from their respective viewpoints using calibrated pairs of stereo cameras (see Figure 8.9). The matching algorithm used for depth extraction is assisted by projectors illuminating the scene with binary structured light patterns. Alternating projection of a pattern and its inverse allows for concurrent acquisition of the scene texture using appropriately synchronized color cameras.

The depth maps are postprocessed to optimize discontinuities, and the results from different viewpoints are unified into a view-independent, point-based scene representation consisting of Gaussian ellipsoids. During merging, outliers are removed by ensuring photo consistency of the point cloud with all acquired images from the texture cameras. Editing operations like compositing and spatio-temporal effects can then be applied to the view-independent geometry. Novel viewpoints of the dynamic scene are rendered using EWA splatting 6.1.

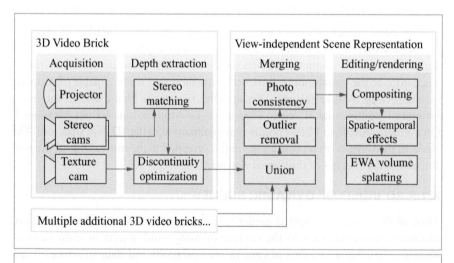

Figure 8.9: Overview of the scalable 3D video framework.

Scalable 3D Video Bricks

The basic building blocks of the scalable 3D video setup are movable bricks containing three cameras and a projector illuminating the scene with alternating patterns. Two grayscale cameras are responsible for depth extraction, while a color camera acquires the texture information of the scene. Figure 8.10 shows a single brick prototype. The prototype setup operates with three bricks, each consisting of a standard PC with a genlock graphics board (NVIDIA Quadro FX3000G), a projector synchronizing to the input signal (NEC LT240K), and cameras having XGA resolution (Point Grey Dragonfly). The components are mounted on a portable aluminum rig as shown in Figure 8.10. The system is complemented by a synchronization microcontroller (MCU) connected to the cameras and the genlock-capable graphics boards.

At a certain point in time, each brick can only capture depth information from a particular fixed position. In order to span a wider range of viewpoints and reduce occlusion effects, multiple movable bricks can be combined and individually oriented to cover the desired working space as illustrated in Figure 8.11. Scalability of multiple bricks is guaranteed, because overlapping projections are explicitly allowed by the depth reconstruction and because the computation load of each brick does not increase during real-time recording.

Simultaneous Texture and Depth Acquisition

Each brick concurrently acquires texture information with the color camera and depth information using the stereo pair of grayscale cameras. Stereo vision generally

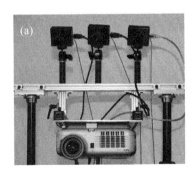

Figure 8.10: Scalable 3D video brick with cameras and projector (*a*), simultaneously acquiring textures (*b*), and structured-light patterns (*c*).

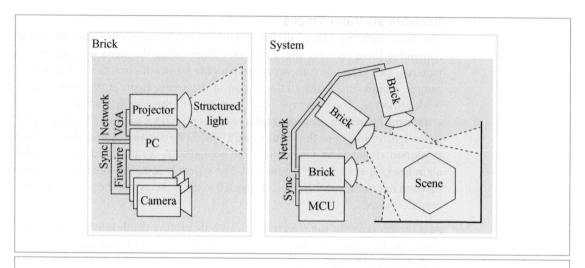

Figure 8.11: Configuration of the scalable 3D video prototype system.

requires a highly texturized scene to find good correlations between different views. It generally fails in reconstructing simple geometry of uniformly colored objects (e.g., white walls). As a consequence, artificial textures are added to the scene by projecting structured-light patterns. Binary vertical stripe patterns are used with randomly varying stripe widths. It supports strong and unique correlations in the horizontal direction and is at the same time insensitive to vertical deviations that may occur from inaccuracies in the camera calibration. To avoid untexturized shadows, the scene is illuminated by patterns from all bricks at the same time.

Alternating projections of structured-light patterns and the corresponding inverses enable simultaneous acquisition of the scene textures using an appropriately synchronized texture camera as illustrated in Figure 8.12. Note that this camera does not see the patterns emanating from the projector, but only a constant white light, which preserves the original scene texture (see Figure 8.10). Since the patterns are changing at a limited rate of 60 Hz (projector input frequency), flickering is slightly visible to the human eye. Alternative solutions using imperceptible structured light [CNGF04] do not show any flickering, but require faster, more sensitive, and, therefore, more expensive cameras for reliable stereo depth extraction.

Each brick acquires the scene geometry using a depth from stereo algorithm. Depth maps are computed for the images of the left and right grayscale cameras by searching for corresponding pixels. To reduce occlusion problems between the views, the

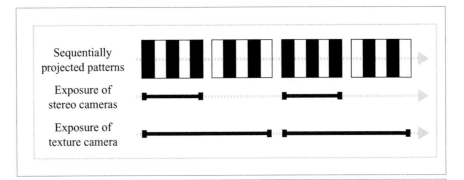

Figure 8.12: Camera exposure with inverse pattern projection.

cameras are mounted at a small horizontal baseline of 20 cm. Depth is acquired by space-time stereo [ZCS03], which exploits time coherence to correlate the stereo images and computes disparities with subpixel accuracy. However, because correlation algorithms assume continuous surfaces, some artifacts arise at depth discontinuities. For moving scenes, discontinuities in image space are extended into the temporal domain, making correlation computation even more difficult. Hence, adaptive correlation windows covering multiple time steps are only employed in static parts of the images that can be detected by comparing successive frames. Remaining errors can be smoothed out with a discontinuity optimization technique based on color segmentation and disparity extrapolation.

To model the resulting three-dimensional scene, a view-independent, point-based data representation is used. By merging all reconstructed views into a common world-reference frame, a convenient and scalable representation is achieved: additional views can be added very easily by back-projecting their image pixels. To be able to handle noise due to inaccurate 3D reconstruction or camera calibration every point is modeled by a three-dimensional Gaussian ellipsoid. After back-projection, the point model still contains outliers and falsely projected samples. Some points originating from a specific view may look wrong from extrapolated views due to reconstruction errors, especially at depth discontinuities. In the 3D model, they may cover correct points reconstructed from other views, disturbing the overall appearance of the 3D video. Thus, those points are removed by checking the whole model for photo consistency with all texture cameras. The final model can then be rendered by using EWA splatting 6.1, which can be extended by view-dependent blending.

Results and Discussion

For the results presented here, a dynamic scene is recorded with the setup consisting of three sparsely placed bricks covering an overall viewing angle of 70° horizontally and 30° vertically. Figure 8.13 shows novel views of the acquired scene in Figure 8.10, rendered from the reconstructed 3D model.

The re-renderings have an appealing look with a high-quality texture. Acquisition noise is smoothed out by the blending method. Even highly detailed geometry like the folds in the tablecloth can be reconstruced. However, there are still some artifacts at silhouettes that could be reduced by using matting approaches as done by Zitnick et al. [ZKU+04]. Some remaining outliers are also visible in the images. They could be reduced using a combination of multiple outlier removal algorithms 5.1 and by enforcing time coherence in the whole reconstruction pipeline. This system is able to acquire a large viewing range with a relatively low amount of cameras. To support increasingly large ranges, the system is scalable up to full spherical views. To fully cover 360° in all dimensions about 8 to 10 3D video bricks are needed.

The view-independent data model provides possibilities for novel effects and 3D video editing. Once the three-dimensional information is available, selection and compositing issues become straightforward and can be easily implemented using spatial clustering or bounding box algorithms. Such tasks are much harder to achieve on both conventional 2D video and view-dependent 3D video approaches based on light fields or depth maps only. Some example effects are shown in Figure 8.14, and more can be found in Waschbüsch [WWC+05].

Figure 8.13: Rerenderings of the 3D video from novel viewpoints.

Figure 8.14: Special effects: (*a*) actor cloning, and (*b*) motion trails.

8.1.6 CONCLUSION

This section showed some application scenarios for point-sampled 3D video. Due to their unique spatio-temporal properties, point samples feature many advantages as compared to other descriptions, like triangle meshes. Point samples can be employed as a basic primitive for both offline and online free-viewpoint systems for capturing and resynthesizing objects only or complex scenes.

8.2 STATISTICAL REPRESENTATIONS

Aravind Kalaiah and Amitabh Varshney

8.2.1 MOTIVATION

Computer graphics has traditionally assumed crisp representations of geometry. Thus, each point and each triangle's location are assumed to be known accurately and precisely. Recent advances in 3D model-acquisition technologies, such as laser scanning, have led us to a stage where we can now scan more accurately (at submicron levels) as well as at great distances (even entire cities, in some cases). This has led to the emergence of massive and highly detailed 3D point-cloud data. Such large point-cloud datasets have inspired new research directions in their representation and rendering by leveraging statistical tools and techniques.

As the point-cloud datasets grow in complexity, density, and richness of their representation, the importance of any one point is diminished among many. Further, as the spacing between the acquired samples reaches the same order of magnitude as the limits of acquisition precision, crisp representations of geometry become redundant, or worse, misleading. Statistical, or nondeterministic, representations of geometry provide a valuable alternative to the traditional models of representation. The central idea in the statistical representation of points is to represent the aggregate shape of a collection of points as a probability distribution. Statistical representation of points lends itself naturally to a multiresolution representation by building probability distributions over a hierarchy of points. It also provides a graceful transition from crisp representations of points to those with uncertainty. Finally, it lends itself to efficient transmission and rendering on modern graphics processors (GPUs).

8.2.2 RELATED WORK

Various chapters of this book have already covered much of the related point-based representations. Here we focus on related work in the context of fuzzy geometry and the connections between statistics and graphics.

Fuzzy geometry has its origins in the very first paper on fuzzy sets [Zad65] where the notion of their convexity was explored. Since then an impressive body of literature has covered a number of fuzzy-set properties including geometric properties (such as proximity, medial axis, and convexity), topological properties (such as connectedness of topological spaces, relationship to mathematical morphology, and adjacency), and metric properties (such as area, perimeter, and diameter). The interested reader can refer a series of survey articles on these by Rosenfeld [Ros84, Ros98].

Some of the earliest work in computer graphics that involves statistical distributions and their uses includes Fournier et al.'s [FFC82] stochastic procedural modeling, Reeve's [Ree83] particle systems, and Cook's [Coo86] distributed ray tracing. Recent work includes stochastic displacement mapping [SBCR05], stereological textures [JDR04], and photon mapping [Jen01]. Most of this work however does not involve statistical representations of given 3D objects. A notable exception is recent work by Pauly et al. [PMG04] that elegantly incorporates uncertainty of point samples into a unified representation of shape.

8.2.3 STATISTICAL POINT GEOMETRY

Statistical models can efficiently represent data coherence and patterns [DHS01]. *Principal component analysis* (PCA) [DHS01] is one of the simplest methods of statistical analysis, and yet is powerful enough to model an adequate class of point-cloud distributions. In addition, a PCA-based ellipsoidal representation is compact and simple enough to be used for efficient rendering and transmission.

Principal Component Analysis

The principal component analysis of a set of points, $\mathcal{P} = \{\mathbf{p}_i | i = 0, \ldots, N - 1\}$, in a d-dimensional space gives us the mean μ, an orthogonal frame Ψ, and the standard deviation σ of the data [DHS01]. The terms μ and σ are d-dimensional vectors and we refer to their i-th component as μ_i and σ_i respectively, where $\sigma_i \geq \sigma_j$ if $i > j$. The frame Ψ consists of d vectors with the i-th vector referred to as Ψ_i. In a three-dimensional space we simply refer to the individual components by the x, y, z subscripts (for example, $\mu = (\mu_x, \mu_y, \mu_z)$). In our case, the input is a set of N points with three attributes: spatial position $\mathbf{x}$, normal $\mathbf{n}$, and color $\mathbf{c}$. We refer to the mean, standard deviation, and the frame of the position attribute of the points by $\mu(\mathbf{x})$, $\sigma(\mathbf{x})$, and $\Psi(\mathbf{x})$, respectively. We determine these values through a PCA analysis of the (x, y, z) values of the points. This gives us an anisotropic Gaussian distribution centered at $\mu(\mathbf{x})$, aligned along the directions $\Psi_x(\mathbf{x})$, $\Psi_y(\mathbf{x})$, and $\Psi_z(\mathbf{x})$, with the standard deviation along these directions being $\sigma_x(\mathbf{x})$, $\sigma_y(\mathbf{x})$, and $\sigma_z(\mathbf{x})$, respectively. Such a distribution can be effectively visualized as an oriented ellipsoid with intercepts proportional to $\sigma_x(\mathbf{x})$, $\sigma_y(\mathbf{x})$, and $\sigma_z(\mathbf{x})$ (see Figures 8.15a and b).

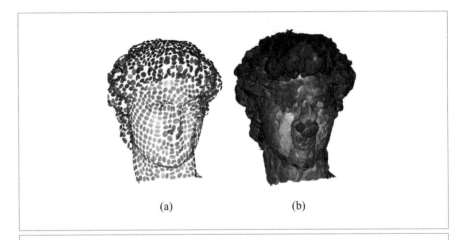

(a)   (b)

Figure 8.15: (a) The nodes at the midlevel resolution of the hierarchy built for the *David's* head model. Each ellipsoid in this figure represents an anisotropic Gaussian distribution of the geometry with their intercepts being their corresponding standard deviation $\sigma(\mathbf{x})$. The ellipsoids are colored by their mean color, $\mu(\mathbf{c})$. (b) Scaling the ellipsoids by a factor $\gamma = 3.5$ ensures that the geometry is represented up to a confidence index (*CI*) of at least 99.7% (i.e., the ellipsoids enclose at least 99.7% of the cumulative Gaussian distribution of the statistical points).

We refer to the mean, variance, and the basis of other attributes such as normal and color with the appropriate term in parentheses (e.g., $\mu(\mathbf{n})$, $\Psi(\mathbf{n})$, and $\sigma(\mathbf{n})$ for the normal).

PCA for Multiple Attributes

PCA analysis is straightforward for spatial coordinates of points that admit well-defined distance metrics, such as the Euclidean. Generalization of PCA to other point attributes such as normals, colors, and textures is possible, but requires extra care due to nonlinearities in defining distances in these other spaces. Let us consider PCA for point normals as an example.

The unit normals can be considered as points on a unit sphere. Therefore, PCA of normals can be viewed as performing PCA directly in a spherical geometry. Another possibility is to use the logarithmic map approach as outlined by Buss and Fillmore [BF01] as follows. Consider a set of point normals $\mathbf{n}_i = (\theta_i, \phi_i)$, $\forall i = 0, \dots,$ $N - 1$. Here the normals are represented by their angles $(\theta, \phi) \in ([0, \pi], (-\pi, \pi])$. We can compute the mean normal using weighted averages on spheres based on least squares minimization that respects spherical distances by using the logarithmic map and its inverse, the exponential map. We represent the mean normal by its angles, $\mu(\mathbf{n}) = (\mu(\theta), \mu(\phi))$. The next step in the PCA analysis is the computation of the covariance matrix. This requires us to define the difference $\mathbf{n}_i - \mu(\mathbf{n})$ between a normal and the mean normal. The difference in the normal space can be represented by the difference vector between the 2D coordinates of the mean normal and the i-th normal in the logarithmic space defined on the plane tangent to the unit sphere centered at the mean normal $\mu(\mathbf{n}) = (\mu(\theta), \mu(\phi))$ [BF01]. The rest of the PCA analysis proceeds as usual. The eigenanalysis of the covariance matrix gives us the eigenvectors and the variances of the Gaussian distribution along these vectors.

The geometry of color and texture spaces is more involved since it involves perceptual assessments. In absence of a clear consensus on the correct way to carry out a perceptually meaningful PCA analysis in the space of color or textures, one possibility is to simply treat these additional point attributes in the same way as spatial coordinates and perform the straightforward PCA analysis for them. In such a case, the (r, g, b) color values are treated as points in a three-dimensional space and a PCA in this space gives us its mean, $\mu(\mathbf{c})$, principal components, $\Psi(\mathbf{c})$, and the standard deviations, $\sigma(\mathbf{c})$. Another possibility is to convert the RGB color space to a more perceptually uniform color space, such as the hue, saturation, and value (HSV), and then carry out the PCA analysis.

We have discussed above how one can perform PCA independently for the attribute spaces of location, orientation, color, and textures. This has several advantages for real-time rendering that we will discuss later. However, the approach of carrying out PCA independently for every attribute has the disadvantage that it does not decorrelate *across* the attribute spaces. One possibility is to address this by performing PCA in the unified space of all the attributes. Consider a PCA analysis of the points, $\mathbf{p}_i = (x_i, \ y_i, \ z_i, \ \theta_i, \ \phi_i, \ r_i, \ g_i, \ b_i)$, $\forall i = 0, \ldots, \ N - 1$, in the 8D space of position (3D), normal (2D), and color (3D). This requires computing the mean and the covariance matrix in the unified 8D space. One can use the Buss and Fillmore [BF01] approach to compute the normal components of the mean and the difference vectors used in the 8D eigenanalysis. Performing PCA in the unified space of all attributes is more effective at representing the data, especially at lower resolutions, but suffers from increased computations and storage required for 8D eigenanalysis. The covariance analysis done here can also be used for the pointsimplification technique discussed in Section 4.3.2.

Statistical Hierarchies

A variety of hierarchical schemes may be used to organize points [Sam05]. These include spatial hierarchies such as octrees and K-d-trees, as well as bounding volume hierarchies such as bounding spheres. Some of these are discussed in Section 4.4. Statistical hierarchies represent data at different levels of detail by using either a spatial or a bounding volume hierarchy. Points that are classified as belonging to a single node of the hierarchy are then collectively represented by their PCA parameters. As discussed above, these PCA parameters could be computed independently on an attribute-by-attribute basis or in a unified space of all attributes. Hierarchies built from isotropic nodes, such as regular grids, octrees, and bounding spheres, require less storage per node and are faster to traverse. Anisotropic hierarchies, such as K-d-trees and ellipsoidal hierarchies, approximate the underlying data distributions more succinctly. Similar observations hold for statistical hierarchies. Kalaiah and Varshney report binary hierarchies based on two-means clustering [KV05] superior to those based on octrees [KV03b].

The *distortion* of a partitioning is defined as the sum of the distances of the points from the partition's mean [DHS01]. A partitioning scheme that aims to represent the constituent points well would strive to reduce the distortion under some appropriate distance metric. The approach of k-means clustering achieves this in a natural fashion. Consider the case for $k = 2$. Kalaiah and Varshney [KV05] initialize the two starting means (centers) for the k-means algorithm by doing a PCA over the points and choosing $\mu(\mathbf{x}) + \frac{\sigma_x(\mathbf{x})}{2}\Psi_x(\mathbf{x})$ and $\mu(\mathbf{x}) - \frac{\sigma_x(\mathbf{x})}{2}\Psi_x(\mathbf{x})$ as the initial guesses. This is a reasonable assumption since the data vary maximally along $\Psi_x(\mathbf{x})$. The k-means clustering algorithm then iterates over the twin steps of partitioning the point set according to the proximity of each point to the two means and then updating the two means according to this partitioning. Figure 8.16 illustrates three iterations of the clustering algorithm. Pauly et al. [PGK02a] use a geometric method to separate the point set for their point-based simplification hierarchy (see Section 4.3.2).

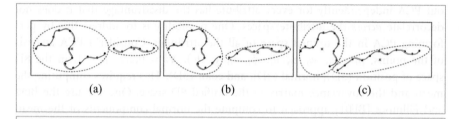

(a) (b) (c)

Figure 8.16: These figures illustrate three iterations of the clustering algorithm used for spatial partitioning of a set of points. Successive iterations reduce the distortion between the original set of points and the cluster centers (shown as blue crosses).

They separate along the principal direction $\Psi_x(\mathbf{x})$ with the separating plane passing through the mean $\mu(\mathbf{x})$. A similar strategy is used by Brodsky and Watson [BW00] for hierarchical mesh partitioning. This approach is equivalent to the first iteration of the clustering scheme. The subsequent iterations then successively reduce the distortion. One can stop iterating when the difference in the average distortion between two successive iterations is sufficiently small or when the number of iterations is more than an upper bound. This clustering step can be made more efficient using the technique proposed by Kanungo et al. [KMN+02]. The hierarchical partitioning may be terminated for nodes that have less than a user-specified number of points (say 30).

Distance Metrics

Choosing the distance metric is a crucial issue when building a hierarchy over points. The Euclidean distance metric is a good metric in most instances and also produces a balanced hierarchy. However, it has a tendency to merge disjoint parts of the surface if they are close enough. The Mahalanobis distance metric [DHS01] can address this by warping the space such that distances along the local normal direction computed by PCA are weighed higher than the distances along the tangential directions. Consider a PCA node defined by the pair $(\mu(\mathbf{x}), \Psi(\mathbf{x}))$. The Mahalanobis distance $\xi(\mathbf{p}_0)$ between a point $\mathbf{p}_0$ (with a spatial attribute $\mathbf{x}_0$) and $\mu(\mathbf{x})$ is given by $\xi(\mathbf{p}_0) = \| S(\mathbf{x})\, T(\mathbf{x})\, \mathbf{x}_0 \|_2$, where $T(\mathbf{x})$ is the affine transformation matrix that transforms $\mathbf{x}_0$ to the coordinate frame $\Psi(\mathbf{x})$, and $S(\mathbf{x})$ scales the result by $\left(\frac{1}{\sigma_x(\mathbf{x})}, \frac{1}{\sigma_y(\mathbf{x})}, \frac{1}{\sigma_z(\mathbf{x})} \right)$. This is shown in Figure 8.17.

The Mahalanobis distance metric generally leads to partitions that most would classify as being more natural and intuitive. This is because the Mahalanobis distance metric measures distances respecting the local anisotropy of the partitions that the Euclidean metric cannot. Still, the Mahalanobis metric remains a heuristic for partitioning, although generally a better one than the Euclidean metric. When the surface is too complex to be neatly partitioned into two clearly disjoint surfaces, the use of the Mahalanobis distance metric can produce an imbalanced partitioning. Here one can use a hybrid strategy: first try a k-means clustering based on the Mahalanobis metric, and if that partitioning turns out to be imbalanced, switch to a Euclidean distance-based partitioning. Figure 8.18 illustrates the Lucy model at various resolutions of the hierarchy.

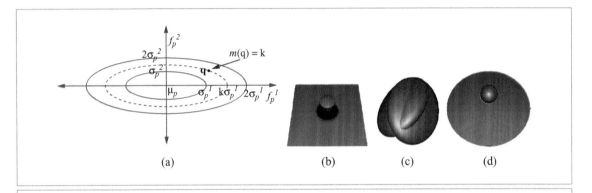

(a)   (b)   (c)   (d)

Figure 8.17: (*a*) The Mahalanobis distance. (*c*) The partitioning of the sphere and plane model of (*b*) obtained by a partitioning plane-based approach while (*d*) is the partitioning obtained by the Mahalanobis distance-based approach. The partitions have been rendered by the ellipsoids corresponding to their respective PCA attributes.

Figure 8.18: The Lucy model at various resolutions. Each ellipsoid in this figure represents an anisotropic Gaussian distribution of the geometry with their intercepts being their corresponding standard deviation $\sigma(\mathbf{x})$. The ellipsoids are colored by their mean color, $\mu(\mathbf{c})$.

Classification and Quantization

Compact representation of a hierarchy is essential for reducing the geometry bandwidth required for its transmission and rendering. Compression methods for meshes can reconstruct the original geometry up to a given level of quantization [Dee95, IS00, TR98, TG98]. Such methods have been extended for progressive compression and reconstruction [AD01, COLR99, GD02a, TGHL98]. Higher compression rates can be obtained by using representations that approximate the given input without necessarily trying to reproduce the original samples [KSS00], with spectral compression [KG00], or with view-dependent quantization [HV01].

Classification and quantization are two powerful techniques that can be used to efficiently encode the coherence in the statistical parameters of a point hierarchy. In the PCA hierarchy discussed above, the standard deviations σ exhibit a high level of coherence. Classification based on a k-means clustering algorithm on the standard deviations ($\sigma(\mathbf{x})$, $\sigma(\mathbf{n})$, and $\sigma(\mathbf{c})$) can be used to generate a lookup table with a small number of representative variances. Kalaiah and Varshney [KV05] use only 12 bits each for $\sigma(\mathbf{x})$ and $\sigma(\mathbf{n})$, and 6 bits for $\sigma(\mathbf{c})$. They quantize $\mu(\mathbf{x})$ in 32 bits using a 10-11-11 quantization, where the dimension of minimum width uses a 10-bit quantization. The value of $\mu(\mathbf{c})$ is encoded in 16 bits using a 5-6-5 quantization of its red, green, and blue values [RL00].

Quantization of a coordinate frame (such as $\Psi(\mathbf{x})$, $\Psi(\mathbf{n})$, or $\Psi(\mathbf{c})$) can be carried out by quantizing the quaternion coefficients representing its rotation from the principal axes. However, this gives equal weights to each of the three axes of the frame. In practice, encoding the normal ($\Psi(\mathbf{n})$) more carefully could be justified on the grounds that it is the primary influence on the appearance, at least for isotropic illumination models. One possibility is to, therefore, quantize θ and ϕ angles representing $\Psi(\mathbf{n})$ in more bits, say 8 and 10, and the third angle ω that will fix the entire frame $\Psi(\mathbf{n})$ in fewer bits, say 6. Thus, the frame $\Psi(\mathbf{n})$ can be quantized into 24 bits. We refer the reader to Kalaiah and Varshney [KV05] for the details of fast decoding of the encoded frame. Overall, each node can be represented with 13 bytes of spatial and normal information with 4 extra bytes required for color. A complete single-precision floating-point representation would have required 96 bytes. Figure 8.19 illustrates the effectiveness of this method.

8.2.4 STATISTICAL RENDERING

The statistical hierarchy is used in identifying an appropriate set of nodes representing a view-dependent level of detail. Each node of the hierarchy provides a set of statistical parameters that govern the generation of a set of well-distributed points. These points are used for the final rendering.

$\mu_p(32)$	$f_p(24)$	$\sigma_p(12)$	$f_n(24)$	$\sigma_n(12)$	$\mu_c(16)$	$f_c(10)$	$\sigma_c(6)$

(a)

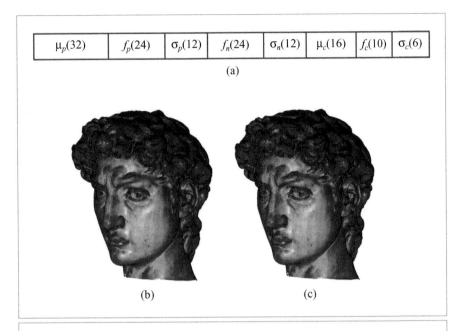

(b)   (c)

Figure 8.19: (*a*) A node is quantized into 13 bytes for the spatial and normal information. Four extra bytes are used for the optional color information. The breakdown is shown in bits. (*b*) View-dependent rendering on a 512 × 512 window from about 191,000 unencoded nodes and about 824,000 generated points. (*c*) The same rendering from encoded nodes. We encode each node to 17 bytes using quantization and classification. Notice that there is little difference between rendering with encoded and unencoded data.

Statistical Regeneration of Points

Each node of the statistical hierarchy gives a probability distribution of the points that it represents. For a PCA-based hierarchy, the distribution is Gaussian:

$$p(x) = \frac{1}{(2\pi)^{d/2} \left|\sum\right|^{1/2}} e^{-(x-\mu)^T \sum^{-1} (x-\mu)}, \tag{8.1}$$

where d is the dimensionality of the attribute and $\sum$ is the covariance matrix of the attribute values. Points respecting this distribution can be generated using a 3D extension of the Box-Muller transform [BM58, SG69, WLH97]:

$$\begin{bmatrix} x \\ y \\ z \end{bmatrix} = \begin{bmatrix} \sigma_x(\mathbf{x}) & 0 & 0 \\ 0 & \sigma_y(\mathbf{x}) & 0 \\ 0 & 0 & \sigma_z(\mathbf{x}) \end{bmatrix} \begin{bmatrix} \tau \sqrt{1 - r_2^2} \cos(2\pi r_1) \\ \tau \sqrt{1 - r_2^2} \sin(2\pi r_1) \\ \tau r_2 \end{bmatrix}, \tag{8.2}$$

where r_0, r_1, and r_2 are uniformly distributed random numbers in $(0, 1]$, $[0, 1]$, and $[-1, 1]$, respectively, and $\tau = \sqrt{-2\ln(r_0)}$. Normals for points can be generated by using the 2D Box-Muller transform to sample the logarithmic map plane discussed by Buss and Fillmore [BF01], and then using the exponential map to revert them back to the surface of a sphere.

Working with a unified representation of location, orientation, and color (as discussed in Section 8.2.3), will require us to generate Gaussian random numbers in an 8D space. We can do this by first sampling points uniformly on a 8D hypersphere [Ma172] and then radially distort them according to a Gaussian distribution of unit variance. We can then use these Gaussian numbers and distort them according to the 8D PCA parameters of the node (mean, standard deviation, and basis). Note that the points generated this way have the proper position and color attributes. However, the normals are still in the 2D Lie space. We convert these values to normals in 3D by using the logarithmic map with respect to the mean $(\mu(\theta), \mu(\phi))$ [BF01].

The above scheme for sampling assumes that all the variances are nonzero. However, in practice one often finds several nodes with one or more zero variances. An easy way to deal with such special cases of zero variances of $\sigma_i(\mathbf{x})$ is to simply set a minimum threshold value (say of the order 10^{-15}). This allows a uniform treatment of all ellipsoids (even if they vanish along some dimensions).

Quasirandom Sampling

Regeneration of points satisfying a certain probability distribution requires uniformly distributed random numbers as an input. Usually such random numbers are generated using a pseudorandom number generator. However, as seen in Figure 8.20a the distribution of pseudorandom numbers does not cover the space equally. In other words, they have a high discrepancy owing to the independent sampling of each pseudorandom number [Nie92]. Quasirandom numbers generated from algebraic sequences such as the Sobol sequence [PFTV03] have a low discrepancy as successive random numbers are aware of the random numbers that were generated earlier and hence are placed so as to minimize the discrepancy (see Figure 8.20b). Quasirandom numbers have been used successfully in computer graphics, for instance, in the Monte Carlo integration for global illumination [Kel96]. Another nice property of the quasirandom numbers generated from algebraic sequences is that smaller sequences are a strict subset of larger sequences. This allows a one-time precomputation of a sufficiently large quasirandom number sequence, from which one can use a suitable subset as needed based on view and display parameters.

To determine how many quasirandom samples are needed to render a given statistical node, we set up an empirical test-bed that links the number of generated points to the screen-space dimensions of the node. This is similar in spirit to the

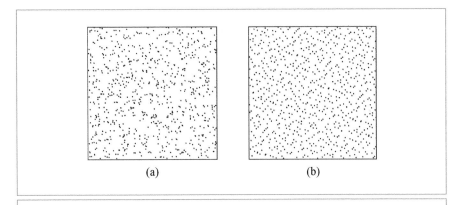

Figure 8.20: (*a*) Eight hundred points generated in a two-dimensional space from a pseudorandom sequence while (*b*) shows 800 points generated using quasirandom numbers. Quasirandom numbers are preferable since they show low discrepancy that results in a more uniform distribution.

randomized z-buffer idea by Wand et al. [WFP$^+$01]. It is easy to empirically establish a relationship between $\sigma(\mathbf{x})$ and the number of points to be generated to completely cover the projection of an ellipsoid with dimensions of $\gamma \times \sigma(\mathbf{x})$. The multiplicative factor of γ is important here. The Gaussian distribution never really goes to zero and one will have to generate an infinite number of points to cover the entire distribution. However, it can be shown that the region enclosed by $\gamma = 3.5$ has a confidence index (CI) of at least 99.7% (i.e., it covers at least 99.7% of the distribution). Hence, we limit ourselves to generating enough points so that the screen-space area occupied by this enclosed region is covered. At render time we estimate the z-distance of the mean $\mu(\mathbf{x})$ from the camera and estimate the dimensions on the screen to be $\lceil F\sigma(\mathbf{x})/z \rceil$, where F is the distance between the center of projection and the view plane. We use this to index the table for determining the number of points to generate. A representative sampling table appears in Kalaiah and Varshney [KV05].

Client-server Rendering
Statistical representations are well suited for rendering over a client-server setup, including a GPU-CPU system, or remote rendering. In a client-server setting the server sends the statistical nodes to the client that generates points based on the probability distribution parameters specified in the node. This is shown in Figure 8.21.

Transmission to the client involves two phases: the initial *startup* phase and the per-frame *update* phase. In the startup phase the client receives initialization information about the geometry, such as the classification and quantization parameters for all the attributes of the statistical nodes. This information is used in the update phase to decode and render the statistical nodes. We present two scenarios in client-server rendering: *on-demand* and *view-dependent* rendering. In on-demand rendering the user selects a subset of the model using a refinement window. The client requests the server to update the nodes in that window. The server sends back the encoded statistical information of the refined nodes (see Figure 8.22). This framework is better suited for remote rendering over low-bandwidth communication channels.

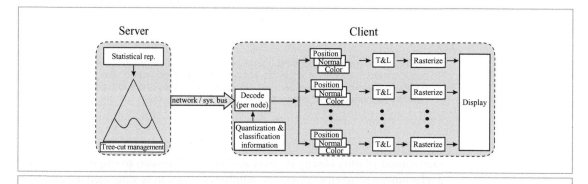

Figure 8.21: Client-server rendering. The server selects the level of detail to be used for rendering in a view-dependent manner. The nodes of the appropriate level of detail are transmitted to the client, which is either the graphics card or a remote-rendering device. The client renders each node by generating points and their attributes from the statistical information of the node.

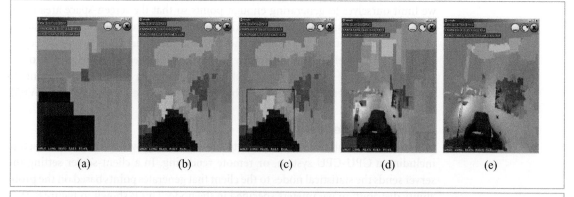

Figure 8.22: On-demand rendering. Rendering of PCA nodes on a remote PC with (*a*) square splats and (*b*) with quasirandom sampling. The client selects a refinement window in (*c*). (*d and e*) The rendering of the refined nodes with square splats and quasirandom sampling, respectively. The figures show that quasirandom sampling conveys more information for the same number of nodes. However, (the software rendering at the client) was twice as slow.

Our view-dependent rendering algorithm is similar to the ones used for view-dependent rendering of triangle meshes. An appropriate level of detail in the hierarchy is maintained as a level cut across the hierarchy tree or a *tree cut*. Thus, in regions where higher detail is desired the tree cut is close to the leaves of the hierarchy and in regions of low detail the cut is closer to the root. The level of detail is updated at each frame depending on the proximity of the object to the user (see Figure 8.23).

GPU Considerations

Statistical hierarchies of points can be used for rendering on modern graphics processors (GPUs). Rendering the nodes of a statistical hierarchy requires their decoding and generation of points. Both of these can be easily implemented using vertex shaders. Ongoing improvements in the programmability of the GPUs will further ease the mapping of rendering of statistical hierarchies of points.

Decoding a PCA node requires communicating the values of σ, μ, and Ψ for each of the attributes from the CPU to the GPU. We currently send raw values of $\sigma(\mathbf{x})$, $\sigma(\mathbf{n})$, $\sigma(\mathbf{c})$ as well as $\mu(\mathbf{x})$, $\mu(\mathbf{n})$, and $\mu(\mathbf{c})$ from the CPU to the GPU without any classification or quantization since the requisite support for their decoding is currently not available on GPUs. To decode the frames $\Psi(\mathbf{x})$, $\Psi(\mathbf{n})$, and $\Psi(\mathbf{c})$ we send the values of the sine and cosine of their respective θ, ϕ, and ψ values. The latest GPUs do allow sine and cosine computations at the vertex shaders and on such GPUs we only need to send the angles.

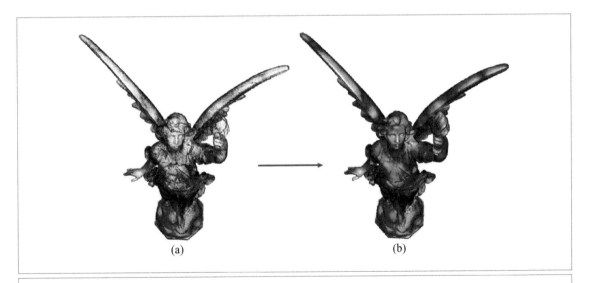

(a)   (b)

Figure 8.23: Figure (*a*) shows the means of the nodes of the tree cut during view-dependent rendering. Figure (*b*) shows the rendering of the model using quasirandom sampling at the GPU.

Quasirandom sequences are highly appropriate for GPU-based generation of points. We can generate a 3D quasirandom sequence of, say, 500 points, and store it on the GPU as the vertex coordinates of a unit Gaussian distribution in a vertex array range (VAR). We also store an equal number of 2D quasirandom numbers as normals of the VAR vertices. During rendering, the PCA attributes of the node are sent as texture coordinates and the function `glDrawArrays( )` is invoked to render the required number of (generated) points from the VAR array. The GPU delivers the quasirandom numbers to the vertex shaders as a sequence of normal and vertex coordinates. For each incoming vertex at the vertex shader, we reconstruct the PCA information of the node, use the quasirandom numbers to determine the attributes of the point, and let the GPU rasterize them. Since OpenGL is a state machine the PCA parameters that we send before the invocation of `glDrawArrays( )` are available for all the generated points. Hence, we only send the PCA attributes to the GPU once for each node as opposed to sending them for every generated point. We, however, have the computational overhead of decoding the PCA attributes for each sample point. Overall, we are able to achieve a 30% speedup in the rendering time compared to the strategy of sampling points at the CPU. This speedup is mainly due to the reduced bus bandwidth and the SIMD nature of the shaders.

8.2.5 CONCLUSION

The rise in the power and resolution of modern-day three-dimensional scanning has diminished the relative importance of the individual points. This section discusses a statistical model that represents the point geometry as a probability distribution. One of the advantages of this model is that it efficiently scales to a hierarchical representation that can represent the point geometry from the coarsest to the finest resolution. The statistical model can be efficiently stored using classification and quantization and it can be rendered with good quality using quasirandom sampling. The statistical model extends easily for remote rendering on resource-constrained devices.

8.3 VISUALIZATION OF ATTRIBUTED 3D POINT DATASETS

Guido Reina, Thomas Klein, and Thomas Ertl

8.3.1 MOTIVATION

Since the available computational power is steadily growing, more and more science areas rely on simulations of ever-growing problem sizes producing a respectively huge amount of data output. Simulation and experimental measurement in life sciences, physics, chemistry, materials, and thermodynamics yield large and often also time-dependent datasets. Interactive visualization is the key service that facilitates the analysis of such datasets and thus enables the researchers in those fields to quickly assess and compare the results of a simulation or measurement, verify and improve their models, and in so doing coming ever closer to understanding how dynamic processes work. An example for such large supercomputer simulations is the galaxy formation calculations done by the VIRGO Supercomputing Consortium [VIR05]. Figure 8.24 shows a rendering of such a simulation dataset. It is the result of a multibody simulation consisting of 134 million data elements and shows a snapshot from a simulation of the matter distribution in the early universe.

The main challenge in visualizing such datasets is two-fold. First, containing the necessary storage capacity and the bandwidth requirements caused by the sheer data size, and second, reducing the processing load caused by the visualization itself. The approach that will be described here aims for distributing the load between the available computational units by leveraging the parallel processing power of the GPU for the actual rendering, thus freeing up the CPU for the data-processing groundwork.

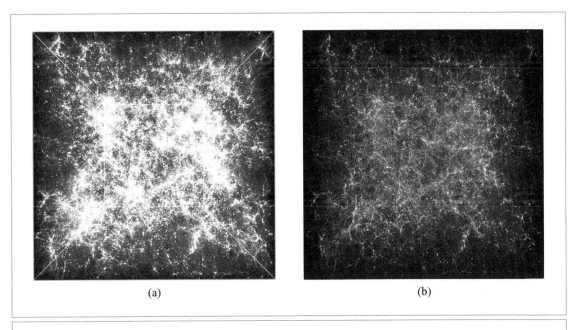

(a)   (b)

Figure 8.24: Rendering of a galaxy formation simulation dataset containing 134 million data points: (*a*) point splatting, and (*b*) high-dynamic range rendering of the same dataset using high-precision floating point blending and a local tone-mapping operator.

Point-based methods have been in use in visualization for a long time. There are numerous examples where points were used as a rendering primitive, including scatter plots, as are widely used in information visualization [Cle85, PKH04], or splatting techniques that are common in volume visualization [Wes90, LH91, MMC99, ZPvBG01a]. Due to space restrictions, these methods will not be discussed here. Instead this section will focus on the more specific topic of application-tailored point-based methods for GPU-based glyph visualization.

Scattered 3D Data

Scattered data, in the context of this section, are defined as a set of discrete attributed points which, unlike typical visualization datasets and the point-sampled geometry data discussed in Chapters 3 through 6, do not contain any topological information since they are not part of a sampled surface or manifold. Often it is possible to infer connectivity in a dataset in order to be able to use traditional visualization techniques, such as direct or indirect volume rendering, relying on interpolation to derive the assumed continuity. A typical approach would be to generate an unstructured grid based on a Voronoi tesselation. In the datasets in question, however, there is no implicitly defined grid structure or continuity and neither is it reasonable to impose these properties because of the strictly discrete nature of the data points. In fact, those points do not represent coordinates where continuous values are sampled, but distinct entities with attributes such as spatial extent and simulation-pertinent properties like particle type, impulse, orientation, age, etc. Therefore, in the following, we like to refer to the data elements not as points but as individual particles that can be represented by application-specific glyphs.

Multiple Levels of Semantic Density

The semantic density of a particle (i.e., the number and diversity of associated attributes) varies depending on the origin of the data. This can be either physical attributes captured from measurements of real objects, or properties derived from the physical model underlying a numerical simulation. In the simplest case this information will comprise only a spatial position. However, if the generation process yields more attributes for the particles, like a certain shape and spatial extent, there is the need to include such information in the visualization as well. If the glyph representing the particle is not infinitely small, it can also exhibit an orientation, but to display this orientation, an anisotropic shape or surface quality is needed that allows the user to perceive this orientation. In the following sections different primitives will be described that allow for an increasing number of attributes to be displayed making use of different kinds of glyph representations. Starting with the description of a generic framework for point-based glyph rendering in Section 8.3.2 the discussion will be continued by multiple sections on different glyphs appropriate for the visualization of particles of varying semantic density. Section 8.3.3 describes the visualization of isotropic particles as found in most multibody simulations, Section 8.3.4 deals with oriented ellipsoidal particles used in tensor field visualization, and Section 8.3.5 details the rendering of dipole glyphs for the visualization of nanoscale simulations in thermodynamics.

Complex Primitives

The rendering of complex glyphs for a large number of particles naturally is a performance problem, since the processing power for generating and the bandwidth for transmitting polygonized complex primitives to the GPU are limited. This is especially problematic when dealing with dynamic or time-dependent data. Thus, the challenge is to minimize the amount of data that has to be transferred from the CPU to the graphics processor. The second general goal is to minimize processing on the CPU by shifting as much computational load as possible to the GPU. The most bandwidth-efficient geometric primitive being the point, it is straightforward to use a parameterized representation of the different shapes and render just a single, attributed point primitive. As will be shown in the following for simple, unshaded isotropic shapes it may be sufficient to use basic point-splatting techniques or precalculated texture sprites (see Section 6.2.2); anisotropic and shaded surfaces, however, require more elaborate GPU processing. This is accomplished by working with implicit surface representations directly in the vertex-processing units and fragment-processing units of the GPU which, in addition, allows for per-pixel surface precision and shading. This choice is further supported by the currently very short product life cycle of GPUs, leading to the creation of more optimized GPUs with ever-increasing parallelism and processing power. The algorithms that will be shown in the remainder of this section can directly benefit from such innovation, since in the past a speedup between 100 and 700% for complex shaders has been observed when switching from one generation of GPUs to the next.

8.3.2 A FRAMEWORK FOR POINT GLYPH VISUALIZATION

In Section 4.4 methods for efficient storage and access of points and their attributes have been discussed. The framework used for implementing the different particle-rendering methods discussed in this section is based on a generic and flexible rendering infrastructure for large, time-dependent particle datasets [HE03] and employs a hierarchical organization of the data, similar to the bounding volume hierarchies described in Section 4.4.2.

The data hierarchy is depicted in Figure 8.25a. At the lowest level it contains the raw particle data used as input for the visualization. For each consecutive hierarchy level i, a number of elements of the next lower level $i+1$ are grouped into a cluster. This process is repeated until only a single cluster remains, which defines the root of the tree (level 0). For each cluster node a representative particle is generated

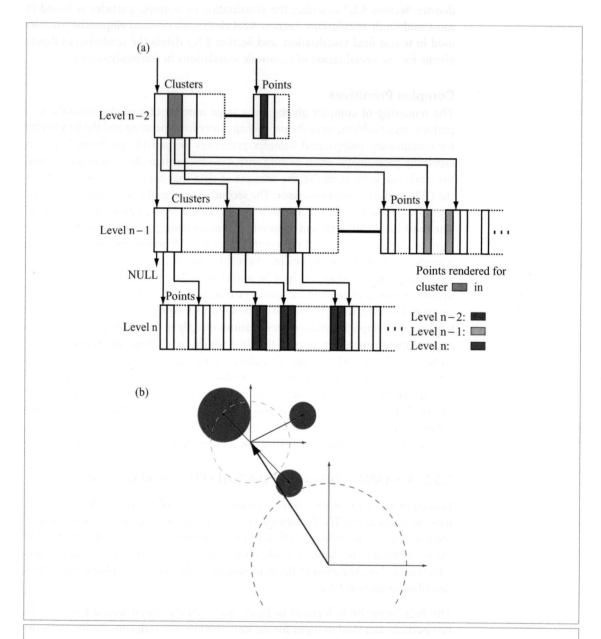

that summarizes the elements contained therein. These representatives are stored in parallel to the cluster hierarchy. A cluster node always contains pointers to its subcluster nodes as well as to the representatives of the subclusters, but no pointer to its own representative. Level 0 and level n are exceptions to the structure since level 0 contains only the root cluster and level n contains no cluster nodes at all. Using flat data structures (see Section 4.4.5) for storing the particles and the representatives enables us to take advantage of OpenGL *Vertex Arrays* to transfer the data in large contiguous chunks. Such a hierarchy can be generated, for example, by the repeated application of a PCA-split with subsequent aggregation of subclusters.

During rendering the hierarchy is traversed and for each level either the representative points are rendered or the recursion is continued by descending deeper into the hierarchy by visiting the subclusters on the next level. Criteria used to steer the recursion process could be the projected screen size of the cluster representative, user-specified error thresholds, the relative contribution to the final color of a pixel, or the available time budget for rendering a single frame while still ensuring interactivity.

To minimize the space requirements for storing the particle cloud and to further reduce the bandwidth requirements for transferring the data to the GPU, the framework allows the user to store the positional data using relative coordinates and make use of the cluster information to calculate the absolute coordinates. Thus, less accuracy is needed for storing the relative coordinates since the clusters of higher levels have logarithmically decreasing extent. Reconstruction of the correct absolute coordinates from the quantized values (see Section 4.4.4) can be easily accomplished on the GPU. Using the float coordinate of the cluster center this reduces to scaling by the cluster extent and offsetting by the cluster origin, as shown in Figure 8.25b.

8.3.3 VISUALIZATION OF ISOTROPIC PARTICLES

The primary goal for the rendering framework [HE03] used is to enable interactive exploration of extremely large point datasets without resorting to volume-rendering techniques and the subsequent loss of detail. This application is geared especially toward datasets originating from cosmological multibody simulation and SPH simulation datasets. For this purpose, particles as well as clusters are represented either as transparent disks or hollow spheres. This is justified by the assumption that the geometry of a distant star can be approximated as isotropic. Both types of primitives are prerendered into a texture and output as point sprites supported by most modern graphics hardware. Since display resolution is relatively low compared to the immense number of particles, a high number of stars will be rendered into the same framebuffer pixel. Therefore, blending is used to achieve the optical impression of such densely packed clusters with hundreds of stars.

Rendering

Several considerations have to be made about the brightness of the particles and how to achieve a consistent rendering output [HE03]. The overall goal is to minimize popping artifacts during the adaptive rendering by ensuring that all cluster representatives offer sufficient visual continuity to allow them to replace the cluster children on the fly without changing the overall visual appearance. The following rules are applied:

- If a particle is smaller than the pixel it must occupy, its brightness will be accordingly attenuated in a vertex program.
- A single point representing a cluster of particles must have an area that matches the extents of the cluster.
- The radiant flux Φ of a cluster representative must match the total radiant flux of all its children, so its brightness has to be adjusted according to the relation of the areas covered by the children and the area of the cluster representative:

$$\Phi = \frac{\sum \phi_i A_i}{A_{\text{cluster}}} . \tag{8.3}$$

Since at the time of the original publication by Hopf and Ertl [HE03] only eight-bit framebuffers were available, it has to be ensured that the resulting radiant flux Φ does not exceed the representable range, otherwise the particle size has to be increased beyond its original extents to be able to correctly emit enough radiance. Even with all these precautions taken, blending operations can still cause overflows in the framebuffer. Due to the fact that large particle cloud datasets have an extremely high overdraw, the utilized dynamic range is severely limited and much contrast is lost. Therefore, user interaction was required to adjust the brightness. Another problem of the original particle representation is that it allows single points to have a big screen-space footprint for compensating high radiance, even if they were not cluster representatives.

As we like to think about each particle as a small star in a huge environment, it would be more appropriate if the objects representing stars were always at most two or three pixels in size. Cluster representatives, on the other hand, cannot be limited in size because visual continuity has to be preserved. Removing the sizing rules from the vertex program and replacing them with a constant size meant that the irradiance of a single point could not be represented with eight-bit precision. Fortunately, modern GPUs like the NVIDIA GeForce 6800 series feature a complete 32-bit precision floating-point-rendering pipeline. Working with floating-point precision allows us to work with a greater numerical range to improve the rendering quality of the original work. Unfortunately, the current generation of graphics cards supports at most 16-bit floating-point precision blending. However, this still provides a much higher relative precision and data range.

Using tone mapping [RSSF02] makes it possible to dynamically adapt to the properties of the current image and rescale its brightness for optimum contrast on output, which is still limited to eight bits per channel. That way the user does not need to adjust any parameters of the visualization to explore the fine details of a dataset. Figure 8.24 shows two renderings of a 134 million point galaxy simulation dataset. The left image was generated using the original point-splatting algorithm described in Hopf and Ertl [HE03]. The right image shows the result of the rendering algorithm that takes the high dynamic range of the input data into account.

8.3.4 VISUALIZATION OF ANISOTROPIC PARTICLES ON THE GPU

The simplest closed anisotropic particle shape that can be described analytically is the ellipsoid. It also is an intuitive glyph widely used in tensor field visualization. Examples are the visualization of the strain tensor in engineering or geomechanics applications or the visualization of diffusion tensor imaging data in the medical setting [SZF+91, PB96]. Furthermore, ellipsoids have been used as a modeling primitive [BK02] for the representation and efficient transmission of geometrical models. In this section we will concentrate on the use of ellipsoidal glyphs for the visualization of symmetric tensor fields that originate, for example, as diffusion tensors from MRI measurements. However, the method presented here is not limited to this application.

Figure 8.26 shows an example of a diffusion tensor MRI dataset of the human brain visualized using ellipsoid glyphs. The dataset contains about 1.4 million tensors.

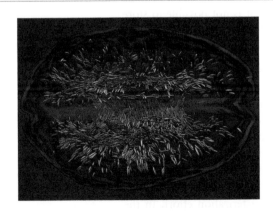

Figure 8.26: Visualization of a diffusion tensor MRI dataset of the human brain with a combination of glyphs and volume rendering. On a NVIDIA GeForce 7800 GTX using a 512^2 viewport, these images can be rendered at about 40 frames per second; 230 frames per second can be achieved by rendering only the glyphs.

Of these only approximately 9,000 glyphs corresponding to tensors of highly linear diffusion are shown, since they correspond to white matter neuronal pathway structures that are of special interest in this setting. Additional color coding was done according to the fractal anisotropy of the diffusion tensors. In order to provide some context of the spatial relationship, the glyph visualization is combined with a semi-transparent volume ray casting of the same data. The image to the right shows a detailed view of a central part of the brain, known as the corpus callosum. This part is especially rich in nerve fibers since it connects the left and right hemispheres of the brain.

Diffusion tensors are typically represented by symmetric 3×3 matrices. Since a symmetric matrix A has three real eigenvalues and a corresponding orthonormal system of eigenvectors, it can be factored into a diagonal matrix Ω of its eigenvalues and a rotation matrix R of the eigenvector basis (i.e., $A = R\Omega R^T$). Thus, the eigenvalues and eigenvectors of A can be identified with the shape parameters of an ellipsoid, where the absolute values of the eigenvalues correspond to the length of principal axes of the ellipsoid and the eigenvector system specifies its orientation with respect to the standard basis.

Traditionally, the resulting ellipsoid representations are rendered either using ray tracing or by tessellating them into a triangle mesh subsequently rendered using the graphics processor. But rendering several hundred thousands of tensor glyphs at interactive rates is a performance problem because there is a lot of geometry data involved. Even when OpenGL display lists or vertex arrays are employed, the frame rates that can be achieved for reasonably smooth tessellated ellipsoids are far from being interactive. Furthermore, since it is often not possible to select or filter the data directly on the GPU (e.g., for time-dependent datasets), it is not possible to store the data in video memory. Instead, they have to be transferred to the GPU for every rendered frame.

A first approach for rendering perspectively correct ellipsoidal shapes that does not depend on tessellated geometry was presented by Gumhold [Gum03]. However, this approach differs from the point-based method [KE04] that will be described in the following, as it uses quadrilateral splats as the basis for the rendering. The presented approach instead reduces the amount of information that has to be transferred over the graphics bus to the GPU to the necessary minimum to avoid this potential bottleneck. The required geometric data per-rendered ellipsoid are broken down to the vertex position and few additional per-vertex attributes of a single OpenGL point primitive in exchange of higher vertex processing and rasterization effort. In the following sections the GPU-based ellipsoid rendering algorithm will be described, which allows the computation of the perspectively correct projection of a Phong-shaded ellipsoidal shape from this data.

Particle Representation

Each ellipsoid is represented by the center point $\mathbf{p}_i$ of the glyph, the spatial extent given by a vector $\mathbf{h}_i$ of the lengths of its principal axes, and a quaternion $\mathbf{q}_i$ describing the orientation of the local coordinate system spanned by the principal axes. These three properties can be easily encoded into the 3D vertex position, the normal vector, and the four element vertex color attributes of a single `GL_POINT` primitive. Thus, no more than ten floating point values, or 40 bytes, per ellipsoid have to be transferred over the system bus to the GPU. Of course, this number can be further reduced if relative coordinates and quantized values are used (see Section 8.3.2).

The boundary surface of an ellipsoid can be represented implicitly by the quadratic form

$$\left\{ \mathbf{x} \mid \| M_i^{-1} (\mathbf{x} - \mathbf{p}_i) \|^2 = 1 \right\}, \tag{8.4}$$

where $M_i = Q_i H_i$ is a symmetric, positive definite matrix given by the scaling matrix $H_i = \frac{1}{2}\mathrm{diag}(\mathbf{h}_i)$ and the rotation matrix $Q_i = R(\mathbf{q}_i)$ that describes the orientation with respect to the local coordinate system of the ellipsoid. Thus, an affine mapping $M_i\mathbf{x} + \mathbf{p}_i$ from the local parameter space of the ellipsoid—in the case of tensor glyphs spanned by the eigensystem of the tensor—to the world coordinate system can be defined.

Rendering the Implicit Geometry

In this section a brief outline of the rendering algorithm will be given. For each ellipsoid an OpenGL point primitive is rendered, either by specifying the above described properties using immediate mode OpenGL calls or using vertex arrays for reduced CPU overhead. The actual rendering of the particle shapes takes place in a combination of a vertex and a fragment program. Since only a single point primitive is drawn, the screen-space footprint covered by the perspective projection of the ellipsoid's shell has to be determined and the screen-space size of the rendered base point has to be adapted accordingly. This is done in the vertex program, by projecting the ellipsoids' bounding box into clip-space. Since OpenGL points are always square, the final point size is defined by the longer edge of the axis-aligned rectangle enclosing the projection. This is clearly a drawback of the presented approach, because many fragments have to be considered in the following steps that could be excluded if a non-axis-aligned rectangular area were used. But in fact this is only a problem if the ellipsoid projects to a rather large, non-axis-aligned screen area. In many applications where large numbers of objects have to be rendered, including ours, the number of pixels that are covered by a single object is often quite small. In addition, all values that are needed in the fragment program and remain constant for all fragments covered by the respective ellipsoid are precomputed in the vertex program. Passing these as vertex attributes, they get automatically replicated for each fragment of the rasterized point by the linear interpolation of vertex attributes. Precomputing as many values as possible reduces the rasterization cost (i.e., the operation count) in the subsequent fragment program.

The next steps are implemented in the fragment program. First, a ray-casting approach is used to compute the resulting shape of the ellipsoid's 2D projection according to the current view parameters. For each fragment covered by the rasterized point primitive a ray $\mathbf{x} = \mathbf{p}_v + \lambda\mathbf{d}$ from the eye point through the object-space position on the view plane of the rasterized fragment is computed. Since the origin of the eye ray in object space is constant for all fragments of the projection it has to be computed only once per ellipsoid, which is also done in the vertex program. In contrast, the ray direction $\mathbf{d}$ has to be computed for each fragment separately. Because only a single point is rendered it is not possible, for example, to exploit the linear interpolation of vertex attributes during the rasterization for the computation of $\mathbf{d}$, as it is done in Gumhold [Gum03]. Instead $\mathbf{d}$ has to be computed from the current viewing parameters given by the model-view-projection matrix available as a fragment state variable by unprojecting the 2D screen-space coordinates of the fragments.

All fragments of the point splat can be classified to lie either inside or outside the silhouette of the projection by intersecting the eye rays with the implicit representation of the ellipsoid. Intersecting a straight line with an ellipsoid is not difficult, but it is even simpler when working in the local coordinate system of the ellipsoid. Since all necessary transformations are affine, and therefore preserve straight line segments, it is quite obvious to transform the eye ray into object space and do a simple ray-sphere intersection computation. Then, the actual intersection computation is straightforward. Inserting the ray equation into the object-space expression $\|\mathbf{x}\| = 1$ of the ellipsoid yields the condition

$$\mathbf{d}^T\mathbf{d}\lambda^2 + 2\mathbf{p}_v^T\mathbf{d}\lambda + \mathbf{p}_v^T\mathbf{p}_v - 1 = 0 \tag{8.5}$$

which only then has real solutions if the determinant

$$D = (\mathbf{p}_v^T\mathbf{d})^2 - \mathbf{d}^T\mathbf{d}(\mathbf{p}_v^T\mathbf{p}_v - 1) \tag{8.6}$$

is greater or equal to zero. Depending on the sign of D the fragment is either discarded (i.e., killed) or the intersection point and the ellipsoid normal necessary for shading the resulting pixel are computed. Solving Equation (8.5) for the actual intersection parameter

$$\lambda_s = \frac{-\mathbf{p}_v^T\mathbf{d} - \sqrt{(\mathbf{p}_v^T\mathbf{d})^2 - \mathbf{d}^T\mathbf{d}(\mathbf{p}_v^T\mathbf{p}_v - 1)}}{\mathbf{d}^T\mathbf{d}} \tag{8.7}$$

allows us to compute the intersection point $\mathbf{s} = \mathbf{p}_v + \lambda_s\mathbf{d}$, and since the whole computation is taking place in the local parameter space of the ellipsoid, the position vector of this point is also identical to the normalized surface normal. With this information per-fragment correct Phong lighting of the ellipsoid surface can be computed. There are only two things missing: the light vector pointing from the point of intersection to the light source position and its reflection about the surface normal. Both can be computed with only a few instructions in the fragment program.

As a last step, the correct depth sorting of the rendered objects has to be ensured. For each fragment, the correct depth value has to be computed and written to the z-buffer. Thereto the point of ray-surface intersection **s** is transformed to world space and the modelview and projection transforms are applied accordingly. After that, perspective division and depth-range mapping yield the corrected depth value for the fragment that allows for the correct depth sorting of both the ellipsoid glyphs and traditionally-rendered geometry.

Deferred Shading

Since for large numbers of objects the depth complexity is often very high (i.e., there is much occlusion taking place), it is beneficial to defer the shading of the glyphs as long as possible. Doing the shading only once per pixel can save a huge amount of per-pixel computations.

Therefore, instead of computing the shading for each fragment directly in the afore-mentioned fragment program, the world-space position and normal of the intersection point are stored into offscreen render buffers using, for example, the OpenGL `ARB_draw_buffers` and `EXT_framebuffer_object` extensions and an additional shading pass is done that computes the actual color values for the pixels. This can be achieved by rendering a screen-sized polygon using a fragment program that fetches the intersection parameters from textures bound to the respective render buffers of the first render pass. Of course, the shading computation is only meaningful for pixels that are actually covered by a glyph. But this can be easily accomplished by using an alpha mask, for example.

8.3.5 VISUALIZATION OF COMPLEX GLYPHS ON THE GPU

The ellipsoid-based representation works very well for relatively simple particles with only few parameters, like in tensor visualization. However, in other application areas, where more attributes are available per particle, more advanced glyphs are required. Thermodynamics researchers, for example, work with molecules of different complexity in molecular dynamics simulations. One particular aspect of research in this area is the simulation of the mechanism of droplet formation in gases for mono-, di-, and quadrupolar molecules. With ellipsoid particles, it is not possible to represent all parameters of such molecules. Specifically, one cannot tell one end of the longest principal axis from the other. Furthermore, the (even symbolic) geometry of a dipole is quite unlike an ellipsoid barring acceptance of this visualization by the involved researchers. To remedy, a specialized glyph for this specific case can be implemented [RE05].

Particle Representation

The shape of the new application-tailored glyph is borrowed from the classic ball-and-stick representation that is widely used in chemistry. Since thermodynamicists usually visualize di- and quadrupoles in the same style, the final representation consists of two Lennard-Jones centers with adjustable radii r_1, r_2 and an adjustable distance d between them (see Figure 8.27a). Some dipolar molecules might not necessarily have visually distinguishable radii, and thus it might not be possible to distinguish one end from the other. So we opted for adding a cylindrical bar magnet with adjustable radius along the distance axis to represent the dipole polarity by color and the charge by the cylinder's radius r_3. The cylinder length l is currently just set in proportion to the two spheres, but could be used to encode another attribute of the molecule as well. The resulting glyph additionally shows the distance between the Lennard-Jones centers and the value of the charge magnitude.

Rendering

To render the dipole glyphs, we take a similar approach as for the ellipsoids. To simplify the ray casting of the surfaces in the fragment program, all calculations are

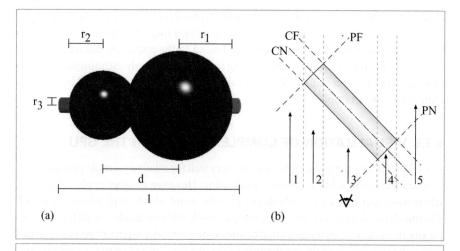

Figure 8.27: (*a*) The different parameters of the dipole glyph. (*b*) The five possible cases to hit a cylinder.

performed in the local coordinate system of each glyph, thus zeroing out several variables in the generic surface representation. This simplified surface can be described as

$$
(\begin{pmatrix} p_x - \frac{d}{2} \\ p_y \\ p_z \end{pmatrix}^2 - r_1^2)(\begin{pmatrix} p_x + \frac{d}{2} \\ p_y \\ p_z \end{pmatrix}^2 - r_2^2)(\begin{pmatrix} 0 \\ p_y \\ p_z \end{pmatrix}^2 - r_3^2) = 0. \qquad \text{(8.8)}
$$

Note that this geometry still contains an infinitely long cylinder. So we need two additional planes to confine the cylinder to a defined length. The different stages of the algorithm are quite similar to the algorithm described in Section 8.3.4. Then, similarly to Section 8.3.4, a combination of a vertex and a fragment program is used to compute the shape and the shading of the glyph from the implicit representation given by Equation (8.8). The actual computation differs only in the following aspects. First, the size of the point primitive is calculated from the projection of a bounding box enclosing the two spheres and adjusted by the projection of the axis of the cylinder extended by its radius.

In the fragment program the eye ray $\mathbf{x} = \mathbf{p}_v + \lambda \mathbf{d}$ passing through the current fragment is computed and intersected with the five surfaces representing the glyph. This yields six significant values for the ray parameter λ, namely the two nearest hits for the spheres, both intersections with the infinite cylinder boundary, and two intersections for the cylinder caps. These have to be sorted in order to decide whether a surface has been hit, and which one. According to Figure 8.27, there are five different cases that have to be considered:

1. $\lambda_{CF} > \lambda_{CN} > \lambda_{PF} > \lambda_{PN}$ *Sphere/Kill*
2. $\lambda_{CF} > \lambda_{PF} > \lambda_{CN} > \lambda_{PN}$ *Cylinder*
3. $\lambda_{PF} > \lambda_{CF} > \lambda_{CN} > \lambda_{PN}$ *Cylinder*
4. $\lambda_{PF} > \lambda_{CF} > \lambda_{PN} > \lambda_{CN}$ *Cap*
5. $\lambda_{PF} > \lambda_{PN} > \lambda_{CF} > \lambda_{CN}$ *Sphere/Kill*

Then, the conditions $\lambda_{PF} < \lambda_{CN}$ and $\lambda_{CF} < \lambda_{PN}$ can be used to distinguish whether the cylinder is missed and then either the sphere has to be intersected or the fragment has to be discarded if none of the spheres was hit. To detect the nearest cap, we use $\lambda_{CN} < \lambda_{PN}$. This works well except for the case when the eye ray is parallel to the cylinder's axis, which can cause floating point specials for the intersection calculations. This can be avoided, for example, by checking if the distance from the intersection with the nearest cap plane PN to the intersection of the cylinder axis and PN is smaller than the cylinder radius. If this condition is fulfilled, we can be sure that the cap is hit. Another problem is floating-point special values resulting from the square-root operation needed to solve the quadratic equations, and the invalid lambda values resulting from roots with negative discriminant are replaced by values that lie beyond the far clipping plane. Once the correct intersection is found, the corresponding color is selected and Phong shading is applied. An example for this rendering style can be seen in Figure 8.28.

In this figure you can see two droplets at low pressure in void, at a temperature of 160 K. The left droplet consists of methane molecules (color-coded red) that quickly start to evaporate because the droplet's boiling point is 111.55 K. The right droplet consists of ethane (color-coded green) in stable fluid state; the molecules exhibit two Lennard-Jones centers but no polarity. These droplets collide at a speed of about 200 m/s. With the point-based visualization, researchers can interactively explore simulations of this size, while the straightforward polygon-based approach they used before did not scale beyond several thousand molecules. One interesting effect that can be observed easily in this simulation—but cannot be deduced without visualizing the dataset—is the fact that the methane molecules form a thin coating around the ethane droplet and the excess molecules evaporate. It can also be seen that the surface tension makes the droplet return to its spherical form after the force of the impact has dissipated.

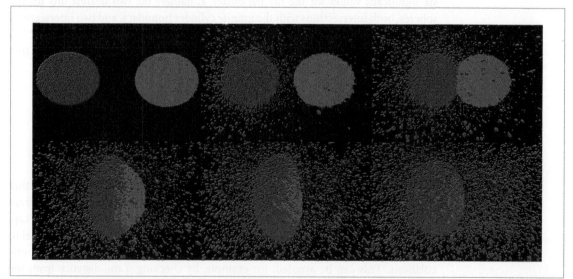

Figure 8.28: Visualization of the methane-ethane collision simulation dataset with 82,000 molecules rendered with the dipole glyph shader. The ethane molecules are shown in green. On a NVIDIA GeForce 7800 GTX using a 512^2 viewport, these images can be rendered at about 42 frames per second.

8.3.6 CONCLUSION

In this chapter an approach has been presented that allows the rendering of complex glyphs directly on the GPU. The aim of this approach is to minimize the amount of data transmitted from the CPU to the GPU, reducing the load on the graphics bus and the CPU. However, this advantage has to be traded for a higher processing load on the GPU, but fortunately the high parallelism and short product cycle of GPU technology allows for higher performance improvements than can be expected for the CPU and, more importantly, the graphics bus. Using recent generations of graphics hardware, the presented algorithms allow the user to interactively explore large, time-dependent simulations containing several hundreds of thousands of semantically dense particles using complex application-specific glyph representations.

Acknowledgments

We would like to thank Matthias Hopf for providing us with his implementation of the point-cloud framework and helpful discussion. The galaxy formation simulations were carried out by the VIRGO Supercomputing Consortium using computers based at the Computing Centre of the Max-Planck Society in Garching and at the Institute for Computational Cosmology. The data are publicly available at www.mpa-garching.mpg.de/NumCos. The brain dataset is courtesy of Gordon Kindlmann at the Scientific Computing and Imaging Institute, University of Utah, and Andrew Alexander at the W. M. Keck Laboratory for Functional Brain Imaging and Behavior, University of Wisconsin at Madison. We also would like to thank Jadran Vrabec from the Institute of Thermodynamics and Thermal Process Engineering in Stuttgart for providing the molecular simulation results.

8.4 POINT CLOUDS AND BRICK MAPS FOR MOVIE PRODUCTION

Per Christensen

8.4.1 MOTIVATION

Collections of 3D point data (point clouds) are getting used more and more as a tool for movie production. It is useful to compute data once and write them out as point clouds. The data can then be reused later—either directly as written or in some manipulated form.

In the past, such data were often generated as 2D textures, which have some desirable properties such as MIP mapping, tiling, and efficient caching. But 2D textures are either tied to the screen parameterization (in which case they are view dependent and can't be reused for different views of the same scene) or tied to the surface parameterization (which requires that the surfaces must have a parameterization).

Three-dimensional point clouds are often more efficient, flexible, and user friendly than 2D textures. They are independent of the viewing direction, surface type, and parameterization. Point clouds truly add another dimension to the process of data generation and reuse. However, point clouds are unstructured and, therefore, not mipmapped, tiled, or cache friendly.

We have introduced a data format called *brick map* that combines the best properties of 3D point clouds and 2D textures: a 3D representation independent of the surface type and parameterization, and also mipmapped, tiled, and cacheable.

Here we first briefly describe Pixar's RenderMan renderer and point-cloud API, and show some examples where it can be advantageous to store data as 3D point clouds. We then describe the use of point clouds for the calculation of subsurface scattering, approximate ambient occlusion, and global illumination, and show how computation of a radiosity point cloud can speed up photon-mapping global illumination. Next is a description of brick maps: how to generate them and look up data in them, how to efficiently cache the bricks, and how to render and ray trace brick maps as geometry. Armed with the powerful tool of brick maps, we then describe how to compute single-bounce and multibounce global illumination in very complex scenes. In the end, we look at the generation and use of volume data and provide a conclusion.

Some of the methods described in this section are used in everyday movie production at Pixar and elsewhere; other methods are new and promising but have not yet been adopted in production.

8.4.2 PIXAR'S RENDERMAN™

Most of the images in this section are rendered with Pixar's RenderMan renderer (PRMan). PRMan is used for rendering all of Pixar's movies, for example, *Toy Story*, *The Incredibles*, and *Cars*. PRMan is also used for rendering special effects in movies such as *Terminator 2, Jurassic Park, Star Wars* episodes 1–3, the *Harry Potter* and *The Lord of the Rings* movies, and many more.

The rendering algorithm used by PRMan tessellates all surfaces into micropolygons. Each micropolygon can be thought of as a surface element. The micropolygons are shaded and composited into a 2D image. More details about PRMan and its rendering algorithm can be found in Cook et al., Upstill, Apodaca and Gritz, and Christensen et al. [CCC87, Ups90, AG00, CLF+03].

Instead of only generating a 2D image as output, it is simple to augment the rendering algorithm to also write out 3D data for each micropolygon, for example, the shaded color or some other shading results that may prove useful later on. Each micropolygon is approximated as a microdisk—a surfel.

As a part of the PRMan package we also provide an application programmer's interface (API) for point-cloud files. The API makes it simple to read and write point-cloud files in PRMan's format. This makes it possible to write stand-alone programs to process and manipulate point clouds, for example, to compute subsurface scattering or approximate ambient occlusion.

8.4.3 BAKING 3D INFORMATION AS POINT CLOUDS

The term *baking* is often used to describe the computation and storage of data for later reuse. Baking data as view-independent 2D textures require a (u, v) parameterization of the surfaces. Some surfaces such as subdivision surfaces, implicit surfaces, and dense polygon meshes do not have an inherent parameterization, so they have to be manually assigned parameter values. This can be cumbersome. Also, the (u, v) ranges can be irregular, for example, the "pinched" areas around the poles of a sphere. In contrast, 3D point clouds have a natural, simple, and ever-present parameterization—3D position (x, y, z).

We distinguish between two types of point clouds: surface point clouds and volume point clouds. Surface point clouds contain data associated with surfaces, and each data point typically contains a surface normal along with the position, radius, and stored data. Surface data points are often referred to as *surfels* [PZvBG00]. Volume point clouds contain data associated with volumes, so the data points don't have normals.

Example 1: Baking Specular Reflections
Let's look at an example of 3D baking of surface data. Figure 8.29a shows a Fiat 500L "Topolino" with reflective paint. This model is from early preproduction ray-tracing tests for the Disney Pixar movie *Cars* [DP06]. The car is modeled as subdivision surfaces and is surrounded by a sphere with an environment map. The image shows reflection of the environment map and interreflections on the car, for example, the reflection of the eyes in the hood. During rendering of this image, the reflection and interreflection data were baked out to a surface point cloud. The point cloud contains approximately 850,000 points, each point containing position (three floats), unit normal (two spherical coordinates—each a short integer), radius (one float), and reflection color (three floats). Some of these points are shown in Figure 8.29b. The point cloud

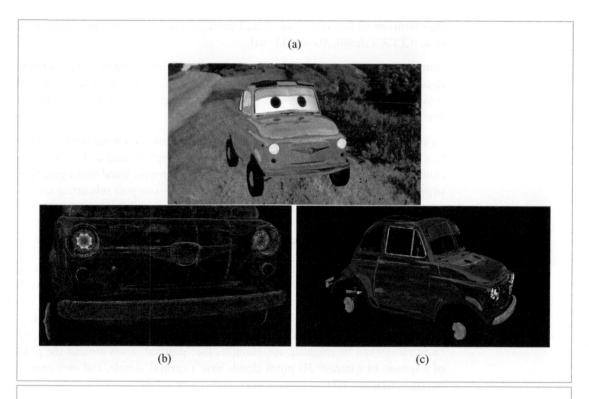

Figure 8.29: Baked reflection on a Fiat Topolino: (*a*) original image, (*b*) surface points with reflection data, (*c*) surface points with reflection data rendered as disks. (Copyright © Disney/Pixar.)

is also shown in Figure 8.29c with the data points rendered as disks. The density of the point cloud is determined by the image resolution and micropolygon tessellation rate (shading rate).

Now that the reflection data have been baked they can be reused. Since reflection data are view dependent they cannot be reused for other viewing directions—we would get images with the reflections in the wrong locations, similar to Figure 8.29c. However, we can re-render the same image without shooting any reflection rays at all. Furthermore, the point-cloud data can be postprocessed. A useful example of this is blurring the reflections by low-pass filtering the point data. Such blurring is much cheaper than computing glossy reflections using ray tracing.

Example 2: Baking Ambient Occlusion

The previous example showed baking of reflection data. Another quantity that is often baked is *ambient occlusion*—a representation of how much of the hemisphere

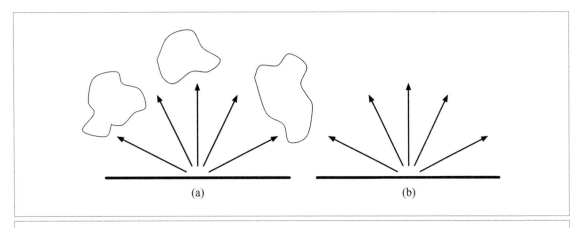

Figure 8.30: Ambient occlusion: (*a*) surface point with high ambient occlusion, and (*b*) surface point with no ambient occlusion.

above each point is occluded by geometry [ZIK98, Lan02]. Figure 8.30 shows two examples of ambient occlusion. In 8.30a most of the hemisphere above the point is covered by geometry, and hence the ambient occlusion is high and the point is rather dark. In Figure 8.30b none of the hemisphere above the point is covered by geometry, and hence the ambient occlusion is low and the point is bright. Ambient occlusion is quite time consuming to compute since it involves shooting lots of rays, so baking and reusing it is a good idea.

Figure 8.31a shows the Topolino car on a plane with baked ambient occlusion values. Now the ambient occlusion can be re-rendered fast—just looking up the baked 3D data is much faster than recomputing the ambient occlusion. Since ambient occlusion is view independent, it can even be re-rendered from a different viewpoint, as shown in Figure 8.32. Furthermore, if the car is deforming (e.g., squashing or stretching), the data can be reused if the deformed car has associated undeformed reference geometry, and if the difference between the correct occlusion on the deformed car and the baked occlusion from the undeformed car is deemed sufficiently small.

Example 3: Baking Diffusely Reflected Direct Illumination

Direct illumination can be expensive to compute, for example, due to many light sources and ray-traced shadows. Likewise, the surface reflection properties can be surprisingly expensive to compute due to procedural textures, dozens of texture maps, and very complex and general shaders. Figure 8.33 shows an example of a directly illuminated scene with a single light source and purely diffuse reflection.

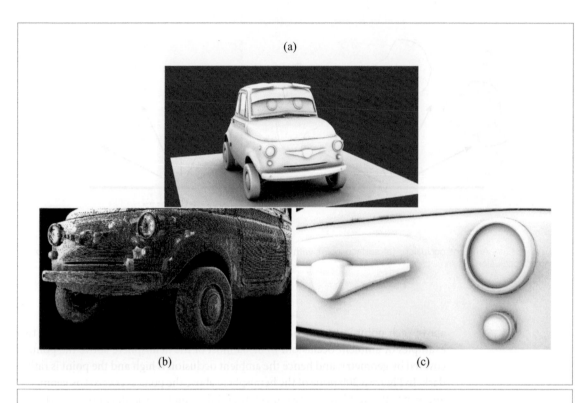

Figure 8.31: Baked ambient occlusion on a Fiat Topolino: (*a*) original image, (*b*) surface points with ambient occlusion data, and (*c*) surface points with ambient occlusion data rendered as disks.

Figure 8.32: Re-rendering of the Fiat Topolino using ambient occlusion from a point-cloud file: (*a*) ambient occlusion, and (*b*) ambient occlusion times diffuse color.

Figure 8.33: Monstropolis city block rendered with direct illumination from the sun and diffuse reflection. (Copyright © Disney/Pixar.)

The scene geometry is from the Pixar movie *Monsters, Inc.* [DP01]: a city block of Monstropolis with many individually modeled buildings, trees, cars, etc. The scene consists of 36,000 high-level primitives, mostly NURBS patches and subdivision surfaces. The shaders have been changed from the original for these tests. In this image large parts of the scene are completely black since no direct light reaches them.

For these tests, the objects were manually divided into 40 groups: each street, building, and car is a group and has a separate point-cloud file. Rendering at resolution $1,024 \times 768$ resulted in 39 million data points being generated. The points were stored in 40 point-cloud files with a total size of 1.3 GB (uncompressed). Figure 8.34 shows all the baked points. The points are so dense that this image looks quite similar to the rendered image in Figure 8.33.

Figure 8.35 shows a more detailed view of two of the point clouds. The point cloud for the car contains 686,000 points (file size 22 MB uncompressed), and the point cloud for the building, tree, and two lampposts contains 2.1 million points (68 MB).

We can reuse the stored reflected illumination values for later re-rendering of this scene. However, as mentioned already, the raw, unorganized point-cloud file format has the drawback that when data are needed from it, the entire point cloud has to be

Figure 8.34: Monstropolis point clouds with diffusely reflected direct illumination.

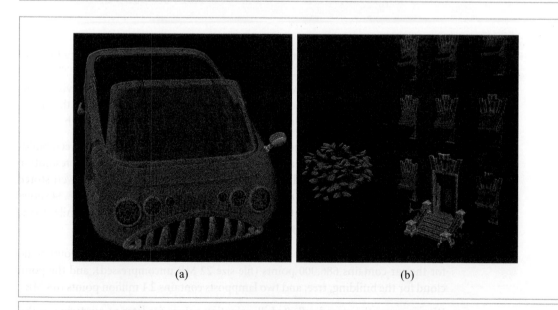

(a)   (b)

Figure 8.35: Point clouds with diffusely reflected direct illumination: (*a*) car, and (*b*) building with a tree and two lampposts (partial view).

read or the entire point cloud must be stored in memory. This can be prohibitive for complex scenes with many huge point-cloud files, such as in this example. We will return to this issue in Section 8.4.8.

8.4.4 SUBSURFACE SCATTERING

Subsurface scattering is an important effect for realistic rendering of translucent materials such as skin, flesh, fat, fruits, milk, marble, and many others. Subsurface scattering is light that enters a material, is scattered one or more times inside the material, and then leaves the material. Subsurface scattering is responsible for effects like color bleeding inside materials and the diffusion of light across shadow boundaries. The photograph in Figure 8.36 shows an example of some real translucent objects.

Subsurface scattering is used on computer-generated characters like Gollum in *The Lord of the Rings* trilogy and Dobby in *Harry Potter and the Chamber of Secrets*. Seeing the light scattered through, for example, the ears and nose, adds subtle but significant realism. The subsurface scattering on those two movie characters was computed using a precursor to the method described here; that method used a z-buffer instead of point clouds.

Figure 8.36: Translucent grapes and leaves. (Photo by Wayne Wooten.)

Figure 8.37 illustrates a simple example of computed subsurface scattering. The scene consists of a teapot made of a uniform, diffuse material. The teapot is illuminated by two area lights. There is no subsurface scattering in the first image, so the parts of the teapot that are not directly illuminated are completely black. In the second image, the material of the teapot has subsurface scattering with a relatively short mean path length, so the light can penetrate thin parts such as the handle, knob, and spout, but very little light makes it through the teapot body. In the third image, the mean path length is longer, so more light can penetrate the material and even the teapot body is brighter.

We use point clouds for the computation of subsurface scattering. The first pass is the generation of a point cloud containing transmitted direct illumination values: For each micropolygon generated during rendering we write out the position, normal, radius, and transmitted radiance. The next step takes that point cloud as input and computes subsurface scattering results in the form of another point cloud; in this point cloud the point colors represent the light that has been scattered through the volume. The final step is to render an image with the subsurface scattering results.

Step 1: Baking Transmitted Direct Illumination

In the first step, the object is rendered with direct illumination, and we bake out the light that is transmitted through the surface. We will use the translucent teapot as the main example in this section. The rendered image looks like Figure 8.37a. The point-cloud file has approximately 170,000 points with transmitted radiance values and is shown in Figure 8.38.

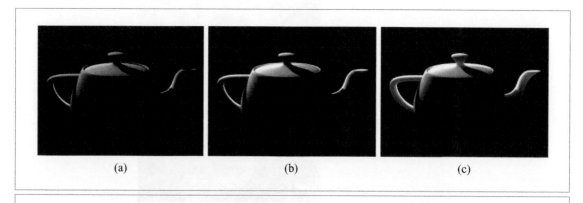

(a)   (b)   (c)

Figure 8.37: Teapots with varying degrees of subsurface scattering: (*a*) no subsurface scattering, (*b*) some subsurface scattering, and (*c*) strong subsurface scattering.

Figure 8.38: Point cloud with transmitted illumination values.

In this example, the illumination is direct illumination from two area lights, but it could just as well be high dynamic range illumination from an environment map or global illumination of the teapot.

Step 2: Diffusion Simulation

The subsurface scattering is approximated as a volume diffusion process; this computation is done using a stand-alone program that reads one point-cloud file and generates another. The subsurface scattering properties of the material can be specified in three equivalent ways: by specifying a material name from a built-in table of data values; by specifying the reduced scattering coefficients, absorption coefficients, and index of refraction; or by specifying the diffuse color (BRDF albedo), diffuse mean free-path lengths, and index of refraction. The diffusion approximation follows the dipole method described by Jensen et al. [JMLH01, JB02] and Hery [Her03].

The algorithm proceeds as follows. First the scattering properties are converted to diffuse albedo, diffuse mean free-path length, and index of refraction if they are not already in that form. Then we read the input point-cloud file with the baked transmitted direct illumination data, and organize the points into an octree, as described in Section 4.4. Each octree node contains information about the centroid of the points in it, the sum of the point areas, and the sum of the power (transmitted radiance times area) of the points. Each node also contains eight pointers to its child nodes. Furthermore, leaf nodes also contain a pointer to a list of the points in it. Then we loop over all the points in the point cloud. For each point, we traverse the octree from its root. If an octree node is deemed sufficiently small and far away from the point, we compute the dipole approximation from the node centroid. If not, we recurse to the children of the node. When a leaf node is reached, the dipole approximation is computed from each of the points in that node.

The result is a point cloud with a subsurface scattering color at every point. Figure 8.39 shows the subsurface scattering values for the teapot example.

Step 3: Rendering Subsurface Scattering

We are now finally ready to render an image with subsurface scattering. The subsurface scattering is looked up in the computed subsurface scattering point cloud and the resulting image is shown in Figure 8.40 without and with direct illumination. If desired, one can of course multiply the subsurface color by a texture and also add specular highlights, etc.

Extensions

The example above had a uniform albedo and uniform diffuse mean free-path length. It is simple to multiply the transmitted radiance by a varying diffuse surface color prior to baking it. For another effect, we can also specify varying albedos and diffuse mean free-path lengths for the diffusion simulation. This means that the diffusion parameters vary over the surface and can give a nice and textured appearance. This requires that the albedo and diffuse mean free paths are baked as data in the point-cloud file along with the transmitted radiance. A few examples are shown in Figure 8.41.

The diffusion approximation described above cannot take blocking internal geometry into account. But sometimes we would like to fake the effect of reduced subsurface scattering near blocking geometry, for example, in skin regions near a bone.

Figure 8.39: Point cloud with subsurface scattering values.

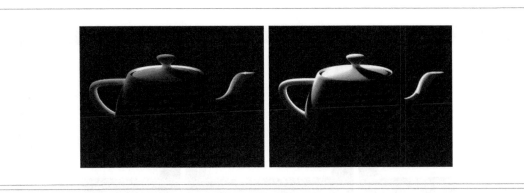

Figure 8.40: Subsurface scattering without and with direct illumination.

Figure 8.41: Subsurface scattering with varying albedo. (Mushroom image by Dylan Sisson.)

This can be done by baking negative illumination values on the internal geometry; these negative values will then make the nearby regions darker.

Figure 8.42 shows three images of a thin translucent box with varying degrees of blocking by a torus embedded in the box. See Hery [Her03] for more discussion and examples of blocking geometry.

8.4.5 POINT-BASED APPROXIMATE AMBIENT OCCLUSION

The standard method for computing ambient occlusion is quite time consuming since it requires tracing of many rays [Lan02]. But there is a faster way to compute ambient occlusion—a method that does not involve ray tracing, but only operates on a point cloud. The computed ambient occlusion values are not entirely correct

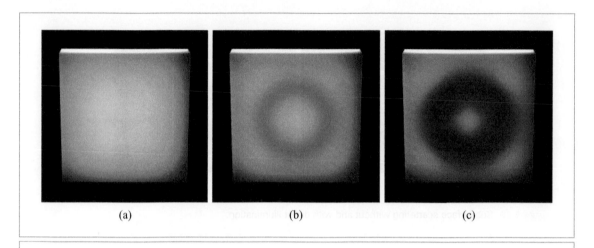

(a)   (b)   (c)

Figure 8.42: Subsurface scattering with blocking geometry: (a) no blocking, (b) blocking by torus with color (-2 -2 -2), and (c) blocking by torus with color (-5 -5 -5).

since some occlusion will be overestimated, but for many applications the speed of the point-based approximate computation will make up for the incorrectness.

The computation method is similar to the methods used for efficient n-body simulation in astrophysics and electrostatics [App85, BH86, Gre87] and clustering in global illumination [SAG94, CLSS97]. The difference from the n-body problem is that gravity and electrostatic forces are independent of direction (they are isotropic) and can simply be combined using the superposition principle, while occlusion does depend on direction (it is anisotropic) and the superposition principle does not apply.

Our method is similar to that of Bunnell [Bun05] in that both methods approximate the surfaces of the scene with disks. The biggest differences are that we use clustering and spherical harmonics and that our algorithm is not implemented on a GPU.

The input is a point cloud of surface data; each point consists of a position, normal, and radius (or, equivalently, area). We treat each data point as a disk. The occlusion contributed by a disk at position $\mathbf{p}_i$ with area A_i and normalized normal $\mathbf{n}_i$ to a point $\mathbf{p}_j$ with normalized normal $\mathbf{n}_j$ is

$$o_{ij} = A_i \frac{(\mathbf{d}_{ij} \cdot \mathbf{n}_i)_+ (\mathbf{d}_{ji} \cdot \mathbf{n}_j)_+}{\mathbf{r}_{ij}^2 + A_i/\pi}, \tag{8.9}$$

where $\mathbf{r}_{ij} = |\mathbf{p}_j - \mathbf{p}_i|$ is the distance between $\mathbf{p}_i$ and $\mathbf{p}_j$, $\mathbf{d}_{ij} = (\mathbf{p}_j - \mathbf{p}_i)/\mathbf{r}_{ij}$ is the normalized direction from $\mathbf{p}_i$ to $\mathbf{p}_j$, and $\mathbf{d}_{ji} = -\mathbf{d}_{ij}$ is the opposite direction. Note that we use the clamped dot product $(\,\cdot\,)_+$, which is 0 if the dot product is negative. This is to ensure that disks below the horizon at $\mathbf{p}_j$ do not contribute occlusion to $\mathbf{p}_j$, and that back sides of surfaces don't occlude (although the latter choice is a matter of taste).

For efficient calculation, we don't want to compute the occlusion from every single point to every other point. So we group nearby points together in clusters and treat them as a single point if they are sufficiently far away.

We first construct an octree by recursively dividing the points, as described in Section 4.4 and Chapter 6. The subdivision stops when an octree node contains only a few points (e.g., less than 10). We then represent the projected area of the points/disks in each node, as viewed from different directions, using spherical harmonics Y_{lm} [PFTV03, RH01b].

The projected front-side area of a single disk as seen from direction $\mathbf{d}$ is $A_i(\mathbf{d}\cdot\mathbf{n}_i)_+$. The coefficients of the spherical harmonic representation of the projected front-side area of a disk are

$$c_{lm} = \int_{\theta=0}^{\pi} \int_{\phi=0}^{2\pi} A_i\,(\mathbf{d}\cdot\mathbf{n}_i)_+ \, Y_{lm}(\theta,\phi)\, \sin\theta\, d\theta\, d\phi, \qquad (8.10)$$

where θ and ϕ are spherical coordinates (the azimuth and polar angle, respectively) and $\mathbf{d} = (\sin\theta\,\cos\phi, \sin\theta\,\sin\phi, \cos\theta)$.

Like Ramamoorthi and Hanrahan [RH01b] we found that using just the first nine spherical harmonics $(Y_{00}, Y_{1,\,-1\ldots1}, Y_{2,\,-2\ldots2})$ gives sufficient accuracy. (If backsides are allowed to occlude, we use the absolute value of the dot product, $|\mathbf{d}\cdot\mathbf{n}_i|$. In this case, the coefficients of the three spherical harmonics with $l=1$ are always zero due to the symmetry of the absolute dot product and the antisymmetry of those three spherical harmonics.) The projected area of a leaf octree node is represented with nine coefficients that are the sums of the coefficients for the disks in that node. For a nonleaf node, the coefficients are the sums of the coefficients of its child nodes.

To compute the occlusion at a point $\mathbf{p}_j$, we recursively traverse the octree from its root. If $\mathbf{p}_j$ is inside the octree node bounding box or if the projected area of the cluster is larger than a user-specified maximum solid angle ω_{max}, we go to the child nodes. When a leaf node is reached, we compute the disk-to-point occlusion for the disks in the node. If a nonleaf node is deemed acceptable, we use the projected area from the spherical harmonics representation. With this approach, the occlusion is computed as disks from nearby points and as clusters for more distant points. The ω_{max} parameter provides a simple time versus quality trade-off.

Figure 8.43 shows a comparison between ray-traced ambient occlusion and three examples of approximate ambient occlusion computed from a point cloud. Notice that with the raw approximate occlusion some areas are overoccluded, as shown

Figure 8.43: Fiat Topolino with ambient occlusion: (*a*) ray-traced ambient occlusion, (*b*) point-based approximate ambient occlusion, (*c*) point-based approximate ambient occlusion with reduced overocclusion, and (*d*) point-based approximate ambient occlusion with maximum distance 100.

in Figure 8.43b. At the root of this problem is that we treat the occlusion as if it could be simply added using the superposition principle as, for example, gravity and electrostatic forces. But in reality some geometry might block other geometry, and such blocked geometry should not contribute to the occlusion. For example, a point on the ground receives occlusion not only from the car body, but also from the car interior, engine, and suspension. We can reduce this problem by dividing the hemisphere into n parts and only allowing each part to occlude by at most $1/n$. This is shown in Figure 8.43c. Furthermore, we can choose to attenuate occlusion from distant objects; an example of this is shown in Figure 8.43d. The point-based computation of approximate occlusion is typically three to eight times faster than ray-traced computation. For this scene, the ray-traced ambient occlusion in Figure 8.43a took 18.5 minutes to render while the point-based approximate ambient occlusion in Figure 8.43c took 7 minutes.

8.4.6 POINT-BASED APPROXIMATE GLOBAL ILLUMINATION

The point-based approximate ambient occlusion method can be extended to compute one or more bounces of diffuse indirect illumination. Diffuse indirect illumination is responsible for color-bleeding effects. The first work on extending ambient occlusion with fast, approximate global illumination was done by Garcia et al. [GSIK01] and Méndez et al. [MSC03].

First we bake a point cloud of diffusely reflected direct illumination. This is the same data type as in the Monstropolis example in Section 8.4.3; however, here we will use another example: the Cornell box with spheres shown in Figure 8.44a. In many cases it is sufficient to generate a rather sparse point cloud like the one shown in Figure 8.44b.

Then we read those data points in, create an octree, and represent the power (radiosity times area) from each octree node using 27 spherical harmonics coefficients—9 for each of the three color bands. The same hierarchical algorithm that was used for approximate ambient occlusion is also used for color bleeding. A point-based color-bleeding computation takes only a few seconds for a simple scene such as the Cornell box with 100,000 points, and it is often more than an order of magnitude faster than computing a decent solution using ray tracing and shader evaluation at the ray hit points. The resulting point cloud is shown in Figure 8.45.

(a)   (b)

Figure 8.44: Cornell box with diffusely reflected direct illumination: (*a*) rendered image, and (*b*) point cloud.

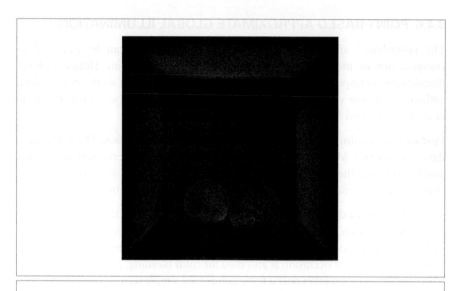

Figure 8.45: Cornell box point cloud with approximate single-bounce global illumination values.

The point-based approximate approach will often compute too much color bleeding, just as there is often too much ambient occlusion. And colors from near and far objects in the same direction will be mixed. However, as Figure 8.46 shows, in some cases this is not too objectionable. The main visible difference for this scene is that the areas under the spheres are a bit too bright in the approximate solution.

Extending this method to handle multiple bounces is simple, but requires that we also store the diffuse surface colors in the point clouds. The workflow then is as follows. Bake diffusely reflected direct illumination and diffuse colors. Run the approximate global illumination algorithm to compute indirect illumination values, then multiply the computed indirect illumination values by the diffuse color at each point, run the approximate global illumination algorithm again, and so on.

Discussion
The point-based approximate global illumination computation is much faster than the standard ray-tracing method. The speed is due to the fact that there is no tessellation, no ray tracing, and no shaders involved in the computation.

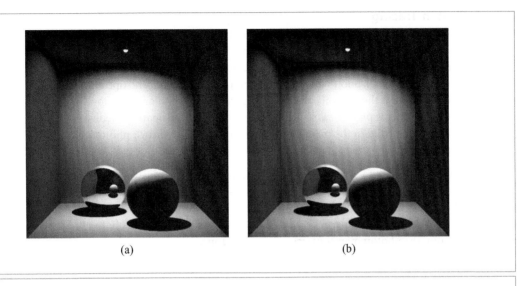

(a)   (b)

Figure 8.46: Cornell box with single-bounce global illumination: (*a*) ray-traced global illumination, and (*b*) point-based approximate global illumination.

8.4.7 PHOTON MAPS AND RADIOSITY POINT CLOUDS

The photon-mapping method [Jen96, Jen01] is a popular global illumination method that can compute caustics, multiple bounces of diffuse indirect illumination (color bleeding), and multiple scattering in participating media. It can handle reasonably complex scenes since the photon maps are independent of the representation of the geometry.

The original photon-mapping method consists of three passes: photon tracing, photon map sorting, and rendering. A significant speed optimization can be obtained by augmenting the second pass to estimate the irradiance at the photon positions [Chr99]. This irradiance estimation is quick, and makes the rendering five to seven times faster for typical scenes without degrading the image quality. A further optimization is to store the local diffuse surface color with each photon, and estimating radiosity instead of irradiance at the photon positions [Chr02]. Estimating radiosity takes no more time than estimating irradiance (only a few extra multiplications per photon), but makes it faster to compute the indirect illumination, especially if the scene has complex shaders and many textures.

Step 1: Photon Tracing

In the photon-tracing step, photons are emitted from the light sources and traced through the scene using Monte Carlo simulation. When a photon hits a diffuse surface, it is stored in the *global photon map*—a point cloud containing the following data: position, surface normal, photon incident direction, photon power, and optionally diffuse surface color. If the photon came from a specular reflection or refraction, it is also stored in a *caustic photon map*. If the scene contains participating media, photons can also be scattered in the media; the scattering positions of such photons are stored in a *volume photon map*.

In the following example we focus on diffuse global illumination of surfaces and only consider the global photon map. Figure 8.47a shows a simple test scene, an orange interior with approximately one million polygons. This image only contains direct illumination and ray-traced specular reflections. Figure 8.47b shows a global photon map for the room; the photon map contains 500,000 photons.

Step 2: Photon Map Sorting and Radiosity Estimation

In the second step the photons in the photon map are sorted into a K-d-tree (K-d-trees are described in Section 4.4). We also estimate the radiosity at all or some of the photon positions. Each radiosity estimate is computed by locating the nearest photons, adding up their power, dividing by the area they cover, and multiplying by the diffuse surface color. As part of this computation, an approximate radius is

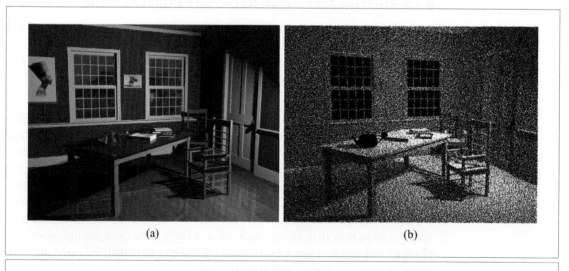

(a)   (b)

Figure 8.47: Orange interior: (*a*) rendered with traditional ray tracing (direct illumination and specular reflections), and (*b*) photon map (photon powers shown).

determined at each photon position; this radius is determined from the area covered by the nearest photons divided by the number of nearest photons. The use of this radius will become apparent later.

The result of this step is a new point cloud with position, normal, radius, and radiosity data. Figure 8.48 shows the scene rendered using the radiosity values.

The point positions divide the surfaces into a Voronoi diagram with constant radiosity inside each Voronoi cell. These radiosity values can be visualized directly for a rough estimate of the global illumination in the scene, as in Figure 8.48, or can be used as the basis for a high-quality rendering of the global illumination, as discussed below.

Step 3: Rendering

For high-quality rendering, the diffuse indirect illumination is computed by shooting rays to sample the hemisphere above each point. This particular use of distribution ray tracing [CPC84] is often called *final gathering* [Rei92]. Final gathering is a time-consuming computation, but it is made much more efficient by interpolation of the computed diffuse indirect illumination results using irradiance gradients

Figure 8.48: Orange interior with radiosity estimates.

Figure 8.49: Orange interior with global illumination: direct illumination, specular reflection, and diffuse indirect illumination.

[WRC88, WH92]. At the ray hit points we look up the precomputed radiosity of the nearest photon with a suitable surface normal. Figure 8.49 shows the orange interior rendered with global illumination using the radiosity estimates shown above.

Discussion

The photon map method (including the extensions used in this section) is limited by memory: It can only run efficiently if the entire photon map fits in memory at the same time as all the geometry, a texture cache, etc. However, Section 8.4.10 describes a method to handle photon map global illumination in very complex scenes with huge photon maps.

8.4.8 BRICK MAPS

Point clouds are generated as unorganized collections of data points. In order to read in these 3D data more efficiently (i.e., on demand and at the appropriate resolution), we have introduced a 3D mipmap representation [Wil83] called a *brick map*—a tiled, adaptive octree suitable for caching. The brick map representation can be used for both surface and volume data, and is independent of the parameterization of the surface. This is convenient if the surface doesn't have an inherent parameterization. The brick map format is inspired by the adaptive octrees used by DeBry et al.

[DGPR02] and Benson and Davis [BD02]. The tiling, caching, and filtering aspects are 3D generalizations of the handling of standard 2D textures in PRMan.

A *brick* always has 8^3 voxels in our implementation. We call the brick *dense* if most of the brick voxels contain data, and *sparse* otherwise. There are two types of brick maps: brick maps for surface data and brick maps for volume data. Surface data points have associated normals, and to avoid mixing, for example, data from the two sides of one surface, we divide the points into six groups depending on the dominant direction of the normal ($+x$, $-x$, $+y$, $-y$, $+z$, and $-z$). Each of the six groups is stored in a separate octree. Volume data points do not have surface normals, so one octree is sufficient.

Figure 8.50 shows an example of a brick map of surface data. The figure shows the three coarsest levels of a brick map of a textured surface. The coarsest brick map level consists of a single brick, the second level consists of up to 2^3 bricks, the third level contains up to 4^3 bricks, etc. All the bricks in this figure are sparse.

Figure 8.51 shows an example of a brick map of volume data. The volume data represent a marble volume texture, and all the bricks are dense.

Advantages of the Brick Map Representation
The brick map format combines the best properties of 3D point clouds and 2D textures:

- The brick map is independent of the original surface type: it doesn't matter whether the surface is a polygon mesh, a collection of NURBS patches, a subdivision surface, or whatever.

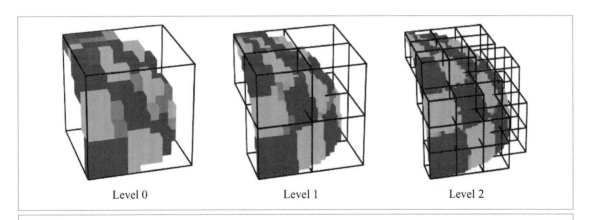

| Level 0 | Level 1 | Level 2 |

Figure 8.50: Brick map of a textured surface.

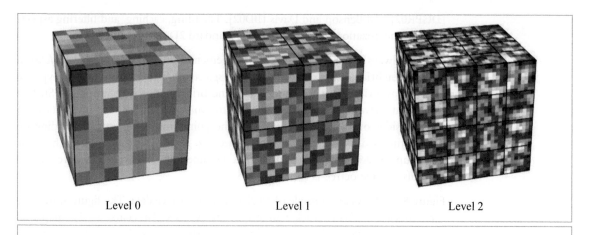

Level 0   Level 1   Level 2

Figure 8.51: Brick map of a marble volume texture.

- No 2D surface parameterization is necessary. This is an advantage since specifying a 2D parameterization for surfaces, such as subdivision surfaces, implicit surfaces, and dense polygon meshes, can be cumbersome.
- Brick maps automatically adapt to the data density and variation. If, for example, a fairly smooth 3D texture has only one small region with a lot of detail, there will only be many bricks in that one small region. This is in contrast to traditional 2D textures where the entire texture has to have high resolution if just a small part of it has a lot of detail.
- The mipmap representation is suitable for efficient filtering at various scales.
- Bricks are ideal for caching. This makes it possible to deal efficiently with huge brick maps—even collections of brick maps much larger than the available memory.
- The user can specify the required accuracy when the brick map is created. This makes it simple to trade-off data precision versus file size.

Creating a Brick Map

Given a set of points with associated radii, data, and possibly normals, we want to create a brick representation of the data. We do this in three steps.

First, the bounding volume of the entire dataset is found. Then, as mentioned already, we divide the data points into seven groups, depending on their normals: one group for points with no normal, and one group for each of the six major directions. Data for points with normals close to 45° are assigned to two (or even three) groups. This is to facilitate fast lookups: given a normal we can just look up in a single octree.

The second step is to store each data group in a sparse octree structure. The octree nodes and bricks are created on the fly as data points are inserted. Each octree node consists of nine pointers: eight pointers to child nodes and one pointer to a brick. For each data point $\mathbf{p}$, we first compute a small volume V_p based on its position and radius. For each octree node, starting at the appropriate root, the data are recursively inserted into the bricks of those octree nodes that V_p overlaps. When a point's data are inserted into a brick, we determine which brick voxels the point volume overlaps, and add the data values to the data in those voxels. When added, the data are multiplied by a weight $(V_p \cap V_v)/V_p$ that indicates how large a fraction of the point volume V_p overlaps the voxel volume V_v. We also increase the voxel weights.

When all the data have been inserted, we proceed to the third step. First, the data values in all voxels are divided by the weight of the voxel. We then determine the data variation of all $2 \times 2 \times 2$ voxel groups of the brick. If the voxel group data variation is smaller than a user-specified maximum error, we eliminate the data in those eight voxels. If all voxel data in a brick are eliminated, that entire brick can be eliminated. If any voxel data of the brick survive, we write the remaining voxel data of the brick to disk. Empty voxels are not written; this saves a lot of disk space for sparse brick maps. We don't write the weights either, since all data have already been divided by their weights.

To reduce the peak memory use during brick map construction, we construct and write out one octant of each octree at a time. Furthermore, brick voxels and voxel data are dynamically allocated and enlarged as needed during construction—this way, we avoid allocating 512 voxels for sparse bricks.

Figure 8.52 shows the five coarsest levels of the brick map constructed for the ambient occlusion data on the Fiat Topolino.

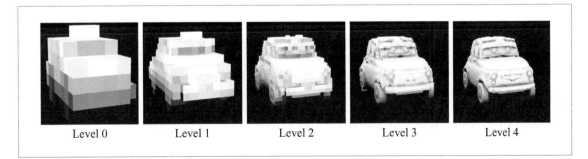

Level 0   Level 1   Level 2   Level 3   Level 4

Figure 8.52: Brick map of ambient occlusion data on the Fiat Topolino.

Looking Up in a Brick Map

Given a position, normal, and filter size, we want to find the interpolated value of the data at that point—smoothed as appropriate for the given filter size.

We first determine which one of the seven octrees to look up in based on the lookup normal. Then we construct a lookup volume V_l from the lookup point position and filter size. The lookup volume is an axis-aligned box (i.e., not necessarily a cube). Then, we recursively traverse the octree, starting at the root and visiting all children that the lookup volume overlaps (usually just one child, but it can be up to eight children). This recursive traversal continues until the node contains voxels of approximately the same size as the lookup volume or a leaf node has been reached.

When we have reached the appropriate level in the octree, we determine which voxels overlap the lookup volume. We increment the lookup result by the voxel data multiplied by the fractional overlap of V_v and V_l (i.e., $(V_l \cap V_v)/V_l$). Empty voxels do not contribute to the lookup results.

If the lookup volume overlaps a neighbor octree branch that does not have as much detail as the branch that contains the lookup point **p**, we use the data at the available resolution. The weights of the data are still determined by the ratio of the overlap volume and the (fine or coarse) voxel volume. More information about lookups that overlap different levels of detail can be found in Benson and Davis [BD02].

Generally the lookup volume size will fall between two levels in the octree. In this case, we can choose to look up in both levels and linearly interpolate the resulting values; this ensures smooth transitions between different resolutions.

Figure 8.53 shows the result of re-rendering the Fiat Topolino by looking up the ambient occlusion in the brick map. These images are indistinguishable from the re-rendered images using the point cloud (see Figure 8.32) but use much less memory since the bricks are read on demand and stored in a fixed-size cache.

Brick Map Caching—3D Texture on Demand

Bricks are read from disk on demand and cached in memory. If the cache lookups are coherent, the cache has a high hit rate and caching is very efficient. Note that even though the individual bricks can be sparse, the cache slots need to have space for all 8^3 potential voxels in a brick since the same cache slot may be filled later with a dense brick. Our cache uses a least-recently used (LRU) replacement strategy. In our implementation, the brick map cache size can be selected by the user. The default size is 10 MB, corresponding to a capacity of 1,574 bricks if the brick data consist of three floats per voxel.

Brick Map Rendering

In addition to using the brick map data as textures to color surfaces, we can also render the brick maps directly. This has appealing properties since the brick map is

(a)   (b)

Figure 8.53: Re-rendering of the Fiat Topolino using ambient occlusion from a brick map: (*a*) ambient occlusion, and (*b*) ambient occlusion times diffuse color.

an inherent level-of-detail representation of the geometry. Since the bricks are stored in a fixed-size cache and only loaded on demand, we can render very, very complex scenes with this approach. As an extreme example, imagine a complex object defined as a very dense polygon mesh or a large collection of NURBS patches. Even if the object only covers a single pixel in the image, we still have to read the entire object definition into memory—and must keep it there until we are certain we won't need it anymore. In contrast, if the object is represented as a brick map, only the very coarsest brick will be read in.

The appropriate brick map level is determined from the screen size of the object. A reasonable convention is to choose the brick map level such that the brick voxels are approximately the size of an image pixel. Figure 8.54 shows a direct rendering of the Fiat Topolino ambient occlusion brick map at three different sizes, hence using different levels of the brick map.

Brick Map Ray Tracing

In addition to rendering directly visible brick maps, we can also ray trace them. The appropriate brick map level is determined from the ray differential. The ray differential describes the difference between a ray and its (real or imaginary) neighbor rays. Ray differentials were introduced for specular reflection by Igehy [Ige99] and extended to diffuse reflection by Suykens and Willems [SW01]. More information about the use of ray differentials can also be found in Christensen et al. [CLF+03]. We choose the brick map level where the brick voxels are approximately the size of the ray differential cross section.

Figure 8.54: Direct rendering of the Fiat Topolino ambient occlusion brick map at three different sizes.

The ray-brick intersection test can be done in several ways. A brute-force approach simply tests for intersection with each of the (up to 512) nonempty voxels in the brick. This is in fact the most efficient approach for bricks with very few nonempty voxels. For denser bricks it is more efficient to recursively subdivide the brick into octants and test the octants for intersection before recursing. The recursion stops after at most three levels when we reach the level of individual voxels. A voxel grid-stepping approach similar to Bresenham's [Bre65] line-drawing algorithm is also possible. Figure 8.55 shows ray tracing of the Fiat Topolino brick map using three different levels of the brick map.

Discussion

The description here of brick map construction and lookups is a more up-to-date version of the description in Christensen and Batali [CB04]. One major difference is that we now divide brick maps for surface data into six separate octrees instead of dealing with incoherent normals at the brick voxel level. We have also changed from box-shaped bricks (with a shape that followed the aspect ratio of the bounding box of the point cloud) to enforcing cubic bricks. The advantage is that each data point now typically gets inserted into fewer voxels since the volume we assign to each point is also cubic. We also improved the lookups to allow noncubic lookup volumes (i.e., anisotropic filtering).

An interesting area of future work would be to develop a brick map API and an interactive tool for editing brick maps.

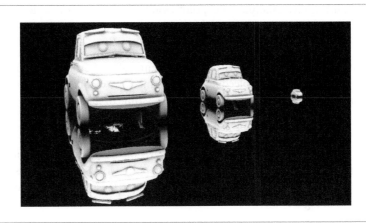

Figure 8.55: Direct rendering and ray-traced reflection of the Fiat Topolino ambient occlusion brick map at three different sizes. (Ray-traced reflection at bottom.)

8.4.9 SINGLE-BOUNCE GLOBAL ILLUMINATION

Tabellion and Lamorlette [TL04] presented a method for computing single-bounce global illumination. Their method is implemented in the PDI/Dreamworks proprietary in-house renderer and was first used in the production of the movie *Shrek 2*. It is exciting that global illumination is finally being used for mainstream computer-generated movie production.

Their method bakes diffusely reflected direct illumination into 2D surface textures. It then samples the hemisphere above each point using final gathering and irradiance interpolation (similar to the photon map description in Section 8.4.7) and uses the 2D texture values at the ray hit points. Here we present a similar, but easier to use, workflow based on point clouds and brick maps.

Step 1: Baking Diffusely Reflected Direct Illumination
The first step in this method is to bake the diffusely reflected direct illumination as in the Monstropolis example in Section 8.4.3. However, we need to ensure that points are being baked out for every surface that should bleed color onto the surfaces that are visible in the final image—even surfaces are not themselves visible in the final image. To ensure this, we zoom out to include the entire scene in the view. We also need to ensure that all surfaces are rendered, even if they are obscured by other objects or are facing away from the camera. The result is a collection of point clouds similar to the ones in Figures 8.34 and 8.35.

In the Monstropolis example, the point-cloud files now have a total size of 4.5 GB—more than the memory of our current desktop PC. So the point clouds obviously wouldn't fit if we were to read them all in.

The point clouds can be manipulated independently after they are generated. If, for example, we want more color bleeding from an object, we could load the point cloud into an interactive 3D paint package and increase some or all of the colors.

Step 2: Generating Brick Maps

The next step is to generate a brick map for each of the direct illumination point clouds. In the Monstropolis example, there are 40 point clouds and 40 corresponding brick maps. Figure 8.56 shows two of the brick maps; these correspond to the two point clouds in Figure 8.35.

The total size of the 40 brick map files is 230 MB—a significant reduction from the 4.5 GB for the point-cloud files. We call this collection of brick maps a *brick atlas of diffusely reflected direct illumination.*

Step 3: Rendering

Figure 8.57 shows a final gather rendering of the entire scene. We look up in the brick atlas of diffusely reflected direct illumination at the final gather ray hit points. Note

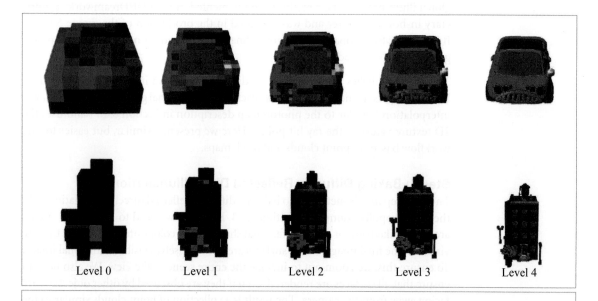

Level 0   Level 1   Level 2   Level 3   Level 4

Figure 8.56: Brick maps for a car and a building.

Figure 8.57: Monstropolis city block with single-bounce global illumination: direct illumination from the sun and sky, and indirect illumination computed using final gathering and the brick atlas of diffusely reflected direct illumination. (Copyright © Disney/Pixar.)

the high quality of the indirect illumination in the shaded areas, for example, the houses on the left side of the street. There is also subtle color bleeding from the red car onto the street. Rendering this image took 5.6 hours on a 2 GHz Apple G5 with 2 GB memory and required 429 million final gather rays and 3.8 million shadow rays. During rendering, the scene was divided into 636,000 surface patches, which corresponds to 325 million triangles at maximum tessellation rate. The brick cache size was set to 100 MB, corresponding to around 13,600 brick slots in the cache. There were 2.7 billion brick cache lookups with a hit rate of 99.8%.

Discussion
The method presented here is easier to use than Tabellion and Lamorlette's method since it does not require parameterized surfaces and the appropriate texture resolution is chosen automatically.

8.4.10 THE RADIOSITY ATLAS FOR GLOBAL ILLUMINATION

Photon mapping provides a more general global illumination method with multiple bounces of global illumination. Here we extend the optimized photon-mapping method discussed in Section 8.4.7 to enable it to handle more complex scenes.

Step 1: Photon Tracing

In the first step, we divide the objects into groups, just as in the previous section. Each group gets a separate photon map. Let's look at the Monstropolis scene again. Photon tracing results in 52 million photons stored in total. Figure 8.58 shows the photon maps for the Monstropolis scene. For clarity, the figure only shows 0.1% of the photons in the photon maps. We call a collection of photon maps a *photon atlas*.

Figure 8.59 shows two of the photon maps for the Monstropolis scene in more detail. Both the photon powers and the diffuse surface colors are shown. The photon map for the car contains 76,000 photons, while the photon map for the building contains 2.2 million photons. The photon powers get a green tint when refracted through the windshield. Also notice the red and blue diffusely reflected photons on the building.

Step 2: Photon Map Sorting and Radiosity Estimation

As in Section 8.4.7, we sort the photons and precompute the radiosity at each photon location. We do this independently for each photon map. Figure 8.60 shows two of the radiosity point clouds for the Monstropolis scene.

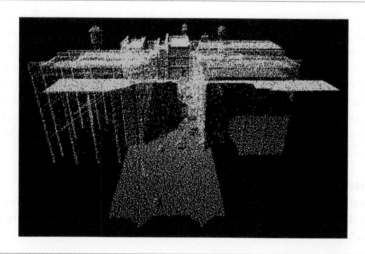

Figure 8.58: Coarse photon atlas for the Monstropolis scene. The photon powers are shown.

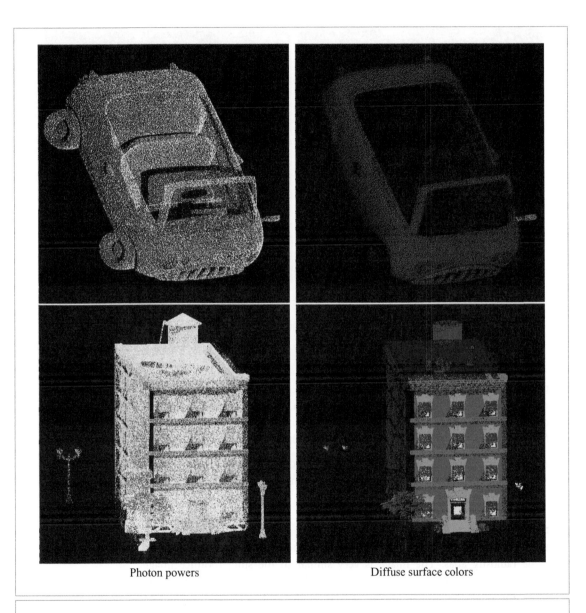

Photon powers   Diffuse surface colors

Figure 8.59: Photon maps for the car and building.

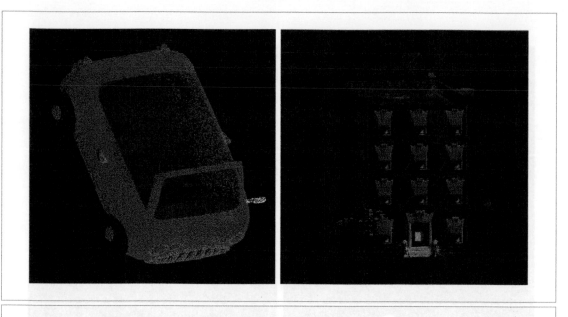

Figure 8.60: Radiosity point clouds for the car and building.

Step 3: Generating Brick Maps

The next step is to compute a brick map representation of each of the radiosity point clouds. We call this collection of radiosity brick maps a *radiosity brick atlas* or simply a *radiosity atlas*.[1] Two of the radiosity brick maps are shown in Figure 8.61.

Figure 8.62 shows the entire scene rendered with radiosity from the radiosity atlas. This image gives a rough indication of the global illumination in the scene, but it is far too noisy for use in a movie.

Step 4: Rendering

Figure 8.63 shows a final gather rendering of the scene. This image was computed using the radiosity atlas. The image is very similar to the single-bounce image in Figure 8.57, but a bit brighter due to the multiple bounces of illumination. Rendering this image took 5.7 hours on a 2 GHz Apple G5. It required the shooting of 413 million final gather rays and 3.8 million shadow rays. There were 3.4 billion brick cache lookups with a hit rate of 99.9%.

---

1   The radiosity terminology denotes that the data in the point clouds and brick maps are radiosities; it does not imply that they have been computed with a finite element radiosity method.

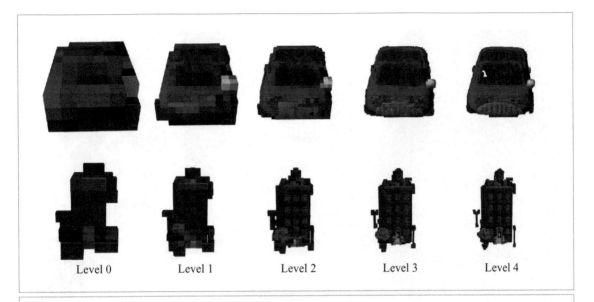

Level 0   Level 1   Level 2   Level 3   Level 4

Figure 8.61: Radiosity brick maps for the car and building.

Figure 8.62: The Monstropolis scene rendered with radiosity from the radiosity atlas.

Figure 8.63: Monstropolis city block with global illumination: direct illumination from the sun and sky, and indirect illumination computed using final gathering and the radiosity atlas. (Copyright © Disney/Pixar.)

Discussion

As shown in this section, the use of radiosity brick maps allows us to extend the photon-mapping method to compute multibounce global illumination in very complex scenes. The radiosity-atlas method presented here is a slight extension of the irradiance-atlas method introduced by Christensen and Batali [CB04].

It is our hope that this method, along with the method presented in Section 8.4.9, will contribute to more widespread use of global illumination in movie production.

8.4.11 VOLUME DATA

The previous sections have been concerned with data on surfaces. However, point clouds and brick maps are also immensely useful for volume data. This section shows an example of the computation of illumination in a volume.

Step 1: Baking Volume Data

Computing illumination and light scattering in a nonhomogeneous volume can be very time consuming. The computation can be accelerated significantly by precomputing the volume scattering coefficients and direct illumination at sample points in the volume.

Figure 8.64a shows a point cloud of turbulent smoke density values. The data have been generated by a ray marcher that computes the smoke density and writes it out for each ray step. But the data could come from a number of other sources as well. Figure 8.64b shows a point cloud of illumination values inside a cube. The cube is illuminated by a spotlight, and there is a sphere inside the cube casting a shadow. Each point cloud has around 1.2 million data points.

Step 2: Generating Brick Maps

These point clouds are then converted to volume brick maps using the same algorithm as for surface brick maps. These brick maps are shown in Figure 8.65. The bricks are dense since there are data points in the entire volume.

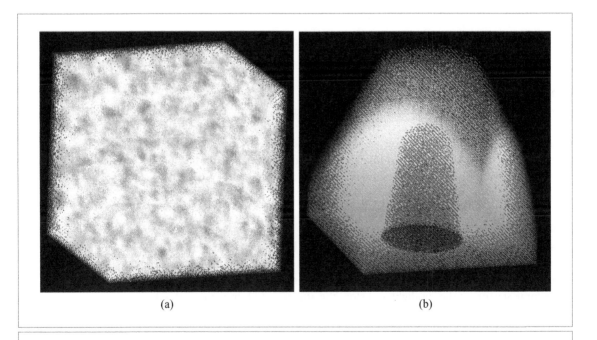

(a)   (b)

Figure 8.64: Volume point clouds: (*a*) turbulent smoke density, and (*b*) direct illumination by spotlight.

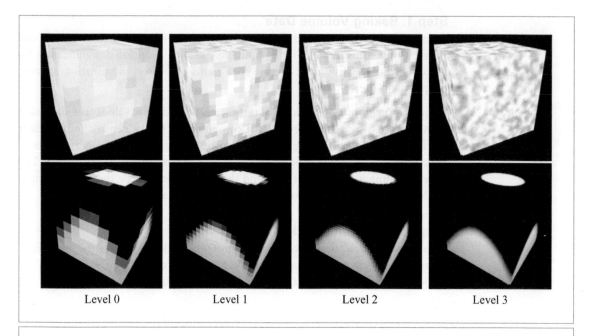

Level 0   Level 1   Level 2   Level 3

Figure 8.65: Volume brick maps of smoke density and direct illumination values.

Step 3: Rendering

Now we can render the illuminated smoky volume using ray marching and brick map lookups along the way. Each ray is marched from the camera through the volume in small steps. At each step we attenuate the contribution of the following steps (depending on the local smoke density) and add the contribution of the illumination from the light source being scattered in this little part of the volume. The resulting image is shown in Figure 8.66.

Discussion

This example does not take into account that the light from the spotlight gets attenuated as it passes through the smoke before it is scattered toward the camera. In order to compute that effect, the most efficient approach is to ray march through the volume starting at the spotlight and store the attenuated illumination value for each ray step.

Another application of volume point clouds is for photon map global illumination in volumes. Details about this are described in Jensen and Christensen [JC98].

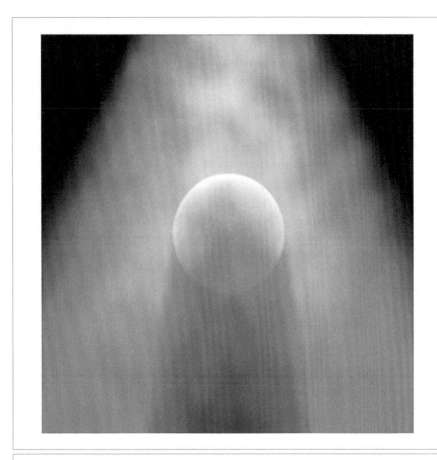

Figure 8.66: Illuminated smoky volume.

8.4.12 CONCLUSION

The production of computer-generated movies and special effects requires tools that can handle very complex scenes and very large datasets. Recently 3D point data are being used more and more in movie production. In this section I have provided an overview of some of the current methods that use 3D point data, and have also described some new methods that seem promising.

Point clouds are used for storing information independent of the view direction, surface type, and surface parameterization. They are used for subsurface scattering and can be used for fast, approximate ambient occlusion and global illumination. Photon maps and radiosity point clouds are other examples of useful point clouds.

Point clouds are simple to generate but not ideal for reading back in. In contrast, brick maps combine the best properties of 3D point clouds and 2D textures, and are much more suitable for reading large datasets than point clouds are. Brick maps can also be rendered and ray traced directly, providing a new geometric primitive that is inherently well suited to level-of-detail representation of objects. Brick maps are useful for storing any kind of surface data, for example, global illumination values. Using a radiosity (brick) atlas enables global illumination computation in very complex scenes.

More details about point clouds, brick maps, ambient occlusion, global illumination, and subsurface scattering, as well as scene files and shader examples, can be found in the PRMan application notes. Another good source of information is the SIGGRAPH 2003 RenderMan course notes [Bat03].

Copyright

All images from *Monsters, Inc.* and *Cars* are copyright © Disney Enterprises, Inc. and Pixar Animation Studios.

BIBLIOGRAPHY

[AA03a]   Anders Adamson and Marc Alexa. Approximating and intersecting surfaces from points. In *SGP 2003: Proceedings of the Eurographics/ACM SIGGRAPH Symposium on Geometry Processing*, pages 230–239. Eurographics Association, 2003.

[AA03b]   Anders Adamson and Marc Alexa. Ray-tracing point-set surfaces. In *Proceedings of Shape Modeling International*, pages 272–279, 2003.

[AA04a]   Anders Adamson and Marc Alexa. Approximating bounded, nonorientable surfaces from points. In *Proceedings of Shape Modeling International 2004*. IEEE Computer Society, 2004, accepted for publication.

[AA04b]   Anders Adamson and Marc Alexa. On normals and projection operators for surfaces defined by point sets. In *Proceedings of the Eurographics/ACM SIGGRAPH Symposium on Point-based Graphics*, pages 149–156. Eurographics Association, 2004.

[aaa]   *DIVA—Double Interferometer for Visual Astrometry.* http://astro.uni-tuebingen.de/groups/diva/.

[AB99]   Nina Amenta and Marshall Bern. Surface reconstruction by Voronoi filtering. *Discrete and Computational Geometry*, 22:481–504, 1999.

[ABCO+01]   Marc Alexa, Johannes Behr, Daniel Cohen-Or, Shachar Fleishman, David Levin, and Cláudio T. Silva. Point set surfaces. In *Proceedings of the Conference on Visualization 2001*, pages 21–28, 2001.

[ABCO+03]   Marc Alexa, Johannes Behr, Daniel Cohen-Or, Shachar Fleishman, David Levin, and Cláudio T. Silva. Computing and rendering point set surfaces. *IEEE Transactions on Computer Graphics and Visualization*, 9(1):3–15, 2003.

[ABK98]   Nina Amenta, Marshall Bern, and Manolis Kamvysselis. A new Voronoi-based surface-reconstruction algorithm. In *Computer Graphics*, SIGGRAPH 1998 Proceedings, pages 415–421, 1998.

[ABL95]   Maneesh Agrawala, Andrew C. Beers, and Marc Levoy. 3D painting on scanned surfaces. In *1995 Symposium on Interactive 3D Graphics*, pages 145–150, April 1995.

[ACDL02]   Nina Amenta, Sunghee Choi, Tamal K. Dey, and Naveen Leekha. A simple algorithm for homeomorphic surface reconstruction. *International Journal of Computational Geometry and Its Applications*, 12(1–2):125–141, Feb, Apr 2002.

[ACK01a]   Nina Amenta, Sunghee Choi, and Ravi Kolluri. The power crust. In *Proceedings of the ACM Symposium on Solid Modeling*, pages 249–260, 2001.

[ACK01b]   Nina Amenta, Sunghee Choi, and Ravi Kolluri. The power crust, unions of balls, and the medial axis transform. *Computational Geometry: Theory and Applications*, 19(2–3):127–153, 2001.

[AD01]   Pierre Alliez and Mathieu Desbrun. Progressive compression for lossless transmission of triangle meshes. In *Computer Graphics*, SIGGRAPH 2001 Proceedings, pages 195–202. ACM, August 2001.

[AD03]   Bart Adams and Philip Dutré. Interactive Boolean operations on surfel-bounded solids. In *ACM Transactions on Graphics*, SIGGRAPH 2003 Proceedings, 22(3):651–656, July 2003.

[AF00]   Sunil Arya and Ho-Yam Addy Fu. Expected-case complexity of approximate nearest-neighbor searching. In *Proceedings of the Eleventh Annual ACM-SIAM Symposium on Discrete Algorithms*, pages 379–388. Society for Industrial and Applied Mathematics, 2000.

[AG00]   Anthony A. Apodaca and Larry Gritz. *Advanced RenderMan: Creating CGI for Motion Pictures*. Morgan Kaufmann Publishers, San Francisco, CA, 2000.

[AH05]   Arul Asirvatham and Hugues Hoppe. Terrain rendering using GPU-based geometry clipmaps *GPU Gems 2*. Addison-Wesley, Boston, MA, pages 109–122, March 2005.

[AK89]   James Arvo and David Kirk. A survey of ray-tracing acceleration techniques. pages 201–262, 1989.

[AK04]   Nina Amenta and Yong Kil. Defining point-set surfaces. In *ACM Transactions on Graphics*, SIGGRAPH 2004 Proceedings, 23(3):264–270, 2004.

[AKP+05]   Bart Adams, Richard Keiser, Mark Pauly, Leonidas J. Guibas, Markus Gross, and Philip Dutré. Efficient ray tracing of deforming point-sampled surfaces. *Computer Graphics Forum*, 24(3):677–684, 2005.

[Ali01]   Alias Wavefront. Maya. http://www.aliaswavefront.com, 2001, cited October 2005.

[AM93]   Sunil Arya and David M. Mount. Algorithms for fast vector quantization. *Data Compression Conference*, pages 381–390. IEEE Computer Society Press, 1993.

[AMH02]   Tomas Akenine-Möller and Eric Haines. *Real-time Rendering*, 2nd ed. A. K. Peters Ltd., 2002.

[AMS90]   Steven Ashby, Thomas Manteuffel, and Paul Saylor. A taxonomy for conjugate gradient methods. *J. Numer. Anal.*, 27:1542–1568, 1990.

[And95a]   John D. Anderson. *Computational Fluid Dynamics*. McGraw-Hill, 1995.

[And95b]   Ted L. Anderson. *Fracture Mechanics*. CRC Press, 1995.

[App85]   Andrew W. Appel. An efficient program for many-body simulation. *SIAM Journal on Scientific and Statistical Computing*, 6(1):85–103, 1985.

[ARR⁺97]   Tetsuo Asano, Desh Ranjan, Thomas Roos, Emo Welzl, and Peter Widmayer. Space-filling curves and their use in the design of geometric data structures. *Theoretical Computer Science*, 181:3–15, 1997.

[AS94]   Pankaj K. Agarwal and Subhash Suri. Surface approximation and geometric partitions. In *Proceedings of the Fifth Annual ACM-SIAM Symposium on Discrete Algorithms*, pages 24–33. Society for Industrial and Applied Mathematics, 1994.

[AWD⁺04]   Bart Adams, Martin Wicke, Phil Dutré, Markus Gross, Mark Pauly, and Matthias Teschner. Interactive 3D painting on point-sampled objects. In *Proceedings of the Eurographics Symposium on Point-based Graphics*, pages 57–66, 2004.

[Bar84]   Alan H. Barr. Global and local deformations of solid primitives. In *Computer Graphics*, SIGGRAPH 84 Proceedings, pages 21–30. ACM Press, New York, NY, 1984.

[Bat03]   Dana Batali, ed. *SIGGRAPH 2003 Course Note #9: RenderMan, Theory and Practice*. ACM SIGGRAPH, 2003.

[BBM⁺01]   Chris Buehler, Michael Bosse, Leonard McMillan, Steven J. Gortler, and Michael Cohen. Unstructured lumigraph rendering. In *Computer Graphics*, SIGGRAPH 2001 Proceedings, pages 425–432, 2001.

[BC00]   Jean-Daniel Boissonnat and Frédéric Cazals. Smooth shape reconstruction via natural neighbor interpolation of distance functions. In *Proceedings of the 16th Annual Symposium on Computational Geometry (SCG-00)*, pages 223–232. ACM Press, New York, NY, June 12–14, 2000.

[BC02a]   William A. Barrett and Alan S. Cheney. Object-based image editing. In *ACM Transactions on Graphics*, SIGGRAPH 2002 Proceedings, 21(3):777–784, July 2002.

[BC02b]   Jean-Daniel Boissonnat and Frédéric Cazals. Smooth surface reconstruction via natural neighbour interpolation of distance functions. *Computational Geometry: Theory and Applications*, 22(1–3):185–203, 2002.

[BD02]   David Benson and Joel Davis. Octree textures. In *ACM Transactions on Graphics*, SIGGRAPH 2002 Proceedings, 21(3):785–790, 2002.

[Bea02]   Paul Beardsley. Calibration of stereo cameras for a turntable 3D scanner. Technical report, TR 2002/20, MERL, 2002.

[Ben75]   Jon Louis Bentley. Multidimensional binary search trees used for associative searching. *Communications of the ACM*, 18(9):509–517, 1975.

[BER76]   James R. Bitner, Gideon Erlich, and Edward M. Reingold. Efficient generation of the binary-reflected Gray code and its applications. *Communications of the ACM*, 19(9):517–521, 1976.

[Bes88]   Paul Besl. Active optical-range imaging sensors. *Machine Vision and Applications*, 1:127–152, 1988.

[BF01]   Samuel R. Buss and Jay P. Fillmore. Spherical averages and applications to spherical splines and interpolation. *ACM Transactions on Graphics*, 20(2):95–126, 2001.

[BGTG03]   Daniel Bielser, Pascal Glardon, Matthias Teschner, and Markus Gross. A state machine for real-time cutting of tetrahedral meshes. *Pacific Graphics*, pages 377–386, 2003.

[BH86]   Josh Barnes and Piet Hut. A hierarchical $O(N \log N)$ force-calculation algorithm. *Nature*, 324(4):446–449, 1986.

[BHZK05]   Mario Botsch, Alexander Hornung, Matthias Zwicker, and Leif Kobbelt. High-quality surface splatting on today's GPUs. In *Proceedings of Symposium on Point-based Graphics 2005*, pages 17–24, 2005.

[BK87]   Kim L. Boyer and Avinash C. Kak. Color-encoded structured light for rapid active ranging. *IEEE Transactions on Pattern Analysis and Machine Intelligence (PAMI)*, 9(1):14–28, January 1987.

[BK02]   Stephan Bischoff and Leif Kobbelt. Ellipsoid decomposition of 3D models. In *Proceedings of 3D Data-processing Visualization and Transmission*, pages 480–488, 2002.

[BK03]   Mario Botsch and Leif Kobbelt. High-quality point-based rendering on modern GPUs. *Pacific Graphics 2003*, pages 335–343, 2003.

[BK04]   Mario Botsch and Leif Kobbelt. An intuitive framework for real-time freeform modeling. In *ACM Transactions on Graphics*, SIGGRAPH 2004 Proceedings, 23(3):630–634, 2004.

[BK05]   Mario Botsch and Leif Kobbelt. Real-time shape editing using radial basis functions. In *Computer Graphics Forum*, Eurographics 2005 Proceedings, 24(3):611–621, 2005.

[BKMK01]   Peter N. Belhumeur, Melissa Koudelka, Sebastian Magda, and David J. Kriegman. Image-based modeling and rendering of surfaces with arbitrary BRDFs. In *Proceedings of Computer Vision and Pattern Recognition*, Kauai, HI, pages 568–575, December 2001.

[BKO+96]   Ted Belytschko, Y. Krongauz, D. Organ, Michael Fleming, and Petr Krysl. Meshless methods: An overview and recent developments. *Computer Methods in Applied Mechanics and Engineering*, 139(3):3–47, 1996.

[BLG94]   Ted Belytschko, Y. Lu, and L. Gu. Element-free galerkin methods. *Int. J. Numer. Meth. Eng.*, 37:229–256, 1994.

[Bli78]   James Frederick Blinn. *Computer display of curved surfaces*. Ph.D. thesis, 1978.

[Bli82a]   James Frederick Blinn. A generalization of algebraic surface drawing. *ACM Transactions on Graphics*, 1(3):235–256, 1982.

[Bli82b]   James Frederick Blinn. Light-reflection functions for simulation of clouds and dusty surfaces. In *Computer Graphics*, SIGGRAPH 1982 Proceedings, pages 21–29. ACM Press, New York, NY, 1982.

[BLL03]   William Baxter, Yuanxin Liu, and Ming C. Lin. A viscous paint model for interactive applications. Technical report, University of North Carolina at Chapel Hill, 2003.

[BM58]   George E. P. Box and Mervin E. Muller. A note on the generation of random normal deviates. *Annals of Mathematical Statistics*, 28:610–611, 1958.

[BM92]   Paul J. Besl and Neil D. McKay. A method for registration of 3D shapes. *IEEE Transactions on Pattern Analysis and Machince Intelligence*, 14(2):239–256, 1992.

[BM97]   I. Babuska and Jens M. Melenk. The partition of unity method. *International Journal of Numerical Methods in Engineering*, 40:727–758, 1997.

[BMR+99]   Fausto Bernardini, Joshua Mittleman, Holly Rushmeir, Cláudio Silva, and Gabriel Taubin. The ball-pivoting algorithm for surface reconstruction. *IEEE Transactions on Vision and Computer Graphics*, 5(4):349–359, 1999.

[BMR01a, b]   Fausto Bernardini, Ioana M. Martin, and Holly Rushmeier. High-quality texture reconstruction from multiple scans. *IEEE Transactions on Visualization and Computer Graphics*, 7(4):318–332, 2001.

[BMS98]   Joan Batlle, El Mustapa Mouaddib, and Joaquim Salvi. Recent progress in coded structured light as a technique to solve the correspondence problem: A survey. *Pattern Recognition*, 31(7):963–982, July 1998.

[Boi84]   Jean-Daniel Boissonnat. Geometric structures for three-dimensional shape reconstruction. *ACM Transactions on Computer Graphics*, 3:266–286, 1984.

[BR86]   J. U. Brackbill and H. M. Ruppel. Flip: A method for adaptively zoned, particle-in-cell calculations of fluid flows in two dimensions. *J. Comput. Phys.*, 65(2):314–343, 1986.

[Bre65]   Jack E. Bresenham. Algorithm for computer control of a digital plotter. *IBM Systems Journal*, 4(1):25–30, July 1965.

[BSGL96]   Robert Bergevin, Marc Soucy, Hervé Gagnon, and Denis Laurendeau. Towards a general multiview registration technique. *IEEE Transactions on Pattern Analysis and Machine Intelligence (PAMI)*, 18(5):540–547, May 1996.

[BSK04]   Mario Botsch, Michael Spernat, and Leif Kobbelt. Phong splatting. In *Proceedings of Symposium on Point-based Graphics 2004*, pages 25–32, 2004.

[BSLM01]   William Baxter, Vincent Scheib, Ming C. Lin, and Dinesh Manocha. DAB: Interactive haptic painting with 3D virtual brushes. In *Computer Graphics*, SIGGRAPH 2001 Proceedings, pages 461–468, 2001.

[Buh03]   Martin D. Buhmann, *Radial Basis Functions: Theory and Implementations*. Cambridge University Press, 2003.

[Bun05]   Michael Bunnell. Dynamic ambient occlusion and indirect lighting, *GPU Gems 2*, pages 223–233. Addison-Wesley, Boston, MA, 2005.

[BVZ01]   Yuri Boykov, Olga Veksler, and Ramin Zabih. Fast approximate energy minimization via graph cuts. *IEEE Transactions on Pattern Analysis and Machine Intelligence (PAMI)*, 23(11):1222–1239, November 2001.

[BW00]   Dmitry Brodsky and Benjamin Watson. Model simplification through refinement. *Graphics Interface*, pages 221–228, May 2000.

[BWK02]   Mario Botsch, Andreas Wiratanaya, and Leif Kobbelt. Efficient high-quality rendering of point-sampled geometry. In *Proceedings Eurographics Workshop on Rendering*, pages 53–64, 2002.

[BWL04]   William Baxter, JeremyWendt, and Ming C. Lin. IMPaSTo, a realistic, interactive model for paint. In *Proceedings of the Third International Symposium on Non-Photorealistic Animation and Rendering (NPAR) for Art and Entertainment*, 2004.

[Car80]   Loren Carpenter. Rendering of fractal curves and surfaces. In *Computer Graphics*, SIGGRAPH 1980 Proceedings, pages 9–15, 1980.

[Car84]   Loren Carpenter. The A-buffer, an antialiased hidden surface method. In *Computer Graphics*, SIGGRAPH 1984 Proceedings, pages 103–109, 1984.

[Cat74]   Edwin E. Catmull. *A Subdivision Algorithm for Computer Display of Curved Surfaces*. Ph.D. thesis, Department of Computer Science, University of Utah, December 1974.

[Cat78]   Edwin E. Catmull. A hidden-surface algorithm with antialiasing. In *Computer Graphics*, SIGGRAPH 1978 Proceedings, pages 6–11, 1978.

[CAZ01]   Jonathan D. Cohen, Daniel G. Aliaga, and Weiqiang Zhang. Hybrid simplification: Combining multiresolution polygon and point rendering. *IEEE Visualization 2001*, pages 37–44, October 2001.

[CB04]   Per H. Christensen and Dana Batali. An irradiance atlas for global illumination in complex production scenes. In *Rendering Techniques*, Proceedings of the 2004 Eurographics Symposium on Rendering, pages 133–141, 2004.

[CBC+01]   Jonathan C. Carr, Richard K. Beatson, Jon B. Cherrie, Tim J. Mitchell, W. Richard Fright, Bruce C. McCallum, and Tim R. Evans. Reconstruction and representation of 3D objects with radial basis functions. In *Computer Graphics*, SIGGRAPH 2001 Proceedings, pages 67–76, July 2001.

[CBCG02]   Wei-Chao Chen, Jeans-Yves Bouguet, Michael H. Chu, and Radek Grzeszczuk. Light field mapping: Efficient representation and hardware rendering of surface light fields. In *ACM Transactions on Graphics*, SIGGRAPH 2002 Proceedings, 21(3):447–456, July 2002.

[CC78]   Edwin E. Catmull and James H. Clark. Recursively generated b-spline surfaces on arbitrary topological meshes. *Computer Aided Design*, 10(6):350–355, 1978.

[CCC87]   Robert L. Cook, Loren Carpenter, and Edwin Catmull. The Reyes image-rendering architecture. In *Computer Graphics*, SIGGRAPH 87 Proceedings, pages 95–102, 1987.

[CDL+96]   Bradford Chamberlain, Tony DeRose, Dani Lischinski, David Salesin, and John Snyder. Fast rendering of complex environments using a spatial hierarchy. In *Proceedings of Graphics Interface 1996*, pages 132–141, 1996.

[CH85]   Brain Carrihill and Robert Hummel. Experiments with the intensity ratio depth sensor. *Computer Vision, Graphics, and Image Processing*, 32:337–358, 1985.

[CH99]   Chu-Song Chen and Yi-Ping Hung. RANSAC-based DARCES: A new approach to fast automatic registration of partially overlapping range images. *IEEE Transactions on Pattern Analysis and Machine Intelligence (PAMI)*, 21(11):1229–1234, November 1999.

[CH02]   Liviu Coconu and Hans-Christian Hege. Hardware-oriented point-based rendering of complex scenes. In *Proceedings Eurographics Workshop on Rendering*, pages 43–52, 2002.

[Che95]   Shenchang Eric Chen. Quicktime VR—an image-based approach to virtual environment navigation. In *Computer Graphics*, SIGGRAPH 1995 Proceedings, pages 29–38. ACM Press, Addison-Wesley, 1995.

[CHP+79]   Charles Csuri, Ronald Hackathorn, Rick Parent, Wayne Carlson, and Marc Howard. Towards an interactive high visual complexity animation system. In *Computer Graphics*, SIGGRAPH 1979 Proceedings, pages 289–299, 1979.

[Chr99]   Per H. Christensen. Faster photon map global illumination. *Journal of Graphics Tools*, 4(3):1–10, 1999. (Reprinted with additional comments in Ronen Barzel, ed., *Graphics Tools—the jgt Editors' Choice,* pages 241–251. A. K. Peters, 2005.)

[Chr02]   Per H. Christensen. Photon mapping tricks. In Henrik Wann Jensen, ed., *SIGGRAPH 2002 Course Note #43: A Practical Guide to Global Illumination Using Photon Mapping*, pages 93–121, 2002.

[Chu96]   T. J. Chung. *Applied Continuum Mechanics.* Cambridge University Press, UK, 1996.

[CKS98]   Dalit Caspi, Nahum Kiryati, and Joseph Shamir. Range imaging with adaptive color structured light. *IEEE Transactions on Pattern Analysis and Machine Intelligence (PAMI)*, 20(5):470–480, May 1998.

[CL95]   Brian Curless and Marc Levoy. Better optical triangulation through space-time analysis. In *ICCV 1995: Proceedings of the Fifth International Conference on Computer Vision*, pages 987–994, IEEE Computer Society, Washington, DC, 1995.

[CL96]   Brian Curless and Marc Levoy. A volumetric method for building complex models from range images. In *Computer Graphics*, SIGGRAPH 1996 Proceedings, pages 303–312, 1996.

[CL05]   Frederic Chazal and Andre Lieutier. Topology guaranteeing surface reconstruction and medial axis approximation from noisy data. Preprint 429, Institut de Mathmatiques de Bourgogne, France, May 2005.

[Cla76]   James Clark. Hierarchical geometric models for visible surface algorithms. *Communications of the ACM*, 19(10):547–554, 1976.

[Cla79]   James Clark. A fast scan-line algorithm for rendering parametric surfaces. In *Computer Graphics*, SIGGRAPH 1979 Proceedings, 13:7–11, 1979.

[Cle85]   William S. Cleveland. *The Elements of Graphing Data.* Wadsworth Inc., Boston, MA, 1985.

[CLF+03]   Per H. Christensen, David Laur, Julian Fong, Wayne L. Wooten, and Dana Batali. Ray differentials and multiresolution geometry caching for distribution ray tracing in complex scenes. In *Computer Graphics Forum*, Eurographics 2003 Proceedings, 22(3):543–552, 2003.

[CLL+88]   Harvey E. Cline, William E. Lorensen, Siegwalt Ludke, Carl R. Crawford, and Bruce C. Teeter. Two algorithms for the three-dimensional reconstruction of tomograms. *Medical Physics*, 15(3):320–327, June 1988.

[CLRS01]   Thomas Cormen, Charles Leiserson, Ronald L. Rivest, and Clifford Stein. *Introduction to Algorithms*, 2nd ed., MIT Press, Boston, MA, 2001.

[CLSS97]   Per H. Christensen, Dani Lischinski, Eric J. Stollnitz, and David H. Salesin. Clustering for glossy global illumination. *ACM Transactions on Graphics*, 16(1):3–33, January 1997.

[CM92]   Yang Chen and Gérard Medioni. Object modeling by registration of multiple range images. *Image and Vision Computing*, 10(3):145–155, 1992.

[CM94]   Yang Chen and Gérard Medioni. Surface description of complex objects from multiple range images. In *Proceedings of Computer Vision and Pattern Recognition*, pages 153–158, Seattle, WA, June 1994.

[CN01]   Baoquan Chen and Minh Xuan Nguyen. POP: A hybrid point and polygon rendering system for large data. Proceedings of *IEEE Visualization 2001*, pages 45–52, October 2001.

[CNGF04]   Daniel Cotting, Martin Naef, Markus Gross, and Henry Fuchs. Embedding imperceptible patterns into projected images for simultaneous acquisition and display. Proceedings of *ISMAR 2004*, pages 100–109, 2004.

[CNW87]   John G. Cleary, Radford M. Neal, and Ian H. Witten. Arithmetic coding for data compression. *Communications of the ACM*, 30(6):520–540, June 1987.

[COCK+01]   Daniel Cohen-Or, Yiorgos Chrysanthou, Vladlen Koltun, Fredo Durand, Ned Greene, and Cláudio T. Silva. Visibility, problems, techniques, and applications. SIGGRAPH 2001 Course Notes, Los Angeles, CA, 2001.

[COLR99]   Daniel Cohen-Or, David Levin, and Offir Remez. Progressive compression of arbitrary triangular meshes. In *Proceedings of IEEE Visualization 1999*, pages 67–72, 1999.

[Coo84]   Robert L. Cook. Shade trees. In *Computer Graphics*, SIGGRAPH 84 Proceeding, pages 223–231, 1984.

[Coo86]   Robert L. Cook. Stochastic sampling in computer graphics. *ACM Transactions on Graphics*, 5(1):51–72, 1986.

[CPC84]   Robert L. Cook, Thomas Porter, and Loren Carpenter. Distributed ray tracing. In *Computer Graphics*, SIGGRAPH 1984 Proceedings, pages 137–145, 1984.

[CRS98]   Paulo Cignoni, Claudio Rocchini, and Roberto Scopigno. Metro: Measuring error on simplified surfaces. In *Computer Graphics Forum*, pages 167–174, 1998.

[CSAD04]   David Cohen-Steiner, Pierre Alliez, and Mathieu Desbrun. Variational shape approximation. *ACM Transactions on Graphics*, SIGGRAPH 2004 Proceedings, 23(3):905–914, 2004.

[CSM03]   David Cohen-Steiner and Jean-Marie Morvan. Restricted Delaunay triangulations and normal cycle. In *19th Annual ACM Symposium on Computational Geometry*, pages 312–321, 2003.

[CTMS03]   Joel Carranza, Christian Theobalt, Marcus A. Magnor, and Hans-Peter Seidel. Free-viewpoint video of human actors. *ACM Transactions on Graphics*, SIGGRAPH 2003 Proceedings, 22(3):569–577, 2003.

[CW93]   Shenchang Eric Chen and Lance Williams. View interpolation for image synthesis. In *Computer Graphics*, SIGGRAPH 1993 Proceedings, pages 279–288, Anaheim, CA, August 1993.

[CZH+00]   Yung-Yu Chuang, Douglas E. Zongker, Joel Hindordd, Brian Curless, David H. Salesin, and Richard Szeliski. Environment matting extensions: Towards higher accuracy and real-time capture. In *Computer Graphics*, SIGGRAPH 2000 Proceedings, pages 121–130, 2000.

[dB00]   Willem H. de Boer. Fast terrain rendering using geometrical mipmapping. FlipCode, http://www.flipcode.com/articles/ article_geomipmaps.pdf, 2000, cited March 2005.

[dC76]   Manfredo Perdigao do Carmo. *Differential Geometry of Curves and Surfaces*. Prentice Hall, 1976.

[DC96]   Mathieu Desbrun and Marie-Paule Cani. Smoothed particles: A new paradigm for animating highly deformable bodies. In *6th Eurographics Workshop on Computer Animation and Simulation 1996*, pages 61–76, 1996.

[DC01]   James Davis and Xing Chen. A laser-range scanner designed for minimum calibration complexity. In *Proceedings of the International Conference on 3D Digital Imaging and Modeling (3DIM)*, pages 91–98, 2001.

[DCG98]   Mathieu Desbrun and Marie-Paule Cani-Gascuel. Active implicit surface for animation. In *Proceedings of Graphics Interface*, pages 143–150, 1998.

[DCH88]   Robert A. Drebin, Loren Carpenter, and Pat Hanrahan. Volume rendering. In *Computer Graphics*, SIGGRAPH 1988 Proceedings, pages 65–71, 1988.

[DDG00]   Matthew Dickerson, Christian A. Duncan, and Michael T. Goodrich. K-d-trees are better when cut on the longest side. In *Proceedings European Symposium on Algorithms ESA 2000*, pages 179–190, 2000.

[Deb98]   Paul Debevec. Rendering synthetic objects into real scenes: Bridging traditional and image-based graphics with global illumination and high dynamic range photography. In *Computer Graphics*, SIGGRAPH 1998 Proceedings, pages 189–198, 1998.

[Dee95]   Michael F. Deering. Geometry compression. In *Computer Graphics*, SIGGRAPH 1995 Proceedings, ACM Press, pages 13–20, August 1995.

[DG00]   Olivier Devilliers and Pierre-Marie Gandoin. Geometric compression for interactive transmission. In *Proceedings of IEEE Visualization Conference*, pages 319–326. Computer Society Press, 2000.

[DG01]   Tamal K. Dey and Joachim Giesen. Detecting undersampling in surface reconstruction. In *Proceedings of the ACM Symposium on Computational Geometry*, pages 257–263, 2001.

[DG03]   Tamal K. Dey and Samrat Goswami. Tight cocone: A water-tight surface reconstructor. *Journal of Computing and Information Science in Engineering*, 3:302–307, 2003.

[DG04]   Tamal K. Dey and Samrat Goswami. Provable surface reconstruction from noisy samples. In *Proceedings of the Symposium on Computational Geometry*, pages 330–339, 2004.

[DGPR02]   David DeBry, Jonathan Gibbs, Devorah Petty, and Nate Robins. Painting and rendering textures on unparameterized models. *ACM Transactions on Graphics*, SIGGRAPH 2002 Proceedings, 21(3):763–768, 2002.

[DHS01]   Richard O. Duda, Peter E. Hart, and David G. Stork. *Pattern Classification*, 2nd ed., John Wiley & Sons, New York, NY, 2001.

[DHT+00]   Paul Debevec, Tim Hawkins, Chris Tchou, Haarm-Pieter Duiker, Westley Sarokin, and Mark Sagar. Acquiring the reflectance field of a human face. In *Computer Graphics*, SIGGRAPH 2000 Proceedings, pages 145–156, July 2000.

[DLS04]   Tamal Dey, Gang Li, and Jian Sun. Normal estimation for point clouds: A comparison study for a Voronoi-based method. In *Symposium on Geometry Processing*, pages 39–46, 2005.

[DM84]   Dan E. Dudgeon and Russel M. Mersereau. *Multidimensional Digital Signal Processing*. Prentice-Hall, Englewood-Cliffs, NJ, 1984.

[DM97]   Paul E. Debevec and Jitendra Malik. Recovering high-dynamic range-radiance maps from photographs. In *Computer Graphics*, SIGGRAPH 1997 Proceedings, pages 369–378, Los Angeles, CA, 1997.

[DMGL02]   James Davis, Stephen Marschner, Matt Garr, and Marc Levoy. Filling holes in complex surfaces using volumetric diffusion. In *Proceedings of the International Symposium on 3D Data Processing, Visualization, and Transmission (3DPVT)*, pages 428–438, 2002.

[DN96]   C. J. Davies and M. S. Nixon. Sensing surface discontinuities via coloured spots. In *Proceedings of the International Workshop on Image and Signal Processing*, pages 573–576, 1996.

[DNRR05]   James Davis, Diego Nehab, Ravi Ramamoorthi, and Szymon Rusinkiewicz. Spacetime stereo: A unifying framework for depth from triangulation. *IEEE Transactions on Pattern Analysis and Machine Intelligence (PAMI)*, 27(2):296–302, February 2005.

[DP01]   Disney Enterprises, Inc. and Pixar Animation Studios. *Monsters, Inc.,* 2001.

[DP06]   Disney Enterprises, Inc. and Pixar Animation Studios. *Cars,* 2006.

[DS05]   Tamal K. Dey and Jian Sun. An adaptive MLS surface for reconstruction with guarantees. In *IEEE Symposium on Geometry Processing*, pages 43–52, Vienna, Austria, July 2005.

[DST01]   Huong Quynh Dinh, Greg Slabaugh, and Greg Turk. Reconstructing surfaces using anisotropic basis functions. In *International Conference on Computer Vision (ICCV) 2001*, pages 606–613, Vancouver, Canada, July 2001.

[DTM96]   Paul E. Debevec, Camillo J. Taylor, and Jitendra Malik. Modeling and rendering architecture from photographs: A hybrid geometry- and image-based approach. In *Computer Graphics*, SIGGRAPH 1996 Proceedings, pages 11–20, August 1996.

[DTS02]   Huong Quynh Dinh, Greg Turk, and Greg Slabaugh. Reconstructing surfaces by volumetric regularization using radial basis functions. *IEEE Transactions on Pattern Analysis and Machine Intelligence*, 24(10): 1358–1371, October 2002.

[DVS03]   Carsten Dachsbacher, Christian Vogelgsang, and Marc Stamminger. Sequential point trees. In *ACM Transactions on Graphics*, SIGGRAPH 2003 Proceedings, pages 657–662. ACM Press, New York, NY, 2003.

[DWS⁺88]   Michael Deering, Stephanie Winner, Bic Schediwy, Chris Duffy, and Neil Hunt. The triangle processor and normal vector shader: A VLSI system for high-performance graphics. In *Computer Graphics*, SIGGRAPH 1988 Proceedings, pages 21–30, 1988.

[DYB98]   Paul Debevec, Yizhou Yu, and George Boshokov. Efficient view-dependent image-based rendering with projective texture-mapping. In *Proceedings of the 9th Eurographics Workshop on Rendering*, pages 105–116, Vienna, Austria, June 1998.

[Dyn87]   Nira Dyn. Interpolation of scattered data by radial basis functions. *Topics in Multivariate Approximation*. Academic Press, Boston, MA, 1987.

[Dyn89]   Nira Dyn. Interpolation and approximation by radial and related
             functions. *Approximation Theory VI*, vol. 1, pages 211–234. Academic
             Press, Boston, MA, 1989.

[Ede05]   Herbert Edelsbrunner. Surface reconstruction by wrapping finite point sets
             in space. *Ricky Pollack and Eli Goodman Festschrift*, pages 379–404.
             Springer-Verlag, New York, NY, 2005.

[ELF97]   David W. Eggert, Adele Lorusso, and Robert B. Fisher. Estimating 3D rigid
             body transformations: A comparison of four major algorithms. *Machine
             Vision and Applications*, 9:272–290, 1997.

[ELF05]   Douglas Enright, Frank Losasso, and Ronald Fedkiw. A fast and accurate
             semi-Lagrangian particle level set. *Computers and Structures*, 83:479–490,
             2005.

[EM94]   Herbert Edelsbrunner and Ernst P. Mücke. Three-dimensional alpha
             shapes. *ACM Transactions on Computer Graphics*, 13:43–72, 1994.

[EMF02]   Douglas Enright, Stephen Marschner, and Ronald Fedkiw. Animation and
             rendering of complex water surfaces. In *ACM Transactions on Graphics*,
             SIGGRAPH 2002 Proceedings, pages 736–744, 2002.

[Fau93]   Olivier Faugeras. *Three-dimensional Computer Vision: A Geometric
             Viewpoint*. MIT Press, Boston, MA, 1993.

[FBF77]   Jerome H. Friedman, Jon Louis Bentley, and Raphael Ari Finkel. An
             algorithm for finding best matches in logarithmic expected time. *ACM
             Transactions on Mathematical Software*, (3):209–226, 1977.

[FBLS05]   Martin Fuchs, Volker Blanz, Hendrik Lensch, and Hans-Peter Seidel.
             Reflectance from images: A model-based approach for human faces.
             Research Report MPI-I-2005-4-001, Max-Planck-Institut für Informatik,
             Stuhlsatzenhausweg 85, 66123 Saarbrücken, Germany, 2005. Accepted for
             publication in IEEE TVCG.

[FCOAS03]   Shachar Fleishman, Daniel Cohen-Or, Marc Alexa, and Cláudio T. Silva.
             Progressive point-set surfaces. *ACM Transactions on Graphics*, 22(4):
             997–1011, 2003.

[FCOS05]   Shachar Fleishman, Daniel Cohen-Or, and Cláudio T. Silva. Robust moving
             least squares fitting with sharp features. In *ACM Transactions on Graphics*,
             SIGGRAPH 2005 Proceedings; 24(3):544–552, 2005.

[FF01]   Nick Foster and Ronald Fedkiw. Practical animation of liquids. In
             Computer Graphics, SIGGRAPH 2001 Proceedings, pages 23–30, 2001.

[FFC82]   Alain Fournier, Donald Fussell, and Loren Carpenter. Computer rendering
             of stochastic models. *Communications of the ACM*, 25(6):371–384, 1982.

[FI96]   M. S. Floater and A. A. Iske. Multistep scattered data interpolation using
             compactly supported radial basis functions. *Journal of Comp. Appl. Math.*,
             73:65–78, 1996.

[FK03]   Randima Fernando and Mark J. Kilgard. *The Cg Tutorial: The Definitive Guide to Programmable Real-time Graphics.* Addison-Wesley Boston, MA, 2003.

[FM97]   Nick Foster and Dimitri Metaxas. Modeling the motion of hot, turbulent gas. In *Computer Graphics*, SIGGRAPH 1997 Proceedings, pages 181–188, 1997.

[FM03]   Thomas P. Fries and Hermann G. Matthies. Classification and overview of meshfree methods. Technical report, TU Brunswick, Germany Nr. 2003–03, 2003.

[FN80]   Richard Franke and Gregory M. Nielson. Smooth interpolation of large sets of scattered data. *International Journal of Numerical Methods in Engineering*, 15:1691–1704, 1980.

[FOA03]   Bryan E. Feldman, James F. O'Brien, and Okan Arikan. Animating suspended particle explosions. In *ACM Transactions on Graphics*, SIGGRAPH 2003 Proceedings, 22(3):708–715, 2003.

[FOK05]   Bryan E. Feldman, James F. O'Brien, and Bryan M. Klingner. Animating gases with hybrid meshes. In *Proceedings of ACM SIGGRAPH 2003*, pages 904–909, 2005.

[FP03a]   David A. Forsyth and Jean Ponce. *Computer Vision: A Modern Approach.* Prentice-Hall, Englewood Cliffs, NJ, 2003.

[FP03b]   Sarah Frisken and Ron Perry. Simple and efficient traversal methods for quad-trees and octrees. *Journal of Graphics Tools*, 7(3):1–11, May 2003.

[FR89]   Christos Faloutsos and Shari Roseman. Fractals for secondary key retrieval. In *Proceedings of the ACM Conference on the Principles of Database Systems*, pages 247–252. ACM Press, New York, NY, 1989.

[FR01]   Michael S. Floater and Martin Reimers. Meshless parameterization and surface reconstruction. *Comput. Aided Geom. Des.*, 18(2):77–92, 2001.

[FS80]   B. Fishman and B. Schachter. Computer display of height fields. *Computer & Graphics*, 5:53–60, 1980.

[FW60]   George E. Forsythe and Wolfgang R. Warsow. *Finite-difference Methods for Partial Differential Equations.* Dover Publications, 1960.

[GAI05]   GAIA. *ESA's Space Astrometry Mission.* http://sci.esa.int/gaia, 2005.

[Gar85]   Geoffrey Y. Gardner. Visual simulation of clouds. In *Computer Graphics*, SIGGRAPH 1985 Proceedings, pages 297–303, 1985.

[Gar99a]   Michael Garland. Multiresolution modeling: Survey and future opportunities. EUROGRAPHICS 1999 Proceedings, State-of-the-Art Report, 1999.

[Gar99b]   Michael Garland. *Quadric-based Polygonal Surface Simplification.* Ph.D. thesis, Computer Science Department, Carnegie Mellon University, Pittsburg, PA, 1999.

[GB90]   Oliver Günther and Alejandro P. Buchmann. Research issues in spatial
                databases. *SIGMOD Records*, 19(4):61–68, 1990.

[GBBF00]   Jens Guehring, Claus Brenner, Jan Boehm, and Dieter Fritsch. Data
                processing and calibration of a cross-pattern stripe projector. *IAPRS*, 33,
                2000.

[GBK99]   A. Georghiades, P. Belhumeur, and D. Kriegman. Illumination-based image
                synthesis: Creating novel images of human faces under differing pose and
                lighting. In *IEEE Workshop on Multiview Modeling and Analysis of Visual
                Scenes*, pages 47–54, April 1999.

[GBP04]   Gaël Guennebaud, Loïc Barthe, and Mathias Paulin. Dynamic surfel set
                refinement for high-quality rendering. *Computers & Graphics*, 28:827–838,
                2004.

[GBP05]   Gaël Guennebaud, Loïc Barthe, and Mathias Paulin. Interpolatory
                refinement for real-time processing of point-based geometry. In
                Proceedings of Eurographics 2005, pages 657–666, 2005.

[GBR⁺01]   Guy Godin, J.-Angelo Beraldin, Marc Rioux, Marc Levoy, Luc Cournoyer,
                and Francois Blais. An assessment of laser-range measurements on marble
                surfaces. In *Proceedings of the Conference on Optical 3D Measurement
                Techniques*, pages 49–56, 2001.

[GD98]   J. P. Grossman and W. J. Dally. Point-sample rendering. In *Rendering
                Techniques 1998*, Proceedings of the Eurographics Workshop on Rendering,
                pages 181–192, July 1998.

[GD02a, b]   Pierre-Marie Gandoin and Olivier Devilliers. Progressive lossless compres-
                sion of arbitrary simplicial complexes. In *ACM Transactions on Graphics*,
                SIGGRAPH 2002 Proceedings, pages 372–379. ACM Press, New York, NY,
                2002.

[GGSC96]   Steven J. Gortler, Radek Grzeszczuk, Richard Szeliski, and Michael
                F. Cohen. The lumigraph. In *Computer Graphics*, SIGGRAPH 1996
                Proceedings, pages 43–54, New York, NY. ACM Press, 1996.

[GH97]   Michael Garland and Paul S. Heckbert. Surface simplification using
                quadric error metrics. In *Computer Graphics*, SIGGRAPH 1997
                Proceedings, pages 209–216. ACM Press, 1997.

[GIRL03]   Natasha Gelfand, Leslie Ikemoto, Szymon Rusinkiewicz, and Marc Levoy.
                Geometrically stable sampling for the ICP algorithm. In *Proceedings of the
                International Conference on 3D Digital Imaging and Modeling (3DIM)*,
                pages 260–267, 2003.

[GJ02]   Joachim Giesen and Matthias John. Surface reconstruction based on a
                dynamical system. *Computer Graphics Forum*, 21:363–363, 2002.

[GJ03]   Joachim Giesen and Matthias John. The flow complex: A data structure for
                geometric modeling. In *ACM/SIAM Symposium on Discrete Algorithms*,
                pages 285–294, 2003.

[GJP93]   Federico Girosi, Michael Jones, and Tomaso Poggio. Priors, stabilizers and basis functions: From regularization to radial, tensor, and additive splines. AI Memo 1430, MIT Artificial Intelligence Laboratory, Cambridge, MA, 1993.

[Gla89]   Andrew S. Glassner, ed. *An Introduction to Ray Tracing*. Academic Press, Boston, MA, 1989.

[Gla95]   Andrew S. Glassner. *Principles of Digital Image Synthesis*, vol. 1. Morgan Kaufmann Publishers, San Francisco, CA, 1995.

[GM77]   Robert A. Gingold and Joe J. Monaghan. Smoothed particle hydrodynamics: Theory and application to nonspherical stars. *Monthly Notices of the Royal Astronomical Society*, 181:375–389, 1977.

[GM95]   Leonidas J. Guibas and David H. Marimont. Rounding arrangements dynamically. In *SCG 1995: Proceedings of the Eleventh Annual Symposium on Computational Geometry*, pages 190–199. ACM Press, New York, NY, 1995.

[GM04]   Enrico Gobbetti and Fabio Marton. Layered point clouds. In *Proceedings Symposium on Point-based Graphics*, pages 113–120. Eurographics, 2004.

[Gos90]   Michael E. Goss. Motion simulation: A real-time particle system for display of ship wakes. *IEEE Computer Graphics and Applications*, 10(3):30–35, 1990.

[GP03]   Gaël Guennebaud and Mathias Paulin. Efficient screen space approach for Hardware Accelerated Surfel Rendering. In *Vision, Modeling and Visualization*, pages 485–495. IEEE Signal Processing Society, November 2003.

[GRB94]   Guy Godin, Marc Rioux, and Réjean Baribeau. Three-dimensional registration using range and intensity information. In *Proceedings of SPIE: Videometrics III*, vol. 2350, pages 279–290, 1994.

[Gre87]   Leslie F. Greengard. *The Rapid Evaluation of Potential Fields in Particle Systems*. Ph.D. thesis, Yale University, New Haven, CT, 1987.

[GS00]   Michael Griebel and Marc A. Schweitzer. A particle-partition of unity method for the solution of elliptic, parabolic, and hyperbolic PDE. *SIAM J. Sci. Comp.*, 22(3):853–890, 2000.

[GS02a]   Michael Griebel and Marc A. Schweitzer. A particle-partition of unity method—part II: Efficient cover construction and reliable integration. *SIAM J. Sci. Comp.*, 23(5):1655–1682, 2002.

[GS02b]   Michael Griebel and Marc A. Schweitzer. A particle-partition of unity method—part III: A multilevel solver. *SIAM J. Sci. Comp.*, 24(2):377–409, 2002.

[GSIK91]   Margarita Garcia, Mateu Sbert, Andrei Iones, and Anton Krupkin. Improved obscurances with color bleeding. Technical Report IIiA 01-12-RR, University of Girona, Spain, 1991.

[GSLF05]   Eran Guendelman, Andrew Selle, Frank Losasso, and Ronald Fedkiw.
             Coupling water and smoke to thin deformable and rigid shells. *ACM
             Transactions on Graphics*, 24(3):973–981, 2005.

[Gue01]   Jens Guehring. Reliable 3D surface acquisition, registration, and validation
             using statistical error models. In *3rd International Conference on 3D Digital
             Imaging and Modeling*, pages 224–231, 2001.

[Gum03]   Stefan Gumhold. Splatting illuminated ellipsoids with depth correction.
             In Thomas Ertl, Bernd Girod, Günther Greiner, Heinrich Niemann,
             Hans-Peter Seidel, Eckehard Steinbach, and Rüdiger Westermann, eds.,
             *Proceedings of Workshop on Vision, Modelling, and Visualization (VMV)
             2003*, pages 245–252, 2003.

[Gut84]   Antonin Guttman. R-tree: A dynamic index structure for spatial searching.
             In *Proceedings ACM SIGMOD Conference on Management of Data*, pages
             47–57. ACM Press, New York, NY, 1984.

[GWN⁺03]   Markus Gross, Stephan Würmlin, Martin Naef, Edouard Lamboray,
             Christian Spagno, Andreas Kunz, Andrew Vande Moere, Kai Strehlke, Silke
             Lang, Tomas Svoboda, Esther Koller-Meier, Luc Van Gool, and Oliver
             Staadt. blue-c: A spatially immersive display and 3D video portal for
             telepresence. *ACM Transactions on Graphics*, SIGGRAPH 2003 Proceedings,
             22(3):819–827, 2003.

[Har64]   Francis H. Harlow. The particle in cell computing methods for fluid
             dynamics. *Methods of Computational Physics*, 3:319–343, 1964.

[Har96]   John C. Hart. Sphere tracing: A geometric method for the antialiased ray
             tracing of implicit surfaces. *The Visual Computer*, 12(10):527–545,
             December 1996.

[Har03]   Mark Harris. *Real-time Cloud Simulation and Rendering*. Ph.D. thesis, The
             University of North Carolina at Chapel Hill, 2003.

[HCD01]   Tim Hawkins, Jonathan Cohen, and Paul Debevec. A Photometric
             approach to digitizing cultural artifacts. In *2nd International Symposium
             on Virtual Reality, Archaeology, and Cultural Heritage*, Glyfada, Greece,
             pages 333–342, November 2001.

[HDD⁺92]   Hugues Hoppe, Tony DeRose, Tom Duchamp, John McDonald, and
             Werner Stuetzle. Surface reconstruction from unorganized points. In
             Edwin E. Catmull, ed., *Computer Graphics*, vol. 26 of SIGGRAPH 1992
             Proceedings, pages 71–78, July 1992.

[HDD⁺94]   Hugues Hoppe, Tony DeRose, Tom Duchamp, Mark Halstead, Hubert Jin,
             John McDonald, Jean Schweitzer, and Werner Stuetzle. Piecewise smooth
             surface reconstruction. In *Computer Graphics*, SIGGRAPH 1994
             Proceedings, pages 295–302, 1994.

[HE03]   Matthias Hopf and Thomas Ertl. Hierarchical splatting of scattered data.
             In *Proceedings IEEE Visualization*, pages 433–440. Computer Society Press,
             2003.

[Hec89]   Paul S. Heckbert. Fundamentals of texture mapping and image warping. M.Sc. thesis, Department of Electrical Engineering and Computer Science, University of California, Berkeley, June 1989.

[Hec97]   Paul S. Heckbert. Fast surface particle repulsion. Technical report, CMU Computer Science, 1997.

[Her03]   Christophe Hery. Implementing a skin BSSRDF. In Dana Batali, ed., *SIGGRAPH 2003 Course Note #9: RenderMan, Theory and Practice*, pages 73–88, 2003.

[HG97]   Paul S. Heckbert and Michael Garland. Survey of polygonal surface simplification algorithms. SIGGRAPH 1997 Course Notes, 1997.

[HH03]   Daniel Huber and Martial Hebert. Fully automatic registration of multiple 3D datasets. *Image and Vision Computing*, 21(7):637–650, July 2003.

[HHR01]   Olaf Hall-Holt and Szymon Rusinkiewicz. Stripe boundary codes for real-time structured-light range scanning of moving objects. In *Proceedings of the International Conference on Computer Vision*, pages 359–366, 2001.

[Hil91]   David Hilbert. Über die stetige Abbildung einer Linie auf ein Flächenstück. *Mathematische Annalen*, pages 459–460, 1891.

[Hof89]   Christoph M. Hoffmann. *Geometric and Solid Modeling*. Morgan Kaufmann, San Francisco, CA, 1989.

[Hop96]   Hugues Hoppe. Progressive meshes. In *Computer Graphics*, SIGGRAPH 1996 Proceedings, pages 99–108. ACM Press, New York, NY, 1996.

[HS94]   Richard Hartley and Peter Sturm. Triangulation. *Image Understanding Workshop*, II:957–966, 1994.

[HS97]   Janne Heikkilä and Olli Silvén. A four-step camera calibration procedure with implicit image correction. In *Proceedings of the Conference on Computer Vision and Pattern Recognition*, pages 1106–1112, 1997.

[HTK98]   Koichi Hirota, Yasuyuki Tanoue, and Toyohisa Kaneko. Generation of crack patterns with a physical model. *The Visual Computer*, 14:126–137, 1998.

[Hun93]   Robert W. G. Hunt. Color reproduction and color vision modeling. In *Proceedings Color Imaging Conference: Transforms and Transportability of Color*, pages 1–5. Society for Imaging Science & Technology (IS&T) and Society for Information Display (SID), 1993.

[HV01]   Xuejun Hao and Amitabh Varshney. Variable-precision rendering. In *Proceedings of ACM Symposium on Interactive 3D Graphics*, pages 149–158, March 2001.

[Ige99]   Homan Igehy. Tracing ray differentials. In *Computer Graphics*, SIGGRAPH 1999 Proceedings, pages 179–186, 1999.

[INS]   The institute for study and implementation of graphical heritage techniques (INSIGHT), http://www.insightdigital.org/.

[IS00]   Martin Isenburg and Jack Snoeyink. Face fixer: Compressing polygon
              meshes with properties. In *Computer Graphics*, SIGGRAPH 2000
              Proceedings, pages 263–270. ACM, 2000.

[ISO05]   ISO/IEC JTC1/SC29/WG11 (MPEG). Text of ISO/IEC 14496–16/FDAM1:
              Animation Framework eXtension (AFX). Doc. N7400, Poznan, Poland,
              July 2005.

[Jac89]   Guy Jacobson. Space-efficient static trees and graphs. In *30th Annual
              Symposium on Foundations of Computer Science*, pages 549–554. IEEE
              Computer Society Press, 1989.

[Jag90]   H. V. Jagadish. Linear clustering of objects with multiple attributes. In
              Proceedings ACM SIGMOD Conference on Management of Data, pages
              332–342. ACM Press, New York, NY, 1990.

[Jai88]   Anil K. Jain. *Algorithms for Clustering Data*. Prentice-Hall, Englewood
              Cliffs, NJ, 1988.

[Jai89]   Anil K. Jain. *Fundamentals of Digital Image Processing*. Prentice-Hall,
              Englewood Cliffs, NJ, 1989.

[JB02]   Henrik Wann Jensen and Juan Buhler. A rapid hierarchical rendering
              technique for translucent materials, pages 576–581, 2002.

[JC98]   Henrik Wann Jensen and Per H. Christensen. Efficient simulation of light
              transport in scenes with participating media using photon maps. In
              Computer Graphics, SIGGRAPH 1998 Proceedings, pages 311–320, 1998.

[JDR04]   Robert Jagnow, Julie Dorsey, and Holly Rushmeier. Stereological tech-
              niques for solid textures. *ACM Transactions on Graphics*, SIGGRAPH 2004
              Proceedings, 23(3):329–335, 2004.

[Jen96]   Henrik Wann Jensen. Global illumination using photon maps. In
              Rendering Techniques 1996, Proceedings of the 7th Eurographics Workshop
              on Rendering, pages 21–30. Springer-Verlag, New York, NY, 1996.

[Jen01]   Henrik Wann Jensen. *Realistic Image Synthesis Using Photon Mapping*. A. K.
              Peters, Natick, MA, 2001.

[JH99]   Andrew Johnson and Martial Hebert. Using spin-images for efficient
              multiple model recognition in cluttered 3D scenes. *IEEE Transactions on
              Pattern Analysis and Machine Intelligence (PAMI)*, 21(5):433–449, May
              1999.

[JMLH01]   Henrik Wann Jensen, Stephen R. Marschner, Marc Levoy, and Pat
              Hanrahan. A practical model for subsurface light transport. In *Computer
              Graphics*, SIGGRAPH 2001 Proceedings, pages 511–518, 2001.

[Jol86]   I. T. Jolliffe. *Principal Component Analysis*. Springer-Verlag, New York, NY,
              1986.

[JP04]   Doug L. James and Dinesh K. Pai. B-d-tree: Output-sensitive collision
              detection for reduced deformable models. In *ACM Transactions on
              Graphics*, SIGGRAPH 2004 Proceedings, 23(3):393–398, 2004.

[KAG⁺05]   Richard Keiser, Bart Adams, Dominique Gasser, Paolo Bazzi, Philip Dutré, and Markus Gross. A unified lagrangian approach to solid-fluid animation. In *Proceedings of the Eurographics Symposium on Point-based Graphics*, 125–148, 2005.

[Kaj83]   James T. Kajiya. New techniques for ray tracing procedurally-defined objects. *ACM Transactions on Graphics*, 2(3):161–181, 1983.

[Kaz04]   Michael Kazhdan. *Shape Representations and Algorithms for 3D Model Retrieval*. Ph.D. thesis, Princeton University, NJ, 2004.

[Kaz05]   Michal Kazhdan. Reconstruction of solid models from oriented point sets. In *Symposium on Geometry Processing*, pages 73–82, Vienna, Austria, July 2005.

[KB04]   Leif Kobbelt and Mario Botsch. A survey of point-based techniques in computer graphics. *Computers & Graphics*, 28(6):801–814, 2004.

[KBH06]   Michael Kazhdan, Matthew Bolitho, and Hugues Hoppe. Poisson surface reconstruction. In *Symposium on Geometry Processing*, pages 43–52, 2006, in press.

[KCVS98]   Leif Kobbelt, Swen Campagna, Jens Vorsatz, and Hans-Peter Seidel. Interactive multiresolution modeling on arbitrary meshes. In *Computer Graphics*, SIGGRAPH 1998 Proceedings, pages 105–114. ACM Press, New York, NY, 1998.

[KE04]   Thomas Klein and Thomas Ertl. Illustrating magnetic field lines using a discrete particle model. In *Workshop on Vision, Modelling, and Visualization (VMV) 2004*, pages 387–394, 2004.

[Kei03]   Richard Keiser. Collision detection and response for interactive editing of point-sampled models. Master's thesis, ETH, Zürich, Switzerland, 2003.

[Kel96]   Alexander Keller. Quasi–Monte Carlo methods in computer graphics: The global illumination problem. In *Lectures in Applied Mathematics*, vol. 32, pages 455–469. SIAM, 1996.

[KF94]   Ibrahim Kamel and Christos Faloutsos. Hilbert R-tree: An improved r-tree using fractals. In *Proceedings of the 20th VLDB Conference*, pages 500–509, 1994.

[KG00]   Zachi Karni and Craig Gotsman. Spectral compression of mesh geometry. In *Computer Graphics*, SIGGRAPH 2000 Proceedings, pages 279–286. ACM Press, 2000.

[KLMV05]   Shankar Krishnan, Pei Yean Lee, John Moore, and Suresh Venkatasubramanian. Simultaneous registration of multiple 3D point sets via optimization on a manifold. In *Proceedings of the Symposium on Geometry Processing*, pages 187–196, 2005.

[KM97]   Shankar Krishnan and Dinesh Manocha. An efficient surface intersection algorithm based on lower-dimensional formulation. *ACM Transactions on Graphics*, 16(1):74–106, 1997.

[KMGL96]   Subodh Kumar, Dinesh Manocha, William Garrett, and Ming Lin.
             Hierarchical back-face computation. In *Rendering Techniques 1996,
             Eurographics Workshop on Rendering*, pages 231–240. Springer-Verlag
             Wien, New York, NY, 1996.

[KMH+04]   Richard Keiser, Matthias Müller, Bruno Heidelberger, Matthias Teschner,
             and Markus Gross. Contact handling for deformable point-based objects.
             In *Proceedings of Vision, Modeling, Visualization (VMV) 2004*, pages
             339–347, November 2004.

[KMN+02]   Tapas Kanungo, David M. Mount, Nathan S. Netanyahu, Christine Piatko,
             Ruth Silverman, and Angela Y. Wu. An efficient k-means clustering
             algorithm: Analysis and implementation. *IEEE Transactions on Pattern
             Analysis and Machine Intelligence*, 24:881–892, 2002.

[KO96]   Seiichi Kochizuka and Yoshiaki Oka. Moving particle semi-implicit method
             for fragmentation of incompressible fluid. *Nuclear Science Engineering*,
             123:421–434, 1996.

[Kob00]   Leif Kobbelt. $\sqrt{3}$ subdivision. In *Computer Graphics*, SIGGRAPH 2000
             Proceedings, pages 103–112, 2000.

[Kol05]   Ravikrishna Kolluri. Provably good moving least squares. In *ACM-SIAM
             Symposium on Discrete Algorithms*, pages 1008–1018, San Francisco, CA,
             January 2005.

[KPDG05]   Thomas Koninckx, Pieter Peers, Philip Dutré, and Luc van Gool.
             Scene-adapted structured light. In *Proceedings of the Conference on
             Computer Vision and Pattern Recognition*, pages 611–619, 2005.

[KSS00]   Andrei Khodakovsky, Peter Schröder, and Wim Sweldens. Progressive
             geometry compression. In *Computer Graphics*, SIGGRAPH 2000
             Proceedings, pages 271–278. ACM Press, 2000.

[Kuh62]   Thomas S. Kuhn. *The Structure of Scientific Revolutions*. University of
             Chicago Press, 1962.

[KV01]   Aravind Kalaiah and Amitabh Varshney. Differential point rendering.
             In *Proceedings of Eurographics Workshop on Rendering Techniques 2001*,
             pages 139–150, 2001.

[KV03a]   Aravind Kalaiah and Amitabh Varshney. Modeling and rendering points
             with local geometry. *IEEE Transactions on Visualization and Computer
             Graphics*, 9(1):30–42, 2003.

[KV03b]   Aravind Kalaiah and Amitabh Varshney. Statistical point geometry. In Leif
             Kobbelt, Peter Schröder, and Hugues Hoppe, eds., *Eurographics Symposium
             on Geometry Processing*, pages 107–115, June 2003.

[KV05]   Aravind Kalaiah and Amitabh Varshney. Statistical geometry representa-
             tion for efficient transmission and rendering. *ACM Transactions on
             Graphics*, 24(2):348–373, 2005.

[Lan02]   Hayden Landis. Production-ready global illumination. In Larry Gritz, ed.,
            SIGGRAPH 2002 Course Note #16: RenderMan in Production, pages 87–102,
            2002.

[Lau94]   A. Laurentini. The visual hull concept for silhouette-based image
            understanding. *PAMI*, 16(2):150–162, February 1994.

[LC87]   William E. Lorensen and Harvey E. Cline. Marching cubes: A high
            resolution 3D surface construction algorithm. In *Computer Graphics*,
            SIGGRAPH 1987 Proceedings, pages 163–169, San Francisco, CA,
            October 1987.

[LCWB80]   Jeffrey M. Lane, Loren C. Carpenter, Turner Whitted, and James F. Blinn.
            Scan-line methods for displaying parametrically defined surfaces.
            Communications of the ACM, 23(1):23–34, 1980.

[Lee00]   In-Kwon Lee. Curve reconstruction from unorganized points. *Computer
            Aided Geometric Design*, 17(2):161–177, February 2000.

[Lev88]   Marc Levoy. Display of surfaces from volume data. 8(3):29–37, May 1988.

[Lev98]   David Levin. The approximation power of moving least squares. *Math.
            Comput.*, 67(224):1517–1531, 1998.

[Lev01a]   David Levin. Mesh-independent surface interpolation. *Advances in
            Computational Mathematics*, 9(1):3–15, 2001.

[Lev01b]   Bruno Levy. Constrained texture mapping for polygonal meshes. In
            Computer Graphics, SIGGRAPH 2001 Proceedings, pages 417–424. ACM
            Press, New York, NY, 2001.

[Lev03]   David Levin. Mesh-independent surface interpolation. *Geometric Modeling
            for Scientific Visualization*, pages 181–187, 2003.

[Lev04]   David Levin. Mesh-independent surface interpolation. In Guido Brunnett,
            Bernd Hamann, Heinrich Müller, and Lars Linsen, eds., *Geometric
            Modeling for Scientific Visualization*. Springer-Verlag, New York, NY, 2004.

[LFTG97]   Eric P. F. Lafortune, Sing-Choong Foo, Kenneth E. Torrance, and Donald
            P. Greenberg. Nonlinear approximation of reflectance functions. In
            Computer Graphics, SIGGRAPH 1997 Proceedings, pages 117–126, 1997.

[LGF04]   Frank Losasso, Frédéric Gibou, and Ronald Fedkiw. Simulating water and
            smoke with an octree data structure. *ACM Transactions on Graphics*,
            SIGGRAPH 2004 Proceedings, 23(3):457–462, 2004.

[LGK⁺01a]   Hendrik Lensch, Michael Goesele, Jan Kautz, Wolfgang Heidrich, and
            Hans-Peter Seidel. Image-based reconstruction of spatially varying
            materials. In *Proceedings of the 12th Eurographics Workshop on Rendering*,
            pages 104–115, June 2001.

[LGK⁺01b]   Hendrik P. A. Lensch, Michael Goesele, Jan Kautz, Wolfgang Heidrich, and
            Hans-Peter Seidel. Image-based reconstruction of spatially varying

          materials. In *Proceedings of the 12th Eurographics Workshop on Rendering Techniques*, pages 103–114. Springer-Verlag, London, UK, 2001.

[LH91]   David Laur and Pat Hanrahan. Hierarchical splatting: A progressive refinement algorithm for volume rendering. In *Computer Graphics*, SIGGRAPH 1991 Proceedings, pages 285–288. ACM Press, 1991.

[LH96]   Marc Levoy and Pat Hanrahan. Light-field rendering. In *Computer Graphics*, SIGGRAPH 1996 Proceedings, pages 31–42. ACM Press, New York, NY, 1996.

[Lin01]   Lars Linsen. Point-cloud representation. Technical Report 2001-3, Faculty for Computer Science, Universität Karlsruhe, 2001.

[Liu02]   Gui-Rong Liu. *Mesh-free Methods*. CRC Press, Boca Raton, FL, 2002.

[LK81]   Bruce Lucas and Takeo Kanade. An iterative image registration technique with an application to stereo vision. In *Proceedings of the International Joint Conference on Artificial Intelligence*, pages 674–679, 1981.

[LL03]   Gui-Rong Liu and M. B. Liu. *Smoothed Particle Hydrodynamics*. World Scientific, 2003.

[LM98]   Bruno Levy and Jean-Laurent Mallet. Nondistorted texture mapping for sheared triangulated meshes. In *Computer Graphics*, SIGGRAPH 1998 Proceedings, pages 343–352, 1998.

[Loo87]   Charles T. Loop. *Smooth subdivision surfaces based on triangles*. Department of Mathematics, University of Utah, 1987.

[LPC⁺00] Marc Levoy, Kari Pulli, Brian Curless, Szymon Rusinkiewicz, David Koller, Lucas Pereira, Matt Ginzton, Sean Anderson, James Davis, Jeremy Ginsberg, Jonathan Shade, and Duane Fulk. The digital Michelangelo project: 3D scanning of large statues. In *Computer Graphics*, SIGGRAPH 2000 Proceedings, pages 131–144. ACM Press/Addison-Wesley, 2000.

[LPFH01] Jerome Edward Lengyel, Emil Praun, Adam Finkelstein, and Hugues Hoppe. Real-time fur over arbitrary surfaces. In *Symposium on Interactive 3D Graphics*, pages 227–232, 2001.

[LR98]   Dani Lischinski and Ari Rappoport. Image-based rendering for nondiffuse synthetic scenes. In *Proceedings Eurographics Workshop on Rendering*, pages 301–314, 1998.

[LRC⁺03] David Luebke, Martin Reddy, Jonathan D. Cohen, Amitabh Varshney, Benjamin Watson, and Robert Huebner. *Level of Detail for 3D Graphics*. Morgan Kaufmann Publishers, San Francisco, CA, 2003.

[LS81]   Peter Lancaster and Kes Salkauskas. Surfaces generated by moving least squares methods. *Mathematics of Computation*, 37:141–158, 1981.

[LS86]   Peter Lancaster and Kes Salkauskas. *Curve and Surface Fitting: An Introduction*. Academic Press, Boston, MA, 1986.

[Luc77]   L. B. Lucy. A numerical approach to the testing of the fission hypothesis. *Astronomical Journal*, 82(12):1013–1024, 1977.

[LW85]   Marc Levoy and Turner Whitted. The use of points as a display primitive. Technical report, Computer Science Department, University of North Carolina at Chapel Hill, January 1985.

[LWW+04]   Edouard Lamboray, Stephan Würmlin, Michael Waschbüsch, Markus Gross, and Hanspeter Pfister. Unconstrained free-viewpoint video coding. In *Proceedings of ICIP 2004*, vol. 5, pages 3261–3264, 2004.

[Mar72]   George Marsaglia. Choosing a point from the surface of a sphere. *Ann. Math. Stat.*, 43(2):645–646, April 1972.

[Mar98]   Stephen Robert Marschner. *Inverse Rendering for Computer Graphics*. Ph.D. thesis, Cornell University, Ithaca, NY, 1998.

[Max81]   Nelson L. Max. Vectorized procedural models for natural terrain: Waves and islands in the sunset. In *Computer Graphics*, SIGGRAPH 1981 Proceedings, pages 317–324, 1981.

[MB93]   Jasna Maver and Ruzena Bajcsy. Occlusions as a guide for planning the next view. *IEEE Transactions on Pattern Analysis and Machine Intelligence (PAMI)*, 15(5):417–433, May 1993.

[MB95]   Leonard McMillan and Gray Bishop. Plenoptic modeling: An image-based rendering system. In *Computer Graphics,* SIGGRAPH 1995 Proceedings, pages 39–46, Los Angeles, CA, 1995.

[MBF04]   Neil Molino, Zhaosheng Bao, and Ron Fedkiw. A virtual node algorithm for changing mesh topology during simulation. *ACM Transactions on Graphics*, SIGGRAPH 2004 Proceedings, 23(3):385–392, 2004.

[MBR+00]   Wojciech Matusik, Chris Buehler, Ramesh Raskar, Steven J. Gortler, and Leonard McMillan. Image-based visual hulls. In *Computer Graphics*, SIGGRAPH 2000 Proceedings, pages 369–374, 2000.

[MC98]   Klaus Mueller and Roger Crawfis. Eliminating popping artifacts in sheet buffer-based splatting. In *IEEE Visualization 1998*, pages 239–246. IEEE, October 1998.

[MCG03]   Matthias Müller, David Charypar, and Markus Gross. Particle-based fluid simulation for interactive applications, pages 154–159, 2003.

[MD03]   Carsten Moenning and Neil A. Dodgson. A new point-cloud simplification algorithm. In *Proceedings 3rd IASTED Conference on Visualization, Imaging and Image Processing*, 2003.

[MG04]   Matthias Müller and Markus Gross. Interactive virtual materials. In *Proceedings of the 2004 conference on Graphics Interface*, pages 239–246. Canadian Human-Computer Communications Society, 2004.

[MGAK03]   William R. Mark, R. Steven Glanville, Kurt Akeley, and Mark J. Kilgard. Cg: A system for programming graphics hardware in a C-like language. *ACM*

Transactions on Graphics, SIGGRAPH 2003 Proceedings, 22(3):896–907, July 2003.

[MGPG04]   Niloy Mitra, Natasha Gelfand, Helmut Pottmann, and Leonidas Guibas. Registration of point-cloud data from a geometric optimization perspective. In *Proceedings of the Symposium on Geometry Processing*, pages 23–32, 2004.

[MGW01]   Tom Malzbender, Dan Gelb, and Hans Wolters. Polynomial texture maps. In *Computer Graphics*, SIGGRAPH 2001 Proceedings, pages 519–528, Los Angeles, CA, 2001.

[MHTG05]   Matthias Müller, Bruno Heidelberger, Matthias Teschner, and Markus Gross. Meshless deformations based on shape matching. *ACM Transactions on Graphics*, SIGGRAPH 2005 Proceedings, 24(3):471–478, 2005.

[MKN+04]   Matthias Müller, Richard Keiser, Andrew Nealen, Mark Pauly, Markus Gross, and Marc Alexa. Point-based animation of elastic, plastic, and melting objects, pages 141–151, 2004.

[MMC99]   Klaus Mueller, Thomas Moeller, and Roger Crawfis. Splatting without the blur. In *IEEE Visualization 1999*, pages 363–370, October 1999.

[MMDJ01]   Matthias Müller, Leonard McMillan, Julie Dorsey, and Robert Jagnow. Real-time simulation of deformation and fracture of stiff materials. *EUROGRAPHICS 2001 Computer Animation and Simulation Workshop*, pages 27–34, 2001.

[MNG04]   Niloy J. Mitra, An Nguyen, and Leonidas Guibas. Estimating surface normals in noisy point-cloud data. *International Journel of Computational Geometry and Applications*, 14(4–5):261–276, 2004.

[Mon92]   Joe J. Monaghan. Smoothed particle hydrodynamics. *Annu. Rev. Astron. Physics*, 30:543, 1992.

[Mon94]   Joe J. Monaghan. Simulating free surface flows with SPH. *J. Comput. Phys.*, 110(2):399–406, 1994.

[Mon05]   Joe J. Monaghan. Smoothed particle hydrodynamics. *Reports on Progress in Physics*, 68:1703–1759, 2005.

[MP79]   David Marr and Tomaso Poggio. A computational theory of human stereo vision. In *Proceedings of the Royal Society of London B*, 204(1156):301–328, May 1979.

[MP04]   Wojciech Matusik and Hanspeter Pfister. 3D TV: A scalable system for real-time acquisition, transmission, and autostereoscopic display of dynamic scenes. *ACM Transactions on Graphics*, SIGGRAPH 2004 Proceedings, 23(3):814–824, 2004.

[MR95]   Rajeev Motwani and Prabhakar Raghavan. *Randomized Algorithms*. Cambridge University Press, UK, 1995.

[MS04]   Morgan McGuire and Peter G. Sibley. A heightfield on an isometric grid. Poster presentation, SIGGRAPH 2004, July 2004.

[MSC03]   Alex Méndez, Mateu Sbert, and Jordi Catà. Real-time obscurances with color bleeding. In *Proceedings of the Spring Conference on Computer Graphics SCCG 2003*, 2003.

[MSKG05] Matthias Müller, Barbara Solenthaler, Richard Keiser, and Markus Gross, Particle-based fiuid-fluid interaction, pages 237–244, 2005.

[MST⁺04] Matthias Müller, Simon Schirm, Matthias Teschner, Bruno Heidelberger, and Markus Gross. Interaction of fluids with deformable solids. In *Proceedings of Computer Animation and Virtual Worlds*, pages 159–171, 2004.

[MTSA97] Y. Matsumoto, H. Terasaki, K. Sugimoto, and T. Arakawa. A portable three-dimensional digitizer. In *Proceedings of the International Conference on 3D Digital Imaging and Modeling (3DIM)*, pages 197–204, 1997.

[Mur91]   Shigeru Muraki. Volumetric shape description of range data using "Blobby Model." In *Computer Graphics*, SIGGRAPH 1991 Proceedings, 22(4):227–235, July 1991.

[MYR⁺01] Brain S. Morse, Terry S. Yoo, Penny Rheingans, David T. Chen, and K. R. Subramanian. Interpolating implicit surfaces from scattered surface data using compactly supported radial basis functions. In *Shape Modeling International 2001*, pages 89–98, Genova, Italy, May 2001.

[MYW05]   Talya Meltzer, Chen Yanover, and Yair Weiss. Globally optimal solutions for energy minimization in stereo vision using reweighted belief propagation. In *Proceedings of the International Conference on Computer Vision*, pages 428–435, 2005.

[Nie89]   Jürg Nievergelt. 7 ± 2 criteria for assessing and comparing spatial data structures. In *Proceedings of the 1st Symposium on the Design and Implementation of Large Spatial Databases*, vol. 409 of *Lecture Notes in Computer Science*, pages 3–27. Springer-Verlag, New York, NY, 1989.

[Nie92]   Harald Niederreiter. *Random number generation and quasi–Monte Carlo methods*. Society for Industrial and Applied Mathematics, 1992.

[Nie04]   Gregory M. Nielson. Radial Hermite operators for scattered point-cloud data with normal vectors and applications to implicitizing polygon mesh surfaces for generalized CSG operations and smoothing. In *Proceedings of IEEE Visualization*, pages 203–210, Austin, TX, 2004.

[NMK⁺05] Andrew Nealen, Matthias Müller, Richard Keiser, Eddy Boxerman, and Mark Carlson. Physically based deformable models in computer graphics. *Eurographics 2005 State-of-the-Art Report (STAR)*, 2005.

[NN94]   Shree Nayar and Yasuo Nakagawa. Shape from focus. *IEEE Transactions on Pattern Analysis and Machine Intelligence (PAMI)*, 16(8):824–831, August 1994.

[NRD05]   Diego Nehab, Szymon Rusinkiewicz, and James Davis. Improved subpixel stereo correspondences through symmetric refinement. In *Proceedings of the International Conference on Computer Vision*, pages 557–563, 2005.

[NRDR05]   Diego Nehab, Szymon Rusinkiewicz, James Davis, and Ravi Ramamoorthi. Efficiently combining positions and normals for precise 3D geometry. In *ACM Transactions on Graphics*, SIGGRAPH 2005 Proceedings, 24(3):536–543, 2005.

[NSI99a]   Ko Nishino, Yoichi Sato, and Katsushi Ikeuchi. Appearance compression and synthesis based on 3D model for mixed reality. In *Proceedings of IEEE ICCV 1999*, pages 38–45, September 1999.

[NSI99b]   Ko Nishino, Yoichi Sato, and Katsushi Ikeuchi. Eigen-texture method: Appearance compression based on 3D model. In *Proceedings of Computer Vision and Pattern Recognition*, pages 618–624, June 1999.

[NW97]   Jürg Nievergelt and Peter Widmayer. Spatial data structures: Concepts and design choices. In Marc van Kreveld, Jürg Nievergelt, Thomas Roos, and Peter Widmayer, eds., *Algorithmic Foundations of Geographic Information Systems, Summerschool, Udine,* vol. 1340 of *Lecture Notes in Computer Science*, pages 153–197. Springer-Verlag, New York, NY, 1997.

[OBA⁺03]   Yutaka Ohtake, Alexander Belyaev, Marc Alexa, Greg Turk, and Hans-Peter Seidel. Multilevel partition of unity implicits. *ACM Transactions on Computer Graphics*, SIGGRAPH 2003 Proceedings, 22(3):463–470, 2003.

[OBH02]   James F. O'Brien, Adam W. Bargteil, and Jessica K. Hodgins. Graphical modeling and animation of ductile fracture. *ACM Transactions on Graphics*, SIGGRAPH 2002 Proceedings, pages 291–294, 2002.

[OBS03]   Yutaka Ohtake, Alexander Belyaev, and Hans-Peter Seidel. A multiscale approach to 3D scattered data interpolation with compactly supported basis functions. In *Proceedings of Shape Modeling International 2003*, page 153, May 2003.

[OCDD01]   Byong Mok Oh, Max Chen, Julie Dorsey, and Fredo Durand. Image-based modeling and photo editing. In *Computer Graphics*, SIGGRAPH 2001 Proceedings, pages 433–442, 2001.

[OFTB96]   D. Organ, M. Fleming, T. Terry, and Ted Belytschko. Continuous meshless approximations for nonconvex bodies by diffraction and transparency. *Computational Mechanics*, 18:1–11, 1996.

[OH99]   James F. O'Brien and Jessica K. Hodgins. Graphical modeling and animation of brittle fracture. In *Computer Graphics*, SIGGRAPH 1999, Proceedings, pages 287–296. ACM Press, 1999.

[OK93]   Masatoshi Okutomi and Takeo Kanade. A multiple-baseline stereo. *IEEE Transactions on Pattern Analysis and Machine Intelligence (PAMI)*, 15(4):353–363, April 1993.

[OLG⁺05]   John D. Owens, David Luebke, Naga Govindaraju, Mark Harris, Jens
             Krüger, Aaron E. Lefohn, and Timothy J. Purcell. A survey of general-
             purpose computation on graphics hardware. In *Eurographics 2005, State
             of the Art Reports*, pages 21–51, 2005.

[O'N66]   Barrett O'Neill. *Elementary Differential Geometry*. Academic Press, 1966.

[OP99]   Michael Ortiz and Anna Pandolfi. Finite-deformation irreversible cohesive
             elements for three-dimensional crack-propagation analysis. *Int. J. Num.
             Meth. Eng.*, 44:1267–1282, 1999.

[OS88]   Stanley Osher and James A. Sethian. Fronts propagating with
             curvature-dependent speed: Algorithms based on Hamilton-Jacobi
             formulations. *Journal of Computational Physics*, 79:12–49, 1988.

[PA82]   J. L. Posdamer and M. D. Altschuler. Surface measurement by
             space-encoded projected beam systems. *Computer Graphics and Image
             Processing*, 18:1–17, 1982.

[Paj03]   Renato Pajarola. Efficient level of details for point-based rendering. In
             *Proceedings IASTED International Conference on Computer Graphics and
             Imaging (CGIM)*, pages 141–146, 2003.

[Paj05]   Renato Pajarola. Stream-processing points. In *Proceedings IEEE
             Visualization*, pages 239–246. Computer Society Press, 2005.

[Pas00]   Valerio Pascucci. Multiresolution indexing for hierarchical out-of-core
             traversal of rectilinear grids. NSF/DoE Lake Tahoe Workshop on
             Hierarchical Approximation and Geometrical Methods for Scientific
             Visualization, 2000.

[Pau03]   Mark Pauly. *Point Primitives for Interactive Modeling and Processing of 3D
             Geometry*. Ph.D. thesis, Department of Computer Science, ETH Zürich,
             2003.

[PB96]   C. Pierpaoli and P. J. Basser. Toward a quantitative assessment of diffusion
             anisotropy. *Magnetic Resonance in Medicine*, 36:893–906, 1996.

[PCD⁺97]   Kari Pulli, Michael Cohen, Tom Duchamp, Hugues Hoppe, Linda Shapiro,
             and Werner Stuetzle. View-based rendering: Visualizing real objects from
             scanned range and color data. In *Eurographics Rendering Workshop* 1997,
             pages 23–34, June 1997.

[PD84]   Thomas Porter and Tom Duff. Compositing digital images. In *Computer
             Graphics*, SIGGRAPH 1984 Proceedings, pages 253–259, 1984.

[PDH⁺97]   Kari Pulli, Tom Duchamp, Hugues Hoppe, John McDonald, Linda Shapiro,
             and Werner Stuetzle. Robust meshes from multiple range maps. In *NRC
             1997: Proceedings of the International Conference on Recent Advances in 3D
             Digital Imaging and Modeling*, page 205. IEEE Computer Society,
             Washington, DC, 1997.

[Pea90]   Giuseppe Peano. Sur une courbe, qui remplit toute une aire plane.
             Mathematische Annalen, pages 157–160, 1890.

[Pea86]   Darwyn R. Peachey. Modeling waves and surf. In *Computer Graphics*,
            SIGGRAPH 1986 Proceedings, pages 65–74, 1986.

[Ped95]   Hans Køhling Pedersen. Decorating implicit surfaces. In *Computer
            Graphics*, SIGGRAPH 1995 Proceedings, pages 291–300, 1995.

[PF01]   Ronald N. Perry and Sarah F. Frisken. Kizamu: A system for sculpting
            digital characters. In *Computer Graphics*, SIGGRAPH 2001 Proceedings,
            pages 47–56, 2001.

[PFTV03]   William H. Press, Brian P. Flannery, Saul A. Teukolsky, and William
            T. Vetterling. *Numerical Recipes in C : The Art of Scientific Computing*,
            2nd ed., Cambridge University Press, UK, January 2003.

[PG01]   Mark Pauly and Markus Gross. Spectral processing of point-sampled
            geometry. In *Computer Graphics*, SIGGRAPH 2001 Proceedings, pages
            379–386. ACM Press, New York, NY, 2001.

[PGK02a]   Mark Pauly, Markus Gross, and Leif P. Kobbelt. Efficient simplification of
            point-sampled surfaces. In *Proceedings of the Conference on Visualization
            2002*, pages 163–170, 2002.

[PGK02b]   Mark Pauly, Markus Gross, and Leif P. Kobbelt. Efficient simplification of
            point-sampled surfaces. In *Proceedings IEEE Visualization*, pages 163–170.
            Computer Society Press, 2002.

[PGO96]   Marc Proesmans, Luc Van Gool, and A. Oosterlinck. One-shot active 3D
            shape acquisition. In *Proceedings of the International Conference on Pattern
            Recognition*, pages 336–340, 1996.

[PGV+04]   Marc Pollefeys, Luc Van Gool, Maarten Vergauwen, Frank Verbiest, Kurt
            Cornelis, Jan Tops, and Reinhard Koch. Visual modeling with a handheld
            camera. *International Journal of Computer Vision*, 59(3):207–232, 2004.

[PKA+05]   Mark Pauly, Richard Keiser, Bart Adams, Philip Dutré, Markus Gross, and
            Leonidas J. Guibas. Meshless animation of fracturing solids. *ACM
            Transactions on Graphics*, SIGGRAPH 2005 Proceedings, 24(3):957–964,
            2005.

[PKG02]   Mark Pauly, Leif Kobbelt, and Markus Gross. Multiresolution modeling of
            point-sampled geometry. Technical report, Department of Computer
            Science, ETH Zürich, 2002.

[PKG03]   Mark Pauly, Richard Keiser, and Markus Gross. Multiscale feature
            extraction on point-sampled surfaces. *Computer Graphics Forum*,
            22:281–289, 2003.

[PKG06]   Mark Pauly, Leif Kobbelt, and Markus Gross. Point-based multiscale
            surface representation. In *ACM Transactions on Graphics*, 25(2):177–193,
            2006, in press.

[PKH04]   Harald Piringer, Robert Kosara, and Helwig Hauser. Interactive focus +
            context visualization with linked 2D/3D scatterplots. In *Proceedings of 2nd*

International Conference on Coordinated and Multiple Views in Exploratory Visualization, 2004.

[PKKG03]   Mark Pauly, Richard Keiser, Leif P. Kobbelt, and Markus Gross. Shape modeling with point-sampled geometry. In *ACM Transactions on Graphics*, SIGGRAPH 2003 Proceedings, 22(3):641–650, 2003.

[PL90]   Przemyslaw Prusinkiewicz and Aristid Lindenmayer. New York, NY, Springer-Verlag, 1990.

[PMG04]   Mark Pauly, Niloy J. Mitra, and Leonidas Guibas. Uncertainty and variability in point-cloud surface data. In *Symposium on Point-based Graphics*, pages 77–84, 2004.

[Poi]   Pointshop3D, URL: http://www.pointshop3d.com/.

[PR05]   Joshua Podolak and Szymon Rusinkiewicz. Atomic volumes for mesh completion. In *Proceedings of the Symposium on Geometry Processing*, pages 33–41, 2005.

[PS97]   Enrico Puppo and Roberto Scopigno. Simplification, LOD, and multiresolution—principles and applications. EUROGRAPHICS 97 Tutorial Notes, 1997.

[PSG04]   Renato Pajarola, Miguel Sainz, and Patrick Guidotti. Confetti: Object-space point blending and splatting. *IEEE Transactions on Visualization and Computer Graphics*, 10(5):598–608, Sept.–Oct. 2004.

[PSL05]   Renato Pajarola, Miguel Sainz, and Roberto Lario. XSplat: External memory multiresolution point visualization. In *Proceedings IASTED International Conference on Visualization, Imaging and Image Processing (VIIP)*, pages 628–633, 2005.

[PT89]   William H. Press and Saul A. Teukolsky. Quasi- (that is, sub-) random numbers. *Computers in Physics*, 3(6):76–79, 1989.

[PTB+03]   Simon Premoze, Tolga Tasdizen, James Bigler, Aaron Lefohn, and Ross Whitaker. Particle-based simulation of fluids. In *Proceedings of Eurographics 2003*, pages 401–410, 2003.

[PTVF92]   William H. Press, Saul A. Teukolsky, William T. Vetterling, and Brain P. Flannery. *Numerical Recipes in C: The Art of Scientific Computing*, 2nd ed., Cambridge University Press, UK, 1992.

[Pul99]   Kari Pulli. Multiview registration for large datasets. In *International Conference on 3D Digital Imaging and Modeling*, pages 160–168, Ottawa, Canada, 1999.

[PZvBG00]   Hanspeter Pfister, Matthias Zwicker, Jeroen van Baar, and Markus Gross. Surfels: Surface elements as rendering primitives. In Kurt Akeley, ed., *Computer Graphics*, SIGGRAPH 2000 Proceedings, pages 335–342. ACM, 2000.

[RB93]   Jarek Rossignac and Paul Borrel. Multiresolution 3D approximations for
             rendering complex scenes. In B. Falcidieno and T. L. Kunii, eds., *Modeling
             in Computer Graphics: Methods and Applications*, pages 455–465.
             Springer-Verlag, New York, NY, 1993.

[RBMT98]   Holly Rushmeier, Fausto Bernardini, Joshua Mittleman, and Gabriel
             Taubin. Acquring input for rendering at appropriate levels of detail:
             Digitizing a pietà. In *Proceedings of the 9th Eurographics Workshop on
             Rendering*, pages 81–92,Vienna, Austria, June 1998.

[RE05]   Guido Reina and Thomas Ertl. Hardware-accelerated Glyphs for Mono-
             and Dipoles in Molecular Dymamics Visualization. In K. W. Brodlie,
             D. J. Duke, and K. I. Joy, eds., *Procceedings of EUROGRAPHICS-IEEE
             VGTC Symposium on Visualization 2005*, 2005.

[Ree83]   William T. Reeves. Particle systems—a technique for modeling a class of
             fuzzy objects. *ACM Transactions on Graphics*, 2(2):91–108, 1983.

[Ree85]   William T. Reeves. Approximate and probabilistic algorithms for shading
             and rendering structured particle systems. In *Computer Graphics*,
             SIGGRAPH 1985 Proceedings, pages 313–322, 1985.

[Ree99]   L. Jack Reese. Intelligent paint: Region-based interactive image segmenta-
             tion. Master's thesis, Department of Computer Science, Brigham Young
             University, Provo, UT, 1999.

[Rei92]   Mark C. Reichert. A two-pass radiosity method driven by lights and viewer
             position. Master's thesis, Cornell University, Ithaca, NY, 1992.

[Rey87]   Craig W. Reynolds. Flocks, herds, and schools: A distributed behavioral
             model. In *Computer Graphics*, SIGGRAPH 1987 Proceedings, pages 25–34,
             1987.

[RH01a]   Ravi Ramamoorthi and Pat Hanrahan. A signal-processing framework for
             inverse rendering. In *Computer Graphics*, SIGGRAPH 2001 Proceedings,
             pages 117–128, 2001.

[RH01b]   Ravi Ramamoorthi and Pat Hanrahan. An efficient representation for
             irradiance maps. In *Computer Graphics*, SIGGRAPH 2001 Proceedings,
             pages 497–500, 2001.

[RHHL02]   Szymon Rusinkiewicz, Olaf Hall-Holt, and Marc Levoy. Real-time 3D
             model acquisition. *ACM Transactions on Graphics*, SIGGRAPH 2002
             Proceedings, 21(3):438–446, 2002.

[Rig01]   Right Hemisphere. DeepPaint3D. http://www.us.deeppaint3d.com, 2001,
             cited October 2005.

[Rit90]   Jack Ritter. Fast 2D-3D rotation. In Andrew Glassner, ed., *Graphics Gems*,
             pages 440–441. Academic Press, Boston, MA, 1990.

[RL00]   Szymon Rusinkiewicz and Marc Levoy. QSplat: A multiresolution
             point-rendering system for large meshes. In *Computer Graphics*,
             SIGGRAPH 2000 Proceedings, pages 343–352. ACM SIGGRAPH, 2000.

[RL01a] Szymon Rusinkiewicz and Marc Levoy. Efficient variants of the ICP algorithm. In *Proceedings of the International Conference on 3D Digital Imaging and Modeling (3DIM)*, 2001.

[RL01b] Szymon Rusinkiewicz and Marc Levoy. Streaming QSplat: A viewer for networked visualization of large, dense models. In *Proceedings Symposium on Interactive 3D Graphics*, pages 63–68. ACM SIGGRAPH, 2001.

[RMP98] Steven Rubin, Gavin Miller, and Dulce Ponceleon. Lazy decompression of surface light fields for precomputed global illumination. In *Proceedings of the 9th Eurographics Workshop on Rendering*, pages 281–292, Vienna, Austria, June 1998.

[Ros84] Azriel Rosenfeld. The fuzzy geometry of image subsets. *Pattern Recognition Letters*, 2:311–317, 1984.

[Ros98] Azriel Rosenfeld. Fuzzy geometry: An updated overview. *Inf. Sci*, 110(3–4):127–133, 1998.

[Ros04] Randi J. Rost. *The OpenGL Shading Language*. Addison-Wesley, Boston, MA, 2004.

[RP94] Matthew Regan and Ronald Pose. Priority rendering with a virtual reality address recalculation pipeline. In *Computer Graphics*, SIGGRAPH 1994 Proceedings, pages 155–162, 1994.

[RPZ02] Liu Ren, Hanspeter Pfister, and Matthias Zwicker. Object space EWA surface splatting: A hardware-accelerated approach to high-quality point rendering. In *Eurographics 2002*, pages 461–470, September 2002.

[RSSF02] Erik Reinhard, Michael Stark, Peter Shirley, and James Ferwerda. Photographic tone reproduction for digital images. *ACM Transcations on Graphics*, 21(3):267–276, 2002.

[RTG97] Holly Rushmeier, Gabriel Taubin, and André Guéziec. Applying shape from lighting variation to bump map capture. In *Proceedings of the Eurographics Workshop on Rendering*, pages 35–44, 1997.

[RW80] Steven M. Rubin and Turner Whitted. A 3-dimensional representation for fast rendering of complex scenes. In *Computer Graphics*, SIGGRAPH 1980 Proceedings, pages 110–116, 1980.

[SA98] Ioannis Stamos and Peter Allen. Interactive sensor planning. In *Proceedings of the Conference on Computer Vision and Pattern Recognition*, pages 489–494, 1998.

[SACO04] Andrei Sharf, Marc Alexa, and Daniel Cohen-Or. Context-based surface completion. *ACM Transactions on Graphics*, SIGGRAPH 2004, Proceedings, 23(3):878–887, 2004.

[SAE93] Leon A. Shirman and Salim S. Abi-Ezzi. The cone of normals technique for fast processing of curved patches. In *Proceedings of Eurographics 1993*, pages 261–272, 1993. Also in Computer Graphics Forum 12(3).

[SAG94]   Brian Smits, James Arvo, and Donald Greenberg. A clustering algorithm for radiosity in complex environments. In *Computer Graphics*, SIGGRAPH 1994 Proceedings, pages 435–442, 1994.

[Sam84]   Hanan Samet. The quad-tree and related hierarchical data structures. *Computing Surveys*, 16(2):187–260, June 1984.

[Sam89a]   Hanan Samet. *Applications of Spatial Data Structures: Computer Graphics, Image Processing, and GIS*. Addison Wesley, Reading, MA, 1989.

[Sam89b]   Hanan Samet. *The Design and Analysis of Spatial Data Structures*. Addison Wesley, Reading, MA, 1989.

[Sam05]   Hanan Samet. *Foundations of Multidimensional and Metric Data Structures*. Morgan Kaufmann Publishers, San Francisco, CA, 2005.

[SB96]   Alvy Ray Smith and James F. Blinn. Blue screen matting. In *Computer Graphics*, SIGGRAPH 1996 Proceedings, pages 259–268, 1996.

[SBCR05]   Craig A. Schroeder, David E. Breen, Christopher D. Cera, and William C. Regli. Stochastic microgeometry for displacement mapping. In *Proceedings of Shape Modeling International*, pages 164–173, June 2005.

[SD99]   Steven Seitz and Charles Deyer. Photorealistic scene reconstruction by voxel coloring. *International Journal of Computer Vision*, 35(2):151–173, 1999.

[SD01a]   Marc Stamminger and George Drettakis. Efficient simplification of point-sampled surfaces. In *Rendering Techniques 2001*, Eurographics Workshop on Rendering, pages 163–170, 2001.

[SD01b]   Marc Stamminger and George Drettakis. Interactive sampling and rendering for complex and procedural geometry. In K. Myskowski and S. Gortler, eds., *Rendering Techniques 2001, Proceeding of the Eurographics Workshop on Rendering 2001*. Eurographics, Springer-Verlag, 2001.

[SDB97]   Francois Sillion, Georage Drettakis, and Beniot Bodelet. Efficient impostor manipulation for real-time visualization of urban scenery. EUROGRAPHICS 1997 Proceedings, pages 207–218, 1997.

[Sed98]   Robert Sedgewick. *Algorithms in C++, 3rd ed*. Addison-Wesley, Reading, MA, 1998.

[SF95]   Jos Stam and Eugene Fiume. Depicting fire and other gaseous phenomena using diffusion processes. In *Computer Graphics*, SIGGRAPH 1995 Proceedings, pages 129–136, 1995.

[SG69]   Jerome Spanier and Ely M. Gelbard. *Monte Carlo Principles and Neutron Transport Problems*. Addison-Wesley, New York, NY, 1969.

[SG01]   Eric Shaffer and Michael Garland. Efficient adaptive simplification of massive meshes. In *Proceedings of the Conference on Visualization 2001*, pages 127–134. IEEE Computer Society, 2001.

[SGG⁺00]   Pedro V. Sander, Xianfeng Gu, Steven J. Gortler, Hugues Hoppe, and John
            Snyder. Silhouette clipping. In *Computer Graphics*, SIGGRAPH 2000
            Proceedings, pages 327–334, 2000.

[SGwHS98]   Jonathan Shade, Steven Gortler, Li wei He, and Richard Szeliski. Layered
            depth images. In *Computer Graphics*, SIGGRAPH 1998 Proceedings, pages
            231–242, 1998.

[She68]   D. Shepard. A two-dimensional interpolation function for irregular spaced
            data. In *Proceedings of 23rd ACM National Conference*, pages 517–524, 1968.

[Shi00]   Peter Shirley. *Realistic Ray Tracing*. A. K. Peters, Ltd., 2000.

[SJ00]   Gernot Schaufler and Henrik Wann Jensen. Ray-tracing point-sampled
            geometry. In *Rendering Techniques 2000: 11th Eurographics Workshop on
            Rendering*, pages 319–328, June 2000.

[SLS⁺96]   Jonathan Shade, Dani Lischinski, David H. Salesin, Tony DeRose, and John
            Snyder. Hierarchical image caching for accelerated walkthroughs of
            complex environments. In *Computer Graphics*, SIGGRAPH 1996
            Proceedings, pages 75–82, 1996.

[SLW02]   Gregory Sharp, Sang Lee, and David Wehe. ICP registration using invariant
            features. *IEEE Transactions on Pattern Analysis and Machine Intelligence
            (PAMI)*, 24(1):90–102, January 2002.

[SLW05]   Gregory Sharp, Sang Lee, and David Wehe. Multiview registration of 3D
            scenes by minimizing error between coordinate frames. *IEEE Transactions
            on Pattern Analysis and Machine Intelligence (PAMI)*, 26(8):1037–1050,
            August 2005.

[SM04]   Aljoscha Smolic and David McCutchen. 3DAV exploration of video-based
            rendering technology in MPEG. *IEEE Transactions on Circuits and Systems
            for Video Technology, Special Issue on Immersive Communications*,
            14(9):348–356, 2004.

[Smi79]   Alvy Ray Smith. Painting tutorial notes (SIG79 tutorial), May 1979.

[Sny92]   John M. Snyder. *Generative Modeling for Computer Graphics and CAD:
            Symbolic Shape Design Using Interval Analysis*. Academic Press, San Diego,
            CA, 1992.

[SOS04]   Chen Shen, James F. O'Brien, and Jonathan R. Shewchuk. Interpolating
            and approximating implicit surfaces from polygon soup. *ACM Transactions
            on Graphics*, SIGGRAPH 2004 Proceedings, pages 896–904, July 2004.

[SP86]   Thomas W. Sederberg and Scott R. Parry. Free-form deformation of solid
            geometric models. In *Computer Graphics*, SIGGRAPH 1986 Proceedings,
            pages 151–160. ACM Press, New York, NY, 1986.

[SP04]   Miguel Sainz and Renato Pajarola. Point-based rendering techniques.
            Computers & Graphics, 28(6):869–879, 2004.

[SPL04]   Miguel Sainz, Renato Pajarola, and Roberto Lario. Points reloaded:
             Point-based rendering revisited. In *Proceedings Symposium on Point-based
             Graphics*, pages 121–128. Eurographics Association, 2004.

[SPMS04]   Miguel Sainz, Renato Pajarola, Albert Mercade, and Antonio Susin.
             A simple approach for point-based object capturing and rendering. *IEEE
             Comput. Graph. Appl.*, 24(4):24–33, 2004.

[SPOK95]   Vladimir V. Savchenko, Alexander A. Pasko, Oleg G. Okunev, and Tosiyasu
             L. Kunii. Function representation of solids reconstructed from scattered
             surface points and contours. *Computer Graphics Forum*, 14(4):181–188,
             1995.

[Spr91]   Robert F. Sproull. Refinements of nearest-neighbour searching in
             K-dimensional trees. *Algorithmica*, 6:579–589, 1991.

[SS98]   Daniel Scharstein and Richard Szeliski. Stereo matching with nonlinear
             diffusion. *International Journal of Computer Vision*, 28(2):155–174,
             June 1998.

[SSS74]   Ivan E. Sutherland, Robert F. Sproull, and Robert A. Schumacker.
             A characterization of ten hidden-surface algorithms. *ACM Computing
             Surveys*, 6(1), 1974.

[ST92]   Richard Szeliski and David Tonnesen. Surface modeling with oriented
             particle systems. In *Computer Graphics*, SIGGRAPH 1992 Proceedings,
             pages 185–194. ACM Press, New York, NY, 1992.

[Sta99]   Jos Stam. Stable fluids. In *Computer Graphics*, SIGGRAPH 1999
             Proceedings, pages 121–128, ACM Press, 1999.

[SW01]   Frank Suykens and Yves D. Willems. Path differentials and applications.
             In *Rendering Techniques 2001*, Proceedings of the 12th Eurographics
             Workshop on Rendering, pages 257–268. Springer-Verlag, New York, NY,
             2001.

[SWB00]   Jeffrey Smith, Andrew Witkin, and David Baraff. Fast and controllable
             simulation of the shattering of brittle objects. In *Graphics Interface*, pages
             27–34, May 2000.

[SWI97]   Yoichi Sato, Mark D. Wheeler, and Katsushi Ikeuchi. Object-shape and
             reflectance modeling from obsevation. In *Computer Graphics*, SIGGRAPH
             1997 Proceedings, pages 379–387, 1997.

[SWND03]   Dave Shreiner, Mason Woo, Jackie Neider, and Tom Davis. *OpenGL
             Programming Guide: The Official Guide to Learning OpenGL, Version 1.4*,
             4th ed. Addison-Wesley, Boston, MA, 2003.

[SWPG05]   Filip Sadlo, Tim Weyrich, Ronald Peikert, and Markus Gross. A practical
             structured-light acquisition system for point-based geometry and texture.
             In *Eurographics Symposium on Point-based Graphics*, pages 89–98, 2005.

[SZF⁺91]   Deborah Silver, Norman Zabusky, Victor Fernandez, Ming Gao, and Ravi Samtaney. Ellipsoidal quantification of evolving phenomena. *Scientific visualization of physical phenomena*, pages 573–588, 1991.

[Tau95]   Gabriel Taubin. A signal-processing approach to fair surface design. In *Computer Graphics*, SIGGRAPH 1995 Proceedings, pages 351–358, 1995.

[TF88]   Demetri Terzopoulos and Kurt Fleischer. Modeling inelastic deformation: Viscolelasticity, plasticity, fracture. In *Computer Graphics*, SIGGRAPH 1988 Proceedings, pages 269–278. ACM Press, New York, NY, 1988.

[TG98]   Costa Touma and Craig Gotsman. Triangle mesh compression. In *Graphics Interface*, pages 26–34, June 1998.

[TGHL98]   Gabriel Taubin, André Gueziec, William Horn, and Francis Lazarus. Progressive forest split compression. In *Computer Graphics*, SIGGRAPH 1998 Proceedings, pages 123–132. ACM Press, July 1998.

[THM⁺03]   Matthias Teschner, Bruno Heidelberger, Matthias Müller, Danat Pomerantes, and Markus Gross. Optimized spatial hashing for collision detection of deformable objects. In *Proceedings of Vision, Modeling, Visualization VMV*, pages 47–54, 2003.

[TK92]   Carlo Tomasi and Takeo Kanade. Shape and motion from image streams under orthography: A factorization method. *International Journal of Computer Vision*, 9(2):137–154, November 1992.

[TK96]   Jay Torborg and James T. Kajiya. Talisman: Commodity real-time 3D graphics for the PC. In *Computer Graphics*, SIGGRAPH 1996 Proceedings, pages 353–363, 1996.

[TL94]   Greg Turk and Marc Levoy. Zippered polygon meshes from range images. In *Computer Graphics*, SIGGRAPH 1994 Proceedings, pages 311–318. ACM Press, New York, NY, 1994.

[TL04]   Eric Tabellion and Arnauld Lamorlette. An approximate global illumination system for computer-generated films. *ACM Transactions on Graphics*, SIGGRAPH 2004 Proceedings, 23(3):469–476, 2004.

[TO99]   Greg Turk and James O'Brien. Shape transformation using variational implicit functions. In *Computer Graphics*, SIGGRAPH 1999, Proceedings, pages 335–342, July 1999.

[TO02]   Greg Turk and James O'Brien. Modelling with implicit surfaces that interpolate. *ACM Transactions on Graphics*, 21(4):855–873, October 2002.

[Ton92]   David Tonnesen. Spatially coupled particle systems. In *SIGGRAPH 1992 Course 16 Notes: Particle System Modeling, Animation, and Physically Based Techniques*, pages 4.1–4.21, 1992.

[TPBF87]   Demetri Terzopoulos, John Platt, Alan Barr, and Kurt Fleischer. Elastically deformable models. In *Computer Graphics*, SIGGRAPH 1987 Proceedings, pages 205–214, July 1987.

[TR98]   Gabriel Taubin and Jarek Rossignac. Geometric compression through
              topological surgery. *ACM Transactions on Graphics*, 17(2):84–115, April
              1998.

[TRS04]   Ireneusz Tobor, Patrick Reuter, and Christophe Schlick. Multiresolution
              reconstruction of implicit surfaces with attributes from large unorganized
              point sets. In *Proceedings of Shape Modeling International (SMI 2004)*, pages
              19–30, 2004.

[Tsa86]   Roger Tsai. An efficient and accurate camera calibration technique for 3D
              machine vision. In *Proceedings of the Conference on Computer Vision and
              Pattern Recognition*, pages 364–374, 1986.

[Tur91]   Greg Turk. Generating textures on arbitrary surfaces using reaction
              diffusion. In *Computer Graphics*, SIGGRAPH 1991 Proceedings, pages
              289–298, 1991.

[Tur92]   Greg Turk. Retiling polygonal surfaces. In *Computer Graphics*, SIGGRAPH
              1992 Proceedings, pages 55–64. ACM Press, New York, NY, 1992.

[Tur01]   Greg Turk. Texture synthesis on surfaces. In *Computer Graphics*,
              SIGGRAPH 2001 Proceedings, pages 347–354. ACM Press, New York, NY,
              2001.

[TWLG99]   Kenneth E. Torrance, Stephen H. Westin, Eric P. F. Lafortune, and Donald
              P. Greenberg. Image-based BRDF measurement including human skin. In
              Proceedings of the 10th Eurographics Workshop on Rendering, pages 139–152,
              Granada, Spain, June 1999.

[TV98]   Emanuele Trucco and Alessandro Verri. *Introductory Techniques for 3D
              Computer Vision*. Prentice-Hall, Englewood Cliffs, NJ, 1998.

[UO93]   Jayaram K. Udupa and Dewey Odhner. Shell rendering. *IEEE Computer
              Graphics & Applications*, 13(6):58–67, November 1993.

[Ups90]   Steve Upstill. *The RenderMan Companion*. Addison-Wesley, Reading, MA,
              1990.

[VCBS03]   J. Verdera, V. Caselles, M. Bertalm, and G. Sapiro. Inpainting surface holes.
              In *Proceedings of IEEE International Conference on Image Processing (ICIP)*,
              pages II: 903–906, September 2003.

[VIR05]   VIRGO. *The Virgo Consortium for Cosmological Supercomputer Simulations*,
              http://www.virgo.dur.ac.uk/, 2005.

[VPBM01]   Alex Vlachos, Jörg Peters, Chas Boyd, and Jason L. Mitchell. Curved PN
              triangles. *Proceedings of the 2001 Symposium on Interactive 3D Graphics*,
              pages 159–166, 2001.

[WAA+00]   Daniel N. Wood, Daniel I. Azuma, Ken Aldinger, Brian Curless, Tom
              Duchamp, David H. Salesin, and Werner Stuetzle. Surface light fields for
              3D photography. In *Computer Graphics*, SIGGRAPH 2000 Proceedings,
              pages 287–296, Los Angeles, CA, July 2000.

[Wal81]   Bruce Wallace. Merging and transformation of raster images for cartoon animation. In *Computer Graphics*, SIGGRAPH 1981 Proceedings, pages 253–262, 1981.

[Wan04]   Michael Wand. *Point-based Multiresolution Rendering*. Ph.D. thesis, University of Tuebingen, Wilhelm Schickard Institute for Computer Science, 2004.

[Wat70]   Gary Scott Watkins. A real-time visible surface algorithm. Technical Report UTECH-CSc-70-101, 1970.

[WBWS01]   Ingo Wald, Carsten Benthin, Markus Wagner, and Philipp Slusallek. Interactive rendering with coherent ray-tracing. *Computer Graphics Forum*, EUROGRAPHICS 2001, 20(3):153–164, 2001.

[Wel91]   Emo Welzl. *Smallest enclosing disks (balls and ellipsoids)*, vol. 555 of *Lecture Notes in Computer Science*. Springer-Verlag, New York, NY, 1991.

[Wen95]   Holger Wendland. Piecewise polynomial, positive definite, and compactly supported radial basis functions of minimal degree. *Advances in Computational Mathematics*, 4:389–396, 1995.

[Wes90]   Lee Westover. Footprint evaluation for volume rendering. In *Computer Graphics*, SIGGRAPH 1990 Proceedings, pages 367–376, August 1990.

[WFP$^+$01]   Michael Wand, Matthias Fischer, Ingmar Peter, Friedhelm Meyer auf der Heide, and Wolfgang Straßer. The randomized z-buffer algorithm: Interactive rendering of highly complex scenes. In *Computer Graphics*, SIGGRAPH 2001 Proceedings, pages 361–370, August 2001.

[WH92]   Gregory J. Ward and Paul S. Heckbert. Irradiance gradients. In *Proceedings of the 3rd Eurographics Workshop on Rendering*, pages 85–98, 1992.

[WH94]   Andrew P. Witkin and Paul S. Heckbert. Using particles to sample and control implicit surfaces. In *Computer Graphics*, SIGGRAPH 1994 Proceedings, pages 269–277. ACM Press, New York, NY, 1994.

[WH03]   Matthias Wloka and Richard Huddy. Directx 9 performance: Where does it come from, and where does it all go? Game Developers Conference 2003 Presentation. Available online at http://www.ati.com/developer, 2003.

[WHDS04]   Zoë Wood, Hugues Hoppe, Mathieu Desbrun, and Peter Schröder. Removing excess topology from iso-surfaces. *ACM Transactions on Graphics*, 23(2):190–208, April 2004.

[Whi78]   Turner Whitted. A scan-line algorithm for computer display of curved surfaces. In *Computer Graphics*, SIGGRAPH 1978 Proceedings, page 26, 1978.

[Whi80]   Turner Whitted. An improved illumination model for shaded display. *Communications of the ACM*, 23(6):343–349, 1980.

[Whi83]   Turner Whitted. Antialiased line drawing using brush extrusion. In *Computer Graphics*, SIGGRAPH 1983 Proceedings, pages 151–156, 1983.

[Wil79]   Robert Williams. *Geometrical Foundation of Natural Structure: A Source Book of Design*. Dover Publications, New York, NY, 1979.

[Wil83]   Lance Williams. Pyramidal parametrics. In *Computer Graphics*, SIGGRAPH 1983 Proceedings, pages 1–11, 1983.

[WK04]   Jianhua Wu and Leif Kobbelt. Optimized subsampling of point sets for surface splatting. *Computer Graphics Forum*, EUROGRAPHICS 2004 Proceedings, 23(3):643–652, 2004.

[WLG04]   Stephan Würmlin, Edouard Lamboray, and Markus Gross. 3D video fragments: Dynamic point samples for real-time free-viewpoint video. *Computers & Graphics*, 28(1):3–14, 2004.

[WLH97]   Tien-Tsin Wong, Wai-Shing Luk, and Pheng-Ann Heng. Sampling with Hammersley and Halton points. *Journal of Graphics Tools*, 2(2):9–24, 1997.

[WLSG02]   Stephan Würmlin, Edouard Lamboray, Oliver G. Staadt, and Markus Gross. 3D video recorder. In *Proceedings of Pacific Graphics 2002*, pages 325–334. IEEE Computer Society Press, 2002.

[WLW02]   Cliff Woolley, David Luebke, and Benjamin Watson. Interruptible rendering. In *SIGGRAPH 2002 Technical Sketches*, page 205, 2002.

[WLW+05]   Stephan Würmlin, Edouard Lamboray, Michael Waschbüsch, Peter Kaufmann, Aljoscha Smolic, and Markus Gross. Image-space free-viewpoint video. In *Vision, Modeling, Visualization VMV 2005*, 2005.

[WNDS99]   Mason Woo, Jackie Neider, Tom Davis, and Dave Shreiner. *OpenGL Programming Guide*, 3rd ed. Addison-Wesley, Reading, MA, 1999.

[Woo80]   Robert Woodham. Photometric method for determining surface orientation from multiple images. *Optical Engineering*, 19(1):139–144, 1980.

[WPK+04]   Tim Weyrich, Mark Pauly, Richard Keiser, Simon Heinzle, Sascha Scandella, and Markus Gross. Postprocessing of scanned 3D surface data. In *Proceedings of Eurographics Symposium on Point-based Graphics 2004*, pages 85–94, Zürich, Switzerland, June 2004.

[WRC88]   Gregory J. Ward, Francis M. Rubinstein, and Robert D. Clear. A ray-tracing solution for diffuse interreflection. In *Computer Graphics*, SIGGRAPH 1988 Proceedings, pages 85–92, 1988.

[WS02]   Michael Wand and Wolfgang Straßer. Multiresolution rendering of complex animated scenes. EUROGRAPHICS 2002 Proceedings, pages 483–483, 2002.

[WS04]   Michael Wand and Wolfgang Straßer. Multi-resolution sound rendering. In *Proceedings of the Symposium on Point-based Graphics 2004*, 2004.

[WS05]   Ingo Wald and Hans-Peter Seidel. Interactive ray tracing of point-based models. In *Proceedings of 2005 Symposium on Point-based Graphics*, pages 9–16, 2005.

[WSG05]   Martin Wicke, Denis Steinemann, and Markus Gross. Efficient animation of point-based thin shells. In *Proceedings of Eurographics 2005*, pages 667–676, 2005.

[WTG04]   Martin Wicke, Matthias Teschner, and Markus Gross. CSG tree rendering of point-sampled objects. In *Proceedings of Pacific Graphics 2004*, pages 160–168, 2004.

[Wür04]   Stephan Würmlin. *Dynamic Point Samples as Primitives for Free- viewpoint Video*. Ph.D. thesis, 2004.

[WW94]   William Welch and Andrew Witkin. Free-form shape design using triangulated surfaces. In *Computer Graphics*, SIGGRAPH 1994 Proceedings, pages 247–256, 1994.

[WWC⁺05]   Michael Waschbüsch, Stephan Würmlin, Daniel Cotting, Filip Sadlo, and Markus Gross. Scalable 3D video of dynamic scenes. In *The Visual Computer (Pacific Graphics 2005)*, vol. 21, pages 629–638. Springer-Verlag, New York, NY, 2005.

[WZK05]   Jianhua Wu, Zhuo Zhang, and Leif Kobbelt. Progressive splatting. In *Eurographics Symposium on Point-based Graphics*, pages 25–32, 2005.

[XWH⁺03]   Hui Xie, Jianning Wang, Jing Hua, Hong Qin, and Arie E. Kaufman. Piecewise C1 continuous surface reconstruction of noisy point clouds via local implicit quadric regression. In *Proceedings of the 14th IEEE Visualization Conference*, pages 91–98, 2003.

[YDMH99]   Yizhou Yu, Paul Debevec, Jitendra Malik, and Tim Hawkins. Inverse global illumination: Recovering reflectance models of real scenes from photographs. In *Computer Graphics*, SIGGRAPH 1999 Proceedings, pages 215–224, Los Angeles, CA August 1999.

[Zad65]   Lotfi A. Zadeh. Fuzzy sets. *Information and Control*, 8:338–353, 1965.

[ZB05]   Yongning Zhu and Robert Bridson. Animating sand as a fluid. *ACM Transactions on Graphics*, SIGGRAPH 2005 Proceedings, 24(3):965–972, 2005.

[ZBK02]   Todd Zickler, Peter Belhumeur, and David Kriegman. Helmholtz stereopsis: Exploiting reciprocity for surface reconstruction. *International Journal of Computer Vision*, 49(2–3):215–227, September 2002.

[ZCS03]   Li Zhang, Brian Curless, and Steven Seitz. Spacetime stereo: Shape recovery for dynamic scenes. In *Proceedings of the Conference on Computer Vision and Pattern Recognition*, pages 367–374, 2003.

[ZH97]   Hansong Zhang and Kenneth E. Hoff, III. Fast backface culling using normal masks. In *1997 Symposium on Interactive 3D Graphics*, pages 103–106, April 1997.

[Zha00]   Zhengyou Zhang. A flexible new technique for camera calibration. *IEEE Transactions on Pattern Analysis and Machine Intelligence*, 22(11):1330–1334, 2000.

[ZIK98]   Sergei Zhukov, Andrei Iones, and Gregorij Kronin. An ambient light
               illumination model. In *Rendering Techniques 1998, Proceedings 9th
               Eurographics Workshop on Rendering*, pages 45–55, 1998.

[ZKU+04]   C. Lawrence Zitnick, Sing Bing Kang, Matthew Uyttendaele, Simon
               Winder, and Richard Szeliski. High-quality video view interpolation using
               a layered representation. *ACM Transactions on Graphics*, SIGGRAPH 2004
               Proceedings, 23(3):600–608, 2004.

[ZOF01]   Hong-Kai Zhao, Stanley Osher, and Ronald Fedkiw. Fast surface recon-
               struction using the level-set method. In *Proceedings of IEEE Workshop on
               Variational and Level Set Methods in Computer Vision (VLSM 2001)*, pages
               194–202, July 2001.

[ZOMK00]   Hong-Kai Zhao, Stanley Osher, Barry Merriman, and Myungjoo Kang.
               Implicit and nonparametric shape reconstruction from unorganized points
               using variational level-set method. *Computer Vision and Image
               Understanding*, 80:295–319, 2000.

[ZPKG02a, b]   Matthias Zwicker, Mark Pauly, Oliver Knoll, and Markus Gross.
               Pointshop3D: An interactive system for point-based surface editing.
               ACM Transactions on Graphics, SIGGRAPH 2002 Proceedings,
               21(3):322–329, July 2002.

[ZPvBG01a]   Matthias Zwicker, Hanspeter Pfister, Jeroen van Baar, and Markus Gross.
               Ewa volume splatting. *IEEE Visualization 2001 Proceedings*, pages 29–36,
               October 2001.

[ZPvBG01b]   Matthias Zwicker, Hanspeter Pfister, Jeroen van Baar, and Markus Gross.
               Surface splatting. In *Computer Graphics*, SIGGRAPH 2001 Proceedings,
               pages 371–378. ACM Press, New York, NY, 2001.

[ZPvBG02]   Matthias Zwicker, Hanspeter Pfister, Jeroen van Baar, and Markus Gross.
               EWA splatting. *IEEE Transactions on Visualization and Computer Graphics*,
               8(3):223–238, 2002.

[ZRB+04]   Matthias Zwicker, Jussi Räsänen, Mario Botsch, Carsten Dachsbacher, and
               Mark Pauly. Perspective accurate splatting. In *Proceedings of Graphics
               Interface*, pages 247–254, 2004.

[ZSCS04]   Li Zhang, Noah Snavely, Brian Curless, and Steven Seitz. Space-time faces:
               High-resolution capture for modeling and animation. *ACM Transactions
               on Graphics*, SIGGRAPH 2004 Proceedings, 23(3):548–558, 2004.

[ZSS96]   Denis Zorin, Peter Schröder, and Wim Sweldens. Interpolating subdivision
               for meshes with arbitrary topology. In *Computer Graphics*, SIGGRAPH
               1996 Proceedings, pages 189–192, 1996.

[ZWCS99]   Douglas E. Zongker, Dawn M. Werner, Brian Curless, and David H. Salesin.
               Environment matting and compositing. In *Computer Graphics*, SIGGRAPH
               1999 Proceedings, pages 205–214, August 1999.

[Zwi03]   Matthias Zwicker. *Continuous Reconstruction, Editing, and Rendering of
               Point-sampled Surfaces*. Ph.D. thesis, ETH Zürich, Switzerland, 2003.

Index

About the Companion Website

This book is accompanied by a companion website (*www.pointbasedgraphics.com*) that contains a library of source code to implement the techniques and demonstrations found in this book. The website library is designed to be relatively easy to read and includes copious comments and demonstration programs. Other support materials for this book such as updates, errata, and additional features will be available at an additional companion site for this book: *http://textbooks.elsevier.com/ 9780123706041*.

SOFTWARE LICENSE

IMPORTANT: PLEASE READ THE FOLLOWING AGREEMENT CAREFULLY. BY COPYING OR OTHERWISE USING THIS SOURCE CODE, YOU ARE DEEMED TO HAVE AGREED TO THE TERMS AND CONDITIONS OF THIS LICENSE AGREEMENT.

All material on the companion website falls under the GPL and LGPL licenses. These licenses are included on the companion website. Each source file contains explicit information about its specific type of license. More information can also be found at:

http://www.gnu.org/licenses/

For legal reasons we are not permitted to add the Pointshop3D executable to the companion website. It can be downloaded from the Pointshop3D web site at:

http://graphics.ethz.ch/pointshop3d/

Printed and bound by CPI Group (UK) Ltd, Croydon, CR0 4YY

03/10/2024

01040312-0006